D0163520

A Comprehensive Guide to the Cannabis Literature

A Comprehensive Guide to the Cannabis Literature

Compiled by
ERNEST L. ABEL

GREENWOOD PRESS
WESTPORT, CONNECTICUT • LONDON, ENGLAND

Library of Congress Cataloging in Publication Data

Abel, Ernest L., 1943-
A comprehensive guide to the cannabis literature.

Includes index.
1. Cannabis—Bibliography. 2. Marihuana—Bibliography. I. Title.
Z7164.N17A23 [BF209.C3] 016.6138 78-20014
ISBN 0-313-20721-6

Library of Congress Catalog Card Number: 78-20014
ISBN: 0-313-20721-6

First published in 1979

Greenwood Press, Inc.
51 Riverside Avenue, Westport, Connecticut 06880

Printed in the United States of America

10 9 8 7 6 5 4 3 2 1

To my father, Jack, who instilled in
me a love of books

CONTENTS

PREFACE

Marihuana, hashish, bhang, dagga, kif, grass, and hemp are but a few of the terms that refer to preparations made from the plant *cannabis sativa L.* This bibliography includes references to the literature dealing not only with the psychotomimetic properties of this plant but also with other topics such as industrial usage, cultivation, history, and legal status published prior to 1978. Although comprehensive, this bibliography is by no means exhaustive. Many items, especially those in general newspapers and drug-related newsletters, were regretfully omitted. Although these are valuable source material, a decision had to be made as to what to incorporate and what to leave out, and these materials were passed by. It is also likely that many items from the chemical, historical, and sociological journals and popular magazines were inadvertently omitted, although every effort was made to be as thorough as possible.

Many of these entries were taken from my personal collection of materials on cannabis. Entries were also collected from the reference lists included in these publications. Previous bibliographies on the subject as well as bibliographies dealing with the drug literature were likewise consulted. Chemical, psychological, historical, and legal abstracts and periodical guides to the popular literature were, of course, invaluable reference sources. Although a great many of the citations were not originally in English, I have translated these or have used the translation provided in the same materials to render these into English. The original language is indicated in parentheses following the title of the article or book.

Entries are arranged alphabetically according to author. A supplementary "Addendum" at the back of the book is also arranged in this manner. These latter entries contain items that were inadvertently omitted in the initial listing or represent materials published after that listing. All items, however, are numbered consecutively and are referred to by number in the subject index.

In producing a work such as this, the services and cooperation of a great many individuals are to be gratefully acknowledged. Among those who deserve special thanks are the librarians of the Health Sciences Library at the State University of New York at Buffalo, *High Times* magazine, which supplied me with copies of all their publications, and last, but certainly not least, my wife, Barbara Ellen Buckley, without whose encouragement and help in collecting and collating entries this bibliography might not have been written.

INTRODUCTION

HISTORICAL BACKGROUND

The oldest known record of man's use of cannabis is believed to be about 10,000 B.C. in China, where fragments of pottery have been found bearing the imprint of cordlike material. Although no one can be sure that these imprints were made by hempen cord, the fact that hemp was an important ingredient in Chinese clothes and ropes in the early history of that country makes it probable that indeed the Chinese were using hempen fiber that long ago. While fibrous material from the past has rarely been preserved except in very dry climates like Egypt, in 1972 an ancient burial site dating back to the Chou dynasty (1122-256 B.C.) was discovered containing fragments of cloth. Upon examination, the cloth was found to be impregnated with cannabis fibers, making it the oldest preserved specimen of hemp in existence.

Although the ancient Chinese relied heavily on the fiber of the cannabis plant for their clothes and their ropes, they also were familiar with its potential uses as a medicine and an intoxicant. The person generally credited with teaching the Chinese about cannabis's medicinal virtues is the legendary emperor, Shen-Nung, who lived around the twenty-eighth century B.C. Shen-Nung was said to have ingested as many as seventy different poisons in a single day and to have discovered the antidotes for each one of them. After he finished these experiments, he wrote the *Pen Ts'ao*, an herbal or Materia Medica, which listed hundreds of drugs he had experimented with, among them cannabis, which he called *ma*. The *Pen Ts'ao* eventually became the standard manual on drugs in China, and so highly regarded was its author that he was accorded the title of Father of Chinese Medicine. Not too long ago, China's drug guild used to show its veneration to this patron of Chinese medicine by offering a 10 percent discount on any medicines sold on the first and fifteenth of each month, days that were set aside in honor of the great emperor.

As physicians became more and more familiar with the actions of various drugs, they discovered that cannabis was a painkiller when mixed with alcohol, and in the second century A.D. Chinese physicians were reputedly performing complicated surgical procedures with minimal pain to their patients, thanks to cannabis's analgesic properties. Hand in hand with cannabis's use as a medicine went its abuse as an intoxicant; however, it was not until about 600 B.C. that the drug began to be mentioned with special disdain. The low opinion of the drug apparently was associated with the growing spirit of the Taoist religion, which preached a back-to-nature philosophy. Anything that enfeebled the body such as *ma* was not highly regarded, and both the medicinal and the pleasurable usages of the drug began to disappear.

In India, an ancient legend tells of how the god Siva became so angry after a family row that he went off into the fields by himself. After he was out walking for several hours, the heat began to bother him and he looked for some refuge to hide from the sun's blazing rays. Finally he discovered a tall plant, and he hid under its leaves until the sun finally went to sleep. Curious about this plant that had brought him such relief, he ate some of its leaves. So refreshed did he feel after this meal that he adopted it as his favorite food. From then on Siva was known as the Lord of *bhang*, an Indian term for one of the popular beverages made from cannabis.

The earliest reference to *bhang*'s mind-altering influence in the writings of the ancient Indians comes from the fourth book of the Vedas, the "Science of Charms." Written some time between 2,000 and 1,400 B.C., the book calls *bhang* one of the "five kingdoms of herbs . . . which release us from anxiety." It appears that *bhang* has been one of India's favorite beverages almost from the beginning of its history. The ancient people of India used to say that those who spoke badly of *bhang* were doomed to suffer the torments of hell as long as the sun shone in the heavens.

At the turn of the twentieth century, the Indian Hemp Commission, which had been summoned in the 1890s to examine the influence of the plant on the people of India, concluded that cannabis was so much a part of the way of life of that country that to limit or outlaw its usage would certainly lead to unhappiness, resentment, and suffering:

> The supporting power of bhang has brought many a Hindu family safe through the miseries of famine. To forbid or even seriously to restrict the use of so holy and gracious an herb . . . would cause widespread suffering and annoyance to large bands of worshipped ascetics, and deep-seated anger. It would rob the people of a solace in discomfort, of a cure in sickness, of a guardian whose gracious protection saves them from the attacks of evil influences . . . . So grand a result, so tiny a sin![1]

Around the seventh century B.C., a swarm of Aryan warriors who were related to the Arians who invaded India came out of central Siberia in search of new grazing lands. Known as the Scythians, these people were no strangers to the intoxicating effects of cannabis. According to Herodotus, who lived in the fifth century B.C., cannabis played an integral part in the funereal ceremonies in which the Scythians honored their dead chieftains. On the first anniversary of the death of a chief, fifty of his former bodyguards and their horses were impaled on stakes arranged in a circle around the chief's grave. Following this grisly rite came a cleansing rite for all those who had taken part in the ceremony. After first washing their bodies with oil, the participants climbed into a tent containing red hot stones and then threw cannabis seeds onto the fire. As the seeds heated, they threw off a vapor which in Herodotus's words, caused the Scythians to "howl with joy."

Although the Scythians had contacts with people as far west as Babylonia, there is no indication that the plant was known beyond the land of Turkey until the time of the Greeks. When the Greeks became familiar with cannabis is not known for certain. In the *Odyssey*, Homer refers to the mysterious drug *nepenthe* ("against sorrow") which causes forgetfulness of all sad things, but he never identifies it by name. Scholars have tried in vain to discover what this mysterious drug might have been and, not surprisingly, cannabis has had many champions. The poet Samuel Taylor Coleridge, for one, coaxed a friend to visit him with the promise that they would "give fair trial to opium, henbane, and nepenthe," adding that he always considered Homer's account of nepenthe a "banging lie."[2] The latter was a reference to the Indian term *bhang*. The fact is that the Greeks remained largely ignorant of cannabis's intoxicating effects. Not until the sixth century B.C. did the plant become familiar to the Greeks, and then it was as a source of fiber, not as a drug, that it gained importance. At first Greek merchants obtained their cannabis fiber from their Milesian colonies, which served as trading centers between mainland Greece and Asia Minor. But by the third century B.C., Hiero II of Syracuse (270-215 B.C.) had become so knowledgeable about cannabis fiber that he preferred to obtain his supplies from the Rhone valley in France. His efforts at procuring these supplies constitute the earliest reference to the presence of cannabis in western Europe.

Like the Greeks, the Romans were primarily interested in cannabis because of its fiber. Roman physicians such as Dioscorides, Galen, and Oribasius noted several of the psychotomimetic effects of the plant, and wealthy Romans used to serve cannabis seeds as a dessert specialty for their guests, but most Romans were ignorant of these properties of the plant. Cannabis fiber, on the other hand, was unsurpassed for its strength, and to expand the Roman navy and keep control of the seas, Rome needed strong rope. Most of Rome's hemp was not grown locally but raised in Babylonia. The city of Sura was particularly renowned for its hempen ropes. Such Milesian cities as Colchis and Ephesus, which had been prominent distributors of cannabis fiber under the Greeks, retained their prominence as cannabis exporters under the Romans.

According to one Arab legend, the discovery of hashish dates back to the twelfth century A.D. when Haydar, the Persian founder of the religious order of Sufi, came across the cannabis plant while wandering in the Persian mountains. Usually a reserved and silent man, when he returned to his monastery after eating some cannabis leaves, his disciples were amazed at how talkative and animated he seemed. After cajoling Haydar into telling them what he had done to make him feel so happy, his disciples went out into the mountains and tried some cannabis for themselves. So it was, according to the legend, that the Sufis came to know the pleasures of hashish. Although entertaining, the story of Haydar and the Sufis is not the earliest evidence of hashish use among the Arabs. Two centuries earlier, the Arab physician Ibn Wahshiyah had described some of the effects of hashish, and it is likely that some knowledge of cannabis was known to the Arabs even earlier.

By the thirteenth century hashish was a commonly used drug in the Arab lands, and one of the favorite haunts for hashish users at that time was the "gardens" of Cafour in Cairo. The "gardens" were also the scene of one of the first attempts by a government to suppress usage of hashish. Alarmed by the growing rabble that had been collecting in what had once been the city's showplace, in 1253 A.D. the governor of Cairo ordered his soldiers to throw the hashish users out of the gardens and burn all the cannabis plants in the vicinity. "A just punishment of God," was how some of the more pious citizens of Cairo reacted to the news of the governor's actions. Deprived of their favorite gathering place, the hashish users had to find other locales to enjoy their drug. The entrepreneurs outside of Cairo were quick to take advantage of the hashish users' plight, and it was not long until cannabis was growing in the outskirts of Cairo and hashish inns began sprouting up to cater to the displaced users. This enterprise flourished for about a hundred years. In 1324 A.D. the authorities once again decided that hashish was not good for the community, and troops were called out to eradicate the hashish inns and raze the cannabis fields. Similar actions were taken at least twice more during the century, but to no avail. Hashish had become too ingrained in the Arab world for it to be eradicated. Said the Egyptian historian Maqrizi of the triumph of hashish: "as a consequence, general corruption of sentiments and manners ensued, modesty disappeared, every base and evil passion was openly indulged in, and nobility of external form alone remained in these infatuated beings."[3]

Throughout the Middle Ages exaggerated tales of hashish's effects were circulated throughout the Arab world, but none gripped the imagination and lived as long as the story of the "Old Man of the Mountains" and his cutthroat band of followers known as the "Assassins." According to Marco Polo who recorded the legend of these terrorists, the Assassins were kept in tow by a leader known as the Old Man of the Mountains, who induced his men to follow him and who made them do his bidding thereafter by feeding them hashish. While a group of terrorists known as the Assassins did control much of the Middle East during the Middle Ages, and while their first leader, Hasan-ibn-Sabah, was known as the Old Man of the Mountains, the link between them and hashish has long since been forgotten, and all that remains is conjecture. Although the Assassins were users of hashish, so were countless others in the Arab world. The issue around which most of the emotional ink has been spilt is whether the Assassins took hashish to fortify themselves before going out on their errands of death. While there is no evidence that this was the case (and had they done so, it is unlikely that they would have been able to plan and execute their terrorist acts), lurid and outrageous stories about the Assassins and their hashish-induced killings have been exploited in western literature and have served as the basis for anti-cannabis laws for centuries.

In the United States, for example, the image of the demented, knife-wielding frenzied hashish user was used by Commissioner Harry Anslinger of the Federal Bureau of Narcotics in his personal vendetta against the drug. Writing in 1937, he told readers of *American Magazine*:

> In the year 1090, there was founded in Persia the religious and military order of the Assassins, whose history is one of cruelty, barbarity, and murder, and for good reason. The members were confirmed users of hashish, or marihuana, and it is from the Arab "hashshashin" that we have the English word "assassin."[4]

Curiously, the Arabs themselves have rarely regarded hashish as a drug that inspires violence. Perhaps they are too familiar with the apathy and lethargy of chronic users to think of them as violent.

Although cannabis was no stranger to Europe during the Middle Ages, Europeans had little awareness that the plant they so heavily relied on for their ropes was also capable of inebriation. During the fifteenth century, the French writer-physician François Rabelais did describe some of the psychotomimetic effects of the cannabis plant, which he called Pantagruelion, but all his information was taken from Pliny and Galen. Not all of Europe was ignorant of the peculiar properties of the plant, however. In secret gathering places, hidden from the peering eyes of the authorities, sorcerers and witches were accused of compounding mysterious drugs, including those made of cannabis, as part of their Devil worship. In condemning witchcraft and other Satanic practices in 1484, for example, Pope Innocent VIII included cannabis as one of the compounds used to summon the Prince of Darkness. In 1615, Giovanni De Ninault, the Italian physician and demonologist, likewise included cannabis among the drugs used by the Devil's followers.

There is also some indication that the people of Eastern Europe and Russia relied on cannabis as a medicinal aid in the sixteenth century, although for the most part it was the seeds of the plant that entered into their remedies. Toothaches and infected gums, for example, were often treated by inhaling the vapor given off by smoldering cannabis seeds. It was not until the beginning of the nineteenth century, however, that appreciable numbers of western Europeans became familiar with cannabis as a drug.

In the wake of Napoleon's retreat from Egypt came incredible stories of hashish and its strange mind-altering effects. Captivated by these tales to the point of wanting to experiment with the drug themselves were the writers, poets, and artists who gathered, for the most part, in Paris's Latin Quarter.

One of the earliest literary figures to use hashish was Pierre Jules Theophile Gautier, who at the age of twenty-four was credited with writing "the most daring novel . . . that ever a full fledged Romanticist could write." It was Gautier's belief that "enjoyment . . . [was] the end of life, and the only useful thing in the world." To that end, said Gautier, a special award should be given to those who invented new pleasures.[5] Had he been in a position to grant such an award, no doubt Gautier's first choice for the prize would have been Dr. Jacques-Joseph Moreau, who first introduced him to hashish. So intrigued was Gautier by this drug that he subsequently founded the Club des Hashischins, where he had Moreau dispense hashish to such notables as Alexander Dumas, Gerard de Nerval, and Victor Hugo. Charles Baudelaire, the best known member of this club, however, was merely an observer and not a participant in the drug-oriented gatherings. Yet it was Baudelaire's book, *The Artificial Paradises*, in which he describes the hashish experience at great length, that captured the imagination of the West. As late as the 1960s it was regarded as the most comprehensive analysis of hashish's effects.

Although cannabis was imported to British North America shortly after the first permanent settlements, Americans were not aware of the peculiar effects that lay hidden in the plant's resin. In fact, it was not until they read the adventures of one of the best-known literary figures of mid-nineteenth-century America, Bayard Taylor, that the country became aware that the cannabis plant was more than it seemed. Taylor's first encounter with hashish was in Egypt, an experience he recounted in his *Journey to Central Africa* (1854). A year later he published a second book, *The Land of the Saracens*, which explored the hashish experience more fully. These accounts were intentionally sensationalistic and played to an audience hungry for vicarious adventure. The impressions Taylor left in the American mind concerning hashish were lurid and not very positive.

Among those to be excited by Taylor's writings on hashish was a teenager from Poughkeepsie, New York, Fitz Hugh Ludlow. Unlike Taylor, however, Ludlow had to content himself with sampling the cannabis products that were available on the neighborhood pharmacist's shelf. It was to become a pastime that would last for years, one Ludlow subsequently documented in his own book, *The Hasheesh Eater: Being Passages from the Life of a Pythagorean* (1857). Ludlow claims to have become psychologically dependent on cannabis and, as a result, he states that he spent much of his teenage years in a perpetual state of cannabis intoxication. He finally was able to give up his habit but not without a great deal of suffering. Although his untimely death at the age of thirty-four was attributed by many to his overindulgence in hashish, the actual cause was tuberculosis. Ludlow's book is now regarded as a minor classic of the American drug literature, equivalent in insight to Baudelaire's *Artificial Paradises.* Besides alerting his readers to the relationship between dose and effect, Ludlow also stressed the importance of set and setting as factors affecting the cannabis experience. During his own lifetime, however, Ludlow's book was largely ignored, and when it was reviewed in 1857, the reviewer passed judgment on Ludlow's experience with the prophetically ironic observation that Americans were fortunately "in no danger of becoming a nation of hasheesh eaters."

By the 1860s, however, the number of Americans using hashish had risen to such a point that even in far-off England a writer such as Mordecai Cubitt Cooke was predicting that cannabis would replace alcohol as the popular form of intoxication. In 1869, *Scientific American* noted that hashish was being used in the country but claimed that usage was still "limited." In 1883, *Harper's New Monthly Magazine* ran an anonymously written article that claimed there were about 600 hashish houses in New York City and comparable dens in Boston, Philadelphia, Chicago, and New Orleans. The medical journals of the era were also filled with countless reports of "cannabis poisonings."

By the early decades of the twentieth century, however, the popularity of the drug had begun to wane considerably, and the most visible users of the drug were Mexicans and Negroes. At the same time the popular name for the drug was no longer hashish but marihuana, a term more closely connected with the Mexicans. During the years when the economy was strong and viable, comparatively little attention was paid to the use of marihuana by minority groups in America. In states where there were large numbers of Mexicans, however, state laws were adopted against the use of marihuana, beginning with California in 1915. References to the drug in the local newspapers in these states show, however, that very little was known about the drug. The *Austin Texas Statesman*, for example, informed its readers that "marihuana is a Mexican herb and is said to be sold on the Texas Mexican border."[6]

On the national level, however, there was little interest in outlawing marihuana until the 1930s. Short on tax monies, Congress was trimming all fat from some already lean federal agencies, and the Bureau of Narcotics was no exception. To meet the threat to the bureau's life, its Commissioner Harry J. Anslinger decided he had to create an issue that would convince Congress not to cut the bureau's budget. If he could prove that there was a new drug menacing the country, then Congress could not very well tamper with the bureau's resources to eradicate the threat. Mustering all the resources at his disposal, Anslinger initiated a media campaign that played up atrocities committed by people who were allegedly under the influence of marihuana. Anslinger also tried to pressure Congress into adopting national marihuana legislation by persuading the League of Nations to adopt international measures against marihuana. If the United States signed such an international agreement, Anslinger felt that Congress could not very easily refuse to adopt comparable national legislation. The ploy at the League did not work, however, and Anslinger had to devise other means of putting such a law on the books.

Anslinger next concentrated his efforts on convincing the Treasury Department, which had control over the Bureau of Narcotics, to prepare arguments for making marihuana illegal. As his part in the campaign, Anslinger was advised to collect as many lurid marihuana-related crimes as he could gather for presentation to Congress. So-called experts were called in to back the Treasury Department's case. The House Committee heard several days' testimony about the dangers of the drug to American society as a whole and to school children in particular. Most of this testimony, however, was taken from newspapers and magazines, which in many instances had relied on the Bureau of Narcotics for its information in the first place! After hearing all the evidence against marihuana, the committee recommended that the House pass a law outlawing the drug, even though most members of Congress did not even have an inkling of what marihuana was. When Speaker of the House Sam Rayburn was asked what Congress was being asked to outlaw, Rayburn replied that "I believe it is a narcotic of some kind." Nevertheless, the House passed the bill and after a few minor changes, so did the Senate. President Roosevelt signed it without much notice being taken, and in 1937 marihuana became a nationally outlawed substance in the United States.

CHEMISTRY

The chemical compounds in *cannabis sativa* that are characteristic of that plant are called *cannabinoids*. The first cannabinoid to be isolated from cannabis was cannabinol, but it was soon found to be biologically inactive (although recent studies indicate it may affect the actions of other cannabinoids). The principal cannabinoid responsible for the psychotomimetic effects associated with the plant is 1-delta-9-trans-tetrahydrocannabinol.* Other cannabinoids that exert biological effects or else modify the effects of delta-9-tetrahydrocannabinol are delta-8-tetrahydrocannabinol, cannabidiol, cannabicyclol, cannabichromene, cannabigerol, cannabivarol, cannabidivarol, and their corresponding acids.

Several different terms referring to the same cannabinoids are used depending on the system used to number the molecules in the chemical structure. The two most common systems are the pyran and the monoterpenoid. The former refers to the principle psychotomimetic cannabinoid as delta-9-tetrahydrocannabinol (abbreviated $\triangle^9$-THC) and to its secondary isomer as delta-8-tetrahydrocannabinol (abbreviated $\triangle^8$-THC); the latter refers to these same two compounds as delta-1-tetrahydrocannabinol ($\triangle^1$-THC) and delta-1(6)-tetrahydrocannabinol (or delta-6-tetrahydrocannabinol) respectively (abbreviated $\triangle^{1(6)}$-THC or $\triangle^6$-THC).

*Henceforth the trans is omitted.

In addition to the cannabinoids, *cannabis sativa* also contains several non-cannabinoid compounds, among them certain alkaloids, terpenes, phenols, flavonoids, and sugars. Whether or how these compounds affect the biological activities of cannabis awaits further study.

There are also several cannabinoid compounds that have been synthesized in the laboratory and that are not found naturally in cannabis. Of these, the delta-3-tetrahydrocannabinols have been shown to be quite biologically active, and one of these compounds, known as pyrahexyl (also synhexyl), has been used clinically.

ANALYSIS

One of the oldest concerns about cannabis is the discovery and implementation of ways of identifying the plant and the preparations made from it. This is an especially important issue in the courts today, since identification is a sine qua non for prosecution.

The earliest test procedures were color tests such as the Beam and Duquenois tests. In the Beam Test, a purple color forms when cannabis is mixed with a mixture of alcohol and potassium hydroxide. The Duquenois Test uses a mixture of vanillin, acetaldehyde, alcohol, and hydrochloric acid and forms a violet color on contact with cannabis. Both tests have their shortcomings. The Beam Test is more sensitive to some of the cannabinoids than others, and the mixture will not turn purple if these cannabinoids are missing, even if added to known cannabis samples. The Duquenois Test is more sensitive than the Beam Test, but it is not as specific—the mixture will turn violet when mixed with coffee, for example.

Other color tests that have in the past or are presently being used to identify cannabis are the Ghamrawy Test, and the Fast Blue Salt B Test. The latter is a mixture of sodium hydroxide and Fast Blue Salt B and forms different colors depending on which cannabinoid it is mixed with.

At present, the most common methods of analysis for the cannabinoids are chromatographic. These methods rely on the separation of materials according to how strongly they are absorbed by a solvent. Substances that are strongly absorbed move slowly along a paper or column containing the solvent; substances less strongly absorbed move faster. Separation of the cannabinoids thus occurs because of different affinities of each cannabinoid for the solvent used to separate them.

Another technique often used in conjunction with chromatography is mass spectrometry. This is a qualitative method of analysis that causes ions to leave the sample material and sorts these ions according to their mass-to-charge ratio.

A third method, nuclear magnetic resonance, relies on the fact that many nuclei have magnetic properties and can be separated on the basis of those properties.

A fourth method, radioimmunoassay, involves binding cannabinoid material to radioactively labeled protein. The amount of radioactivity present in the protein-bound is used to estimate the amount of a given substance present in the compound.

PHARMACOLOGY

Delta-9-tetrahydrocannabinol, the principal active constituent of marihuana, was isolated in 1964 and subsequently synthesized. Once it became available for laboratory investigation, researchers began to rely on it instead of crude marihuana preparations. Although this procedure avoided the difficult problems associated with potency and ingredient differences between batches of crude marihuana, later studies indicated that cannabinol and other cannabinoids present in marihuana could affect the actions of delta-9-tetrahydrocannabinol. As a result, it became apparent that studies in man and animals using delta-9-tetrahydrocannabinol might not reflect the action of the crude plant material. Nevertheless, the availability of pure cannabinoid compounds meant that the reliability of various studies was greatly enhanced.

Due to assay problems, it was not possible at first to determine whether delta-9-tetrahydrocannabinol or its metabolite, 11-hydroxy-delta-9-tetrahydrocannabinol, was responsible for the effects associated with marihuana. This difficulty was subsequently overcome with the identification and subsequent synthesis of these metabolites and by the availability of radiolabeled compounds that enabled investigators to trace the course of these compounds during their passage through the body.

The principal route of administration in man is by smoking. This method produces a rapid onset of drug action but only 50 to 75 percent of the delta-9-tetrahydrocannabinol present in marihuana is absorbed into the body. Differences in individual smoking habits also result in considerable differences in the amount of cannabinoids absorbed into the body.

The smallest amount of delta-9-tetrahydrocannabinol present in a marihuana cigarette that will produce reliable effects in man is around 5 mg. For a man weighing about 70 kg., this would be equivalent to a dose of approximately 0.07 mg./kg. However, since only about 50 percent of this amount is absorbed under normal smoking conditions, this dose should be halved to 0.035 mg./kg.

When smoked, the onset of drug action is about five to fifteen minutes; peak effect occurs around sixty minutes; the duration of action is often four hours or longer. Interestingly, while the peak psychological effect or "high" occurs around sixty minutes after smoking, the peak increase in pulse rate associated with marihuana occurs at fifteen minutes and then rapidly declines.

In animals such as the rat and mouse, the cannabinoids are generally administered by intraperitoneal, oral, or subcutaneous injection, although some investigators have placed animals in chambers where they are forced to inhale the smoke from burning marihuana. Not surprisingly, route of administration is an important consideration in assessing the effects of the cannabinoids in animals. For example, a dose of 10 mg./kg. of delta-9-tetrahydrocannabinol has no observable effect on key-pecking behavior in pigeons when the drug is administered orally. After intramuscular ingestion, key pecking is suppressed about ninety minutes after injection. When injected intravenously, however, suppression is immediate.

A major problem in administering the cannabinoids to animals is that these drugs are very insoluble in water. As a result, organic solvents, surfactants, or suitable suspending agents have to be used. However, many of these solvents have effects of their own, and depending on the nature of the vehicle, quantitative as well as qualitative differences in the effects of the cannabinoids may occur.

In the last few years water-soluble derivatives of delta-9-tetrahydrocannabinol have been synthesized, although they have not as yet been widely tested, so that there have not been many comparisons between these derivatives and the water-insoluble compound.

Studies of drug distribution have shown that tissues richly invested with blood such as the liver, lung, kidney, and spleen attain relatively high levels of drug concentration. An exception is the brain. Although it too receives a high blood flow, brain cannabinoid levels remain far below blood levels.

It has now been well established that delta-9-tetrahydrocannabinol is hydroxylated by the liver to 11-hydroxy-delta-9-tetrahydrocannabinol. Following its metabolism to this metabolite, it is then further converted to 8, 11-dihydroxy-delta-9-tetrahydrocannabinol, which is then transformed to other metabolites. Most of the cannabinoids that are excreted from the body are in the form of these metabolites rather than the parent compound.

Studies of the elimination of delta-9-tetrahydrocannabinol and its metabolites from the body in man and animals indicate that excretion occurs very slowly. The main route of elimination is through the bile and feces. Comparatively little drug passes through the kidney. About 50 percent of the delta-9-tetrahydrocannabinol content taken into the body is eliminated in the first twenty-four hours. In man, traces of the drug can still be found as long as eight days after usage. In animals, traces of the drug have been detected in the brain as long as thirty days after a single administration. Other studies in animals have shown that the cannabinoids and/or their metabolites accumulate in the brain following repeated administration. This accumulation could increase the length of time the cannabinoids remain in the brain and might account for such long-lasting phenomena as learning/memory impairment and flashbacks that have been reported in long-time users of marihuana.

On the other hand, there is no doubt that tolerance develops to a great many of the effects of delta-9-tetrahydrocannabinol. In general, tolerance to a drug is recognized as having developed when, after repeated administrations, a given dose of that drug produces less of an effect than was initially produced. Alternatively, tolerance is said to have developed when greater amounts of the drug must be administered to produce the effects initially observed. Closely related to the phenomenon of tolerance is physical dependence. Physical dependence on a drug is said to have developed when a characteristic abstinence syndrome is observed when use of that drug is discontinued. Although drug dependence is always associated with tolerance, tolerance need not result in drug dependence.

Among the behavioral effects for which tolerance has been observed in animals are: suppression of aggressiveness in fish, loss of righting reflex in frogs, suppression of heat escape in chicks, suppression of key pecking for food reward in pigeons, catelepsy in mice, anticonvulsant effects in rats, shock avoidance in rats, analgesia in rats, ataxia in dogs, and impairment of temporal responding in monkeys. Among the physiological effects in which tolerance has been observed are: hypothermia, reduction of electrocorticogram and EEG activity, bradycardia, changes in plasma corticosterone, and rate of brain tissue respiration.

Tolerance to the cannabinoids occurs in a wide variety of species and occurs to some of the drug's effects but not all (for example, depression of isolation-induced fighting in mice, delayed matching-to-sample performance in chimpanzees, tachycardia in man), and when tolerance does occur, the rate of development is rapid and often long-lasting. The magnitude of tolerance development is also noteworthy. In one experiment, pigeons chronically treated with delta-9-tetrahydrocannabinol were not affected by an intramuscular injection of 1,800 mg./kg., a dose that is 6,000 to 18,000 times greater than the minimally effective dose for suppression of behavior in a drug-naive pigeon.

Although cross tolerance occurs among the tetrahydrocannabinols, their metabolites, and their synthetic analogues, there is no evidence for cross tolerance between the cannabinoids and drugs such as mescaline, LSD, or chlorpromazine. The evidence for cross tolerance with alcohol and morphine is equivocal. However, cross tolerance has reliably been shown between the cannabinoids and the barbiturates.

No differences in the time course of disappearance of the cannabinoids or their metabolites has been observed between tolerant and nontolerant animals or between naive and chronic marihuana users in man, indicating that the observed tolerance to the cannabinoids does not result from differential absorption or metabolism. This suggests that cannabinoid tolerance is "functional" rather than "dispositional" in nature.

To account for the observation that many users of marihuana do not become "high" when they first use the drug, the concept of "reverse tolerance" has been postulated. However, there is little evidence to support this concept. Rather than exhibiting an increased pharmacological sensitivity to marihuana, it appears that naive users learn to discriminate the sought-after effects. In other words, users learn to get "high" with repeated usage.

Although tolerance develops rather rapidly to many of the behavioral and physiological effects of the cannabinoids in animals, marked physical dependence has not been observed. An exception to this general finding are some studies using monkeys. Upon termination of chronic drug treatment, abstinence symptoms appeared within twelve hours and lasted for twelve days. Among the symptoms observed were yawning, piloerection, scratching, biting and licking fingers, pulling hair, twitches, shaking, photophobia, coprophagia, penile erection, and masturbation. There are few reports of cannabis-related withdrawal in man. However, a report from South Africa noted that in chronic users undergoing withdrawal, abstinence was followed by anxiety, restlessness, nausea, sweating, headache, increased pulse rate, low blood pressure, and acute abdominal cramps that lasted from one to three days and disappeared with the arrival of a new supply of the drug.

Studies of the acute toxicity of cannabis and its derivatives in animals indicate that huge doses of these compounds can be administered without producing death.

The LD_{50}—i.e., the dose that kills 50 percent—in animals varies, not surprisingly, as a function of route of administration, species, and vehicle used to administer the drug. The LD_{50}s for rats given delta-9-tetrahydrocannabinol dissolved in Tween are approximately 42.5 mg./kg. (intravenous injection), 454.5 mg./kg. (intraperitoneal injection), and 482 mg./kg. (oral administration). These values are approximately twice as great if bovine serum albumin or sesame seed oil are used as vehicles for drug administration. When administered via smoke inhalation, the LD_{50} was calculated as being approximately 106 mg./kg. in the rat. Toxicity has not been observed in dogs or monkeys given up to 3 and 9 g./kg. respectively of delta-9-tetrahydrocannabinol orally.

Death associated with administration of the cannabinoids is thought to be caused by respiratory failure. Gross observations of animals injected with lethal doses reveal a pattern of initial hypersensitivity, followed by depression, loss of righting reflex, dyspnea, and finally apnea. Chronic oral administration of various cannabinoids for up to 104 days at doses between 50 and 500 mg./kg. produced a biphasic pattern of toxicity in rats. Animals appeared behaviorally depressed during the first week of drug treatment and most of the animals died at this time. Depression was accompanied by weight loss, hypothermia, and bradypnea. After the first week, surviving animals became hyperactive, irritable, and aggressive, and continued to lose weight.

There are, however, few reports of death due to overdosing with cannabinoids in man. In one suicide attempt allegedly associated with cannabis, nine to ten large pipefuls of hashish and tobacco were smoked before a loss of consciousness occurred. The rareness of cannabinoid-related deaths in humans is noteworthy. The absence of such reports indicates that as far as toxicity is concerned, marihuana and its derivatives are relatively safe drugs. One estimate places the lethal oral dose in humans at about 4,000 times greater than the behaviorally active dose.

Closely related to the issue of toxicity is teratogenesis. There are clinical reports of birth defects in infants born to mothers who used marihuana during pregnancy. However, along with marihuana, these mothers also admitted to use of

LSD and probably used other drugs as well. If teratogenesis is connected with the use of marihuana during pregnancy, it has not been noticed by clinicians. This does not necessarily mean that marihuana is not a teratogen. Clinical notice of alcohol's teratogenicity occurred only in 1973 (more correctly, the rediscovery of its potential as a teratogen), and it is possible that marihuana's effects on the unborn are also awaiting discovery. There are suggestions from the animal literature, however, that marihuana does have teratogenic effects depending on dose, species, and route of administration.

Although chromosomal aberrations have been reported in heavy marihuana users, these individuals often tend to be users of other illicit drugs as well. When allowance is made for the confounding effects of multiple drug use, there is no good evidence that cannabis or its derivatives produce chromosomal damage in animals or man.

The issue of drug interactions between cannabis and other drugs is one that has received a good deal of attention, because chronic users of cannabis drugs are often polydrug users. As a result, there is the possibility of unpredictable drug interactions that could arise as a consequence of various drug combinations. The effects of alcohol, for example, have been found to be enhanced by the cannabinoids. As previously noted, there is some evidence to suggest cross tolerance between the two. Since blood alcohol levels are not affected by pretreatment with cannabinoid drugs, the cannabinoid potentiation and cross tolerance to ethanol are apparently not metabolic in origin but rather are due to changes at the level of the central nervous system.

Barbiturate action is also potentiated by the cannabinoids, although in this case the potentiation appears to be both metabolic and central in origin. The interaction between the cannabinoids and amphetamines, on the other hand, has not been clearly delineated. In some cases potentiation occurs; in other cases antagonism has been observed.

Although a great deal of effort has been directed at identifying the effects of the cannabinoids, very little is known concerning the mechanism and site of action of these compounds.

One area of research that has received a great deal of attention concerns the effects of the cannabinoids on various putative neurotransmitters. However, for the most part, these data are rather contradictory. Most studies indicate that the cannabinoids do not affect whole brain levels of serotonin in rats but do so in mice. The data with respect to localized changes is confusing. Some investigators have reported increases in serotonin content in the hypothalamus, cerebellum, and midbrain; others have reported decreases or no changes in these same areas. Similarly, there is no agreement as to the effects of the cannabinoids on the rate of turnover of serotonin in the brain.

As with serotonin, most studies of norepinephrine and dopamine levels in the rat brain indicate that the cannabinoids do not affect whole brain levels of the catecholamines. In the mouse, the data are equally divided between no changes and decreases in whole brain levels. On the other hand, there is a great deal of evidence suggesting that the cannabinoids significantly increase the rate of turnover of the catecholamines.

In contrast to the amount of attention directed at serotonin and the catecholamines, relatively little attention has been directed at acetylcholine. These data are too insufficient to discern any patterns as yet.

A second area of research concerning the mechanism of action of the cannabinoids that has begun to receive attention concerns the interaction of these compounds at the level of the cell membrane. Recent evidence suggests that cannabinoid action is related to changes that these compounds produce in cell membrane characteristics such as membrane stabilization, expansion, and disorganization. Such changes are similar to those produced by general anesthetics and by alcohol. The synergism and cross tolerance observed between the cannabinoids and alcohol is also suggestive of a common site, if not mechanism of action. However, even though they resemble the general anesthetics in their action on cell membranes, the cannabinoids are not good general anesthetics. It has been suggested that the cannabinoids cannot produce deep anesthesia because their tendency toward self-cohesion is greater than that allowing for a thorough saturation of all nerve cell membranes. As a result, they are able to depress the more vulnerable but not all nerve fibers of the brain.

PHYSIOLOGICAL EFFECTS

In general, the occasional use of cannabis has no damaging effects on the body. Although many changes do occur, rarely do they have clinical significance.

One of the most reliable physiological changes associated with cannabis use is an increase in pulse rate, which has been shown to be dose-dependent. In animals, the cannabinoids reliably cause a decrease in blood pressure and heart rate, whereas in man blood pressure and heart rate are reliably increased. However, these effects are affected by various factors, for example, posture.

Another fairly reliable effect is reddening of the eyes caused by dilation of conjunctival blood vessels. (Effects on blood vessels and blood flow in other areas of the body are less reliable.)

As far as the eye itself is concerned, cannabis has been found to cause a significant reduction in the fluid pressure within the eye (intraocular pressure), an effect that has been the subject of increasing clinical study. (*See* Therapeutic Uses.) Although a narrowing of pupil size is often reported in the annecdotal literature, laboratory studies often report the contrary effect, namely pupilary dilation.

In the lung, the most reliable acute effect of cannabis is bronchodilation, and on the basis of this effect, cannabis has been tested for its therapeutic action in asthmatics. (*See* Therapeutic Uses.) However, chronic cannabis usage has been associated with bronchoconstriction. In animals, breathing rate is reliably slowed, although this effect is not often observed in man.

Although there are some reports of liver damage in chronic cannabis users, the subjects of these reports were typically polydrug users and therefore liver damage cannot be unequivocally attributed to cannabis. Reports of hepatitis have also not been substantiated.

An increase in appetite is one of the more reliably reported effects associated with cannabis smoking in the annecdotal literature. However, this effect has not been reliably observed in laboratory studies. In animals, cannabis typically depresses food intake. No relationship between cannabis use and blood glucose levels, which could possibly underlie the changes in man or in animals, has been reported.

One area of study that has begun to attract interest is cannabis's effects on hormones, particularly testosterone. Although there is some contradictory evidence, it appears that cannabis does depress plasma testosterone levels, although the clinical significance of this effect on sexual or aggressive behavior has not been determined. In male animals, cannabis has been found to disrupt sexual activity (although this may be a result of general malaise), suppress spermatogenesis, and cause regression of Leydig cells. There are also reports in humans of gynecomastia in heavy male cannabis smokers, which may be related to suppression of testosterone.

The effects of cannabis on the pituitary-adrenal axis has also been the subject of several studies. Cannabis has been shown to increase pituitary output, as indicated by rising levels of adrenal steroids. Chronic administration of cannabis in animals also causes increases in adrenal weight.

Although much work has been directed at cannabis's effects on the immune system, the nature of this effect still awaits clarification. While chronic cannabis smokers tend to have lower thymus-dependent lymphocytes (T-cells), there is little evidence linking cannabis to susceptibility to colds, infections, and cancer, which might be expected if cannabis reduced the effectiveness of the immune system.

Perhaps the most controversial aspect of cannabis's actions on the body concerns how it affects the brain. In the early 1970s a great deal of attention was directed at a study that reported gross and irreversible brain damage for a number of chronic cannabis users in England. However, these cannabis users were also all frequent users of LSD as well as other drugs so that the observed brain damage could not be attributed unequivocally to cannabis. Subsequent studies conducted on chronic cannabis users in countries such as Jamaica give no support to the possibility of serious cannabis-related brain damage.

THERAPEUTIC USES

Cannabis is one of man's oldest medicaments. According to Chinese legend, its medicinal properties were discovered more than 2,500 years B.C., and it was part of the Chinese materia medica up to about 500 A.D. In India, its medicinal properties have been extolled for centuries by the native physicians, and it is still a widely used medicament in parts of that country.

Although some physicians in the West were knowledgeable about cannabis's use as a therapeutic agent, wide-scale attention was not drawn to the drug until the mid-1800s, when an Irish physician, Dr. William B. O'Shaughnessy, reported his experiences with the drug while he was serving as professor of chemistry at the Medical College of Calcutta. Among the conditions for which he found cannabis to be a valuable therapeutic agent were rheumatism, tetanus, epilepsy, cholera, and rabies. Although it did not cure these disorders, O'Shaughnessy found that it gave sufferers considerable relief. When O'Shaughnessy returned to England, he gave pharmacist Peter Squire a large supply of Indian cannabis to prepare for medical usage. This preparation came to be known as Squire's extract and became one of the commonest cannabis preparations among England's physicians. Soon after it became available, physicians began using it to treat a wide variety of conditions from childbirth, loss of appetite, insomnia, migraine, and excessive coughing, to alcoholism.

Despite a number of enthusiastic clinical reports, however, the drug fell into general medical disuse because of a number of difficulties physicians experienced in its usage. For one thing, the potency of the compounds available to them varied greatly. The same amount of drug at one time would have the desired effect; at another time it was too weak; and at a third time it was too strong and caused undesirable side effects. Physicians were also unhappy with the fact that the drug was not soluble in water. Therefore it had to be taken orally. In the meantime other drugs were available that were soluble in water and could therefore be administered by injection. Since these proved as useful as cannabis, there was little incentive to use the insoluble drug.

With the availability of pure cannabinoid compounds, cannabinoid derivatives have once again become the subject of medical attention. Thus far cannabis has been found to have therapeutic potential in the relief of glaucoma because of its dilating effect on blood vessels in the eye. Another condition for which cannabis has been found to have potential therapeutic value is asthma. Although other drugs exert a greater effect on bronchoconstriction, the cannabis effect is often longer lasting. Cannabis has also been used as a sedative-hypnotic, as an antiemetic, as an adjunct in the treatment of alcoholism, and in the treatment of pain associated with cancer and phantom-limb sensations.

PREVALENCE

Literally hundreds of surveys have now been conducted concerning the use of marihuana in the United States. These studies are directed at determining how much marihuana is being used, who is using it, and the correlates of drug use.

One of the grossest means used by governmental agencies to estimate usage is based upon seizures of the drug. Estimating that these confiscations represent approximately 10 percent of total drug use, a rough figure of total consumption is arrived at. However, this method is very misleading. For one thing, there is no basis for the 10 percent estimate. For another, total consumption says nothing about the frequency of use by individuals.

Surveys of actual users often specify frequency of drug usage as "ever, infrequently, occasional, casual, moderate, and heavy" within a given time and may also ask how much is used at a time. On the basis of such surveys, it is estimated that about twenty million Americans have used marihuana at least once. Among these users, about 3 percent are estimated to use marihuana daily.

For the most part, introduction to marihuana occurs during the school years. About 15 percent of the junior high school population has used marihuana at least once. By high school, almost 40 percent of the graduating class has had some experience with the drug. In college, about 50 percent of the student body has tried it at least once. The number of adults who have tried the drug at least once is estimated to be around 15 percent. However, as the high school and college population moves into the adult classification, this latter figure will obviously increase.

Studies of marihuana users suggest that boys are much more likely to have tried marihuana than girls (although this finding may reflect female reluctance to admit usage rather than actual usage). Those living in urban areas are also more likely to have tried marihuana than rural dwellers. Urban dwellers are much more likely to be heavy users than rural dwellers.

Although marihuana first came into general usage through minority-group influence, the survey evidence indicates that whites are far more likely to have tried marihuana than blacks. Among those that have experimented with marihuana, whites are also much more likely than blacks to be heavy users.

A variable closely related to marihuana usage is family income. The higher the family income, the more likely are the adolescents in that family to have tried marihuana.

Marihuana users are also much more likely to have used other drugs than nonusers. A very good indicator of marihuana use is cigarette smoking: Whereas only 10 to 25 percent of nonmarihuana users smoke, 60 to 90 percent of those using marihuana have also smoked at least once. Among heavy marihuana users, 80 to 90 percent smoke cigarettes. Marihuana users are also much more likely to have used other drugs such as LSD, heroin, barbiturates, and amphetamines.

Not surprisingly, peer group influence is an important factor affecting marihuana usage. The more often an individual uses marihuana, the more likely he (or she) is to have close friends who are also frequent users. Among adolescents, frequency of marihuana use is also positively correlated with attendance at school. About three times as many truancies occur among marihuana users as among nonusers.

In addition to peer influence, marihuana use is also related to parental drug use. Parents who smoke, drink alcohol, and/or use prescription drugs are more likely to have children who use marihuana than are parents who do not use these substances.

Political attitudes and religion are two more factors associated with marihuana use. Typically, the more politically liberal an individual, the more likely he is to have used marihuana. As far as religion is concerned, those who do not attend religious services are more likely to be marihuana users than are those who do. When religious background is considered, one generally finds more experimental and casual use among Jews.

In general, the usual reason for trying marihuana is to satisfy curiosity. Curiosity seekers continue to use marihuana for any of a number of different reasons, among which are its pleasurable and (for many) its anti-anxiety effects.

There are also many reasons users stop indulging in marihuana. Among the reasons frequently mentioned are fear of physical damage and psychological dependence.

BEHAVIORAL EFFECTS

Most people use cannabis because it gives them a feeling of well-being. It makes them relaxed and/or euphoric. However, these feelings are not always associated with the drug, and to some extent they have to be "learned." The subjective feelings accompanying cannabis usage also depend to a large extent on the user's "set"—his expectations—and the "setting" drug use occurs in.

Although used primarily because it instills a pleasurable sensation, cannabis can also induce unpleasurable sensations such as anxiety, panic, apprehension, paranoia, nausea, headache, and vomiting. In the older clinical literature these latter effects were often referred to as "poisonings." In addition to the factors of "set" and "setting," these reactions were often due to excess doses and inexperience with the effects of the drug.

General motor activity tends to decline following drug usage, although verbal activity often increases. Conversations, however, are difficult to follow by people who are not under the drug influence, although those who are often claim to derive great insight from what others say. Speech itself is often slurred and rapid.

In some cases motor activity increases. Users become restless and begin moving about. Muscles may jerk involuntarily. This increased motor activity may have been the basis for the expression "running amok," which was often associated with the older clinical literature from the East Indies. Accompanying the effects on motor activity are a loss of coordination, loss of manual dexterity, and an increase in reaction time. The more complex the task, the greater the impairment.

Related to the general lethargy and various motor effects is an alleged lack of interest in work, referred to as the "amotivational syndrome." However, studies from countries such as Jamaica, where cannabis is used on a daily basis, do not support the notion that cannabis reduces work output.

Numerous changes in perception are reported to occur in connection with cannabis use. The most commonly mentioned of these changes is a distortion of time. In most cases, time sense seems to slow down so that individuals underestimate actual clock time. However, the opposite also occurs in some individuals so that instead of slowing down, time seems to go faster.

Visual perceptual changes are also commonly linked with cannabis use, especially color perception, which is often reported to increase in vividness. Hearing is often said to increase in acuity, although laboratory studies do not bear this out.

Given cannabis's effects on psychomotor activity and perception, it is not surprising that driving skills have been found to be significantly impaired after smoking cannabis. Although users usually admit that their driving performance is adversely affected, many believe that they can compensate for cannabis's effects on driving skills by driving at slower speeds and with greater caution. Because of this belief, users often admit driving while still under the influence of the drug. With the general trend toward decriminalization of cannabis use, it is not unrealistic to anticipate an increase in marihuana-related traffic accidents.

In the past, a great deal has been written about cannabis's alleged aphrodisiac properties. Many contemporary users also claim that cannabis either increases their desire for sex or increases the pleasures of sexual behavior. Sexual dysfunction, however, is often reported in chronic users or users of large doses. As far as the enhancement of sexuality is concerned, this effect is likely only in the case of small doses and is probably the result of increased relaxation, altered time perception, and diminished inhibitions, rather than some direct action on the libido.

In recent years the effects of cannabis on memory have been the subject of increasing attention. In general, these studies indicate that cannabis has a negligible effect on information already stored in memory (long-term memory). Short-term memory, on the other hand, is significantly incapacitated. As a result, information does not become permanently stored. The effects on short-term memory are more pronounced the more difficult the task. Several hypotheses have been advanced to account for the effects on short-term memory. On a behavioral level, individuals may simply not be concentrating on material to be learned or may be unable to concentrate because of the intrusion of extraneous information not pertinent to the problem. Motivation may be reduced, although this possibility has not received experimental support. On the physiological level, cannabis may affect memory by influencing neural processes—amine production or protein synthesis—connected with the processing and storage of information.

Considerable attention has also been directed at cannabis's effects on aggressive behavior. The drug's alleged propensity for increasing such behavior was based in large part on the long-discredited story of the Assassins' use of hashish to fortify themselves prior to their terrorist activities. This alleged relationship served as the basis for the many anticannabis laws passed in the United States and other countries. The available evidence indicates, however, that with the exception of certain individuals already predisposed toward violence, cannabis has a tranquilizing rather than stimulating action on aggression.

As far as criminality is concerned, there is little evidence to indicate that cannabis in any way provokes criminal behavior. Studies that purport to show such a relationship have typically been found to be biased and unacceptable by contemporary standards of scientific rigor and evaluation.

PSYCHIATRIC CONSIDERATIONS

Although there are numerous reports of psychiatric illnesses associated with cannabis use, many of these reports come from nonwestern countries where malnutrition and various unfavorable environmental factors undoubtedly contribute to the incidence of psychopathology. Nevertheless, there is some indication that in certain individuals cannabis may precipitate psychiatric illness, although it may not be a unique drug in this respect.

By far the most common adverse response to cannabis is acute panic. Disorientation, depersonalization, confusion, and loss of control sometimes occur in naive users or following large doses causing the individual to feel intense panic and anxiety. These effects disappear as the drug is eliminated from the body and can also be assuaged through assurance from other more experienced individuals.

A number of users also experience feelings of paranoia on occasion. Quite often, this response is a reaction to the fear of discovery by police.

Although psychosis has been attributed to chronic cannabis use in many eastern and middle-eastern countries, several recent studies have not corroborated this finding and it is likely that factors in addition to, or other than, cannabis are involved in the reports of cannabis-precipitated psychosis.

NOTES

1. Indian Hemp Drugs Commission, *Report* (London: Government Printing Office, 1893-1894).

2. In D. Ebin, *The Drug Experience* (New York: Grove Press, 1965), p. 103.

3. In W. D. Drake, *The Connoisseur's Handbook of Marihuana* (New York: Straight Arrow Press, 1970), pp. 69-70.

4. H. J. Anslinger and C. R. Cooper, "Marihuana, assassin of youth," *American Magazine* 124 (1937), p. 18.

5. In L. Grinspoon, *Marihuana Reconsidered* (Cambridge, Mass.: Harvard University Press, 1971), p. 64.

6. In R. J. Bonnie and C. H. Whitebread, *The Marihuana Conviction: A History of Marihuana Prohibition in the U. S.* (Charlottesville, Va.: University of Virginia Press, 1974), p. 38.

ABBREVIATIONS OF JOURNALS CITED

A. B. A. J.	American Bar Association Journal
Abs. Criminol. Penol.	Abstracts of Criminology and Penology
Accid. Anal. Prevent.	Accident Analysis and Prevention
Act. Chem. Scand.	Acta Chemica Scandinavica
Act. Criminol.	Acta Criminologica
Act. Endocrinol.	Acta Endocrinologica
Act. Fac. Rerum Nat. Univ. Comen. Bot.	Acta Facultatis Rerum Naturalium Universitis Comenianae Botanica
Act. Lus.-Espagnol. Neurol. Psiquiat.	Actas Lus-Espagnoloas de Neurologia y Psiquiatria
Act. Med. Turc.	Acta Medica Turcica
Act. Nerv. Super.	Activitas Nervosa Superior
Act. Paedopsychiat.	Acta Paedopsychiatrica
Act. Pharmaceut. Suecica	Acta Pharmaceutica Suecica
Act. Pharmacol. Toxicol.	Acta Pharmacologica et Toxicologica
Act. Physiol. Acad. Sci. Hung.	Acta Physiologica Academiae Scientiarum Hungaricae
Act. Physiol. Lat. Amer.	Acta Physiologica Latino Americana
Act. Psiquiat. Psicol. Am. Lat.	Acta Psiquiatrica y Psicologica de America Latina
Act. Psychiat. Scand.	Acta Psychiatrica Scandinavica
Act. Univ. Palachi Olumuc. Fac. Med.	Acta Universitatis Palachi Olumucensis
Addict.	Addictions
Adv. Chromatog.	Advances in Chromatography
Adv. Expt'l. Med. Biol.	Advances in Experimental Medicine and Biology
Adv. Pharmacol.	Advances in Pharmacology
Advert. Age	Advertising Age
Aggressive Behav.	Aggressive Behavior

Agric. J. India	Indian Journal of Agriculture
Agricult. Biol. Chem.	Agricultural and Biological Chemistry
Agricult. Hist.	Agricultural History
Agrobiol.	Agrobiologiya
Agron. J.	Agronomy Journal
Alaska Med.	Alaska Medicine
Alberta J. Educat. Res.	Alberta Journal of Educational Research
Allahabad.	Allahabad University Studies
Alien. Neurol.	Alienist and Neurologist
Allgem. Med. Cent. Zeit.	Allgemeine Medizinische Central Zeitung
Allgem. Zeit. Psychiat.	Allgemeine Zeitschrift fur Psychiatrie
All. Zeit. Psychiol. Psych-gericht.	Allgemeine Zeitschrift fur Psychiatrie und Psychische-gerichtlische Medicine
Am. Crim. Law Quart.	American Criminal Law Quarterly
Am. Drug.	American Druggist
Am. Drug. Merch.	American Druggist Merchandising
Am. Fam. Phys./GP	American Family Physician/GP
Am. Heart J.	American Heart Journal
Am. J. Bot.	American Journal of Botany
Am. J. Clin. Hypnosis	American Journal of Clinical Hypnosis
Am. J. Clin. Med.	American Journal of Clinical Medicine
Am. J. Clin. Pathol.	American Journal of Clinical Pathology
Am. J. Drug Alcohol Abuse	American Journal of Drug and Alcohol Abuse
Am. J. Insan.	American Journal of Insanity
Am. J. Med.	American Journal of Medicine
Am. J. Med. Sci.	American Journal of the Medical Sciences
Am. J. Nurs.	American Journal of Nursing
Am. J. Obstet. Gynecol.	American Journal of Obstetrics and Gynecology
Am. J. Opthalmol.	American Journal of Opthalmology
Am. J. Optom. Physiol. Optics	American Journal of Optometry and Physiological Optics
Am. J. Orthopsychiat.	American Journal of Orthopsychiatry
Am. J. Pharmaceut. Educat.	American Journal of Pharmaceutical Education

Am. J. Pharmacol.	American Journal of Pharmacology
Am. J. Pol. Sci.	American Journal of Police Science
Am. J. Psychiat.	American Journal of Psychiatry
Am. J. Psychoanal.	American Journal of Psychoanalysis
Am. J. Pub. Hlth.	American Journal of Public Health
Am. J. Sociol.	American Journal of Sociology
Am. Legion	American Legion
Am. Mercury	American Mercury
Am. Polit. J.	American Political Journal
Am. Pol. Sci. Rev.	American Political Science Review
Am. Practition.	American Practitioner
Am. Rev. Respirat. Dis.	American Review of Respiratory Disease
Am. Sociol. Rev.	American Sociological Review
Am. Speech	American Speech
Amer. Hist. Illus.	American History Illustrated
Amer. Mag.	American Magazine
Amer. Schol.	American Scholar
An. Acad. Brazil. Cienc.	Anais da Academia Brazileira de Ciencias
An. Acad. Med. Stetin.	Annales Academiae Medicae Stetinensis
An. Fac. Farm. Univ. Recife	Anais da Faculdada de Farmacia da Universidada do Recife
An. Fac. Quim. Farm.	Anales de la Facultad de Quimica y Farmacia
An. Paul. Med. Ciurg.	Anais Paulistas de Medicina e Ciurgia
Anat. Anz.	Anatomischer Anzeiger
Anesth. Analges.	Anesthesia and Analgesia
Ang. Bot.	Angewandte Botanik
Ang. Chem.	Angewandte Chemie
Ann. Am. Acad. Pol. Soc. Sci.	Annals of the American Academy of Political and Social Science
Ann. Amelior. Plant.	Annales de l'Amelioration des Plantes
Ann. Biol. Clin.	Annales de Biologie Clinique
Ann. Bot.	Annals of Botany
Ann. Chim. Appl.	Annales de Chimie
Ann. Epiphyt.	Annales des Epiphyties
Ann. Fac. Med. Pharm. Beyrouth	Annales de la Faculté de Pharmacie de Beyrouth
Ann. Falsif. Fraudes	Annales des Falsifications et des Fraudes
Ann. Fals. Expert. Chim.	Annales des Falsifications et de l'Expertise Chimique

Ann. Geog.	Annales de Geographie
Ann. Int. Med.	Annals of Internal Medicine
Ann. Med. Psychol.	Annales Medico-Psychologiques
Ann. Med. Leg. Criminol.	Annales de Medecine Legale
Ann. N. Y. Acad. Sci.	Annals of the New York Academy of Sciences
Ann. Pharmaceut. Fran.	Annales Pharmaceutiques Francaises
Ann. Physiol. Veget.	Annales de Physiologie Vegetale
Ann. Rev. Med.	Annual Review of Medicine
Ann. Rev. Pharmacol.	Annual Review of Pharmacology and Toxicology
Ann. Sc. Nat.	Annales des Sciences Naturelles
Ann. Soc. Bot. Lyon	Annales de la Societe Botanique de Lyon
Ann. Tec. Agr.	Annales de Technologie Agricole
Ann. Therapeut. Mat. Med.	Annuaire de Therapeutique et de Materia Medicale
Ann. Univ. Mariae Curie-Skold.	Annales Universitatis Mariae Curie Sklodowska
Ann. Univ. Madagascar	Annales Universitatis Madagascar
Ant. Med.	Antioquia Medica
Apoth.-Ztg.	Apotheker-Zeitung
Appl. Ther.	Applied Therapeutics
Arbeit. Pharmazeut. Inst. Univ. Berlin	Arbeitsgemeinschaft fuer Pharmazeutische Verfarhrenstednik
Arch. Belg. Med. Soc.	Archives Belges de Medecine Sociale, Hygiene, Medecine du Travail
Arch. Biochem. Biophys.	Archives of Biochemistry and Biophysics
Arch. Biol. Med.	Archivos de Biologia y Medicina Experimentales
Arch. Exper. Pathol. Pharmakol.	Archiv fuer Experimentelle Pathologie und Pharmakologie
Arch. Fac. Med. Madrid	Archivos de la Facultad de Medicina de Madrid
Arch. Farmacol. Sperim.	Archivio di Farmacologia Sperimentale e Scienze Affini
Arch. Gen. Med.	Archives Generales de Medicine
Arch. Gen. Psychiat.	Archives of General Psychiatry
Arch. Inst. Pasteur Tunis	Archives de l'Institut Pasteur de Tunis
Arch. It. Sci. Farmacol.	Archivio Italiano di Scienze Farmacologiche

Arch. Internat'l. Pharmacodyn. Ther.	Archives Internationales de Pharmacodynamie et de Therapie
Arch. Kriminol.	Archiv fur Kriminologie
Arch. Mal Coeur	Archives des Maladies du Coeur et des Vaisseaux
Arch. Otolaryng.	Archives of Otolaryngology
Arch. Pharm. Ber. Deut. Pharm.	Archiv der Pharmazie und Berichte der Deutshen Pharmazeutischer Gesellschaft
Arch. Psychiat. Nerven.	Archiv fur Psychiatrie und Nervenkrankheiten
Arch. Schiffs Tropenhyg.	Archiv fur Schiffs und Tropenhygiens
Arch. Toxicol.	Archives of Toxicology
Archiv. Environ. Health	Archives of Environmental Health
Archiv. Psychiat. Zeit.	Archiv fur Psychiatrie und Nervenkrankheiten, Vereinigt mit Zeitschrift fur die Gesamte Neurologie und Psychiatrie
Arkansas Law Rev.	Arkansas Law Review
Arquiv. Assist. Psicopat.	Arquivos da Assistencia a Psicopatas de Pernambuco
Arquiv. Hig.	Arquivos de Higiene e Saude Publica
Arquiv. Manicom Judic.	Arquivos do Manicomio Judicario Heitor Carrilho
Arquiv. Pol. Sao Paulo	Arquivos de Policia Civil de Sao Paulo
Arzneim-Forsch.	Arzneimittel-Forschung
Arzt. Rund.	Arztliche Rundschau
Assoc. Physicians	Association of Physicians of India
Asthma Res.	Asthma Research
At. Inst. Bot Univers. Pavia	Atti Istituto Botanico della Universita Pavia
At. Soc. Natural Matemat. Modina	Atti della Societa Dei Naturalisti e Matematici di Modina
At. Soc. Pelo. Sci. Fis. Mat. Nat.	Atti della Societa Peloritana di Scienze Fisiche, Matematiche Naturali
Atlantic Mon.	Atlantic Monthly
At. Soc. Pelo. Sci. Fis. Mat. Nat.	Atti della Societa Peloritana di Scienze Fisiche Matematiche e Naturali
Aust. J. Forens. Sci.	Australian Journal of Forensic Sciences

Aust. J. Pharmaceut. Sci.	Australian Journal of Pharmaceutical Sciences
Aust. J. Soc. Is.	Australian Journal of Social Issues
Aust. N.Z. J. Criminol.	Australian and New Zealand Journal of Criminology
Aviat. Space Environ. Med.	Aviation, Space and Environmental Medicine
Bangladesh Pharm. J.	Bangladesh Pharmaceutical Journal
Behav. Neuropsychiat.	Behavioral Neuropsychiatry
Behav. Biol.	Behavioral Biology
Beitr. Gericht. Med.	Beitraege zur Gerichtlichen Medizin
Belg. Tid. Geneesk.	Belgisch Tidschrift voor Geneeskunde
Bericht. Deut. Bot. Gesell.	Bericht der Deutschen Botanishen Gesellschaft
Berlin Klin. Woch.	Berliner Klinische Wochenscrift
Biochem. Med.	Biochemical Medicine
Biochem. Pharmacol.	Biochemical Pharmacology
Biochim. Biophys.	Biochimica et Biophysica Acta
Biokhim. Mikrob.	Biokhimia Mikrobiologia
Biol. Plant.	Biologia Plantarum
Biol. Zent.	Biologisches Zentralblatt
Biol. Psychiat.	Biological Psychiatry
Biomed. Mass Spectrom.	Biomedical Mass Spectrometry
Bioquim. Clin.	Bioquimica Clinica
Biul. Inst. Ros. Lecz.	Biuletyn Instytuta Rosln Leczniczych
Blackwood's Mag.	Blackwood's Magazine
Bol. Agric. Pecur.	Boletim de Agricola i Pecurario
Bol. Chim. Farm.	Bollettino Chimico Farmaceutico
Bol. Inst. Catal. Hist. Nat.	Boletin de la Institucion Catalana de Historia Natural
Bol. Of. Sanit. Pan Am.	Boletin de la Oficina Sanitaria PanAmericana
Bol. Orto Bot. Realle Univ. Napoli	Bolletino dell'orto Botanico della Realle Universita di Napoli
Bol. Soc. Ital. Biol. Sper.	Bollettino della Societa Italiana di Biologica Sperimentale
Bost. Med. Surg. J.	Boston Medical and Surgical Journal
Bot. Gaz.	Botanical Gazette
Bot. Mus. Harv.	Botanical Museum Leaflets (Harvard)
Bot. Zh.	Botanicheskii Zhurnal
Brain Res.	Brain Research
Brain Res. Bull.	Brain Research Bulletin
Br. Columb. Med. J.	British Columbia Medical Journal

Br. J. Addict.	British Journal of Addiction
Br. J. Clin. Practice	British Journal of Clinical Practice
Br. J. Criminol.	British Journal of Criminology
Br. J. Indust. Med.	British Journal of Industrial Medicine
Br. J. Inebriety	British Journal of Inebriety
Br. J. Pharmacol.	British Journal of Pharmacology
Br. J. Social Psychiat.	British Journal of Social Psychiatry
Br. J. Sociol.	British Journal of Sociology
Br. J. Vener. Dis.	British Journal of Venereal Diseases
Br. Med. J.	British Medical Journal
Br. Quart. Rev.	British Quarterly Review
Brazil-Med.	Brazil-Medico
Brux.-Med.	Bruxelles-Medical
Buffalo Med. J.	Buffalo Medical Journal
Bull. Acad. Nation. Med.	Bulletin de l'Acadamie Nationale de Medecine
Bull. Acad. Roy. Med.	Bulletin de l'Academie Royale de Medicine de Belgique
Bull. Agricult. Chem. Soc. Jap.	Bulletin of the Agricultural Chemical Society of Japan
Bull. Am. Pharmaceut. Assoc.	Bulletin of the American Pharmaceutical Association
Bull. Appl. Bot. Plant. Breed.	Bulletin of Applied Botany, of Genetics and Plant Breeding
Bull. Bur. Crim. Invest.	Bulletin of the Bureau of Criminal Investigation
Bull. Econ. Indochine	Bulletin Economique de l'Indo-Chine
Bull. Gen. Ther.	Bulletin General de Therapeutics
Bull. Geol. Soc. China	Bulletin of the Geological Society of China
Bull. Hist. Med.	Bulletin of the History of Medicine
Bull. Los Angeles County Med. Assoc.	Bulletin of the Los Angeles County Medical Association
Bull. Mem. Soc. Ther.	Bulletin et Memoires de la Societé de Therapeutique
Bull. Menninger Clin.	Bulletin of the Menninger Clinic
Bull. Narc.	Bulletin on Narcotics
Bull. Nat'l. Hyg. Sci.	Bulletin of National Institute of Hygienic Sciences
Bull. Needle Bobbin Club	Bulletin of the Needle and Bobbin Club
Bull. N.Y. Acad. Med.	Bulletin of the New York Academy of Medicine

Bull. N.Y. Acad. Sci.	Bulletin of the New York Academy of Sciences
Bull. Psychol.	Bulletin de Psychologie
Bull. Schweiz. Akad. Med. Wissen.	Bulletin der Schweizerischen Akademie der Medizinishen Wissenschaften
Bull. Sci. Med.	Bulletin des Sciences Medicales
Bull. Sci. Pharmacol.	Bulletin des Sciences Pharmacologiques
Bull. Soc. Bot.	Bulletin de la Societé Botanique de France
Bull. Soc. Clin. Ment.	Bulletin de la Societé Clinique de Medecine Mentale
Bull. Soc. Pathol. Exot.	Bulletin de la Societé de Pathologie Exotique
Bull. Soc. Roy. Botan. Belg.	Bulletin de la Societé Royale de Botanique de Belgique
Bull. Soc. Prof. Invest.	Bulletin of the Society of Professional Investigators
Bull. Torrey Bot. Club	Bulletin of the Torrey Botanical Club
Bull. Trav. Soc. Pharm.	Bulletin des Travaux de la Societé de Pharmacie de Bordeaux
C. R. Acad. Sci.	Comptes Rendus des Seances de la Societé de Biologie et de Ses Filiales
Cah. Etude Africa	Cahiers d'Etudes Africaines
Cah. Psychol.	Cahiers de Psychologie
Cairo Sci. J.	Cairo Scientific Journal
Cal. Hlth.	California's Health
Cal. Clin.	California Clinician
Cal. Law Rev.	California Law Review
Cal. S. B. J.	California State Bar Journal
Calcutta Rev.	Calcutta Review
Can. Bar J.	Canadian Bar Journal
Can. J. Behav. Sci.	Canadian Journal of Behavioral Sciences
Can. J. Biochem.	Canadian Journal of Biochemistry
Can. J. Chem.	Canadian Journal of Chemistry
Can. J. Correct.	Canadian Journal of Corrections
Can. J. Criminol.	Canadian Journal of Criminology and Corrections
Can. J. Otolaryng.	Canadian Journal of Otolaryngology

Can. J. Pharmaceut. Sci.	Canadian Journal of Pharmaceutical Sciences
Can. J. Physiol. Pharmacol.	Canadian Journal of Physiology and Pharmacology
Can. J. Pub. Hlth.	Canadian Journal of Public Health
Can. Med. Assoc. J.	Canadian Medical Association Journal
Can. Med. Rec.	Canadian Medical Record
Can. Ment. Hlth.	Canada's Mental Health
Can. Psychol. Assoc. J.	Canadian Psychiatric Association Journal
Can. Practitioner	Canadian Practitioner
Can. Wel.	Canadian Welfare
Cancer Res.	Cancer Research
Carbohyd. Res.	Carbohydrate Research
Caryol.	Caryologia
Cas. Lek. Cesk.	Casopis Lekaru Ceskych
Cath. Sch. J.	Catholic School Journal
Cath. U. Law Rev.	Catholic University Law Review
Cat. Select. Doc. Psychol.	Catalogue of Select Documents in Psychology
Cent. Af. J. Med.	Central Africa Journal of Medicine
Cent. Med. Pharmaceut.	Centre Medicale et Pharmaceutique
Cesk. Stomat.	Ceskoslovenska Stomata
Ceylon Med. J.	Ceylon Medical Journal
Chamber's Edin. J.	Chamber's Edinburgh Journal
Chem. Abs.	Chemical Abstracts
Chem. Brit.	Chemistry in Britain
Chem-Biol. Interact.	Chemical-Biological Interactions
Chem. Commun.	Chemical Communications
Chem. Engin. News	Chemical and Engineering News
Chem. Indust.	Chemical Industries
Chem. News J. Phys. Sci.	Chemical News and Journal of Physical Science
Chem. Pharmaceut. Bull.	Chemical and Pharmaceutical Bulletin
Chem. Zent.	Chemisches Zentralblatt
Chicago Med. Times	Chicago Medical Times
Chim.	Chimia
Chitty's Law Rev. J.	Chitty's Law Review Journal
Christ. Cent.	Christian Century
Chromatog.	Chromatographia
Chron. High. Educat.	Chronicle of Higher Education
Chron. Med.	Chronique Medicale

Chron. Pharmaceut.	Chronique Pharmaceutique
Ciba Found. Sympos.	Ciba Foundation Symposium
CIBA Rev.	CIBA Review
Cience Cult.	Ciencia e Cultura
Civil Lib. Rev.	Civil Liberties Review
Clin. Chim. Act.	Clinical Chimica Acta
Clin. Ped.	Clinical Pediatrics
Clin. Proc. Child. Hosp.	Clinical Proceedings of the Children's Hospital
Clin. Res.	Clinical Research
Clin. Sketch.	Clinical Sketches
Clin. Toxicol.	Clinical Toxicology
Coll. Internat'l. Neuropsychopharmacol.	Collegium International Neuropsychopharmacologia
Coll. Stud. J.	College Student Journal
Coll. Stud. Surv.	College Student Survey
Columb. For.	Columbia Forum
Columbia J. Transnat'l. Law	Columbia Journal of Transnational Law
Com. Nac. Fiscal. Entor.	Comissao Nacional de Fiscalizacao de Entorpecentes
Comm. Behav. Biol.	Communications in Behavioral Biology
Comm. Ment. Hlth. J.	Community Mental Health Journal
Comm. Prob. Drug Depend.	Committee on Problems of Drug Dependence
Comp. Psychiat.	Comprehensive Psychiatry
Comp. Rend. Cong. Internat'l. Pharm.	Comptes Rendus du Congrès International de Pharmacie
Concours Med.	Concours Medical
Cong. Quart. Wkly. Rep.	Congressional Quarterly Weekly Report
Congress. Dig.	Congressional Digest
Conn. Law Rev.	Connecticut Law Review
Conn. Med.	Connecticut Medicine
Consum. Rep.	Consumer Reports
Contemp. Drug Prob.	Contemporary Drug Problems
Correct. Proc.	Correctional Process
Correct. Psychol. J. Soc. Ther.	Corrective Psychiatry and Journal of Social Therapy
Crime Delinquen.	Crime and Delinquency
Crime Law Bull.	Criminal Law Bulletin
Crime Law Quart.	Criminal Law Quarterly

Crime Punish. Correct.	Crime, Punishment and Corrections
Criminol.	Criminology
Cur. Med. Drugs	Current Medicine and Drugs
Cur. Ther. Res.	Current Therapeutic Research
Cur. Sci.	Current Science
Dan. Tid. Farm.	Dansk Tidsskriftfortegnelse
Danish Med. Bull.	Danish Medical Bulletin
Delinq. Soc.	Delinquency and Society
Del. State Med. J.	Delaware State Medical Journal
De Paul Law Rev.	De Paul Law Review
Der Zucht.	Der Zuchter
Deut. Apoth.	Deutsche Apotheker-Zeitung
Deut. Arzt	Deutsche Arzt
Deut. Bot. Ges.	Deutsche Botanische Gesellschaft
Deut. Med. J.	Deutsche Medizisches Journal
Deut. Med. Woch.	Deutsche Medizisches Wochenschrift
Deut. Milit.	Deutsche Militararzt
Deut. Zahnaerztl.	Deutsche Zahnaerzliche Zeitschrift
Die Pharm.	Die Pharmazie
Dis. Nerv. Syst.	Diseases of the Nervous System
Diss. Abs.	Dissertation Abstracts
Diss. Pharm. Pharmacol.	Dissertationes Pharmaceuticae et Pharmacologicae
Doklady Akad. Nauk. Azerbaidzhan	Doklady Akademii Nauk Azerbaidzhan
Dok. Soob. Uzhgor Gosud.	Doklady I Soobshcheniya Uzhgorodskogo Gosudarstvennogo
Dok. Vses. Akad. Sel'sk. Nauk Lenin.	Doklady Vsesoyuznol Akademie Sel'skokhoyyaistvennykh Nauk Imeni V I Lenina
Downstate Med. Ctr.	Downstate Medical Center Report
Drug. Circ.	Druggist's Circular
Drug Cosmet. Indust.	Drug and Cosmetic Industry
Drug Enforce.	Drug Enforcement
Drug For.	Drug Forum
Drug Metabol. Disposit.	Drug Metabolism and Disposition
Drug Res. J.	Drug Research Journal
Drug Soc.	Drugs and Society
Drug. Ther. Bull.	Drug and Therapeutic Bulletin
Duke Law Rev.	Duke Law Review
E. Af. J. Pharmacol. Pharmaceut. Sci.	East African Journal of Pharmacology and Pharmaceutical Science
E. Af. Med. J.	East African Medical Journal

Econ. Bot.	Economic Botany
Econ. Geog.	Economic Geography
Edinburgh Med. J.	Edinburgh Medical Journal
Educat. Rec.	Educational Record
Ed. Res. Rep.	Educational Research Reports
EEG Clin. Neurophysiol.	Electroencephalography and Clinical Neurophysiology
Eisei Kag.	Eisei Kagaku
Elelmis Kozlem	Elelmis Zerhizsgalati Kozlemenyek
Elemez.Ip.	Elelmezesi Ipar
Emerg. Med.	Emergency Medicine
Endocrinol.	Endocrinology
Endocrinol. Exper.	Endocrinologia Expermentatis
Ergeb. Physiol. Biol. Chem. Exper. Pharmakol.	Ergebnisse der Physiologie, Biologishen Chemie und Experimentellen Pharmakologie
Eur. J. Cardiol.	European Journal of Cardiology
Eur. J. Toxicol.	European Journal of Toxicology
Evergreen Rev.	Evergreen Review
Evol. Ther. Medicochirug.	Evolution Therapeutique Medico-chirurgicale
Exper.	Experientia
Expt'l. Eye Res.	Experimental Eye Research
Expt'l. Neurol.	Experimental Neurology
Fam. Hlth.	Family Health
Far East. Assoc. Trop. Med.	Far Eastern Association of Tropical Medicine
Farm.	Farmaco
Farm. Chil.	Farmacia Chilena
Farm. Ed. Sci.	Farmaco Edizione Scientifica
Farm. Glasnik	Farmaceutski Glasnik
Farm. Vest.	Farmaceutski Vestnik
Farmaceut. Tid.	Farmaceutski Tidende
Farmikol. Toksikol.	Farmakologiya i Toksikologiya
Farmer's Bull.	Farmer's Bulletin
Farmer's Week.	Farmer's Weekly
Faserforsch.	Faserforschung und Textilechnik
F.B.I. Law Enforce. Bull.	F.B.I. Law Enforcement Bulletin
Febs. Let.	Febs Letters
Fed. Bar J.	Federal Bar Journal
Fed. Proc.	Federation Proceedings
Fertil. Steril.	Fertility and Sterility

First Cong. Panam. Legal-med. Crim.	First Congress PanAmericana da Legal-medicina y Criminologia
First Lat. Am. Cong. Psycho-biol.	First Latin American Congress of Psychobiology
Fiz. Rast. Akad. Nauk.	Fiziologiya Rastenii Akademiya Nauk
Florida J. Educat. Res.	Florida Journal of Educational Research
Fog. Med.	Foglia Medica
Fol. Pharmacol. Jap.	Folia Pharmacologica Japanica
Foreign Psychiat.	Foreign Psychiatry
Forshung.	Forshungsberichte des Wirtschafts und Venkehrministeriums
Fortsch. Chem. Organ. Natur.	Fortschritte der Chemie Organischer Naturstoffe
Fortsch. Med.	Fortschritte der Medizin
Front. Hosp. Psychiat.	Frontiers of Hospital Psychiatry
Frat. Ord. Pol. J.	Fraternal Order of Police Journal
Gac. Med. Mex.	Gaceta Medica de Mexico
Gaz. Chim. Ital.	Gazzetta Chimica Italiana
Gaz. Hop. Civil. Milit.	Gazette des Hopitaux Civils et Militaires de l'Empire Ottoman
Gaz. Med. Lombard.	Gazzetta Medica di Lombardia
Gaz. Nat. Moniteur Univ.	Gazette Nationale; ou le Moniteur Universel
Genet. Iber.	Genetica Iberica
Genet. Ned. Tijd. Afstammings.	Genetica; Nederlandsch Tijdschrift voor Erfeliskheids en Afstammingsleer
Gen. Practition.	General Practitioner
Genet. Psychol. Monog.	Genetic Psychology Monographs
Georgia Law Rev.	Georgia Law Review
Georgia State Bar J.	Georgia State Bar Journal
Ger. Med.	German Medicine
Gigiena Sanitar.	Gigiena i Sanitariia
Giorn. Farm. Chem. Sci. Affin.	Giornale di Farmacia di Chemica e di Science Affini
Good House.	Good Housekeeping
Gov't. Exec.	Government Executive
Greenhouse—Garden Grass	Greenhouse—Garden Grass
Guys Hosp. Gaz.	Guy's Hospital Gazette
Harper's Baz.	Harper's Bazaar
Harper's New Month. Mag.	Harper's New Monthly Magazine

Hast. Law J.	Hastings Law Journal
Hawaii Med. J.	Hawaii Medical Journal
Hearst's Internat'l. Cosmopol.	Hearst's International Cosmopolitan
Hefter's Hdbh. Expt'l. Pharmakol.	Hefter's Handbuch Der Experimentellen Pharmakologie
Heil.-Gewurz.	Heil.-und Gewurzpflanzen
Helv. Chim. Act.	Helvetica Chimica Acta
Hlth. Officer	Health Officer
Hokkaid. Eisei Kenkyush.	Hokkaidoritsu Eisei Kenkyusho-ito
Hosp. Phys.	Hospital Physician
Houston Law Rev.	Houston Law Review
Howard Law J.	Howard Law Journal
Human Behav.	Human Behavior
Human Fact.	Human Factors
Human Relat.	Human Relations
Hyg. Med. Pharmaceut. Manad.	Hygiea, Medicensk Och Pharmaceutisk Manadskrift
Hyg. Ment.	Hygiene Mentale au Canada
Il Farm. Scienz. Tecn.	Il Farmaco Scienza e Tecnica
Ill. Med. J.	Illinois Medical Journal
Illus. Rund. Gendarm.	Illustrierte Rundschau der Gendarmerie
Imprensa Med.	Imprensa Medica
Improv. Coll. Univ. Teach.	Improving College and University Teaching
Ind. Hist. Quart.	Indian Historical Quarterly
Ind. J. Appl. Chem.	Indian Journal of Applied Chemistry
Ind. J. Biochem. Biophys.	Indian Journal of Biochemistry and Biophysics
Ind. J. Chem.	Indian Journal of Chemistry
Ind. J. Med. Res.	Indian Journal of Medical Research
Ind. J. Pharm.	Indian Journal of Pharmacy
Ind. Med. Gaz.	Indian Medical Gazette
Ind. Med. Rec.	Indian Medical Record
Indust. Engin. Chem.	Industrial and Engineering Chemistry
Ind. Soap. J.	Indian Soap Journal
Indust. Med.	Industrial Medicine and Surgery
Inst. Cercet. Pentic. Cereal Plant.	Institutul de Cercetari Pentru Cereale Plante Technice
Internat'l. J. Addict.	International Journal of the Addictions
Internat'l. J. Clin. Expt'l. Hypnosis	International Journal of Clinical and Experimental Hypnosis

Internat'l. J. Clin. Pharmacol.	International Journal of Clinical Pharmacology and Biopharmacy
Internat'l. J. Soc. Psychiat.	International Journal of Social Psychology
Internat'l. Med. Dig.	International Medical Digest
Internat'l. Pharmacopsychiat.	International Pharmacopsychiatry
Internat'l. Rev. Neurobiol.	International Review of Neurobiology
Iowa Med. J.	Iowa Medical Journal
Iowa State Coll. J. Sci.	Iowa State College Journal of Science
Irish Phys. Surg.	Irish College of Physicians and Surgeons Journal
Isr. J. Chem.	Israel Journal of Chemistry
Israel Ann. Psychiat.	Israel Annals of Psychiatry
Israel J. Med. Sci.	Israel Journal of Medical Sciences
Iss. Criminol.	Issues in Criminology
Jahr. Prak. Pharm.	Jahrbuch der Praktischen Pharmacie
Jamaic. Pub. Hlth.	Jamaican Public Health
Jap. J. Genet.	Japanese Journal of Genetics
J.A.M.A.	Journal of the American Medical Association
J. Am. Chem. Soc.	Journal of the American Chemical Society
J.A.P.A.	Journal of the American Pharmaceutical Association
J. Abn. Psychol.	Journal of Abnormal Psychology
J. Abn. Soc. Psychol.	Journal of Abnormal and Social Psychology
J. Agric. Food. Chem.	Journal of Agricultural and Food Chemistry
J. Agricult. Res.	Journal of Agricultural Research
J. Alcohol Educat.	Journal of Alcohol Education
J. Allergy Clin. Immunol	Journal of Allergy and Clinical Immunology
J. Am. Acad. Child Psychiat.	Journal of the American Academy of Child Psychiatry
J. Am. Acad. Psychiat. Neurol	Journal of the American Academy of Psychiatry and Neurology
J. Am. Coll. Hlth Assoc.	Journal of the American College Health Association
J. Am. Optom. Assoc.	Journal of the American Optometric Association

J. Am. Osteopath. Assoc.	Journal of the American Osteopathic Association
J. Am. Psychoanal. Assoc.	Journal of the American Psycho-analytical Association
J. Am. Soc. Agron.	Journal of the American Society of Agronomy
J. Am. Vet. Med. Assoc.	Journal of the American Veterinary Medical Association
J. Anesthesiol.	Journal of Anesthesiology
J. Appl. Psychol.	Journal of Applied Psychology
J. Arnold Arbor.	Journal of the Arnold Arboretum
J. Asian Af. Stud.	Journal of Asian and African Studies
J. Assoc. Off. Agricult. Chem.	Journal of the Association of Official Agricultural Chemists
J. Assoc. Pub. Anal.	Journal of the Association of Public Analysts
J. Asthma Res.	Journal of Asthma Research
J. Attitude Res.	Journal of Attitude Research
J. Bacteriol.	Journal of Bacteriology
J. Behav. Ther. Psychiat.	Journal of Behavior Therapy and Experimental Psychiatry
J. Biol. Chem.	Journal of Biological Chemistry
J. Bot.	Journal Botanique
J. Brazil Psiquiat.	Journal Braziliero de Psiquiatria
J. Cannab. Res.	Journal of Cannabis Research
J. Ceylon Branch Br. Med. Assoc.	Journal of the Ceylon Branch of the British Medical Association
J. Chem. Soc.	Journal of the Chemical Society
J. Chromatog.	Journal of Chromatography
J. Chromatog. Sci.	Journal of Chromatographic Science
J. Clin. Endocrinol. Metab.	Journal of Clinical Endocrinology and Metabolism
J. Clin. Med.	Journal of Clinical Medicine
J. Clin. Psychol.	Journal of Clinical Psychology
J. Clin. Psychopathol.	Journal of Clinical Psychopathology
J. Coll. Univ. Hous.	Journal of College University Housing
J. Consult. Clin. Psychol.	Journal of Consulting and Clinical Psychology
J. Counsel. Psychol.	Journal of Counseling Psychology
J. Crim. Law. Criminol.	Journal of Criminal Law and Criminology
J. Crim. Psychopathol.	Journal of Criminal Psychopathology
J. Drug Abuse	Journal of Drug Abuse

J. Drug Abuse Educat.	Journal of Drug Abuse Education
J. Drug Educat.	Journal of Drug Education
J. Eur. Toxicol.	Journal of European Toxicology
J. Econ. Bus. Hist.	Journal of Economic and Business History
J. Egypt. Med. Assoc.	Journal of the Egyptian Medical Association
J. Endocrinol.	Journal of Endocrinology
J. Florida Med. Assoc.	Journal of the Florida Medical Association
J. Forens. Sci.	Journal of Forensic Sciences
J. Forens. Sci. Soc.	Journal of the Forensic Science Society
J. Franklin Inst.	Journal of the Franklin Institute
J. Genet. Psychol.	Journal of Genetic Psychology
J. Higher Educ.	Journal of Higher Education
J. Histochem. Cytochem.	Journal of Histochemistry and Cytochemistry
J. Hillside Hosp.	Journal of the Hillside Hospital
J. Hlth. Soc. Behav.	Journal of Health and Social Behavior
J. Human Relat.	Journal of Human Relations
J. Home Econ.	Journal of Home Economics
J. Hyg. Chem.	Journal of Hygienic Chemistry
J. Imp. Inst.	Journal of the Imperial Institute
J. Indian Med. Assoc.	Journal of the Indian Medical Association
J. Indiv. Psychol.	Journal of Individual Psychology
J. Iowa Med. Soc.	Journal of the Iowa Medical Society
J. Irish Med. Soc.	Journal of the Irish Medical Society
J. Kansas Med. Assoc.	Journal of the Kansas Medical Association
J. Korean Med. Assoc.	Journal of the Korean Medical Association
J. Label. Comp.	Journal of Labelled Compounds and Radiopharmaceuticals
J. Linn. Soc. (Bot.)	Journal of the Linnean Society (Botany)
J. Louisiana State Med. Soc.	Journal of the Louisiana State Medical Society
J. Magnet.	Journal du Magnetisme
J. Marriage Fam.	Journal of Marriage and the Family
J. Med. Bord.	Journal de Medecine de Bordeaux et du Sud-Ouest
J. Med. Educat.	Journal of Medical Education

J. Med. Liban.	Journal Medical Libanais
J. Med. Soc. N. J.	Journal of the Medical Society of New Jersey
J. Ment. Sci.	Journal of Mental Science
J. Mich. Med. Soc.	Journal of the Michigan Medical Society
J. Microbiol. Immunol.	Journal of Hygiene, Epidemiology, Microbiology and Immunology
J. Minnesota Coll. Person. Assoc.	Journal of the Minnesota College Personnel Association
J. Mond. Pharm.	Journal Mondial de Pharmacie
J. Nat'l. Assoc. Women Deans Counsel.	Journal of the National Association for Women Deans, Administrators, and Counsellors
J. Nat'l. Med. Assoc.	Journal of the National Medical Association
J. Neuropsychiat.	Journal of Neuropsychiatry
J. Nerv. Ment. Dis.	Journal of Nervous and Mental Disease
J. Oral Surg.	Journal of Oral Surgery
J. Org. Chem.	Journal of Organic Chemistry
J. Pediat.	Journal of Pediatrics
J. Person. Assess.	Journal of Personality Assessment
J. Person. Soc. Psychol.	Journal of Personality and Social Psychology
J. Pharmaceut. Sci.	Journal of Pharmaceutical Sciences
J. Pharmacol. Exper. Ther.	Journal of Pharmacology and Experimental Therapeutics
J. Pharm. Anvers	Journal de Pharmacie d'Anvers
J. Pharm. Belg.	Journal de Pharmacie de Belgique
J. Pharm. Chem.	Journal de Pharmacie et de Chemie
J. Pharm. Pharmacol.	Journal of Pharmacy and Pharmacology
J. Physiol.	Journal of Physiology
J. Pol. Sci. Adminst.	Journal of Police Science and Administration
J. Pub. Hlth.	Journal of Public Health
J. Reprod. Fert.	Journal of Reproduction and Fertility
J. Res. Crime Delinquency	Journal of Research in Crime and Delinquency
J. Royal Coll. Phys.	Journal of the Royal College of Physicians
J. Safe. Res.	Journal of Safety Research

J. Sch. Hlth.	Journal of School Health
J. S. Carolina Med. Assoc.	Journal of the South Carolina Medical Association
J. Second. Educat.	Journal of Secondary Education
J. Sex Res.	Journal of Sex Research
J. Soc. Agric. Forest	Journal of the Society of Agriculture and Forestry
J. Soc. Iss.	Journal of Social Issues
J. Soc. Psychiat.	Journal of Social Psychiatry
J. Suisse Pharm.	Journal Suisse de Pharmacie
J. Tennessee Med. Assoc.	Journal of the Tennessee Medical Association
J. Toxicol. Environ. Hlth.	Journal of Toxicology and Environmental Health
J. Wash. Acad. Sci.	Journal of the Washington Academy of Sciences
Juris Doc.	Juris Doctor
Just. Lieb. Annal. Chem.	Justus Liebigs Annalen der Chemie
Juv. Court J.	Juvenile Court Judges Journal
Kem. Tidskr.	Kemisk Tidskrift
Kentucky Folk Rec.	Kentucky Folk Record
Khim. Sel'sk Khoz.	Khimiya V Sel'skom Khozyaistve
Klepzig. Textil.	Klepzigs Textil-zeitschrift
Lab. Med.	Laboratory Medicine
Lakartid.	Lakartidningen
Law Soc. Rev.	Law and Society Review
Lek. List.	Lekarske Listy
Lek. Obzor	Lekarske Obzor
Life Sci.	Life Sciences
Lit. Dig.	Literary Digest
Louisiana Law Rev.	Louisiana Law Review
Louisiana State Med. Soc. J.	Louisiana State Medical Society Journal
Madras Quart. Med. J.	Madras Quarterly Medical Journal
Marihuana Month.	Marihuana Monthly
Marihuana Rev.	Marihuana Review
Maroc-Med.	Maroc-Medical
Marseilles Med.	Marseilles Medical
Mass. Phys.	Massachusetts Physician
Mater. Med. Nordmank.	Materia Medica Nordmank
Measure Eval. Guid.	Measurement and Evaluation in Guidance
Med	Medycyna

Med. Ann. D.C.	Medical Annals of the District of Columbia
Med. Aspects Human Sex.	Medical Aspects of Human Sexuality
Med. Bull. U.S. Army	Medical Bulletin of the U.S. Army
Med. Chirurg. Trans.	Medico-Chirurgical Transactions
Med. Counterpoint	Medical Counterpoint
Med. Dig.	Medical Digest
Med. Econ.	Medical Economics
Med. Insight	Medical Insight
Med. J. Aust.	Medical Journal of Australia
Med. J. Rec.	Medical Journal and Record
Med. Lat.	Medicina Latina
Med. Leg. Dom. Corp.	Medicine Legale et Dommage Corporel
Med. Leg. J.	Medico-Legal Journal
Med. Lett. Drugs Ther.	Medical Letter on Drugs and Therapeutics
Med. Norsk.	Medicin Nordisk
Med. Pharmacol. Exper.	Medicina et Pharmacologia Experimentalis
Med. Rec.	Medical Record
Med. Rev. Rev.	Medical Review of Reviews
Med. Sci. Sports	Medicine and Science in Sports
Med. Surg. J.	Medical and Surgical Journal
Med. Surg. Report.	Medical and Surgical Reporter
Med. Time.	Medical Times
Med. Trial Tech. Quart.	Medical Trial Technique Quarterly
Med. Trib. Med. News	Medical Tribune and Medical News
Med. Welt	Medizinische Welt
Med. Wld. News	Medical World News
Mem. Cognit.	Memory and Cognition
Mem Soc. Sci. Nat. Maroc	Memoires dela Societa des Sciences Naturels et Physique du Maroc
Ment. Hlth. Dig.	Mental Health Digest
Metro Detroit Sci. Rev.	Metropolitan Detroit Science Review
Mich. Law Rev.	Michigan Law Review
Mich. Quart. Rev.	Michigan Quarterly Review
Mikrochim. Act.	Mikrochimica Acta
Microchem J.	Microchemical Journal
Mil. Pol. J.	Military Police Journal
Milit. Med.	Military Medicine
Milit. Surg.	Military Surgeon
Min. Med.	Minnesota Medicine
Minerva Med.	Minerva Medica

Miss. Law J.	Mississippi Law Journal
Missouri Hist. Rev.	Missouri Historical Review
Mitteil Deut. Landwirtschaft	Mitteilungen der Deutschen Landwirtschafts Gesellschaft
Mod. Med.	Modern Medical Monographs
Modern Rev.	Modern Review
Mol. Pharmacol.	Molecular Pharmacology
Mon. Far. Terapeut.	Monitor de la Farmacia y de la Terapeutica
Month. J. Med. Sci.	Monthly Journal of Medical Science
Montpell. Med.	Montpellier Medical
Munch. Med. Woch.	Munchener Medizinische Wochenschrift
Mutation Res.	Mutation Research
Nation's Sch.	Nation's Schools
Nat'l. Drug	National Drug Reporter
Nat'l Inst. Hlth. Rec.	National Institute of Health Record
Nat'l. Rev.	National Review
Nat's Bus.	Nation's Business
Naturwissen.	Naturwissenschaften
Nauch. Tr. Smarkand Med. Inst.	Nauchmye Trudy Samarkandskogo Gosudarstvennogo Meditsinskogo Instututa
Naval Res.	Naval Research Review
N.C.C.D. News	National Council on Crime and Delinquency News
N.C. Central Law J.	North Carolina Central Law Journal
Neb. State Med. J.	Nebraska State Medical Journal
Ned. Mil. Geneesk. Tijd.	Nederlands Militair Geneeskundig Tijdschrift
Ned. T. Criminol.	Nederlands Tijdschrift voor Criminologie
Ned. Tijd. Geneesk.	Nederlands Tijdschrift voor Geneeskunde
Neue Pliz.	Neue Polizei
Neurobiol.	Neurobiology
Neurol. Neurocirurg. Psiquiat.	Neurologie Neurocirurgie i Psiquiatrie
Nevropatol. Psikhiat.	Nevropatologiia i Psikhiatriia
Neuropharmacol.	Neuropharmacology
Neuropsichiat. Infant.	Neuropsichiatria Infantile
New Orleans Med. Surg. J.	New Orleans Medical and Surgical Journal

New Phys.	New Physician
New Pol.	New Politics
New Repub.	New Republic
New Rev.	New Review
New Scient.	New Scientist
New Soc.	New Society
New States.	New Statesman
New York.	New Yorker
Newport Hist.	Newport History
Nigerian Bar J.	Nigerian Bar Journal
N.J. Med. Soc. J.	New Jersey Medical Society Journal
Nord. Hyg. Tid.	Nordisk Hygienisk Tidskrift
Nord. Kriminol. Tid.	Nordisk Kriminalteknisk Tidskrift
Nord. Med.	Nordisk Medicin
Nord. Psykiat.	Nordisk Psykiatrisk Tidskrift
Notre Dame Law Rev.	Notre Dame Law Review
Nouv. Presse Med.	Nouvelle Presse Medicale
Nouv. Rem.	Nouveaux Remedes
Nov. Icon. Salpetr.	Nouvelle Iconographie de la Salt-petriere
Nurs. Times	Nursing Times
N.Y. Law Forum	New York Law Forum
N.Y. Med. J.	New York Medical Journal
N.Y. Med. Press.	New York Medical Press
N.Z. Med. J.	New Zealand Medical Journal
Oeffent. Gesundheit.	Oeffentliche Gesundheitswesen
Oestereich Monat.	Oesterreichische Monatshefte
Office Internat'l. Hyg. Pub. Bull. Men.	Office Internationel d'Hygiene Publique Bulletin Mensuel
Ohio State Med. J.	Ohio State Medical Journal
Oil Fat Indust.	Oil and Fat Industries
Ons Gezin	Ons Gezin
Oregon Ment. Hlth. Div.	Oregon Mental Health Division
Organ. Mond. Sante	Organisation Mondiale de la Santé Chronique
Orient. Mod.	Oriente Moderna
Orthomol. Psychiat.	Orthomolecular Psychiatry
Orv. Hetil.	Orvosi Hetilap
Osgoode Hall Law J.	Osgoode Hall Law Journal
Ost. Arzt	Oesterreichische Arzt
Otago Law Rev.	Otago Law Review
Pacific Law J.	Pacific Law Journal
Pacific Med. Surg. J.	Pacific Medicine and Surgery Journal

Pa. Pharmacist	Pennsylvania Pharmacist
Pa. Psychiat. Quart.	Pennsylvania Psychiatric Quarterly
Parent's Mag.	Parent's Magazine and Better Homemaking
Partisan Rev.	Partisan Review
Peabody J. Educat.	Peabody Journal of Education
Pediat.	Pediatrics
Ped. News	Pediatric News
Penn. Med.	Pennsylvania Medical Journal
Penn. Psychiat. Quart.	Pennsylvania Psychiatric Quarterly
Percept. Psychophys.	Perception and Psychophysics
Person. Guid. J.	Personnel and Guidance Journal
Perspect. Psychiat.	Perspectives in Psychiatric Care
Pflug. Arch. Gesant. Physiol. Mensch.	Pflugers Archiv fuer die Gesamte Physiologie der Menshen und die Tiere
Pharm. Act. Helv.	Pharmaceutica Acta Helvetiae
PharmChem News.	PharmChem Newsletter
Pharm. Hist.	Pharmacy in History
Pharm. Indust.	Pharmazeutische Industrie
Pharmaceut. Cent.-Blat	Pharmaceutisches Central-Blat
Pharmaceut. Era	Pharmaceutical Era
Pharmaceut. J.	Pharmaceutical Journal
Pharmaceut. J. Pharmacist	Pharmaceutical Journal and Pharmacist
Pharmaceut Weekbl.	Pharmaceutisch Weekblad
Pharmacol.	Pharmacology
Pharmacol. Biochem. Behav.	Pharmacology Biochemistry and Behavior
Pharmacol. Res. Commun.	Pharmacological Research Communications
Pharmacol. Toxicol.	Pharmacologiya i Toxicologiya
Pharmakopsychiat. NeuroPsycho-pharmakol.	Pharmakopsychiatrie NeuroPsycho-pharmakologie
Pharmazeut. Prax.	Pharmazeutische Praxis
Pharmazeut. Zeit. Russland	Pharmazeutische Zeitschrift fuer Russland
Pharmazeut. Zentral.	Pharmazeutische Zentralle fuer Deutschland
Phil. Med.	Philadelphia Medicine
Phys. Cult.	Physical Culture
Physiol. Behav.	Physiology and Behavior
Physiol. Plant.	Physiologia Plantarum

Physiol. Psychol.	Physiological Psychology
Phytochem.	Phytochemistry
Phytomorphol.	Phytomorphology
Phyton Ann. Bot.	Phyton Annales Rei Botanica
Phytopath.	Phytopathologische Zeitschrift
Plant. Dis. Rep.	Plant Disease Reporter
Plant. Med.	Planta Medica
Plant. Med. Phyto.	Plantes Medicinales et Phytotherapie
Pol. Chron. Constab. Wld.	Police Chronicle and Constabulary World
Pol. Esp.	Policia Espanola
Pol. Gaz. Lek.	Polska Gazeta Lekarska
Pol. J. Pharmacol.	Polish Journal of Pharmacology and Pharmacy
Pop. Sci. Month.	Popular Science Monthly
Pol. Sec. Nacion.	Policia Secreta Nacional
Port. Act. Biol. Morfal. Fisiol.	Portugaliae Acta Biologica Morfalogia Fisiologia Genetica et Biologia Geral
Postgrad. Med.	Postgraduate Medicine
Poznan. Tow. Przyjac. Nauk	Poznanski Towarzystwo Przjacio Nauk
Prax. Kinderpsychol.	Praxis der Kinderpsychologie und Kinderpsychiatrie
Pren. Med. Argentina	Prensa Medica Argentina
Prep. Biochem.	Preparative Biochemistry
Presse Med.	Presse Medicale
Priv. Pract.	Private Practice
Proc. Am. Drug Manufact. Assoc.	Proceedings of the American Drug Manufacturers Association
Proc. Am. Pharmaceut. Soc.	Proceedings of the American Pharmaceutical Society
Proc. Am. Psychol. Assoc.	Proceedings of the American Psychological Association
Proc. Cam. Phil. Soc.	Proceedings of the Cambridge Philosophical Society
Proc. Can. Forens. Sci.	Proceedings of the Canadian Forensic Sciences
Proc. Chem. Soc.	Proceedings of the Chemical Society
Proc. 5th Internat'l Cong. Pharmacol.	Proceedings of the 5th International Congress on Pharmacology
Proc. Internat'l Flax Hemp Cong.	Proceedings of the International Flax and Hemp Congress

Proc. Nat'l Acad. Sci.	Proceedings of the National Academy of Sciences
Proc. Pharmaceut. Soc. Egypt	Proceedings of the Pharmaceutical Society of Egypt
Proc. Nat'l Sympos. Marihuana	Proceedings of the National Symposium on Marihuana
Proc. Roy. Medicopsychol. Assoc.	Proceedings of the Royal Medico-psychological Associations
Proc. Roy. Soc. Edin.	Proceedings of the Royal Society of Edinburgh
Proc. Roy. Soc. Med.	Proceedings of the Royal Society of Medicine
Proc. Rud. Virchow Med. Soc. N.Y.	Proceedings of the Rudolf Virchow Medical Society in the City of New York
Proc. Soc. Anal. Chem.	Proceedings of the Society of Analytical Chemists
Proc. Soil Crop Sci. Soc.	Proceedings of the Soil and Crop Sciences Society
Prog. Brain Res.	Progress in Brain Research
Prog. Chem. Toxicol.	Progress in Chemical Toxicology
Prog. Clin. Neurophysiol.	Progress in Clinical Neurophysiology
Prog. Med.	Progrès Medicale
Prog. Org. Chem.	Progress in Organic Chemistry
Prov. Med. J. Retro. Med. Sci.	Provincial Medical Journal and Retrospect of the Medical Sciences
Psyched. Rev.	Psychedelic Review
Psychiat.	Psychiatria
Psychiat. An.	Psychiatric Annals
Psychiat. Dig.	Psychiatry Digest
Psychiat. Neurol. Blad.	Psychiatrische en Neurologische Bladen
Psychiat. Opin.	Psychiatric Opinion
Psychiat. Quart.	Psychiatric Quarterly
Psychoanal. Forum	Psychoanalytic Forum
Psychoanal. Study Child	Psychoanalytic Study of the Child
Psychol.	Psychology
Psychol. Bull.	Psychological Bulletin
Psychol. Rep.	Psychological Reports
Psychol. Today	Psychology Today
Psychon. Sci.	Bulletin of the Psychonomic Sciences Society
Psychopharmacol.	Psychopharmacology

Psychopharmacol. Commun.	Psychopharmacology Communications
Psychophysiol.	Psychophysiology
PTA Mag.	PTA Magazine
Pub. Hlth. Rep.	Public Health Reports
Pub. Opin. Quart.	Public Opinion Quarterly
Pupil Person.	Pupil Personnel Services
Putnam's Month. Mag. Am. Lit. Sci. Ant.	Putnam's Monthly Magazine of American Literature, Science and Art
Quad. Criminol. Clin.	Quaderni di Criminologia Clinica
Qual. Plant. Mater. Veg.	Qualitas Plantarum et Materiae
Quart. J. Crude Drug Res.	Quarterly Journal of Crude Drug Research
Quart. J. Ineb.	Quarterly Journal of Inebriety
Quart. J. Stud. Alcohol	Quarterly Journal of Studies on Alcohol
Quart. Rev.	Quarterly Review
R. Soc. Hlth.	Royal Society of Health Journal
Rass. Med. Appl. Lavon Indust.	Rassegna di Medicina Applicata al Lavaro Industriale
Reader's Dig.	Reader's Digest
Rec. Med. Vet.	Recueil de Medecine Veterinaire
Recht. Jugend.	Recht der Jugend und des Bildungswessen
Ref. Zh. Otd. Vyp. Farmakol. Khim. Tokschaf.	Referativnyi Zhurnal Otdel ny Vypusk Farmakologiya I Toksikoliya
Rend. R. Inst. Lombardo	Rendiconti Instituto Lombardo
Rep. Pharm.	Repertorium fuer die Pharmazie
Res. Comm. Chem. Path. Pharmacol.	Research Communications in Chemical Pathology and Pharmacology
Res. High. Educat.	Research in Higher Education
Res. Nat'l. Mus. Bloem.	Researches of the National Museum, Bloemfontain
Res. Rep. Fac. Text. Sericult. Shinshu Un.	Research Reports of the Faculty of Sericulture Shinshu University
Rev. Assoc. Med. Brazil.	Revista da Associacao Medica Braziliera
Rev. Assyr. Archeol. Mid East	Review of Assyriology and Archeology of the Middle East
Rev. Assyr. Orient.	Revue d'Assyriologie et d'Archeologie Orientale

Rev. Atheroscler.	Revue de l'Atherosclerose et Arteriopathies Peripheriques
Rev. Brasil. Med.	Revista Brasileira de Medicina
Rev. Brasil. Odont.	Revista Brasileira de Odontologia
Rev. Can. Biol.	Revue Cannadienne de Biologie
Rev. Cent. Estud. Farm. Bioquim.	Revista del Centro de Estudiantes de Farmacia y Bioquimica
Rev. Cent. Med.	Revista del Centro Medico
Rev. Chil. Higien. Med. Prevent.	Revista Chilena de Higiene y Medicina Preventiva
Rev. Clin. Espan.	Revista Clinica Espanola
Rev. Criminal.	Revista de Criminalistica do Rio Grande do Sol
Rev. Deux-Mondes	Revue des Deux-Mondes
Rev. Econ. Stat.	Review of Economics and Statistics
Rev. Ecuat. Hig. Med. Trop.	Revista Ecuatoriana de Higiene y Medicina Tropical
Rev. Educat. Res.	Review of Educational Research
Rev. Espan. Tuber.	Revista Espanola de Tuberculosis
Rev. Farm. Cuba	Revista Farmaceutica de Cuba
Rev. Flor. Med.	Revista de Flora Medicinal
Rev. Frenopat. Espan.	Revista Frenopatica Espanola Therapeutique
Rev. Hist. Litt. France	Revue d'Histoire Litteraire de la France
Rev. Hypnotisme	Revue d'Hypnotisme
Rev. Iber. Endocrinol.	Revista Iberica de Endocrinologia
Rev. Inst. Adolfo Lutz	Revista do Instituto Adolfo Lutz
Rev. InterAm. Psicol.	Revista InterAmericana de Psicologia
Rev. Med. Chile	Revista Medica de Chile
Rev. Med. Ciurg. Habana	Revista de Medicina y Ciurgia de la Habana
Rev. Med. Franc. Etrang.	Revue Medicale Française et Etrangère
Rev. Med. Hyg. Trop.	Revue de Medicine et d'Hygiene Tropicales
Rev. Med. Cirerg. Colombia	Revista de Medicina y Cirergia Colombia
Rev. Med. Mex.	Revista de Medicina de Mexico
Rev. Med. Pernam.	Revista de Medicina de Pernambuco
Rev. Med. Yucatan	Revista de Medicina de Yucatan
Rev. Metap.	Revue de Metaphysique et de Morale
Rev. Neuropsiquiat.	Revista de Neuropsiquiatria

Rev. Paris	Revue de Paris
Rev. Philosoph.	Revue de Philosophie
Rev. Psiquiat. Criminol.	Revista de Psiquiatria y Criminologia
Rev. Psychol. Peuples	Revue de Psychologie des Peuples
Rev. Sanidad Milit.	Revista de Sanidad Militar
Rev. Sci. Humain.	Revue des Sciences Humaines
Rev. Sci. Hypnot.	Revue des Sciences Hypnotiques
Rev. Scientif.	Revue Scientifique
Rev. Special.	Revue des Specialities
Rev. Tec. Pol.	Revista de Tecnica Policia
Rhode Is. Med. J.	Rhode Island Medical Journal
Riv. Agron.	Rivista di Agronomia
Riv. Am. Brazil	Revista Americana Braziliera
Riv. Chim. Med. Farm.	Revista de Chimica Medica e Farmaceutica
Rocky Mt. Med. J.	Rocky Mountain Medical Journal
Rocky Mt. Soc. Sci. J.	Rocky Mountain Social Science Journal
Roy. Asiat. Soc. Brit.	Royal Asiatic Society of Great Britain and Ireland
Roy Melbourne Hosp. Clin. Rep.	Royal Melbourne Hospital Clinical Reports
S. Af. J. Sci.	South African Journal of Science
S. Af. Med. J.	South African Medical Journal
S. C. Law Rev.	South Carolina Law Review
S. Dak. Law Rev.	South Dakota Law Review
Salub. Asist.	Salubridad y Asistencia Social
Salud Pub. Mex.	Salud Publica de Mexico
San Diego Law Rev.	San Diego Law Review
Sat. Even. Post	Saturday Evening Post
Sat. Rev.	Saturday Review
Sat. Rev. Educat.	Saturday Review of Education
Sborn. Cesk. Akad. Zemedel. Ved.	Sborník Ceskoslovenske Akademie Zemedelske Ved Rostlinna Vyroba
Scand. J. Clin. Lab. Invest.	Scandinavian Journal of Clinical and Laboratory Investigation
Scand. J. Soc. Med.	Scandinavian Journal of Social Medicine
Scanlan's Month.	Scanlan's Monthly
Sch. Mgt.	School Management
Schiz. Bull.	Schizophrenia Bulletin

Schmidt's Jahrbuch.	Schmidt's Jahrbucher der in und Auslandischen Medicin
Schrift. Gesel. Psychol. Forsch.	Schriften der Gesellschaft fuer Psychologische Forschung
Schweiz. Arch. Neurol. Psychiat.	Schweizer Archiv Fuer Neurologie und Psychiatrie
Schweiz Brau.-Rundsch.	Schweizer Brauerei-Rundschau
Schweiz. Med. Woch.	Schweizer Medizinische Wochenshrift
Schwest. Rev.	Schwestern Revue
Sci. Cult.	Science and Culture
Sci. J. Roy. Coll. Sci.	Scientific Journal of the Royal College of Science
Sci. Stud. St. Bonavent. Coll.	Science Studies St. Bonaventure College
Science Dig.	Science Digest
Scientif. Amer.	Scientific American
Scripta Med.	Scripta Medica
Ser. Techn. Mas. Kult.	Serie Technicheskie i Maslichnye Kultur
Sel'skokhoz. Biol.	Sel'skokhozyaistvennaya Biologiya
Sem. Hop. Paris	Semaine des Hopitaux de Paris
Semaine Med.	Semaine Medicale
Seminars Drug Treat.	Seminars in Drug Treatment
Sen. Schol.	Senior Scholastic
Seton Hall Law Rev.	Seton Hall Law Review
Sex. Behav.	Sexual Behavior
Slown. Towaroz.	Slownik Towaroznawczy
Soc.	Sociology
Soc. Casework	Social Casework
Soc. Econ. Stud.	Social and Economic Studies
Soc. Forces	Social Forces
Soc. Prob.	Social Problems
Soc. Sci. Med.	Social Science and Medicine
Soc. Sci. Quart.	Social Science Quarterly
Soc. Work Technique	Social Work Technique
Sociol. Med.	Journal of Sociologic Medicine
Sociol. Methods Res.	Sociological Methods and Research
Sociol. Soc. Res.	Sociology and Social Research
South. Med. J.	Southern Medical Journal
South. Med. Rec.	Southern Medical Record
South. Pract.	Southern Practitioner
Southwest. Med.	Southwestern Medicine

Sovet. Psikhoneurol.	Sovetska Psikhoneurologiia
Sovet. Zdrav. Kirgiz.	Sovetsko Zdravookhranenie Kirgizii
Soz. Arbeit.	Sozialistiche Arbeitswissenschaft
Soz. Praeventimed.	Sozial und Praeventivmedizin
Sr. Scholast.	Senior Scholastic
St. Andrews Med. Grad. Assoc. Trans.	St. Andrews Medical Graduates Association Transactions
St. Barth. Hosp. J.	St. Bartholomew's Hospital Journal
St. Louis Med. Surg. J.	St. Louis Medical and Surgical Journal
Stan. Law Rev.	Stanford Law Review
Stanford Univ. Pub. Med. Sci. Ser.	Stanford University Publications Medical Sciences Series
Staz. Sper. Ag. It.	Stazione Sperimentali Agrarie Italiane
Sudeteten. Apot.	Sudetendeutscher Apotekerzeitung
Suffolk Univ. Law Rev.	Suffolk University Law Review
Surg. Forum	Surgical Forum
Sv. Fam. Tidskr.	Svensk Farmaceutisk Tidskrift
Sven. Kem. Tid.	Svensk Kemisk Tidskrift
Sydo. Ann. Mycol.	Sydowia Annales Mycologici
Sympos. Soc. Exp. Biol.	Symposia of the Society for Experimental Biology
T. Norsk. Laegeforen.	Tidsskrift for den Norske Laegeforenings
T. Soc. Geneesk.	Tijdschrift voor Social Geneeskunde
Tekstil. Prom.	Tekstil'naya Promyshlennost
Tend. Temps	Tendences du Temps
Tetrahed.	Tetrahedron
Tetrahed. Let.	Tetrahedron Letters
Tex. Manufact.	Textile Manufacturing World
Texas Bar J.	Texas Bar Journal
Texas Med.	Texas Medicine
Texas Med. News	Texas Medical News
Ther.	Therapie
Ther. Monat.	Therapeutische Monatsberichte
Ther. Soc. Trans.	Therapeutic Society of London Transactions
Ther. Record	Therapeutic Record
Thromb. Haemorrhag.	Thrombosis et Diathesis Haemorrhagica
Tid. Samfunn.	Tidskrift for Samfunnsforskning
Tid. Sygepeljersk	Tidsskrift for Sygeplejersk

Tid. Ziekenver.	Tijdschrift vor Ziekenverplegning
Today's Ed.	Today's Education
Today's Hlth.	Today's Health
Toxicol. Ann.	Toxicology Annual
Toxicoman.	Toxicomanies
Traffic Safe.	Traffic Safety
Trans. Am. Microscop. Soc.	Transactions of the American Microscopical Society
Trans. Am. Philosoph. Soc.	Transactions of the American Philosophical Society
Trans. Ill. State Acad. Sci.	Transactions of the Illinois State Academy of Science
Trans. N.Y. Acad. Sci.	Transactions of the New York Academy of Sciences
Trans. Med. Phys. Soc. Bombay	Transactions of the Medical and Physical Society of Bombay
Trans. Med. Phys. Soc. Calcutta	Transactions of the Medical and Physical Society of Calcutta
Trans. Roy. Soc. S. Africa	Transactions of the Royal Society of South Africa
Trial Mag.	Trial Magazine
Trud. Ricklad. Bot. Genet. Selek.	Trudy Po Rickladnoi Botanike Genetike I Selektsi
Trud. Zoovet.	Trudy Zoologischeskogo Institutu Akademii Nauk USSR
Turk Ijiyen Tecrub. Biyol. Derg.	Turk Ijiyen Ve Tecrubi Biyoloji Dergisi
Tyg. Lek.	Tygodnik Lekarski
U.B.C. Law Rev.	University of British Columbia Law Review
Uch. Zap. Azerb. Med. Inst.	Uchenye Zapiski Azerbaidzbanskogo Meditsinskogo Instituta
U.C.L.A. Law Rev.	University of California at Los Angeles Law Review
Ugeskr. Laeg.	Ugeskrift for Laeger
Ukran. Bio. Zh.	Ukrayinskyi Biokhimichnyi Zhurnal
U.N. Doc.	United Nations Document
U.N. Secretariat	United Nations Secretariat
Un. Med. Can.	Union Medicale du Canada
Union Pharmaceut.	Union Pharmaceutique
Union Sig.	Union Signal
Univ. Med.	University Medical

Univ. Miami Law Rev.	University of Miami Law Review
Univ. Mich. Med. Ctr.	University of Michigan Mental Health Center
Univ. Penn. Law Rev.	University of Pennsylvania Law Review
Univ. San Francisco Law Rev.	University of San Francisco Law Review
U.S. Pub. Hlth. Serv.	U.S. Public Health Service
Verhand. Gesell. Deut. Natur. Aerz.	Verhandlungen der Gesellschaft Deutscher Naturfoerscher und Aerzte
Vest. Dermat. Venerol.	Vestnik Dermatologii I Venerologii
Vest. Selskokhoz. Nauk.	Vestnik Sol'skokhozyaistvennoi Nauk USSR
Vest. Sotsial. Rastenievart.	Vestnik Sotsialisticheskogo Raskeniev Odstva
Vet. Med.	Veterinaria Medicina
Vet. Rec.	Veterinary Record
Vie Med. Can. Fran.	Vie Medicale au Canada Francais
Villanova Law Rev.	Villanova Law Review
Virginia Law Rev.	Virginia Law Review
Vop. Psikhoneurol.	Voprosy Psikhoneurologii
War Med.	War Medicine
Wash. Census Rep.	Washington Census Reports
Week. Compil. President. Doc.	Weekly Compilation of Presidential Documents
West. Ind. Med. J.	West Indian Medical Journal
West. Virginia Med. J.	West Virginia Medical Journal
Western Univ. Law Rev.	Western University Law Review
W.H.O. Tech. Rep. Ser.	World Health Organization Technical Report Series
Wien. Med. Wschr.	Wiener Medizinische Wochenschrift
Wien. Pharmazeut. Woch.	Wiener Pharmazeutische Wochenschrift
Wiscon. Law Rev.	Wisconsin Law Review
Wiscon. Pharm.	Wisconsin Pharmacist
Yak. Zassh.	Yakugaku Zasshi
Yale Alum. Mag.	Yale Alumni Magazine
Yale Rev.	Yale Review
Yearbook Med. Publish	Yearbook of Medicine
Yearbook Pharm.	Yearbook of Pharmacy
Yearbook U.S. Dept. Agricult.	Yearbook of the U.S. Department of Agriculture

Youth Soc.	Youth and Society
Zahnarzl. Prax.	Zahnaerzliche Praxis
Zbornik Rad. Belgrade Univ. Poljo Fac.	Zbornik Radova Belgrade Universitia Poljuprivrednog Fakultika
Zdrav. Kaz.	Zdravookhramenie Kazakhstana
Zeit. Augenheil.	Zeitschrift fur Augenheilkunde
Zeit. Exp. Ang. Psychol.	Zeitschrift fuer Experimentelle und Angewandte Psychologie
Zeit. Expt'l. Path. Ther.	Zeitschrift fur Experimentelle Pathologie und Therapie
Zeit. Ges. Expt'l. Med.	Zeitschrift fuer die Gesamte Experimentalle Medizin
Zeit. Ges. Neurol. Psychiat.	Zentralblatt fuer die Gesamte Neurologie und Psychiatrie
Zeit. Hang.	Zeitschrift fur Hangzuchtung
Zeit. Klin. Psychol. Psychother.	Zeitschrift fur Klinishce Psychologie und Psychotherapie
Zeit. Naturfor.	Zeitschrift fuer Naturforschung
Zeit. Offentl. Sorge	Zeitschrift Offentliche Sorge
Zeit. Pflanz.	Zeitschrift fur Pflanzenphysiologie
Zeit. Plan. Dun. Bod.	Zeitschrift fuer Pflanzenernaehrung Duengung Bodenkunde
Zeit. Psychiat.	Zeitschrift fuer Psychiatrie
Zeit. Rechtsmed.	Zeitschrift fuer Rechtsmedizin
Zeit. Sozialpsychol.	Zeitschrift fuer Sozial Psychologie
Zent. Neurol. Psychiat.	Zentralblatt fur die Gesamte Neurologie und Psychiatrie

A Comprehensive Guide to the Cannabis Literature

BIBLIOGRAPHY

A

1. Aal'Tsman,G.I. and Lenskii,G.P. "The effect of hashish on the mind."(Rus.). Zdrav. Kaz. 1962, 22, 30-35.

2. Aaron,H.S. and Ferguson,C.P. "Synthesis of the eight stereoisomers of a tetrahydrocannabinol congener." J. Org. Chem. 1968, 33, 684-689.

3. Aarons,B. and Osmond,H.(eds.). Psychedelics: Uses and Implications of Hallucinogenic Drugs. Doubleday, N.Y., 1970.

4. Abbott,S.R., Abu-shumays,A., Loeffler,K.O., and Forest,I.S. "High pressure liquid chromatography of cannabinoids as their fluorescent dansyl derivatives." Res. Comm. Chem. Path. Pharmacol. 1975, 10, 9-19.

5. Abdel-Nabi,A.A. and El-Nagdi,A. "Drug addiction in Egypt and its sociological aspects." Med.-Leg. J. 1960, 28, 200-208.

6. Abdulla,A. "Cannabis indica as a national epidemic in Egypt."(Ger.). Schwiz. Med. Woch. 1953, 83, 541-543.

7. Abel,E.L. "Cannabis and aggression in animals." Behav. Biol. 1975, 14, 1-20.

8. Abel,E.L. "Cannabis: Effects on hunger and thirst." Behav. Biol. 1975, 15, 255-281.

9. Abel,E.L. "Changes in anxiety feelings following marihuana smoking: The alternation in feelings of anxiety resulting from the smoking of marihuana(Cannabis sativa L.)." Br. J. Addict. 1971, 66, 185-187.

10. Abel,E.L. "Chronopharmacology of delta-9-tetrahydrocannabinol hypothermia in mice." Exper. 1973, 29, 1528-1529.

11. Abel,E.L. "Development of tolerance to delta-9-THC in the frog." Exper. 1973, 29, 1528-1529.

12. Abel,E.L. "Effects of marihuana on the solution of anagrams, memory and appetite." Nature 1971, 231, 260-261.

13. Abel,E.L. "Effects of the marihuana homologue, pyrahexyl, on a conditioned emotional response." Psychon. Sci. 1969, 16, 27.

14. Abel,E.L. "Effects of the marihuana homologue, pyrahexyl, on open field behavior." J. Pharm. Pharmacol. 1970, 22, 785.

15. Abel,E.L. "Marihuana and memory." Nature 1970, 227, 1151.

16. Abel,E.L. "Marihuana and memory: Acquisition or retrieval?" Science 1971, 173, 1038-1040.

17. Abel,E.L. "Marihuana and motivation." Science 1972, 176, 8.

18. Abel,E.L. "Marihuana, learning and memory." Internat'l. Rev. Neurobiol. 1975, 18, 329-356.

19. Abel,E.L. "Marihuana vs. the work ethic: The amotivational syndrome." Science Dig. 1973, 74, 29-30.

20. Abel,E.L. "Studies of tolerance to delta-9-tetrahydrocannabinol in neonatal chicks." Fed. Proc. 1972, 32, 1712.

21. Abel,E.L. "Suppression of maternal behavior in the mouse by delta-9-tetrahydrocannabinol." Fed. Proc. 1975, 34, 1532.

22. Abel,E.L. "Suppression of pup retrieving behavior in rats following administration of delta-9-tetrahydro-cannabinol." Exper. 1973, 29. 1527-1528.

23. Abel,E.L. "'That valuable article': Hemp." Amer. Hist. Illus. 1976, 11, 27-33.

24. Abel,E.L.(ed.). The Scientific Study of Marihuana. Nelson-Hall, Chicago, 1975.

25. Abel,E.L. "The relationship between cannabis and violence. A review." Psychol. Bull. 1977, 84, 194-211.

26. Abel,E.L., Cooper,C.W., and Harris,L.S. "Effects of delta-9-tetrahydrocannabinol on body weight and brain electrolytes in the chicken." Psychopharmacol. 1974, 35, 335-339.

27. Abel,E.L., McMillan,D.E., and Harris,L.S. "Delta-9-tetrahydrocannabinol: Effects of route of administration on onset and duration of activity and tolerance development." Psychopharmacol. 1974, 35, 29-34.

28. Abel,E.L., McMillan,D.E., and Harris,L.S. "Tolerance to the behavioral and hypothermic effects of delta-9-tetrahydrocannabinol in neonatal chicks." Exper. 1972, 28, 1188.

29. Abel,E.L., McMillan,D.E., and Harris,L.S. "Tolerance to the hypothermic effects of delta-9-tetrahydrocannabinol as a function of age in the chicken." Br. J. Pharmacol. 1973, 47, 452-456.

30. Abel,E.L. and Schiff,B.B. "Effects of the marihuana homologue, pyrahexyl, on food and water intake and curiosity in the rat." Psychon. Sci. 1969, 16, 38.

31. Abel,E.L. and Siemens,A.J. "Response to delta-9-tetrahydrocannabinol, barbiturates and ethanol in lactating, virgin female, and male mice." Fed. Proc. 1976, 35, 1658.

32. Abelson,H., Cohen,R., and Schrayer,D. Public Attitudes toward Marihuana. Response Analysis Corp., Princeton, N.J., 1972.

33. Abelson,H., Cohen,R., Schrayer,D., and Rappeport, M. Drug Experience, Attitudes, and Related Behavior among Adolescents and Adults. Response Analysis Corp., Princeton, N.J., 1973.

34. Abelson,H., Cohen,R., Schrayer,D., and Rappeport, M. "Drug experience, attitudes and related behavior among adolescents and adults." In National Commission on Marihuana and Drug Abuse. Drug Use in America: Problem in Perspective. Gov't. Print. Office, Washington, D.C., 1973, I, 489-867.

35. Abelson,P.H. "LSD and marihuana." Science 1968, 159, 1189.

36. Ablon,S.L. and Goodwin,F.K. "High frequency of dysphoric reactions to tetrahydrocannabinol among depressed patients." Am. J. Psychiat. 1974, 131, 448-453.

37. Abou Zeid,Y.M. and El Ghamrawy,M.A. "Examination of cannabis resin and its reactions by ultra-violet rays." Proc. Pharmaceut. Soc. Egypt 1952, 115.

38. Abrahm,P.M. "Snakes in the grass, or the worm turns on." J.A.M.A. 1972, 221, 917.

39. Abrams,A.L., Dessauer,B.L., and Shenker,I.R. "Marihuana and the pediatrician: An attitude survey." Pediat. 1970, 46, 462-464.

40. Abrams,S. "The Oxford scene and the law." In Andrews,G. and Vinkenoog,S.(eds.). The Book of Grass. Grove Press, N.Y., 1967, 235-242.

41. Abramson,H.A. "Respiratory disorders and marihuana use." Asthma Res. 1974, 11, 97.

42. Abruzzi,W. "Drug-induced psychosis." Internat'l. J. Addict. 1977, 12, 183-193.

43. Abu-Eittah,R. and Mobarak,Z. "Absorption spectra of iron(III)-cannabidiolic acid solutions in organic solvents." Nuc. Chem. 1972, 34, 2283-2293.

44. Acock,A.C. and Defleur,M. "A configurational approach to contingent consistency on the attitude-behavior relationship. Am. Sociol. Rev. 1972, 3, 714-726.

45. Adam,C. "Talk about pot." New States. 1970, 80, 674.

46. Adamek,C., Pihl,R.O., and Leiter,L. "An analysis of the subjective marihuana experience." Internat'l. J. Addict. 1976, 11, 295-307.

47. Adams,A.J., Brown,B., Flom,M.C., Jones,R.T., and Jampolsky,A. "Alcohol and marihuana effects on static visual acuity." Am. J. Opthamol. Physiol. 1975, 52, 729-735.

48. Adams,A.J., Brown,B. Haegerstrom-Portnoy,G. and Flom,M.C. "Evidence for acute effects of alcohol and marihuana on color discrimination." Percept. Psychophys. 1976, 20, 119-124.

49. Adams,H.R. and Sofia,R.D. "Interaction of chloramphenicol and delta-1-tetrahydrocannabinol in barbital-anesthetized mice." Exper. 1973, 29, 181-182.

50. Adams,M.D., Chait,L.D., and Earnhardt,J.T. "Tolerance to the cardiovascular effects of delta-9-tetrahydrocannabinol in the rat." Br. J. Pharmacol. 1976, 56, 43-48.

51. Adams,M.D., Dewey,W.L., and Harris,L.S. "Cardiovascular effects of delta-8- and delta-9-tetrahydrocannabinol in rats." J. Pharmacol. Exper. Ther. 19

52. Adams,M.D., Earnhardt,J.T., Dewey,W.L., and Harris,L.S. "Vasoconstrictor actions of delta-8- and

delta-9-tetrahydrocannabinol in the rat. J. Pharmacol. Exper. Ther. 1976, 196, 649-656.

53. Adams,P.M. and Barratt,E.S. "Effects of acute and chronic marihuana on complex operant performance by the squirrel monkey." In Singh,J.M. and Lal,H.(eds.). Drug Addiction. Intercontinental Med. Book Corp., N.Y., 1974, III, 169-180.

54. Adams,P.M. and Barratt,E.S. "Effects of chronic marihuana administration on states of primate sleep-wakefulness." Biol. Psychiat. 1975, 10, 315-322.

55. Adams,P.M. and Barratt,E.S. "Effects of chronic marihuana administration on stages of primate sleep-wakefulness." Fed. Proc. 1974, 19, 540.

56. Adams,P.M. and Barratt,E.S. "Effects of a marihuana extract on performance and EEG's in squirrel monkeys." In Singh,J.M., Miller,L., and Lal,H.(eds.). Drug Addiction: Experimental Pharmacology. Futura Pub. Co., Mount Kisco,, N.Y., 1974, 123-132.

57. Adams,P.M. and Barratt,E.S. "Role of biogenic amines in the effects of marihuana on EEG patterns in cats." EEG and Clin. Neurophysiol. 1975, 39, 621-625.

58. Adams,P.M. and Barratt,E.S. "The effects of a marihuana extract on the general motor activity of the squirrel monkey." Psychon. Sci. 1971, 25, 279-280.

59. Adams,P.M. and Barratts,E.S. "The effects of a marihuana extract on two-choice discrimination learning in the squirrel moneky." Physiol. Psychol. 1976, 4, 155-158.

60. Adams,R. "Marihuana." Bull. N. Y. Acad. Med. 1942, 18, 705-730.

61. Adams,R. "Marihuana." Harvey Lectures 1941-1942, 37, 168-195.

62. Adams,R. "Marihuana." Science 1940, 92, 115-119.

63. Adams,R., Aycock,B.F., and Loewe,S. "Tetrahydrocannabinol homologs." J. Am. Chem. Soc. 1948, 70, 662-664.

64. Adams,R. and Baker,B.R. "Structure of cannabinol. IV. Synthesis of two additional isomers containing a resorcinol residue." J. Am. Chem. Soc. 1940, 62, 2208-2215.

65. Adams,R. and Baker,B.R. "Structure of cannabinol. A second method of synthesis of cannabinol." J. Am. Chem. Soc. 1940, 62, 2401.

66. Adams,R. and Baker,B.R. "Structure of cannabinol. VII. A method of synthesis of a tetrahydrocannabinol which possesses marihuana activity." J. Am. Chem. Soc. 1940, 62, 2405-2408.

67. Adams,R., Baker,B.R., and Wearn,R.B. "Structure of cannabinol. III. Synthesis of cannabinol, 1-hydroxy-3-n-amy-6,6,9-trimethyl-6-dibenzopyran." J. Am. Chem. Soc. 1940, 62, 2204-2207.

68. Adams,R., Cain,C.K., and Baker,B.R. "Structure of cannabinol. II. Synthesis of two new isomers, 3-hydroxy-4-n-amyl- and 3-hydroxy-2-amy 6,6,9-trimethyl-6-dibenzopyrans." J. Am. Chem. Soc. 1940, 62, 2201-2204.

69. Adams,R., Cain,C.K., and Loewe,S. "Tetrahydrocannabinol analogs with marihuana activity. XI." J. Am. Chem. Soc. 1941, 63, 1977-1978.

70. Adams,R., Cain,C.K., McPhee,W.D., and Wearn,R.B. "Structure of cannabidiol: Isomerization to tetrahydrocannabinols." J. Am. Chem. Soc. 1941, 63, 2209-2213.

71. Adams,R., Cain,C.K., and Wolff,H. "Structure of cannabidiol. Absorption spectra compared with those of various dihydric phenols." J. Am. Chem. Soc. 1940, 62, 732-734.

72. Adams,R., Chen,K.H., and Loewe,S. "Tetrahydrocannabinol homologs with a s-alkyl group in the 3-position." J. Am. Chem. Soc. 1945, 67, 1534-1537.

73. Adams,R., Harfenist,M., and Loewe,S. "New analogs of tetrahydrocannabinol. XIX." J. Am. Chem. Soc. 1941, 63, 1624-1628.

74. Adams,R., Hunt,M., and Clark,J.H. "Structure of cannabinol, a product isolated from the marihuana extract of Minnesota wild hemp." J. Am. Chem. Soc. 1940, 62, 196-200.

75. Adams,R., Hunt,M., and Clark,J.H. "Structure of cannabidiol. III. Reduction and cleavage." J. Am. Chem. Soc. 1940, 62, 735-737.

76. Adams,R., Loewe,S., Jelinek,C., and Wolff,H. "Tetrahydrocannabinol homologs with marihuana activity." IX. J. Am. Chem. Soc. 1941, 63, 1971-1976.

77. Adams,R., Loewe,S., Pease,D.C., Cain,C.K., Wearn,R.N., Baker,R.B., and Wolff,H. "Structure of cannabidiol. III. Position of the double bonds in cannabidiol. Marihuana activity of tetrahydrocannabinols." J. Am. Chem. Soc. 1940, 62, 2566-2567.

78. Adams,R., Loewe,S., Smith,C.M., and McPhee,W.D. "Tetrahydrocannabinol homologs and analogs with marihuana activity." J. Am. Chem. Soc. 1940, 64, 694-697.

79. Adams,R., Loewe,S., Theobold,C.W., and Smith, C.M. "Tetrahydrocannabinol analogs with marihuana activity." J. Am. Chem. Soc. 1942, 64, 2653-2655.

80. Adams,R., MacKenzie,S., and Loewe,S. "Tetrahydrocannabinol homologs with doubly branched alkyl groups in the 3-position." J. Am. Chem. Soc. 1948, 70, 664-668.

81. Adams,R., Pease,D.C., Cain,C.K., Baker,B.R., Clark, J.H., Wolff,H., and Wearn,R.B. "Conversion of cannabidiol to a product with marihuana activity. A type reaction for synthesis of analogous substances. Conversion of cannabidiol to cannabinol." J. Am. Chem. Soc. 1940, 62, 2245-2246.

82. Adams,R., Pease,D.C., Cain,C.K. and Clark,J.H. "Structure of cannabidiol. VI. Isomerization of cannabidiol to tetrahydrocannabinol, a physiologically active product. Conversion of cannabidiol to cannabinol." J. Am. Chem. Soc. 1940, 62, 2402-2405.

83. Adams,R., Pease,D.C., and Clark,J.H. "Isolation of cannabinol, cannabidiol and quebrachitrol from red oil of Minnesota wild hemp." J. Am. Chem. Soc. 1940, 62, 2194-2196.

84. Adams,R., Pease,D.C., Clark,J.H., and Baker,B.R. "Structure of cannabinol. I. Preparation of an isomer, 3-hydroxy-1-n-amyl-6,6,9-trimethyl-6-dibenzopyran." J. Am. Chem. Soc. 1940, 62, 2197-2200.

85. Adams,R., Smith,C.M., and Loewe,S. "Tetrahydrocannabinol homologs and analogs with marihuana activity." J. Am. Chem. Soc. 1941, 63, 1973-1976.

86. Adams,R., Smith,C.M., Loewe,S. "Chemically active synthetic tetrahydrocannabinols; d- and l-hydroxy-3-n-amyl-6,9,9-trimethyl-7,8,9,10-tetrahydro-6-dibenzopyrans." J. Am. Chem. Soc. 1942, 64, 2087-2089.

87. Adams,R., Wolff,H., Cain,C.K., and Clark,J.H. "Structure of cannabidiol. IV. The position of the linkage between the two rings." J. Am. Chem. Soc. 1940, 62, 1770-1775.

88. Adams,R., Wolff,H., Cain,C.K., and Clark,J.H. "Structure of cannabidiol. V. Position of the alicyclic double bonds." J. Am. Chem. Soc. 1940, 62, 2215-2219.

89. Adams,T.C. and Jones,L.A. "Long-chain hydrocarbons of cannabis and its smoke."Agric. Food Chem. 1973, 21, 1129-1131.

90. Adrian,C. "Note concerning Indian hemp."(Fr.). J. Pharm. Chim. 1891, 24, 27-28, 31-32.

91. A.G.N. "Marihuana." Can. Med. Assoc. 1934, 31, 544-546.

92. Agnew,W.F., Rumbaugh,C.L., and Cheng,J.T. "The uptake of delta-9-tetrahydrocannabinol in choroid plexus and brain cortex in vitro and in vivo." Brain Res. 1976, 109, 355-366.

93. Aguar,O. "Examination of cannabis extracts for alkaloid components." U.N. Doc. ST/SOA/Ser.S, May 24, 1971.

94. Agurell,S. "Constituents of male and female cannabis." In Joyce,C.R.B. and Curry,S.H.(eds.). The Botany and Chemistry of Cannabis. J. A. Churchill, London, 1970, 57-61.

95. Agurell,S. "Chemical and pharmacological studies of cannabis." In Joyce,C.R.B. and Curry,S.H.(eds.). The Botany and Chemistry of Cannabis. J. A. Churchill, London, 1970, 175-193.

96. Agurell,S. "Determination of cannabis components in blood." Ciba Found. Sympos. 1974, 26, 125-131..

97. Agurell,S., Binder,M., Fonseka,K., Lindgren,J.E., Leander,K., Martin,B., Nilsson,I.M., Nordquist, M., Ohlsson,A., and Widman,M. "Cannabinoids: Metabolites hydroxylated in the pentyl side chain." In Nahas,G.G., Paton,W.D.M., and Idanpaan-Heikkila,J.E.(eds.). Marihuana. Springer Verlag, N.Y., 1976, 141-159.

98. Agurell,S., Dahmen,J., Gustafsson,B., Johansson,U.B., Leander,K., Nilsson,I., Nilsson,J.L.G., Nordquist,M., Ramsay,C.H., Ryrfeldt,A., Sandberg,F., and Widman,M. "Metabolic fate of tetrahydrocannabinol." In Paton,D.W.M. and Crown,J.(eds.). Cannabis and its Derivatives. Oxford Univ. Press, London, 1972, 16-39.

99. Agurell,S., Gustafsson,B., Gosztonyi,T., Hedman,K., and Leander,K. "Synthesis of tritium labeled tetrahydrocannabinol and cannabidiol." Act. Chem. Scand. 1973, 27, 1090-1091.

100. Agurell,S., Gustafsson,B., Holmstedt,B., Leander,K., Lindgren,J., Nilsson,I. Sandberg,F., and Asberg,M. "Quantitation of delta-1-tetrahydrocannabinol in plasma from cannabis smokers." J. Pharm. Pharmacol. 1973, 25, 554-568.

101. Agurell,S. and Leander,K. "Stability, transfer and absorption of cannabinoid constituents of cannabis(hashish) during smoking." Act. Pharmaceut. Suec. 1971, 8, 391-402.

102. Agurell,S., Leander,S., Binder,M., Bader-Bartfai,A., Gustafsson,B., Leander,K., Lindgren,J.E., Ohlsson,A., and Tobisson,B. "Pharmacokinetics of delta-8-tetrahydrocannabinol in man after smoking: Relations to physiological and psychological effects." In Braude,M.C. and Szara,S. (eds.). Pharmacology of Marihuana. Raven Press, N.Y., 1976, I, 49-63.

103. Agurell,S. and Nilsson, J.L.G. "The chemistry and biological activity of cannabis." Bull. Narc. 1972, 24, 35-37.

104. Agurell,S., Nilsson,I., Lars,J., Nilsson,G., Ohlsson, A., Olofsson,K., Sandberg,F., Wahlquist,M., and Lindgren,J. "Constituents of male and female cannabis." In Joyce,C.R.B. and Curry,S.H.(eds.). The Botany and Chemistry of Cannabis. J. & A. Churchill, London, 1970, 57-59.

105. Agurell,S., Nilsson,I.M., Nilsson,J.L.G., Ohlsson,A., Widman,M., and Leander,K. "Metabolism of 7-hydroxy-delta-1(6)-THC and CBN." Act. Pharmaceut. Suec. 1971, 8, 698-699.

106. Agurell,S., Nilsson,I.M., Ohlsson,A., and Sandberg,F. "Elimination of tritium-labelled cannabinols in the rat with special reference to the development of tests for the identification of cannabis users." Biochem. Pharmacol. 1969, 18, 1195-1201.

107. Agurell,S., Nilsson,I.M., Ohlsson,A., and Sandberg,F. "On the metabolism of tritium-labelled delta-1-tetrahydrocannabinol in the rabbit." Biochem. Pharmacol. 1970, 19, 1333-1339.

108. Agurell,S., Nilsson,I.M., and Sandberg,F."Cannabis. Biochemical and chemical properties."(Swed.). Sv. Fam. Tidskr. 1968, 20, 662-670.

109. Ahlenstiel,H. and Kauffmann,R. "Geometrical images in visual halluncinations."(Ger.). Archiv. Psychiat. Zeit. Neurol. 1953, 190, 503-529.

110. Aitken,D. "Going to pot?" Paper presented at 9th annual convention of Student Humanist Federation. London, 1968.

111. Ainslie,W. "Materia medica of Hindustan." Madras

1813, 1, 21-80.

112. Albrecht,S.L. "Verbal attitudes and significant others' expectations as predictors of marihuana use." Sociol. Soc. Res. 1973, 57, 196-207.

113. Albretsen,C.S. and Odegard,J. "Narcomania--immediate help."(Nor.). Tid. Norsk. Laeg. 1962, 6, 356-368.

114. Alcott,L.M. "Perilous play." In Leslie, F.(ed.). Chimney Corner. N.Y., 1869.

115. Alden,J.P. "One wrong to justify another." Science 1968, 160, 604-605.

116. Aldrich,C.K. "The effect of a synthetic marihuana-like compound on musical talent as measured by the Seashore test." Pub. Hlth. Rep. 1944, 59, 431-435.

117. Aldrich,M.R. A Brief Legal History of Marihuana. Do It Now Foundation, Phoenix, Ariz. 1971.

118. Aldrich,M.R. Cannabis Myths and Folklore. State Univ. of New York, Buffalo, N.Y., 1970.

119. Aldrich,M.R. "Delta-9-tetrahydrocannabinol research." Marihuana Rev. 1968, 1, 14.

120. Aldrich,M.R. Drugs: a seminar. LEMAR, Buffalo, 1967.

121. Aldrich,M.R. "LEMAR international: The time is now." Marihuana Rev. 1968, 1, 2.

122. Aldrich,M.R. "Marihuana and the military: a complete report." Marihuana Rev. 1968, 1, 3-5.

123. Aldrich,M.R. "Marihuana mantras." Incense 1968, 16, 18-22.

124. Aldrich,M.R. "Soma: A solid year's work." Marihuana Rev. 1968, 1, 13.

125. Aldrich,M.R. Soma Dionysos: Worldwide Psychedelic Religion in 1500 B.C. LEMAR, Buffalo, 1968.

126. Aldrich,M.R. The Iguana Clock and other Notes on Marihuana Legislation. LEMAR, Buffalo, 1968.

127. Aldrich,M.R. "The old man of the mountain and translation from Mandeville." Incense 1967, 13, 10-14.

128. Aldrich,M.R. "The pentheus approach." Humanist 1968, 28, 16-19.

129. Aldrich,M.R. "Statement to the National Commission on Marihuana and Drug Abuse." Clin. Toxicol. 1971, 4, 643-653.

130. Aldrich,M.R. "Wichita precedes the U.S.A.. The Wichita decision." Marihuana Rev. 1968, 1, 11.

131. Aleksandrov,G.N. "A characterization of the vascular disturbances of the brain in experimental hashish poisoning in dogs."(Rus.). Nauch Tr. Samarkand Med. Inst. 1966, 36, 76-80.

132. Alexander,D.G. "Drugs: Where do we stand on enforcement? A status report on the growing drug control crisis, marihuana controversy, and administration proposals." Nations' Cities 1969, 7, 8-11.

133. Alexander,R.J. "Benactyzine and marihuana." Am. J. Psychiat. 1974, 131, 607.

134. Alexander,S. "Case of the pot-smoking school principal; Mrs. G. Brennan of Nicasio, Calif." Life 1967, 63, 25.

135. Alhanaty,E. and Livne,A. "Osmotic fragility of liposomes as affected by antihemolytic compounds." Biochim. Biophys. Acta 1974, 339, 146-155.

136. Alioto, J.T. "The effects of the expectancy of receiving either marihuana or alcohol on subsequent aggression in provoked high and low users of these drugs." Diss. Abs .1975, 35, 4637.

137. Allain,P. Hallucinogens and Society.(Fr.). Payot, Paris, 1973.

138. Allen,C. "Legalization of cannabis." Br. Med. J. 1973, 1, 550.

139. Allen,J.L. The Reign of Law; A Tale of the Kentucky Hemp Fields. MacMillan Co., N.Y., 1900.

140. Allen,J.R. and West,L.J. "Flight from violence: Hippies and the green rebellion." Am. J. Psychiat. 1968, 125, 364-378.

141. Allen,R.C. "Drug abuse on campus: The role of the university." In Wittenborn,J.R., Brill,H., Smith,J.P., and Wittenbron,S.A.(eds.). Drugs and Youth. C.C. Thomas, Springfield, Ill., 1969, 362-371.

142. Allen,R.C. "Drug laws and enforcement policies as communication." In Wittenborn,J.R., Smith,J.P. and Wittenborn,S.A.(eds.). Communication and Drug Abuse. C.C. Thomas, Springfield, Ill., 1970, 485-500.

143. Allen,T.F., Huges,R., Hering,C., Dunham,C., and Lippe,A. "Cannabis indica." In Allen,T.F.(ed.). The Encyclopedia of Pure Materia Medica. MacMillan Co., N.Y., 1875, 448-505.

144. Allentuck,S. and Bowman,K.M. "The psychiatric aspects of marihuana intoxication." Am. J. Psychiat. 1942, 99, 248-251.

145. Alles,G.A., Haagen-Smith,J.J., Geigen,G.A., and Danliker,W.B. "Evidence of another physiologically active principle in cannabis sativa." J. Pharmacol. Exper. Ther. 1942, 76, 21-26.

146. Alles,G.A., Icke,R.N., and Feigen,G.A. "Some analogs of synthetic tetrahydrocannabinol." J. Am. Chem. Soc. 1942, 64, 2031-2035.

147. Allman,J.D. "Cannabis indica." Med. Times 1911, 39, 765-766.

148. Allwardt,W.H., Babcock,P.A., Segelman,A.B., and Cross,J.M. "Photochemical studies of marihuana(cannabis) constituents." J. Pharmaceut. Sci. 1972, 61, 1994-1996.

149. Allyn,L.B. "How a seed supplemented chemical analysis." J.A.M.A. 1933, 101, 947.

150. Al-Magraby,S. The Phenomenon of Hashish Use. (Arab.). Dar-el-Maaref, Cairo, 1963.

151. Almeida,A.G. "Poisonous and medicinal plants indigenous to Mozambique."(Port.). Bol. Agric. Pecur. 1930, 1, 29.

152. Alpinus, P. Concerning the Medicines of the Egyptians.(Lat.). Venice, 1591.

153. Alsever,W.D. "An evaluation of marihuana for school physicians, nurses and educators." J. Sch. Hlth. 1968, 38, 629-638.

154. Altman,H. and Evenson,R.C. "Marihuana use and subsequent psychiatric symptoms: A replication." Comp. Psychiat. 1973, 14, 415-420.

155. Alvarez Tostado,E. Brief Study on Cannabis Indica.(Sp.). Editorial Cultura, Mexico, 1930.

156. Alves,C.N. and Carlini,E.A. "Effects of acute and chronic administration of cannabis sativa extract on the mouse-killing behavior of rats." Life Sci. 1973, 13, 75-85.

157. Alves,C.N., Goyos,A.C., and Carlini,E.A.

"Aggressiveness induced by marihuana and other psychotropic drugs in REM sleep deprived rats." Pharmacol. Biochem. Behav. 1973, 1, 183-189.

158. Alves,D. On Certain Indigenous and Foreign Textile Plants and Fibers.(Sp.). Bahia, 1927.

159. Amaral Da Cunha,I. The Roller Test of White Mice Under the Influence of Cannabis Sublimate.(Port.). Com. Nac. Fiscal. Entor., Rio de Janeiro, 1965.

160. Amaral Da Cunha,I. A Cannabis Identified by the Beam Reaction Has Proved Inactive.(Port.). Com. Nac. Fiscal. Entor., Rio de Janeiro, 1965.

161. Amaral Vieira,F.J. and Aguiar,M.B. The Action of Maconha(cannabis sativa) in Cases of Weakened Breathing Caused by High Doses of Nesdonal.(Port.). Imprensa Univ. Ceara, Fortaleza, 1964.

162. Amaral Vieira,F.J., Aguiar,M.B., and Ferreira Filho,F.M. "The relationship between the anticurare action and the excitant effects of 'maconha'(cannabis sativa)." Paper presented at the 16th reunion of the Brazilian society for the progress of science. Brazil, 1964.

163. American Academy of Pediatrics. "Effects of marihuana on man." Pediat. 1975, 56, 134-143.

164. American Academy of Pediatrics. Committee on Youth. "Drug abuse in adolescence: The use of harmful drugs--a pediatric concern." Pediat. 1969, 44, 131-141.

165. American Drug Manufacturers Association. "Report of the subcommittee on cannabis." Proc. Am. Drug Manufact. Assoc. 1921, 1, 323-326.

166. American Drug Manufacturers Association. "Report of the subcommittee on cannabis." Proc. Am. Drug Manufact. Assoc. 1922, 1, 144-146.

167. American Medical Association. "Dependence on cannabis(marihuana)." J.A.M.A. 1967, 201, 108-111, 368-371.

168. American Medical Association. "Dependence on LSD and other hallucinogens." J.A.M.A. 1967, 202, 47-50.

169. American Medical Association. "Marihuana and society." J.A.M.A. 1968, 204, 1181-1188.

170. American Medical Association. "Report of

committee on legislative activities--medical use of narcotics." J.A.M.A. 1937, 108, 2214.

171. American Medical Association. Bureau of Legal Medicine and Legislation. "Federal cannabis regulations approved." J.A.M.A. 1937, 109, 63B-64B.

172. American Psychiatric Association. "Position statement on marihuana laws." Am. J. Psychiat. 1970, 126, 1553.

173. American School Health Association. "Statement concerning the use of marihuana; 1972." J. Sch. Hlth. 1972, 42, 213.

174. Ames,F. "A clinical and metabolic study of acute intoxication with cannabis sativa and its role in the model psychoses." J. Ment. Sci. 1958, 104, 972-999.

175. Ames,O. Economic Annuals and Human Cultures. Harvard Univ. Press, Cambridge, Mass., 1939.

176. Amit,Z., Corcoran,M.E., Charness,M.E., and Shizgal,P. "Intake of diazepam and hashish by alcohol preferring rats deprived of alcohol." Physiol. Behav. 1973, 10, 523-527.

177. Ammar,S. and Barek,E.M. "Study of the evolutive aspects of toxicophilia in Tunisia." Proc. 3rd Wld. Cong. Psychiat. 1961, 1, 407-412.

178. Amo,M.F. and Bittner,J.R. "College student attitudes toward marihuana." Coll. Stud. Surv. 1970, 4, 52-54.

179. Anderes,T. On The Strengthening of the Diuretical Effects of the Species Diuretica Zyma through Cannabis Sativa. Gerschwiler, Berne, Switzerland, 1944.

180. Andersen,J., Morkholdt,N.E., Schou,J., Steentoft, A., and Worm,K. "A specific method for the demonstrating of cannabis intake by TLC of urine." Act. Pharmacol. Toxicol. 1971, 29, 111-112.

181. Anderson,F.E. "Marihuana flashbacks." Am. J. Psychiat. 1973, 130, 1399.

182. Anderson,G.S.D. "Remarks on the remedial virtues of cannabis indica, or Indian hemp." Med. Surg. J. 1863, 67, 426-430.

183. Anderson,L.C. "A study of systematic wood anatomy in cannabis." Bot. Mus. Harv. Leaf. 1974, 24, 29-36.

184. Anderson,P.F., Jackson,D.M., and Chesher,G.B.

"Interaction of delta-9-tetrahydrocannabinol and cannabidiol on intestinal motility in mice." J. Pharm. Pharmacol. 1974, 26, 136-137.

185. Anderson,P.F., Jackson,D.M., Chesher,G.B., and Malor,R. "Tolerance to the effects of delta-9-tetrahydrocannabinol in mice on intestinal motility, temperature and locomotor activity." Psychopharmacol. 1975, 43, 31-36.

186. Anderson,R. Some Tribal Customs in Eastern Bahr-El-Ghazal. Fourth report of Welcome Trop. Res. Lab., Gordon Memorial Coll., 1972.

187. Andersson,J.G. "An early Chinese culture." Bull. Geol. Surv. China 1923, 5, 26.

188. Andrade,L.P. Medicinal Plants of Goa. Their History, Description, Chemical Analysis, Therapeutic and Economic Uses.(Port.). Bastora, 1899.

189. Andrade,O.M. "The criminogenic action of cannabis(marihuana) and narcotics." Bull. Narc. 1964, 16, 23-28.

190. Andre,Cl. and Vercruysse,A. "Histochemical study of the stalked glandular hairs of the female cannabis plants, using fast blue salt." Plant. Med. 1976, 29, 361-366.

191. Andrews,G. and Vinkenoog,S.(eds.). The Book of Grass--An Anthology of Indian Hemp. Grove Press, N.Y., 1967.

192. Ange De Saint Joseph,Le. P. Persian Pharmacopoea Translated from Persian into Latin.(Lat.). Paris, 1681.

193. Angel,K. "No marihuana for adolescents." N. Y. Times Mag. 1969, 170.

194. Angel,K. "No marihuana for adolescents." N. Y. Times Mag. 1970, 9.

195. Angel,K. "Reflections on the psychological dangers of marihuana." Chitty's Law J. 1970, 18, 229.

196. Angelico,I. and Brown,J. "Marihuana and angina pectoris." New Eng. J. Med. 1974, 291, 800.

197. Angelo,A.J.S., Ordy,R.L., and Hansen,J.J. "Properties of a purified proteinase from hempseed." Phytochem. 1970, 9, 1933-1938.

198. Angst,J. and Woggon,B.Z. "Psychological and clinical aspects of cannabis abuse."(Ger.). A. Alleg. 1972, 48, 94-99.

199. Anker,J.L. and Milman,D.H. "Patterns of nonmedical drug usage among university students; student attitudes toward drug usage." In Keup,W.(ed.). Drug Abuse, Current Concepts and Research. C.C. Thomas, Springfield, Il., 1972, 202-214.

200. Anker,J.L., Milman,D.H., Kahan,S.A., and Valenti,C. "Drug usage and related patterns of behavior in university students: I. General survey and marihuana use." J. Am. Coll. Hlth. Assoc. 1971, 19, 124-132.

201. Annis,H.M. and Smart,R.G. "Adverse reactions and recurrences from marihuana use." Br. J. Addict. 1973, 68, 315-319.

202. Anonymous. "A blood test for marihuana metabolite." Chem. Engin. News 1973, 51, 9.

203. Anonymous. "A cannabis concoction." Bull. Narc. 1968, 20, 55.

204. Anonymous. "A case for cannabis?" Br. Med. J. 1967, 3, 258-259.

205. Anonymous. "A hashish-house in New York; the curious adventures of an individual who indulged in a few pipefuls of the narcotic hemp." Harper's New Month. Mag. 1883, 67, 944-949.

206. Anonymous. "A new preparation of cannabis indica." J.A.M.A. 1896, 26, 1145.

207. Anonymous. "A note from the underground." In Simmons,J.L.(ed.). Marihuana Myths and Realities. Brandon House, Hollywood, Calif., 1967, 15-23.

208. Anonymous. "A study of American grown cannabis in comparison with samples from other various sources." Eighth Internat'l Cong. Appl. Chem. 1912, 17, 23-30.

209. Anonymous. "A synthetic form of marihuana lowers blood pressure and body temperature in humans." Chem. Engin. News 1970, 48, 43.

210. Anonymous. "A Unesco inquiry on the harmfulness of cannabis." Unesco Courier 1973, 5, 23-26.

211. Anonymous. "Active compound." Chem. Engin. News 1971, 49, 14.

212. Anonymous. "Adolescence and marihuana."(Fr.). Concours Med. 1972, 94, 2385-2392.

213. Anonymous. "Addiction and tolerance." In Mayor's Committee on Marihuana. The Marihuana Problem in the City of New York. Jacques Cattell Press, Lancaster, Pa.,

1944, 144-146.

214. Anonymous. "Administrator's forum. This month's problem; program on drugs backfired when six students were picked up by juvenile authorities." Sch. Mgt. 1967, 11, 25.

215. Anonymous. "Advisory committee's report on cannabis." Lancet 1969, 1, 268-269.

216. Anonymous. "After chronic marihuana exposure, behavior and brain function change." Chem. Engin. News 1971, 49, 24.

217. Anonymous. "Aggressiveness and pot." Science Dig. 1976, 79, 19.

218. Anonymous. "Alcohol and marihuana exert many differences in action." Chem. Engin. News 1971, 49, 24.

219. Anonymous. "Alcohol and marihuana: Spreading menace among the teenagers." U.S. News 1975, 79, 28-30.

220. Anonymous. "AMA: Switch on to pot." Newsweek 1972, 80, 50.

221. Anonymous. Amphetamines, Barbiturates, LSD and Cannabis: Their Use and Misuse. Her Majesty's Stationery Office, London, 1970.

222. Anonymous. "An analgesic from pot." Med. Wld. News 1970, 11, 11.

223. Anonymous. "Analysis of hashish and Indian hemp using thin-layer chromatography." Acta Univ. Palachi. Olomuc. Fac. Med. 1966, 43, 111-124.

224. Anonymous. "Appendix to Victor Robinson's essay on hasheesh." Med. Rev. Med. 1929, 35, 313-318.

225. Anonymous. "Application of thin-layer chromatography in analysis of cannabis."(Fr.). U. N. Doc. ST/SOA/SER.S/13, Dec. 6, 1965.

226. Anonymous. "Aqueous extract of cannabis indica." Med. Rec. 1896, 50, 650.

227. Anonymous. "Argot of marihuana."(Sp.). Rev. Tec. Pol. 1955, 1, 13.

228. Anonymous. "As common as chewing gum; problem in Vietnam." Time 1971, 97, 14-15.

229. Anonymous. "Authorities respond to growing drug use among high school students." Phi Delta Kappan 1968, 50, 213.

230. Anonymous. "Background on the addicting drugs most frequently used in Canada." Addict. 1961, 8, 15-19.

231. Anonymous. "B.C. rejects drug laws report." Can. Bar J. 1970, 1, 20.

232. Anonymous. "Behavior and biological concomitants of chronic marihuana use." Contemp. Drug. Prob. 1975, 4, 447-448.

233. Anonymous. "Being busted: L. Fiedler arrested for maintaining premises where marihuana was used." Time 1972, 100, 50.

234. Anonymous. "Bibliography. Cannabis sativa." Bull. Narc. 1951, 3, 42-48, 59-78.

235. Anonymous. "Bibliography. Scientific publications on narcotic drugs in 1967." Bull. Narc. 1968, 20, 21-63.

236. Anonymous. "Biological dosage of cannabis indica cultivated near Pavia."(It.). Boll. Soc. Ital. Biol. Sper. 1940, 15, 8.

237. Anonymous. "Boston pot party: Research sponsored by Boston University Medical Center." New Repub. 1968, 159, 8.

238. Anonymous. Brazilian Cannabis--Brief Notes.(Port.). Com. Nac. Fiscal. Entor., Rio de Janeiro, 1959.

239. Anonymous. "Bust insurance; organiation. Free weed, dedicated to legalization of marihuana." Time 1970, 96, 15.

240. Anonymous. "Call for a change of attitudes toward drugs." Science News 1973, 103, 207.

241. Anonymous. "Campaign against marihuana cigarettes." J.A.M.A. 1934, 102, 850.

242. Anonymous. Campaign of Repression Against Use of and Trade in 'Maconha'."(Port.). Com. Nac. Fiscal. Entor., Rio de Janeiro, 1947.

243. Anonymous. "Can marihuana cause bronchitis and cancer." Am. Drug. 1970, 161, 53.

244. Anonymous. "Cannabinoid research may yield new drugs." Chem. Engin. News 1974, 52, 15-16.

245. Anonymous. "Cannabinoids released hydrolytic enzymes." Chem. Engin. News 1974, 52, 13.

246. Anonymous. "Cannabinon." Ther. Gaz. 1885, 9, 286-287.

247. Anonymous. "Cannabinum tannicum." J.A.M.A. 1883, 1, 210.

248. Anonymous. "Cannabis." Drug Ther. Bull. 1967, 5, 97-99.

249. Anonymous. "Cannabis." J.A.P.A. 1912, 1, 634-635.

250. Anonymous. "Cannabis." J.A.P.A. 1913, 2, 863-864.

251. Anonymous. "Cannabis." J.A.P.A. 1913, 2, 1088.

252. Anonymous. "Cannabis." J.A.P.A. 1920, 9, 615-616.

253. Anonymous. "Cannabis." Lancet 1969, 1, 139-140.

254. Anonymous. "Cannabis." Med. J. Aust. 1968, 1, 99-101.

255. Anonymous. "Cannabis." Med-Leg. J. 1969, 37, 3-5.

256. Anonymous. "Cannabis." Proc. Am. Drug Manufact. Assoc. 1897, 45, 417-418.

257. Anonymous. "Cannabis." Proc. Am. Drug Manufact. Assoc. 1897, 45, 216-219.

258. Anonymous. "Cannabis and driving skills." Can. Med. Assoc. J. 1972, 107, 269-270.

259. Anonymous. "Cannabis and LSD." Practitioner 1972, 209, 71.

260. Anonymous. "Cannabis and road accidents." Med. J. Aust. 1976, 1, 771.

261. Anonymous. "Cannabis and the brain." J. Irish Med. Assoc. 1972, 65, 493.

262. Anonymous. "Cannabis and the cardiovascular system." J.A.M.A. 1973, 2, 26-27.

263. Anonymous. "Cannabis and the med student." Human Behav. 1973, 2, 26-17.

264. Anonymous. "Cannabis and violence." Bull. Narc. 1968, 20, 44.

265. Anonymous. "Cannabis; as you were." Economist 1970, 236, 26.

266. Anonymous. "Cannabis causes chromosome breaks." Drugs Soc. 1973, 2, 3.

267. Anonymous. "Cannabis continued." Lancet 1969, 1, 246.

268. Anonymous. "Cannabis control bill." J.A.P.A. 1937, 26, 459.

269. Anonymous. "Cannabis conundrum." MD 1967, 11, 19.

270. Anonymous. "Cannabis debate continued." Br. Med. J. 1973, 1, 371.

271. Anonymous. "Cannabis encephalopathy." Lancet 1971, 2, 1240-1241.

272. Anonymous. "Cannabis habit scheduled for discussion in Geneva." J.A.P.A. 1936, 25, 373.

273. Anonymous. "Cannabis--harmless or dangerous?" Ceylon Med. J. 1971, 16, 67-68.

274. Anonymous. "Cannabis in early pregnancy." Bull. Narc. 1968, 20, 8.

275. Anonymous. "Cannabis indica." Br. Med. J. 1883, 1, 992.

276. Anonymous. "Cannabis indica." Lancet 1943, 2, 296-297.

277. Anonymous. "Cannabis indica." Pharmaceut. J. 1902, 15, 171.

278. Anonymous. "Cannabis indica." Proc. Am. Pharmaceut. Assoc. 19764, 22, 160-161.

279. Anonymous. "Cannabis indica and belladonna in whooping-cough." Ther. Gaz. 1887, 11, 47.

280. Anonymous. "Cannabis indica--examination in reference to active constituent." Proc. Am. Pharmaceut. Assoc. 1885, 33, 193-194.

281. Anonymous. "Cannabis indica in chorea and pertussis." Chicago Med. Times 1902, 35, 500.

282. Anonymous. "Cannabis indica in diarrhoea." Ther. Gaz. 1887, 11, 554-555.

283. Anonymous. "Cannabis indica in diseases of the stomach." Ther. Gaz. 1890, 14, 684-685.

284. Anonymous. "Cannabis indica in dysentery." Practitioner 1887, 124, 290-291.

285. Anonymous. "Cannabis indica in gastric disorders." Lancet 1890, 2, 631-632.

286. Anonymous. "Cannabis indica in headache." Pharmaceut. J. Trans. 1887, 17, 608.

287. Anonymous. "Cannabis indica in melancholia and mental depression with sleeplessness." Can. Med. Rec. 1884, 13, 65.

288. Anonymous. "Cannabis indica in pharmaceuticals." J. Med. Soc. New Jersey 1938, 35, 51-52.

289. Anonymous. "Cannabis indica in smoking tobacco." Pharmaceut. J. 1923, 111, 353-354.

290. Anonymous. "Cannabis indica. Materia medica of Pharmacopoeia." Pharmaceut. J. 1900, 10, 275.

291. Anonymous. "Cannabis indica--value in facial neuralgia, etc.." Proc. Am. Pharmaceut. Assoc. 1890, 30, 500-501.

292. Anonymous. "Cannabis. Lords debate drugs." Nature 1969, 222, 8.

293. Anonymous. "Cannabis regulations approved." J.A.M.A. 1937, 109, 63B-64B.

294. Anonymous. Cannabis Resin and the Elimination of the Corneal Reflex in the Rabbit. Com. Nac. Fiscal. Entor., Rio de Janeiro, 1965.

295. Anonymous. "Cannabis sativa, Indian hemp, or ganja." J. Imp. Inst. 1896, 2, 105-106.

296. Anonymous. "Cannabis sativa var. indica." Proc. Am. Pharmaceut. Assoc. 1864, 12, 112.

297. Anonymous. "Cannabis: The first controlled experiment." New Society, 1969, 13, 84-86.

298. Anonymous. "Cannabis--Yet another teratogen?" Br. Med. J. 1969, 1, 797.

299. Anonymous. "Carter's grass roots appeal." Time 1977, 110, 8.

300. Anonymous. "Cerebral atrophy in marihuana smokers." Science News 1971, 100, 406.

301. Anonymous. "Cerebral atrophy in young cannabis smokers." Conn. Med. 1972, 36, 285-286.

302. Anonymous. "Chemical and pharmacological research on cannabis indica cultivated in Italy."(It.). Il Farm. Scienz. Tecn. 1948, 3, 8-12.

303. Anonymous. "Chronic cannabis use and psychomotor function." Med. J. Aust. 1977, 1, 201-202.

304. Anonymous. "Classification of marihuana." Contemp. Drug Prob. 1973, 2, 303.

305. Anonymous. Clinical Studies of Narcotic Remedies. (Ger.). Erlangen, 1969.

306. Anonymous. "CMA issues brief on cannabis to senate committee; calls for process to 'decriminalize' offence." Can. Med. Assoc. J. 1975, 112, 503-504.

307. Anonymous. Colloquies on the Simples and Drugs of India and also on some Fruit Growing There. (Port.). Imprensa Nacional, Lisbon, 1872.

308. Anonymous. "Comparison between users and nonusers from the standpoint of mental and physical deterioration." In Mayor's Committee on Marihuana. The Marihuana Problem in the City of New York. Jacques Cattell Press, Lancaster, Pa., 1944, 140-143.

309. Anonymous. "Computers in medicine." Br. Med. J. 1967, 3, 430.

310. Anonymous. "Concerning hashish and its active substance."(Ger.). Verhand. Gesell. Deut. Natur. Aerz. 1909, 82, 2.

311. Anonymous. "Concurrent state and local regulation of marihuana: The validity of the Ann Arbor marihuana ordinance." Mich. Law Rev. 1972, 71, 400.

312. Anonymous. "Confessions of a campus pot dealer." Esquire 1967, 68, 100-101.

313. Anonymous. Confessions of an English Hashish-Eater. George Redway, London, 1884.

314. Anonymous. "Confusion over effects." Science News 1967, 92, 345-346.

315. Anonymous. "Constitutional law--eighth ammendment--statutory penalty for possession of marihuana violates cruel and unusual punishment clause." Miss. Law J. 1974, 45, 1297-1304.

316. Anonymous. "Constitutional law--eighth amendment--the harmlessness of marihuana must be conclusively proven by the defendant as the basis for an eighth amendment appeal or challenge to a sentence for possession." Cath. U. Law Rev. 1975, 24, 648-657.

317. Anonymous. "Constitutional law federal marihuana statutes on empirical appraisal of criminal statutory presumptions." De Paul Law Rev. 1969, 19, 184.

318. Anonymous. "Constitutional law: Self-incrimination: Transfer tax and order forms required by marihuana tax act not in violation of fifth amendment." Law Soc. Order 1969, 125, 69.

319. Anonymous. "Continuing battle over pot." Science News 1971, 99, 277.

320. Anonymous. "Crackdown; sentence of 3½ years in state prison for possession of marihuana." Nation 1969, 208, 293-294.

320a. Anonymous. "Crime of marihuana." New Repub. 1967, 157, 9-10.

321. Anonymous. "Criminal law--marihuana--conviction for possession for personal use held not violative of substantive due process." N. Y. Law Forum 1968, 14, 182.

322. Anonymous. "Cultivation of hemp(cannabis sativa L.) for its fiber content."(Ger.). Der Zucht. 1942, 14, 201-213.

323. Anonymous. "Dagga."(Dut.). Huisgenoot 1945, 30, 19, 23, 37.

324. Anonymous. "Dagga." S. Af. Med. J. 1951, 25, 284-286.

325. Anonymous. "Dagga--opium of the west."(Dut.). Huisgenoot 1948, 33, 28-29.

326. Anonymous. "Dagga smoking." S. Af. Med. J. 1938, 12, 71.

327. Anonymous. "Dagga smoking in Rhodesia." Cent. Af. J. Med. 1966, 12, 215-216.

328. Anonymous. "Decriminalization of marihuana." Med. Trib. Med. News 1972, 13, 15.

329. Anonymous. "Dependence on cannabis(marihuana)." J.A.M.A. 1967, 201, 368-371.

330. Anonymous. "Deportation of an alien for a marihuana conviction can constitute cruel and unusual punishment." San Diego Law Rev. 1976, 13, 454-466.

331. Anonymous. "Detecting cannabis in drivers; work of Joe Vinson." Science Dig. 1976, 80, 22-23.

332. Anonymous. "Detection of hashish in saliva." (Ger.). Kriminalistik 1972, 26, 456.

333. Anonymous. Determination of the Physiological Activity of the Cannabis Resin using the Dog Ataxia Test. (Port.). Com. Nac. Fiscal. Entor., Rio de Janeiro, 1965.

334. Anonymous. Determination of the Quality of the Cannabinolic Constituents; of the Degree of Maturity and Acitivity of the Cannabis Resin. (Port.). Com. Nac. Fiscal. Entor., Rio de Janeiro, 1965.

335. Anonymous. "Diagnostic interview with a disturbed college student." Front. Hosp. Psychiat. 1968, 5, 5-6,8.

336. Anonymous. "Doctor builds a case against marihuana." Mod. Med. 1972, 40, 24, 26,

337. Anonymous. "Dope cigarette peddling among British musicians." Melody Maker 1936, 12.

338. Anonymous. "Doubt as to sanity or insanity--opinions as to smoking of marihuana--evidence as to syphilis." J.A.M.A. 1923, 2, 1553-1554.

339. Anonymous. "Draft refusal, marihuana and bar admission." A.B.A. J. 1971, 57, 140.

340. Anonymous. "Dream farm; field of marihuana destroyed by narcotic agents." Time 1967, 90, 17-18.

341. Anonymous. "Drop that pot!" Newsweek 1968, 72, 61.

342. Anonymous. "Drug abuse in business." Nature 1970, 227, 331-332.

343. Anonymous. "Drug abuse: Tobacco a precursor." Chem. Engin. News 1971, 36, 20.

344. Anonymous. "Drug abuse up in Australia." N.C.C.D. News 1970, 49, 3.

345. Anonymous. "Drug addiction among adolescents." Sat. Rev. 1953, 36, 20.

346. Anonymous. Drug Dependence. A Guide for Physicians. Am. Med. Assoc., Chicao, 1969.

347. Anonymous. "Drug dependence--marihuana." Med. Ann. D.C. 1969, 38, 105.

348. Anonymous. "Drug smokers are on the increase." Pol. Chron. Constab. Wld. 1951, 33, 4.

349. Anonymous. "Drug-taking by the young." Br. Med. J. 1967, 2, 67.

350. Anonymous. "Drug use and analysis results; 1973-1975." Pharm. Chem. News 1976, 5, 1-8.

351. Anonymous. "Drugged artists paint better." Science Dig. 1955, 38, 35.

352. Anonymous. "Drugged future?" Time 1958, 71, 35-36.

353. Anonymous. "Drugs affect artists." Science News Letter 1955, 68, 4.

354. Anonymous. "Drugs--hard and soft distinguished." Nature 1970, 225, 1089.

355. Anonymous. "Drugs of addiction--2." Br. Med. J. 1964, 2, 1119-1120.

356. Anonymous. "Easing up on pot?" Newsweek 1972, 79, 17.

357. Anonymous. "Effects of alcohol and cannabis during labor." J.A.M.A. 1930, 94, 1165.

358. Anonymous. "Effects of cannabis." J.A.M.A. 1933, 100, 601.

359. Anonymous. "Effects of hashish." Scientif. Amer. 1869, 21, 183.

360. Anonymous. "Effects of marihuana and alcohol on simulated driving performance." Med. J. Aust. 1969, 2, 732.

361. Anonymous. "Effects of marihuana; findings of scientific tests." Time 1968, 92, 52.

362. Anonymous. "Effects of marihuana use." Science 1973, 180, 1121.

363. Anonymous. "Effects of the single convention on narcotic drugs upon the regulation of marihuana." Hast. Law J. 1968, 19, 848.

364. Anonymous. "Egypt. Hasheesh lunatics." Lancet 1897, 1, 415-416.

365. Anonymous. "End of the pot-watch?" Newsweek 1974, 84, 113.

366. Anonymous. "End penalties for private cannabis use recommends U.S. Commission." Drugs Soc. 1972, 1, 2.

367. Anonymous. "Enquiry on drug abuse." Correct. Process 1969, 10, 8.

368. Anonymous. Ether, Cocaine, Haschich, Peyote and Dementia Praecox.(Fr.). Vega, Paris, 1932.

369. Anonymous. "Evils of marihuana, more fantasy than fact?" U.S. News 1972, 72, 37.

370. Anonymous. "Experimental psychoses which mimic schizophrenia." Neb. State Med. J. 1956, 41, 455-459.

371. Anonymous. "Facts and fancies about marihuana." Lit. Dig. 1936, 122, 7-8.

372. Anonymous. "Federal regulation of medicinal use of cannabis." J.A.M.A. 1937, 108, 1543-1544.

373. Anonymous. "Federal statutes governing traffic in marihuana--the grass is still greener on the other side." U. Miami Law Rev. 1969, 24, 184.

374. Anonymous. "Fiedler affair; Buffalo university group aims to legalize marihuana." Newsweek 1967, 69, 29.

375. Anonymous. "Find how drugs build up addiction." Science News Letter 1956, 69, 200.

376. Anonymous. "First double-blind findings on marihuana." Med. Wld. News 1969, 10, 18-20.

377. Anonymous. "First report of the international narcotics control board." Bull. Narc. 1969, 21, 33-38.

378. Anonymous. "First year: few surprises." Science News 1971, 99, 114.

379. Anonymous. "For the record." Med. Wld. News 1972, 13, 6.

380. Anonymous. "For those using brown-wrapped smokes there's now a magasine sent the same way." Advert. Age 1974, 45, 20.

381 Anonymous. "Fresh disclosures on drugs and GI's Senate investigation." U.S. News 1970, 68, 32-33.

382. Anonymous. "Ganja--threat to health in Jamaica." J.A.M.A. 1974, 229, 1521.

383. Anonymous. "GC nails marihuana isomers." Chem. Engin. News 1966, 44, 14.

384. Anonymous. "Getting established." Economist 1976, 258, 42.

385. Anonymous. "Getting tough with pot; marihuana smokers discovered at New Jersey's preparatory school." Time 1967, 90, 110.

386. Anonymous. "GH poll: should marihuana laws be changed?" Good House. 1968, 167, 10.

387. Anonymous. "Going to pot in Washington; a hippie party." U.S. News 1967, 62, 63.

388. Anonymous. "Graduate students as marihuana users." School Soc. 1968, 96, 392.

389. Anonymous. "Grass and poison."(Fr.). Concours Med. 1972, 94, 2379-2380.

390. Anonymous. "Grass clippings." New Repub. 1972, 166, 7.

391. Anonymous. "Grass grows more acceptable." Time 1973, 102, 67.

392. Anonymous. "Grass on campus." Alaska Med. 1972, 14, 16.

393. Anonymous. "Grass roots: People's pot conference of 1972." Newsweek 1972, 80, 18.

394. Anonymous. "Haschisch. Cannabinon." Pharmaceut. J. Trans. 1887, 17, 685-686.

395. Anonymous. "Hasheesh." Med. Rec. 1935, 142, 488.

396. Anonymous. "Hasheesh(cannabis indica) inebriety." Quart. J. Ineb. 1897, 19, 402-404.

397. Anonymous. "Hashish." Br. Med. J. 1964, 2, 1348-1349.

398. Anonymous. "Hashish." Littell's Living Age 1858, 56, 449-461.

399. Anonymous. "Hashish." Sciences 1966, 5, 14.

400. Anonymous. "Hashish." Once a Week 1868, 18, 350-351.

401. Anonymous. "Hashish and insanity." Lancet 1896, 2, 545-546.

402. Anonymous. "Hashish-marihuana: a worldwide problem."(Ger.). Neue Polizei 1971, 25, 182.

403. Anonymous. "Hashish--regulations regarding sale of it in Constantinople." Br. Med. J. 1864, 1, 372.

404. Anonymous. "Have a high holiday; user of marihuana on campus." Newsweek 1968, 72, 50-51.

405. Anonymous. "Hemp industry." Scientif. Amer. 1903, 56, 3343-3344.

406. Anonymous. "Hemp the barometer of war." Lit. Dig. 1923, 76, 26-27.

407. Anonymous. "How pot-smokers start." Science Dig. 1969, 66, 57-58.

408. Anonymous. "How to spoil the 'hash' market." (Ger.). Neue Polizei 1971, 25, 183-185.

409. Anonymous. "How to use pot; course description from the bulletin of the Midpeninsula free university; Stanford California." Sat. Rev. 1968, 51, 62.

410. Anonymous. Identification of Active Maconha. (Port.). Com. Nac. Fiscal. Entor., Rio de Janeiro, 1965.

411. Anonymous. Identification of cannabis by Spectrophotometry. Com. Nac. Fiscal. Entor., Rio de Janeiro, 1965.

412. Anonymous. Identifying and Controlling Wild Hemp. Agricultural Experiment Station, Kansas State Univ. of Agriculture and Applied Sciences, Manhattan, Kansas, 1972.

413. Anonymous. "If pot were legal." Time 1970, 96, 41.

414. Anonymous. "Illegal transportation of marihuana: Recent judicial construction of the California statute." Pacific Law J. 1972, 3, 670.

415. Anonymous. "In Vietnam: mama saw pushers." Newsweek 1969, 73, 108.

416. Anonymous. "Indian hemp." Amer. Drug. 1884, 13, 122.

417. Anonymous. "Indian hemp."(Sp.). Mon. Farm. Ter. 1953, 56, 71.

418. Anonymous. "Indian hemp and belladonna in whooping cough." Ther. Gaz. 1887, 11, 124.

419. Anonymous. "Indian hemp in persistent headache." J.A.M.A. 1887, 9, 731-732.

420. Anonymous. Indian Hemp with Particular Regard to its Narcotic Properties. (Ger.). Prague, 1860.

421. Anonymous. "Indian hemp--physiological effects." Proc. Am. Pharmaceut. Assoc. 1900, 48, 665-666.

422. Anonymous. "Indian hemp poisoning." Br. Med. J. 1896, 2, 1619.

423. Anonymous. Indigenous Drugs of India. Art Press, Calcutta, 1933.

424. Anonymous. "Intoxicants." Maroc med. 1955, 34, 1493.

425. Anonymous. Intoxicants in Legal Medicine.(Sp.). Havana, 1947.

426. Anonymous. "Is marihuana all that harmless." Rhode Is. Med. J. 1972, 55, 49.

427. Anonymous. "Is marihuana harmful."(Sp.). Med. 1971, 31, 244-246.

428. Anonymous. "Is marihuana the best drug for glaucoma." Med. Wld. News 1973, 14, 19-21.

429. Anonymous. "Is the pot user driver, or in the driver's seat?" Time 1969, 94, 64-65.

430. Anonymous. "Justice department gets into marihuana research." Med. Wld. News 1970, 11, 4.

431. Anonymous. "Juvenile delinquency; narcotic factor." Cong. Dig. 1954, 33, 292.

432. Anonymous. "Keep off the grass." Nature 1969, 224 205-206.

433. Anonymous. "Keep off the grass." New Repub. 1967, 156, 5-6.

434. Anonymous. "Last week was a bad week for the narcs; eventual decriminalization of marihuana." Science News 1972, 101, 117-118.

435. Anonymous. "Latest findings on marihuana." U.S. News 1971, 70, 26-27.

436. Anonymous. "Latest medical facts about marihuana." Good House. 1971, 172, 185-186.

437. Anonymous. "Law 'n order in Dallas; use of 4 black students from University of California." Nation 1970, 211, 582.

438. Anonymous. "Lebanon and hashish." Lancet 1943, 2, 745.

439. Anonymous. "Lebanon: hash is for others." Economist 1971, 240, 34.

440. Anonymous. "Legality of cannabis experiments." Nature 1968, 220, 1265.

441. Anonymous. "Legalize marihuana?" Med. J. Aust. 1970, 1, 1237-1238.

442. Anonymous. "Legislative note--legal analysis of marihuana legislation in Illinois." De Paul Law Rev. 1972, 22, 277.

443. Anonymous. "Let liquor stores sell marihuana?" Am. Drug. 1971, 163, 36.

444. Anonymous. "Licensed federal municipal-cop-prosecuted nathless--Harry Herman M.D. busted." Marihuana Rev. 1968, 1, 19.

445. Anonymous. "Little less legal." New Repub. 1969, 161, 11.

446. Anonymous. "Lords debate cannabis." Nature 1969, 222, 8.

447. Anonymous. Maconha, a Hallucinogenic Plant. (Port.). Com. Nac. Fiscal. Entor., Rio de Janeiro, 1963.

448. Anonymous. "Make marihuana laws easier? Most people say no." Sen. Schol. 1971, 99, 7.

449. Anonymous. "Magic garden." Time 1970, 96, 14.

450. Anonymous. "Male and female marihuana." Drug Cosmet. Indust. 1969, 105, 117-118.

451. Anonymous. "Marihuana." Bull. Bur. Crim. Invest. 1951, 16, 1.

452. Anonymous. "Marihuana." Can. Med. Assoc. J. 1934, 31, 544-546.

453. Anonymous. "Marihuana." Crim. Law Quart. 1967, 10.

454. Anonymous. "Marihuana." Del. State Med. J. 1944, 16, 15.

455. Anonymous. "Marihuana." J.A.M.A. 1953, 151, 1247.

456. Anonymous. "Marihuana." Med. Lett. Drugs Ther. 1967, 9, 73-76.

457. Anonymous. "Marihuana." Med. Lett. Drugs Ther. 1970, 12, 33-35.

458. Anonymous. "Marihuana." Med. Lett. Drugs Ther. 1976, 18, 69-70.

459. Anonymous. "Marihuana." N. Z. Med. J. 1969, 70, 195.

460. Anonymous. "Marihuana." N. Z. Med. J. 1973, 78, 362-363.

461. Anonymous. "Marihuana." Rhode Is. Med. J. 1969, 52, 337-338.

462. Anonymous. "Marihuana."(Ger.). Schweiz. Med. Woch. 1940, 5, 109-110.

463. Anonymous. "Marihuana: A red herring?" Med. J. Aust. 1973, 2, 203-204.

464. Anonymous. "Marihuana: A weapon against cancer?" Chem. Engin. News 1974, 52, 6.

465. Anonymous. Marihuana Addiction. Practitioner's Library of Medicine and Surgery, N.Y., 1941.

466. Anonymous. "Marihuana addictive." Chem. Engin. News 1971, 49, 14.

467. Anonymous. "Marihuana affects sleep EEG." Ped. News 1972, 6, 67.

468. Anonymous. "Marihuana and diabetic coma." Med. J. Aust. 1971, 1, 360.

469. Anonymous. "Marihuana and Health: A report to the Congress." Am. J. Psychiat. 1971, 128, 189-193.

470. Anonymous. "Marihuana and Health. A report to the Congress from the Secretary, Department of Health Education and Welfare." J. Drug Is. 1971, 1, 167-176.

471. Anonymous. "Marihuana and Health, latest government findings." U.S. News 1975, 72, 75.

472. Anonymous. "Marihuana and its effects: an assessment of current knowledge." Addict. 1968, 15, 1-7.

473. Anonymous. "Marihuana and LSD." Med. J. Aust. 1969, 2, 165-166.

474. Anonymous. "Marihuana and LSD. Effects and dangers."(Sp.). Rev. Pol. Tecn. 1971, 36, 40-46.

475. Anonymous. "Marihuana and our youth." Clin. Ped. 1969, 8, 253-254.

476. Anonymous. "Marihuana and the law." Can. Med. Assoc. J. 1967, 97, 1359-1361.

477. Anonymous. "Marihuana and the law." Nature 1970, 227, 1186.

478. Anonymous. "Marihuana and the law: A judicial opinion." Suff. Univ. Law Rev. 1968, 3, 23-41.

479. Anonymous. "Marihuana and the law: problem of education and enforcement." U.S.F.V. Law Rev. 1968, 1, 139.

480. Anonymous. "Marihuana and the law: The constitutional challenges to marihuana laws in light of marihuana use." Villanova Law Rev. 1968, 13, 851.

481. Anonymous. "Marihuana and the narcotic control act." U.B.C. Law Rev. 1967, 3, 250.

482. Anonymous. "Marihuana and the tax law." Lincoln Law Rev. 1970, 5, 176.

483. Anonymous. "Marihuana as cigarette filler." (Sp.). Rev. Tec. Pol. 1955, 1, 8.

484. Anonymous. "Marihuana before the bench." Time 1967, 90, 77.

485. Anonymous. "Marihuana brain damage." Chem. Engin. News 1971, 49, 29.

486. Anonymous. "Marihuana: Buyer beware." J.A.M.A. 1972, 222, 84.

487. Anonymous. "Marihuana causes mental harm." Am. Drug. 1971, 164, 62.

488. Anonymous. "Marihuana causes psychic dependence, says physician." Today's Hlth. 1967, 45, 13.

489. Anonymous. "Marihuana, chromosomes, teratogenicity: An overview." J. Cannab. Res. 1974, 2, 1-4.

490. Anonymous. "Marihuana cigarettes." Lancet 1935, 1, 38.

491. Anonymous. "Marihuana clouded their recent memory." Med. Wld. News 1972, 13, 18.

492. Anonymous. "Marihuana: Cultural and clinical studies." Science News 1975, 108, 374.

493. Anonymous. Marihuana: Dangerous as alcohol." New Repub. 1967, 157, 7-8.

494. Anonymous. "Marihuana: Decriminalization, deemphasizes discouragement." Science News 1972, 101, 197.

495. Anonymous. "Marihuana: Detection in urine." Chem. Engin. News 1971, 49, 8.

496. Anonymous. "Marihuana effect on speech." Marihuana Rev. 1968, 1, 13.

497. Anonymous. "Marihuana--evidence for the prosecution." Med. J. Aust. 1975, 1, 767.

498. Anonymous. "Marihuana evil." Fifth Estate 1972, 7, 14.

499. Anonymous. "Marihuana evils." Frat. Ord. Pol. J. 1933, 10-11, 21-22.

500. Anonymous. "Marihuana for better breathing." Science News 1976, 110, 55.

501. Anonymous. "Marihuana grown on vacant lots." J.A.M.A. 1935, 105, 891.

502. Anonymous. "Marihuana harmful? The dispute goes on." U.S. News 1971, 70, 68.

503. Anonymous. "Marihuana--it's big business now; house select committee on crime report." U.S. News 1970, 68, 103.

504. Anonymous. "Marihuana laws: A need for reform." Arkansas Law Rev. 1968, 22, 359.

505. Anonymous. "Marihuana laws: An empirical study of enforcement and administration in a Los Angeles country." U.C.L.A. Law Rev. 1968, 15, 1501-1585.

506. Anonymous. "Marihuana legislation." America 1969, 121, 378.

507. Anonymous. "Marihuana: Making its presence felt." Yale Alum. Mag. 1967, 30, 10-11.

508. Anonymous. "Marihuana may lurk in window boxes." Science News Letter 1951, 60, 60.

509. Anonymous. "Marihuana may yield agents having therapeutic benefits." Med. Trib. Med. News 1972, 13, 3.

510. Anonymous. "Marihuana or alcohol, which harms most?" U.S. News 1968, 64, 15.

511. Anonymous. "Marihuana persistence in the body." Science News 1970, 98, 476.

512. Anonymous. "Marihuana possession and the California constitutional prohibition of cruel or unusual punishment." U.C.L.A. Law Rev. 1974, 21, 1136-1171

513. Anonymous. "Marihuana: Possible use as a medicine." Science News 1975, 108. 262-263.

514. Anonymous. "Marihuana: Pot luck." Economist 1974, 253, 56.

515. Anonymous. "Marihuana problem; symposium" Newsweek 1967, 70, 46-50.

516. Anonymous. "Marihuana problems." J.A.M.A. 1945, 127, 1129.

517. Anonymous. "Marihuana program advances at NIMH." Chem. Engin. News 1970, 48, 30-33.

518. Anonymous. "Marihuana relieves severe cancer-caused depression." Am. Drug 1975, 171, 36.

519. Anonymous. "Marihuana report; another approach." Science News 1976, 109, 119.

520. Anonymous. "Marihuana report. First year: few surprises." Science News 1971, 99, 114.

521. Anonymous. "Marihuana report leaves legal problems unsolved." J.A.M.A. 1972, 220, 338-339.

522. Anonymous. "Marihuana research still to come." Nation's Sch. 1970, 85, 51.

523. Anonymous. "Marihuana smoking and the onset of heroin use." Bull. Narc. 1968, 20, 29.

524. Anonymous. "Marihuana smoking decreases intra-ocular pressure." Chem. Engin. News 1972, 50, 25.

525. Anonymous. "Marihuana studies." Med. J. Aust. 1971, 2, 1261-1264.

526. Anonymous. "Marihuana tax and the privilege against self-incrimination." Univ. Penn. Law Rev. 1969, 117, 432.

527. Anonymous. "Marihuana, the law and the courts." Osgoode Hall Law J. 1970, 8, 215.

528. Anonymous. "Marihuana: The legal question." Consum. Rep. 1975, 40, 265-266.

529. Anonymous. "Marihuana--the other enemy in Vietnam." U.S. News 1970, 68, 68-69.

530. Anonymous. "Marihuana the unromantic." Can. Med. Assoc. J. 1967, 97, 132-133.

531. Anonymous. "Marihuana: Truth on health problems." Science News 1975, 107, 117.

532. Anonymous. "Marihuana: U.S. army study." Contemp. Drug Prob. 1975, 4, 447-448.

533. Anonymous. "Marihuana vote--impact for White House; California votes on legalizing use and cultivation of marihuana." U.S. News 1972, 73, 50.

534. Anonymous. "Marihuana warning." Time 1968, 91, 6.

535. Anonymous. "Marihuana: What it is and isn't" U.S. News 1969, 67, 48-50.

536. Anonymous. "Marines and marihuana." Newsweek 1951, 38, 17.

537. Anonymous. "Materia medica and therapeutics." N.Y. Med. J. 1870, 11, 437-439.

538. Anonymous. Materia Medica of North Africa.(Fr.). Vigot, Paris, 1921.

539. Anonymous. "Medical group favors milder marihuana laws." J.A.M.A. 1974, 227, 262.

540. Anonymous. "Medical research council report on marihuana." N. Z. Med. J. 1972, 75, 370-373.

541. Anonymous. "Mental effects of hasheesh." Lancet 1896, 2, 1776-1777.

542. Anonymous. "Mental symptoms associated with the smoking of dagga." S. Af. Med. J. 1938, 12, 85-88.

543. Anonymous. "Metabolism of cannabis." Br. Med. J. 1970, 4, 610.

544. Anonymous. "Metabolism of cannabis." Br. Med. J. 1971, 2, 332-333.

545. Anonymous. "Mexico's war on marihuana." U.S. News 1969, 67, 21-23.

546. Anonymous. "Mild intoxicant." Scientif. Amer. 1969, 220, 43-44.

547. Anonymous. "Miscellaneous intelligence." Nature 1970, 225, 991.

548. Anonymous. "Modern medicine poll on socio-medical issues, abortion--homosexual practices--marihuana." Mod. Med 1969, 37, 18-25.

549. Anonymous. "Morality of marihuana." Time 1968, 92, 58.

550. Anonymous. "More controversy about pot." Time 1971, 97, 65.

551. Anonymous. "More flexibility on drugs." Nature 1970, 225, 485-486.

552. Anonymous. "More light on marihuana." Lancet 1940, 2, 370.

553. Anonymous. "Multilingual list of narcotic drugs under international control." U.N. Doc. E/CN.7/513, 1968.

554. Anonymous. "Narcotic enforcement in the U.S.A.." F.B.I. Law Enforce. Bull. 1938.

555. Anonymous. "Narcotics and glucosuria." J.A.M.A. 1958, 167, 2162.

556. Anonymous. "National affairs." Newsweek 1969, 71, 82.

557. Anonymous. "Nationwide survey on marihuana." Science Dig. 1972, 71, 63.

558. Anonymous. "Navy study indicates regular marihuana use disrupts sleep patterns." Naval Res. 1972, 1 25-26.

559. Anonymous. "New allies for marihuana reform." Christ. Cent. 1972, 89, 1311-1312.

560. Anonymous. "New awareness points to softer marihuana laws." Cong. Quart. Wkly. Rep. 1969, 27, 2651-2654.

561. Anonymous. "New color tests for hashish." Proc. Pharmaceut. Soc. Egypt 1952, 77.

562. Anonymous. "New contributions to the study of cannabis."(Fr.). Arch. Inst. Pasteur Tunis 1938, 27, 368-443.

563. Anonymous. "New dope on pot." Human Behav. 1973, 2, 75.

564. Anonymous. "New report on marihuana use and its hazards." Soc. 1974, 11, 6.

565. Anonymous. "New research on cannabis." Br. Med. J. 1971, 2, 293-294.

566. Anonymous. "New test for marihuana." J.A.M.A. 1972, 221, 722.

567. Anonymous. "New test for marihuana smoker." J.A.M.A. 1941, 116, 2640.

568. Anonymous. "New view on pot." Time 1971, 97, 45-46.

569. Anonymous. "News about cannabis."(Nor.). Tidsskr. Norske Laege. 1970, 90, 323.

570. Anonymous. "Nixon drug law; a crucial fault." Life 1969, 67, 32.

571. Anonymous. "Nixon's new plan to deal with the marihuana problem." U.S. News 1969, 67, 14.

572. Anonymous. "No martyr to marihuana: New Goddard line." New Repub. 1967, 157, 6.

573. Anonymous. "Note on the extracts of cannabis indica." Mont. Med. 1890, 15, 461-465.

574. Anonymous. "Notes from a campus pot smoker." Yale Alum. Mag. 1967, 31, 27-28.

575. Anonymous. "Nocious effects of marihuana and danger from the marihuana drug addict."(Sp.). Pol. Sec. Nacion. 1941, 8, 3-11.

576. Anonymous. "Oberlin's revised policy." Sch. Soc. 1968, 96, 167.

577. Anonymous. "Of pot and rats." Time 1971, 98, 71.

578. Anonymous. "On sativa."(Ger.). Schweiz. Med. Woch. 1943, 73, 1259.

579. Anonymous. "On smoking pot; report of the Indian Hemp Drugs Commission." Trans-action 1969, 7, 8.

580. Anonymous. "On some other intoxicants." In Albutt,T.C.(ed.). A System of Medicine. Macmillan Co., N.Y., 1900, 900-903.

581. Anonymous. "On the use of marihuana."(Dut.) Ned. Mil. Geneesk. Tijd. 1960, 13, 108-112.

582. Anonymous. "Operation showboat: Mexican border crackdown." Nation 1969, 209, 365-366.

583. Anonymous. "Our home hasheesh crop." Lit. Dig. 1926, 89, 64-65.

584. Anonymous. "Paraphernalia for marihuana and hashish use: possession statutes and Indiana's pipe dream." Valparaiso Univ. Law Rev. 1976, 10, 353-383.

585. Anonymous. "Penalties and programs; national drive against narcotics and other drugs." Time 1969, 94, 65.

586. Anonymous. "Penalty provision for possession of marihuana." Today's Ed. 1972, 61, 36-37.

587. Anonymous. "Perils of pot." Time 1974, 104, 94.

588. Anonymous. "Perils of pot start showing up." U.S. News 1974, 76, 58.

589. Anonymous. "Personal business; if your teen-ager uses pot." Bus. Wld. 1969, 137-138.

590. Anonymous. "Personal business(marihuana and your children)." Bus. Week 1971, 87.

591. Anonymous. "Pharmacology of marihuana remains obscure." Chem. Engin. News 1970, 48, 36-38.

592. Anonymous. "Physical damage of pot yet unproven, says the Department of Health, Education and Welfare." Psychiat. News 1971, 6, 3.

593. Anonymous. "Pills of extract cannabis." Pharmaceut. Rec. 1891, 11.

594. Anonymous. "Pinning down the weed." Science News 1969, 96, 263-264.

595. Anonymous. "Polemics of pot." Newsweek 1971, 77, 109.

596. Anonymous. "Pondering pot: Effects of pot smoking." Christ. Cent. 1969, 86, 1270.

597. Anonymous. "Pop drugs: The high as a way of life." Time 1969, 94, 68-70.

598. Anonymous. "Pop 'Pot'." Lancet 1963, 2, 989-990.

599. Anonymous. "Position of preparations of narcotic drugs under narcotic treaties." Bull. Narc. 1959, 11, 17.

600. Anonymous. "Position statement of the use of drugs in schools." Am. J. Psychiat. 1970, 126, 1552-1553.

601. Anonymous. "Possession of marihuana in San

Mateo county, some social costs of criminalization." Stan. Law Rev. 1969, 22, 101.

602. Anonymous. "Possession of marihuana in Texas." S. T. Law Rev. 1971, 13, 194.

603. Anonymous. "Possible therapeutic applications." In Mayor's Committee on Marihuana. The Marihuana Problem In The City Of New York. Jacques Cattell Press, Lancaster,

604. Anonymous. "Pot and alcohol: Some new brews." Time 1972, 99, 51.

605. Anonymous. "Pot and health." Nature 1972, 235, 415-416.

606. Anonymous. "Pot and parents; high school students smoking marihuana." Time 1968, 92, 44-45.

607. Anonymous. "Pot and performance." Time 1974, 104, 83.

608. Anonymous. "Pot and potency." Br. Med. J. 1974, 4, 4.

609. Anonymous. "Pot and sex." Time 1975, 106, 54.

610. Anonymous. "Pot and sexuality." Newsweek 1974, 83, 57.

611. Anonymous. "Pot and the penalty of death." Human Behav. 1974, 3, 53.

612. Anonymous. "Pot bust." Newsweek 1970, 75, 92.

613. Anonymous. "Pot can harm, but does prison help? HEW report." U.S. News 1974, 77, 80.

614. Anonymous. "Pot picking time: Boys arrested for growing marihuana in Carpinteria, California." Newsweek 1965, 65, 42.

615. Anonymous. "Pot-pourri." Fam Hlth. 1976, 8, 22.

616. Anonymous. "Pot problem; college students use marihuana." Time 1965, 85, 49.

617. Anonymous. "Pot proves hazardous to researchers." Med. Wld. News 1969, 10, 15-16.

618. Anonymous. "Pot report: Still inconclusive." Time 1971, 97, 46.

619. Anonymous. "Pot: Safer than alcohol?" Time 1968, 91, 52-53.

620. Anonymous. "'Pot' samplers may be dabbling with psychosis." Today's Hlth. 1970, 48, 71.

621. Anonymous. "Pot-smokers' charter?" Economist 1969, 230, 45.

622. Anonymous. "Pot smoking and the manly bosom." Med. Wld. News 1974, 15, 39.

623. Anonymous. "Pot spotters; U.S. Mexican border." Newsweek 1969, 74, 81-82.

624. Anonymous. "Pot: Year of the famine; Mexican border crackdown." Newsweek 1969, 74, 36-37.

625. Anonymous. "Pot: Your kids will encounter it, so be prepared." Bus. Wld. 1971, 87.

626. Anonymous. "Pot's luck; Mass. ban." Newsweek 1968, 71, 14.

627. Anonymous. "Potted dreams." Br. Med. J. 1969, 1, 133-134.

628. Anonymous. "Potted ivy; alienated students smoking marihuana." Time 1967, 89, 98.

629. Anonymous. "Potty laws in the U.S." Economist 1967, 225, 160.

630. Anonymous. "Preparations that intoxicate made with cannabis."(Fr.). Bull. Sci. Med. 1809, 4, 204.

631. Anonymous. "Presumption that marihuana is illegally imported is unconstitutional and the transfer tax provisions of the marihuana tax act violate the fifth amendment against self-incrimination." Houston Law Rev. 1970, 7, 378.

632. Anonymous. "Private use. Pot--a growing public issue." U.S. News 1975, 78, 37-38.

633. Anonymous. "Procedure adopted for marihuana research." J.A.P.A. 1974, 14, 681.

634. Anonymous. "Psychiatry in drug dependence." Br. Med. J. 1968, 2, 486.

635. Anonymous. "Pursuit of pot; Nixon eases proposals." Sen. Schol. 1969, 95, 14.

636. Anonymous. "Putting drugs in their places." Nature 1971, 230, 135-136.

637. Anonymous. "Questioning the legal status." Science News 1971, 99, 349.

638. Anonymous. Quick Identification of Cannabis by Ferric Hydrochloride.(Port.). Com. Nac. Fiscal. Entor., Rio de Janeiro, 1965.

639. Anonymous. "Ravin v State(Alaska): Marihuana in the home protected by right of privacy." N.C. Central Law J. 1975, 7, 163-174.

640. Anonymous. "Reaction of cannabis resin with aldehydes and certain ketones(preparation of certain aromatic aldehydes and ketones containing active groups." (Arab.). Proc. Pharmaceut. Soc. Egypt 1952, 34, 49.

641. Anonymous. "Recommendations on cannabis." Br. Med. J. 1969, 1, 178.

642. Anonymous. "Reefers on KPFA." Newsweek 1954, 43, 92.

643. Anonymous. "Report of the International Narcotics Control Board on its work in 1970." Bull. Narc. 1971, 23, 31-36.

644. Anonymous. "Report of the International Narcotics Control Board on its work in 1971." Bull. Narc. 1972, 24, 29-33.

645. Anonymous. "Reports on the therapeutic progress--the therapeutic value of cannabinon." Ther. Gaz. 1885, 9, 329-330.

646. Anonymous. "Research on the absorption of nutritive substances and on the need for such substances by hemp(cannabis sativa L)."(Ger.). Zeit. Pflan. 1950, 9, 7.

647. Anonymous. "Resolution of the United Nations General Assembly. Assistance to end illegal or uncontrolled production of raw narcotic drugs; technical assistance in the field of narcotics." Bull. Narc. 1969, 21, 1-2.

648. Anonymous. "Respiratory disorders and marihuana use." J. Asthma Res. 1974, 11, 97.

649. Anonymous. "Reverse uncertainty." Scientif. Amer. 1977, 236, 64.

650. Anonymous. "Review of the 22nd session of the Commission on Narcotic Drugs and the 44th session of the Economic and Social Council." Bull. Narc. 1968, 20, 37-41.

651. Anonymous. "Review of the 23rd session of the Commission on Narcotic Drugs and the 46th session of the Economic and Social Council." Bull. Narc. 1969, 21, 23-31.

652. Anonymous. "Rivera chafes as ABC cuts scene of his smoking marihuana legally." Broadcasting 1974, 86, 56.

653. Anonymous. "Saw-toothed; marihuana in the back yards of the city." New York. 1951, 27, 18-19.

654. Anonymous. "Scarcity, higher prices, crooks: Effects of crackdown on drug trade." U.S. News 1969, 67, 48-49.

655. Anonymous. "Scientific publications on narcotic drugs in 1966." Bull. Narc. 1967, 19, 19-50.

656. Anonymous. "Seal of approval; consumers union recommends legalization." Newsweek 1972, 80, 30.

657. Anonymous. "Search for data on marihuana." Bus. Wld. 1971, 50, 4.

658. Anonymous. "Sent to the gallows by dagga." Zonk 1956, 11-13.

659. Anonymous. "Sentences for marihuana offences." Crim. Law Quart. 1969, 11, 263-266.

660. Anonymous. "Should Congress de-criminalize marihuana? 'Yes,' by Edward I. Koch; 'No,' by La Mar Baker." Amer. Legion 1972, 93, 14-15.

661. Anonymous. "Should marihuana be legalized? Yes, by Michael R. Aldrich. No, by Henry L. Giordano." Humanist 1968, 28, 16-23.

662. Anonymous. "Simian viruses again." Lancet 1975, 1, 667.

663. Anonymous. "Single Convention on narcotic drugs vs. decriminalization of marihuana: a beginning or an end." Cal. S.B. J. 1974, 49, 524-527.

664. Anonymous. "Smoking cannabis." Br. Med. J. 1965, 2, 310.

665. Anonymous. "'Softer' line on cannabis proposed." Pharmaceut. J. 1969, 202, 32.

666. Anonymous. "Some comments on drugs and CU's position; concerning book Licit and Illicit Drugs." Consum. Rep. 1973, 38, 134-135.

667. Anonymous. "Some observations on cannabis sativa cultivated in Egypt."(Arab.). Rep. Pharmaceut. Soc. Egypt 1936, 35-36.

668. Anonymous. "Some questions and answers on marihuana. _Sen. Schol._ 1969, _94_, 11-13.

669. Anonymous. "South Dakota's 1968 Uniform Narcotic Drug law--marihuana and its constitutional questions." _S. Dak. Law Rev._ 1969, _14_, 303.

670. Anonymous. "Sparks fly over pot." _Nat's. Bus._ 1970, _58_, 24.

671. Anonymous. "Special: The alarming new evidence about marihuana's effects." _Good House._ 1975, _180_, 161-162.

672. Anonymous. "Spectrophotometric study of extracts from Japanese cannabis sativa L." _Bull. Nat'l. Hyg. Lab._ 1957, _75_, 117-122.

673. Anonymous. "Spot light on pot." _Sen. Schol._ 1971, _98_, 16-17.

674. Anonymous. "Standard marihuana." _Science News_ 1967, _91_, 461.

675. Anonymous. "Structure of cannabinol. V. A second method of synthesis of cannabinol." _J. Am. Chem. Soc._ 1940, _62_, 2401.

676. Anonymous. "Students re marihuana." _Am. Drug Merch._ 1973, _168_, 67.

677. Anonymous. "Students, young pharmacists rally on marihuana issue." _Am. Drug._ 1974, _170_, 42.

678. Anonymous. "Studies of marihuana and teenage drug users." _Pub. Hlth. Rep._ 1969, _84_, 76.

679. Anonymous. "Studies on hashish. I. The structure of the cannabinols and their effects."(Ger.). In _Festschrift for Alexander Tschirch on his 70th Birthday._ (Ger.). Tauchnitz, Leipzig, 1926.

680. Anonymous. "Substantive due process and felony treatment of pot smokers: the current conflict." _Georgia Law Rev._ 1968, _2_, 247.

681. Anonymous. _Suggestions made during a meeting of delates of the Police of Minas Geraes, Sao Paulo and Rio de Janeiro._(Port.). Imprensa Naval, Rio de Janeiro, 1958.

682. Anonymous. _Suggestions proposed during a meeting of delegates on publication no. 1 of the Comissao Nacional de Fiscalizacao de Entorpecentes._(Port.). Com. Nac. Fiscal. Entor., Rio de Janeiro, 1959.

683. Anonymous. "Survey of drug use among Michigan students." Pub. Hlth. Rep. 1969, 84, 1084.

684. Anonymous. "Survey reports marihuana use has increased." Psychol. Today 1975, 8, 39-40.

685. Anonymous. Symposium in Sao Paulo on the Problems of Maconha.(Port.). Com. Nac. Fiscal. Entor., Rio de Janeiro, 1960.

686. Anonymous. "Synthesis gives active marihuana component." Chem. Engin. News 1970, 48, 43.

687. Anonymous. "Synthesis gives active marihuana component. Tetrahydrocannabinol isomer is identical to physiologically active compound from hashish." Chem. Engin. News 1966, 44, 38-39.

688. Anonymous. "Taming a tough county; marihuana smuggling in Starr county Texas." Time 1977, 109, 58-59.

689. Anonymous. "Tannate of cannabin." Ther. Gaz. 1884, 8, 164.

690. Anonymous. "Tant v State(Georgia), possession of marihuana, and Georgia's appellate process: a call for additional reform." Georgia State Bar J. 1973, 9, 490.

691. Anonymous. "Tar level found high in pot." J. Drug Abuse 1972, 1, 6.

692. Anonymous. "Technical questions--narcotic drugs." Internat'l Crim. Pol. Rev. 1966, 203, 290-296.

693. Anonymous. "Telepharmedics: a more cautious approach to marihuana use." Am. Drug. 1972, 166, 41.

694. Anonymous. "Tetrahydrocannabinol and chemotherapy." N. Eng. J. Med. 1976, 294, 168.

695. Anonymous. "Tetrahydrocannabinols and analgesia." Bull. Narc. 1969, 21, 29.

696. Anonymous. The Action of Ordinary and Sublimate Cannabis on Motor Paralysis and Ataxia in White Mice. (Port.). Com. Nac. Fiscal. Entor., Rio de Janeiro, 1965.

697. Anonymous. "The actual state of intoxication produced by cannabis from British India."(Fr.). Office Internat'l. Hyg. Pub. Bull. Men. 1944, 36, 303-310.

698. Anonymous. "The California marihuana possession statute: An infringement on the right of privacy or

other peripheral constitutional rights?" Hast. Law J. 1968, 19, 758.

699. Anonymous. "The cannabis debate." Wld. Med. J. 1972, 19, 20.

700. Anonymous. "The cannabis problem: A note on the problem and the history of international control." Bull. Narc. 1962, 14, 27-31.

701. Anonymous. "The clinical study." In Mayor's Committee on Marihuana. The Marihuana Problem in the City of New York. Jacques Cattell Press, Lancaster, Pa., 1944, 26-34.

702. Anonymous. "The concurrent state and local regulation of marihuana: The validity of the Ann Arbor marihuana ordinace." Mich. Law Rev. 1972, 400, 291-318.

703. Anonymous. "The Custom's Bureau: Making a trip more difficult." Gov't. Exec. 1969, 1, 2.

704. Anonymous. "The 'dagga' smokers."(Ger.). Med. Welt 1938, 40, 1442.

705. Anonymous. "The dangers of cannabis indica." Ther. Gaz. 1890, 14, 355.

706. Anonymous. "The effects of cannabis." Bull. Narc. 1968, 20, 38.

707. Anonymous. The Effect of Cannabis Sublimate on the Swimming of White Mice.(Port.). Com. Nac. Fiscal. Entor., Rio de Janeiro, 1965.

708. Anonymous. "The effects of hash." Med. J. Aust. 1969, 1, 584-585.

709. Anonymous. "The effects of hashish." N.Y. Med. J. 1869, 9, 107-108.

710. Anonymous. "The effects of marihuana on consciousness." In Tart,C.T.(ed.). Altered States of Consciousness. J. Wiley and Sons, N.Y., 1969, 335-355.

711. Anonymous. "The federal drug abuse program." Pub. Hlth. Rep. 1970, 85, 565-568.

712. Anonymous. "The first blood test for marihuana in humans." New Scient. 1973, 59, 181.

713. Anonymous. "The grass and poison."(Fr.). Concours Med. 1972, 94, 2379-2380.

714. Anonymous. "The hash over hash." Can. Med. Assoc. J. 1969, 100, 627-628.

715. Anonymous. "The hashish." Chamber's Edin. J. 1848, 10, 341-343.

716. Anonymous. "The increasing menace of marihuana." Can. Med. Assoc. J. 1934, 31, 561.

717. Anonymous. "The legalization of marihuana: a realistic approach. Pt. 1." Vanderbilt Law Rev. 1968, 21, 517.

718. Anonymous. The Marihuana Consumer's and Dealer's Guide. Chton Press, N.Y., 1968.

719. Anonymous. "The Marihuana Control Act of 1975." Clin. Toxicol. 1975, 8, 645-648.

720. Anonymous. "The marihuana issue: still burning." Med. Econ. 1973, 50, 89-92.

721. Anonymous. "The marihuana myth." Louis. State Med. Soc. 1974, 126, 445-447.

722. Anonymous. "The marihuana problem." Can. Med. Assoc. J. 1946, 54, 58-59.

723. Anonymous. "The marihuana problem." J.A.M.A. 1945, 129, 1108-1109.

724. Anonymous. "The menace of marihuana." Internat'l. Med. Dig. 1937, 31, 183-187.

725. Anonymous. "The new mood on campus." Newsweek 1969, 77, 42-45.

726. Anonymous. "The new pharmacologic attack in psychiatry." Drug Cos. Ind. 1956, 78, 32-33, 125-129.

727. Anonymous. "'The one'." Newsweek 1972, 80, 62-63.

728. Anonymous. "The pharmacology of cannabis indica." Br. Med. J. 1899, 2, 1354-1357, 1517.

729. Anonymous. "The pharmacology of Indian hemp." Year Book of Pharm. 1900, 1, 28-29.

730. Anonymous. "The problem of maconha." Bol. Of. San. Pan. 1949, 28, 509-510.

731. Anonymous. "The psychiatric aspects of marihuana intoxication." J.A.M.A. 1943, 121, 212-213.

732. Anonymous. "The role of 'Indian hemp' in causation of insanity in India." Far East. Assoc. Trop. Med. 1928, 1, 400-407.

733. Anonymous. "The surprising extinction of the

charas traffic." Bull. Narc. 1953, 5, 1-7.

734. Anonymous. "The United Nations narcotics laboratory." Bull. Narc. 1967, 19, 7-14.

735. Anonymous. "The use of cannabis." Bull. Narc. 1972, 24, 11-19.

736. Anonymous. The Use of Cannabis. World Health Organization, Geneva, 1971.

737. Anonymous. "The use of cannabis." W.H.O. Chron. 1972, 26, 20-28.

738. Anonymous. "The use of cannabis. Report of WHO scientific group, World Health Organization, Geneva, Switzerland, 1971. Book Report." J. Pharmaceut. Sci. 1972, 61, 1509.

739. Anonymous. "The use of hashish in a cult." Ciba Symposium 1946, 8, 401.

740. Anonymous. "The use of marihuana: a brief for the John Howard Society." Can. Wel. 1969, 45, 14-16.

741. Anonymous. "The use of marihuana and LSD on the college campus." J. Nat'l. Assoc. Women Deans Counsel. 1967, 30, 124.

742. Anonymous. "The vision of hashish." Putnam's Month. Mag. Am. Lit. Sci. Art 1854, 3, 402-408.

743. Anonymous. "The Wootton Report on cannabis." Med. J. Aust. 1969, 1, 545.

744. Anonymous. "To parents: plain talk on marihuana." Bus. Wld. 1970, 121.

745. Anonymous. "To seal a border." Time 1969, 91, 70.

746. Anonymous. "Today's drugs: drugs of addiction." Br. Med. J. 1964, 2, 1119-1120.

747. Anonymous. "Toronto school drug survey." Addict. 1969, 16, 1-7.

748. Anonymous. "Toxic effects of cannabis indica." Lancet 1890, 1, 621.

749. Anonymous. Toxic Plants of Brazil.(Port.). Tipografia Perseveranca, Rio de Janeiro, 1871.

750. Anonymous. "Triple standard: Report findings." Newsweek 1972, 79, 27-28.

751. Anonymous. "Twenty years of narcotics control under the United Nations." Bull. Narc. 1966, 18, 2-60.

752. Anonymous. "UN likes Mississippi marihuana research." Am. Drug. 1974, 170, 42.

753. Anonymous. "United Nations Commission on narcotic drugs." U.N. Doc. E/CN.7/479, Sept. 15, 1965.

754. Anonymous. "United Nations Commission on narcotic drugs." U.N. Doc. E/CN/7/476, Sept. 25, 1965.

755. Anonymous. "United States assumes control of cannabis." J.A.M.A. 1937, 107, 31B-32B.

756. Anonymous. "Unwanted effects of cannabis." Lancet 1970, 2, 1350.

757. Anonymous. "Urticacae--cannabis indica--distinction of the drug as supplied under different names." Proc. Am. Pharmaceut. Assoc. 1903, 51, 803-804.

758. Anonymous. "Urticaceae--cannabis indica--U.S.P. requirements." Proc. Am. Pharmaceut. Assoc. 1911, 59, 261-264.

759. Anonymous. "Use of Indian hemp in chronic chloral and chronic opium poisoning." Am. J. Med. Sci. 1889, 98, 69.

760. Anonymous. Use of Maconha in Brazil. Medical and Police Measures of Repression. (Port.). Coletanea de Trabalhos brasileiros. Servico Nacional de Educacao Sanitaria, Rio de Janeiro, 1958.

761. Anonymous. "Use of marihuana disrupts sleep, studies reveal." Med. Trib. Med. News 1972, 13, 28.

762. Anonymous. "Use of satellites in detecting marihuana is studied by U.S." Aviat. Wld. 1972, 96, 35-36.

763. Anonymous. "Values of some hashish constituents." J. Chromatog. 1961, 1, D8.

764. Anonymous. "Verdict on marihuana; findings of team of Boston line investigators." Newsweek 1968, 72, 48.

765. Anonymous. "War on drugs comes under fire." U.S. News 1973, 74, 62.

766. Anonymous. "What works are to be published on the differences between German and Indian hemp?"(Ger.). Die Pharm. 1950, 3, 126.

767. Anonymous. "What about marihuana?" Nature 1969, 21, 268.

768. Anonymous. "What is marihuana?" Today's Ed. 1969, 58, 39-41.

769. Anonymous. "What? Pot? Not Laredo." Forbes 1970, 106, 48.

770. Anonymous. "What the drug trade has done to win the war." J.A.P.A. 1918, 7, 528-529.

771. Anonymous. "What to do about marihuana?" Reader's Dig. 1970, 97, 88-92.

772. Anonymous. "What's it like to smoke marihuana?" Science Dig. 1970, 68, 18-19.

773. Anonymous. "What's wrong with pot?" Newsweek 1967, 70, 30.

774. Anonymous. "Where the grass isn't greener." Emerg. Med. 1972, 4, 152.

775. Anonymous. "Whiskey versus grass: Ethanol or tetrahydrocannabinol." Mag. Wall St. 1972, 129, 29-32.

776. Anonymous. "Who's for pot?" Economist 1972, 243, 45.

777. Anonymous. "Will cigarettes take to pot?" Bus. Wld. 1969, 28.

778. Anonymous. "Woodstock rocked." Economist 1969, 232, 31.

779. Anonymous. "World Health Organization expert committee on addiction-producing drugs." Bull. Narc. 1964, 16, 53-55.

780. Anonymous. "WPA workers assigned to marihuana eradication." J.A.M.A. 1936, 107, 437.

781. Anonymous. "Youth and drugs." Cent. Af. Med. J. 1968, 14, 229.

782. Anslinger,H.J. "Criminal and psychiatric aspects associated with marihuana." Union Sig. 1944, 70, 77-78.

783. Anslinger,H.J. "Marihuana." Union Sig. 1939, 28, 5-12. 5-12.

784. Anslinger,H.J. "More on marihuana and Mayor La Guardia's committee report." J.A.M.A. 1945, 128, 1187

785. Anslinger,H.J. "The psychiatric aspects of marihuana intoxication." J.A.M.A. 1943, 121, 212.

786. Anslinger,H.J. "The traffic in narcotics." Bull. Narc. 1954, 6, 1-6.

787. Anslinger,H.J. and Cooper,C.R. "Marihuana, assassin of youth." Amer. Mag. 1937, 124, 18-19, 150-153.

788. Anslinger,H.J. and Tompkins,W.F. The Murderers: The Story of the Narcotics Gangs. Funk and Wagnalls, N.Y., 1961.

789. Anslinger,H.J. and Ousler,R.A. The Traffic in Narcotics. Funk and Wagnalls, N.Y. 1953.

790. Anstie,F.E. Stimulants and Narcotics; Their Mutual Relations. Lindsay and Blakiston, Phil., 1865.

791. Anton,A.H., Serrano,A., Beyer,R.D., and Lavappa, K.S. "Tetrahydrocannabinol, sesame oil and biogenic amines: a preliminary report." Life Sci. 1974, 14, 1741-1746.

792. Antone,E.J. "A study of the relationship of the use of various drugs to the visual-motor performance of college students." Diss. Abs. 1972, 33, 1963.

793. Anumonye,A. and McClure,J.L. "Adolescent drug abuse in a North London suburb." Br. J. Addict. 1970, 65, 25-33.

794. Anziferow,S. Hashish Addiction in Turkestan. (Rus.). Univ. of Moscow, Moscow, 1929.

795. Apter,J.T. and Pfeiffer,C.C. "Effects of hallucinogenic drugs on the electroretinogram." Am. J. Opthalmol. 1956, 42, 206-211.

796. Arafat,I. and Yorburg,B. "Drug use and the sexual behavior of college women." J. Sex Res. 1973, 9, 21-29.

797. Aramaki,H., Tomiyasu,N., Yoshimura,H., and Tsukamoto,H. "Forensic chemical study on marihuana. I. A detection method of the principle constituents by thin-layer gas chromatographies." Chem. Pharmaceut. Bull. 1968, 16, 822-826.

798. Aramaki,H., Tomiyasu,N., Yoshimura,H., and Tsukamoto,H. "Forensic chemical studies on marihuana. II. Application of the new detection method of marihuana constituents to the practical identification of marihuana." Eisei Kag. 1968, 14, 262-265.

799. Archer,R.A. "The cannabinoids: therapeutic potential." Ann. Rep. Med. Chem. 1974, 9, 253-259.

800. Archer,R.A., Boyd,D.B., Demarco,P.V., Tyminski, I.J., and Allinger,N.L. "Structural studies of cannabinoids. A theoretical and proton magnetic resonance analysis." J. Am. Chem. Soc. 1970, 92, 5200-5206.

801. Ardila Rodriguez,F. Legal-medical and Sociomedical Aspects of Marihuana.(Sp.). Univ. of Madrid, Madrid, 1965.

802. Arey,S.L. "Cannabis for asthma." N. Eng. J. Med. 1973, 289, 980.

803. Argeri,N.J. and Relva,C.R. "A new thin layer chromatographic method for the identification of marihuana(cannabis sativa L.)." Bioquim. Clin. 1971, 5, 38-46.

804. Argota,G. and Guerra,A. "Effects of marihuana on brain amine levels."(Sp.). Colombian Seminar on Pharmacol. n.d., 3, 66.

805. Arinshteyn,A. and Senchenko,M. "Monoecious hemp. Exchange of experience in a rural economy." (Czech.). Ser. Techn. Mas. Kult. 1956, 10, 1-3.

806. Armand,J.P., Hsu,J.T. and Nahas,G.G. "Inhibition of blastogenesis of T lymphocytes by delta-9-tetrahydrocannabinol." Fed. Proc. 1974, 33, 539.

807. Armitage,A.K., Hall,G.H. and Heneage,E. "A smoking simulator for the controlled presentation of tobacco smoke to laboratory animals." Br. J. Pharmacol. 1969, 36, 211-212.

808. Armstrong,W.D. and Parascandola,J. "American concern over marihuana in the 1930's." Pharm. Hist. 1972, 14, 25-34.

809. Arnao,G. "Drugs and marihuana." Min. Med. 1974, 65, 2647-2663.

810. Aneson,L.A. "The problem of marihuana--an introduction." Southwest. Med. 1970, 51, 162-164.

811. Arnold,D.O. "The meaning of the La Guardia Report: The effects of marihuana." In Simmons,J.E.(ed.). Marihuana; Myths and Realities. Brandon House, California, 1967, 111-135.

812. Arnone,A., Merlini,L., and Servi,S. "Hashish: Synthesis of (±)-delta-4-tetrahydrocannabinol." Tetrahed. 1975, 31, 3093-3096.

813. Arnoux,M. "The influence of environment on sexual expression in monoecious hemp(cannabis sativa.). II. The effect of nitrogen nutrition."(Fr.). Ann. Amelior. Plant. 1966, 16, 123.

814. Arnoux,M. "The influence of environment on sexual expression in monoecious hemp(cannabis sativa). III. Note on the effect of photoperiod and nitrogen supply." (Fr.). Ann. Amelior. Plant. 1966, 16, 259.

815. Arnoux,M., Castiaux,J., and Mathieu,G. "On the improvement of productivity in hemp fibers (cannabis sativa)." (Fr.). Ann. Amelior. Plant. 1969, 19, 405-418.

816. Arnoux,M. and Mathieu,G. "Environmental influences on sexual phenotype of progeny F_1 resulting from crosses between dioecious and monoecious hemp varieties(cannabis sativa L.)."(Fr.). Ann. Amelior. Plant. 1969, 19, 53-58.

817. Aronow,W.S. and Cassidy,J. "Effect of marihuana and placebo-marihuana smoking on angina pectoris." N. Eng. J. Med. 1974, 291, 66-67.

818. Aronow,W.S. and Cassidy,J. "Marihuana and angina pectoris." New Eng. J. Med. 1974, 291, 800-801.

819. Aronow,W.S. and Cassidy,J. "Effect of smoking marihuana and of a high-nicotine cigarette on angina pectoris." Clin. Pharmacol. Ther. 1975, 17, 549-554.

820. Aronson,H. "New facts about marihuana." Seventeen 1975, 34, 96.

821. Arora,S. and Hardman,H.F. "Analysis of hypothermic actions of delta-9-tetrahydrocannabinol in mice." Pharmacol. 1974, 16, 282.

822. Artamonov,M.I. "Frozen tombs of the Scythians." Scientif. Amer. 1965, 212, 101-109.

823. Artbauer,O. The Rif Pirates and Their Country. (Ger.). Stuttgart, 1911.

824. Arutinyantz,S.M. "Chemical investigation of Indian hemp."(Rus.). Paper presented at Conference of Imperial Medico-Surgical Academy, St. Petersburg, 1881, 80.

825. Asahina,H. "Studies on cannabis obtained from hemp plants grown in Japan." Bull. Narc. 1957, 9, 17-20.

826. Asahina,H. and Mizumachi,S. "Spectrophotometric study of 'charas', an Indian hemp preparation."(Jap.). Bull. Nat'l Inst. Hyg. Sci. 1958, 76, 113-114.

827. Asahina,H. and Mizumachi,S. "Spectrophotometric study of extracts from Japanese cannabis sativa L." (Jap.). Bull. Nat'l. Inst. Hyg. Sci. 1957, 75, 117-122.

828. Asahina,H., Shimamine,M., and Takahashi,K. "Studies on cannabis. I. Separation of cannabis constituents by means of thin-layer and gas chromatography." (Jap.). Bull. Nat'l Hyg. Sci. 1968, 86, 21-25.

829. Asahina,H., Shimamine,M., and Takahashi,K. "Studies on cannabis. II. Separation of tetrahydrocannabinol."(Jap.). Bull. Nat'l Inst. Hyg. Sci. 1968, 86, 25-28.

830. Asahina,H. and Shiuchi,Y. "Paper chromatography of extracts from Japanese hemp."(Jap.). Bull. Nat'l. Inst. Hyg. Sci. 1957, 75, 123-125.

831. Asahina,H. and Shiuchi,Y. "The color reaction and paper chromatography of 'charas'."(Jap.). Bull. Nat'l. Hyg. Sci. 1958, 76, 115-117.

832. Asahina,H. and Takashasi,K. "Microscopic identification of cannabis leaves."(Jap.). Bull. Nat'l. Inst. Hyg. Sci. 1966, 84, 54-59.

833. Ash,A.L. "Hemp--production and utilization." Econ. Bot. 1948, 2, 158-169.

834. Askew,W.E. "Neurochemical role of adenosine 3,5-cyclic monophosphate and guanosine 3,5-cyclic monophosphate and their relation to neurotransmitters; effect of tetrahydrocannabinols." Diss. Abs. 1974, 34, 5397.

835. Askew,W.E. and Ho,B.T. "Effects of tetrahydrocannabinols on cyclic AMP levels in rat brain areas." Exper. 1974, 30, 879-880.

836. Askew,W.E., Kimball,A.P., and Ho,B.T. "Effect of tetrahydrocannabinols on brain acetylcholine." Brain Res. 1974, 69, 375-378.

837. Asuni,T. "Socio-psychiatric problems of cannabis in Nigeria." Bull. Narc. 1964, 16, 17-28.

838. Atal,C.K. "Sex reversal in hemp by application of gibberellin." Cur. Sci. 1959, 28, 408-409.

839. Atal,C.K. and Sethi,J.K. "Increased fiber content in hemp(cannabis sativa) and sunn(crotalaria juncea) by application of gibberellins." Cur. Sci. 1961, 30, 177-179.

840. Atkins,R.D. "Marihuana reconsidered." In Levin, P.A.(ed.). Contemporary Problems of Drug Abuse. Publish. Science Group, Acton, Mass., 1974, 130-134.

841. Atkyns,R.L. and Hanneman,G.J. "Illicit drug distribution and dealer communicative behavior."

J. Hlth. Soc. Behav. 1974, 15, 36-43.

842. Atkyns,R.L., McEwen,W.J. and Hanneman,G.J. "Sources of drug information among adults." J. Drug Educat. 1975, 5, 161-169.

843. Attlee,J. "A case of poisoning by cannabis indica." Br. Med. J. 1896, 2, 948.

844. Attlee,J. "Case of poisoning by cannabis indica." Lancet 1896, 2, 1078.

845. Aubert-Roche,L. Documents and Observations Concerning the Pestilence of Typhus of the Orient Followed by an Essay on the Use of Hashish in the Treatment of the Pestilence.(Fr.). J. Rouvier, Paris, 1843.

846. Aubin,J. "The evaluative test in chronic kif intoxication."(Fr.). Ann. Med-psychol. 1945, 1, 487-488.

847. Aulde,J. "Studies in therapeutics--cannabis indica." Ther. Gaz. 1890, 6, 523-526.

848. Austin,C.G. "Marihuana." J. Higher Educat. 1969, 40, 477-479.

849. Avison,A.W.D., Morrison,A.L., and Parkes,M.W. "Tetrahydrodibenzopyran derivatives isomeric with tetrahydrocannabinols." J. Chem. Soc. 1949, 2, 952-955.

850. Ayalon,D., Tsafriri,A., Cordova,T., and Lindner,H.R. "Suppression of the cyclic surge of luteinizing hormone secretion and of ovulation in the rat by delta-1-tetrahydrocannabinol." Nature 1973, 243, 470-471.

851. Ayd,F.J. "The Marihuana Smokers. Book Review." J.A.M.A. 1971, 215, 1828.

852. Azadian,A. "A study of hashish and its different preparations."(Fr.). J. Pharm. Belg. 1922, 4, 28-29, 489-492, 505-507.

853. Azadian,A. "Examination of hashish and preparations containing it." Analyst 1923, 48, 77.

B

854. Babayev,A.Z. and Goldberg,I.K. "Materials for medico-legal determination of anasha."(Rus.). Doklady Akad. Nauk. Azerbaidzhan 1956, 12, 749-751.

855. Babor,T.F., Mendelson,J.H., Greenberg,I. and Kuehnle,J.C. "Marihuana consumption and tolerance to physiological and subjective effects." Arch. Gen. Psychiat. 1975, 32, 1548-1552.

856. Babor,T.F., Mendelson,J.H., and Kuehnle,J. "Marihuana and human physical activity." Psychopharmacol. 1976, 50, 11-19.

857. Babor,T.F., Rossi,A.M., Sagotsky,G., and Meyer,R.E. "Group behavior: Patterns of smoking." In Mendelson,J.H., Rossi,A.M., and Meyer,R.E.(eds.). The Use of Marihuana. Plenum Press, N.Y., 1974, 47-57.

858. Babor,T.F., Rossi,A.M., Sagotsky,G., and Meyer,R.E. "Group behavior: Problem solving efficiency." In Mendelson,J.H., Rossi,A.M., and Meyer,R.E.(eds.). The Use of Marihuana. Plenum Press, N.Y., 1974, 81-86.

859. Babor,T.F., Rossi,A.M., Sagotsky,G., and Meyer,R.E. "Group behavior: Verbal interaction." In Mendelson,J.H., Rossi,A.M., and Meyer,R.E.(eds.). The Use of Marihuana. Plenum Press, N.Y., 1974, 61-71.

860. Babst,D.V., Mirin,M., and Koval,M. "The relationship between friends' marihuana use, family cohesion, school interest and drug abuse prevention." J. Drug Abuse Educat. 1976, 6, 23-41.

861. Bach,D., Raz,A., and Goldman,R. "The effect of hashish compounds on phospholipid transition." Biochim. Biophys. 1976, 436, 889-894.

862. Bach,D., Raz,A., and Goldman,R. "The interaction of hashish compounds with planar lipid bilayer membranes." Biochem. Pharmacol. 1976, 25, 1241-1244.

863. Backer,R.C., Jensen,W.N., Beck,A.G., and Barnett, R.J. "A simple method for the infrared identification of cannabinoids of marihuana resolved by gas chromatography." J. Forens. Sci. 1970, 15, 287-291.

864. Baden,M.M., Valanju,N.N., Verma,S.K., and Valanju,S.N. "Confirmed identification of biotransformed drugs of abuse in urine." Am. J. Clin. Pathol. 1972, 57, 43-51.

865. Baeckstrom,P. and Sundstrom,G. "A simple synthesis of olivetol." Act. Chem. Scand. 1970, 24, 716-717.

866. Baer,D.J. "Attitudes about marihuana and political views." Psychol. Rep. 1973, 32, 1051-1054.

867. Baer,D.J. "Political views of high school and college students and attitudes about legalization of marihuana." Proc. Am. Psychol. Assoc. 1971, 6, 337-338.

868. Baer,D.J. and Ordway,D. "Alcoholics Anonymous members' attitudes toward marihuana and its users." Psychol. Rep. 1973, 32, 950.

869. Baeyer,V.W. "Clinic for hashish users. II. Psychomotor effects."(Ger.). Nervenarzt 1932, 5, 342-346.

870. Bailey,K. "Progress in cannabis research, 1972." Can. J. Pharmaceut. Sci. 1974, 9, 1-7.

871. Bailey,K. and Gagne,D. "Distinction of synthetic cannabidiol, cannabichromene, and cannabivarin by GLC using on-column methylation. J. Pharmaceut. Sci. 1975, 64, 1719-1720.

872. Bailey,K., Legault,D., and Verner,D.J. "Identification of synthetic cannabinoids by gas chromatography." Chromatography 1973, 87, 263-266.

873. Bailey,K. and Toft,P. "Difference spectra of rat hepatic microsomes induced by cannabinoids and related compounds." Biochem. Pharmacol. 1973, 22, 2780-2783.

874. Bailey,K. and Verner,D.J. "C-glucosidation of delta-8-tetrahydrocannabinol." J. Chem. Soc. 1972, 2, 89-90.

875. Bailey,K. and Verner,D. "Delta-9- and delta-8-1-n-amyl-3-hydroxy-6,6,9-trimethyl-6a,10a-trans-tetrahydrodiobenzo-(b,d)pyran, position isomers of and major side products in synthesis of delta-8-tetrahydrocannabinol." Can. J. Pharmaceut. Sci. 1972, 7, 51-53.

876. Bailey,P.T. and Pradhan,S.N. "Action and interaction of abusive drugs on reward system." Proc. 5th Internat'l. Cong. Pharmacol. 1972, 1, 12.

877. Bailey,P.T. and Pradhan,S.N. "Effects of delta-9-tetrahydrocannabinol and mescaline on self-stimulation." Neuropharmacol. 1972, 11, 831-838.

878. Bailey,P.T., Pradhan,S.N., and Ghosh,B. "Some behavioral effects of delta-9-tetrahydrocannabinol." Fed. Proc. 1971, 30, 279.

879. Bailey,W.C. and Koval,M. "Differential patterns of drug abuse among white activists and nonwhite militant college students." Internat'l. J. Addict. 1972, 7, 191-199.

880. Baiter,J.T., Mizner,G.L., and Werme,P.H. "Patterns of drug use among college students: An epidemiological and demographic survey of student attitudes and practices." Unpub. ms., Dept. of Psychiatry, Univ. Colorado Medical School, 1970.

881. Baitlon,D. "Causes of myocardial infarction." J.A.M.A. 1975, 233, 1357.

882. Bakal,D., Milstein,S.L., and Rootman,I. "Trends in drug use among rural students in Alberta." Can. Ment. Hlth. 1975, 23, 8-9.

883. Baker,A.A. and Lucas,E.G. "Some hospital admissions associated with cannabis." Lancet 1969, 1, 148.

884. Baker,J.R. and Rosenkrantz,H.J. "A simple method for demonstrating tetrahydrocannabinols in fresh or frozen sections." J. Histochem. Cytochem. 1972, 20, 827-829.

885. Baker,S.L. "Drug abuse in the United States army." Bull. N.Y. Acad. Sci. 1971, 47, 541-549.

886. Baker-Bates,E.T. "A case of cannabis indica intoxication." Lancet 1935, 1, 811.

887. Bakhireva,A. "A new method for the determination of the end point in the steeping of hemp straw."(Rus.). Leni Knoplya 1940, 6, 38-39.

888. Bakker,P., van der Meulen,J., van der Veen,H., Holtzer,G.J., Hoetmer,K., and Polak,F. "The marihuana problem."(Dut.). Ned. Tijd. Geneesk. 1972, 116, 535-536.

889. Bakopoulos,I. Cultivation of Cannabis Indica (Hashish) in Mantinia.(Grk.). Georgikon and Dasikon Deltion Ministry for National Economy, Athens, 1914.

890. Baldinger,R., Capel,W.C., Goldsmith,B.M., and Stewart,G.T. "Pot smokers, junkies, and squares: A comparative study of female values." Internat'l. J. Addict. 1972, 7, 153-166.

891. Ball,J.C. "Marihuana smoking and the onset of heroin use." In Cole,J.O. and Wittenborn,J.R.(eds.). Drug Abuse: Social and Psychopharmacological Aspects. C.C. Thomas, Springfield, Ill., 1969, 117-128.

892. Ball,J.C. "Onset of marihuana and heroin use among Puerto Rican addicts." Br. J. Criminol. 1967, 7, 408-413.

893. Ball,J.C. and Chambers,C.D.(eds.). The Epidemiology of Opiate Addiction in the United States. C.C. Thomas, Springfield, Ill., 1970.

894. Ball,J.C., Chambers,C.D., and Ball,M.J. "The association of marihuana smoking with opiate addiction in the United States." J. Crim. Law, Criminol. Pol. Sci. 1968, 59, 171-182.

895. Ball,M.V. "Marihuana--Mexican name for cannabis, also called Loco Weed in certain parts of Texas." In Report of Committee Appointed by the Governor of the Canal Zone, April 1, 1925, for the purpose of Investigating the Use of Marihuana and Making Recommendations Regarding Same and Related Papers. Balboa Heights, Canal Zone, 1925, 55-60.

896. Ball,M.V. "The effects of haschisch not due to cannabis indica." Ther. Gaz. 1910, 34, 777-780.

897. Ballante,A. "Marihuana. The symbol and the ritual." J. Second. Educat. 1968, 43, 218-222.

898. Ballard,C.W. and Phar,A.M. "Notes on the histology of an American cannabis." J.A.P.A. 1915, 4, 1299-1303.

899. Ballas,C.N. The Delirium of the Prophet of Pythia.(Grk.). Soteropoulos, Athens, 1968.

900. Balozet,L. "Physiological activity of crude resin of cannabis extract."(Fr.). Archiv. Instit. Pasteur Tunis 1937, 26, 318-325.

901. Balthasar,W., Gartner,F., and Denbsky,G. "Studies on the analysis of cannabis constituents in the mouth using chromatography."(Ger.). Deut. Zahnaerztl. 1974, 29, 623-626.

902. Bandaranayake,W.M., Begley,M.J., Brown,B.O., Clarke,D.G., Crombie,L., and Whiting,D.A. "Synthesis of acridone and carbazole alkaloids involving pyridine-catalysed chromen formation: Crystal and molecular structure of dibromocannibicyclol and its bearing on the structures of the 'cyclol' alkaloids." J. Chem. Soc. 1974, 1, 998-1007.

903. Banel,M. "Note on the extracts of cannabis indica."(Fr.). Mont. Med. 1890, 15, 461-465.

904. Banerjee,A., Poddar,M.K., Saha,S., and Ghosh,J.J. "Effect of delta-9-tetrahydrocannabinol on monoamine oxidase activity of rat tissues in vivo." Biochem. Pharmacol. 1975, 24, 1435-1436.

905. Banerjee,B.N., Galbreath,C., and Sofia,R.D. "Teratologic evaluation of synthetic delta-9-tetrahydrocannabinol in rats." Teratology 1975, 11, 99-102.

906. Banerjee,B.N., Sofia,R.D., Enkson,D., and Ivins,N.J. "Toxicity of delta-9-tetrahydrocannabinol (THC) administered subcutaneously for 13 days to female rabbits." J. Toxicol. Environ. Hlth. 1976, 1, 769-776.

907. Banerjee,S.P., Snyder,S.H., and Mechoulam,R. "Cannabinoids: Influence on neurotransmitter uptake in rat brain synaptosomes." J. Pharmacol. Exper. Ther. 1975, 194, 74-81.

908. Baquar,S.R. and Askari,S.H.A. "Chromosome studies in some flowering plants of West Pakistan. II." Genet. Iber. 1970, 22, 41-51.

909. Barash,L., Stankiewica,H., and Farmilo,R.C. "A review of hemp cultivation in Canada. The romance and statistics of cannabis in Canada." Unpub. ms., 1971.

910. Barbee,E.L. "Marihuana. A social problem." Perspect. Psychiat. Care 1971, 9, 194-199.

911. Barber,T.X. LSD, Marihuana, Yoga, and Hypnosis. Aldine, Chicago, 1970.

912. Barbero,A.C. and Flores,M.R. "Cannabis in hemp workers."(Sp.). Rev. Clin. Espan. 1944, 13, 395-399.

913. Barbero,A.C. and Flores,M.R. "Dust disease in hemp workers." Archiv. Environ. Hlth. 1967, 14, 529-532.

914. Barbosa,M. and Moraes Andrade,O. "Problems of drug addiction."(Sp.). Arquiv. Manicom. Judic. n.d., 26, 119-124.

915. Barbosa,O. 'Diamba' Vice.(Port.). Servico Nacional de Educacao Sanitaria, Rio de Janeiro, 1958.

916. Bard,L. "Clinical observation of chronic marihuana intoxication."(Sp.). Pren. Med. Argent. 1941, 28, 171-179.

917. Bardet,G. "Use of various alkaloids as hypnotics and tranquilizers."(Fr.). Nouv. Rem. 1893, 9, 130-135.

918. Barenque,O. Marihuana in Psychiatry and the Penal Code.(Sp.). Migaris, Mexico, 1931.

919. Bargman,G.J. and Gardner,L.I. "Approach to the study of the effects of marihuana." J. Pediat. 1969, 75, 342.

920 Barloy,J. and Pelhate,J. "Initial phyto-pathological observations relative to the cultivation of hemp in Anjou."(Fr.). Ann. Epiphyt. 1962, 13, 117-149.

921. Barnard,M. "Mechanism of the negative chronotropic and inotropic effects of delta-l-tetra-hydrocannabinol." Fed. Proc. 1973, 32, 755.

922. Barnard,M. "The god in the flowerpot." Amer. Schol. 1963, 32, 578-586.

923. Barnes,C. and Fried,P.A. "Tolerance to delta-9-THC in adult rats with differential delta-9-THC exposure when immature or during early adulthood." Psychopharmacol. 1974, 34, 181-190.

924. Barnett,J. "Dietary requirements for reproduction. III. The existence of reproductive dietary complex (vitamin E) in the ethereal extracts of yellow corn, wheat embryo and hemp-seed." J. Biol. Chem. 1924, 62, 371-396.

925. Barnett,W.L. Ganja(resin of Cannabis sativa). Department of Government Chemist, Kingston, Jamaica, 1951.

926. Barnett-Bentlif,P. "A case of poisoning by extract of cannabis indica." Clin. Sketch. 1896, 3, 70.

927. Baron,P.A. "Some points on 'College Student Drug Use'." Am. J. Psychiat. 1970, 127, 706.

928. Barona,J. "Some aspects of narcotics control in Mexico." Bull. Narc. 1964, 16, 1-5.

929. Barral,M. "Hashish."(Fr.). Rev. Sci. Hypnot. 1887, 20-26, 58-63, 99-103.

930. Barral,M "Note on the extracts of cannabis indica."(Fr.). Mont. Med. 1890, 15, 461-465.

931. Barratt,E.S. and Adams,P.M. "Chronic marihuana usage and sleep-wakefulness cycles in cats." Biol. Psychiat. 1973, 6, 207-214.

932. Barratt,E.S. and Adams,P.M. "The effects of chronic marihuana administration on brain functioning in cats." In Singh,J.M. and Lal,H.(eds.). Drug Addiction: Experimental Pharmacology. Futura Pub. Co., Mount Kisco, N.Y., 1972, 145-157.

933. Barratt,E.S., Beaver,W., and White,R. "The effects of marihuana on human sleep patterns." Biol. Psychiat. 1974, 8, 47-54.

934. Barratt,E.S., Beaver,W., White,R., Blakeney,P., and Adams,P. "The effects of the chronic use of marihuana on sleep and perceptual-motor performance in humans." In Lewis,M.F.(ed.). Current Research in Marihuana. Academic Press, N.Y., 1972, 163-193.

935. Barrett,R.T. "Stoned assents." Nature 1970, 227, 101.

936. Barron,F. "The relationship of ego diffusion to creative perception." In Taylor,C.W.(ed.). Widening Horizons in Creativity. J. Wiley and Sons, N.Y., 1964, 8-86.

937. Barron,F., Jarvik,M.E., and Bunnell,S. "The hallucinogenic drugs." Scientif. Amer. 1964, 210, 29-37.

938. Barry,H. and Krimmer,E.C. "Discriminative delta-9-THC stimulus tested with several doses, routes, intervals, and a marihuana extract." In Braude,M.C. and Szara,S.(eds.). Pharmacology of Marihuana. Raven Press, N.Y., 1976, II, 535-539.

939. Barry,H. and Krimmer,E.C. "Discriminable stimuli produced by alcohol and other CNS depressants." Psychopharmacol. Commun. 1976, 2, 323-326.

940. Barry,H. and Kubena,R.K. "Acclimation to laboratory alters response of rats to delta-1-tetrahydrocannabinol." Proc. Am. Psychol. Assoc. 1969, 4, 865-866.

941. Barry,H. and Kubena,R.K. "Discriminative stimulus characteristics of alcohol, marihuana and atropine." In Singh,J.M., Miller,L., and Lal,H.(eds.) Drug Addiction: Experimental Pharmacology. Futura Pub. Co., N.Y., 1974, 3-16.

942. Barry,H. and Kubena,R.K. "Effects of delta-1-tetrahydrocannabinol on avoidance by rats and monkeys." Proc. Am. Psychol. Assoc. 1970, 5, 805-806.

943. Barry,H. and Kubena,R.K. "Repeated high doses of delta-1-tetrahydrocannabinol enhance acquisition of shock avoidance by rats." Proc. Am. Psychol. Assoc. 1971, 6, 747-748.

944. Barry,H., Kubena,R.K., and Perhach,J.L. "Pituitary-adrenal activation and related responses to delta-1-tetrahydrocannabinol." Prog. Brain Res. 1973, 39, 323-330.

945. Barry,H., Perlach,J.L., and Kubena,R.K. "Delta-1-tetrahydrocannabinol activation of pituitary-adrenal function." Pharmacologist 1970, 12, 258.

946. Barter,J.T., Mizner,G.L., and Werme,P.H. "Patterns of drug use among college students: An epidemiological and demographic survey of student attitudes and practices." Unpub. ms., Department of Psychiatry, Univ. of Colorado School of Medicine, 1970.

947. Barter,J.T., Mizner,G.L., and Werme,P.H. Patterns of Drug Abuse Among College Students in the Denver-Boulder Metropolitan Area. Bureau of arcotics and Dangerous Drugs, Washington, D.C., 1971.

948. Bartholomew,A.A. "Drug addiction or drug dependence?" Med. J. Aust. 1973, 1, 710.

949. Bartholomew,A.A. and Reynolds,W.S. "Four cases of progressive drug abuse." Med. J. Aust. 1967, 1, 653-657.

950. Bartimo,F.A. and Hopson,E.G. "Marihuana." Internat'l. Crime Pol. Rev. 1972, 27, 182-188.

951. Bartley, D. "Palaeobotanical evidence." In Sawyer,P.H.(ed.). Medieval Settlement. Edward Arnold, London, 1976, 226-235.

952. Bartolucci,G., Fryer,L., Perris,C., and Shagass,C. "Marihuana psychosis: A case report." Can. Psychiat. Assoc. J. 1969, 14, 77-79.

953. Barton,W. "Drug usage and the law. The adolescent and an archaic concept." Clin. Proc. Child. Hosp. 1968, 24, 180-184.

954. Bartova,A. and Birmingham,M.K. "Effect of tetrahydrocannabinol and deoxycorticosterone(DOC) on brain and adrenal NADH-oxidase activity." Fed. Proc. 1972, 31, 481.

955. Bartunek,R. "Differences between cotton, flax, and hemp on dyeing." Cellulosechemie 1924, 5, 33-44.

956. Bartunek,R. "Differences in the structure of cotton, flax and hemp fiber." Cellulosechemie 1924, 5, 25-26.

957. Baruk,H. "Life and work of Moreau de Tours." (Fr.). Ann. Med. Psychol. 1970, 128, 27-32.

958. Baruk,H. "The problem of the drug. Causes, prevention and dose."(Fr.). Ann. Med. Psychol. 1970, 128, 136-139.

959. Baskett,G.D. and Nysewander,R.W. "Drug use correlates." Psychol. 1973, 10, 54-66.

960. Baslavaskaya,S.S. "The relation of hemp to the pH of the soil."(Rus.). Trans. Sci. Inst. Fertil. Insect. 1936, 130, 34-38.

961. Basson,G. "Victims of the 'weed'."(Swed.). Justitia 1962, 2, 3, 47.

962. Bates,G.M. "Marihuana." J.A.M.A. 1970, 214, 1566.

963. Bates,R.C. "Psychedelics and the law: A prelude in question marks." Psychedel. Rev. 1964, 1, 4.

964. Bates,T. "Marihuana, clinical, psychological and legal aspects." Pediat. 1970, 45, 129.

965. Bates,T. "The pediatrician and the marihuana question." Pediat. 1970, 45, 1041.

966. Batho,R. "Cannabis indica." Br. Med. J. 1883, 1, 1002.

967. Batista,E.L. "Subsidies for the sociomedical study of maconha."(Port.). Rev. Brasil. Med. 1959, 16, 648-650.

968. Battaglia,B. "Action of hashish on man."(It.). Psichiatria 1887, 5, 1-38.

969. Battandier,A. The drug from Mozambique to Algeria, en 1882." Union Pharmaceut. 1882, 249, 254.

970. Battegay,R., Baumler,J., Gniras,F., and Ladewig,G. "Drug dependence of the cannabis type (hashish, marihuana)."(Ger.). Schweiz. Med. Woch. 1969, 99, 965-971.

971. Battegay,R. and Ladewig,D. "Comparative studies on amphetamines, cannabis and hallucinogenic dependents." Coll. Internat'l. Neuro-psychopharmacol. 1970, 8, 11-15.

972. Battig,K. "Use of psychoactive drugs and illegal drugs by Zurich university students."(Ger.). Schweiz. Med. Woch. 1970, 100, 1887-1893.

973. Battista,O. Mental Drugs: Chemistry's Challenge to Psychotherapy. Chilton, Phil., 1960.

974. Baudelaire,C. The Artificial Ideal.(Fr.). La Revue Contemporaine, Paris, 1858.

975. Baudelaire,C. Artificial Paradises.(Fr.). Poulet-Malassis, Paris, 1860.

976. Bauder,R. "Problem of hashish from the angle of police activity." Praxis 1971, 60, 497-499.

977. Bauer,G. "Current narcotics abuse from the viewpoint of criminality."(Ger.). Munch. Med. Woch. 1970, 112, 1562-1569.

978. Bauer,G. "Hashish use."(Ger.). Recht Jugend. 1970, 18, 122-126.

979. Bauer,G. "Psychological and social consequences of hashish addiction."(Ger.). Nachrichhendienst 1970, 50, 183-185.

980. Bauman,M.R. "Kenaph-seed oil." Separate 1926, 5.

981 Baumann,F. "Hypnosis and the adolescent drug abuser." Am. J. Clin. Hypnot. 1970, 13, 17-21.

982. Baumler,J. "The prompt identification of hashish."(Ger.). Arch. Kriminol. 1964, 134, 92.

983. Baxter-Tyrie,C.C. "A case of poisoning by cannabis indica." Lancet 1897, 1, 1452.

984. Bayer,A.E., Astin,A.W., and Baruch,R.F. "College students' attitudes toward social issues. 1967-1970." Educat. Rec. 1971, 51, 52-59.

985. Bayer,A.E. and Dutton,J.E. "Trends in attitudes on political, social and collegiate issues among college students: Mid 1960's to mid 1970's." Paper presented to Amer. College Personnel Assoc., Atlanta, 1975.

986. Bayer,I. "Report on drug abuse in Hungary." Addict. Dis. 1977, 3, 53-54.

987. Baytop,T. Medicinal and Toxic Plants of Turkey. (Fr.). University of Istambul, Istambul, 1963.

988. Bazzaz,F.A. and Dusek,D. "Photosynthesis, respiration, transpiration and delta-9-THC content of tropical and temperate populations of cannabis sativa." Am. J. Bot. 1971, 58, 462.

989. Bazzil,M. "Biological dosage of cannabis indica cultivated near Pavia."(It.). Boll. Soc. It Biol. Speriment. 1940, 14, 858-860.

990. Beaconsfield,P. "Some cardiovascular effects of cannabis." Am. Heart J. 1974, 87, 143-146.

991. Beaconsfield,P., Carpi,A., Cartoni,C., Basso,P., and Rainsbury,R. "Effect of delta-9-tetrahydrocannabinol on cerebral circulation and function." Lancet 1972, 2, 1146.

992 Beaconsfield,P., Ginsburg,J., and Rainsbury,R. "Marihuana smoking; cardiovascular effects in man and possible mechanisms." N. Eng. J. Med. 1972, 287, 209-212.

993. Beaconsfield,P., Ginsburg,J., and Rainsbury,R. "Therapeutic potential of marihuana." N. Eng. J. Med. 1973, 289, 1315.

994. Beaconsfield,P., Oakley,C., Capri,A., Rainsbury,R., and del Basso,P. "Cardiac effects of delta-9-tetrahydrocannabinol on a heart-lung preparation and on the intact animal." Eur. J. Cardiol. 1974, 2, 167-173.

995. Beaconsfield,P., Rainsbury,R., Ginsburg,J., and Carpi,A. "Marihuana smoking: Effects on blood and urine in man." Br. J. Clin. Practice 1973, 27, 207-210.

996. Beahrs,J.O., Carlin,A.S., and Shelhorn,J. "Impact of psychoactive drugs on hypnotizability." Am. J. Clin. Hypnosis 1974, 16, 267-179.

997. Beam,W. Tests for Hashish. Fourth Report of the Wellcome Tropical Research Laboratories, Gordon Memorial College, Khartoum, Anglo-Egyptian Sudan, 1911.

998. Beane,F.D. "An experience with cannabis indica." Buffalo Med. J. 1883, 23, 445-451.

999. Bear,L.A. "Of drugs and the lonely crowd." In Wittenborn,J.R., Smith,J.P., and Wittenborn,S.A.(eds.). Communication and Drug Abuse. C.C.Thomas, Springfield, Ill., 1970, 15-22.

1000. Bear,L.A. "Proposal and guide for a law school seminar in drug abuse and and the law." In Wittenborn,J.R., Brill,H., Smith,J.P., and Wittenborn,S.A. (eds.). Drugs and Youth. C.C.Thomas, Springfield, Ill., 1969, 423-446.

1001. Beaubrun,M.H. "Cannabis or alcohol: The Jamaican experience." In Rubin,V.(ed.). Cannabis and Culture. Mouton, The Hague, 485-497.

1002. Beaubrun,M.H. and Knight,F. "Psychiatric assessment of 30 chronic users of cannabis and 30 matched controls." Am. J. Psychiat. 1973, 130, 309-311.

1003. Beaugrand,G. "Sharing the blame for the hashish wave."(Ger.). Jugendwohl 1972, 53, 64-66.

1004. Beautrais,A.L. and Marks,D.F. "A test of state dependency effects in marihuana intoxication for the learning of psychomotor tasks." Psychopharmacol. 1976, 46, 37-40.

1005. Bech,P. "Cannabis and alcohol: Effects on simulated driving." In Van Praag,H.M.(ed.). Biochemical and Pharmacological Aspects of Dependence and Reports on Marihuana Research. Erven F. Bohn, Harlem, the Netherlands, 1972, 160-167.

1006. Bech,P., Rafaelsen,L and Rafaelsen,O.J. "Cannabis: A psychopharmacological review." Danish Med. Bull. 1974, 21, 106-120.

1007. Bech,P., Rafaelsen,L., and Rafaelsen,O.J. "Cannabis and alcohol: Effects on estimation of time and distance." Psychopharmacol. 1973, 32, 373-381.

1008. Beck,S.M. "Marihuana." Crim. Law Quart. 1967, 10, 1-3.

1009. Beckelhymer,H. "Grams and damns." Christ. Cent. 1970, 87, 267-268.

1010. Becker,H.S. "Becoming a marihuana user." Am. J. Sociol. 1953, 59, 235-242.

1011. Becker,H.S. "Ending campus drug incidents." Trans-action 1968, 5, 4-8.

1012. Becker,H.S. "History, culture and subjective experience: An exploration of the social bases of drug-induced experiences." J. Hlth. Soc. Behav. 1967, 8, 163-176.

1013. Becker,H.S. The Outsiders; Studies in the Sociology of Deviance. Free Press, N.Y., 1963.

1014. Beckett,D. "Should we legalize pot?" New Society 1967, 11, 720-721.

1015. Beckett,P.G.S. "Cannabis and medical practice--1970." J. Irish Med. Assoc. 1970, 63, 387-390.

1016. Beckler,H. "Poisoning symptoms produced by cannabis indica balsam."(Ger.). Munch. Med. Woch. 1886, 33, 544.

1017. Beddoe,J. "Cannabis indica." Br. Med. J. 1883, 1, 1064.

1018. Beedle,P. "The Patterns of Drug Abuse in the United Kingdom." In Btesh,S.(ed.). Drug Abuse. Plenum Press, N.Y., 1972, 114-117.

1019. Begley,M.J., Clarke,D.G., Crombie,L. and Whiting,D.A. "The X-ray structure of dibromocannabicyclol: Structure of bicyclomahanimbine." Chem. Commun. 1970, 22, 1547-1548.

1020. Beidleman,B. "Hazards of marihuana." New Eng. J. Med. 1971, 284, 920.

1021. Belesasso,G."Some general observations on the drug problem in Mexico." Foreign Psychiat. 1973, 2, 36-41.

1022. Beliaev,N.V. "General toxicodermatitis following acute poisoning by Indian hemp."(Rus.). Vest. Dermat. Venerol. 1964, 38, 77-78.

1023. Bell,D.S. "The present status of drug dependence in Australia." Addict. Dis. 1977, 3, 115-118.

1024. Bell,J. "On the Haschisch or cannabis indica." Bost. Med. Surg. J. 1857, 61, 209-216.

1025. Bellanger,J.L. The Pursuit of the Dragon.(Fr.). Del Duca, Paris, 1961.

1026. Bellemore,K.L. "Marihuana and addiction." Med. J. Aust. 1970, 2, 252.

1027. Bellinger,L. "Textiles from Gordion." Bull. Needle Bobbin Club 1962, 46, 5-20.

1028. Bellville,J.W., Gasser,J.C., Miyake,T., and Aqleh,K. "Tolerance to the respiratory effects of marihuana in man." J. Pharmacol. Exper. Ther. 1976, 197, 326-331.

1029. Bellville,J.W., Swanson,G.D., and Aqleh,K.A. "Respiratory effects of delta-9-tetrahydrocannabinol." Clin. Pharmacol. Ther. 1975, 17, 541-548.

1030. Bellville,J.W., Swanson,G.D., Haldemann,G., Aqleh,K., and Sato,T. "Respiratory effects of tetrahydrocannabinol, pentobarbital and alcohol." Proc. West. Pharmacol. Soc. 1974, 17, 215-218.

1031. Bel'tyukova,K.I. "Antibiotic substances from cannabis sativa and its effect on phytopathogenic bacteria."(Rus.). Antibiotiki 1958, 49-51.

1032. Bembry,T.H. and Powell,G. "Compounds of the cannabinol type. I. Synthesis of some compounds related to tetrahydrocannabinol." J. Am. Chem. Soc. 1941, 63, 2766-2768.

1033. Benabud,A. "Psycho-pathological aspects of the cannabis situation in Morocco: Statistical data for 1956." Bull. Narc. 1957, 9, 1-12.

1034. Bender,L. "Drug addiction in adolescence." Comprehens. Psychiat. 1963, 4, 181-194.

1035. Bender,P.E. and Loev,B. "6-norcannabinols and some related xanthenes." Paper presented at Am. Chemical Soc. 1974.

1036. Benedict,A.L. "Cannabis indica." Ther. Gaz. 1916, 40, 758-759.

1037. Benet,S. "Early diffusion and folk uses of hemp." In Rubin,V.(ed.). Cannabis and Culture. Mouton, The Hague, 1975, 39-51.

1038. Benetowa,S. "Tracing one word through different language names of the plant." In Andrews,G. and Vinkenoog,S.(eds.). The Book of Grass. Grove Press, N.Y., 1967, 15-18.

1039. Benforado,J.M. "Catnip and related psychedelic compounds." J.A.M.A. 1969, 208, 1190-1191.

1040. Benforado,J.M. "Hallucinogens and marihuana." Wiscon. Pharm. 1968, 37, 221-223.

1041. Benforado,J.M. "The cannabis controversy." N. Eng. J. Med. 1969, 281, 1371-1372.

1042. Benigni,R., Capra,C., and Cattorini,P.E. "Indian hemp, medicinal plant, chemical pharmacology and therapeutics.."(It.). Inverni Dell. Beff. 1962, 1, 206-215.

1043. Benjamin,F.B. "The effect of marihuana on driving performance." In Lewis,M.(ed.). Current Research in Marihuana. Academic Press, N.Y., 1972, 205-214.

1044. Bennett,A.E. "Compulsive, addictive personality problem." Med. Times 1964, 92, 433-442.

1045. Bennett,W.L. "Marihuana." J.A.M.A. 1972, 222, 1424.

1046. Benoist,J. "Reunion: Cannabis in a pluricultural and polyethnic society." In Rubin,V.(ed.). Cannabis and Culture. Mouton, The Hague, 1975, 227-235.

1047. Benowitz,N.L. and Jones,R.T. "Cardiovascular effects of prolonged delta-9-tetrahydrocannabinol ingestion." Clin. Pharmacol. Ther. 1975, 18, 287-297.

1048. Benowitz,N.L. and Jones,R.T. "Effects of delta-9-tetrahydrocannabinol on drug distribution and metabolism. Antipyrine, pentobarbital, and ethanol." Clin. Pharmacol. Ther. 1977, 22, 259-268.

1049. Benowitz,N.L. and Jones,R.T. "Prolonged delta-9-tetrahydrocannabinol ingestion." Clin. Pharmacol. Ther. 1977, 21, 336-342.

1050. Benowitz,N.L., Jones,R.T., and Lerner,C.B. "Depression of growth hormone and cortisol response to insulin-induced hypoglycemia after prolonged oral delta-9-tetrahydrocannabinol administration in man." J. Clin. Endocrinol. Metab. 1976, 42, 938-941.

1051.Bensemana,D. and Gascon,A.L. "Effect of delta-9-THC on the distribution, uptake, and release of catecholamine in rats." Rev. Can. Biol. 1974, 33, 269-278.

1052. Benson,H., Wallace,R.K., Dahl,E.C., and Cooke, D.P. "Decreased drug abuse with transcendental meditation--A study of 1,862 subjects." In Zarafonetis, C.J.D.(ed.). Drug Abuse. Lea and Febiger, Phil., 1972, 369-376.

1053. Benson,R.E. and Martine,J.G. "An educational program on drug usage." J. Am. Coll. Hlth. Assoc. 1970, 18, 270-273.

1054. Benson,V.A. "Marihuana 'Study' Critique." J.A.M.A. 1971, 217, 1391.

1055. Bensusan,A.D. "Intense headache as a symptom of dagga withdrawal." S. Af. Med. J. 1972, 46, 1461.

1056. Bensusan,A.D. "Marihuana withdrawal symptoms." Br. Med. J. 1971, 1, 112.

1057. Bentley,G.A. "The pharmacology of cannabis." Aust. N. Z. J. Criminol. 1969, 2, 83-86.

1058. Bentlif,P.B. "A case of poisoning by extract of cannabis indica." Clin. Sketch. 1896, 3, 70.

1059 Ben-Zvi,Z., Bergen,J.R., and Burstein,S. "Cannabinol-7-oic acid: A metabolite of delta-1-tetrahydrocannabinol in the rhesus monkey." Res. Comm. Chem. Pathol. Pharmacol. 1974, 9, 201-204.

1060. Ben-Zvi,Z., Bergen,J.R., Burstein,S., Sehgal,P.K., and Varanelli,C. "The metabolism of delta-1-tetrahydrocannabinol in the rhesus monkey." In Braude,M.C. and Szara,S. (eds.). Pharmacology of Marihuana. Raven Press, N.Y., 1976, I, 63-77.

1061. Ben-Zvi,Z. and Burstein,S. "7-oxo-delta-1-tetrahydrocannabinol: A novel metabolite of delta-1-tetrahydrocannabinol." Res. Comm. Chem. Pathol. Pharmacol. 1974, 8, 223-229.

1062. Ben-Zvi,Z. and Burste-n,S. "Transformation of delta-1-tetrahydrocannabinol(THC) by rabbit liver microsomes." Biochem. Pharmacol. 1975, 24, 1130-1131.

1063. Ben-Zvi,Z., Burstein,S., and Zikopoulos,J. "Metabolism of delta-1-tetrahydrocannabinol by mouse hepatic microsomes: Identification of 6 alpha-hydroxy-tetrahydrocannabinol." J. Pharmaceut. Sci. 1974, 63, 1173-1174.

1064. Ben-Zvi,Z., Mechoulam,R., and Burstein,S. "Identification through synthesis of an active delta-1(6)-tetrahydrocannabinol metabolite." J. Am. Chem. Soc. 1970, 92, 3468-3469.

1065. Ben-Zvi,Z., Mechoulam,R., and Burstein,S.H. "Synthesis of delta-1-and delta-1(6)-tetrahydrocannabinol metabolites." Tetrahed. Let. 1970, 51, 4495-4497.

1066. Ben-Zvi,Z., Mechoulam,R., Edery,H. and Porath,G. "6 beta-hydroxy-delta-1-tetrahydrocannabinol synthesis and biological activity." Science 1971, 174, 951-952.

1067. Bercht,C.A.L., Kuppers,F.J.E.M., Lousberg,R.J.J., and Salemink,C.A. "Analysis of the so-called green hashish oil." U.N. Doc. ST/SOA/SER.S/46, Oct. 29, 1973.

1068. Bercht,C.A.L., Lousberg,R.J.J., Kuppers,J.E.M., and Salemink,C.A. "Cannabicitran: A new naturally occurring tetracyclic diether from Lebanese cannabis sativa." Phythochem. 1974, 13, 619-121.

1069. Bercht,C.A.L., Lousberg,R.J.J., Kuppers,J.E.M., and Salemink,C.A. "L(+)-Isoleucine betaine in cannabis seeds." Phytochem. 1973, 12, 2457-2459.

1070. Bercht,C.A.L.,Lousberg,R.J.J, Kuppers,F.J.E.M., Salemink,C.A., Vree,T.B. and Van Rossum,J.M. "Cannabis. VII. Identification of cannabinol methyl ether from hashish." J. Chromatog. 1973, 81, 163-166.

1071. Berg,D. "The nonmedical use of dangerous drugs in the United States: a comprehensive review." Internat'l. J. Addict. 1970, 5, 777-834.

1072. Berg,D.F. and Broecker,L.P. Illicit Use of Dangerous Drugs in the United States: A Compilation of Studies, Surveys and Polls. Bureau of Narcotics and Dangerous Drugs, Washington, D.C., 1972.

1073. Berg,R.H. "Pot and booze." N. Eng. J. Med. 1969, 280, 1077.

1074. Berg,R.H. "Warning: Steer clear of the THC." Look 1969, 33, 46.

1075. Bergel,F. "Keep off the grass." Nature 1970, 225, 979.

1076. Bergel,F. "Some contributions to the cannabinol constituents in hashish."(Ger.). Lieb. Ann. Chem 1930, 482, 55-74.

1077. Bergel,F., Morrison,A.L., Rinderknecht,H., Todd,A.R., MacDonald,A.D., and Woolfe,G. "Cannabis indica. XII. Some analogues and a water-soluble derivative of tetrahydrocannabinol." J. Chem. Soc. 1943, 1, 286-287.

1078. Bergel,F., Todd,A.R., and Work,T.S. "Observations on the active principles of cannabis indica resin." Chem. Indust. 1938, 16, 86.

1079. Bergel,F. and Voegele,K. "Synthesis of cannabinolactons and isomeric compounds(cannabinol constituents. II.)."(Ger.). Lieb. Ann. Chem. 1932, 493, 250-258.

1080. Bergel,F. and Wagner.R. "Contributions to the structure of cannabinol, the active principle of hashish."(Ger.). Lieb. Ann. Chem. 1930, 482, 55-74.

1081. Berger,F.R. An Experimental Study of the Effects of Marihuana on Memory, Depth Perception, Mood and Thinking. University of California, Los Angeles, Cal., 1971.

1082. Berger,H.J. and Krantz,J.C. "Phenitrone: Ineffective blockade of (-)-trans-delta-9-tetrahydrocannabinol in mice and dogs." J. Pharm. Pharmacol. 1972, 24, 492-493.

1083. Berger,M. "Tea for a viper." New York. 1938, 14, 40-42.

1084. Bergersen,B.. "Oslo--marihuana or hashish."(Nor.) Tid. Samfunn. 1968, 9, 232-233.

1085. Beringer,K. "Clinical signficance experiments with narcotics."(Ger.). Schweitz. Arch. Neurol. Psyhciat. 1931, 28, 1-17.

1086. Beringer,K. "Clinical study of effects of hashish."(Ger.). All. Zeit. Psychiat. Psych.-gericht. Med. 1933, 99, 233-234.

1087. Beringer,K., Baeyer,W., and Marx,H. "Clinical study of effects of hashish."(Ger.). Nervenarzt 1932, 5, 337-350.

1088. Berkhan,H. "Visit to a hashish booth in Cairo."(Ger.). All. Zeit. Psychiat. Psych.-gericht. Med. 1901, 58, 748-749.

1089. Berkman,A.H. Seedling Anatomy of Cannabis Sativa L. Univ. of Chicago, Chicago, 1936.

1090. Berlu,J. Treasury of Drugs. J.Haris, London, 1690.

1091. Berman,G. and Benierakis,C. "Characteristics of student marihuana users." J. Can. Psychiat. Assoc. 1972, 17, 37-40.

1092. Berman,M.L. and Bochantin,J.F. "Effect of delta-9-tetrahydrocannabinol(marihuana) on liver microsomal dechlorinase activity: A preliminary report." Cur. Res. 1972, 51, 929-932.

1093. Berman,S. "Marihuana: A study of toxic drug reaction among adolescents." Med. Ann. D.C. 1971, 40, 742-744.

1094. Bernath,Z.C. and Martini Herrera,P. "Pathogenesis of hemp worker's disease."(Sp.). Rev. Chil. Higien. Med. Prevent. 1943, 6, 11-20.

1095. Berner,P., Hoff,H., and Krypspin-exner,K. "On the psychopathology of the disease."(Ger.). Wien. Med. Wschr. 1963, 113, 759-765.

1096. Bernhardson,G. "Cannabis psychoses."(Swed.). Lakart. 1969, 66, 1230-1234.

1097. Bernhardson,G. and Gunne,L. "Forty-six cases of psychosis in cannabis abusers." Internat'l. J. Addict. 1972, 7, 9-16.

1098. Bernstein,B. and Shkuda,A.N. The Young Drug Abuser: Attitudes and Obstacles to Treatment. Center for N.Y. City Affairs, New School for Social Research, N.Y., 1974.

1099. Bernstein,J.G. "Physiological effects of marihuana." Psychopharmacol. Bull. 1973, 9, 50-51.

1100. Bernstein,J.G., Becker,D., Babor,T.F., and Mendelson,J.H. "Physiological assessments: Cardiopulmonary function." In Mendelson,J.H., Rossi,A.M., and Meyer,R.E. (eds.). The Use of Marihuana. Plenum Press, N.Y., 1974, 147-160.

1101. Berstine,J.G., Kuehnle,J.C., and Mendelson,J.H. "Medical implications of marihuana use." Am. J. Drug Alcohol Abuse 1976, 3, 347-361.

1102. Berstein,J.G., Meyer,R.E., and Mendelson,J.H. "Physiological assessments: General medical survey." In Mendelson,J.H., Rossi,A.M., and Meyer,R.E.(eds). The Use of Marihuana. Plenum Press, N.Y., 1974, 135-145.

1103. Berntsen,K. "Social attitudes of users." In Connell,P.H. and Dorn,N. Cannabis and Man. Churchill Livingstone, Edinburgh, 1975, 183-189.

1104. Berry,E.C. Nosing Around--Canine Marihuana Expert. Police Department, Richmond, Va., 1970.

1105. Berthault,J.M.E. Hashish, Its History, Physiological and Therapeutic Effects.(Fr.). Faculty of Medicine, Sorbonne, Paris, 1854.

1106. Bertherand,P.I.D.E. "Concerning the prohibition of hashish in Turkey."(Fr.). J. Med. Pharm. Alquie 1876, 1, 76-77.

1107. Berthier,M. "Hashish-induced sleep. Hashish as a hypnotic."(Fr.). Gaz. Hop. Civil Milit. 1867, 40, 387.

1108. Berti,F. Cultivation of Hemp. Instructions by Fabrizio Berti. Bologna, 1741.

1109. Bertulli,G. "Rapid method for the detection and identification of cannabinols in cannabis."(It.). Boll. Chim. Farm. 1976, 115, 14-19.

1110. Besch,N.F., Smith,C.G., Besch,P.K., and Kaufman,R.H. "The effect of marihuana(delta-9-tetrahydrocannabinol) on the secretion of luteinizing hormone in the ovariectomized rhesus monkey." Am. J. Obstet. Gynecol. 1977, 128, 635-642.

1111. Bessey,E.A. "Effect of the age of pollen upon the sex of hemp." Am. J. Bot. 1928, 15, 405-411.

1112. Betts,E.M.(ed.). Thomas Jefferson's Farm Book. Princeton Univ. Press, Princeton, N.J., 1953.

1113. Betts,T.J. and Holloway,P.J. "Chromatographic identification of cannabis." J. Pharm. Pharmacol. 1967, 19, 97S-102S.

1114. Beuthin,F. "Marihuana: Can it hurt you?" J.A.M.A. 1975, 233, 1357.

1115. Bewley,T.H. "Discussion in drug addiction." Practitioner 1967, 198, 842.

1116. Bewley,T.H. "Drug abuse in the United Kingdom." Addict. Dis. 1977, 3, 27-32.

1117. Bewley,T.H. "Drug addiction." Br. Med. J. 1967, 3, 603-605.

1118. Bewley,T.H. "Drugs and driving." Criminol. 1969, 4, 7-16.

1119. Bewley,T.H. "Recent changes in the incidence in all types of drug dependence in Great Britain." Proc. Roy. Soc. Med. 1968, 61, 175-177.

1120. Bewley,T.H. "Slang terms associated with drugs in the United Kingdom." Bull. Narc. 1966, 18, 10-13.

1121. Bewley,T.H. "The cannabis problem in the United Kingdom." J.A.P.A. 1969, NS9, 613-614.

1122. Bey,D.R. and Zecchinelli,V.A. "Marihuana as a coping device in Vietnam." Milit. Med. 1971, 14, 448-450.

1123. Bey,D.R. and Zecchinelli,V.A. "Marihuana as a coping device in Vietnam." U.S. Army Viet. Med. Bull. 1969, 40, 21-28.

1124. Bharati,A. The Tantric Tradition. Rider and Co., London, 1965.

1125. Bhargava,H.N. "Effect of some cannabinoids on naloxone-precipitated abstinence in morphine-dependent mice." Psychopharmacol. 1970, 49, 267-270.

1126. Bhargava,H.N. "Inhibition of naloxone-induced withdrawal in morphine dependent mice by 1-trans-delta-9-tetrahydrocannabinol." Eur. J. Pharmacol. 1976, 36, 259-262.

1127. Bialos,D.S. "Adverse marihuana reactions: A critical examination of the literature with selected case material." Am. J. Psychiat. 1970, 127, 819-820.

1128. Bianchi,A. and Malatesta,G. "Contribution to the analysis of substances contained in linen and hemp."(It.). Ann. Chim. Appl. 1914, 1, 297-302.

1129. Bianchi,A. and Malatesta,G. "Naturally colored material in the fiber of linen and hemp."(It.). Ann. Chim. Appl. 1914, 1, 281-291.

1130. Bibra,E. Narcotic Drugs and Man.(Ger.). Nuremberg, 1885.

1131. Bicher,H.I. and Mechoulam,R. "Pharmacological effects of two active constituents of marihuana." Arch. Internat'l. Pharmacodyn. Ther. 1968, 172, 24-31.

1132. Bicknell,R.C. "Ingestion of extract of cannabis indica." Univ. Med. Mag. 1897, 10, 323-325.

1133. Bicknell,R.C. "Some effects of cannabis indica in large doses." Ther. Gaz. 1898, 22, 13-15.

1134. Biegeleisen,H. Polish Folk Medicine.(Pol.). Crackow, 1929.

1135. Bieger,D. and Hockman,C.H. "Differential effects produced by delta-1-tetrahydrocannabinol on lateral geniculate neurones." Neuropharmacol. 1973, 12, 269-273.

1136. Bieniek,D., Gau,W. and Korte,F. "Hashish-chemistry and problems."(Ger.). Naturwissen. 1974, 61, 117-121.

1137. Bier,M.M. and Steahly,L.P. "Emergency treatment of marihuana complicating diabetes." In Bourne,P.E.(ed.). Acute Drug Abuse Emergencies. Academic Press, N.Y., 1976, 163-173.

1138. Bier,W.C. Problems in Addiction: Alcohol and Drug Addiction. Fordham Univ. Press, N.Y., 1962.

1139. Biggs,A.L. "The spectrophotometric detection of cannabis sativa resin." J. Pharm. Pharmacol. 1953, 5, 18-25.

1140. Biggs,D.A., Orcutt,J.B., and Bakkenist,N. "Correlates of marihuana and alcohol use among college students." J. Coll. Stud. Person. 1974, 15, 22-30.

1141. Bijlsma,U.G. "Addiction poisoning."(Dut.). Ned. Tijd. Geneesk. 1959, 103, 1694-1696.

1142. Bilash,I.S., Arnold,M., and Zell,C. "Marihuana and suggestibility." J. Can. Psychiat. Assoc. 1972, 17, 327-329.

1143. Bilodeau,L. and Jacob,A. Prevalence and Usage of Drugs from 1969 to 1971 Among Students of Secondary and College on Montreal Island.(Fr.). Office of Prevention and Treatment of Alcohol and other Intoxicants, Quebec, Quebec, 1971.

1144. Bindelglas,P.M. "'Conclusive evidence' and marihuana." Br. J. Addict. 1973, 68, 51-56.

1145. Binder,A. "An experimental approach to driver evaluation using alcohol drinkers and marihuana smokers." Accid. Ann. Prevent. 1971, 3, 237-256.

1146. Binder,M. "Identification of hydroxylated cannabinoids by PMR and mass spectroscopy." In Nahas,G.G., Paton,W.D.M., and Idanpaan-Heikkila,J.E. (eds.). Marihuana. Springer Verlag, N.Y., 1976, 159-169.

1147. Binder,M. "Microbial transformation of (-)-delta-1-3,4,-trans-tetrahydrocannabinol." Helv. Chim. Act. 1976, 59, 1674-1684.

1148. Binder,M., Agurell,S., Leander,K., and Lindgren,J.E. "Identification of potential metabolites of cannabis-containing substances. Nuclear resonance and mass spectroscopic investigation of side-chain hydroxylated cannabinoids."(Ger.). Helv. Chim. Act. 1974, 57, 1626-1641.

1149. Binet-Sangle,C. "Effect of hashish on neurons."(Fr.). Rev. Scientif. 1901, 15, 270-274.

1150. Binitie,A. "Psychosis following ingestion of hemp in children." Psychopharmacol. 1975, 44, 301-302.

1151. Binnie,H.L. "The attitudes to drugs and drug takers of students at the university and colleges of higher education in an English midland city." In Jones,H.A.(ed.). Vaughan Papers. Department of Adult Education, University of Leicester, Leicester, England, 1969, 1-29.

1152. Bino,T., Chari-Bitron,A., and Shahar,A. "Biochemical effects and morphological changes in rat liver mitochondria exposed to delta-1-tetrahydrocannabinol." Biochim. Biophys. Act. 1972, 288, 195-202.

1153. Birch,E.A. "The use of Indian hemp in the treatment of chronic chloral and chronic opium poisoning." Lancet 1889, 1, 625.

1154. Birmingham,M.K. "Reduction by delta-9-tetrahydrocannabinol in the blood pressure of hypertensive rats bearing regenerated adrenal glands." Br. J. Pharmacol. 1973, 48, 169-171.

1155. Birmingham,M.K. and Bartova,A. "Effects of cannabinol derivatives on blood pressure, body weight, pituitary-adrenal function and mitochrondrial respiration in the rat." In Nahas,G.G., Paton,W.D.M., and Idanpaan-Heikkila,J.E.(eds.) Marihuana. Springer Verlag, N.Y., 1976, 425-441.

1156. Birmingham,M.K., Oliver,J.T., Possanza,G.J., Langlois,Y., and Stewart,P.B. "Reduction in blood pressure of hyptertensive rats by marihuana extract and tetrahydrocannabinol." Fed. Proc. 1972, 31, 393.

1157. Bischoff,W.H. The Ecstacy Drugs. University Circle Press, 1966.

1158. Biswas,B., Deb,C., and Ghosh,J.J. "Acute and chronic effects of cannabis extract administration on hypothalamo-neurohypophysial neurosecretory activity in the rat." U.N. Doc. ST/SOA/SER.S.45, Oct. 12, 1973.

1159. Biswas,B., Deb,G., and Ghosh,J.J. "Adrenocortical changes in rats during acute and chronic administration of delta-9-tetrahydrocannabinol." Endocrin. Exper. 1976, 10, 139-148.

1160. Biswas,B., Deb,G., and Ghosh,J.J. "Changes in rat adrenal medulla following delta-9-tetrahydrocannabinol treatment. A histochemical study." Act. Endocrin. 1975, 80, 329-338.

1161. Biswas,B. and Ghosh,J.J. "Delta-9-tetrahydrocannabinol and lysergic acid diethylamide: comparative changes in the supraoptic and paraventricular neurosecretory activities in rat hypothalamus." Anat. Anz. 1975, 138, 324-331.

1162. Biswas,B. and Bhosh,J.J. "Long-term effects of delta-9-tetrahydrocannabinol on testicular function in rats." U.N. Doc. ST/SOA/SER.SS/44, Oct. 8, 1973.

1163. Bittner,J.R. and Cash,W.B. "A comparison of student leader and non-leader attitudes toward legalizing marihuana." Coll. Stud. J. 1971, 5, 45.

1164. Bizzaria Mamede,E. "Maconha, opium of the poor."(Sp.). Neurobiol. 1945, 8, 71-93.

1165. Blachly,P.H. "Effects of decriminalization of marihuana in Oregon." Ann. N. Y. Acad. Sci. 1976, 282, 416-421.

1166. Blachly,P.H. "Use of amphetamines, marihuana, and LSD by students." New Physician 1966, 15, 88-93.

1167. Black,C.A. "Effect of commercial fertilizers on the sex expression of hemp." Bot. Gaz. 1945, 107, 114-120.

1168. Black,C.A. and Vessel,A.J. "The response of hemp fertilizers in Iowa." Proceed. Soil Crop Sci. Soc. 1944, 9, 179-184.

1169. Black,M.B., Woods,J.H., and Domino,E.F. "Some effects of (-)-delta-9-trans-tetrahydrocannabinol and other cannabis derivatives on schedule-controlled behavior." Pharmacol. 1970, 12, 258.

1170. Black,S., Owens,K.L., and Wooff,R.P. "Patterns of drug use: a study of 5,482 subjects." Am. J. Psychiat. 1970, 127, 62-65.

1171. Blackford,L.S. "Trends in student drug use in San Mateo country." Cal. Hlth. 1969, 27, 3-6,11.

1172. Blackie,W.J. "New color reactions for cannabis sativa resin." Indust. Engin. Chem. 1941, 13, 96-97.

1173. Blakeney,P.E. "Differentiation of individuals who use only marihuana from non-drug users and multiple drug users." Diss. Abs. 1973, 33, 4500.

1174. Blakey,D. "Is the grass greener?" J. Miss. State Med. Assoc. 1975, 16, 153-154.

1175. Blaine,J.D., Lieberman,C.M., and Hirsh,J. "Preliminary observations on patterns of drug consumption among medical students." Internat'l. J. Addict. 1968, 3, 389-396.

1176. Blaine,J.D., Meacham,M.P., Janowsky,D.S., Schoor,M., and Bozzetti,L.P. "Marihuana smoking and simulated flying performance." In Braude,M.C. and Szara,S. (eds.). Pharmacology of Marihuana. Raven Press, N.Y., 1976, I, 445-449.

1177. Blanco Juste,J. "'Grifa' from Morocco."(Sp.). Mon. Farm. Terapeut. 1952, 58, 199-202.

1178. Blatt,A.H. "A critical survey of the literature dealing with the chemical constituents of cannabis sativa." J. Wash. Acad. Sci. 1938, 28, 465-477.

1179. Bleibtreu,J.N. "Marihuana and the new American hedonism." Psychedel. Rev. 1967, 9, 72-79.

1180. Blevins,R.D. and Regan,J.D. "Delta-9-tetrahydrocannabinol: Effect on macromolecular synthesis in human and other mammalian cells." Arch. Toxicol. 1976, 35, 127-135.

1181. Blevins,R.D. and Reagan,J.D. "Delta-9-tetrahydrocannabinol: Effect on macromolecular synthesis in human and other mammalian cells." In Nahas,G.G., Paton,W.D.M., and Idanpaan-Heikkila,J.E.(eds.). Marihuana. Springer Verlag, N.Y., 1976, 213--23.

1182. Bloch,H.S. "Army clinical psychiatry in the combat zone--1967-1968." Am. J. Psychiat. 1969, 126, 289-298.

1183. Bloom,A.S., Dewey,W.L., Harris,LS., and Brosius, K.K. "9-nor-9 beta-hydroxyhexahydrocannabinol, a cannabinoid with potent antinociceptive activity: comparisons with morphine." J. Pharmacol. Exper. Ther. 1977, 200, 263-270.

1184. Bloom,R. "The effects of tetrahydrocannabinol on aggression in humans." Diss. Abs. 1973, 33, 4500.

1185. Bloom,R., Hays,J.R., and Winburn,G.M. "Marihuana use in urban secondary schools: A three-year comparison." Internat'l. J. Addict. 1974, 9, 329-335.

1186. Bloomquist,E.R. Marihuana. Glencoe Press, Beverly Hills, Cal., 1968.

1187. Bloomquist,E.R. "Marihuana: Social benefit or social detriment?" Cal. Med. 1967, 106, 346-353.

1188. Bloomquist,E.R. Marihuana: The Second Trip. Glencoe Press, Beverly Hills, Cal., 1971.

1189. Bloomquist,E.R. "Some observations on the contemporary use of cannabis." In Wittenborn,J.R., Brill,H., Smith,J.P., and Wittenborn,S.A.(eds.). Drugs and Youth, C.C.Thomas, Springield, Ill., 1969, 178-186.

1190. Blum,A. On the Origin of Paper. R.R. Bowker Co., N.Y., 1934.

1191. Blum,D., Hudson,K. and Wallace,J.E. "Tetrahydrocannabinol blockage of alcohol-induced withdrawal symptoms in mice." Clin. Toxicol. 1974, 7, 291.

1192. Blum,K., Briggs,A.H., Feinglass,S.J., Domey,R., and Wallace,J.E. "Effects of delta-9-tetrahydrocannabinol on amphetamine-aggregate toxicity in mice." Cur. Ther. Res. 1977, 21, 241-244.

1193. Blum,K., Hudson,K.C., Friedman,R.N., and Wallace,J.E. "Tetrahydrocannabinol: Inhibition of alcohol-induced withdrawal symptoms in mice." In Singh,J.M. and Lal,H.(eds.). Drug Addiction: Neurobiology and Influences on Behavior. Stratton Intercontinental Medical Book Co., N.Y., 1974, 39-53.

1194. Blum,R.H. and Associates. Horatio Alger's Children: The Role of the Family in the Origin and Prevention of Drug Risk. Jossey-Bass, San Francisco, 1972.

1195. Blum,R.H. and Associates. Society and Drugs. Jossey-Bass, San Francisco, 1970.

1196. Blum,R.H. and Associates. Students and Drugs. Jossey-Bass, San Francisco, 1969.

1197. Blum,R.K.and Wahl,J. "Police views on drug use." In Blum,R., Alpert,R., Blum,E., and Comber,E.(eds.). Utopiates. Atherton Press, N.Y., 1964, 224-251.

1198. Blumenfield,M., Riester,A.E., Serrano,A.C., and Adams,R.L. "Marihuana use in high school students." Dis. Nerv. Syst. 1972, 33, 603-610.

1199. Blumer,H. The World of Youthful Drug Use. Add Center Project, Oakland, Cal., 1967.

1200. Boe,S. "Drugs: What factor in juvenile crime?" Juv. Court J. 1971, 22, 40-44.

1201. Boer,D.D. "A modified Beam-test for detection of cannabis resin."(Ger.) Pharm. Weekbl. 1955, 90, 321-323.

1202. Boer,D.D. "Thin-layer chromatography in toxicological analysis." Pharm. Weekbl. 1969, 104 606-610.

1203. Boeren,E.G., Elsohly,M.A., Turner,C.E., and Salemink,C.A. "Beta-cannabispiranol: A new non-cannabinoid phenol from cannabis sativa L." Exper. 1977, 33, 848.

1204. Boericke,W. "Materia Medica (A dictionary of homeopathic substances)." In Andrews,G. and Vinkenoog,S.(eds.). The Book of Grass. Grove Press, N.Y., 1967, 149-150.

1205. Boericke,W. Pocket Manual of Homeopathic Materia Medica Comprising the Characteristic and Guiding Symptoms of All Remedies. Boericke and Runyon, Phil., 1927.

1206. Boettcher,A. "On the use of Indian hemp in psychiatry."(Ger.). Berlin. Klin. Woch. 1866, 3, 166-168.

1207. Bogg,R.A. "Drinking as a precursor to hallucinogenic drug usage." Drug Forum 1975, 5, 55-67.

1208. Bogg,R.A. and Hughes,J.W. "Correlates of marihuana usage at a Canadian technological institute." Internat'l. J. Addict. 1973, 8, 489-504.

1209. Bogg,R.A., Smith,R.G., and Russell,S. Drugs and Michigan High School Students. Michigan House of Representatives, Special Committee on Narcotics, Lansing, Mich., 1968.

1210. Boggan,W.O., Steele,R.A., and Freedman,D.X. "Delta-9-tetrahydrocannabinol effect on audiogenic seizure susceptibility." Psychopharmacol. 1973, 29, 101-106.

1211. Bohlig,J.F "Chemical analysis of cannabis sativa and urtica dioica."(Ger.). Jahr. Prak. Pharm. 1840, 1-58.

1212. Boissier,E. "Flora orientalis."(Lat.). Lugduni, 1879, 4, 1152-1153.

1213. Boissier,J.R. "Clinical pharmacological study and EEG changes of delta-9-tetrahydrocannabinol effects in human volunteers." In Usdin,E. and Snyder,S.H.(eds.). Frontiers in Catecholamine Research. Pergamon Press, N.Y., 1973, 911-915.

1214. Boiteau,P. "Two autochthonous plants from Madigascar used in the manner of hemp as narcotics." (Fr.). C. R. Acad. Sci. 1967, 264, 41-42.

1215. Bolas,T. and Francis,E.E.H. "On the products of the action of nitric acid on the resinous extract of Indian hemp." Chem. News J. Phys. Sci. 1869, 22, 417-419.

1216. Bolas,T. and Francis,E.E.H. "Preliminary note on oxy-cannabin." Chem. News J. Phys. Sci. 1871, 24, 77.

1217. Boldt,R.F., Reilly,R.R., and Haberman,P.W. "A survey and assessment of the current status of drug-related instructional programs in secondary and elementary educational institutions." In U.S. National Commission on Marihuana and Drug Abuse. Drug Use in America: Problem in Perspective. Gov't. Print. Office, Washington, D.C., 1973, II, 455-547.

1218. Bombelon,E. "Cannabinon."(Ger.). Pharmazeut. Zeit. Russ. 1884, 29, 322-323.

1219. Bond,F.F. and Edwards,B.E. "Cannabis indica in diarrhea." J.A.M.A. 1887, 9, 115.

1220. Bonier,R. and Hymowitz,P. "Marihuana and college students: set, setting and personality." Proc. Am. Psychol. Assoc. 1972, 7, 213-214.

1221. Bonnasies,M. "Suggestion in hashish."(Fr.). Rev. Philosoph. 1886, 21, 673-674.

1222. Bonnefin,F.H. "Short notes on a method for rendering creosote and cannabis indica soluble, and some little known medicinal plants." Ther. Soc. Trans. 1907, 5, 99-105.

1223. Bonnie,R.J. and Sonnerich,M.R.(eds.). Legal Aspects of Drug Dependence. CRC Press, Cleveland, 1975.

1224. Bonnie,R.J. and Whitebread,C.H. "The forbidden fruit and the tree of knowledge: An inquiry into the legal history of American marihuana prohibition." Virginia Law Rev. 1970, 56, 971-1203.

1225. Bonnie,R.J. and Whitebread,C.H. The Marihuana Conviction; A History of Marihuana Prohibition in the U.S. Univ. of Virginia Press, Charlottesville, Va., 1974.

1226. Booij,J. "The marihuana problem."(Dut.). Ned. Tijd. Geneesk. 1971, 115, 650-651.

1227. Boolsen,M.V. and Knipschildt,H.E. "Who uses what drugs in Denmark and some principles behind drug treatment programs." J. Drug Issues 1975, 5, 33-42.

1228. Boothroyd,W.E. "Marihuana research." Can. Med. Assoc. J. 1973, 108, 825.

1229. Borg,J., Gershon,S., and Alpert,M. "Dose effects of smoked marihuana on human cognitive and motor functions." Psychopharmacol. 1975, 42, 211-218.

1230. Borgen,L.A. "Operant behavioral studies of delta-9-tetrahydrocannabinol in the rat." Diss. Abs. 1973, 34, 1662-1663.

1231. Borgen,L.A. and Davis,W.M. "Cannabidiol (CBD) attenuation of effects of delta-9-tetrahydro-cannabinol." Pharmacol. 1973, 15, 201.

1232. Borgen,L.A. and Davis,W.M. "Cannabidiol interaction with delta-9-tetrahydrocannabinol." Res. Comm. Chem. Path. Pharmacol. 1974, 7, 663-670.

1233. Borgen,L.A. and Davis,W.M. "Delta-9-tetra-hydrocannabinol dose effects compared on three schedules of food reinforced operant performance." Fed. Proc. 1973, 32, 725.

1234. Borgen,L.A. and Davis,W.M. "Effects of chronic delta-9-tetrahydrocannabinol on pregnancy in the rat." Pharmacol. 1970, 12, 329.

1235. Borgen,L.A. and Davis,W.M. "Vehicle and route of administration as parameters affecting operant behavioral effects of delta-9-tetrahydrocannabinol." J. Pharmaceut. Sci. 1973, 62, 479-480.

1236. Borgen,L,A., Davis,W.M., and Pace,H.B. "Effects of prenatal delta-9-tetrahydrocannabinol on the development of rat offspring." Pharmacol. Biochem. Behav. 1973, 1, 203-206.

1237. Borgen,L.A., Davis,W.M., and Pace,H.B. "Effects of synthetic delta-9-tetrahydrocannabinol on pregnancy and offspring in the rat." Toxicol. Appl. Pharmacol. 1971, 20, 480-486.

1238. Borgen,L.A., Lott,G.C., and Davis,W.M. "Cannabis-induced hypothermia: A dose-effect comparison of crude marihuana extract and synthetic delta-9-tetra-hydrocannabinol in male and female rats." Res. Comm. Chem. Pathol. Pharmacol. 1973, 5, 621-625.

1239. Borgen,L.A. and Shumway,J. "Comparative effects of delta-9-tetrahydrocannabinol, cannabidiol, and cannabinol on timing behavior in rats." Pharmacol. 1974, 16, 260.

1240. Borkowski,B., Raszeja,W., and Szpunar,K. "Research on the narcotic properties of the varieties of cannabis cultivated in Poland."(Pol.). Biul. Inst. Ros. Lecz. 1958, 4, 230-236.

1241. Borkowski,T. and Chrobok,F. "Marihuana--a new problem?"(Pol.). Zag. Kryminal. 1970, 5, 96-106.

1242. Boroffka,A. "Mental illness and Indian hemp in Lagos." E. Af. Med. J. 1966, 43, 377-384.

1243. Borrison,J.G., Commons,M.L., and Molino,J.A. "Performance of rats on random interval schedules of reinforcement as a function of amount of combusted cannabis inhabled." Psychon. Sci. 1969, 17, 63.

1244. Borthwick,H.A. and Scully,N.J. "Photoperiodic responses of hemp." Bot. Gaz. 1954, 116, 14-29.

1245. Bosc De Venze,E. Theoretical and Practical Treatise on Hashish and Other Psychic Substances.(Fr.). Chaumel, Paris, 1895.

1246. Bosca,I., Pozzar,B., and Majko,Z. "Breeding a southern hemp variety with light-colored stems."(Ger.). Zeit. Pflan. 1969, 62, 231-240.

1247. Bose,B.C. and Mukerji,B. "Observations on the physiologically active fraction of Indian hemp, cannabis sativa Linn." Ind. J. Med. Res. 1945, 33, 265-270.

1248. Bose,B.C. and Mukerji,B. "Physiologically active fractions of Indian hemp." Analyst 1943, 68, 311.

1249. Bose,B.C. and Mukerji,B. "Physiologically active fraction of Indian hemp." Nature 1943, 152, 109-110.

1250. Bose,B.C., Saifi,A.Q., and Bhagwat,A.W. "Effect of cannabis indica on hexobarbital sleeping time and tissue respiration of rat brain." Arch. Internat'l. Pharmacodyn. Ther. 1963, 141, 520-524.

1251. Bose,B.C., Saifi,A.Q., and Bhagwat,A.W. "Observations on the pharmacological actions of cannabis indica. Part II." Arch. Internat'l. Pharmacodyn. Ther. 1964, 147, 285-289.

1252. Bose,B.C., Saifi,A.Q., and Bhagwat,A.W. "Studies on pharmacological actions of cannabis indica (Linn). Part III." Arch. Internat'l. Pharmacodyn. Ther. 1964, 147, 291-297.

1253. Bose,B.C., Vijayvargiya,R., Saifi,A.Q., and Bhagwat,A.W. "Chemical and pharmacological investigations of cannabis indica(Linn). Part I." Arch. Internat'l. Pharmacodyn. Ther. 1963, 146, 99-105.

1254. Bose,R.D. "A study of sex in the Indian hemp." Ag. J. India 1930, 25, 495-507.

1255. Botelho,A. and Pernambuco,P. "Diamba vice." (Port.). In Anonymous. Maconha. Serv. Nac. Educac. Sanit., Rio de Janeiro, 1958.

1256. Bottcher,H. "Concerning the use of Indian hemp in psychiatry."(Ger.). Berl. Klin.Woch. 1866, 1, 166-168.

1257. Bottcher,L.J. "Addiction to euphoriants in young people."(Nor.) Nord. Psykiat. 1967, 21, 202-215.

1258. Boucher,F., Cosson,L., Unger,J., and Paris, M.R. "Cannabis sativa. Chemical races or varieties."(Fr.). Plant. Med. Phytother. 1974, 8, 20-31.

1259. Boucher,F., Paris,M., and Cosson,L. "Evidence for two chemical types of cannabis sativa from South Africa."(Fr.). Phytochem. 1977, 16, 1445-1448.

1260. Boudreau,A. Knowledge of Drugs.(Fr.). Editions du Jour, Montreal, 1972.

1261. Boughey,H. "Pot scenes east and west." In Simmons,J.L.(ed.). Marihuana; Myths and Realities. Brandon House, Cal., 1967, 24-44.

1262. Bouhuys,A., Barbero,A., Lindell,S.E., Roach,S.A., and Schilling,R.S.F. "Byssinosis in hemp workers." Arch. Environ. Hlth. 1967, 14, 533-544.

1263. Bouhuys,A., Barbero,A., Schilling,S.F., and van de Woestljne,K.P. "Chronic respiratory disease in hemp workers." Am. J. Med. 1969, 46, 526-537.

1264. Bouhuys,A. and van de Woestljne,K.P. "Respiratory mechanics and dust exposure in byssinosis." J. Clin. Invest. 1970, 49, 106-118.

1265. Boulougouris,J.C., Liakos,A., and Stefanis,C. "Social traits of heavy hashish users and matched controls." Ann. N. Y. Acad. Sci. 1976, 282, 17-23.

1266. Boulougouris,J.C., Panayiotopoulos,C.P., Antypas,E., Liakos,A., and Stefanis,C. "Effects of chronic heavy hashish use on medical status in 44 users compared with 38 controls." Ann. N. Y. Acad. Sci. 1976, 282, 168-172.

1267. Bouquet,G. and Perronel,M "Cannabis usage in Tunis."(Fr.). Arch. Instit. Pasteur Tunis 1925, 14, 404.

1268. Bouquet, J. Aliens in Tunis.(Fr.). Univ. of Lyon, Sch. of Med., Lyon, France, 1909.

1269. Bouquet,J. "Cannabis." Bull. Narc. 1950, 2, 14-30.

1270. Bouquet,J. "Cannabis in Tunisia. I Medical data on hemp(origin, composition, legislation."(Fr.). Arch. Instit. Pasteur Tunis 1925, 14, 404-421.

1271. Bouquet,J. "Marihuana intoxication." J.A.M.A. 1944, 124, 1010-1011.

1272. Bouquet,J. Materia Medica of North Africa.(Fr.). (Fr.). Vigot, Paris, 1921.

1273. Bouquet,J. "New contributions to the study of cannabis."(Fr.). Arch. Instit. Pasteur Tunis 1937, 26, 288-317.

1274. Bouquet,J. "New contributions to the study of cannabis."(Fr.) Arch. Instit. Pasteur Tunis 1938, 27, 368-443.

1275. Bouquet,J. "Some investigations on Indian hemp."(Fr.). Bull. Sci. Pharmacol. 1938, 45, 107-122, 161-173.

1276. Bouquet,J. The Herb of the Fakirs(Hashish). Univ. of Lyons, Sch. of Pharm., Lyon, France, 1912.

1277. Bourassa,M. "Anxiety as an undesirable effect of marihuana."(Fr.). Toxicoman. 1972, 5, 293-306.

1278. Bourassa,M. "Marihuana and research."(Fr.) Toxicoman. 1971, 4, 19-50.

1279. Bourassa,M. "Personality characteristics of adult cannabis users."(Fr.). Toxicoman. 1975, 8, 295-310.

1280. Bourassa,M. "The psychological effects of cannabis."(Fr.). Bull. Psychol. 1971, 5, 393-401.

1281. Bourdon,R. "Fluorimetric dosage of delta-9-tetrahydrocannabinol and its metabolites in urine."(Fr.). Ann. Biol. Clin. 1975, 33, 105-113.

1281. Bourdon,R. "Fluorimetric dosage of delta-9-tetrahydrocannabinol and its metabolites in urine." Eur. J. Toxicol. 1976, 9, 11-21.

1282. Bourdon,R. "Identification and quantification of cannabinoids in urine by gallium chelate formation." In Nahas,G.G., Paton,W.D.M., and Idanpaan-Heikkila,J.E. (eds.). Marihuana. Springer Verlag, N.Y., 1976, 111-123.

1283. Bourhill,C.J.G. The Smoking of Dagga(Indian hemp) among the Native Races of South Africa and the Resultant Evils. University of Edinburgh, Dept. of Med., Edinburgh, 1913.

1284. Bourley,J. "Longitudinal organization of external fiber bundles of phoem of hibiscus-cannabis L.(marvacae)."(Fr.). C. R. Acad. Sci. 1971, 272, 1623-1626.

1285. Boutron,A. "Hashish and its preparations." Bull. Sci. Pharmacol. 1922, 29, 89-91.

1286. Bowd,A., Byrom,P., Hudson,J.B., and Turnbull, H.H. "Ultraviolet absorption and luminescence properties of some cannabis constituents." Talanta 1971, 18, 697-705.

1287, Bowd,A., Swann,D.A., and Turnbull,J.H. "Photochemical transformations of cannabinol." J. Chem. Soc. 1975, 1, 797-798.

1288. Bowers,W.J. "Trends in college campus deviance." Coll. Stud. Survey 1971, 5, 20-30.

1289. Bowker,L.H. "The influence of the perceived home drug environment on college student drug use." Addict. Behav. 1976, 1 293-298.

1290. Bowles,P. "Kif: Prologue and compendium of terms." In Andrews,G. and Vinkenoog,S.(eds.). The Book of Grass. Grove Press, N.Y. 1967, 108-114.

1291. Bowman,M.L. "Chronic heavy use of cannabis sativa." Diss. Abs. 1972, 33, 2804.

1292. Bowman,M.L. and Pihl,R.O. "Cannabis: psychological effects of chronic heavy use. A controlled study of intellectual functioning in chronic users of high potency cannabis." Psychopharmacol. 1973, 29, 159-170.

1293. Bowman,R. "Marihuana problems." J.A.M.A. 1945, 128, 889-890.

1294. Boyce,S.S. Hemp(cannabis sativa). A Practical Treatise on the Culture of Hemp for Seed and Fiber with a Sketch of the History and Nature of the Hemp Plant. Orange Judd Co., N.Y., 1912.

1295. Boyd,E.H., Boyd,E.S., and Brown,L.E. "Differential effects of a tetrahydrocannabinol and pentobarbital on cerebral cortical neurones." Neuropharmacol. 1975, 14, 533-536.

1296. Boyd,E.S., Boyd,E.H., and Brown,L.E. "Effects of delta-9-tetrahydrocannabinol and pentobarbital on a cortical response evoked during conditioning. Psychopharmacol. 1976, 47, 119-122.

1297. Boyd,E.S., Boyd,E.H., and Brown,L.E. "The effects of some drugs on an evoked response sensitive to tetrahydrocannabinols." J. Pharmacol. Exper. Ther. 1974, 189, 748-758.

1298. Boyd,E.S., Boyd,E.H., Muchmore,J.S., and Brown,L.E. "Effects of two tetrahydrocannabinols and of pentobarbital on cortico-cortical evoked responses in the squirrel monkey." J. Pharmacol. Exper. Ther. 1971, 176, 480-488.

1299. Boyd,E.S., Hutchinson,E.D., Gardner,L.C., and Meritt,D.A. "Effects of tetrahydrocannabinols and other drugs on operant behavior in rats." Arch. Internat'l. Pharmacodyn. Ther. 1963, 144, 533-554.

1300. Boyd,E.S. and Meritt,D.A. "Effects of barbiturates and a tetrahydrocannabinol derivative on recovery cycles of medial lemniscus, thalamus and reticular formation in the cat." J. Pharmacol. Exper. Ther. 1966, 151, 376-384.

1301. Boyd,E.S. and Meritt,D.A. "Effects of a tetrahydrocannabinol derivative on some motor systems in the cat." Arch. Internat'l. Pharmacodyn. Ther. 1965, 153, 1-12.

1302. Boyd,E.S. and Meritt,D.A. "Effects of thiopental and a tetrahydrocannabinol derivative on arousal and recruiting in the cat." J. Pharmacol. Exper. Ther. 1965, 149, 138-145.

1303. Boyko,E.P. and Rotberg,M.W. "Constitutional objections to California's marihuana possession statute." U.C.L.A. Law Rev. 1967, 14, 773-795.

1304. Bozetti,L., Goldsmith,S., and Ungerleider,T.J. "The great banana hoax." Amer. J. Psychiat. 1967, 124, 678.

1305. Bozner,M. "Paper chromatography in distinguishing hemp varieties in acid and alkaline hydrolyzed solutions and in alcoholic extracts of young plants." (Czech.). Sborn. Cesk. Akad. Zemedel. Ved. 1960, 6, 121-130.

1306. Bozzetti,L. and Blaine,J. "Memories, reflections and myths: The American Marihuana Commission." In Rubin,V.(ed.) Cannabis and Culture. Mouton, The Hague, 1975, 521-531.

1307. Braceland,F.J. "Psychiatry." Med. Wld. News 1968, 9, 156.

1308. Bracs,P., Jackson,D.M., and Chesher,G.B. "The effect of delta-9-tetrahydrocannabinol on brain amine concentration and turnover in whole rat brain and in various regions of the brain." J. Pharm. Pharmacol. 1975, 27, 713-715.

1309. Braden,W., Stillman,R.C., and Wyatt,R.J. "Effects of marihuana on contingent negative variation and reaction time." Arch. Gen. Psychiat. 1974, 31, 537-541.

1310. Bradford,L.W. and Bracket,J.W. "Systematic procedure for the identification of dangerous drugs, poisons and narcotics by ultraviolet spectrophotometry." Mickrochim. Act. 1958, 3, 23.

1311. Bradley,S.G., Munson,A.E., Dewey,W.L. and Harris,S. "Enhanced susceptibility of mice to combinations of delta-9-tetrahydrocannabinol and live or killed gram-negative bacteria." Infect. Immun. 1977, 17, 325-329.

1312. Brady,R.O. and Carbonne,E. "Comparison of the effects of delta-9-tetrahydrocannabinol, 11-hydroxy-delta-9-tetrahydrocannabinol, and ethanol on the electrophysical activity of the giant axon of the squid." Neuropharmacol. 1973, 12, 601-605.

1313. Braenden,O.J. "Cannabis research at the Division of Narcotic Drugs, U.N., Geneva." Act. Pharmaceut. Suec. 1971, 8, 673-674.

1314. Bragman,L.J. "A minor De Quincey." Med. J. Rec. 1925, 121, 43-45.

1315. Bragman,L.J. "The weed of insanity." Med. J. Rec. 1925, 122, 416-418.

1316. Brale,M. Practical Analysis on the Cultivation and Raising of Hemp. Paris, 1790.

1317. Bram,S. and Brachet,P. "Inhibition of proliferation and differentiation of dictyostelium discoideum amoebae by tetrahydrocannabinol and cannabinol." In Nahas,G.G., Paton,W.D.M., and Idanpaan-Heikkila,J.E. (eds.). Marihuana. Springer Verlag, N.Y., 1976, 207-213.

1318. Bramson,A., Yolles,M, and Yolles,S.F. "Psychiatrist and his daughter speak frankly about marihuana." Seventeen 1970, 29, 134-135.

1319. Brand,M. "Flower of hell." This Week 1938, 24.

1320. Brantley,W.G. "Attitudes toward marihuana among law students: The south's future lawyers." J. Drug Educat. 1976, 6, 113-116.

1321. Brantley,W.G. "Marihuana trends at a state university in the deep south." J. Alcohol Drug Educat. 1974, 20, 53-60.

1322. Brau,J.L. Hashish and LSD.(Ger.). Insel-Verlag, Frankfurt, 1969.

1323. Braude,M.C. "Five years of preclinical marihuana research." In Braude,M.C., and Szara,S.(eds.). Pharmacology of Marihuana. Raven Press, N.Y., 1976, 21-27.

1324. Braude,M.C. "The National Institute of Mental Health biomedical program of marihuana research." Act. Pharmaceut. Suec. 1971, 8, 674-675.

1325. Braude,M.C. "Toxicology and teratology of marihuana and constituents." Abstracts of Am. Pharmaceut. Assoc. 1971, 47.

1326. Braude,M.C. "Toxicology of cannabinoids." In Paton,W.D.M. and Crown,J.(eds.). Cannabis and its Derivatives. Oxford Univ. Press, London, 1972, 88-101.

1327. Braude,M.C., Mansaert,R., and Truitt,E.B. "Some pharmacologic correlates to marihuana use." Seminars Drug Treat. 1971, 1, 229-246.

1328. Brecher,E.M. Licit and Illicit Drugs. Little Brown and Co., Boston, 1972.

1329. Brecher,E.M. "Marihuana: The health questions." Consum. Rep. 1975, 40, 143-149.

1330. Brecher,E.M. "Debunking the marihuana researchers." Hosp. Phys. 1975, 1, 12-15.

1331. Bredemann,G. "Contribution to hemp cultivation. III. Further experiments in cultivation for fiber content." (Ger.). Zeit. Pflan. 1927, 12, 259-268.

1332. Bredemann,G. "Contribution to the study of hemp cultivation. II. Selection of male plants having a high fiber content for fertilization by determining the fiber content of the living plant before blossoming." (Ger.). Ang. Bot. 1924, 6, 348-360.

1333. Bredemann,G. "Cultivation of hemp(cannabis sativa L.) for its fiber content."(Ger.). Forshung. 1937, 3, 398-410.

1334. Bredemann,G. "Cultivation of hemp for its fiber. Results for 1937." Faserfor. 1938, 13, 81-87

1335. Bredemann,G. "Cultivation of hemp for its fiber content." Zuchter 1942, 14, 201-213.

1336. Bredemann,G. "Determination of fiber yield in hemp cultivation."(Ger.). Ang. Bot. 1922, 4, 223-233.

1337. Bredemann,G. "Determination of fiber yield in various stems of hemp."(Ger.). Forschung. 1940, 10, 57-67.

1338. Bredemann,G. "Further observations on research on the fiber yield of hemp."(Ger.). Zuchter 1952, 22, 9.

1339. Bredemann,G. "Research on the absorption of nutritive substances and the need for nutrients by hemp(cannabis sativa L)."(Ger.). Zeit. Pflan. 1945, 36, 167-204.

1340. Bredemann,G., Garber,K., Huhnke,W., and von Sengbushch,R. "The selection of monoic and dioic fiber-rich varieties of hemp."(Ger.). Zeit. Pflan. 1961, 46, 235-245.

1341. Bredemann,G., Schwanitz,F., and von Sengbusch,R. "Problems of modern hemp breeding, with particular reference to the breeding of varieties of hemp containing little or no hashish." Bull. Narc. 1956, 8, 31-34.

1342. Breimer,D.D., Vree,T.B., van Ginneken,C.A.M., and van Rossum,J.M. "Some new cannabis constituents." In van Praag,H.M.(ed.). Biochemical and Pharmacological Aspects of Dependence and Reports on Marihuana Research. De Erven F. Bohn, Haarlem, The Netherlands, 1972, 116-118.

1343. Brennan,G.E. "Marihuana witchhunt." Evergreen Rev. 1968, 55, 55-56, 91-95.

1344. Brenner,J.H. "Drugs and society." In Zarafonetis,C.J.D.(ed.). Drug Abuse. Lea and Febiger, Phil., 1971, 115-128.

1345. Breslavec,L. "Research on development of the flower in hemp whose sex has been changed under the influence of photo-periodism." Genetica 1937, 19, 393-412.

1346. Bretschneider,E. "Botanicon Sinicum. Materia medica of the ancient Chinese." Roy. Asiat. Soc. Gr. Brit. 1890, 25, 4-16, 203-208, 345-346, 405-407.

1347. Bretschneider,E. "Botanicon Sinicum. Materia medica of the ancient Chinese." Roy. Asiat. Soc. Gr. Brit. 1894, 29, 376-379.

1348. Bretton,P. Pigeons for Profit. C. Arthur Pearson, London, 1914.

1349. Brickenstein,R. "Dangers of cannabis drugs for adolescents."(Ger.). Allgemeinmed. 1971, 47, 846-847.

1350. Brickman,H.R. "The psychedelic 'hip scene': Return to the death instinct." Am. J. Psychiat. 1968, 125, 766--72.

1351. Brierre de Boismont,A. "Observations of imbecility and alternating spells of exaltation and melancholy for a long number of years--ineffectiveness of quinine sulphate and hashish."(Fr.). Gaz. Hop. Civil. Milit. 1854, 27, 63.

1352. Brigham,A. "Review of Moreau de Tours."(Fr.). Am. J. Insan. 1846, 2, 275-281.

1353. Bright,T.P., Farber,M.O., Brown,D.J., and Forney,R.B. "Cardiopulmonary effects of cannabidiol in anesthetized dogs." Pharmacologist 1974, 16, 281.

1354. Bright,T.P., Farber,M.O., Brown,D.J., and Forney,R.B. "Cardiopulmonary toxicity of delta-9-tetrahydrocannabinol in the anesthetized dog." Toxicol. Appl. Pharmacol. 1975, 31, 100-106.

1355 Bright,T.P., Farber,M.O., Winter,L.W., Brown,D.J., and Forney,R.B. "The effects of delta-9-tetrahydrocannabinol on lung resistance and compliance in the dog." Toxicol. Appl. Pharmacol. 1974, 29, 78.

1356. Bright,T.P., Kiplinger,G.F., Brown,D., Phillips,J., and Forney,R.B. "Effects of beta adrenergic blockade of marihuana induced tachycardia." Comm. Prob. Drug Depend. 1971, 2, 1737-1744.

1357. Brigs,C.J. "Student-father attitudes toward contemporary social issues." Psychol. Rep. 1972, 31, 699-706.

1358. Brill,H. "Drugs and drug users: Some perspectives." In New York State Narcotic Addiction Control Commission. Drugs on Campus. Saratoga Springs, N.Y., 1967, 47-64.

1359. Brill,H. "Pro-drug dialectic communication on drug abuse and the marihuana red herring." In Wittenborn, J.R., Smith,J.P., and Wittenborn,S.A.(eds.). Communication and Drug Abuse. C.C.Thomas, Springfield, Ill., 1970, 25-42.

1360. Brill,H. "Recurrent pattern in the history of drugs of dependence and some interpretations." In Wittenborn,H., Brill,H., Smith,J.P., and Wittenborn, S.A.(eds.). Drugs and Youth. C.C.Thomas, Springfield, Ill., 1969, 8-25.

1361. Brill,H. "The case against marihuana." J. Sch. Hlth. 1968, 38, 522-523.

1362. Brill,H. "Why not pot now? Some questions and answers about marihuana." Psychiat. Opin. 1968, 5, 16-21.

1363. Brill,N.Q. "Marihuana problem." Psychiat. Dig. 1969, 30, 9-19.

1364. Brill,N.Q. "The marihuana problem." Cal. Med. 1971, 114, 54-55.

1365. Brill,N.Q. "The marihuana problem." Milit. Med. 1973, 138, 205-210.

1366. Brill,N.Q. "Marihuana use and psychosocial adaptation." Arch. Gen. Psychiat. 1974, 31, 713-719.

1367. Brill,N.Q., Crumpton,E., Frank,I.M., Hochman,J.S., Lomax,P., McGlothlin,W.H., and West,L.J. "The marihuana problem." Ann. Intern. Med. 1970, 73, 449-465.

1368. Brill,N.Q., Crumpton,E., and Grayson,H.M. "Personality factors in marihuana use." Arch. Gen. Psychiat. 1971, 24, 163-166.

1369. Brillant,L. "Pot: Hobby not habbit." New Physician 1969, 18, 189-190.

1370. Brinkenhoff,J. "Indian hemp."(Pol.). Slown. Towaroz. 1955, 4, 1044-1047.

1371. Briosi,G. and Tognini,F. "Contribution to the study of the comparative anatomy of cannabis. Preliminary note."(It.). At. Inst. Bot. Univers. Pavia 1892, 2, 1-3.

1372. Briosi,G. and Tognini,F. "The anatomy of hemp(cannabis sativa L.). Part 1."(It.). At. Inst. Bot. Univers. Pavia 1894, 3, 91-209.

1373. Briosi,G. and Tognini,F. "The anatomy of hemp(cannabis sativa L.). Part 2."(It.). At. Inst. Bot. Univers. Pavia 1894, 2, 168-329.

1374. British Government. Report of the Inter-departmental Committee, Ministry of Health, Scottish Home and Health Department. H.M. Stationery Office, London, 1961.

1375. British Government. Report on Cannabis Prepared by the Hallucinogens Subcommittee of the Home Office's Advisory Committee on Drug Dependence. H.M. Stationery Office, London, 1968.

1376. British Government. Second Report of the Interdepartmental Committee, Ministry of Health, Scottish Home and Health Department. H.M. Stationery Office, London, 1965.

1377. British Pharmaceutical Society. "Statement on cannabis." Pharmaceut. J. 1967, 199, 142.

1378. Brito,F.D. "Isolation of cannabinol, cannabidiol, and tetrahydrocannabinol from cannabis sativa L."(Port.). Rev. Quim. Ind. 1972, 41, 15-16.

1379. Britton,R.S. and Mellors,A. "Lysis of rat liver lysosomes in vitro by delta-9-tetrahydrocannabinol." Biochem. Pharmacol. 1974, 23, 1342-1344.

1380. Bro,P. and Schou,J. "Cannabis poisoning with analytical verification." New Eng. J. Med. 1975, 293, 1049-1050.

1381. Brodlie,J.F. "Drug abuse and television viewing patterns." Psychol. 1972, 9, 33-36.

1382. Bromberg,W. "Dr. Bromberg replies." Am. J. Psychiat. 1968, 125, 852-852.

1383. Bromberg,W. "Marihuana: A psychiatric study." J.A.M.A. 1939, 113, 4-12.

1384. Bromberg,W. "Marihuana intoxication. A clinical study of cannabis sativa intoxication." Am. J. Psychiat. 1934, 91, 303-330.

1385. Bromberg,W. "Marihuana--Thirty five years later." Am. J. Psychiat. 1968, 125, 391-393.

1386. Bromberg,W. "The effects of marihuana." Nerv. Ment. Dis. 1939, 19, 180-189.

1387. Bromberg,W. "The marihuana hassle: A way out." Med. Insight 1972, 9, 24-33.

1388. Bromberg,W. "The menace of marihuana." Med. Rec. 1935, 142, 309-311.

1389. Bromberg,W. and Rodgers,T.C. "Marihuana and aggressive crime." Am. J. Psychiat. 1946, 102, 825-827.

1390. Bron,B. "Motivation and effect of use of hallucinogens."(Ger.). Prax. Kinderpsychol. Kinder-psychiat. 1976, 25, 128-139.

1391. Brookes,W.L. "A case of recurrent migraine, successfully treated with cannabis indica." Ind. Med. Rec. 1896, 11, 338.

1392. Brooks,A.D. "Marihuana and the constitution: Individual liberties and puritan virtues." In Wittenborn, H., Brill,H, Smith,J.P., and Wittenborn,S.A.(eds.). Drugs and Youth. C.C. Thomas, Springfield, Ill., 1969,280-298.

1393. Brotman,R., Silverman,I., and Suffet,F. "Drug use among affluent high shcool youth." In Goode,E.(ed.). Marihuana. Atherton Press, N.Y., 1969, 128-135.

1394. Brotman,R., Silverman,I., Suffet,F., Hudson,D., and Lightfoot,H. "Suburban towns respond to drugs: A study of decision making in contiguous communities." In U.S. National Commission on Marihuana and Drug Abuse. Drug Use in America: Problem in Perspective. Gov't. Print. Office, Washington, D.C. 1973, II, 288-333.

1395. Brotman,R. and Suffet,F. "Marihuana use and social control." Ann. N. Y. Acad. Sci. 1971, 191, 235-245.

1396. Brotman,R. and Suffet,F. "Marihuana use: Values, behavioral definitions and social control." In U.S. National Commission on Marihuana and Drug Abuse. Drug Use in America: Problem in Perspective. Gov't. Print. Office, Washington, D.C., 1973, I, 1078-1110.

1397. Brotman,R. and Suffet,F. "Marihuana users' views of marihuana use." In Zubin,M.(ed.). The Psycho-pathology of Adolescence. Grune and Stratton, Inc., 1970, 258-272.

1398. Brotteaux,P. Hashish--the Herb of Folly and Dreams.(Fr.). Vega, Paris, 1934.

1399. Brown,A. and Stickgold,A. "Marihuana flashback phenomena." J. Psychedel. Drugs 1976, 8, 275-283.

1400. Brown,A. and Stickgold,A. "Self-diagnosed marihuana flashbacks." Clin. Res. 1974, 22, 316A.

1401. Brown,B.S. "Current needs and future trends in drug abuse research." Clin. Res. 1971, 19, 618-619.

1402. Brown,B. "Marihuana and health." Am. J. Psychiat. 1971, 128, 218-219.

1403. Brown,B., Adams,A.J., Haegerstrom-Portnoy,G., Jones,R.T., and Flom,M.C. "Effects of alcohol and marihuana on dynamic visual acuity." Percept. Psychophys. 1975, 18, 441-446.

1404. Brown,B., Adams,A.J., Jones,R.T. and Flom,M.C. "Pupil size after use of marihuana and alcohol." Am. J. Opthalmol. 1977, 83, 350-354.

1405. Brown,D.J., Miller,F.N., Longnecker,D.E., Greenwald,E.K., Harris,P.D., and Forney,R.B. "The influence of delta-9-tetrahydrocannabinol on cardiovascular and subcutaneous microcirculatory systems in the bat." J. Pharmacol. Exper. Ther. 1974, 188, 624-629.

1406. Brown,F.H. "Case of poisoning by cannabis indica." Bost. Med. Surg. J. 1863, 67, 291-292.

1407. Brown,H. "Possible anticholinesterase-like effects of trans(-)-delta-8- and delta-9-tetrahydrocannabinol as observed in the general motor activity of mice." Psychopharmacol. 1972, 27, 111-116.

1408. Brown,H. "Some anticholinergic-like behavioral effects of trans(-)-delta-8-tetrahydrocannabinol." Psychopharmacol. 1971, 21, 294-301.

1409. Brown,H. and Richards,R.K. "An interaction between drug effects and food reinforcement. (Social behavior in pigeons.)." Arch. Internat'l. Pharmacodyn. Ther. 1966, 164, 286-293.

1410. Brown,J. "Cannabis indica; a valuable remedy in menorrhagia." Br. Med. J. 1883, 1, 1002.

1411. Brown,J.K.and Malone,M.H. "A street drug analysis program--three years later." In Marshman,J.A. (ed.). Street Drug Analysis and Its Social and Clinical Implications. Addiction Res. Found., Toronto, 1974, 19-39.

1412. Brown,J.K. and Malone,M.H. "Qualitative analytical results of a street drug monitoring program--a new aspect of toxicology." Proc. West. Pharmacol. Soc. 1973, 16, 134-137.

1413. Brown,J.W. "A test of a three-stage learning model of drug abuse." Criminol. 1972, 9, 449-466.

1414. Brown,J.W., Glaser,D., Waxer,E., and Geis,G. "Turning off: Cessation of marihuana use after college." Soc. Prob. 1974, 21, 127-138.

1415. Brown,O.M. "Effect of delta-9-tetrahydrocannabinol(THC) on rat brain acetylcholine levels." Pharmacol. 1973, 15, 200.

1416. Brown,T.M. "Differences in attitudes of public school students toward selected drugs and relationship between these attitudes and drug knowledge." Diss. Abs. 1972, 32, 3752-3753.

1417. Brown,T.T. The Enigma of Drug Addiction. C.C.Thomas, Springfield, Ill., 1961.

1418. Browne,E.G. "A chapter from the history of cannabis indica." St. Barth. Hosp. J. 1897, 4, 81-86.

1419. Brubaker,T.H. "A synthesis of current research on marihuana." J. Drug Educat. 1973, 3, 25-30.

1420. Bruce,R. The Pot Report. Award Books, N.Y., 1971.

1421. Bruhn-Petersen,F.and Nimb,M. "Hash or LSD."(Dan.). Ugeskr. Laeg. 1967, 129, 1662.

1422. Bruin Humanist Forum. "A marihuana bibliography." New West 1967, 2, 16.

1423. Bruin Humanist Forum. Documented Facts about Marihuana: First Preliminary Draft. Bruin Humanist Forum, L.A., Cal., 1966.

1424. Bruin Humanist Forum. Documented Facts about Marihuana: Second Preliminary Draft. Bruin Humanist Forum, L.A., Cal., 1966.

1425. Bruin Humanist Forum. Marihuana(cannabis) Fact Sheet. Bruin Humanist Forum, L.A., Cal., 1967.

1426. Brun-Gulbrandsen,S. "How dangerous are dangerous drugs?"(Nor.). In Anonymous. Marihuana and Hashish.(Nor.). Universitetsforlaget, Oslo, 1970.

1427. Brunner,T.F. "Marihuana in ancient Greece and Rome? The literary evidence." Bull. Hist. Med. 1973, 47, 344-355.

1428. Brussel,J. "Marihuana." J.A.M.A. 1959, 171, 1910.

1429. Bruun,K., Pan,L., and Rexed,I. The Gentlemen's Club, International Control of Drugs and Alcohol. Univ. of Chicago Press, Chicago, 1975.

1430. Bruyn,H.B. "Drugs on the college campus." J. Sch. Hlth. 1970, 40, 91-98.

1431. Bruyn,H.B. "Management of drug abuse in the college university." J. Am. Coll. Hlth. Assoc. 1972, 20, 357-363.

1432. Bruyn,H.B. "Marihuana: Mary jane faces the identity crisis or, three blind men study the elephant." J. Am. Coll. Hlth. Assoc. 1970, 18, 323-324.

1433. Bryant,T.E. "Special contribution: National survey of marihuana use and attitudes." J. Sch. Hlth. 1975, 45, 544-546.

1434. Bschor,F. "Marihuana."(Ger.). Kriminal. 1950, 4, 13-14, 152.

1435. Bschor,F. "Youth and the use of drugs."(Ger.). Soz. Arbeit 1970, 19, 525-539.

1436. Bschor,F., Herha,J., and Denmark,N. "Young users of intoxicating drugs in West Berlin."(Ger.). Erkund. Forsch. Inst. Gericht. Soz. Med. 1969, 1-48.

1437. Bschor,F., Klug,E., and Herha,J. "Cannabis problem in Berlin."(Ger.). F.U. Pressed. Wissen. 1971, 5, 31-33.

1438. Buchan,T. "Some aspects of drug abuse in Rhodesia. Part 1." Cent. Af. J. Med. 1975, 21, 235-238.

1439. Buchner,H. "Notes on the effects of 'Hatchy'." (Ger.). Rep. Pharm. 1838, 80-83.

1440. Buchner,H. "Some more on hashish."(Ger.). Rep. Pharm. 1845, 231-237.

1441. Buchwald,A. "Concerning cannabis preparations along with remarks on cannabis poisoning."(Ger.). Bres. Arz. Zeit. 1885, 7, 277-279.

1442. Buckley,J.J. "The case for cannabis sativa (legalization of marihuana)." Ripon Forum 1973, 9, 6.

1443. Buckley,W.F. "Conservatives and marihuana." Nat'l. Rev. 1977, 29, 687.

1444. Buckley,W.F. "Pot -n- prison." Nat'l. Rev. 1970, 22, 221.

1445. Buckley,W.F. "Private enterprise and dope." Nat'l. Rev. 1970, 22, 964.

1446. Buckley,W.F. "Thinking out loud about marihuana." Redbook 1973, 140, 1023.

1447. Budin,J.S., Bargman,G.J., Milman,D.H. "Approach to the study of the effects of marihuana." J. Pediat. 1969, 75, 342-343.

1448. Budzikiewica,H., Alpin,R.T., Lightner,D.A., Djerassi,C., Mechoulam,R., and Gaoni,Y. "Mass spectroscopic investigation of hashish constituents."(Ger.). Tetrahedron 1965, 21, 1881-1888.

1449. Budzikiewica,H., Djerassi,C., and Williams,D.H. Interpretation of Mass Spectra of Organic Compounds. Holden-Day, San Francisco, 1964.

1450. Bueno,F.A. and Carlini,E.A. "Dissociation of learning in marihuana tolerant rats." Psychopharmacol. 1972, 25, 49-56.

1451. Bueno,F.A., Carlini,E.A., Finkelfarb,E., and Suzuki,J.S. "Delta-9-tetrahydrocannabinol, ethanol, and amphetamine as discriminative stimuli--generalization tests with other drugs." Psychopharmacol. 1976, 46, 235-243.

1452. Buentello,Y.V.E. "Some psychologic-psychiatric statistics about marihuana and other safe drugs."(Sp.). Rev. Med. Mex. 1972, 52, 332-338.

1453. Buentello,Y.V.E. "Youth and marihuana."(Sp.). Med. 1973, 53, 1-5, 18-22.

1454. Buikhusen,W. and Timmerman,H. "Drug use and drug policy in youth centers. A pilot study."(Dut.). Ned. T. Criminol. 1972, 14, 141-155.

1454. Bull,J. "Cerebral atrophy in young cannabis smokers." Lancet 1971, 2, 1420.

1455. Bullock,F.J., Bruni,R.J., and Werner,E. "A fluorescence assay of submicrogram amounts of cannabis constituents in biological fluids." Paper presented at Am. Chem. Soc., Chicago, 1970.

1456. Bunkley,J.W. "Marihuana: A signal of misunderstanding. First report of the National Commission on Marihuana and Drug Abuse. Book review." Miss. Law J. 1972, 43, 756-762.

1457. Burbridge,T.N. "Marihuana: An overview." J. Second. Educat. 1968, 15, 197-198.

1458. Burdsal,C., Greenberg,G., Bell,M., and Reynolds,S. "A factor analytic examination of sexual behaviors and attitudes and marihuana usage. J. Clin. Psychol.1975, 31, 568-572.

1459. Burdsal,C., Greenberg,G., and Timpe,R. "The relationship of marihuana usage to personality and motivational factors." *J. Psychol.* 1973, *85*, 45-51.

1460. Burger,A.(ed.). *Drugs Affecting the Central Nervous System.* Marcel Dekker Inc., N.Y., 1968.

1461. Burgi,E. "Indona, a hypnotic combination containing cannabis indica."(Ger.). *Deut. Med. Woch.* 1924, *50*, 1529-1530.

1462. Burke,F.W. "The cannabis controversy." *N. Eng. J. Med.* 1931, *96*, 1225-1226.

1463. Burke,T. *Limehouse Nights.* Robert M. McBride And Co., N.Y., 1926.

1464. Burkett,S.R. and Jensen,E.L. "Conventional ties, peer influence, and the fear of apprehension: A study of adolescent marihuana use." *Sociol. Quart.* 1975, *16*, 522-533.

1465. Burn,H. "Drugs producing hallucinations." In Burn,H.(ed.). *Drugs, Medicines and Man.* Charles Scribner's Sons, N.Y., 1962, 219-224.

1466. Burns,G.C. "Neurosine poisoning." *J.A.M.A.* 1931, *96*, 1225-1226.

1467. Burns,M. and Sharma,S. "Marihuana high--a first time effort." *Psychol. Rep.* 1976, *38*, 543-546.

1468. Burr,C.W. "Two cases of cannabis indica intoxication." *Ther. Gaz.* 1916, *40*, 554-556.

1469. Burroughs,H. *Cannabis Indica.*(Fr.). Univ. of Lyon, Department of Medicine and Pharmacy, Lyon, France, 1896.

1470. Burroughs,W. "Letter from a master addict to dangerous drugs." *Br. J. Addict.* 1957, *53*, 119.

1471. Burroughs,W. "Points of distinction between sedative and consciousness expanding drugs." In Solomon, D.(ed.). *LSD: The Conscious Expanding Drug.* Berkeley Medallion, N.Y., 1966.

1472. Burstein,S.H. "Labeling and metabolism of the tetrahydrocannabinols." In Mechoulam,R.(ed.). *Marihuana, Chemistry, Pharmacology, Metabolism and Clinical Effects.* Academic Press, N.Y., 1973.

1473. Burstein,S. "Prostaglandins and cannabis. IV. A biochemical basis for therapeutic applications." In Cohen,S. and Stillman,R.(eds.). Therapeutic Potential of Marihuana. Plenum Press, N.Y., 1976, 19-34.

1474. Burstein,S. and Kupfer,D. "Hydroxylation of trans-delta-1-tetrahydrocannabinol by hepatic microsomal mono-oxygenase." Ann. N. Y. Acad. Sci. 1971, 191, 61-68.

1475. Burstein,S., Levin,E., and Varanelli,C. "Prostaglandins and cannabis. II. Inhibition of biosynthesis by the naturally occurring cannabinoids." Biochem. Pharmacol. 1973, 22, 2905-2910.

1476. Burstein,S., Martinez,J., Rosenfeld,J., and Wittstruck,T. "The urinary metabolites of delta-1-THC. In Paton,W.D.M. and Crown,J.(eds.). Cannabis and its Derivatives. Oxford Univ. Press, London, 1972, 39-50.

1477. Burstein,S. and Mechoulam,R. "Stereospecifically labeled delta-1(6)-tetrahydrocannabinol." J. Am. Chem. Soc. 1968, 90, 2420-2421.

1478. Burstein,S., Menezes,F., Williamson,E., and Mechoulam,R. "Metabolism of delta-1(6)-tetrahydrocannabinol, an active marihuana constituent." Nature 1970, 225, 87-88.

1479. Burstein,S. and Raz,A. "Inhibition of prostaglandin E_2 biosynthesis by delta-1-tetrahydrocannabinol." Prostaglandins 1972, 2, 369-374.

1480. Burstein,S. and Rosenfeld,J. "The isolation and characterization of a major metabolite of delta-1-THC." Act. Pharmaceut. Suec. 1971, 8, 699-700.

1481. Burstein,S., Rosenfeld,J., and Wittstruck,T. "Isolation and characterization of two major urinary metabolites of delta-1-tetrahydrocannabinol." Science 1972, 176, 422-423.

1482. Burstein,S., Taylor,P., El-Feraly,F.S., and Turner,C. "Prostaglandins and cannabis. V. Identification of p-vinylphenol as a potent inhibitor of prostaglandin synthesis." Biochem. Pharmacol. 1976, 25, 2003-2004.

1483. Burstein,S. and Varanelli,C. "Transformations of cannabinol in the mouse." Res. Comm. Chem. Pathol. Pharmacol. 1975, 11, 343-353.

1484. Burton,E.T. "Cannabis indica in chorea and pertussis." Lancet 1902, 1, 1859.

1485. Busquet,H. "Biological essay on the medicinals in the U.S. Pharmacopoea."(Fr.). Bull. Sc. Pharmacol. 1918, 1, 87.

1486. Butler,B.C. "The identification of marihuana with the aid of a color reaction."(Ger.). Pharm. Weekbl. 1936, 98, 1217.

1487. Butler,J.L. "The effects of expectation and suggestion on immediate memory in subjects under the influence of marihuana." Diss. Abs. 1973, 34, 868-869.

1488. Butler,J.L, Gaines,L.S., and Lenox,J.R. "Effects of marihuana, expectation and 'suggestibility' on cognitive functioning." Percept. Motor Skills 1976, 42, 1059-1065.

1489. Butler,J.R., Peek,L., Regelson,W., Moore,M., and Lubin,L. "Treatment effects of delta-9-THC in an advanced cancer population." In Cohen,S. and Stillman, R.(eds.). Therapeutic Potential of Marihuana. Plenum Press, N.Y., 1976, 313-328.

1490. Butler,J.R., Reid,B.E., and Peek,L.A. "Prediction of drug use using life history antecedents with college populations." Proc. Am. Psychol. Assoc. 1973, 8, 303-304.

1491. Butler,W.O. "Duquenois-Levine test for marihuana." J. Assoc. Off. Ag. Chem. 1962, 45, 597-599.

1492. Butowsky,A. The Means of Improving the Management, Cultivation, and Fabrication of Hemp.(Rus.). St. Petersburg, Rus., 1842.

1493. Butterfield,R.O. "A case of cannabis indica poisoning." Critique 1902, 9, 338-340.

1494. Buxbaum,D.M. "Analgesic activity of delta-9-tetrahydrocannabinol in the rat and mouse." Psychopharmacol. 1972, 25, 275-280.

1495. Buxbaum,D., Sanders-Bush,E., and Efron,D.H. "Analgesic activity of tetrahydrocannabinol(THC) in the rat and mouse." Fed. Proc. 1969, 28, 735.

1496. Byck,R. and Ritchie,J.M. "Delta-9-tetrahydrocannabinol: Effects on mammalian nonmyelinated nerve fibers." Science 1973, 180, 84-85.

1497. Byrd,O.E.(ed.). Medical Readings on Drug Abuse. Addison-Wesley Pub. Co., Reading, Mass., 1970.

C

1498. Caballero,A. "The killing drug." *Pol. Sec. Nac.* 1942, *10*, 182-184.

1499. Cabanes,J. "The death of Baudelaire."(Fr.). *Chron. Med.* 1902, 725-735.

1500. Cabanis,D. "Present problems with narcotics." (Ger.). *Deut. Med. J.* 1970, *21*, 1285-1286, 1288, 1291.

1501. Caddy,B. and Fish,F. "A screening technique for Indian hemp." *J. Chromatog.* 1967, *31*, 584-587.

1502. Caddy,B., Fish,F., and Wilson,W.D.C. "Gas chromatography of Indian hemp." *J. Pharm. Pharmacol.* 1967, *19*, 851-852.

1503. Cahagnet,L.A. *Magnetism: Encyclopedia of Spiritualistic Magnetism.*(Fr.). *Sanctuaire du Spiritualisme, Paris, 1849.*

1504. Cahn,M. "The user and the law." In Simmons,J.L. (ed.). *Marihuana; Myths and Realities.* Brandon House, Cal., 1967, 45-57.

1505. Cahn,R.S. "Cannabis indica resin. I. The constitution of nitrocannabinolactone." *J. Chem. Soc.* 1930, *1*, 986-992.

1506. Cahn,R.S. "Cannabis indica resin. II." *J. Chem. Soc.* 1931, *1*, 630-638.

1507. Cahn,R.S. "Cannabis indica resin. III. The constitution of cannabinol." *J. Chem. Soc.* 1932, *1*, 1342-1353.

1508. Cahn,R.S. "Cannabis indica resin. IV. The synthesis of some 2:2-dimethyldibenzopyrans, and confirmation of the structure of cannabinol." *J. Chem. Soc.* 1933, *1* 1400-1405.

1509. Cais,M., Dani,S., Josephy,Y., Modiano,A., Gerson,H., and Mechoulam,R. "Studies of cannabinoid metabolites--a free radical immunoassay." *Febs Let.* 1975, *55*, 257-160.

1510. Caldas,A. "Chemical identification of cannabis." *Anal. Chim. Act.* 1970, *49*, 194.

1511. Caldwell,D.F., Myers,S.A., and Domino,E.F. "Effects of marihuana smoking on sensory thresholds in man." In Efron,D.H.(ed.). *Psychotomimetic Drugs.* Raven Press, N.Y., 1970, 299-321.

1512. Caldwell,D.F., Myers,S.A., Domino,E.F., and Merriam,P.E. "Auditory and visual threshold effects of marihuana in man." *Percept. Motor Skill.* 1969, *29*, 755-759, 922.

1513. Caldwell,J. and Sever,P.S. "The biochemical pharmacology of abused drugs. III. Cannabis, opiates and synthetic narcotics." *Clin. Pharmacol. Ther.* 1974, *16*, 989-1013.

1514. Caldwell,S.A.G. "Sunn and Bombay hemps." *Tex. Manufact.* 1936, *62*, 455.

1515. Callicchin,J.P. "Effects of magnitude and schedule of reward for counter attitudinal advocacy on subsequent attitude change." *J. Soc. Psychol.* 1973, *91*, 239-249.

1516. Callahan,T.R. "A sampling from recent literature concerning hallucinogenic drugs." *Provo Papers* 1969, *4*, 41-61.

1517. Callan,J.P. and Patterson,C.D. "Patterns of drug abuse among military inductees." *Am. J. Psychiat.* 1973, *130*, 260-264.

1518. Callomb,H., Diop,M., and Ayats,H. "Intoxication by Indian hemp from Senegal."(Fr.). *Cah. Etude. Africa.* 1934, *9*, 139-144.

1519. Cameron,D.C. "An overview of the problem of drug abuse: As a clinical entity." *J. Hillside Hosp.* 1967, *16*, 120-127.

1520. Cameron,D.C. "Youth and drugs. A world view." *J.A.M.A.* 1968, *206*, 1267-1271.

1521. Cameron,G. "Detective Kitty Barry." *Colliers* 1954, *134*, 32.

1522. Caminhoa,J.M. *Elements of General and Medicinal Botany.*(Port.). *Tipografia Nacional, Rio de Janeiro,* 1877.

1523. Caminhoa,J.M. The Poisonous Plants of Brazil. (Port.). Tipografia Perseverana, Rio de Janeiro, 1871.

1524. Camp,W.A. "Antiquity of hemp as an economic plant." J. N. Y. Bot. Garden. 1936, 37, 110-114.

1525. Camp,W.H. Floral Anatomy of Hemp. Ohio State Univ. Press, Columbus, Ohio, 1939.

1526. Camp,W.L. "We are told that marihuana is harmless, except..." Person. Guid. J. 1973, 52, 9-15.

1527. Campbell,A.M.G., Evans,M., Thomson,J.L.G., and Williams,M.J. "Cerebral atrophy in young cannabis smokers." Lancet 1971, 1 1219-1224.

1528. Campbell,A.M.G., Thomson,J.L.G., Evans,M. and Williams,M.J. "Cerebral atrophy in young cannabis smokers." Lancet 1972, 1, 202-203.

1529. Campbell,A.M.G., Thomson,J.L.G., and Williams, M.J. "New research on cannabis." Br. Med. J. 1971, 2, 587.

1530. Campbell,D.R. "The electroencephalogram in cannabis associated psychosis." Can. Psychiat. Assoc. J. 1971, 16, 161-165.

1531. Campbell,I. "The amotivational syndrome and cannabis use with emphasis on the Canadian scene." Ann. N. Y. Acad. Sci. 1976, 282, 33-36.

1532. Campbell,I.L. Non-medical Psychoactive Drug Use at Bishop's University 1965 to 1970. Unpub. ms., Bishop's Univ., Lennoxville, Quebec, Canada, 1970.

1533. Campbell,J.M. "On the religion of hemp." In Indian Hemp Drugs Commision. Report. Gov't. Print. Office, London, England, 1893-1894, II, 250-252.

1534. Campbell,W.W. "Report of an experiment with cannabis indica." Med. Times Gaz. 1863, 2, 194-195.

1535. Campo,R.A. "Development of tolerance in pigeons to behavioral effects of a new benzopyran derivative." J. Pharmacol. Exper. Ther. 1973, 184, 521-527.

1536. Campo,R.A. "Development of tolerance to behavioral effects of a synthetic tetrahydrocannabinol derivative in pigeons." Coll. Internat'l. Neuro-pscyho-pharmacol. 1970, 7, 73.

1537. Camps,F.E. and Laurence,D.R. "Drugs." In Norman,L.G.(ed.). Medical Aspects of Fitness to Drive

Vehicles: A Guide For Medical Practitioners. Medical Commission on Accident Prevention, London, 1968, 29-38.

1538. Canada. *Commission of Inquiry into the Non-medical Use of Drugs. Interim Report*. Information Canada, Ottawa, 1970.

1539. Canada, *Commision of Inquiry into the Non-Medical Use of Drugs. Treatment Report*. Information Canada, Ottawa, 1972.

1540. Canada. *Commission of Inquiry into the Non-medical Use of Drugs. Cannabis Report*. Information Canada, Ottawa, 1972.

1541. Canada. *Commission of Inquiry into the Non-Medical Use of Drugs. Final Report*. Information Canada, 1973.

1542. Cann,F.L. "The identification of drugs of addiction and habituation." *J. Forensic Sci. Soc.* 1962, *3*, 33-36.

1543. Cano Puerta,G. "The dangers of marihuana." (Sp.). *Antioq. Med.* 1961, *11*, 23.

1544. Capek,R. and Esplin,B. "Effects of delta-9-tetrahydrocannabinol on the homosynaptic depression in the spinal monosynaptic pathway: Implications for transmitter dynamics in the primary afferents." In Nahas,G.G., Paton,W.D.M., and Idanpaan-Heikkila,J.E. (eds.). *Marihuana*. Springer Verlag, N.Y., 1976, 383-397.

1545. Capella,A.B. and Puig,F.C. "The Duquenois and Moustapha reaction for identification of the active principles of hashish."(Fr.). *Eur. J. Toxicol.* 1971, *4*, 39-42.

1546. Capelle,N., Treich,I., Ayrault-Jarrier,M., Hoellinger,H., and Schermann,J.M. "Binding of delta-9-tetrahydrocannabinol to human serum protein: Study of fixation and function of the lipoprotien composition." (Fr.). *Eur. J. Toxicol.* 1976, *9*, 5-9.

1547. Capener,N. "A case for cannabis?" *Br. Med. J.* 1967, *3*, 435.

1548. Capone,T. and McGlaughlin,J. *Incidence of Drug Addiction and Usage among School Age Population of New York City: A report to the City Council*. New York City Educational REsearch Bureau, New York, 1970.

1549. Cappell,H., Kuchar,E., and Webster,C.D. "Some correlates of marihuana self administration in man: A study of titration of intake as a function of drug

1550. Cappell,H. and Pliner,P. "Cannabis intoxication: The role of pharmacological and psychological variables." In Miller,L.L.(ed.). Marihuana, Effects on Human Behavior. Academic Press, N.Y., 1974, 233-263.

1551. Cappell,H. and Pliner,P. "Regulation of the self-administration of marihuana by psychological and pharmacological variables." Psychopharmacol. 1974, 40, 65-76.

1552. Cappell,H.D. and Pliner,P.L. "Volitional control of marihuana intoxication: A study of the ability to 'come down' on command." J. Abn. Psychol. 1973, 82, 428-434.

1553. Cappell,H., Webster,C.D., Herring,B.S., and Ginsberg,R. "Alcohol and marihuana: A comparison of effects on a temporally controlled operant in humans." J. Pharmacol. Exper. Ther. 1972, 182, 195-203.

1554. Cappelli,A. and Tuffi,R. "Quantitative chemical determination of hemp."(It.). Ann. Chim. Appl. 1939, 29, 225-231.

1555. Caprio,F.S. Variations in Lovemaking. Richlee Pub., N.Y., 1968.

1556. Carakushansky,G., Neu,R.L., and Gardner,L.I. "Lysergide and cannabis as possible teratogens in man." Lancet 1969, 1, 150-151.

1557. Carbonaro,G. and Imbesi,A. "Action of cannabis sativa cultivated in Messina on the isolated intestine."(It.). Arch. Farmacol. Sperim. Aff. 1948, 77, 57-74.

1558. Carbonaro,G. and Imbesi,A. "Action of the cannabis indica cultivated in Sassari on blood pressure and respiration."(It.). Atti. R. Accad. Pelorit. 1942, 44, 229-272.

1559. Carbonaro,G. and Imbesi,A. "General action of cannabis indica cultivated in Sassari on dogs." Bol. Soc. Ital. Biol. Sperim. 1942, 17, 406.

1560. Carchman,R.A., End,D., Thourson,K., Dewey,W.L., and Harris,L.S. "The inhibition of growth and macromolecular synthesis in neural cells in tissue culture by delta-9-tetrahydrocannabinol." Pharmacologist 1976, 18, 294.

1561. Carchman,R.A., Harris,L.S., and Munson,A.E. "The inhibition of DNA synthesis by cannabinoids." Cancer Res. 1976, 36, 95-100.

1562. Carchman,R.A., Warner,W., White,A.C., and Harris,L.S. "Cannabinoids and neoplastic growth." In Nahas,G.G., Paton,W.D.M., Idanpaan-Heikkila,J.E.(eds.). Marihuana. Springer Verlag, N.Y., 1976, 329-349.

1563. Cardassis,J. "Intoxication of horses by cannabis indica."(Fr.). Rec. Med. Vet. 1951, 127, 971-973.

1564. Cardelle y Penichet,J. "Contribution to the study of the jargon of marihuana users and dealers in Cuba."(Sp.). Pol. Sec. Nac. 1938, 2, 7-20.

1565. Carder,B. "Blockade of morphine abstinence by delta-9-tetrahydrocannabinol." Science 1975, 190, 590-591.

1566. Carder,B. and Deikel,S.M. "Similarities between delta-9-tetrahydrocannabinol and reserpine-like drugs." Behav. Biol. 1976, 17, 313-332.

1567. Carder,B. and Olson,J. "Learned behavioral tolerance to marihuana in rats." Pharmacol. Biochem. Behav. 1973, 1, 73-76.

1568. Carder,B. and Olson,J. "Marihuana and shock induced aggression in rats." Physiol. Behav. 1972, 8, 599-602.

1569. Cardillo,G., Cricchio,R., and Merlini,L. "Synthesis of d,l-cannabichromene, franklinone, and other natural chromenes." Tetrahed. 1968, 24, 4825-4831.

1570. Cardillo,G., Merlini,L., and Servi,S. "Alkylation of resorcinols with monoterpenoids allylic alcohols in aqueous acid: synthesis of new cannabinoid derivatives."(It.). Gazz. Chim. Ital. 1973, 103, 127-139.

1571. Cardos,E. Diambism or Maconhism, Killing Vice. (Port.). Servico Nacional de Educacao Sanitaria, Rio de Janeiro, 1958.

1572. Carew,D.P. "A qualitative study of cannabis from various geographic sources." Lloydia, 1970, 33, 493.

1573. Carew,D.P. "Microscopic, microchemical, and thin-layer chromatographic study of marihuana grown or confiscated in Iowa." J. Forensic Sci. 1971, 16, 87-91.

1574. Carey,E.F. "A new approach to the emergency treatment of sickness cuased by narcotic withdrawl." Ann. N. Y. Acad. Sci. 1955, 61, 222-229.

1575. Carey,J.T. "Marihuana use among the new bohemians." J. Psychedel. Drugs 1968, 2, 79-92.

1576. Carles,P. "Notes on the extracts of Indian hemp."(Fr.). Union Pharmaceut. 1894, 35, 195-196.

1577. Carlier,B. "Illegal drug traffic."(Dan.). Rev. Rijks. 1974, 13, 19-28.

1578. Carlin,A.S. "It can make sex more pleasureable as can perfume and even waterbeds." Sex. Behav. 1972, 2, 51.

1579. Carlin,A.S. "Marihuana and achievement." Int. J. Addict. 1974, 9, 401-410.

1580. Carlin,A.S., Bakker,C.B., Halpern,L., and Post,R.D. "Social facilitation of marihuana intoxication: Impact of social set and pharmacological activity." J. Abn. Soc. Psychol. 1972, 80, 132-140.

1581. Carlin,A.S. and Post,R.D. "Patterns of drug use among marihuana smokers." J.A.M.A. 1971, 218, 867-868.

1582. Carlin,A.S., Post,R.D., Baker,C.B., and Halpern,L.M. "The role of modeling and previous experience in the facilitation of marihuana intoxication." J. Nerv. Ment. Dis. 1974, 159, 275-281.

1583. Carlini,E.A. "Acute and chronic behavioral effects of cannabis sativa." Proc. 5th Internat'l. Cong. Pharmacol. 1972, 1, 31-43.

1584. Carlini,E.A. "Cannabis sativa and aggressive behavior in laboratory animals." Arch. Invest. Med. 1974, 5, 161-172.

1585. Carlini,E.A. "Further studies of the aggressive behavior induced by delta-9-tetrahydrocannabinol in REM sleep-deprived rats." Psychopharmacol. 1977, 53, 135-145.

1586. Carlini,E.A. "Pharmacology of marihuana."(Port.). Arch. Invest. Med. 1974, 5, 151-160.

1587. Carlini,E.A. "Recent research on the psychopharmacology of cannabis sativa(marihuana)."(Port.). Rev. Assoc. Med. Brazil 1969, 15, 223-228.

1588. Carlini,E.A. "Tolerance to chronic administration of cannabis sativa(marihuana) in rats." Pharmacol. 1968, 1, 135-142.

1589. Carlini,E.A. and Gagliarid,R.J. "Comparison of the pharmacological actions of crude extracts of Olmedioperebea calophyllum and cannabis sativa."(Port.). An. Acad. Brazil Cien. 1970, 42, 400-412.

1590. Carlini,E.A. and Goldman,J. "Behavioral effects of chronic administration of 'cannabis sativa' extract in rats."(Port.). Act. Physiol. Lat. Amer. 1968, 18, 275.

1591. Carlini,E.A. and Gonzalez,C. "Aggressive behavior induced by marihuana compounds and amphetamine in rats previously made dependent on morphine." Exper. 1972, 28, 542-544.

1592. Carlini,E.A., Hamaoui,A., Bieniek,D., and Korte,F. "Effects of (-)-delta-9-trans-tetrahydrocannabinol and a synthethic derivative on maze performance of rats." Pharmacol. 1970, 4, 359-368.

1593. Carlini,E.A., Hamaoui,A., and Martz,M.W. "Factors influencing the aggressiveness elicited by marihuana in food-deprived rats." Br. J. Pharmacol. 1972, 44, 794-804.

1594. Carlini,E.A., Karniol,I.G., Renault,P.F., and Schuster,C.R. "Effects of marihuana in laboratory animals and in man." Br. J. Pharmacol. 1974, 50, 299-309.

1595. Carlini,E.A. and Kramer,C. "Effects of cannabis sativa(marihuana) on maze performance of the rat." Psychopharmacol. 1965, 7, 175-181.

1596. Carlini,E.A., Leite,J.R., Tannhauser,M., and Berardi,A.C. "Cannabidiol and cannabis sativa extract protect mice and rats against convulsive agents." J. Pharm. Pharmacol. 1973, 25, 664-665.

1597. Carlini,E.A. and Lindsey,C.J. "Pharmacological manipulations of brain catecholamines and the aggressive behavior induced by marihuana in REM-sleep-deprived rats." Aggressive Behav. 1975, 1, 81-99.

1598. Carlini,E.A., Lindsey,C.J., Musty,R.E., and Monti,J.M. "Marihuana-aggressiveness in REM sleep-deprived rats: Neurochemical and neurophysiological correlates." In Braude,M.C. and Szara,S.(eds.). Pharmacology of Marihuana. Raven Press, N.Y., 1976, II, 515-531.

1599. Carlini,E.A., Lindsey,C.J., and Tufik,S. "Environmental and drug interference with effects of marihuana." Ann. N. Y. Acad. Sci. 1976, 281, 229-242.

1600. Carlini,E.A. and Masur,J. "Development of aggressive behavior in rats by chronic administration of cannabis sativa(marihuana)." Life Sci. 1969, 8, 607-620.

1601. Carlini,E.A. and Masur,J. "Development of fighting behavior in starved rats by chronic administration of (-)-delta-9-tetrahydrocannabinol and cannabis extracts. Lack of action of other psychotropic drugs." Comm. Behav. Biol. 1970, 5, 57-61.

1602. Carlini,E.A., Masur,J., Karniol,I.G., and Leite,J.R. "Cannabis sativa: Is it possible to consider behavioral animal data as experimental models for some effects on humans?" In Paton,W.D.M. and Crown,J.(eds.). Cannabis and its Derivatives. Oxford Univ. Press, London, 1972, 154-175.

1603. Carlini,E.A., Masur,J., Palermo Neto,J., and Gonzalez,S.C. "Aggressive behavior in rats and cannabis sativa." Act. Pharmaceut. Suecica 1971, 8, 687.

1603a. Carlini,E.A., Mechoulam,R., and Lander,N. "Anticonvulsant activity of four oxygenated cannabidiol derivatives." Res. Comm. Chem. Pathol. Pharmacol. 1975, 12, 1-15.

1604. Carlini,E.A. and Santos,M. "Structure activity relationship of four tetrahydrocannabinols and the pharmacological activity of five semi-purified extracts of cannabis sativa." Psychopharmacol. 1970, 18, 82-93.

1605. Carlini,E.A., Santos,M., Claussen,U., Bieniek,D., and Korte,F. "Structure activity relationship of four tetrahydroannabinoids and the pharmacological activity of five semi-purified extracts of cannabis sativa." Psychopharmacol. 1970, 18, 82-93.

1606. Carlini,G.R.S. and Carlini,E.A. "Effects of strychnine and cannabis sativa(marihuana) on the nucleic acid content in brain of the rat." Med. Pharmacol. Exper. 1965, 12, 21-26.

1607. Carlson,E.T. "Cannabis indica in 19th century psychiatry." Am. J. Psychiat. 1974, 131, 1004-1007.

1608. Carlson,J.R. Cairo to Damascus. A. Knopf, N.Y., 1951.

1609. Carneiro,E. Negro Cult.(Port.). Bib. Divulgacao Cientifica, Rio de Janeiro, 1936.

1610. Carney,P.A., Timms,M.W.H., and Stevenson,R.D. "The social and psychological background of young drug abusers in Dublin." Br. J. Addict. 1972, 67, 199-207.

1611. Carr,C.J. "Man and drugs." Arch. Environ. Hlth. 1970, 20, 77-83.

1612. Carr, C.J., Fisher, K.D., and Terzian, L.A. A Review of the Biomedical Effects of Marihuana on Man in the Military Environment. Federation of American Societies for Experimental Biology, Bethesda, Md., 1970.

1613. Carr, R.R. "Oregon's marihuana decriminalization: One year later." Intellect 1975, 104, 235-236.

1614. Carranza-Acevedo, J. "Brain damage and marihuana."(Sp.). Arch. Invest. Med. 1974, 5, 187-194.

1615. Carranza-Acevedo, J. "Cannabis introduction."(Sp.). Arch. Invest. Med. 1974, 5, 125-126.

1616. Carranza-Acevedo, J. "Physiological effects of cannabis."(Sp.). Arch. Invest. Med. 1974, 5, 173-178.

1617. Carson, D.I. and Lewis, J.M. "Factors influencing drug abuse in young people." Texas Med. 1970, 66, 50-57.

1618. Carstairs, G.M. "A land of lotus-eaters?" Am. J. Psychiat. 1969, 125, 1576-1580.

1619. Carstairs, G.M. "Daru and bhang. Cultural factors in the choice of an intoxicant." Quart. J. Stud. Alcohol 1954, 15, 220-232.

1620. Carter, W.E. and Coggins, W.J. "Chronic cannabis use in Costa Rica: A description of research objectives." In Rubin, V.(ed.). Cannabis and Culture. Mouton, The Hague, 1975, 389-401.

1621. Carter, W.E. and Doughty, P.L. "Social and cultural aspects of cannabis use in Costa Rica." Ann. N. Y. Acad. Sci. 1976, 282, 2-16.

1622. Cartwright, L.G. "Cannabis sativa(hemp)." Aust. J. Pharm. 1970, 51, S33-S36.

1623. Carvalho, J.R.G.S. "Identification of cannabinoids by thin-layer chromatography."(Port.). Rev. Port. Farm. 1971, 21, 142-146.

1624. Casamada, S.M. Descriptive Pharmacognosy.(Sp.). Editorial Cientifico-Medica, Barcelona, 1957.

1625. Casanova, E.R. and Lbariola, R.F. "Biogenic amines and marihuana."(Sp.). Orinet. Med. 1973, 22, 141-143.

1626. Casarett, L.J. "A toxologic view of marihuana." Hawaii Med. J. 1971, 30, 262-265.

1627. Casellas Roca,J. "Cellulose from hemp." British 1937, 469, 132.

1628. Casiccia,V. "A case of poisoning by Indian hemp."(It.). Riv. Chim. Med. Farm. 1883, 1, 326-330.

1629. Casini,F., Sbarigia,V., and Schiavone,C. "Identification of cannabis indica from the residue of the incomplete combustion of the drug."(It.). Boll. Chim. Farm. 1969, 108, 330-336.

1630. Casparis,P. "Studies on hashish. 1. Cannabinol and its effects."(Ger.). Pharm. Act. Pharm. 1926, 1, 210-217.

1631. Casparis,P. and Baur,F. "Studies on hashish. 2. Isolation of cannabinol."(Ger.). Pharm. Act. Helv. 1927, 2, 107-129.

1632. Casper,E., Janecek,J., and Martinelli,H. "Marihuana in Vietnam." U.S. Army Viet. Med. Bull. 1968, 11, 60-72.

1633. Casswell,S. "Cannabis intoxication: Effects of monetary incentive on performance. A controlled investigation of behaivoral tollerance in moderate users of cannabis." Percept. Motor Skill. 1975, 41, 423-434.

1634. Casswell,S. and Marks,D.F. "Cannabis and temporal disintegration in experienced and naive subjects." Science 1973, 179, 803-805.

1635. Casswell,S. and Marks,D. "Cannabis induced impairment of performance of a divided attention task." Nature 1973, 241, 60-61.

1636. Casto,D.M. "Marihuana and the assassins--an etymological investigation." Internat'l. J. Addict. 1970, 5, 747-755.

1637. Catania,R.A. "Marihuana: A review of clinical psychopharmacologic aspects." J. Kansas Med. Soc. 1970, 71, 313-317.

1638. Cavalluzzo,P.J. "Marihuana, the law and the courts." Osgood Hall L. J. 1970, 8, 215.

1639. Cavero,I. "Mechanism of action of (-)-delta-9-trans-tetrahydrocannabinol on the cardiovascular system." Diss. Abs. 1973, 34, 336-337.

1640. Cavero,I, Buckley,J.P., and Jandhyala,B.S. "Hemodynamic and myocardial effects of (-)-delta-9-transtetrahydrocannabinol in anesthetized dogs."

Eur. J. Pharmacol. 1973, 24, 243-251.

1641. Cavero,I., Buckley,J.P., and Jandhyala,B.S. "Parasympatholytic activity of (-)-delta-9-trans-tetrahydrocannabinol in mongrel dogs." Eur. J. Pharmacol. 1972, 19, 301-304.

1642. Cavero,I., Ertel,R., Buckley,J.P., and Jandhyala,B.S. "Effects of (-)-trans-tetrahydrocannabinol on regional blood flow in anesthetized dogs." Eur. J. Pharmacol. 1972, 20, 373-376.

1643. Cavero,I. and Jandhyala,B.S. "Further studies on the hemodynamic effects of delta-9-tetrahydrocannabinol." Fed. Proc. 1973, 32, 755.

1644. Cavero,I., Kubena,R.K., Dziak,J., Buckley,J.P., and Jandhyala,B.S. "Certain observations on inter-relationships between respiratory and cardiovascular effects of (-)-delta-9-trans-tetrahydrocannabinol." Res. Comm. Chem. Pathol. Pharmacol. 1972, 3, 483-492.

1645. Cavero,I., Lokhandwala,M.F., Buckley,J.P., and Jandhyala,B.S. "The effect of (-)-delta-9-trans-tetrahydrocannabinol on myocardial contractility and venous return in anesthetized dogs." Eur. J. Pharmacol. 1974, 29, 74-82.

1646. Cavero,I., Lokhandwala,M.F., Jandhyala,B.S., and Gerold,M. "Effects of (-)-delta-9-trans-tetrahydrocannabinol(THC) on venous return in dogs." Exper. 1974, 30, 694.

1647. Cavero,I., Solomon,T., Buckley,J.P., and Jandhyala,B.S. "Role of central autonomic outflow on the cardiovascular effects of (-)-delta-9-trans-tetrahydrocannabinol." Proc. 5th Int. Cong. Pharmacol. 1972, 1, 38.

1648. Cavero,I., Solomon,T., Buckley,J.P., and Jandhyala,B.S. "Studies on the bradycardia induced by (-)-delta-9-trans-tetrahydrocannabinol in anesthetized dogs." Eur. J. Pharmacol. 1973, 22, 263-269.

1649. Cavero,I., Solomon,T., Buckley,J.P., and Jandhyala,B.S. "Studies on the hypotensive activity of (-)-delta-9-trans-tetrahydrocannabinol in anesthetized dogs." Res. Comm. Chem. Pathol. Pharmacol. 1973, 6, 527-540.

1650. Ceapoiu,N. Hemp.(Roum.). Academy of People's Republic of Romania, Bucharest, 1958.

1651. Ceapoiu,N. and Hoffmann,I. "Effect of gamma-rays on hemp(cannabis sativa L.)."(It.). Inst. Cercet. Pentru. Cereal. Plant. 1970, 2, 187-207.

1652. Ceballos,R. "Grass, pot, and better things." J.A.M.A. 1970, 212, 627.

1653. Cely,W., Turkanis,S.A., and Karler,R. "Anticonvulsant properties of cannabidiol." Pharmacologist 1974, 16, 281.

1654. Ceniceros,J.A. "The popular Dona Junaita."(Sp.). Criminalia 1944, 10, 326-328.

1655. Centola,G. "The effect of retting on the chemical-physical properties of hemp fibers." Teintex 1954, 19, 241-253.

1656. Centola,G. "The influence of the maceration on the physical and chemical properties of hemp fiber." Tinctoria 1954, 51, 16.

1657. Ceresia,G.B. and Goldstein,F.J. "Marihuana." In White,W. and Albano,R.F.(eds.). North American Symposium on Drugs and Drug Abuse. North American Pub. Co., Phil., 1974, 49-51.

1658. Cesar,N. "Evils of 'maconha'."(Port.). Rev. Med. Pernam. 1945, 15, 221-228.

1659. Cesario de Melo,A., Carlini,E.A., and Green,J.P. "Cross-tolernace studies among nutmeg compounds, (-)-delta-9-trans-tetrahydrocannabinol and mescaline." (Port.). Cienc. Cult. 1973, 25, 644-647.

1659a. Chailakyan,M.K., Kochankov,V.G., and Zamota,V.P. "Effect of gibberellin on growth and yield of hemp and tobacco."(Rus.). Fiz. Rast. Akad. Nauk 1960, 7, 340-343.

1659b. Chakrabarty,I. and Ghosh,J.J. "Cannabis and the oestrous cycle of adult rats." U.N. Doc. ST/SOA/SER.S/ 38, Feb. 14, 1973.

1659c. Chakrabarty,I., Sengupta,D., Bhattacharya,P., and Ghosh,J.J. "Effect of cannabis extract on the uterine monoamine oxidase activity of normal and estradiol treated rats." Biochem. Pharmacol. 1976, 25, 377-378.

1659d. Chakrabarty,I., Sheth,A.R., and Ghosh,J.J. "Delta-9-tetrahydrocannabinol-induced changes in the serum luteinizing hormone and prolactin levels in rats." U.N. Doc. ST/SOA/SER.S/49, Sept. 12, 1974.

1659e. Chakrabarty,I., Sheth,A.R. and Ghosh,J.J. "Effect of acute delta-9-tetrahydrocannabinol treatment on serum leuteinizing hormone and prolactin levels in adult female rats." Fertil. Steril. 1975, 26, 947-948.

1659f. Chall,M.N. "Patterns of illicit drug use." N. Y. State J. Med. 1973, 73, 329-331.

1659g. Chambers,C.D. Differential Drug Use Within the New York Labor Force. Starch/Hooperating, Mamaroneck, N.Y., 1971.

1659h. Chambers,C.D., Cuskey,W.R., and Moffett,A.D. "Demographic factors in opiate addiction among Mexican Americans." Pub. Hlth. Rep. 1970, 85, 523-531.

1659i. Chambers,C.D., Hinesley,K.R., and Moldestad,M. "Narcotic addiction in females: A race comparison." Internat'l. J. Addict. 1970, 5, 257-278.

1660. Chambers,C.D. and Moffett,A.D. "Negro opiate addiction." In Ball,J.C. and Chambers,C.D.(eds.). The Epidemiology of Opiate Addiction in the United States. C.C. Thomas, Springfield, Ill., 1970, 178-201.

1661. Chambon,P. "On an identification of hidden hashish."(Fr.). Bull. Trav. Soc. Pharm. 1968, 12, 43-48.

1662. Chambon,P. and Chabon-Mougenot,R. "Contribution to the identification of toxic resins of hemp."(Fr.). Ann. Pharm. Franc. 1969, 27, 739-742.

1663. Chambon,P., Netien,G., and Chambon-Mougenot,R. "Problems posed by local cultures of hemp. Determination of principal constituents of hemp resins."(Fr.). Bull. Trav. Soc. Pharm. 1972, 16, 47-52.

1664. Champlin,R.S. "The art, trade, or mystery of the ropemaker." Newport Hist. 1973, 46, 81-95.

1665. Chan,W.R., Magnus, K.E., and Watson,H.A. "The structure of cannabitriol." Exper. 1976, 32, 283.

1666. Chang,K. The Archeology of Ancient China. Yale Univ. Press, New Haven, Conn., 1968.

1667. Chapel,J.L. "Emergency room treatment of the drug-abusing patient." Am. J. Psychiat. 1973, 130, 257-259.

1668. Chaplin,M. I Couldn't Smoke Grass on My Father's Lawn. Ballantine Books, N.Y., 1972.

1669. Chapple,P.A.L. "Cannabis--a toxic and dangerous substance--a study of eighty takers." Br. J. Addict. 1966, 61, 269-282.

1670. Char,J. "Drug abuse in Vietnam." Am. J. Psychiat. 1972, 129, 463-465.

1671. Chardin,J. Journey of Chevalier Chardin to Persia and Other Lands of the Orient.(Fr.). J.L.de Lorme, Amerstam, 1711.

1672. Charen,S. "Facts about marihuana. A survey of the literature." Am. J. Pharm. 1945, 117, 422-430.

1673. Charen,S. and Perelman,L. "Personality studies of marihuana addicts." Am. J. Psychiat. 1946, 102, 674-682.

1674. Chari-Bitron,A. "Effect of delta-1-tetrahydrocannabinol on red blood cell membranes and on alveolar macrophages." In Nahas,G.G., Paton,W.D.M., and Idanpaan-Heikkila,J.E.(eds.). Marihuana. Springer Verlag, N.Y., 1976, 273-283.

1675. Chari-Bitron,A. "Stabilization of rat erythrocyte membrane by delta-1-tetrahydrocannabinol." Life Sci. 1971, 10, 1273-1279.

1676. Chari-Bitron,A. "Swelling of rat liver mitochondria induced by delta-1-tetrahydrocannabinol." Isr. J. Med. Sci. 1975, 11, 1189.

1677. Chari-Bitron,A. and Bino,T. "Effect of delta-1-tetrahydrocannabinol on ATPase activity of rat liver mitochondria." Biochem. Pharmacol. 1971, 20, 473-475.

1678. Charnot,A. "Intoxication."(Fr.). Maroc Med. 1955, 34, 1493.

1679. Charnot,A. "Moroccan toxicology. Cannabis sativa L."(Fr.). Mem. Soc. Sci. Nat. Maroc 1945, 1, 252-276.

1680. Charpy,J.P. and Guey,N. "Experimental and clinical approach to the effects of cannabis."(Fr.). Cah. Psychol. 1973, 16, 31-56.

1681. Chase,A.R., Kelley,P.R., Taunton-Rigby,A., Jones,R.T., and Harwood,T. "Quantitation of cannabinoids in biological fluids by radioimmunoassay." In Willette,P.(ed.). Cannabinoid Assays in Humans. Nat'l Inst. Drug Abuse Res. Monog. Ser. 7, U.S. Dept. H.E.W., Washington, 1976, 1-9.

1682. Chatterjee,M.L. "Mind expanders." J. Indian Med. Assoc. 1969, 53, 201-204.

1683. Chatterji, D.N. and Roy,M.B. "The valuation of charas." Indian Med. Gaz. 1929, 64, 373-374.

1684. Chaumeton,F.P. Flora Medical.(Fr.). Paris, 1815.

1685. Chausow,A.M. and Saper,C.B. "Marihuana and sex." N. Eng. J. Med. 1974, 291, 308.

1686. Chayet,N.L. "Legal aspects of drug abuse." In Wittenborn,J.R., Brill,H., Smith,J.P., and Wittenborn, S.A.(eds.). Drugs and Youth. C.C.Thomas, Springfield, Ill., 1969, 236-249.

1687. Chazan,J.B. and Ourisson,G. "Tetrahydrocannabinol analogs and related compounds. I. Condensation products of pulegone and orcinol in the presence of phosphorous oxychloride."(Fr.). Bull. Soc. Chim. 1968, 4, 1374-1394.

1688. Chazan,J.B. and Ourisson,G. "Tetrahydrocannabinol analogs and related compounds. III. Syntheses in the xanthene series."(Fr.). Bull. Soc. Chim. 1968, 4, 1384-1393.

1689. Cheek,F.E., Sarett-Barrie,M., Holstein,C.M., Newell,S., and Smith,S. "Four patterns of campus marihuana use: Part I. Drug use." Internat'l. J. Addict. 1973, 8, 13-31.

1690. Cheek,F.E., Sarett-Barrie,M., Holstein,C.M., Newell,S., and Smith,S. "Four patterns of campus marihuana use: Part II. Social aspects of use." Internat'l. J. Addict. 1973, 8, 335-351.

1691. Chein,I., Gerard,D., Lee,R.S., and Rosenfeld,E. The Road to H.; Narcotics, Juvenile Delinquency and Social Policy. Basic Books, N.Y., 1964.

1692. Cherek,D.R. and Thompson,T. "Delta-1-tetrahydrocannabinol and schedule-induced aggression: Evidence for possible selectivity of action." Pharmacologist 1973, 15, 250.

1693. Cherek,D.R. and Thompson,T. "Effects of delta-1-tetrahydrocannabinol on schedule-induced aggression in pigeons." Pharmacol. Biochem. Behav. 1973, 1, 493-500.

1694. Cherek,D.R., Thompson,T., and Heistad,G.T. "Effects of delta-1-tetrahydrocannabinol and food deprivation level on responding maintained by the opportunity to attack." Physiol. Behav. 1972, 9, 795-800.

1695. Cheronis,N.D. "Tentative and rigorous proof in the identification of organic compounds and application of these concepts to the detection of the active principles of marihuana." Microchem. J. 1960, 4, 555-567.

1696. Chesher,G.B. "On the dangers of cannabis." Aust. J. Forens. Sci. 1971, 4, 68-92.

1697. Chesher,G.B., Dahl,C.J., Everingham,M., Jackson,D.M., Marchant-Williams,H., and Starmer,G.A. "The effect of cannabinoids on intestinal motility and their antinociceptive effect in mice." Br. J. Pharmacol. 1973, 49, 588-594.

1698. Chesher,G.B., Franks,H.M., Hensley,V.R., Hensley,W.J., Jackson,D.M., Starmer,G.A., and Teo,R.K.C. "The interaction of ethanol and delta-9-THC in man, effects on perceptual, cognitive and motor functions." Med. J. Aust. 1976, 2, 159-163.

1699. Chesher,G.B., Hasleton,S.L., Jackson,D.M., and Starmer,G.A. "The effect of repeated administration of a cannabis extract on operant behavior in the rat." Proc. 5th Internat'l. Cong. Pharmacol. 1971, 1, 12.

1700. Chesher,G.B. and Jackson,D.M. "Anticonvulsant effects of cannabinoids in mice: Drug interactions within cannabinoids and cannabinoid interactions with phenytoin." Psychopharmacol. 1974, 37, 255-264.

1701. Chesher,G.B. and Jackson,D.M. "The effect of withdrawal from cannabis on pentylenetetrazol convulsive threshold in mice." Psychopharmacol. 1974, 40, 129-135.

1702. Chesher,G.B., Jackson,D.M., Malor,R.M. "Interaction of delta-9-tetrahydrocannabinol and cannabidiol with phenobarbitone in protecting mice from electrically induced convulsions." J. Pharm. Pharmacol. 1975, 27, 608-609.

1703. Chesher,G.B., Jackson,D.M., and Starmer,G.A. "Interaction of cannabis and general anaesthetic agents in mice." Br. J. Pharm. 1974, 50, 593-599.

1704. Chet,I., Henis,Y., and Mitchell,R. "Effect of biogenic amines and cananbinoids on bacterial chemotaxis." J. Bacteriol. 1973, 115, 1215-1218.

1705. Cheuvert,C. "Studies on the development of cannabis sativa L. at constant temperatures and under different photoperiods(sexually and foliage pigments)." (Fr.). Bull. Acad. Roy. Med. 1954, 40, 1152-1168.

1706. Chevalier,J. "Pharmacological studies of the galenic preparations of Indian hemp; determination of their potency by the physiological method."(Fr.). Bull. Mem. Soc. Ther. 1907, 1, 478.

1707. Chevannes,B. "Licensing ganja." Soc. Econ. Stud. 1975, 24, 379-380.

1708. Chevers,N. A Manual of Medical Jurisprudence for India. Thacker, Spink and Co., Calcutta, 1870.

1709. Cheymol,J. "Cannabis: hashish or marihuana. I. Statement of the problem."(Fr.). Bull. Acad. Nat. Med. 1969, 153, 523-531.

1710. Cheymol,J., Heuyer,G., and Douady,D. "The problem of cannabis." Internat'l. Crim. Pol. Rev. 1970, 25, 275-285.

1711. Chia,D.T., Fike,S.A., and Nelson,J.T. "Identification of the reaction product of delta-8-tetrahydrocannabinol with KN reagent." J. Forens. Sci. Soc. 1974, 14, 197-200.

1712. Chiesa,E.P., Rondina,R.V.D., and Coussio,J.D. "A rapid thermomicrothin-layer chromatography procedure for the identification of cannabinoids in marihuana. J. Chromatog. 1973, 87, 298-299.

1713. Chiesa,E.P., Rondina,R.V.D., and Coussio,J.D. "Chemical composition and potential activity of Argentine marihuana." J. Pharm. Pharmacol. 1973, 25, 953-956.

1714. Chiesa,E.P., Rondina,R.V.D., and Coussio,J.D. "Chemical composition and potential activity of Argentine marihuana." Lloydia 1973, 36, 437.

1715. Chipman,D.A. "The attitudes, behaviors, characteristics of students at Mocalester college in respect to use of illicit and exotic drugs, with particular emphasis on marihuana." Diss. Abs. 1972, 32, 4342.

1716. Chipman,D.A. and Parker,C.A. "Characteristics of liberal arts college student marihuana users." J. Coll. Stud. Person. 1972, 13, 511-517.

1717. Chiu,P., Karler,R., Craven,C., Olsen,D.M., and Turkanis,S.A. "The influence of delta-9-tetrahydrocannabinol, cannabinol and cannabidiol on tissue oxygen consumption." Res. Comm. Chem. Pathol. Pharmacol. 1975, 2, 267-286.

1718. Chohoki,K. A Handy Guide to Papermaking. Univ. Cal. Press, Berkeley, Cal., 1948.

1719. Cholst,S. "Notes on the use of hashish." In Goode,E.(ed.). Marihuana. Atherton Press, N.Y., 1969, 141-146.

1720. Chopra,G.S. "Man and marihuana." Internat'l. J. Addict. 1969, 4, 215-247.

1721. Chopra,G.S. "Marihuana and adverse psychotic reactions(evaluation of different factors involved)." Bull. Narc. 1971, 23, 15-22.

1722. Chopra,G.S. "Studies on psycho-clinical aspects of long-term marihuana use in 124 cases." Internat'l. J. Addict. 1973, 8, 1015-1026.

1723. Chopra,G.S. and Chopra,P.S. "Studies on 300 Indian drug addicts with special reference to psycho-sociological aspects, etiology and treatment." Bull. Narc. 1965, 17, 1-9.

1724. Chopra,G.S. and Jandu,B.S. "Psychoclinical effects of long-term marihuana use in 275 Indian chronic users. A comparative assessment of effects in Indian and USA users." Ann. N. Y. Acad. Sci. 1976, 282, 95-108.

1725. Chopra,G.S. and Smith,J.W. "Psychotic reactions following cannabis use in East Indians." Gen. Psychiat. 1974, 30, 24-27.

1726. Chopra,I.C. and Chopra,R.N. "The present position of hemp drug addiction in India." Indian Med. Res. Mem. 1939, 31, 1-119.

1727. Chopra,I.C. and Chopra,R.N. "The use of cannabis drugs in India." Bull. Narc. 1957, 9, 4-29.

1728. Chopra,R.N. "Drug addiction in India and its treatment." Indian Med. Gaz. 1935, 70, 121-131.

1729. Chopra,R.N. "Use of hemp drugs in India." Indian Med. Gaz. 1940, 75, 356-367.

1730. Chopra,R.N. and Chopra,G.S. "Present position of hemp drug addiction in India." Br. J. Inebriety 1940, 38, 71-74.

1731. Chopra,R.N., Chopra,G.S., and Chopra,I.C. "Cannabis sativa in relation to mental diseases and crime in India." Indian J. Med. Res. 1942, 30, 155-171.

1732. Chopra,R.N. and Chopra,I.C. "Treatment of drug addiction. Experience in India." Bull Narc 1957, 9, 21-23.

1733. Choulis,N.H. "Separation and quantitation of mixtures of the most commonly abused drugs." J. Pharmaceut. Sci. 1973, 62, 112-114.

1734. Christensen,C.W., Best,J.B., and Herin,R.A. "Changes seen in the electroencephalogram and heart rate in the rat after administration of marihuana intravenously." Fed. Proc. 1971, 30, 375.

1735. Christensen,H.D., Freudenthal,R.I., Gidley, J.T., Rosenfeld,R., Boegli,G., Testino,L., Brine,D.R., PItt,C.G., and Wall,M.E. "Activity of delta-8- and delta-9-tetrahydrocannabinol and related compounds in the mouse." Science 1971, 172, 165-167.

1736. Christiansen,J. and Rafaelsen,O.J. "Cannabis metabolites in urine after oral administration." Psychopharmacol. 1969, 15, 60-63.

1737. Christie,N. "Cross-cultural notes on common problems." In Wittenborn,J.R., Brill,H., Smith,J.P., and Wittenborn,S.A.(eds.). Drugs and Youth. C.C.Thomas, Springfield, Ill., 1969, 452-455.

1738. Christison,A. "On the natural history, action, and uses of Indian hemp." Month. J. Med. Sci. 1851, 13, 26-45.

1739. Christophers,A.J. "Legalize marihuana?" Med. J. Aust. 1970, 2, 100.

1740. Christozov,C. "Cannabis intoxication in Morocco. I. Studies of chronic mental patients."(Fr.). Maroc Med. 1965, 44, 630-642.

1741. Christozov,C. "Cannabis intoxication in Morocco. II. Studies of chronic mental patients."(Fr.). Maroc Med. 1965, 44, 866-889.

1742. Christozov,C. "The Moroccan aspect of cannabis intoxication." Maroc. Med. 1965, 43, 44-65.

1743. Chrusciel,T.L. "Recent progress in long-term pharmacological research on cannabis." Internat'l. J. Clin. Pharmacol. 1975, 12, 57-62.

1744. Chun,G. "Marihuana: A realistic approach." Cal. Med. 1971, 114, 7-13.

1745. Church,A. and Petersen,F. Nervous and Medical Diseases. W.B. Saunders, Phil., 1908.

1746. Church,J. "Cannabis sativa." Provost Parade 1952, 8, 109.

1747. Church,M.A., Truss,C.V., and Martino,E.R. "Trends in psychoactive drug use and in attitudes toward marihuana at a large metropolitan university." J. Counsel. Psychol. 1974, 21, 228-231.

1748. Chusid,M.J., Gelfand,J.A., Nutter,C., and Fauci,A.S. "Pulmonary aspergillosis, inhalation of contaminated marihuana smoke, chronic granulomatous disease." Ann. Intern. Med. 1975, 82, 682-683.

1749. Cintra,A. The Carlota Joaquina Scandal.(Port.). Civilizacao Brasileira, Rio de Janeiro, 1934.

1750. Cisin,I.H., and Manheimer,D.I. "Marihuana use among adults in a large city and suburb." Ann. N. Y. Acad. Sci. 1971, 191, 222-235.

1751. Ciulla,L. "Marihuana users in Porto Alegre." (Port.). In Anonymous. Maconha. Servico Nacionale de Educacao Sanitario, Rio de Janeiro, 1958, 377-381.

1752. Clarac,A. "Hashish and hashishism."(Fr.). In Grall,Ch. and Clarac,A.(eds.). A Practical Treatise of Exotic Pathology.(Fr.). J.B. Bailliere, Paris, 1911, 94-99.

1753. Clark,L.D. "Marihuana and human behavior. A brief review." Rocky Mt. Med. J. 1972, 69, 43-46.

1754. Clark,L.D., Hughes,R., and Nakashima,E.N. "Behavioral effects of marihuana. Experimental studies." Arch. Gen. Psychiat. 1970, 23, 193-198.

1755. Clark,L.D. and Nakashima,E.N. "Experimental studies of marihuana." Am. J. Psychiat. 1968, 125, 135-140.

1756. Clark,R.E., Kowitz,A., and Duckworth,D. "The influence of information sources and grade level on the diffusion and adoption of marihuana." J. Drug Iss. 1975, 177-188.

1757. Clark,S.C. "Marihuana and the cardiovascular system." Pharmacol. Biochem. Behav. 1975, 3, 299-306.

1758. Clark,S.C., Greene,C., Karr,G.W., MacCannell, K.L., and Miestein,S.L. "Cardiovascular effects of marihuana in man." Can. J. Physiol. Pharmacol. 1974, 52, 706-719.

1759. Clark,W.A.G. Linen, Jute and Hemp Industries in the United Kingdon. U.S. Dept. of Commerce, Washington, D.C., 1913.

1760. Clarke,A.G. "On the cannabis indica." Boston Med. Surg. J. 1857, 56, 315-316.

1761. Clarke,D.E. and Jandhyala,B. "Acute and chronic effects of tetrahydrocannabinols on monoamine oxidase activity: Possible vehicle/tetrahydrocannabinol interactions." Res. Commun. Chem. Pathol. Pharmacol. 1977, 17, 471-480.

1762. Clarke,E.G.C., Greatorex,J.C., and Potter,R. "Cannabis poisoning in the dog." Vet. Rec. 1971, 88, 194.

1763. Clarke,E.G.C. and Robinson,A.E. "When is cannabis resin?" Med. Sci. Law 1970, 10, 139-148.

1764. Clarke,J.W. and Levine,E.L. "Marihuana use, social discontent and political alienation: A study of high school youth." Am. Pol. Sci. Rev. 1971, 65, 119-130.

1765. Claus,E.P. and Tyler,V.E. Pharmacognosy. Lea and Bebiger, Phil., 1965.

1766. Claussen,U., Borger,W., and Korte,F. "Gas chromatographic analysis of components of hemp."(Ger.). Just. Lieb. Ann. Chem. 1966, 693, 158-164.

1767. Claussen,U., Borger,W., and Korte,F. "On the chemical classification of plants. XXVII. Hashish VI. Gas chromatographic analysis of hemp components." (Ger.). Just. Lieb. Ann. Chem. 1966, 693, 158-164.

1768. Claussen,U., Fehlhaber,H.W., and Korte,F. "Hashish. XI. Mass spectrometric determination of hashish containing materials."(Ger.). Tetrahed. 1966, 22, 3535-3543.

1769. Claussen,U. and Korte,F. "Chemical classification of plants. XXX. Hashish. IX. Mass spectrometric determination of hashish containing material."(Ger.). Tetrahed. Suppl. 1966, 7, 89-96.

1770. Claussen,U. and Korte,F. "Hashish. XI. Structure of two synthetic isomers of tetrahydrocannabinol." (Ger.). Zeit. Naturfor. 1966, 21b, 594-595.

1771. Claussen,U. and Korte,F. "Hashish. XIII. Behavior of constituents of cannabis sativa during smoking." Tetrahedron Let. 1967, 22, 2067-2069.

1772. Claussen,U. and Korte,F. "Hashish. XV. On the behavior of hemp and of delta-9-6 alpha, 10 alpha, trans-tetrahydrocannabinol duirng smoking." Just. Lieb. Ann. Chem. 1968, 713, 162-165.

1773. Claussen,U. and Korte,F. "Hashish. XVI. Phenolic compounds of the hemp plant and their conversion to hashish compounds."(Ger.). Just. Lieb. Ann. Chem. 1968, 713, 166-174.

1774. Claussen,U. and Korte,F. "On the chemical classification of plants. XXX. Hashish. IX. Mass spectroscopic investigation of hashish constituents."(Ger.). Tetrahed. Suppl. 1966, 7, 89-96.

1775. Claussen,U. and Korte,F. "Origin, action and synthesis of constituents of hashish."(Ger.). Naturwissen. 1966, 53, 541-546.

1776. Claussen,U., Mummenhoff,P., and Korte,F. "Hashish XVIII. Tetrahydrocannabinol synthesis from olivetol and pulegone." Tetrahed. 1968, 24, 2897-2898.

1777. Claussen,U., Spulak,F., Fehlhaber,H.W., and Korte,F. "Hashish XIX. Cannabidiolcarbonsaure-tetrahydrocannabitriol ester, a new hashish inhalant." (Ger.). Tetrahed. 1968, 24, 5379-5383.

1778. Claussen,U., Spulak,F., and Korte,F. "Hashish XIV. Information on the substance of hashish." (Ger.). Tetrahed. 1968, 24, 1021-1023.

1779. Claussen,U., Spulak,F., and Korte,F. "On the chemical classification of plants. XXXI. Hashish-10. Cannabichromene, a new hashish constituent."(Ger.). Tetrahed. 1966, 22, 1477-1479.

1780. Clendinning,J. "Observations on the medicinal properties of the cannabis sativa of India." Med.-Chirug. Trans. 1843, 26, 188-210.

1781. Clerambault,D. "Discussion of L. Livet's article: Marihuana smokers."(Fr.). Ann. Med.-Psychol. 1920, 12, 267-269.

1782. Clouston,T.S. "Observations and experiences on the use of opium, potassium bromide, and Indian hemp in mental disorders."(Fr.). Ann. Med.-Psychol. 1872, 2, 36-51.

1783. Clouston,T.S. "The Cairo asylum. Dr. Warnock on hasheesh insanity." J. Ment. Sci. 1896, 42, 790-795.

1784. Clouston,T.S. "Use of opium, potassium bromide and cannabis indica in mental cases." Br. Quart. Rev. 1870, 46, 493; 47, 203.

1785. Clute,W.M. "Meaning of plant names. XCIII. The nettle family." Am. Bot. 1943, 49, 111-115.

1786. Co,B.T., Goodwin,D.W., Gado,M., Mikhael,M., and Hill,S.Y. "Absence of cerebral atrophy in chronic cannabis users." J.A.M.A. 1977, 237, 1229-1230.

1787. Cockerman,W.C. "Patterns of alcohol and multiple drug use among rural white and American Indian adolescents." Interna't. J. Addict. 1977, 12, 271-285.

1788. Codd,L.E. "Is there dagga on your farm?" Farmer's Week. 1956, 91, 65.

1789. Coddington,R.D. and Jacobsen,R. "Drug use by Ohio adolescents: An epidemiological study." Ohio State Med. J. 1972, 68, 481-484.

1790. Codere,H. "The social and cultural context of cannabis use in Rwanda." In Rubin,V.(ed.). Cannabis and Culture. Mouton, The Hague, 1975, 217-227.

1791. Coffman,C.B. and Gentner,W.A. "Cannabinoid profile and elemental uptake of cannabis sativa L. as influenced by soil characteristics." Agron. J. 1975, 67, 491-497.

1792. Coffman,C.B. and Gentner,W.A. "Cannabis sativa L.: Effect of drying time and temperature on cannabinoid profile of stored leaf tissue." Bull. Narc. 1974, 16, 67-70.

1793. Cofman-Nicoresti,J. "Physiological standardizations." Pharmaceut. J. Pharmacist 1920, 50, 195.

1794. Coggins,W.G. "The Costa Rica cannabis project: An intermim report on the medical aspects." In Braude,M.C. and Szara,S.(eds.). Pharmacology of Marihuana. Raven Press, N.Y., 1976, II, 667-671.

1795. Coggins,W.J., Swenson,E.W., Dawson,W.W., Fernandez-Salas,A., Hernandex-Boulaos,J., and Faerron-Valdez,F. "Health status of chronic heavy cannabis users." Ann. N. Y. Acad. Sci. 1976, 282, 148-161.

1796. Cohen,A.Y. "Psychedelic drugs and the student. Educational strategies." J. Coll. Stud. Person. 1969, 10, 96-101.

1797. Cohen,C. Drug Usage among the Children in the Allegheny Country Juvenile Detention Home, Pittsburgh, Pennsylvania. Allegheny County Juvenile Detenion Home, Pittsburgh, Pa., n.d.

1798. Cohen,C.J. "Marihuana and sex." N. Eng. J. Med. 1974, 29, 308-309.

1799. Cohen,E. "Hashish and hashish users in Acre." (Heb.). Delinq. Soc. 1968, 31, 34-39.

1800. Cohen,G.A. "Personality, cognitive style, and student marihuana use." Diss. Abs. 1972, 33, 2163.

1801. Cohen,G.M., Peterson,D.W., and Mannering,G.J. "Interactions of delta-9-tetrahydrocannabinol with the hepatic microsomal drug metabolizing system." Life Sci. 1971, 10, 1207-1215.

1802. Cohen,H. "Clandestine use of drugs and society." (Dut.). T. Soc. Geneesk. 1968, 46, 714-720.

1803. Cohen,H. "Principal conclusions from the Report: 'Psychology, social-psychology and sociology of illicit drug use'." Br. J. Addict. 1970, 65, 39-44.

1804. Cohen,M. and Klein,D.F. "Drug abuse in a young psychiatric population." Am. J. Orthopsychiat. 1970, 40, 448-455.

1805. Cohen,M. and Shepard,R. "Marihuana." Texas Med. 1972, 68, 71-77.

1806. Cohen,M.J. and Rickles,W.H. "Marihuana and induced changes in GSR activation peaking during paired-associate learning." Pharmacol. Biochem. Behav. 1975, 3, 195-200.

1807. Cohen,M.J. and Rickles,W.H. "Performance on a verbal learning task by subjects of heavy past marihuana usage." Psychopharmacol. 1974, 37, 323-330.

1808. Cohen,S. "Changing concepts of cannabis pharmacology." Act. Pharmaceut. Suec. 1971, 8, 686-687.

1809. Cohen,S. "Drugs and drugged behavior: Medicolegal considerations." J. Clin. Pharmacol. 1969, 9, 5-11.

1810. Cohen,S. "Information and misinformation about drugs." In Wittenborn,J.R., Smith,J.P., and Wittenborn,S.A.(eds.). Communication and Drug Abuse. C.C. Thomas, Springfield, Ill., 1970, 285-293.

1811. Cohen,S. "Pot, acid and speed." Med. Sci. 1968, 19, 30.

1812. Cohen,S. "Psychotomimetic agents." Ann. Rev. Pharmacol. 1967, 7, 301-318.

1813. Cohen,S. "The 94-day cannabis study." Ann. N. Y. Acad. Sci. 1976, 282, 211-220.

1814. Cohen,S. "The psychedelic future: Wire up, plug in, and buzz." In Simmons,J.L.(ed.). Marihuana, Myths and Realities. Brandon House, Berkeley, Cal., 1967, 223-227.

1815. Cohen,S., Lessin,P.J., Hahn,P.M., and Tyrell, E.D. "A 94-day cannabis study." In Braude,M.C. and Szara,S.(eds.). Pharmacology of Marihuana. Raven Press, N.Y., 1976, II, 621-627.

1816. Cohn,R., Barnes,P., Barratt,E., and Pirch,J. "Sex differences in response to marihuana extract in rats." Pharmacologist 1971, 13, 297.

1817. Cohn,R.A., Barratt,E., and Pirch,J.H. "Differences in behavioral responses of male and female rats to marihuana." Proc. Soc. Expt'l. Biol. Med. 1972, 140, 1136-1139.

1818. Cohn,R.A., Barratt,E., and Pirch,J.H. "Effects of alteration of hormonal balance on responses to marihuana extract." Proc. 5th Internat'l. Cong. Pharmacol. 1972, 1, 45.

1819. Cohn,R.A., Barratt,E.S., and Pirch,J.H. "Marihuana responses in rats: Influence of castration or testosterone." Proc. Soc. Expt'l. Biol. Med. 1974, 146, 109-113.

1820. Cohn,R.A., Williams,B.J., Nash,J.B., and Pirch,J.H. "Distribution of ^{14}C-delta-9-THC in male and female rats." Pharmacologist 1974, 16, 260.

1821. Cohodes,A. "Should schoolmen fight to legalize marihuana?" Nation's Schools 1969, 84, 20.

1822. Cohrssen,J.J. and Blain,J.D. "Marihuana,... what it does." Drug Forum 1971, 1, 13-20.

1823. Colaiuta,V. and Breed,G. "Development of scales to measure attitudes toward marihuana and marihuana users." J. Appl. Psychol. 1974, 59, 398-400.

1824. Colasanti,B. and Khazan,N. "Changes in EEG voltage output of the sleep-awake cycle in response to tetrahydrocannabinols in the rat." Pharmaoclogist 1971, 13, 246.

1825. Colasanti,B. and Khazan,N. "Effects of delta-8-tetrahydrocannabinol on the voltage output of the EEG in the rat." Comm. Prob. Drug Depend. 1971, 2, 1728-1736.

1826. Colbach,E. "Marihuana use by GIs in Viet Nam." Am. J. Psychiat. 1971, 128, 204-207.

1827. Colbach,E.M. and Crowe,R.R. "Marihuana associated psychosis in Vietnam." Mil. Med. 1970, 135, 571-573.

1828. Colburn,R.W., Ng,L.K.Y., Lemberger,L., and Kopin,I.J. "Subcellular distribution of delta-9-tetrahydrocannabinol in rat brain." Biochem. Pharmacol. 1974, 23, 873-877.

1829. Coldwell,B.B., Bailey,K., Anderson,G., and Paul,C. "Effect of cannabinoids on pentobarbital metabolism in the rat." Toxicol. Appl. Pharmacol. 1974, 29, 77.

1830. Cole,C.W. Colbert and a Century of French Mercantilism. Columbia Univ. Press, Morningside Heights, N.Y., 1939.

1831. Cole,J.M., Pieper,W.A., and Rumbaugh,D.M. "Effects of delta-9-tetrahydrocannabinol on spaced responding in great apes." Comm. Behav. Biol. 1971, 6, 285-293.

1832. Cole,J.O. "LSD and marihuana: Research needs." In Wittenborn,J.R., Brill,H., Smith,J.P., and Wittenborn,S.A.(eds.). Drugs and Youth. C.C. Thomas, Springfield, Ill., 1969, 212-216.

1833. Coleclough,A. and Hanley,L.G. "Marihuana users in Toronto." In Mann,W.E.(ed.). Deviant Behavior in Canada. Social Science Pub., Toronto, 1968, 257-291.

1834. Coleman,J.H., Tacker,H.C., Esans,W.E., Lemmi,H., and Britton,E.C. "Neurological manifestations of chronic marihuana intoxication. Part I: Paresis of the fourth cranial nerve." Dis. Nerv. Syst. 1976, 37, 29.

1835. Coleman,J.W. Slavery Times in Kentucky. Univ. North Carolina Press, Chapel Hill, N.C., 1940.

1836. Coles,R. "Beyond the pleasure principle." Partisan Rev. 1967, 34, 415-420.

1837. Coles,R. "Drug: Flying high or low(drug addiction on two scenes: the middle class youth and the negro and Puerto Rican poor)." Yale Rev. 1967, 57, 38-46.

1838. Coles,R. The Grass Pipe. Little Brown Co., Boston, 1969.

1839. Coles,W.H. "Cannabis indica." Lancet 1935, 1, 904.

1840. Collet,C.G. "Candidature of Joseph Moreau (of Tours) for the Montyon reward of the Academy of Sciences."(Fr.). Ann. Moreau Tours, 1846, 1, 15-21.

1841. Collier,B. "Grassing of America." Sat. Rev. 1972, 55, 12-14.

1842. Collier,H.O. "The essence of pot." New Scient. 1967, 35, 436-438.

1843. Collin,E. Poisonous Plants.(Fr.). O. Doin, Paris, 1907.

1844. Collins,F.G., Haavik,C.O., and Skibba,J.L. "Depression of oxygen consumption by delta-9-tetrahydrocannabinol: Whole body and perfused liver." Pharmacologist 1976, 18, 300.

1845. Collins,F.G. and Hardman,H.F. "Influence of yeast(Y) induced hyperthermia and 2,4-dinitrophenol (DNP) on the hypothermic action of delta-9-tetrahydrocannabinol in mice." Fed. Proc. 1974, 33, 539.

1846. Collins,J.G. Marihuana Position Paper. Los Angeles Police Department, Los Angeles, Cal., 1974.

1847. Collomb,H., Diop,M., and Ayats,H. "Intoxication for Senegalese Indian hemp."(Fr.). Cah. Etud. Africa. 1936, 9, 139-144.

1848. Collu,R. "Endocrine effects of chronic intraventricular administration of delta-9-tetrahydrocannabinol to prepuberal and adult male rats." Life Sci. 1975, 18, 223-230.

1849. Collu,R., Letarte,J., Leboeuf,G., and Ducharme,J.R. "Endocrine effects of chronic administration of psychoactive drugs to prepuberal male rats. I: delta-9-tetrahydrocannabinol." Life Sci. 1975, 16, 533-542.

1850. Colombini,C.E. "The changes in vitamin B_6 and brain amine metabolism in mice chronically treated with delta-9-tetrahydrocannabinol." Act. Nerv. Super. 1974, 16, 68-69.

1851. Colombini,C.E., Westfall,T.C., and McCoy,E.E. "The changes in vitamine B_6 and brain amine metabolism in mice treated with delta-9-tetrahydrocannabinol" Coll. Internat'l. Neuro-psychopharmacol. 1970, 7, 11-15.

1852. Colomer,L.R. "Botanical and chemical aspects of marihuana."(Sp.). Rev. Tech. Pol. 1955, 1, 3.

1853. Colson,H.C. "Cannabis." J.A.P.A. 1920, 9, 302.

1854. Columella,L.J.M. De Re Rustica. W. Heinemann Ltd., London, 1948.

1855. Combes,G., Montero,J.L., and Winternitz,F. "Synthesis of analogs of cannabichromene derived from phloracetophenone."(Fr.). C. R. Acad. Sci. 1972, 274C, 1313-1316.

1856. Comitas,L. "Cannabis and work in Jamaica: a refutation of the amotivational syndrome." Ann. N. Y. Acad. Sci. 1976, 282, 24-32.

1857. Comitas,L. "The social nexus of ganja in Jamaica." In Rubin,V.(ed.). Cannabis and Culture. Mouton, The Hague, 1975, 119-133.

1858. Comite d'Experts des Drogues Engendrant la Toxicomanie. "Fourth report."(Fr.). Organ. Mond. Sante 1954, 76, 1-12.

1859. Comite d'Experts des Drogues Engendrant la Toxicomanie. "Fifth report."(Fr.). Organ. Mond. Sante 1955, 95, 1-16.

1860. Comite d'Experts des Drogues Engendrant la Toxicomanie. "Sixth report."(Fr.). Organ. Mond. Sante 1956, 102, 1-21.

1861. Comite d'Experts des Drogues Engendrant la Toxicomanie. "Seventh report."(Fr.). Organ. Mond. Sante 1957, 116, 1-15.

1862. Comite d'Experts des Drogues Engendrant la Toxicomanie. "Eighth report."(Fr.). Organ. Mond. Sante 1958, 142, 1-12.

1863. Comite d'Experts des Drogues Engendrant la Toxicomanie. "Ninth report."(Fr.). Organ. Mond. Sante 1960, 160, 1-15.

1864. Comite d'Experts des Drogues Engendrant la Toxicomanie. "Tenth report."(Fr.). Organ. Mond. Sante 1960, 188, 1-16.

1865. Comite d'Experts des Drogues Engendrant la Toxicomanie. "Eleventh report."(Fr.). Organ. Mond. Sante 1971, 211, 1-16.

1866. Comite d'Experts des Drogues Engendrant la Toxicomanie. "Twelth report."(Fr.). Organ. Mond. Sante 1962, 229, 1-16.

1867. Comite d'Experts des Drogues Engendrant la Toxicomanie. "Thirteenth report."(Fr.). Organ. Mond. Sante 1964, 273, 1-20.

1868. Comite d'Experts des Drogues Engendrant la Toxicomanie. "Fourteenth report."(Fr.). Organ. Mond. Sante 1965, 312, 1-16.

1869. Comite d'Experts des Drogues Engendrant la Toxicomanie. "Fifteenth report." Organ. Mond. Sante 1966, 343, 1-18.

1870. Community Service Society of New York. Background Paper for Position Favoring Legalization and Regulation of Marihuana. Dept. Public Affairs, Comm. on Youth and Correction, N.Y., 1975.

1871. Community Service Society of New York. *Reclassification of Marihuana as a Non-narcotic Dangerous Drug: Position Paper*. Dept. Public Affairs, Comm. on Youth and Correction, N.Y., 1970.

1872. Community Service Society of New York. *Statement for the Senate Committee on Codes re Marihuana: A Public Hearing*. Dept. Public Affairs, Comm. on Youth and Corrections, N.Y., 1970.

1873. Community Service Society of New York. *Statement for the Temporary State Commission to Evaluate the Drug Laws. Subcommittee to Evaluate the Marihuana Laws*. Dept. Public Affairs, Comm. on Youth and Corrections, N.Y., 1970.

1874. Condon,A. and Roland,A. "Drug abuse jargon." *Am. J. Nurs*. 1971, *71*, 1738-1739.

1875. Connell,P.H. "Clinical aspects of drug addiction." *J. Royal Coll. Phys*. 1970, *4*, 254-263.

1876. Connell,P.H. "Drug taking in Great Britain: A growing problem." *Roy. Soc. Hlth. J*. 1969, *89*, 92.

1877. Connell,P.H. and Dorn,N. "Asking better questions in cannabis research." In Connell,P.H. and Dorn,N.(eds.). *Cannabis and Man*. Churchill Livingstone, Edinburgh, 1975, 228-235.

1878. Connell,P.H. and Dorn,N.(eds.). *Cannabis and Man*. Churchill Livingstone, Edinburgh, 1975.

1879. Conos,B. "Three cases of cannabis addiction followed by psychosis."(Fr.). *Bull. Soc. Pathol. Exot*. 1925, *18*, 788-793.

1880. Conrad,D.G., Elsmore,T.F., and Sodetz,F.J. "Delta-9-tetrahydrocannabinol: Dose-related effects on timing behavior in chimpanzee." *Science* 1972, *175*. 547-550.

1881. Conrad,H.T. "Heroin and Marihuana."(Sp.). *Arch. Invest. Med*. 1974, *5*, 179-186.

1882. Conrad,K. and Mothes,K. "Sex conditioned differences in auxin-content of dioic hemp plants."(Ger.). *Naturwissen*. 1961, *48*, 26-27.

1883. Conradson,J.M. "Mens rea in relation to drug offences." *Otago Law Rev*. 1970, *2*, 131.

1884. Conroy,R.F. "Marihuana, a psychiatric point of view." *Southwest. Med*. 1970, *51*, 172-177.

1885. Consroe,P.F. "Effect of delta-9-tetrahydrocannabinol on a cholinergic-induced activation of the electroencephalogram in the rabbit." Res. Comm. Chem. Pathol. Pharmacol. 1973, 5, 705-712.

1886. Consroe,P.F. "Hallucinogenic agents, seizures, and drug antagonists." Psychopharmacol. Bull. 1975, 11, 56-57.

1887. Consroe,P.F., Jones,B.C., and Akins,F. "Delta-9-tetrahydrocannabinol-methamphetamine interaction in the rabbit." Neuropharmacol. 1975, 14, 377-383.

1888. Consroe,P.F., Jones,B.C., and Chin,L. "Delta-9-tetrahydrocannabinol, EEG and behavior: The importance of adaptation to the testing milieu." Pharmacol. Biochem. Behav. 1975, 3, 173-177.

1889. Consroe,P., Jones,B., and Laird,H. "EEG and behavioral effects of delta-9-tetrahydrocannabinol in combination with stimulant drugs in rabbits." Psychopharmacol. 1976, 50, 47-52.

1890. Consroe,P., Jones,B., and Laird,H. "Interactions of delta-9-tetrahydrocannabinol with other pharmacological agents." Ann. N. Y. Acad. Sci. 1976, 281, 198-211.

1891. Consroe,P., Jones,B., Laird,H., and Reinking,J. "Anticonvulsant-convulsant effects of delta-9-tetrahydrocannabinol." In Cohen,S. and Stillman,R.(eds.). Therapeutic Potential of Marihuana. Plenum Press, N.Y., 1976, 363-381.

1892. Consroe,P.F., Jones,B., Picchioni,A., and Chin,L. "Neuropharmacological analysis of central adrenergic and cholinergic antagonism of delta-9-tetrahydrocannabinol." Pharmacologist 1974, 16, 281.

1893. Consroe,P.F. and Man,D.P. "Effects of delta-8- and delta-9-tetrahydrocannabinol on experimentally induced seizures." Life Sci. 1973, 13, 429-439.

1894. Consroe,P., Martin,P., and Eisenstein,D. "Anticonvulsant drug antagonism of delta-9-tetrahydrocannabinol-induced seizures in rabbits." Res. Comm. Chem. Pathol. Pharmacol. 1977, 16, 1-13.

1895. Consroe,P. and Wolkin,A. "Cannabidiol-antiepileptic drug comparisons and interactions in experimentally induced seizures in rats." J. Pharmacol. Exper. Ther. 1977, 201, 26-32.

1896. Consroe,P.F., Wood,G.C., and Buchsbaum,H. "Anticonvulsant nature of marihuana smoking." J.A.M.A. 1975, 234, 306-307.

1897. Constantinidis,J. and Miras,C.J. "Effect of hashish smoke sublimate on hypothalamic noradrenaline studied by the fluorescence method." Psychopharmacol. 1971, 22, 80-90.

1898. Contenau,G. Divination among the Assyrians and Babylonians.(Fr.). Payot, Paris, 1940.

1899. Contri,G.F. Instructions for the Cultivation of Hemp.(It.). Bologna, 1841.

1900. Cook,A.B. "Poisoning by cannabis indica." Am. Practition. 1884, 30, 25-30.

1901. Cook,C.E., Hawes,M.L., Amerson,E.W., Pitt,C.G., and Williams,D. "Radioimmunoassay of delta-9-tetrahydrocannabinol." In Willette,P.(ed.). Cannabinoid Assays in Humans. Nat'l. Inst. Drug Abuse Res. Monog. 7, Dept. H.E.W., Washington, D.C., 1976, 15-27.

1902. Cook,C.E., Hawes,M.L., Amerson,E.W., Pitt,C.G., Williams,D.L., and Willette,R.G. "Tetrahydrocannabinol (THC) radioimmunoassay: Immunogen and novel ^{125}I-radioligand based on 5'-substituted delta-8-THC." Pharmacologist 1976, 18, 291.

1903. Cook,M.C. The Seven Sisters of Sleep. James Blackwood, London, 1860.

1904. Cook,S.J. Ideology and Canadian Narcotics Legislation. Dept. Sociology., University of Toronto, Toronto, 1964.

1905. Cook,W.J. "Grass in Eugene: Decriminalizing marihuana use in Oregon." Newsweek 1975, 86, 28.

1906. Cooler,P. and Gregg,J. "The effect of delta-9-tetrahydrocannabinol on intraocular pressure in humans." In Cohen,S. and Stillman,R.(eds.). Therapeutic Potential of Marihuana. Plenum Press, N.Y., 1976, 77-88.

1907. Coon,T.F. "America should not go to pot." Bull. Soc. Prof. Invest. 1969, 8-20.

1908. Cooper,J.T. and Goldstein,S. "Toxicity testing in vitro. I. The effects of delta-9-tetrahydrocannabinol and aflatoxin B_1 on the growth of cultured human fibroblasts." Can. J. Physiol. Pharmacol. 1976, 54, 541-545.

1909. Coopersmith,J. and Dick,L. "Attitude toward alcohol and other drugs expressed by college students and their parents." Paper presented at Internat'l. Cong. on Alcohol and Alcoholism, Washington, D.C., 1969.

1910. Cooperstock,R. "Sex-differences in the use of mood modifying drugs: an explanatory model." J. Hlth. Soc. Behav. 1971, 12, 238-244.

1911. Copeman,P.R. "An investigation into the composition of wild dagga." Sci. Bull. Un. Dept. Agric. 1923, 28, 1-16.

1912. Coper,H. "Clinical pharmacology of drug abuse."(Ger.). Deut. Med. J. 1971, 20, 515-518.

1913. Coper,H. and Fernandes,M. "Interaction between cannabis and other drugs." In Goldberg,L. and Hoffmeister,F.(eds.). Psychic Dependence. Definition, Assessment in Animals and Man, Theoretical and Clinical Implications. Springer Verlag, N.Y., 1973, 135-143.

1914. Coper,H., Fernandes,M., Honecker,H., and Kluwe,S. "The influence of solvent agents on the effects of cannabis." Act. Pharmacol. Toxicol. 1971, 29, 89.

1915. Coper,H. and Hippius,H. "Abuse of hashish (marihuana)."(Ger.). Deut. Arzt. 1970, 67, 1618-1627.

1916. Corcoran,A.M. and Helm,J. "Compilation and analysis of criminal drug laws in the 50 states and five territories." In U.S. National Commission on Marihuana and Drug Abuse. Drug Use in America: Problem in Perspective. Gov't. Print. Office, Washington,D.C., 1973, III, 240-334.

1917. Corcoran,M.E. "Role of drug novelty and metabolism in the aversive effects of hashish injection in rats." Life Sci. 1973, 12, 63-72.

1918. Corcoran,M.E. "Self-administration of cannabis by rats." Diss. Abs. 1972, 33, 2830-2831.

1919. Corcoran,M.E. and Amit,Z. "Reluctance of rats to drink hashish suspensions: Free-choice and forced consumption, and the effects of hypothalamic stimulation." Psychopharmacol. 1974, 35, 129-147.

1920. Corcoran,M.E. and Amit,Z. "The effects of hashish injections on feeding and drinking in rats." Res. Comm. Chem. Pathol. Pharmacol. 1974, 9, 193-196.

1921. Corcoran,M.E., Amit,Z., Malsbury,C.W., and Daykin,S. "Reduction in copulatory behavior of male rats following hashish injections." Res. Comm. Chem. Pathol. Pharmacol. 1974, 7, 779-782.

1922. Corcoran,M.E., Bolotow,I., Amit,Z., and McCaughran,J.A. "Conditioned taste aversions produced by active and inactive cannabinoids." Pharmacol. Biochem. Behav. 1974, 2, 725-728.

1923. Corcoran,M.E., McCaughran,J.A., and Wada,J.A. "Acute antiepileptic effects of delta-9-tetrahydrocannabinol in rats with kindled seizures." Expt'l. Neurol. 1973, 40, 471-483.

1924. Cordeiro de Farias,R. "Campaign against the use of maconha in Northern Brazil."(Port.). Arquiv. Hig. 1942, 12, 177-186.

1925. Cordeiro de Farias,R. Inspection Conducted between November 7 to 9, 1943 in the States of Bahia, Sergipe and Alagoas for Purposes of Studying the Problem of Trade in and Use of Maconha.(Port.). Servico Nacional de Educacacao Sanitaria, Rio de Janeiro, 1958.

1926. Cordeiro de Farias,R. Post-war Addictions. Servico Nacional de Educacao Sanitaria, Rio de Janeiro, 1958.

1927. Cordeiro de Farias,R. "Use of maconha(cannabis sativa L.) in Brazil." Bull. Narc. 1955, 7, 5-19.

1928. Cordeiro de Farias,R., Pernambuco,F., and Parreiras,D. "Experiments conducted on maconha smokers." Servico Nacional de Educacao Sanitaria, Rio de Janeiro, 1958.

1929. Cormier,D., Bourassa,M., and Landreville,I. "Frustration tolerance and the use of marihuana."(Fr.). Toxicomanies 1973, 6, 371-383.

1930. Cormier,D. "Personal characteristics of soft-drug users: A cross-cultural comparison."(Fr.). Toxicomanies 1973, 6, 267-285.

1931. Cormier,D. "Personal inhibitions in the transfer from cannabis to hard drugs."(Fr.). Toxicomanies 1974, 7, 135-145.

1932. Correa,J.J.A. "The problem of marihuana." (Sp.). Medicina 1973, 33, 309-314.

1933. Corrigan,O. "Chorea(use of chloroform fumes in treatment). Use of hashish in the same malady."(Fr.). J. Pharm. Chim. 1855, 27, 312-314.

1934. Corrigan,O. "Treatment of chorea by the use of cannabis indica." Med. Times 1845, 12, 291-292.

1935. Costa,A.F. Pharmacognosy. (Port.). Fundacao Calouste Gulbenkian, Lisbon, 1967.

1936. Costa,C. Treatise on Drugs and Medicines from the East Indies in Which Much of What Dr. Garcia de Orta Wrote is Corroborated.(Port.). Junta de Investigacoes do Ultramar, Lisbon, 1964.

1937. Costa,G. "Effects on brain serotonin in rats subjected to audiogenic stress: Influence of cannabis resin."(It.). Farm. Sci. Tec. 1977, 32, 186-195.

1938. Costa,G., De Pasquale,A., and De Pasquale,R. "On the pharmacological activity of cannabis indica. V." (It.). Lav. Farmagonos. 1965, 4, 139-152.

1939. Costa,G., De Pasquale,A., and De Pasquale,R. "On the pharmacological activity of cannabis indica. VIII." Lav. Farmacognos. 1967, 5, 35-41.

1940. Costello,C.E. "Gas chromatographic-mass spectrometric analysis of street drugs, particularly in the body fluids of overdose victims." In Marshman,J.A. (ed.). Street Drug Analysis and Its Social and Clinical Implications. Addiction Research Found., Toronto, 1974, 67-78.

1941. Cote,G., Boily,M., Benmouyal,E., and Seale,D. "The effects of chronic administration of delta-9-tetrahydrocannabinol(THC) in the guinea pig."(Fr.). Un. Med. 1972, 101, 735.

1942. Cottrell,J.C., Sohn,S.S., and Vogel,W.H. "Toxic effects of marihuana tar on mouse skin." Arch. Environ. Hlth. 1973, 26, 277-278.

1943. Couglan,R. "Chemical mind changes." Life 1963, 54, 81-82.

1944. Courtiere,S. "Indian hemp."(Fr.). Bull. Sci. Pharmacol. 1938, 45, 15-18.

1945. Cousens,K. and DiMascio,A. "(-)-delta-9-THC as an hypnotic. An experimental study of three dose levels." Psychopharmacol. 1973, 33, 355-364.

1946. Coutselinis,A. "Some observations on the action of delta-9-THC on the human organism." Med. Sci. Law 1974, 14, 117-119.

1947. Coutselinis,A. and Miras,C.J. "The effect of the smoking process on cannabinoids." J. Forens. Med. 1971, 18, 108-113.

1948. Coutselinis,A. and Miras,C.J. "The effects of the smoking process on cannabinols." U.N. Doc. ST/SOA/SER.S/23, Oct. 30, 1970.

1949. Covello,M. "Chemical and pharmacological research on cannabis indica cultivated in Italy. II. Biological deterioration as a result of aging and chromatographic separation of the active fraction in alcoholic and ether extracts."(It.). Farm. Sci. Tec. 1947, 2, 503-517.

1950. Covello,M. "Chemical and pharmacological research on cannabis indica cultivated in Italy. I. Relationship between the chemico-analytical character and pharmacological activity."(It.). Farm. Sci. Tec. 1948, 3, 8-12.

1951. Covello,M. "Relationship between the method of preparation and the properties of tinctures."(It.). Ann. Chim. Appl. 1936, 26, 409-414.

1952. Cowan,C.L. "Foreign drug laws and United States citizens abroad." In U.S. National Commission on Marihuana and Drug Abuse. Drug Use in America: Problem in Perspective. Gov't. Print. Office, Washington, D.C., 1973, II, 133-168.

1953. Cowan,R.C. "American conservatives should reverse their position on marihuana." Nat 1972, 24, 1344-1346.

1954. Cowan Lees,R. "Extract of cannabis indica." Br. Med. J. 1895, 1, 300.

1955. Cox,B., ten Ham,M., Loskota,W.J., and Lomax,P. "The anticonvulsant activity of cannabinoids in seizure sensitive gerbils." Proc. West. Pharmacol. Soc. 1975, 18, 154-157.

1956. Cradock,J.C., Davignon,J.P., Litterst,C.L., and Guarino,A.M. "An intravenous formulation of delta-9-tetrahydrocannabinol using a non-ionic surfactant." J. Pharm. Pharmacol. 1973, 25, 345.

1957. Craigmill,A.L. "Potentiation of d-amphetamine by delta-9-tetrahydrocannabinol in aggregated mice." Fed. Proc. 1974, 33, 539.

1958. Craigmill,A.L., Canafax,D.M., and Curtiss,F.R. "The interaction of delta-9-tetrahydrocannabinol and d-amphetamine in aggregated mice." Res. Comm. Chem. Pathol. Pharmacol. 1974, 9, 229-241.

1959. Crain,R. "B. and W's success with Laredo--it's not pot luck." Advert. Age 1971, 42, 56.

1960. Crain,W.C., Ertel,D., and Gorman,B. "Personality correlates of drug preference among college undergraduates." Internat'l. J. Addict. 1975, 10, 849-856.

1961. Crancer,A. "Marihuana and simulated driving." Science 1969, 166, 640.

1962. Crancer,A., Dille,J.M., Delay,J.C., Wallace, J.E., and Haykin,M.D. "Comparison of the effects of marihuana and alcohol on simulated driving performance." Science 1969, 164, 851-854.

1963. Crancer,A. and Quiring,D.L. Driving Records of Persons Arrested for Illegal Drug Use. State of Washington, Dept. of Motor Vehicles, Washington, 1968.

1964. Crawford,A.C. "Notes on 'physiological testing'." Am. J. Pharmacol. 1908, 80, 321-333.

1965. Crawford,H.J. "The effects of marihuana on primary suggestability." Diss. Abs. 1974, 35, 3055-3056.

1966. Crawford,K. "Vogues in vice: views of Margaret Mead." Newsweek 1969, 74, 45.

1967. Creighton,C. "On indications of the hachish-vice in the Old Testament." Janus 1903, 8, 241-246, 297-303.

1968. Crejci,Z. "Hemp(cannabis sativa) antibiotic." Pharm. Indust. 1958, 13, 155-157.

1969. Crescini,F. "Artificial selection and sex ratios in hemp(cannabis sativa)."(It.). Caryologia 1955, 7, 415-419.

1970. Crescini,F. "Association of genetic factors in cannabis sativa L."(It.). Caryologia 1952, 5, 288-296.

1971. Crescini,F. "Different forms of hemp."(Ger.). Zuchter 1940, 12, 105-115.

1972. Crescini,F. "Investigations on the genetic amelioration of fiber hemp grown in Italy."(It.). Caryologia 1954, 6, 284-318.

1973. Crescini,F., Mano,A.D., Bellini,E.P. "Genetic improvement of hemp cultivated in Italy."(It.). Caryologia 1957, 9, 215-225.

1974. Cress,C.R. "The marihuana arguments." Med. Art. Sci. 1974, 28, 34-38.

1975. Crestentius,P. New Field and Agriculture. (Ger.). Frankfort-on-Main, 1583.

1976. Crevost,C. and Lemaire,C. "Catalogue of products from Indochina."(Fr.). Bull. Econ. Indochine 1919, 16.

1977. Crockett,D., Klonoff,H., and Clark,C. "The effects of marihuana on verbalization and thought processes." J. Person. Assess. 1976, 40, 582-587.

1978. Crockett,R. Drug Abuse and Personality in Young Offenders. Butterworths, London, 1971.

1979. Crombie,L. "Numbering systems, formulae, trivial names and suggested abbreviations for various cannabinoids." In Joyce,C.R.B. and Curry,S.H.(eds.). The Botany and Chemistry of Cannabis. J. and A. Churchill, London, 1970, 209.

1980. Crombie,L. and Crombie,W.M.L. "Cannabinoid acids and esters: Miniaturized synthesis and chromatographic study." Phytochemistry 1977, 16, 1413-1420.

1981. Crombie,L. and Crombie,W.M.L. "Cannabinoid formation in cannabis sativa grafted interracially with two Humulus species." Phytochemistry 1975, 14, 409-414.

1982. Crombie,L. and Crombie,W.M.L. "Chemistry of the cannabinoids." In Graham,J.D.P.(ed.). Cannabis and Health. Academic Press, N.Y., 1976, 43-77.

1983. Crombie,L. and Ponsford,R. "Catalysis and the course of cyclisation in phenolic terpenes." Tetrahedron Let. 1968, 43, 4557-4560.

1984. Crombie,L. and Ponsford,R. "Synthesis of cannabinoids by pyridine-catalysed citral-olivetol condensation: Synthesis and structure of cannabicyclol, cannabichromene(hashish extractives), citrylidene-cannabis, and related compounds." J. Chem. Soc. 1971, 4, 796-804.

1985. Crombie,L. and Ponsford,R. "Synthesis of hashish cannabinoids by terpenic cyclisation." Chem. Commun. 1968, 15, 894-895.

1986. Crombie,L., Ponsford,R., Shani,A., Yagnitinsky, B., and Mechoulam,R. "Hashish components. Photochemical production of cannabicyclol from cannabichromene." Tetrahed. Let. 1968, 55, 5771-5772.

1987. Crombie,W.M.L. "The analysis of cannabis." In Graham,J.D.P.(ed.). Cannabis and Health. Academic Press, N.Y., 1976, 21-43.

1988. Crombie,W.M.L. "The influence of photo-synthesis and SKF inhibitors on cannabinoid production in cannabis sativa." Phytochemistry 1977, 16, 1369-1371.

1989. Cronin,J.D. "Cannabis indica." Br. Med. J. 1883, 1, 1117.

1990. Cross,H.J. and Davis,G.L. "College students' adjustment and frequency of marihuana use." J. Counsel. Psychol. 1972, 19, 65-67.

1991. Cross,H.J. and Keir,R.G. "Drug usage and attitude toward drugs among college students." Coll. Stud. Survey 1971, 5, 9-15.

1992. Croudace,T. "Case of catalepsy from an overdose of Indian hemp." Med. Times Gaz. 1859, 18, 135-136.

1993. Crow,I. "Two groups of cannabis users in South London." Drugs Soc. 1973, 2, 10-14.

1994. Crowley,A. The Diary of a Drug Fiend. Lancer Books, N.Y., 1972.

1995. Crowley,A. "The herb dangerous. II. The psychology of hashish." In Regardie,I.(ed.). Roll Away the Stone. Llewellyn, St. Paul, Minn., 1968, 93-151.

1996. Crowshaw,K. and Hardman,H.F. "Effect of delta-9-tetrahydrocannabinol on prostaglandin (PG) synthesis and the relationship of this effect to the hypothermic response in mice." Fed. Proc. 1974, 33, 539.

1997. Crowther,B. "Patterns of drug use among Mexican Americans." Internat'l. J. Addict. 1972, 7, 637-647.

1998. Cruickshank,E.K. "Physical assessment of 30 chronic cannabis users and 30 matched controls." Ann. N. Y. Acad. Sci. 1976, 282, 162-167.

1999. Crumpton,E. and Brill,N.Q. "Personality factors associated with frequency of marihuana use." Cal. Med. 1971, 115, 11-15.

2000. Cuendet,J.F., Shapiro,D., CAlanca,A., Faggioni, R., and Ducrey,N. "Action of delta-9-tetrahydrocannabinol on eye muscle."(Fr.). Ophthalmologica 1976, 172, 122-127.

2001. Cugell,D.W. "Chronic cough and bronchial irritation in teen-age drug addict." J.A.M.A. 1971, 216, 337-338.

2002. Cuk,S., Haasz,A., and Haasz,I. "Appearances of drug abuse in Rijeka."(Ger.). Paper presented at Internat'l. Inst. of Prevent. and Treat. of Drug Depend., Lausanne, Switzerland, 1970.

2003. Culliton,B.J. "Pot facing stringent scientific examination." Sci. News 1970, 97, 102-105.

2004. Culpeper,N. Complete Herbal. Richard Evans, London, 1814.

2005. Culver,C.M. "Neuropsychological assessment of undergraduate marihuana and LSD users." Arch. Gen. Psychiat. 1974, 31, 707-711.

2006. Cunningham,D.D. "On the nature of the effects accompanying the continued treatment of animals with hemp drugs and with dhatura." In Indian Hemp Drugs Commission. Report. Gov't. Print. Office, London, 1893, III, 485-459.

2007. Cunningham,W.H., Cunningham,I.C.M., and English,W.D. "Sociological characteristics of undergraduate marihuana users." J. Genet. Psychol. 1974, 125, 3-12.

2008. Curev,R. "Toxicity of waste waters from flax and hemp retting on fish." Bul. Inst. Cercet. Pisciede 1959, 18, 56-59.

2009. Curran,F.J. "Juveniles and drug abuse: Child psychiatrist looks at drug problem." N.Y. State J. Med. 1971, 71, 1611-1622.

2010. Curran,W.J. "Decriminalization, demythologizing, desymbolizing and deemphasizing marihuana." J. Pub. Hlth. 1972, 62, 1151-1152.

2011. Curray,A.E. "Drugs in jazz and rock music." Clin. Toxicol. 1968, 1, 235-244.

2012. Currie,A.J., Decker,J.F., and Van der Vaart,J. "International control of cannabis sativa--alternate approaches." J. Drug Issues 1973, 3, 240-255.

2013. Currie,F., Perlaman,D., Walker,L. "Marihuana use among Calgary youths as a function of sampling and locus of control." Br. J. Addict. 1977, 72, 159-165.

2014. Curtis,H.C. "Psychosis following the use of marihuana with report of cases." J. Kansas Med. Assoc. 1939, 40, 515-528.

2015. Curtis,H.C. and Wolf,J.R. "Psychosis following the use of marihuana with report of cases." J. Kansas Med. Soc. 1939, 40, 151-157.

2016. Curtis,J.H. "Social control and marihuana use." Clin. Toxicol. 1968, 1, 215-225.

2017. Cushman,A.S. "Growing medicinal plants in America." J. Franklin Inst. 1918, 186, 267-278.

2018. Cushman,M.S. "Stereochemistry, scope and mechanism of the condensation of Schiff bases and cyclic anhydrides; applications to the synthesis of trans-3'-methylnicotine and nitrogen analogs of the tetrahydrocannabinols." Diss. Abs. 1973, 34, 1442.

2019. Cushman,M. and Castagnoli,N. "A novel approach to the synthesis of nitrogen analogs of the tetrahydrocannabinols." J. Org. Chem. 1973, 38, 440-448.

2020. Cushman,M. and Castagnoli,N. "Synthesis of pharmacologically active nitrogen analogs of the tetrahydrocannabinols." J. Org. Chem. 1974, 39, 1546-1550.

2021. Cushman,P. "Plasma testosterone levels in healthy male marihuana smokers." Am. J. Drug Alcohol Abuse 1975, 2, 269-275.

2022. Cushman,P., Grieco,M., and Gupta,S. "Impaired rosette forming T-cells in chronic marihuana smokers." Internat'l J. Clin. Pharmacol. 1974, 10, 154.

2023. Cushman,P., Grieco,M., and Gupta,S. "Reduction in T-lymphocytes forming active rosettes in chronic marihuana smokers." Internat'l. J. Clin. Pharmacol. 1975, 12, 217-220.

2024. Cushman,P. and Khurana,R. "Marihuana and T-lymphocyte rosettes." Clin. Pharmacol. Ther. 1976, 19, 310-317.

2025. Cushman,P., Khurana,R., and Hashim,G. "Tetrahydrocannabinol: Evidence for reduced rosette formation by normal T-lymphocytes." In Braude,M.C. and Szara,S.(eds.). Pharmacology of Marihuana. Raven Press, N.Y., 1976, I, 207-211.

2026. Cuskey,W.R., Klum,D.W., and Krasner,W. Drug Trip Abroad. Univ. Penn. Press, Phil., 1972.

2027. Cutler,M.G. and Mackintosh,J.H. "Effects of delta-9-tetrahydrocannabinol on social behavior in the laboratory mouse and rat." Psychopharmacol. 1975, 44, 287-289.

2028. Cutler,M.G., Mackintosh,J.H., and Chance,M.R.A. "Behavioral changes in laboratory mice during cannabis feeding and withdrawal." Psychopharmacol. 1975, 44, 173-177.

2029. Cutler,M.G., Mackintosh,J.H., and Chance,M.R.A. "Cannabis resin and sexual behavior in the laboratory mouse." Psychopharmacol. 1975, 45, 129-131.

2030. Cutler,M.G., Mackintosh,J.H., and Chance,R.A. "Effects of cannabis resin on social behavior in the laboratory mouse." Psychopharmacol. 1975, 41, 271-276.

2031. Cutting,M., Goodenough,S., Simmons,G., Watson,A., Laguarda,R., and Huber,G. "Marihuana and pulmonary antibacterial defenses: Depression of alveolar macrophage function following experimental exposure to marihuana smoke." Chest 1974, 66, 321-322.

2032. Cutting,M., Watson,A., Goodenough,S., Simmons,G., Laguarda,R., and Huber,G. "The effect of exposure to marihuana smoke on the bactericidal activity of pulmonary alveolar macrophages." Clin. Res. 1974, 22, 501A.

2033. Cwallina,G.E. "Drug use on high school and college campuses." J. Sch. Hlth. 1968, 38, 638-646.

2034. Czerkis,M. "About hashish and the efficacious substances therein."(Ger.). Verhand. Gesell. Deut. Natur. Aerz. 1909, 82, 2.

2035. Czerkis,M. "Concerning cannabinol, the active substance of hashish."(Ger.). Deut. Apoth. Zeit. 1909, 24, 742-743.

2036. Czerkis,M. "Contribution to the knowledge of cannabinol, the active ingredient of hashish."(Ger.). Lieb. Ann. Chem. 1907, 351, 467-472.

2037. Czerkis,M. "On cannabinol, the active ingredient of hashish."(Ger.). Wien. Pharmazeut. Woch. 1907, 38, 49-51, 69-70, 97-98.

D

2038. Dacy,G.H. "Revolutionizing an industry; how modern machinery is minimizing hand labor in hemp production." Scientif. Amer. 1921, 124, 446-448.

2039. Dagirmanjian,R. and Boyd,E.S. "Peripheral effects of a tetrahydrocannabinol." Fed. Proc. 1960, 19, 267.

2040. Dagirmanjian,R. and Boyd,E.S. "Some pharmacological effects of two tetrahydrocannabinols." J. Pharmacol. Exper. Ther. 1962, 135, 25-33.

2041. Dagirmanjian,R. and Hodge,H.C. "Are biogenic amines involved in the mechanism of action of the tetrahydrocannabinols?" Agents Actions 1969, 2, 46-48.

2042. Dahi,M. "Mechanism of action of synthetic tetrahydrocannabinol(pyrahexyl)." Fed. Proc. 1951, 10, 290-291.

2043. Daley,J.D., Branda,L.A., Rosenfeld,J., and Younglai,E. "Increase of serum prolactin in male rats by delta-9-THC." J. Endocrinol. 1974, 63, 415-416.

2044. Dalgado,D.G. Botanical Classification of Plants and Drugs Described in Garcia d'Orta's 'Colloquies of India.(Port.). Nicol's Printing Work, Bombay, 1898.

2045. Dallas,A.M. "Ganja and aphonia." Ind. Med. Rec. 1896, 11, 76.

2046. Dall'Olio,G. "Preliminary experiments on the effects of chlorocholine chloride(CCC) and gibberellin A on vegetative and reproductive development of cannabis sativa L."(It.). Bot. Ital. 1964, 71, 35.

2047. Dally,P. "Undesirable effects of marihuana." Br. Med. J. 1967, 3, 367.

2048. Dalrymple,W. "A doctor speaks of marihuana." J. Am. Coll. Hlth. Assoc. 1966, 14, 218-222.

2049. Dalton,W.S., Martz,R., Lemberger,L., Rodda,B.E. and Forney,R.B. "Effects of marihuana combined with secobarbital." Clin. Pharmacol. Ther. 1975, 18, 298-304.

2050. Dalton,W.S., Martz,R., Lemberger,L, Rodda,B.E., and Forney,R.B. "Influence of cannabidiol on delta-9-tetrahydrocannabinol effects." Clin. Pharmacol. Ther. 1976, 19, 300-309.

2051. Dalton,W.S., Martz,R., Rodda,B.E., Lemberger, L., and Forney,R.B. "Influence of cannabidiol on seco-barbital effects and plasma kinetics." Clin. Pharmacol. Ther. 1976, 20, 695-700.

2052. Dalziel,J.M. The Useful Plants of West Tropical Africa. Crown Agents for Overseas Governments and Administration. London, 1936.

2053. Dana,K. Hashish and Intoxicants in Iran.(Fr.). M. Vigne, Paris, 1938.

2054. Danaceau,P. Pot Luck in Texas. Changing a Marihuana Law. Drug Abuse Council, Washington, D.C., 1974.

2055. Danova,N.S. and Egiazarova,V.C. "On the use of synthomyein in hashish poisoning."(Rus.). Sovet. Zdrav. Kirgiz. 1957, 4, 52-55.

2056. Danzig,F. "Pot users welcome Laredo kit." Advert. Age 1971, 42, 4.

2057. Da Orta,G. Colloquies on the Simples and Aromatics of India.(Port.). Plantin, DeBanque, and Antevaerpiea, Goa, India, 1574.

2058. Daramola,T. and Grange,J.J. "The cannabis problem among prisoners in Lagos." Bull. Narc. 1971, 23, 5-10.

2059. Dardanne,A. "Contribution to the study of Indian hemp."(Fr.). Arch, Inst. Past. 1938, 27, 442.

2060. Darley,C.F. and Tinklenberg,J.R. "Marihuana and memory." In Miller,L.L.(ed.). Marihuana, Effects on Human Behavior. Academic Press, N.Y., 1974, 73-100.

2061. Darley,C.F., Tinklenberg,J.R., Hollister,L.E., and Atkinson,R.C. "Marihuana and retrieval from short-term memory." Psychopharmacol. 1973, 29, 231-238.

2062. Darley,C.F., Tinklenberg,J.R., Roth,W.T., Hollister,L.E., and Atkinson,R.C. "Influence of marihuana on storage and retrieval processes in memory." Mem. Cognit. 1973, 1, 196-200.

2063. Darley,C.F., Tinklenberg,J.R., Roth,W.T., and Atkinson,R.C. "The nature of storage deficits and state-dependent retrieval under marihuana." Psychopharmacol. 1974, 37, 139-149.

2064. D'Arvieus,L. A Journey in Palestine, With the Grand Emir, Chief of the Arab Princes of the Desert Known as the Bedouins.(Fr.). Paris, 1717.

2065. DaSilva,J.B. "Comparative chromatographic analysis of 100 samples of cannabis sativa."(Port.). Rev. Fac. Farm. Bioquim. 1966, 4, 55-69.

2066. DaSilva,J.B. "Identification of cannabinol by chromatographic analysis from the blood, urine and saliva of cannabis addicts."(Port.). Rev. Fac. Farm. Bioquim. 1967, 5, 205-214.

2067. Daskalopoulos,N., Schmidtt,H., and Laubie,M. "Action of delta-9-tetrahydrocannabinol on the central cardiovascular regulation: mechanism and localization." (Fr.). Encephale 1973, 1, 121-132.

2068. Dastur,J.F. Medicinal Plants of India and Pakistan. Taraporvala and Sons, Bombay, n.d.

2069. Daul,C.B. "The effect of chronic marihuana usage on the immunological status of rhesus monkeys." Life Sci. 1975, 17, 875-881.

2070. Davalos,S.D. "Contribution to the study of Mexican marihuana. Preliminary studies: cannabinoids and essential oil."(Fr.). J. Pharm. Belg. 1977, 32, 89-99.

2071. David,D. Essay on the Treatment of Tuberculosis, Cancer and Leprosy.(Fr.). Vigot, Paris, 1940.

2072. Davidson,J. "Observations on Indian hemp and syphilis as causes of mental alienation in Turkey, Asia Minor and Marocco."(Fr.). Ann. Med. Psychol. 1885, 1, 123.

2073. Davidson,S. "Types and treatment of adolescent drug abusers in Israel." Israel Ann. Psychiat. 1973, 11, 210-218.

2074. Davidyan,G.C. "Botanical characteristics of hemp."(Rus.). Trud. Bot. Genet. Selek. 1972, 48, 17-19.

2075. Davidyan,G.C. "Effect of day length on the growth and development of the hemp, cannabis sativa L." (Rus.). Bot. Zh. 1967, 52, 989-995.

2076. Davidyan,G.C. "The effect of gibberellin on growth, development, and sex of hemp." Sel'skokhoz. Biol. 1967, 2, 90-94.

2077. Davidyan,G.C. and Kutuzova,S.N. "Studying organogenesis in hemp(cannabis sativa L.)." Bull. Vses Inst. Rastenievod. 1970, 15, 69-73.

2078. Davies,B.H., Radcliffe,S., Seaton,A., and Graham,J.D.P. "A trial of oral delta-1-(trans)-tetrahydrocannabinol in reversible airway obstruction." *Thorax* 1975, *30*, 80-85.

2079. Davies,B.H., Weatherstone,R.M., Graham,J.D.P., and Griffiths,R.D. "A pilot study of orally administered delta-1-trans-tetrahydrocannabinol in the management of patients undergoing radiotherapy for carcinoma of the bronchos." *J. Clin. Pharmacol.* 1974, *1*, 301-306.

2080. Davies,O.L., Raventos,J., and Wolpole,A.L. "A method for the evaluation of analgesic activity using rats." *Br. J. Pharmacol.* 1946, *1*, 255.

2081. Davis,C.H., Forney,R.B., and Hughes,F.W. "Extraction of the phenolic compounds of cannabis sativa and preparation of a synthetic intermediate." *Pharmacologist* 1962, *4*, 161.

2082. Davis,C.S. "A study of the relationships of value orientations in psychological health, marihuana use, and psychedelic use in a select population." *Diss. Abs.* 1974, *34*, 6379-6380.

2083. Davis,D.J., Cahan,S., and Bashi,J. "Cannabinoids inhibit testosterone secretion by mouse testes in vitro." *Science* 1977, *196*, 1472-1474.

2084. Davis,E.L. "LSD and marihuana: where are the answers?" *Science* 1968, *160*, 1062-1064.

2085. Davis,E.M. "Position paper on marihuana." *Police Chief* 1975, *1*, 34-35.

2086. Davis,F. and Munoz,L. "Heads and freaks: Patterns and meanings of drug use among hippies." *J. Hlth. Soc. Behav.* 1968, *9*, 156-164.

2087. Davis,J.H. "Marihuana and automobile driving." *J.A.M.A.* 1972, *221*, 714.

2088. Davis,J.H. and Ramsey,H.H. "Antiepileptic action of marihuana-active substances." *Fed. Proc.* 1949, *8*, 284-285.

2089. Davis,J.M. and Milte,K.L. "Drug use in Australia--a survey." *Aust. N. Z. J. Criminol.* 1970, *3*, 131-141.

2090. Davis,J.M., Sekerke,H.J., and Janowsky,D.S. "Drug interactions involving the drugs of abuse." In U.S. National Commission on Marihuana and Drug Abuse. *Drug Use in America: Problem in Perspective.* Gov't. Print. Office, Washington, D.C., 1973, 1, 181-208.

2091. Davis,K.H., Martin,N.H., Pitt,C.G., Wildes, J.W., and Wall,M.E. "The preparation and analysis of enriched and pure cannabinoids from marihuana and hashish." Lloydia 1970, 33, 453-460.

2092. Davis,M.A. "Antidepressants, stimulants, hallucinogens." In Cain,C.K.(ed.). Annual Reports in Medicinal Chemistry. Academic Press, N.Y., 1968, 19-20.

2093. Davis,M.A. "Antidepressants, stimulants, hallucingens." In Cain,C.K.(ed.). Annual Reports in Medicinal Chemistry. Academic Press, N.Y., 1969, 18-19.

2094. Davis,T.R.A., Kensler,C.J., and Dews,P.B. "Comparison of behavioral effects of nicotine, d-amphetamine, caffeine and dimethylheptyl tetrahydrocannabinol in squirrel monkeys." Psychopharmacol. 1973, 32, 51-65.

2095. Davis,T.W.M., Farmilo,C.G., and Osadchuk,M. "Identification and origin determinations of cannabis by gas and paper chromatography." Anal. Chem. 1963, 35, 751-755.

2096. Davis,W.G. and Persaud,T.V.N. "Recent studies on the active principles of Jamaican medicinal plants." West. Ind. Med. J. 1970, 19, 101-110.

2097. Davis,W.M. and Borgen,L.A. "Effects of cannabidiol and delta-9-tetrahydrocannabinol on operant behavior." Res. Commun. Chem. Pathol. Pharmacol. 1974, 9, 453-461.

2098. Davis,W.M. and Borgen,L.A. "Tolerance development to the effect of delta-9-tetrahydrocannabinol on conditioned behavior: Role of treatment interval and influence of microsomal metabolism." Arch. Internat'l. Pharmacodyn. Ther. 1975, 213, 97-112.

2099. Davis,W.M., Moreton,J.E., King,W.T., and Pace, H.B. "Marihuana on locomotor activity: Biphasic effect and tolerance development." Res. Commun. Chem. Pathol. Pharmacol. 1972, 3, 29-35.

2100. Davison,K. and Wilson,C.H. "Psychosis associated with cannabis smoking." Br. J. Addict. 1972, 67, 225-228.

2101. Davoli,E. "Drug abuse: Our new challenge." Clin. Proc. Child. Hosp. D.C. 1968, 24, 151-152.

2102. Dawson,W.W. "Cannabis and eye function." Invest. Ophthalmol. 1976, 15, 243-245.

2103. Dayanandan,P. and Kaufman,P.B. "Trichomes of cannabis sativa L.(cannabacea)." Am. J. Bot. 1976, 63, 578-591.

2104. Dayydova,O.N. and Kudrin,A.N. "A pharmacological method for determination of hashish activity." Coll. Internat'l. Neuro-psychopharmacol. 1970, 7, 11-15.

2105. Deakin,S. "Death from taking Indian hemp." Ind. Med. Gaz. 1880, 15, 71.

2106. DeAlmeida,A.G. "Venomous plants and drugs indigenous to Mozambique."(Port.). Bol. Agric. Pecuar. 1930, 1, 9-29.

2107. Dean,M.E. and Stock,B.H. "Propylene glycol as a drug solvent in the study of hepatic microsomal enzyme metabolism in the rat." Toxicol. Appl. Pharmacol. 1974, 28, 44-52.

2108. Deane,H. "Extract of Indian hemp." Year-book Pharm. 1911, 1, 402-411.

2109. Dean,H. "Extract of Indian hemp." Pharmaceut. J. Pharmacist 1911, 87, 160-162.

2110. Dearden,M. "Does marihuana lead to other drugs?" Sch. Mgt. 1972, 16, 31.

2111. Dearden,W. "Sinsemilla." High Times 1976, 11, 55-59, 83.

2112. DeAssis Iglesias,F. "The vice of diamba."(Port.). Ann. Paul. Med. Cirurg. 1918, 9, 274-281.

2113. Debjani,G. and Pradhan,S.N. "Effects of mescaline and delta-9-tetrahydrocannabinol on the auditory evoked response in the cat." Pharmacologist 1973, 15, 200.

2114. DeBoismont,B. "Mechanism of action of quinine and hashish."(Ger.). Schmidt's Jahrb. 1854, 82, 230.

2115. DeBoor,W. Pharmacology and Psychopathology of Hemp.(Ger.). Springer Verglag, Berlin, 1956.

2116. DeBoskey,R. "Youth and drug abuse." Clin. Toxicol. 1968, 1, 187-193.

2117. DeCandolle,A. Origins of Cultivated Plants. (Fr.). Germer-Bailliere,Paris, 1883.

2118. Decherd,J.F. "The medical effects of marihuana." Southwest. Med. 1970, 51, 170-172.

2119. DeCillis,E. "The structure of hemp."(It.). Ann. Tec. Agrar. 1941, 1, 19.

2120. Decker,J.F. "Official report of the National Commission studying marihuana: more misunderstanding." U. San Francisco Law Rev. 1973, 8, 1-28.

2121. DeClercq,H., Massart,D.L., and Vercruysse,A. "A reaction for the fluorimetric identification of cannabis constituents."(Fr.). J. Pharm. Belg. 1973, 28, 437-444.

2122. DeCourtive,E. "Hashish. Historical, chemical and physiological study."(Fr.). Reper. Pharm. 1848, 1, 358-361.

2123. Decourtive,E. "Note on hashish."(Fr.). C. R. Acad. Sci. 1848, 26, 509-510.

2124. DeCourtive,E. "On hashish."(Fr.). J. Pharm. Chim. 1848, 13, 427-444.

2125. DeFaubert Maunder,M.J. "A comparative evaluation of the delta-9-tetrahydrocannabinol content of cannabis plants." J. Assoc. Pub. Anal. 1970, 8, 42-47.

2126. DeFaubert Maunder,M.J. "A simple and specific test for cannabis." J. Assoc. Pub. Anal. 1969, 7, 24-30.

2127. DeFaubert Maunder,M.J. "An improved procedure for the field testing of cannabis." Bull. Narc. 1974, 26, 19-26.

2128. DeFaubert Maunder,M.J. "Preservation of cannabis thin-layer chromatograms." J. Chromatog. 1974, 100, 196-199.

2129. DeFaubert Maunder,M.J. "Simple chromatography of cannabis constituents." J. Pharm. Pharmacol. 1969, 21, 334-335.

2130. DeFaubert Maunder,M.J. "The forensic significance of the age and origin of cannabis." Med. Sci. Law 1976, 16, 78-90.

2131. DeFaubert Maunder,M.J. "The rapid detection of drugs of addiction." Med. Sci. Law 1974, 14, 243-249.

2132. DeFaubert Maunder,M.J. "Two simple color tests for cannabis." Bull. Narc. 1969, 21, 37-43.

2133. Defer,B. and Diehl,M.L. "Mental disorders caused by Indian hemp: Nosography and description of acute psychosis based on 600 cases."(Fr.). Ann. Medico-psychol. 1968, 2, 260-266.

2134. Defer,B., Grasser-Billard,K., and Diehl,M.L. "Epidemiological aspects of cannabism in France."(Fr.). Paper presented at Internat'l. Inst. on Prevent. and Treat. of Drug Dependence, Lausanne, 1970, 329-337.

2135. Defer,B., Grasser-Billard,K., and Diehl,M.L. "Epidemiology of cannabis use in France."(Fr.). *Ann. Med.-Psychol.* 1970, *2*, 113-120.

2136. Defarge,A. *Critical History of Ancient Anesthetics Particularly of Sleep Inducing Sponges Made from Medicinal Plants*. J. Biere, Bordeaux, 1928.

2137. DeFleur,L.B. and Garrett,G.R. "Dimensions of marihuana usage in a land-grant university." *J. Counsel. Psychol.* 1970, *17*, 468-476.

2138. De-Groot,M.H. "The role of hallucinogens in depersonalization and allied syndromes." *Proc. Roy. Medicopsychol. Assoc.* 1963, *1*, 97-100.

2139. Dehay,C. "Medicinal plants from the north of France."(Fr.). *Bull. Soc. Bot.* 1961, *57*, 24.

2140. Deikel,S.M. "Attenuation of precipitated abstinence in methadone-dependent rats by delta-9-THC." *Psychopharmacol. Commun.* 1976, *2*, 61-65.

2141. Delabarre,E.B. and Popplestone,J.A. "A cross cultural contribution to the cannabis experience." *Psychol. Rec.* 1974, *24*, 67-73.

2142. De la Fuente,R. "Psychiatric disorders in relation to the use of drugs."(Sp.). *Gac. Med. Mex.* 1972, *103*, 384-392.

2143. De La Mare,W. *Desert Islands and Robinson Crusoe*. Faber and Faber, London, 1930.

2144. Delamer,E.S. *Flax and Hemp*. G. Routledge and Co., N.Y., 1854.

2145. Delasiuve,M. "Differential diagnosis of delirium tremens."(Fr.). *Rev. Med. Franc. Etrang.* 1850, *1*, 657-679.

2146. Delay,J. "Psychopharmacology and psychiatry: Towards a classification of psychotropic drugs." *Bull. Narc.* 1967, *19*, 1-5.

2147. Delay,J. "The midadventures of a hashish user."(Fr.). *Presse Med.* 1944, *52*, 321.

2148. Delay,J. and Maillard,G. "Oneiro-confused state after hashish intoxication with self-accusation of a fictitious murder." Ann. Med.-Psychol. 1944, 102, 37-40.

2149. DelFavero,E. "Mental effects of hashish on Central African negros."(It.). Pens. Med. 1928, 17, 270-277.

2150. D'Elia,G., Perris,C., and Persson,G. "Psychosis due to cannabis abuse."(Swed.). Lakartid. 1970, 67, 3526-3529.

2151. Delini-Stula,A. "Suppression of conditioned avoidance behavior and the development of tolerance to delta-8-tetrahydrocannabinol and dimethylheptylpyran in rats." Pharmakopsychiat. Neuro-psychopharmakol. 1973, 6, 189-197.

2152. Delkers,H.A. "Mode of action of Indian hemp."(Ger.). Zeit. Ges. Expt'l. Med. 1941, 109, 457.

2153. Dell,D.D. and Snyder,J.A. "Marihuana: Pro and con." Am. J. Nurs. 1977, 21, 630-635.

2154. DeLong,F.L. and Levy,B.I. "A model of attention describing the cognitive effects of marihuana." In Miller,L.L.(ed.). Marihuana, Effects on Human Behavior. Academic Press, N.Y., 1974, 103-117.

2155. DeLong,F.L. and Levy,B.I. "Cognitive effects of marihuana, described in terms of a model of attention." Psychol. Rep. 1973, 33, 907-916.

2156. Delteil,P., Lasserre,P., Abittan,J., Josselin, F., Douche,F., and Prieur,M. "The personality of drug addicts and their treatment."(Fr.). Ann. Med.-Psychol. 1970, 2, 107-113.

2157. DeLuca,S. "The effect of hashish upon the economy of man." C. R. Acad. Sci. 1862, 55, 617-620.

2158. DeMarco,C.T. "Comprehensive drug abuse prevention and control act of 1970." Am. J. Hosp. Pharm. 1971, 28, 290-292.

2159. Dembert,M.L. and Harclerode,J. "Effects of l-delta-9-tetrahdyrocannabinol, dl-amphetamine and pentobarbital on oxygen consumption by mouse brain and heart homogenates." Biochem. Pharmacol. 1974, 23, 947-956.

2160. Dembo,R., Schmerdler,J., Babst,D.V. and Lipton,D.S. "Drug information source credibility among junior and senior high school youths." Am. J. Drug Alcohol Abuse 1977, 4, 43-54.

2161. Dembo,R., Schmeidler,J., and Koval,M. "Demographic, value, and behavior correlates of marihuana use among middle-class youths." J. Hlth. Soc. Behav. 1976, 17, 177-187.

2162. DeMeritt,M. "Differences in the self-concept of drug-abusers, non-users, and former users of narcotics and/or non-narcotic drugs." Diss. Abs. 1970, 31, 1008.

2163. DeMonfreid,H. Pearls, Arms and Hashish. Coward-McCann, Inc., N.Y., 1930.

2164. DeMonfreid,H. The Hashish Crossing.(Fr.). Ferenczi, Paris, 1934.

2165. Demos,W.H. and Frazer,M.P. "Factors leading to drug abuse." J. Am. Coll. Hlth. Assoc. 1968, 16, 345-347.

2166. DeMyttenaere,F. "Note on Indian hemp."(Fr.). J. Pharm. Belg. 1936, 18, 613, 633.

2167. DeMyttenaere,F. "Note on Indian hemp. II."(Fr.). J. Pharm. Belg. 1936, 18, 651.

2168. DeMyttenaere,F. "Note on Indian hemp. V."(Fr.). J. Pharm. Belg. 1939, 21, 571-574, 597-599, 615-617; 1940, 22, 163-168.

2169. DeMyttenaere,F. "Note on Indian hemp. VI. Cannabinol." Bull. Acad. Roy. Med. Belg. 1941, 6, 326-344.

2170. DeMyttenaere,F. "Supplement to O.C. 1724." J. Pharm. Belg. 1938, 20, 683-686, 702-707, 723-728.

2171. Deneau,G.A. and Kaymakcalan,S. "Physiological and psychological dependence to synthetic delta-9-tetrahydrocannabinol(THC) in rhesus monkeys." Pharmacologist 1971, 13, 246.

2172. DeNerval,G. The Women of Cairo, Scenes of Life in the Orient. Harcourt, Brace and Co., N.Y., 1956.

2173. Deniker,P. "Clinical research on dependence-producing drugs." In Betsh,S.(ed.). Drug Abuse. Plenum Press, N.Y., 1972, 70-76.

2174. Deniker,P. "Drugs and modern toxicomania."(Fr.). Ann. Med.-Psychol. 1970, 128, 68-70.

2175. Deniker,P. "Intoxicants and cures for intoxication. Psychiatric aspects of treatment."(Fr.). Ther. Recent. 1956, 107, 99.

2176. Deniker,P., Boissier,J.R., Etevenon,P., Ginestet,D., Peron-Magnan,P., and Verdeaux,G. "Clinical pharmacology of delta-9-tetrahydrocannabinol in healthy volunteers with polygraphic control."(Fr.). Ther. 1974, 29, 185-200.

2177 Deniker,P., Colonna,L., Cottereau,M.J., and Loo,H. "Current toxicomanias; clinical effects of agents."(Fr.). Ann. Med.-Psychol. 1970, 128, 70-78.

2178. Deniker,P., Ginestet,D., Etevenon,P., and Peron-Magnan,P. "Comparison of the clinical effects of delta-9-tetrahydrocannabinol with classical hashish reactions."(Fr.). Encephale 1975, 1, 33-41.

2179. Denzel-Reutlingen,J. "Analysis of Indian hemp."(Ger.). Chem.-Zeit. 1884, 8, 1454.

2180. Denzel-Reutlingen,J. "Constituents of Indian hemp."(Ger.). Pharmazeut. Cent. Deut. 1885, 1, 540-541.

2181. DeOliveira,E. "Marihuana addiction in Brazil."(Port.). Imprensa Med. 1952, 28, 41-48.

2182. DePasquale,A. "Influence of delta-9-tetrahydrocannabinol, cannabis resin, and apomorphine on the brain."(It.). Lav. Ist. Farmacog. Univ. Mess. 1973, 9, 1-35.

2183. DePasquale,A. "Initial electron microscopy observations of Indian hemp."(It.). Lav. Ist. Farmacog. Univ. Mess. 1969, 6, 1-8.

2184. DePasquale,A. "On a color reaction of Indian hemp resin."(It.). Lav. Ist. Farmacog. Univ. Mess. 1964, 3, 101-105.

2185. DePasquale,A. "On the pharmacological activity of Indian hemp. III."(It.). Atti Soc. Pelor. Sc. Fis. Mat. Nat. 1958, 5, 321-325.

2186. DePasquale,A. "Pharmacology of Indian hemp. I. Bibliography."(It.). Lav. Ist. Farmacog. Univ. Mess. 1969, 5, 43-121.

2187. DePasquale,A. "Pharmacology of Indian hemp. II. Morphology."(It.). Lav. Ist. Farmacog. Univ. Mess. 1969, 6, 1-21.

2188. DePasquale,A. "Reaction of Indian hemp resin."(It.). Lav. Ist. Farmacog. Univ. Mess. 1965, 3, 215-219.

2189 DePasquale,A. "Ultrastructure of cannabis sativa glands."(It.). Lav. Ist. Farmacog. Univ. Mess. 1973, 8, 1-10.

2190. DePasqaule,A. "Ultrastructure of the cannabis sativa glands." Plant. Med. 1974, 25, 238-248.

2191. DePasqaule,A. and Costa,G. "On the pharmacological activity of Indian hemp. VII."(It.). Lav. Ist. Farmacog. Univ. Mess. 1968, 5, 9-17.

2192. DePasquale,A. and Costa,G. "On the pharmacological activity of Indian hemp. IX."(It.). Lav. Ist. Farmacog. Univ. Mess. 1958, 5, 160.

2193. DePasquale,A., Costa,G., and DePasquale,R. "On the pharmacological activity of Indian hemp. IV." (It.). Lav. Ist. Farmacog. Univ. Mess. 1966, 4, 11-23.

2194. DePasquale,A., Costa,G., and DeSarro,A. "Cannabis sativa L. Cultivated in Messina. Constituents and active principle in various parts of the male and female plant."(It.). Lav. Ist. Farmacog. Univ. Mess. 1973, 8, 1-10.

2195. DePasquale,A., Tumino,G., and Costa de Pasqual,R. "Micromorphology of the epidermic surfaces of female plants of cannabis sativa L." Bull. Narc. 1974, 26, 27-40.

2196. DePasquale,A., Tumino,A., DePasquale,R., and Costa,R. "Micromorphology of the superficial layer of the female cannabis sativa plant."(It.). Lav. Ist. Farmacog. Univ. Mess. 1973, 8, 11-20.

2197. DePasquale,A., Costa,G., and DePasqaule,A. "On the pharmacological activity of Indian hemp. VI." (It.). Lav. Ist. Farmacog. Univ. Mess. 1967, 4, 153-161.

2198. DePaul,L. and Zitterell,G. "An analysis of proposed therapeutic applications of cannabis sativa." Comm. Prob. Drug Depend. 1970, 3, 6556-6563.

2198a. DePinho,A.R. "Social and medical aspects of the use of cannabis in Brazil." In Rubin,V.(ed.). Cannabis and Culture. Mouton, The Hague, 1975, 293-303.

2199. DePinho,A.R. "Sociopsychological problems from maconha."(Port.). Neurobiologia 1962, 25, 9-19.

2200. Deprez,H. "Extract of cannabis indica." Am. J. Pharmacol. 1878, 50, 518.

2201. DeRemer,R. "9 tons of pot. Seven men and a barge test Florida justice." High Times 1974, 1, 15-16.

2202. DeRios,M.D. "Man, culture and hallucinogens: An overview." In Rubin,V.(ed.). Cannabis and Culture. Mouton, The Hague, 1975, 401-417.

2203. D'Erlanger,B.H. The Last Plague of Egypt. Lovat, Dickson and Thompson, London, 1936.

2204. Der Marderosian,A.H. and Murthy,S.N.S. "Analysis of old samples of cannabis sativa." J. Forens. Sci. 1974, 19, 670-675.

2205. Der Marderosian,A. "International illegal drug traffic." Am. J. Pharm. 1971, 143, 66-71.

2206. Der Marderosian,A.H. "Marihuana madness." J. Second. Educat. 1968, 43, 200-205.

2207. Derobert,L. Intoxication and Professional Illnesses.(Fr.). Flammarion, Paris, 1954.

2208. De Ropp,R.S. "Chromatographic separation of the phenolic compounds of cannabis sativa." J.A.P.A. 1960, 49, 756-758.

2209. De Ropp,R.S. Drugs and the Mind. V. Gollencz, London, 1957.

2210. De Ropp,R.S., Kastl,L.H., and Balbus,L. "Acute effects of marihuana smoke on mice." Proc. West. Pharmacol. Soc. 1972, 15, 21-24.

2211. De Ropp,R.S. "The uptake and metabolism of cannabinoids in smoke of marihuana." Proc. 5th Internat'l. Cong. Pharmacol. 1972, 1, 55.

2212. DeSainte-Marie,C. "On some experiences with hashish."(Fr.). J. Med. Bord. 1850, 1, 565-571.

2213. De Savignac,D. "Obstetric drugs substituted for by ergot, and particularly by antimonial tartar. IV. Indian hemp."(Fr.). Bull. Gen. Ther. Med. Chir. Obstet. Pharmaceut. 1871, 81, 293-294.

2214. Deschamps,A. An Essay on the Pharmacodynamic Exploration of Dementia Praecox.(Fr.). Faculty of Medicine, Univ. Paris, Paris, 1906.

2215. Deschamps,A. Ether, Cocaine, Hashish, Peyote and Dementia Praecox.(Fr.). Vega, Paris, 1932.

2216. Desoize,B., Jardillier,J.C., Leger,C., and Nahas,G.G. "Delta-9-tetrahydrocannabinol(THC) and macromolecular synthesis: mechanisms of action." Br. J. Pharmacol. 1976, , 419P.

2217. Desoize,B. and Nahas,G.G. "Inhibition of protein and nucleic acid syntheses by delta-9-tetrahydrocannabinol."(Fr.). C. R. Acad. Sci., 1975, 281, 475-478.

2218. De Souza,M.R. Karniol,I.G., and Ventura,D.F. "Human tonal preferences as a function of frequency under delta-8-tetrahydrocannabinol." Pharmacol. Biochem. Behav. 1974, 2, 607-611.

2219. De Souza,M.R., Karniol,I.G., and Ventura,D.F. "Measurement of human tonal preferences as a function of frequency under the effects of delta-8-THC." First Lat. Am. Cong. Psychobiol. 1973, 1, 95.

2220. Desser,K.B. "Effects of 'speed' and 'pot' on the juvenile diabetic." J.A.M.A. 1970, 214, 2065.

2221. Detrick,R. and Foltz,R.L. "Quantitation of delta-9-tetrahydrocannabinol in body fluids by gas chromatography-chemical ionization-mass spectrometry." In Willette,P.(ed.). Cannabinoid Assays in Humans. Nat'l. Inst. Drug Abuse Monog. 7, Dept. H.E.W., Washington, D.C., 1976, -8-95.

2222. Devaney,J.R. and Bradford,L.W. "Applications of scanning electron microscopy to forensic science of Jet Propulsion Laboratory." In Johari,O. and Corvin,I. (eds.). Scanning Electron Microscope Symposium. ITT. Res. Inst., Chicago, 1969, 561-568.

2223. Dewey,L.H. "Hemp." Yearbook U. S. Dept. Agricult. 1913, 1, 283-346.

2224. Dewey,L.H. "Hemp fiber losing ground, despite its valuable qualities." Yearbook U. S. Dept. Agricult. 1931, 1, 285-287.

2225. Dewey,W.L., Harris,L.S., Dennis,B., Fisher,S., Kessaris,J., Kerson,L., and Watson,J. "Some acute and chronic interactions between delta-9-THC and ethanol and between delta-9-THC and morphine in mice." Pharmacologist 1971, 13, 296.

2226. Dewey,W.L., Harris,L.S., Howes,J.F., and Kennedy,J.S. "Pharmacological effects of some active constituents of marihuana." Pharmacologist 1969, 11, 278.

2227. Dewey,W.L., Harris,L.S., Howes,J.F., Kennedy,S., and Andersen,R.N. "A pharmacological investigation of some of the peripheral effects of the constituents of marihuana." Comm. Prob. Drug Depend. 1970, 3, 6818-6826.

2228. Dewey,W.L., Harris,L.S., Howes,J.F., Kennedy,J.S., Granchelli,F.E., Pars,H.G., and Razdan,R.K. "Pharmacology of some marihuana constituents and two heterocyclic analogues." Nature 1970, 226, 1265-1267.

2229. Dewey,W.L., Harris,L.S., and Kennedy,J.S. "Some pharmacological and toxicological effects of 1-trans-delta-8- and 1-trans-delta-9-tetrahydrocannabinol in laboratory rodents." Arch. Internat'l. Pharmacodyn. Ther. 1972, 196, 133-145.

2230. Dewey,W.L., Harris,L.S., McMillan,D.E., Frankenheim,J.M., Turk,R., and Ford,R.D. "Pharmacological studies of some constituents of marihuana." Comm. Prob. Drug Depend. 1971, 2, 1692-1711.

2231. Dewey,W.L., Jenkins,J., O'Rourk,T., and Harris,L.S. "The effects of chronic administration of trans-delta-9-tetrahydrocannabinol on behavior and the cardiovascular system of dogs." Arch. Internat'l. Pharmacodyn. Ther. 1972, 198, 118-131.

2232. Dewey,W.L., Johnson,K.M., and Bloom,A.S. "Interactions of active constituents of marihuana with other drugs in the neuron." Ann. N. Y. Acad. Sci. 1976, 281, 190-197.

2233. Dewey,W.L., Kennedy,J.S., and Howes,J.F. "Some autonomic, gastrointestinal and metabolic effects of two constituents of marihuana." Fed. Proc. 1970, 29, 650.

2234. Dewey,W.L., Martin,B.R., Beckner,J.S., and Harris,L.S. "A comparison of the subcellular distribution of cannabinoids in the brains of tolerant and nontolerant dogs, rats, and mice after injecting radiolabeled delta-9-tetrahydrocannabinol." In Nahas,G.G., Paton,W.D.M., and Idanpaan-Heikkila,J.E.(eds.). Marihuana. Springer Verlag, N.Y., 1976, 349-367.

2235. Dewey,W.L., Martin,B.R., and Harris,L.S. "Chronic effects of delta-9-THC in animals: tolerance and biochemical changes." In Braude,M.C. and Szara,S. (eds.). Pharmacology of Marihuana. Raven Press, N.Y., 1976, 585-595.

2236. Dewey,W.L., Martin,B.R., Harris,L.S., and Becker,J.S. "Disposition of H^3-delta-9-tetrahydrocannabinol in brain of pregnant dogs and their fetuses." Pharmacologist 1974, 16, 260.

2237. Dewey,W.L., McMillan,D.E., Harris,L.S., and Turk,R.F. "Distribution of radioactivity in brain of tolerant and nontolerant pigeons treated with ^{3}H-delta-9-tetrahydrocannabinol." Biochem. Pharmacol. 1973, 22, 399-405.

2238. Dewey,W.L., Peng,T.C., and Harris,L.S. "The effect of 1-trans-delta-9-tetrahydrocannabinol on the hypothalamo-hypophyseal-adrenal axis of rats." Eur. J. Pharmacol. 1970, 12, 382-384.

2239. Dewey,W.L. and Turk,R.F. "The excretion and metabolism of ^{3}H-delta-9-tetrahydrocannabinol in intact and bile duct cannulated rats." Fed. Proc. 1972, 31, 506.

2240. Dewey,W.L., Yonce,L.R., Harris,L.S., Reavis, W.M., Griffin,E.D., and Newby,V.E. "Some cardiovascular effects of trans-delta-9-tetrahydrocannabinol." Pharmacologist 1970, 12, 492.

2241. De Wildeman,E. "Hemp in the Belgian Congo." (Fr.). Congo 1920, 1, 534-538.

2242. Dews,P.B. "The pediatrician and the marihuana question." Pediatrics 1970, 45, 1040-1041.

2243. Dews,P.B. "The pharmacologist's dilemma: When is a drug safe for general consumption?" Pediatrics 1970, 45, 3-6.

2244. DeZan,P., Canaff,R.F., and Bianchi,R. "Fluorimetric characteristics of some narcotic and dangerous drugs." J. Assoc. Off. Anal. Chem. 1971, 54, 925-928.

2245. Dezani,S. "On a new Indian hemp preparation." (It.). Giorn. Farm. Chim. Sci. Affin. 1924, 73, 5-6.

2246. De Zeeuw,R.A., Malingre,T.M., and Merkus,F. "Delta-1-tetrahydrocannabolic acid, an important component in the evaulation of cannabis products." J. Pharm. Pharmacol. 1972, 24, 1-6.

2247. De Zeeuw,R.A., Vree,T.B., Breimer,D.D., and van Ginneken,C.A. "Cannabivarichromene, a new cannabinoid with a propyl side chain in cannabis." Exper. 1973, 29, 260-261.

2248. De Zeeuw,R.A., Wijsbeck,J., Brimer,D.D., Vree,T.B., van Ginneken,C.A.M., and van Rossum,J.M. "Cannabinoids with a propyl side chain in cannabis: Occurrence and chromatographic behavior." Science 1972, 175, 778-779.

2249. De Zeeuw,R.A., Wijsbeek,J., and Malingre,T.H. "Interference of alkanes in the gas chromatographic analysis of cannabis products." J. Pharm. Pharmacol. 1973, 25, 21-26.

2250. Dhunjibhoy,J.E. "The role of Indian hemp in causation of insanity in India." Far East. Assoc. Trop. Med. 1966, 103, 400-407.

2251. Dhunjibhoy,J.E. and Bomb,B.S. "A brief resume of the types of insanity commonly met with in India, with a full description of 'Indian hemp insanity' peculiar to the country." J. Ment. Sci. 1930, 76, 254-264.

2252. Diaz,C.J. "Asthma and fibrosis: Considerations on hemp and feather-grass patients."(Sp.). Rev. Clin. Espan. 1966, 103, 182-188.

2253. Diaz Padron,J.A. "Diagnostic value of the 'finger stain' in the marihuana addict."(Sp.). Rev. Criminal. 1954, 1, 25-28.

2254. Diaz Padron,J.A. "Drug addiction in legal medicine."(Sp.). Criminalia 1948, 14, 189-220.

2255. DiCiommo,M. and Merline,L. "Cannabinoid-like benzoxocinols from p-menthadienes and olivetol." (It.). Gaz. Chim. Ital. 1976, 106, 967-969.

2256. Dieckhofer,K. and Goenechea,S. "Toxicity of cannabis."(Ger.). Med. Welt. 1972, 23, 779-782.

2257. Diehl,C.L. "Report on the progress of pharmacy. Urticacaea." Proc. Am. Pharmaceut. Assoc. 1903, 51, 803-804.

2258. Dietrich,H. "Addiction and hashish--from the psychiatrist's point of view."(Ger.). Munch. Med. Woch. 1971, 113, 109-116.

2259. Dietze,L. "Equating hemp products with addicting and narcotic drugs."(Ger.). Kriminalistik 1970, 24, 395-402.

2260. DiMattei,P. "Is hemp always intoxicating?" (It.). La Stampa 1965, 99, 11.

2261. DiMattei,P. "The tremendous vision of hashish."(It.). La Stampa 1967, 101, 163.

2262. Dimijian,G.G. "Differential diagnosis of emergency drug reactions." In Bourne,P.G.(ed.). Acute Drug Abuse Emergencies. Academic Press, N.Y., 1976, 3-13.

2263. Dimijian,G.G. and Radelat,F.A. "Evaluation and treatment of the suspected drug user in the emergency room." Intern. Med. 1970, 125, 162-170.

2264. Dimoff,P. "Concerning a project by Roman De Flaubert: 'The Spirale'."(Fr.). Rev. Hist. Litt. France 1948, 48, 309-335.

2265. Dingell,J.V., Miller,K.W., Heath,E.C., and Klausner,H.A. "The intracellular localization of delta-9-tetrahydrocannabinol in liver and its effects on drug metabolism in vitro." Biochem. Pharmacol. 1973, 22, 949-958.

2266. Dingell,J.V., Wilcox,H.G., and Klausner,H.A. "Biochemical interactions of delta-9-tetrahydrocannabinol." Pharmacologist 1971, 13, 296.

2267. Dinguizli,B. "Hygienic reforms to be introduced among the Moslem population of Tunisia."(Fr.). Bull. Acad. Nation. Med. 1923, 89, 235-236.

2268. Dinnerstein,A.J. "Marihuana and perceptual style: A theoretical note." Percept. Motor Skills 1968, 26, 1016-1018.

2269. Dinshaw,V. "Complete aphonia after ganja-smoking: Recovery." Ind. Med. Rec. 1896, 11, 14.

2270. Diodorus of Sicily. Histories. Harvard Univ. Press, Cambridge, Mass., 1960.

2271. Dionyssiou-Asteriou,A. and Miras,C.J. "Fluorescence of cannabinoids." J. Pharm. Pharmacol. 1975, 27, 135-137.

2272. Dioscorides. The Greek Herbal. R.T. Gunther, Oxford, 1934.

2273. Dittrich,A. "Comparison of altered states of consciousness induced by short term sensory deprivation and (-)-delta-9-trans-tetrahydrocannabinol."(Ger.). Zeit. Exp. Ang. Pschol. 1975, 22, 547-560.

2274. Dittrich,A., Battig,K., and von Zepplin,I. "Effects of (-)-delta-9-trans-tetrahydrocannabinol on memory, attention and subjective state. A double blind study." Psychopharmacol. 1973, 33, 369-376.

2275. Dittrich,A., Battig,K., Woggon,B. and von Zepplin,I. "Development of an auto-estimation scale(DAE-Scale I) for determining the effects of cannabis."(Ger.). Pharmakopsychiat. 1972, 5, 255-268.

2276. Dittrich,A., Bickel,P., Schopf,J., and Zimmer,D. "Comparison of altered states of consciousness induced by the hallucinogen (-)-delta-9-trans-tetrahydrocannabinol and N,N,-dimethyltryptamine(DMT)."(Ger.). Arch. Psychiat. Nervenkrankheit. 1976, 223, 77-87.

2277. Dittrich,A., Bickel,P., and Zimmer,D. "Effect of (-)-delta-9-trans-tetrahydrocannabinol on psychological tests."(Ger.). Psychopharmacol. 1975, 40, 351-358.

2278. Dittrich,A. and Woggon,B. "Experimental studies with delta-9-tetrahydrocannabinol in volunteers--subjective syndromes, physiological changes and after-effects." In Ban,T.A., Boissier,J.R., Gessa,G.J., Heimann,H., and Hollister,L.E.(eds.). Psychopharmacology, Sexual Disorders and Drug Abuse. North-Holland Pub. Co., Amsterdam, 1973, 701-702.

2279. Dittrich,A. and Woggon,B. "Subjective changes under the influence of (-)-delta-9-trans-tetrahydrocannabinol in cannabis-naive subjects."(Ger.). Internat'l. Pharmacopsychiat. 1974, 9, 138-151.

2280. Dittrich,J.P. "Why marihuana?" Alaska Med. 1972, 14, 11-14.

2281. Dixit,V.P., Arya,M., and Lohiya,N.K. "The effect of chronically administered cannabis extract on the female genital tract of mice and rats." Endokrinologie 1975, 66, 365-368.

2282. Dixit,V.P., and Lohiya,N.K. "Effects of cannabis extract on the response of accessory sex organs of adult male mice to testosterone." Ind. J. Physiol. Pharmacol. 1975, 19, 98-100.

2283. Dixit,V.P. and Sharma,V.P. "Mechanism of action of chronically administered cannabis extract on the female genital tract of gerbils Meriones Hurrianae." Ind. J. Physiol. Pharmacol. 1976, 20, 38-41.

2284. Dixit,V.P., Sharma,V.N., and Lohiya,N.K. "The effect of chronically administered cannabis extract on the testicular function of mice." Eur. J. Pharmacol. 1974, 26, 111-114.

2285. Dixon,W.E. "Smoking of Indian hemp and opium." Br. Med. J. 1923, 2, 1179-1180.

2286. Dixon,W.E. "The bio-chemical standardization of drugs." Pharmaceut. J. 1905, 21, 155-157.

2287. Dixon,W.E. "The bio-chemical standardization of drugs." Year-book Pharm. 1905, 1, 387-394.

2288. Dixon,W.E. "The pharmacology of cannabis indica." Br. Med. J. 1899, 2, 1354-1357.

2289. Dixon,W.E. "The pharmacology of cannabis indica." Br. Med. J. 1899, 2, 1517.

2290. Dixon,W.E. "The pharmacology of Indian hemp." Year-book Pharm. 1900, 1, 128-129.

2291. Dmochowski,J. "Quantity of oil in linseed and hemp seed during the different periods of maturation and germination as well as in the birch and linden trees during different phases of winter."(Pol.). Pol. Agr. Forest Ann. 1934, 32, 35-77.

2292. Dobell,H. "On some effects of cannabis indica." Med. Times Gaz. 1863, 2, 245-246.

2293. Dobrin,P.B. "Physiology and control of the circulation." Sex Secret. 1974, 10, 61-88.

2294. Dobrunov,L.G. "Characteristics of the growth and mineral nutrition of hemp with simultaneously maturing male and female plants."(Fr.). C. R. Acad. Sci. 1937, 14, 521-524.

2295. Dobrunov,L.G. "Competitive ability of hemp, flax and oats growing together on soils differing in fertility."(Fr.). Zeit. Pflan. Dun. Bod. 1934, 13B, 510-515.

2296. Dobrunov,L.G. "Relation of plants to the concentration of nitrogen in the nutrient solution." C. R. Acad. Sci. 1934, 3, 527-530.

2297. Doctor,R.M. and Sieveking,N.A. "A comparison of attitudes among heroin addicts, policemen, marihuana users and nondrug users about the drug addict." Internat'l. J. Addict. 1973, 8, 191-199.

2298. Doctor,R.M. and Sieveking,N.A. "Survey of attitudes toward drug addiction." Proc. Am. Psychol. Assoc. 1970, 5, 795-796.

2299. Doctor,R.M. and Sklov,M. "A cross-cultural study of attitudes about marihuana smokers." Br. J. Addict. 1973, 68, 111-115.

2300. Dodge,C.R. A Report on Flax, Hemp, Rame and Jute. Gov't. Print. Office, Washington,D.C., 1890.

2301. Dodge,C.R. A Report on the Culture of Hemp and Jute in the U.S. Gov't. Print. Office, Washington, D.C., 1896.

2302. Dodge,C.R. A Report on the Culture of Hemp in Europe. Gov't. Print. Office, Washington,D.C., 1898.

2303. Dodge,D.L. "Survey of students and drugs at the University of Notre Dame: an overview." J. Am. Coll. Hlth. Assoc. 1976, 25, 102-108.

2304. Dodson,B. "Alas, Katmandu." High Times 1974, 1, 35-39.

2305. Dohner,V. "LSD and marihuana: Where are the answers?" Science 1968, 160, 1061-1062.

2306. Dohner,V. "The pediatrician and the marihuana question." Pediatrics 1970, 45, 1039-1040.

2307. Doit,D.B. "Examination of extract of Indian hemp." Pharmaceut. J. 1922, 108, 63-64.

2308. Doktorov,V. "Application of phytoncide substance from cannabis sativa L. in experimental inflammation of the mouth cavity."(Czech.). Cesk. Stomat. 1961, 61, 81-90.

2309. Doktorov,V. "The biological action of alcoholic extracts of cannabis sativa L."(Czech.). Biologia 1961, 16, 351-358.

2310. Dolan,J.P. "A note on the use of cannabis sativa in the 17th century." J. S. Carolina Med. Assoc. 1971, 67, 424-427.

2311. Dolby,T.W. and Kleinsmith,L.J. "Effects of delta-9-tetrahydrocannabinol on the levels of cyclic adenosine 3'5'-monophosphate in mouse brain." Biochem. Pharmacol. 1974, 23, 1817-1825.

2312. Dominick,J. The Drug Bust. Light Co., Bayshore, N.Y., 1970.

2313. Domino,E.F. "Effects of delta-9-tetrahydrocannabinol and cannabinol on rat brain acetylcholine." In Nahas,G.G., Paton,W.D.M., and Idanpaan-Heikkila,J.E. (eds.). Marihuana. Springer Verlag, N.Y., 1976, 407-415.

2314. Domino,E.F. "Neuropsychopharmacologic studies of marihuana: Some synthetic and natural THC derivatives in animals and man." Ann. N. Y. Acad. Sci. 1971, 191, 166-192.

2315. Domino,E.F. "Pharmacology of madness--the hallucinogens. In Zarafonetis,C.J.D.(ed.). Drug Abuse. Lea and Febiger, Phil., 1972, 307-320.

2316. Domino,E.F. and Bartolini,A. "Effects of various psychotomimetic agents on the EEG and acetylcholine release from the cerebral cortex of brainstem transected cats." Neuropharmacol. 1972, 11, 703-713.

2317. Domino,E.F., Hardman,H.F., and Seevers,M.H. "Central nervous system actions of some synthetic tetrahydrocannabinol derivatives." Pharmacol. Rev. 1971, 23, 317-336.

2318. Domino,E.F., Hardman,H.F., and Seevers,M.H. "Some CNS actions of delta-3-tetrahydrocannabinol derivatives." Univ. Mich. Med. Ctr. J. 1970, 36, 240.

2319. Domino,E.F., Rennick,P., and Pearl,J.H. "Dose-effect relations of marihuana smoking on various physiological parameters in experienced male users." Clin. Pharmacol. Ther. 1974, 15, 514-520.

2320. Domino,E.F., Rennick,P., Pearl,J.H. "Short-term neuropsychopharmacological effects of marihuana smoking in experienced male users." In Braude,M.C. and Szara,S.(eds.). Pharmacology of Marihuana. Raven Press, N.Y., 1976, I, 393-413.

2321. Donnelly,J. "Mary Jane in action; GI's arrested in Vietnam on charges of smoking pot." Newsweek 1967, 70, 40.

2322. Donovan,J.A. "Jargon of marihuana addicts." Am. Speech 1940, 15, 336-337.

2323. Dontas,S. and Zis,P. "Experimental researches on the action of hashish." Arch. Internat'l. Pharmacodyn. Ther. 1928, 35, 30-37.

2324. Dontas,S. and Zis,P. "Narcotic action of potassium chlorate added to tobacco. (Comparison with hashish)."(Ger.). Wien. Klin. Woch. 1928, 41, 161-163.

2325. Doolittle,J. Social Life of the Chinese. Harper and Bros., N.Y., 1865.

2326. Doorenbos,N.J., Fetterman,P., Guerrero,O., Keith,E., Masoud,A., and Quimby,M.V. "Mississippi grown cannabis sativa L. Variations in the content versus age, sex, and plant part." Paper presented at American Pharmaceutical Association, Washington, D.C., 1970.

2327. Doorenbos,N.J., Fetterman,P.S., Quimby, M.W., and Turner,C.E. "Chemical differences between variants of cannabis sativa L." Proc. 31st Internat'l. Cong. Pharmaceut. Sci. 1971, 1, 101.

2328. Doorenbos,N.J., Fetterman,P.S., Quimby,M.W., and Turner,C.E. "Cultivation, extraction, and analysis of cannabis sativa L." Ann. N. Y. Acad. Sci. 1971, 191, 3-14.

2329. Doorenbos,N.J., Fetterman,P.S., Quimby,M.V., and Turner,C.E. "Morphological and chemical differences between variants of cannabis sativa L." Comm. Prob. Drug Depend. 1971, 2, 1666-1670.

2330. Doria,R. "The smokers of machona, effects and evils of the vice."(Port.). Riv. Am. Brazil 1916, 1, 64-85.

2331. Doria,R. The Smokers of Maconha.(Port.). Imprensa Officia, Bahia, Brazil, 1936.

2332. Dornbush,R.L. "Marihuana and the central nervous system." In Tinklenberg,J.R.(ed.). Marihuana and Health Hazards. Academic Press, N.Y., 1975, 103-115.

2333. Dornbush,R.L. "Marihuana and memory: Effects of smoking on storage." Trans. N. Y. Acad. Sci. 1974, 36, 94-100.

2334. Dornbush,R.L., Fink,M., and Freedman,A.M. "Marihuana, memory, and perception." Am. J. Psychiat. 1971, 128, 194-197.

2335. Dornbush,R.L. "The long-term effects of cannabis use." In Miller,L.L.(ed.). Marihuana, Effects on Human Behavior. Academic Press, N.Y., 1974, 221-231.

2336. Dornbush,R.L., Clare,G., Zaks,A., Crown,P., Volavka,J., and Fink,M. "21-day administration of marihuana in male volunteers." In Lewis,M.F.(ed.). Current Research in Marihuana. Academic Press, N.Y., 1972, 115-128.

2337. Dornbush,R.L. and Kokkevi,A. "Acute effects of cannabis on cognitive, perceptual and motor performance in chronic hashish users." Ann. N. Y. Acad. Sci. 1976, 282, 313-322.

2338. Dornbush,R.L. and Kokkevi,A. "The acute effects of various cannabis substances on cognitive, perceptual, and motor performance in very long-term hashish users." In Braude,M.C. and Szara,S.(eds.). Pharmacology of Marihuana. Raven Press, N.Y., 1976, 1, 421-429.

2339. Dorr,M. and Steinberg,H. "Effects of delta-9-tetrahydrocannabinol social behavior in mice. Comparison between two vehicles." Psychopharmacol. 1976, 47, 87-91.

2340. Dorr,M., Steinberg,H., and Shapiro,M. "Stimulation of sexual behavior in rats by a benzodioxane derivative." Exper. 1975, 31, 91-93.

2341. Dorrance,D., Janiger,O., and Teplitz,R.L. "In vivo effects of illicit hallucinogens on human lymphocyte chromosomes." J.A.M.A. 1970, 212, 1488-1491.

2342. Dorvault,F. "On hashish."(Fr.). Bull. Gen. Ther. Med. Chir. Obstet. Pharmaceut. 1848, 35, 360-366.

2343. Dosick,M.L. Drug Abuse In Terms of the Functions of Social Deviance and Social Control. Southern Illinois University Delinquency Study Project, Carbondale, Ill., 1967.

2344. Dott,A.B. "Effect of marihuana on risk acceptance in an automotive simulator." In Singh,J.M. and Lal,H.(eds.). Drug Addiction. Stratton Intercontinental Medical Book Corp., N.Y., 1974, 4, 55-64.

2345. Dott,D.B. "Examination of extract of Indian hemp." Pharmaceut. J. Pharmacist 1922, 108, 63-64.

2346. Dotti,A. "Drug dependence in adolescence." (It.). Neuropsichiat. Infant 1970, 110, 384-400.

2347. Douady,D. "Remarks on the protection of schools and universities."(Fr.). Bull. Acad. Nat'l. Med. 1969, 153, 534-540.

2348. Dougelevich,S. "Stability of bast fiber against the action of micro-organisms occurring in nature."(Rus.). Tekstil Pam. 1960, 9, 9.

2349. Douglas,M. Dealing. Or the Berkeley-to Boston Forty-Brick Lost-Bag Blues. Bantam Books, N.Y., 1972.

2350. Douglas,S. "On the use of Indian hemp in chorea." Edinburgh Med. J. 1869, 4, 777-785.

2351. Douthwaite,A.H. "Hashish." Guy's Hosp. Gaz. 1948, 62, 138-141.

2352. Douthwaite,A.H. "Cannabis indica as a sedative in the ulcer of the duodenum."(Sp.). Prensa Med. Argentina 1948, 35, 812.

2353. Do Valley,J.R. "Pharmacological approaches to the study of the cannabis problem." Internat'l. J. Addict. 1969, 4, 623-647.

2354. Downer,R.L.E. "Cannabis indica in smoking tobacco." Br. Med. J. 1923, 2, 521.

2355. Downing,D.F. "Psychotomimetic compounds. V. Tetrahydrocannabinols." In Gordon,M.(ed.). Psychopharmacological Agents. Academic Press, N.Y., 1964, 1, 585-591.

2356. Downing,D.F. "The chemistry of the psychotomimetic substances." Quart. Rev. 1962, 16, 133-162.

2357. Drachler,D.H. "Hashish and the transmission of hepatitis." N. Eng. J. Med. 1975, 293, 667.

2358. Dragendorff,G. The Medicinal Plants of Different Peoples and Different Times.(Ger.). F. Enke, Stuttgart, 1898.

2359. Drangendorff,G. and Marquiss,A. "Note on the active principle of cannabis indica."(Ger.). Year-book of Pharm. 1878, 1, 248.

2360. Draghetti,A. "The fertilizing value of hemp retting water."(It.). Staz. Sper. Ag. It. 1916, 49, 324-334.

2361. Drake,W.D. The Cultivator's Handbook of Marihuana. Agrarian Reform Co., Eugene, Oregon, 1970.

2362. Drake,W.D. The International Cultivator's Handbook. And/Or Press, Berekeley, Cal., 1972.

2363. Drapkin,I.. and Landau,S.F. "Drug offenders in Israel. A survey." Br. J. Criminol. 1966, 6, 376-390.

2364. Dren,A.T. "Preclinical neuropharmacology of three nitrogen-containing heterocyclic benzopyrans derived from the cannabinoid nucleus." In Cohen,S. and Stilman,R.(eds.). Therapeutic Potential of Marihuana. Plenum Press, N.Y., 1976, 439-456.

2365. Dreury,P.H. "Some psychiatric aspects of marihuana intoxication." Psychiat. Quart. 1936, 10, 232-234.

2366. Drew,W.G., Kiplinger,G.F., Miller,L.L., and Marx,M. "Effects of propranolol on marihuana-induced cognitive dysfunctioning." Clin. Pharmacol. Ther. 1972, 4, 526-533.

2367. Drew,W.G., and Miller,L.L. "Cannabis: Neural mechanisms and behavior--a theoretical review." Pharmacol. 1974, 11, 12-32.

2368. Drew,W.G. and Miller,L.L. "Differential effects of delta-9-THC on locomotor behavior in activity-wheel habituated and nonhabituated rats." Pharmacol. 1973, 9, 41-51.

2369. Drew,W.G., Miller,L.L., Ables,B.M., Marx,D., and Marx,M. "Studies on cognitive function in two samples of temporarily drug-free chronic marihuana users." Comm. Prob. Drug Depend. 1972, 1, 758-779.

2370. Drew,W.G., Miller,L.L., and Baugh,E.L. "Effects of delta-9-THC, LSD-25 and scopolamine on continuous, spontaneous alternation in the Y-maze." Psychopharmacol. 1973, 32, 171-182.

2371. Drew,W.G., Miller,L.L., and Wikler,A. "Effect of delta-9-THC on the open-field activity of the rat." Psychopharmacol. 1972, 23, 289-299.

2372. Drew,W.G. and Slagel,D.E. "Delta-9-THC: Selective impairment of corticosterone uptake by limbic structures of the rat." Neuropharmacol. 1973, 12, 909-914.

2373. Drewnoswski,A. and Gray,J.A. "Influence of delta-9-tetrahydrocannabinol on partial reinforcement effects." Psychopharmacol. 1975, 43, 233-237.

2374. Drewry,P.H. "Some psychiatric aspects of marihuana intoxication." Psychiat. Quart. 1936, 10, 232-242.

2375. Drug Abuse Council. Survey of City/County Drug Abuse Activities: 1972. Drug Abuse Council Inc., Washington, D.C., 1973.

2376. Drug Abuse Council. Survey of Drug Abuse Activities: 1972. Drug Abuse Council Inc., Washington, D.C., 1973.

2377. Drug Abuse Council. "The cannabis controversy." Drug Enforce. 1974, 1, 22-27.

2378. Dube,K.C. "Drug abuse in Northern India." Bull. Narc. 1972, 24, 49-53.

2379. Dube,K.C. "Patterns of drug abuse in India." In Btesh,S.(ed.). Drug Abuse. Plenum Press, N.Y., 1972, 123-127.

2380. Dube,K.C. and Handa,S.K. "Drug use in health and mental illness in an Indian population." Br. J. Psychiat. 1971, 118, 345-346.

2381. Dube,K.C., Jain,S.C., Basu,A.K., and Kumar,N. "Patterns of the drug habit in hospitalized psychiatric patients." Bull. Narc. 1975, 27, 1-10.

2382. Dubinsky,B., Robichaud,R.C., and Goldberg,M.E. "Effects of (-)-delta-9-trans-tetrahydrocannabinol and its selectivity in several models of aggressive behavior." Pharmacol. 1973, 9, 204-216.

2383. Dubinsky,B., Robichaud,R.C., and Goldberg,M. "Effects of (-)-delta-9-trans-tetrahydrocannabinol in several animal models of aggression." Pharmacologist 1973, 32, 725.

2384. Dubinsky,B., Robichaud,R.C., and Goldberg,M.E. "Inhibitory effects of (-)-delta-9-trans-tetrahydrocannabinol and its selectivity in several models of aggressive behavior." Comm. Prob. Drug Depend. 1972, 1, 813-830.

2385. Dubois,L. "John Finlator. The BNDD's former chief speaks frankly on pot, narcs, and other subjects." High Times 1974, 1, 19-21.

2386. Du Chaillou,P.B. Explorations and Adventures in Equatorial Africa. John Murray, London, 1861.

2387. Duckman,R.H. "Marihuana--how it affects visual perception and memory." J. Am. Optom. Assoc. 1972, 43, 160-163.

2388. Duggan,J.F. and Aust,M. "Marihuana psychosis."(Sp.). Act. Psiquiat. Psicol. Amer. Lat. 1976, 22, 63-70.

2389. Duke,E.L. and Reimann,B.E.F. "The extractability of the Duquenois-positive cannabinoids." Toxicol. 1973, 1, 289-300.

2390. Dukerley,I. "Note on the diferences exhibited by common hemp, known in Algeria as kif and tekrouri." (Fr.). Bull. Soc. Bot. 1866, 13, 401-406.

2391. Dumas,A. The Count of Monte Cristo. Spencer Press, N.Y., 1944.

2392. Duncan,D.F. "Marihuana and heroin: a study of initiation of drug use by heroin addicts." Br. J. Addict. 1975, 70, 192-197.

2393. Duncan,D.P. "Hashish--or cannabis indica." South. Pract. 1880, 2, 203-205.

2394. Dunn,M. and Davis,R. "The perceived effects of marihuana on spinal cord injured males." Paraplegia 1974, 12, 75.

2395. Dunncliff,H.B. "Colorimetric method for estimating the narcotic power of hemp drugs." Analyst 1943, 68, 70-74.

2396. Dunstan,W.R. and Henry,T.A. "On oxycannabin from Indian hemp." Proc. Chem. Soc. 1898, 14, 44-45.

2397. Dunsworth,F.A. "Marihuana research." Can. Med. Assoc. J. 1973, 108, 825.

2398. DuPont,R.L. "Just what can you tell your patients about marihuana?" Med. Times 1976, 104, 120-123.

2399. DuPont,R.L. "Marihuana." *Science* 1976, *192*, 647-649.

2400. DuPont,R.L. "Marihuana: An issue comes of age." In Braude,M.C. and Szara,S.(eds.). *Pharmacology of Marihuana*. Raven Press, N.Y., 1, 3-9.

2401. Duquenois,P. "A test for the identification of hashish and hemp through microchromatography."(Fr.). *Ann. Med. Leg. Criminol.* 1954, *34*, 224-225.

2402. Duquenois,P. "Chemical and physiological identification of Indian hemp." *Bull. Narc.* 1950, *2*, 30-33.

2403. Duquenois,P. "Effects of cannabis indica on small fish; physiological experiments."(Fr.). *Bull. Sci. Pharmacol.* 1939, *46*, 222-231.

2404. Duquenois,P. "Factor in the chemical and physiological identification of Indian hemp."(Fr.). *Prod. Pharmaceut.* 1947, *2*, 535-538.

2405. Duquenois,P. and Mustapha Negm,H. "A characteristic color-reaction of hashish."(Fr.). *Bull. Sci. Pharmacol.* 1938, *45*, 203-205.

2406. Duquenois,P. and Mustapha Negm,H. "Contribution to the identification and dosage of sensorial drugs in internal organs."(Fr.). *Ann. Med. Leg. Criminol.* 1938, *18*, 485-506.

2407. Duquenois,P. and Mustapha Negm,H. "Identification and dosage of cannabis indica."(Fr.). *J. Egypt. Med. Assoc.* 1938, *21*, 224-227.

2408. Durand,P. "Note on the Sahara."(Fr.). *Arch. Inst. Pasteur* 1925, *24*, 469-504.

2409. Durand,P. "Note on the Sahara."(Fr.). *Arch. Inst. Pasteur* 1928, *27*, 442.

2410. Durandina,A.I. "Chronic hashish intoxication in dogs produces several physiological symptoms which occur in waves. Neurophysiological changes are similar to those of toxic encephalopathy."(Rus.). *Ref. Zh. Otd. Vyp. Farmakol. Khim. Sred. Toksikol.* 1971, *3*, 843.

2411. Durandina,A.I. "Hashish psychosis lasts several days to six months manifesting a number of symptoms which follow various time courses during the psychotic episode." *Ref. Zh. Otd. Vyp. Farmakol. Khim. Sred. Toksikol.* 1971, *3*, 846.

2412. Durandina,A.I. "Pathomorphological changes in the internal organs in acute and chronic experimental hashish intoxication."(Rus.). Ref. Zh. Otd. Vyp. Farmakol Khim. Sred. Toksikol. 1971, 3, 845.

2413. Durandina,A.I. "Physiological and morphological changes in dogs following acute hashish poisoning. Gross symptoms are similar to those of toxic encephalopathy." (Rus.). Ref. Zh. Otd. Vyp. Farmakol. Khim. Sred. Toksikol.

2414. Durandina,A.I. and Romasendko,V.A. "Functional and morphological changes in experimental acute poisoning by resinous substances prepared from Yujonchuisk cannabis." Bull. Narc. 1971, 23, 1-7.

2415. Durandina,A.I. and Romasenko,V.A. "Functional and morphological disorders in chronic poisoning by resinous substances prepared from Yujonchuisk cannabis. Part 2." Bull. Narc. 1972, 24, 31-37.

2416. Durieux,G.P. Extension of Cannabis Sativa Intoxication.(Fr.). Univ. Paris, Paris, 1953.

2417. Dussen,W. and Metzner,R. "The long-term effects of psychedelics." Clin. Toxicol. 1968, 1, 227-234.

2418. Duster,T. The Legislation of Morality; Law, Drugs, and Moral Judgment. Free Press, N.Y., 1970.

2419. Du Toit,B.M. "Cannabis sativa in sub-Saharan Africa." S. Af. J. Sci. 1974, 70, 266-270.

2420. Du Toit,B.M. "Continuity and change in cannabis use by Africans in South Africa." J. Asian Af. Stud. 1976, 11, 1-16.

2421. Du Toit,B.M. "Dagga: The history and ethnographic setting of cannabis sativa in Southern Africa." In Rubin,V.(ed.). Cannabis and Culture. Mouton, The Hague, 1975, 81-119.

2422. Du Toit,B.M.(ed.). Drugs, Rituals and Altered States of Consciousness. A.A. Balkema, Rotterdam, 1977.

2423. Du Toit,B.M. "Ethnicity and patterning in South African drug use." In Du Toit,B.M.(ed.). Drugs, Rituals and Altered States of Consciousness. A.A. Balkema, Rotterdam, 1977, 75-99.

2424. Du Toit,B.M. "Historical and cultural factors influencing cannabis use among Indians in South Africa." J. Psychedel. Drugs 1977, 9, 235-246.

2425. Dutt,S. "Indian cannabis sativa and essential oils derived from the same." Ind. Soap J. 1957, 22, 242-246.

2426. Dutt,U.D. The Materia Medica of the Hindus. Dwarkanath Mukerjee, Calcutta, 1900.

2427. Dvorak,E.J. "A longitudinal study of nonmedical drug use among university students--a brief survey." Paper presented at American College Health Association, San Francisco, 1971.

2428. Dwarakanath,C. "Use of opium and cannabis in the traditional systems of medicine in India." Bull. Narc. 1965, 17, 15-19.

2429. Dwivedi,C. and Harbison,R.D. "Anticonvulsant activities of delta-8- and delta-9-tetrahydrocannabinol and uridine." Toxicol. Appl. Pharmacol. 1975, 31, 452-458.

2430. Dykstra,L. and McMillan,D.E. "Shock-intensity adjustment by squirrel monkeys under a titration procedure following administration of morphine, nalorphine, pentazocine, propoxyphene, delta-8-tetrahydrocannabinol or chlorpromazine." Fed. Proc. 1974, 33, 516.

2431. Dykstra,L.A., McMillan,D.E., and Harris,L.S. "Effects of delta-9-THC and a water soluble ester of delta-9-THC on schedule-controlled behavior." Pharmacol. Biochem. Behav. 1975, 3, 29-32.

2432. Dziak,J., Chi,C., Sprecher,R., and Cavero,I. "Effects of delta-9-tetrahydrocannabinol on the dog hind limb vasculature." Fed. Proc. 1973, 32, 755.

E

2433. Earley,K.S. "Sex and marihuana." Harper's Baz. 1976, 109, 66.

2434. Easterfield,T.H. and Wood,T.B. "The constituents of Indian hemp resin." Proc. Cam. Phil. Soc. 1896, 9, 144-148.

2435. Eaton,B.J. Identifying and Controlling Wild Hemp. Bulletin of Agricultural Experiment Station, Kansas State University of Agriculture and Applied Science, Lawrence, Kansas, 1972.

2436. Eaton,B.J., Hartowicz,L.E., Latta,R.P., Knutson,H., Paulsen,A., and Eshbaugh,E. Controlling Wild Hemp. Bulletin of Agricultural Experiment Station, Kansas State University of Agriculture and Applied Science, Lawrence, Kansas, 1972.

2437. Eaton,C. A History of the Old South. MacMillan Co., N.Y., 1966.

2438. Ebel,H.C., Katz,D., and Rosen,A. "Effect of a marihuana drug education program: Comparison of faculty-elicited and student-elicited data." J. Drug Educat. 1975, 5, 77-85.

2439. Eberland,W. The Local Cultures of South and East China. E.J. Brill, Leiden, 1968.

2440. Ebin,D. The Drug Experience. Grove Press, N.Y., 1965.

2441. Echeverria,I.R. "A point of view of two problems: I. Student protest. II. Marihuana."(Sp.). Univ. Med. 1972, 14, 15-24.

2442. Eck,F. "Hashish in the classroom?"(Ger.). Concepte 1967, 3, 1-7.

2443. Eckerman,W.C., Bates,J.D., Rachel,J.V., and Poole,W.K. Drug Usage and Arrest Charges, A Study of Drug Usage and Arrest Charges Among Arrestees in Six Metropolitan Areas of the United States. Gov't. Print. Office, Washington, D.C., 1971.

2444. Eckhardt,W. "Drugs, peace and freedom.." J. Human Relat. 1971, 19, 311-318.

2445. Eckler,C.R. and Miller,F.A. "A study of American grown cannabis in comparison with samples from various other sources." Am. J. Pharm. 1912, 84, 488-495.

2446. Eckler,C.R. and Miller,F.A. "On the deterioration of crude Indian cannabis." J.A.P.A. 1917, 6, 872-875.

2447. Eddy,N.B., Halbach,H., Harris,I., and Seevers,M.H. "Drug dependence: its significance and characteristics." Bull. W.H.O. 1965, 32, 721-733.

2448. Edelstein,E. "Doubts on the latest reports concerning hashish."(Heb.). Harefuah 1971, 81, 391.

2449. Eden,C.K. "One more analysis of marihuana and society." Mil. Pol. J. 1971, 21, 22-24.

2450. Edery,H. "Psychopharmacological actions of cannabinoids in experimental animals." Toxicon 1970, 8, 162-163.

2451. Edery,H. and Gottesfield,Z. "The gamma-aminobutyric acid system in rat cerebellum during cannabinoid-induced cateleptoid state." Br. J. Pharmacol. 1975, 54, 406-408.

2452. Edery,H., Grunfeld,Y., Ben-Zvi,Z., and Mechoulam,R. "Structural requirements for cannabinoid activity." Ann. N. Y. Acad. Sci. 1971, 191, 40-54.

2453. Edery,H., Grunfeld,Y., Porath,G., Ben-Zvi, Z., Shani,A., and Mechoulam,R. "Structure-activity relationships in the tetrahydrocannabinol series. Modifications on the aromatic ring and on the side-chain." Arxneim. Forsch. 1972, 22, 1995-2003.

2454. Edes,R.T. "Cannabis indica." Boston Med. Surg. J. 1893, 129, 273.

2455. Edmondson,W.R. "The narcotics addiction epidemic." Crisis 1972, 74, 79-82.

2456. Edmundson,W.F., Davies,J.E., Acker,J.D., and Myer,B. "Patterns of drug abuse epidemiology in prisoners." Indust. Med. 1972, 41, 15-19.

2457. Edwards,A.E., Bloom,M.H., and Cohen,S. "The psychedelics: Love or hostility potion?" Psychol. Rep. 1969, 24, 843-846.

2458. Edwards,G. "An anthology of Indian hemp." Br. Med. J. 1967, 2, 228-229.

2459. Edwards,G. "Cannabis and the criteria for legalization of a currently prohibited recreational drug: Ground for a debate." Act. Psychiat. Scand. 1974, 251, 1-62.

2460. Edwards,G. "Cannabis and the psychiatric position." In Graham,J.D.P.(ed.). Cannabis and Health. Academic Press, N.Y., 1976, 321-343.

2461. Edwards,G. "The problem of cannabis dependence." Practitioner 1968, 200, 226-233.

2462. Edwards,R. "Telltale trash; R. Edwards case." Time 1969, 94, 54.

2463. Eells,K. "A survey of student practices and attitudes with respect to marihuana and LSD." Internat'l. J. Addict. 1969, 4, 259.

2464. Eells,K. "Marihuana and LSD: A survey of one college campus." J. Counsel. Psychol. 1968, 15, 459-467.

2465. Efron,D.H. "Cannabis(marihuana) research." Comm. Prob. Drug Depend. 1967, 2, 4829-4831.

2466. Efron,D.H. "Marihuana." U.S. Pub. Hlth. Serv. 1967, 1836, 1269-1271.

2467. Efron,D.H. "Marihuana: a few problems." In Efron,D.H., Cole,J.O., Levine,J., and Wittenborn,J.R. (eds.). Psychopharmacology. Gov't. Print. Office, Washington, D.C., 1967, 1269-1271.

2468. Efron,D.H.(ed.). Psychotomimetic Drugs. Raven Press, N.Y., 1970.

2469. Egan,S.M., Graham,J.D.P. and Lewis, B. "The uptake of tritiated delta-1-tetrahydrocannabinol by the isolated vas deferens of the rat." Br. J. Pharmacol. 1976, 56, 413-416.

2470. Egasse,E. "Indian hemp."(Fr.). Bull. Gen. Ther. Med. Chirurg. 1890, 118, 119-128, 170-176, 226-233.

2471. Egasse,E. "New drugs: Indian hemp, orexine, pyrodine."(Fr.). Bull. Gen. Ther. Med. Chirurg. 1890, 118, 351-367.

2472. Egun,E. "The effects of cannabis from the horse's mouth." East Af. J. Pharmacol. Pharmaceut. Sci. 1971, 1, 73-75.

2473. Egypt. Committee for the Investigation of Hashish Consumption in Egypt. Hashish Consumption in Egypt. I.(Arab.). Nat'l. Center for Social and Criminological Research, Cairo, 1960.

2474. Egypt. Committee for the Investigation of Hashish Consumption in Egypt. Hashish Consumption in Egypt. II. Hashish Users in Cairo City: A Pilot Study. (Arab.). Nat'l. Center for Social and Criminological Research, Cairo, 1964.

2475. Egypt. Government Central Narcotics Intelligence Bureau. Annual Report on Hashish for 1944. Central Narcotics Intelligence Bureau, Cairo, 1945.

2476. Ehrhardt,H.E. "Drug abuse in Europe: Medical and legal aspects." In Keup,W.(ed.). Drug Abuse, Current Concepts and Research. C.C. Thomas, Springfield, Ill., 1972, 27-35.

2477. Ehrlich,D.A. "Standard marihuana." Sci. News 1967, 91, 461.

2478. Eichholtz,F. "Central stimulants of the adrenalin-ephedrine group."(Ger.). Ang. Chem. 1941, 53, 517-522.

2479. Einstein,R., Hughes,I.E., and Hindmarch,I. "Patterns of use of alcohol, cannabis and tobacco in a student population." Br. J. Addict. 1975, 70, 145-150.

2480. Einstein,S. Beyond Drugs. Pergamon Press, N.Y., 1975.

2481. Eisenberg,H. "Why some of your colleagues are going to pot." Med. Econ. 1972, 49, 96-103.

2482. Ek,N.A., Lonberg,E., Maehly,A.C., and Stromberg,L. "Cannabinoid content of fifty seized hashish samples." J. Forens. Sci. 1972, 17, 456-459.

2483. El-Darawy,Z.I., Abu-Eitah,A., and Mobarak,Z.M. "Studies on hashish. Part 5: Identification of cannabidiol and cannabidiolic acid by ultraviolet spectrophotometry." Pharmazie 1973, 28, 129-133.

2484. El-Darawy,Z.I., Ali,M.I., and Mobarak,Z.M. "Studies on hashish. IV. Color reactions of cannabinols." Qual. Plant. Mater. Veg. 1972, 22, 7-13.

2485. El-Darawy,Z.I., Rizek,A.M., Hammoud,F.M., and Mobarak,Z.M. "Studies on hashish. II. Effect of heat on cannabinols." Ind. J. Appl. Chem. 1972, 35, 9.

2486. El-Darawy,Z.I., Rizek,A.M., and Mobarak,Z.M. "Studies on hashish. III. Colorimetric determination of cannabinols." Diss. Pharm. Pharmacol. 1972, 24, 313-319.

2487. El-Darawy,Z.I., Roushdy,M.I., Rizek,A.M., Hammouda,F.M., and Mobarak,Z.M. "Studies on hashish. I Isolation and identification of cannabinols and effect of certain factors." Qual. Plant. Mater. Veg. 1972, 21, 311-325.

2488. Eldridge,W.B. Narcotics and the Law: A Critique of the American Experiments in Narcotic Drug Control. New York Univ. Press, N.Y., 1962.

2489. Elejalde,B.R. "Marihuana and genetic studies in Colombia: The problem in the city and in the country." In Rubin,V.(ed.). Cannabis and Culture. Mouton, The Hague, 1975, 327-345.

2490. El-Ferlay,F.S., Elsohly,M.A., Boeren,E.G., and Turner,C.E. "Crystal and molecular structure of cannabispiran and its correlation to dehydrocannabis-piran." Tetrahedron 1977, 33, 2373-2378.

2491. El-Feraly,F.S. and Turner,C.E. "Alkaloids of cannabis sativa leaves." Phytochemistry 1975, 14, 2304.

2492. El-Feraly,F.S. and Turner,C.E. "The isolation and characterization of the alkaloid cannabisativine from the leaves of a Thailand variant of cannabis sativa L. " U.N. Secretariat 1975, 1, 1-6.

2493. El-Ghamravy,M.A.and Abou Zeid,Y.M. "Reaction to cannabis resin with aldehydes and certain ketones." Proc. Pharmaceut. Soc. Egypt 1952, 34, 49-61.

2494. El Hadka,A.A. "Forty years of wrestling against narcotics in the United Arab Republic." Bull. Narc. 1965, 17, 1-11.

2495. Ellingstad,U.S., McFarling,L.H., and Struckman,D.L. Alcohol, Marihuana and Risk Taking. Nat'l. Technical Information Service, Springfield, Virginia, 1974.

2496. Ellis,W.G. "The amok of the Malays." J. Ment. Sci. 1893, 39, 325-338.

2497. Ells,K.A. "A survey of student practices and attitudes with respect of marihuana and LSD." Internat'l. J. Addict. 1969, 4, 259.

2498. El Maghrabi,S.Z. Hashish(Cannabis) Consumption--a Psycho-social Study in Egypt.(Arab.). Dar el Maaref, Cairo, 1962.

2499. El Mahi,T. "Picture of the hashish smoker." (Arab.). Salud Mundial 1960, 13, 24-25.

2500. Elshohly,M.A., El-Feraly,F.S., and Turner,C.E. "Isolation and characterization of (+)-cannabitriol and (-)-10-ethoxy-9-hydroxy-delta-6-alpha(10-alpha)-tetrahydrocannabinol: Two new cannabinoids from cannabis sativa L. extract." Lloydia 1977, 40, 275-280.

2501. Elsmore,T.F. "Effects of delta-9-tetrahydrocannabinol on temporal and auditory discrimination performance of monkeys." Psychopharmacol. 1972, 26, 62-72.

2502. Elsmore,T.F. "The role of reinforcement loss in tolerance to chronic delta-9-tetrahydrocannabinol effects on operant behavior of rhesus monkeys." Pharmacol. Biochem. Behav. 1976, 5, 123-128.

2503. Elsmore,T.F. and Fletcher,G.V. "Delta-9-tetrahydrocannabinol: Aversive effects in rat at high doses." Science 1972, 175, 911-912.

2504. Elsmore,T.F. and Manning,F.J. "Time course and dose-response effects of orally administered delta-9-THC on interval schedule performance of the rat." Life Sci. 1974, 15, 481-489.

2505. El-Sourogy,M., Malek,A.Y., Ibrahim,H.H., Farag,A., and El-Shihy,A. "The effect of cannabis indica on carbohydrate metabolism in rabbits." J. Egypt. Med. Assoc. 1966, 49, 626-628.

2506. Ely,D.L., Henry,J.P., and Jarosz,J. "Effects of marihuana on behavior patterns and social roles in colonies of CBA mice." Behav. Biol. 1975, 13, 263-276.

2507. El-Yousef,M.K., Janowsky,D.S., Davis,J.M., and Rosenblatt,J.E. "Induction of severe depression by physostigmine in marihuana intoxicated individuals." Br. J. Addict. 1973, 68, 321-325.

2508. Emboden,W.A. "A botanical history of the genus cannabis with reference to legislation." Cal. Attorn. Crim. Just. Forum 1974, 5, 1-5.

2509. Emboden,W.A. "Cannabis--a polytypic genus." Econ. Bot. 1974, 28, 304-310.

2510. Emboden,W.A. "Ritual use of cannabis sativa L.: A historical-ethnographic survey." In Furst,P.T.(ed.). Flesh of the Gods; The Ritual Use of Hallucinogens. Praeger, N.Y., 1974.

2511. Emmett,G.C. "Synthesis of 6-hydroxy-8,9-dihydrocannabidiol." Diss. Abs. 1974, 34, 4874.

2512. End,D., Carchman,R.A., Thoursen,K., Dewey, W.L., and Harris,L.S. "The uptake and distribution of (^{3}H)-delta-9-tetrahydrocannabinol in cultured neural and glial cells." Pharmacologist 1976, 18, 295.

2513. End,D., Thoursen,K., Dewey,W.L., and Carchman,R.A. "A comparative study of the disposition of (-)-delta-9-tetrahydrocannabinol in neuroblastoma and glioma cells in tissue culture: relation to cellular impairment." Mol. Pharmacol. 1977, 13, 864-871.

2514. Englebrecht,L. "Differences in maturation of male and female hemp plants in relation to hormonal regulation."(Pol.). Inst. Sadown. Skiern. 1973, 3, 389-397.

2515. Engler,L.F., Ho,B.T., and Taylor,D. "The effects of (-)-delta-9-tetrahydrocannabinol on reserpine-induced hypothermia in rats." Br. J. Pharmacol. 1973, 49, 243-252.

2516. English,G.E. and Tori,C.A. "Psychological characteristics of drug abuse clients seen in a community mental health center." J. Commun. Psychol. 1973, 1, 403-407.

2517. Entin,E.E. and Goldzung,P.J. "Residual effects of marihuana usage on learning and memory." Psychol. Rec. 1973, 23, 169-178.

2518. Erdmann,G., Just,W.W., Thel,S., Werner,G., and Wiechmann,M. "Comparative autoradiographic and metabolic study of delta-8- and delta-9-tetrahydrocannabinol in the brain of the marmoset Callithrix jacchus." Psychopharmacol. 1976, 47, 53-58.

2519. Erickson,P.G. "Deterrence and deviance: the example of cannabis prohibition." J. Crim. Law Criminol. 1976, 67, 222-232.

2520. Ertel,R., Vollmer,R.R. and Cavero,I. "Mechanistic study of the cardiovascular effects of (-)-delta-9-trans-tetrahydrocannabinol in alpha-chloralose anesthetized cats." Pharmacologist 1973, 15, 200.

2521. Eskes,D., Verwey,A.M.A., and Witte,A.H. "Thin-layer and gas chromatographic analysis of hashish samples containing opium." Bull. Narc. 1973, 25, 41-47.

2522. Esman,A.H. "Drug use by adolescents: Some valuative and technical implications." Psychoanal. Forum 1967, 2, 340.

2523. Esquivel Medina,R., Gonzales,G., and Miguel,E. "Marihuana, a special study of its problems from their clinical, psychopathological, experimental and medico-legal aspects."(Sp.). Rev. Med. Yucatan 1938, 19, 265-274.

2524. Esse,J. and Kahn,M. "An analysis of hallucinogenic drug use." Paper presented at Southeast. Psychol. Assoc. Atlanta, 1972.

2525. Estevez,V.S., Englert,L.F., and Ho, B.T. "A new methylated metabolite of (-)-11-hydroxy-delta-8-tetrahydrocannabinol in rats." Res. Commun. Chem. Pathol. Pharmacol. 1973, 6, 821-827.

2526. Estevez,V.S., Englert,L.F., Ho,B.T. "Effect of SKF-525A on the metabolism of (-)-delta-9-tetrahydrocannabinol in the rat brain and liver." Res. Commun. Chem. Pathol. Pharmacol. 1974, 8, 389-392.

2527. Etzioni,A. "America's social frontiers; why not smoke pot?" Current 1968, 95, 38-41.

2528. Evang,K. "Abuse of drugs."(Norweg.). T. Norsk. Laegeforen. 1966, 86, 1502-1503.

2529. Evang,K. "Narcotic problems."(Norweg.). T. Norsk. Laegeforen. 1969, 89, 545-549.

2530. Evans,M., Harbison,R.D., Brown,D.J., and Forney,R.B. "Stimulant action of delta-9-tetrahydrocannabinol in mice." Psychopharmacol. 1976, 50, 245-250.

2531. Evans,M.A., Martz,R., Lemberger,L., Rodda, B.E., and Forney,R.B. "Clinical effects of marihuana dextro-amphetamine combination." Pharmacologist 1974, 16, 281.

2532. Evans,M.A., Martz,R., Lemberger,L., Rodda, B.E., and Forney,R.B. "Effects of marihuana-dextro-amphetamine combination." Clin. Pharmacol. Ther. 1976, 20, 350-358.

2533. Evans,M.A., Martz,R., Rodda,B.E., Brown, D.J., Kiplinger,G.F., Lemberger,L., and Forney,R.B. "Impairment of performance with low doses of marihuana." Clin. Pharmacol. Ther. 1973, 14, 136-140.

2534. Evans,M.A., Stevens,S., and Samuel,P. "A random survey of cannabis use in young people." Br. J. Addict. 1974, 69, 231-236.

2535. Evans,M.R. "Cannabis and cerebral atrophy." R. Soc. Hlth. 1974, 94, 15-18.

2536. Evans,W.O. and Evans,M.E. "A neutral language for the drug scene." In Wittenborn,J.R., Smith,J.P., and Wittenborn,S.A.(eds.). Communication and Drug Abuse. C.C. Thomas, Springfield, Ill., 1970, 109-132.

2537. Everingham,D. "Doctors and cannabis." Med. J. Aust. 1972, 1, 87.

2538. Ewens,G.F.W. "Insantiy following the use of Indian hemp." Ind. Med. Gaz. 1904, 39, 401-413.

2539. Ewens,G.F.W. Insanity in India.(Its Symptoms and Diagnosis. With Reference to the Relation of Crime and Insanity.) Thacker, Spink and Co., Calcutta, 1908.

2540. Ewing,J.A. "Students, sex and marihuana." Med. Aspects Human Sex. 1972, 7, 101-117.

2541. Ewing,J.A. "Why students 'turn on', marihuana and other drug use in an undergraduate male population." Paper presented at 2nd Internat'l. Cong. Social Psychiatry, London, 1969.

2542. Ewing,J.A., Rouse,B.A., Keeler,M.H., and Blackwell,W.E. "Why students 'turn on', marihuana and other drug use in an undergraduate male population." Br. J. Social Psychiat. 1970, 4, 255-265.

2543. Ey,H. and Mignot,H. "Psychopathology of J. Moreau(de Tours)."(Fr.). Ann. Med.-Psychol. 1947, 105, 225-241.

F

2544. Faber,S.J. Marihuana: If the Cops Come, Eat This Book. Good Life Press, Burbank, Cal., 1973.

2545. Fagerberg,S. "A comparative study of drug use patterns in three academic settings, university, community college and high schools." J. Alcohol Drug Educat. 1975, 20, 27-34.

2546. Fagerberg,S., Young,M., Sanders,L., McGoskill,C., Leardon,R., and Beach,L. "Illicit drug use in a Florida country." J. Alcohol Drug Educat. 1973, 18, 9-17.

2547. Fago,D.P. and Sedlacek,W.E. A Comparison of Freshmen and Transfer Student Attitudes and Behavior Toward Drugs. Counselling Center, University of Maryland, 1974.

2548. Fago,D.P. and Sedlacek,W.F. Sex Differences in University Freshmen Attitudes and Behavior Toward Drugs: A Three Year Comparison. Counselling Center, University of Maryland, 1974.

2549. Fago,D.P. and Sedlacek,W.E. Trends in University Student Attitudes and Behavior Toward Drugs. Counselling Center, University of Maryland, 1973.

2550. Fahmy,I.R. "Some observations on cannabis sativa L. cultivated in Egypt."(Arab.). Rep. Pharmaceut. Soc. Egypt. 1932, 7, 28-32.

2551. Fahmy,I.R. "Some observations on the action and methods of standardization of hashish."(Arab.). J. Egypt. Med. Assoc. 1936, 19, 1-10.

2552. Fahmy,I.R. and Keiy,A. "Studies of Indian hemp and its preparations."(Fr.). Comp. Rend. Cong. Internat'l. Pharm. 1935, 1, 185-197.

2553. Fahreddin,K. "Psychological problems and use of hashish."(Fr.). Hyg. Ment. 1930, 25, 93.

2554. Fahrenholtz,K.E. "The synthesis of two metabolites of (-)-delta-8-tetrahydrocannabinol." J. Org. Chem. 1972, 37, 2204-2207.

2555. Fahrenholtz,K.E., Lurie,M., and Kierstead, R.W. "The total synthesis of dl-delta-9-tetrahydro-cannabinol and four of its isomers." J. Am. Chem. Soc. 1967, 89, 5934-5941.

2556. Fahrenholtz,K.E., Lurie,M., and Kierstead, R.W. "Total synthesis of dl-delta-9-tetrahydrocannabinol and of dl-delta-8-tetrahydrocannabinol, racemates of active constituents of marihuana." J. Am. Chem. Soc. 1966, 88, 2079-2080.

2557. Faigel,H.C. "Chemistry of marihuana. Background knowledge for the physician." Clin. Pediat. 1970, 9, 713-714.

2558. Fairbairn,J.W. "No one has produced evidence of the safety of cannabis use for the public." Drugs Soc. 1972, 1, 6-7.

2559. Fairbairn,J.W. "The pharmacology of cannabis." In Graham,J.D.P.(ed.). Cannabis and Health. Academic Press, N.Y., 1976, 3-21.

2560. Fairbairn,J.W., Hindmarch,S., Simic,S., and Tylden,E. "Cannabinoid content of some English reefers." Nature 1974, 249, 276-277.

2561. Fairbairn,J.W. and Liebmann,J.A. "The cannabinoid content of cannabis sativa L. grown in England." J. Pharm. Pharmacol. 1974, 26, 413-419.

2562. Fairbairn,J.W. and Liebmann,J.A. "The extraction and estimation of the cannabinoids in cannabis sativa L. and its products." J. Pharm. Pharmacol. 1973, 25, 150-155.

2563. Fairbairn,J.W., Liebmann,J.A., and Rowan,M.G. "The stability of cannabis and its preparations on storage." J. Pharm. Pharmacol. 1976, 28, 1-7.

2564. Fairbairn,J.W., Liebmann,J.A., and Simic,S. "Distribution and stability of the cannabinoids in cannabis sativa." Act. Pharmaceut. Suec. 1971, 8, 679-680.

2565. Fairbairn,J.W., Liebmann,J.A., and Simic,S. "The tetrahydrocannabinol content of cannabis leaf." J. Pharm. Pharmacol. 1971, 23, 558-559.

2566. Fairbairn,J.W. and Rowan,M.G. "Cannabinoid pattern in cannabis sativa L. seedlings as an indication of chemical race." J. Pharm. Pharmacol. 1975, 27, 90P.

2567. Fairlie,K. and Fox,B.L. "Rapid, quantitative determination of tetrahydrocannabinol in marihuana by gas chromatography." J. Chromatog. Sci. 1976, 14, 334-335.

2568. Falek,A. "Genetic studies of marihuana: Current findings and new directions." In Tinklenberg, J.R.(ed.). Marihuana and Health Hazards. Academic Press, N.Y., 1975, 1-17.

2569. Famulener,L.W. and Lyons,A.B. "The psychological assay of cannabis indica and its galencial preparations, with notes on some of the commercial products supposed to represent the active principles of the drug." Proc. Am. Pharmaceut. Assoc. 1903, 51, 240-249.

2570. Fantchenko,I.F. "Brief notes and observations from experience with intoxicated psychotics. A case of intoxication from tincture of cannabis indica."(Rus.). Klin. Med. 1927, 5, 770-773.

2571. Farber,S.J. and Huertas,V.E. "Intravenously injected marihuana syndrome." Arch. Intern. Med. 1976, 136, 337-339.

2572. Farini Duggan,J. "Marihuana psychosis."(Sp.). Act. Psiquiat. Psicol. Am. Lat. 1976, 22, 63-70.

2573. Farlow,J.W. "On the use of belladonna and cannabis indica by the rectum in gynecological practices." Boston Med. Surg. J. 1889, 120, 507-509.

2574. Farmilo,C.G. and Genest,K. "Narcotics and related bases." Prog. Chem. Toxicol. 1963, 1, 199-295.

2575. Farmilo,C.G. and McConnell,D.T.W. "Paper and gas chromatographic analysis of cannabis." J. Pharm. Pharmacol. 1961, 13, 767-768.

2576. Farmilo,C.G., McConnell,D.T.W., Vandenheuvel, F.A., and Lane,R. "Studies on the chemical analysis of marihuana. IV. Biogenesis, paper chromatography, gas chromatography." Proc. Can. Forens. Sci. 1962, 1, 1-50.

2577. Farnsworth,D.L. "Drug dependence among physicians." New Eng. J. Med. 1970, 282, 392-393.

2578. Farnsworth,D.L. "Drug use for pleasure: a complex social problem." J. Sch. Hlth. 1973, 43, 153-158.

2579. Farnsworth,D.L. "Drugs in our society." J. Sch. Hlth. 1970, 40, 110-116.

2580. Farnsworth,D.L. "Legalization of marihuana: pros and cons." Am. J. Psychiat. 1971, 128, 217-218.

2581. Farnsworth,D.L. "Marihuana and the law: A medical approach." Suffolk Univ. Law Rev. 1968, 3, 97-100.

2582. Farnsworth,D.L. "Marihuana: metabolic and social progress." N. Eng. J. Med. 1972, 286, 721-722.

2583. Farnsworth,D.L. "Summary of the report from the National Commission on Marihuana and Drug Abuse:'Marihuana, A Signal of Misunderstanding'." Psychiat. Ann. 1972, 2, 8-25.

2584. Farnsworth,D.L. "The drug problem among young people." West Virginia Med. J. 1967, 63, 433-437.

2585. Farnsworth,D.L. "The drug problem among young people: Use of both LSD and marihuana entails significant risk." Rhode Is. Med. J. 1968, 51, 179-182.

2586. Farnsworth,D.L. "What is the evidence for an amotivational syndrome in cannabis users?" Ann. N. Y. Acad. Sci. 1976, 282, 1.

2587. Farnsworth,N.R. "Hallucinogenic plants." Science 1968, 162, 1086-1092.

2588. Farnsworth,N.R. "Pharmacognosy and chemistry of 'cannabis sativa'." J.A.P.A. 1969, NS9, 410-415.

2589. Farnsworth,N.R. and Coredell,G.A. "New potential hazard regarding use of marihuana treatment of plants with liquid fertilizers." J. Psychedel. Drugs 1976, 8, 151-155.

2590. Farrell,B. "Marihuana famine." Life 1969, 67, 20B.

2591. Farrell,J. "The assassin." High Times 1974, 1, 42.

2592. Fattah,E.A. "Relationship between cannabis and crime: Critical review of criminological writings on cannabis."(Fr.). Toxicomanies 1971, 4, 51-79.

2593. Faugeras,G. and Paris,M. "Quantification of the tetrahydrocannabinols in cannabis by photodensimetry after separation by thin-layer chromatography." Plant. Med. Phyto. 1971, 5, 224-233.

2594. Faure,J. "Contribution to the study of cannabis use in Morocco."(Fr.). Bull. Inst. Hyg. Maroc. 1952, 12, 229-240.

2595. Favazza,A.R. and Domino,E.F. "Recurrent LSD experience(flashbacks) triggered by marihuana." Univ. Mich. Med. Ctr. J. 1969, 35, 214-216.

2596. Favero,F. "Clandestine trade in, or facilitation in the use of, drugs."(Port.). Arquiv. Pol. Civil 1947, 13, 7-27.

2597. Fawcett,W. "The American hemp industry." Scientif. Amer. 1902, 87, 356.

2598. F.B. "Appendix to Victor Robinson's essay on hasheesh." Med. Rev. Rev. 1929, 35, 313-318.

2599. Federn,E. "Socioeducational view of juvenile drug abuse."(Ger.). Prax. Kinderpsychol. 1971, 20, 219-225.

2600. Feeney,D.M. "Marihuana and epilepsy." Science 1977, 197, 1301-1302.

2601. Feeney,D.M. "Marihuana use among epileptics." J.A.M.A. 1976, 235, 1105.

2602. Feeney,D.M. "The marihuana window: A theory of cannabis use." Behav. Biol. 1976, 18, 455-471.

2603. Feeney,D.M., Spiker,M., and Weiss,G. "Marihuana and epilepsy: Activation of symptoms of delta-9-THC." In Cohen,S. and Stillman,R.(eds.). Therapeutic Potential of Marihuana. Plenum Press, N.Y., 1976, 343-362.

2604. Feeney,D.M., Wagner,H.R., McNamara,M.C., and Weiss,G. "Effects of tetrahydrocannabinol on hippocampal evoked afterdischarge in cats." Exp. Neurol. 1973, 41, 357-365.

2605. Fehr,K.O. and Kalant,H. "Analysis of cannabis smoke obtained under different combustion conditions." Can. J. Physiol. Pharmacol. 1972, 50, 761-767.

2606. Fehr,K.O. and Kalant,H. "Fate of ^{14}C-delta-1-THC in rat plasma after intravenous injection and smoking." Eur. J. Pharmacol. 1974, 25, 1-8.

2607. Fehr,K.O., Kalant,H., and LeBlanc,A.E. "Residual learning deficit after heavy exposure to cannabis or alcohol in rats." Science 1976, 192, 1249-1251.

2608. Fehr,K.A., Kalant,H., LeBlanc,A.E., and Knox,G.V. "Permanent learning impairment after chronic heavy exposure to cannabis or ethanol in the rat." In Nahas,G.G., Paton,W.D.M., and Idanpaan-Heikkila,J.E.(eds.). Marihuana. Springer Verlag, N.Y., 1976, 495-507.

2609. Feinberg,I., Jones,R., Walker,J., Cavness,C., and Floyd,T. "Effects of marihuana extract and tetrahydrocannabinol on electroencephalographic sleep patterns." Clin. Pharmacol. Ther. 1975, 19, 782-794.

2610. Feinberg,I., Jones,R., Walker,J.M., Cavness,C., and March,J. "Effects of high dosage delta-9-tetrahydrocannabinol on sleep patterns in man." Clin. Pharmacol. Ther. 1975, 17, 458-466.

2611. Feinglas,S.J. "Marihuana: Standardization, characterization, and potential therapeutic uses." J. Second. Educat. 1968, 43, 206-210.

2612. Fejer,D. and Smart,R.G. Drug Use and Psychological Problems Among Adolescents in a Semirural Area of Ontario: Haldemand County. Addiction Research Foundation, Toronto, 1971.

2613. Fejer,D. and Smart,R.G. "Preferences of students for drug education programs and program elements." J. Alcohol Drug Educat. 1975, 21, 11-20.

2614. Fejer,D., Smart,R.G., and Whitehead,P.C. "Changes in patterns of drug use in two Canadian cities: Toronto and Halifax." Internat'l. J. Addict. 1972, 7, 25-33.

2615. Fejer,D., Smart,R.G., Whitehead,P.C., and LaForest,L. "Sources of information about drugs among high school students." Public Opin. Quart. 1971, 35, 235-241.

2616. Feldman,H. "American way of drugging. Street status and drug users." Society 1973, 10, 32-38.

2617. Feldmann,T.J. Concerning the Toxicity of Cannabis Sativa.(Ger.). Univ. of Bern, Bern, Switzerland, 1945.

2618. Fenimore,D.C., Freeman,R.R., and Loy,P.R. "Determination of delta-9-tetrahydrocannabinol in blood by electron capture gas chromatography." Anal. Chem. 1973, 45, 2331-2335.

2619. Fenimore,D.C. and Loy,P.R. "Injectible dispersion of delta-9-tetrahydrocannabinol in saline using polyvinylpyrrolidone." J. Pharm. Pharmacol. 1971, 23, 310.

2620. Fenselau,C. and Hermann,G. "Identification of phytosterols in red oil extract of cannabis." J. Forens. Sci. 1972, 17, 309-312.

2621. Fenselau,C., Kelly,S., Salmon,M., and Billets,S. "The absence of tetrahydrocannabinol from hops." Food Cosmet. Toxicol. 1976, 14, 35-39.

2622. Fentiman,A.F., Foltz,R.C., and Kinzer,G.W. "Identification of noncannabinoid phenols in marihuana smoke condensate using chemical ionization mass spectrometry." Anal. Chem. 1973, 45, 580-583.

2623. Fenyvesi,T. "The spreading of cannabinomania." (Hung.). Orv. Hetil. 1972, 113, 622-626.

2624 Fere,C. "Note on the influence of hashish on work."(Fr.). C. R. Acad. Sci. 1901, 3, 696-700.

2625 Ferencyzy,L. "Antibacterial substances in seeds of cannabis." Nature 1958, 178, 639.

2626. Ferenczy,L., Gracza,L., and Jakobey,I. "An antibacterial preparation from hemp(cannabis sativa L.)." Naturwissen. 1958, 45, 188.

2627 Ferguson,L.W. and Koury,N.J. "Peer drug use as estimated by current users, ex-users, and non-users of marihuana." Percept. Motor Skill. 1974, 38, 1113-1114.

2628. Ferguson,R.W. Drug Abuse Control. Holbrook Press Inc., N.Y., 1975.

2629. Fernandes,M. "Clinical pharmacology of narcotics."(Ger.). Hippokrates 1972, 43, 157-179.

2630. Fernades,M. and Coper,H. "The role of vehicles in cannabis application and interaction between cannabis and central active drugs." Act. Pharmaceut. Suec. 1971, 8, 692-693.

2631. Fernandes,M., Kluwe,S., and Coper,H. "Cannabinoids and hexobarbital induced loss of righting reflexes." Arch. Pharmacol. 1974, 283, 431-435.

2632. Fernandes,M., Schabarek,A., Coper,H., and Hill,R. "Modification of delta-9-THC actions by cannabinol and cannabidiol in the rat." Psychopharmacol. 1974, 38, 329-338.

2633. Fernandes,M., Warning,N., Christ,W., and Hill,R. "Interactions of several cannabinoids with hepatic drug metabolizing system." Biochem. Pharmacol. 1973, 22, 2981-2987.

2634. Fernandes,M. Warning,N., Christ,W., and Hill,R. "Morphine-cannabinoid interactions in rats and mice." Arch. Pharmacol. 1974, 282, R19.

2635. Fernandez-Guardiola,A., Contreras,C.M., Solis,H.J., Condes,M., and Estrada,T.G. "Polygraphic recording of all night sleep in humans under chronic and acute intoxication with marihuana." Comm. Prob. Drug Depend. 1974, 1, 172-186.

2636. Fernandez-Guardiola,A., Salgado,A., Conteras, C.M., Condes,M., Estrada,T.G., Solis,H., Calvo,J.M., and Ayala,F. "Multiunit activity and polygraphic recordings of the pharmacological effects of delta-9-THC. In Braude,M.C. and Szara,S.(eds.). Pharmacology of Marihuana. Raven Press, N.Y., 1976, i, 335-345.

2637. Fernandez Sanchez,A., and Gonzalez Mas,R. "The clubs of the the hashish smokers in Spanish Morocco."(Sp.). Farm. Chil. 1953, 10, 473-475.

2638. Ferraro,D.P. "A behavioral model of marihuana tolerance." In Braude,M.C. and Szara,S.(eds.). Pharmacology of Marihuana. Raven Press, N.Y., 1976, 2, 475-487.

2639. Ferraro,D.P. "Effects of delta-9-tetrahydrocannabinol on simple and complex learned behavior in animals." In Lewis, M.(ed.). Current Research in Marihuana. Academic Press, N.Y., 1972, 49-95.

2640. Ferraro,D.P. and Billings,D.K. "Comparison of behavioral effects of synthetic (-)-delta-9-trans-tetrahydrocannabinol and marihuana extract distillate in chimpanzees." Psychopharmacol. 1972, 25, 169-174.

2641. Ferraro,D.P. and Billings,,D.K. "Effects of marihuana extract on operant behavior of chimpanzees." Psychopharmacol. 1971, 22, 333-351.

2642. Ferraro,D.P. and Billings,D.K. "Marihuana use by college students: three-year trends, 1970-1972." Internat'l. J. Addict. 1974, 9, 321-327.

2643. Ferraro,D.P. and Gluck,J.P. "Effects of oral delta-9-tetrahydrocannabinol on operant reinforcement schedule performance in rats." Pharmacol. 1974, 11, 65-69.

2644. Ferraro,D.P., Gluck,J.P., and Herndon,G.B. Acquisition and extrinction of variable interval schedule behavior by rats under delta-9-tetrahydrocannabinol." Pharmacol. Biochem. Behav. 1974, 2, 487-491.

2645. Ferraro,D.P., Gluck,J.P., and Morrow,C.W. "Temporally-related stimulus properties on delta-9-tetrahydrocannabinol in monkeys." Psychopharmacol. 1974, 35, 305-316.

2646. Ferraro,D.P. and Grilly,D.M. "Effects of chronic exposure to delta-9-tetrahydrocannabinol on delayed matching-to-sample in chimpanzees." Psychopharmacol. 1974, 37, 127-138.

2647. Ferraro,D.P. and Grilly,D.M. "Lack of tolerance to delta-9-tetrahydrocannabinol in chimpanzees." Science 1973, 179, 490-492.

2648. Ferraro,D.P. and Grilly,D.M. "Marihuana extract in chimpanzees: Absence of long-term effects on operant behavor." Psychol. Rep. 1973, 32, 473-474.

2648a. Ferraro,D.P., Grilly,E.M., and Grisham,M.G. "Delta-9-tetrahydrocannabinol and delayed matching-to-sample in chimpanzees." In Singh,J.M.(ed.). Neurobiology and Influences on Behavior. Stratton Intercontinental Med. Book Corp., N.Y., 1974, 181-207.

2649. Ferraro,D.P. and Grisham,M.G. "Tolerance to the behavioral effects of marihuana in chimpanzees." Physiol. Behav. 1972, 9, 49-54.

2650. Ferraro,D.P., Huthsing,K.B., and Fetterolf,D.J. "Time course of delta-9-THC effects on water consumption in rats." Behav. Biol. 1976, 17, 567-572.

2651. Ferraro,D.P., Lynch,W.C., and Grilly,D.M. "Behavioral effects of small oral doses of marihuana extract in chimpanzees." Pharmacol. 1972, 7, 273-282.

2652. Fetterman,P.S., Doorenbos,J.J., Keith,E.S., and Quimby,M.W. "A simple gas liquid chromatography procedure for determination of cannabinoidic acids in cannabis sativa L." Exper. 1971, 27, 988-990.

2653. Fetterman,P.S., Keith,E.S., Waller,C.W., Guerrero,O., Doorenbos,N.J., and Quimby,M.W. "Mississippi grown cannabis sativa L.: Preliminary observation on chemical definition of phenotype and variations in tetrahydrocannabinol content versus age, sex, and plant part." J. Pharmaceut. Sci. 1971, 60, 1246-1249.

2654. Fetterman,P.S. and Turner,C.E. "Constituents of cannabis sativa L. I.: Propyl homologs of cannabinoids from an Indian variant." J. Pharmaceut. Sci. 1972, 61, 1466-1477.

2655. Ficalho,C. Useful Plants of Portuguese Africa. Agencia Geral do Ultramar, Lisbon, 1947.

2656. Fidaleo,R.A. "Marihuana--social and clinical observations." U.S. Army Vietnam Med. Bull. 1968, 8, 58-59.

2657 Fidler,P.P. and Still,J. Comparison of Freshman Attitudes on Controversial Issues. Division of Student Affairs, Univ. of S. Carolina, 1973.

2658. Fiedler,L. Being Busted. Stein and Day, N.Y., 1970.

2659. Fiedler,L. "In defense of youth." Humanist 1967, 27, 117.

2660. Field,T.F. and Madigan,M. "Personality and social factors of college students involved in drug use." J. Coll Stud. 1974, 8, 23-26.

2661. Fielde,A.M. "An experience in hasheesh-smoking." Ther. Gaz. 1888, 12, 449-451.

2662. Filedt Kok,J.C. and Kamp.G.E. "Analysis of 'black-market' materials used as drugs."(Dut.). Pharm. Weekbl. 1973, 108, 990-999.

2663. Filho,P.P. The Cannabis Problem. General Considerations on the Marihuana Vice in Brazil.(Port.) Grupo Consultivo Interamericano Sobre Fiscalizacion de Estupefacientes, Rio de Janeiro, 1961.

2664. Filipenya,V.M. "Potassium fertilizers for flax and hemp." Kalii 1935, 4, 40-42.

2665. Finestone,H. "Cats, kicks, and color." Soc. Prob. 1957, 5, 3-13.

2666. Fink,M. "Effects of acute and chronic inhalation of hashish, marihuana and delta-9-tetrahydrocannabinol on brain electrical activity in man: Evidence for tissue tolerance." Ann. N. Y. Acad. Sci. 1976, 282, 387-398.

2667. Fink,M., Volavka,J., Dornbush,R., and Crown,P. "Effects of cannabis on human EEG and heart rate--evidence of tolerance development on chronic use." In Ban,T.A., Boissier,J.R., Gessa,G.J., Heimann,H., and Hollister,L.(eds.). Psychopharmacology, Sexual Disorders and Drug Abuse. North-Holland Pub. Co., Amsterdam, 1973, 703-704.

2668. Fink,M., Volavka,J., Panayiotopoulos,C.P., and Stefanis,C. "Quantitative EEG studies of marihuana, delta-9-THC, and hashish in man." In Braude,M.C. and Szara,S.(eds.). Pharmacology of Marihuana. Raven Press, 1976, 1, 383-393.

2669. Finlator,J. "Federal action and inaction." In Levin,P.A.(ed.). Contemporary Problems of Drug Abuse. Publishing Sciences Group Inc., Acton, Mass., 1974, 151-155.

2670. Finnell,W.S. and Jones,J.D. "Marihuana, alcohol, and academic performance." J. Drug Educat. 1975, 5, 13-21.

2671. Fioramonti,F. "Reefer reform comes to America." High Times 1974, 5, 40-41, 63, 66.

2672. Firstenberg,M.L. "Pot is good for business." Marihuana Rev. 1968, 1, 12.

2673. Fischer,H. "Indian pleasure-giving agents." (Ger.). Chem.-Zeit. 1923, 47, 665-666.

2674. Fischer,R. Practicum of Pharmacognosy.(Ger.). Springer Verlag, Wien, Germany, 1968.

2675. Fischlowitz,G.G. "Poisoning by cannabis indica." Med. Rec. 1896, 50, 280-281.

2676. Fish,F. "Gas chromatography of cannabis constituents." Chromatog. 1974, 6, 311-315

2677. Fish,F. and Caddy,B. "Analysis for drugs of abuse." Some applications and limitations." J. Forens. Sci. Soc. 1969, 9, 48-52.

2678. Fish,F. and Wilson,W.D.C. "Identification of cannabis constituents in particulate matter of smoke." J. Forens. Sci. Soc. 1969, 9, 37-40.

2679. Fisher,D. "Experimenter effects in the verbal conditioning of adolescents' responses toward drugs." Diss. Abs. 1972, 32, 3784-3785.

2680. Fisher,D.D. "Marihuana and sex." Paper presented at National Symposium on the Psychedelic Drugs and Marihuana. Chicago, 1968.

2681. Fisher,G. "Harmful effects of marihuana use: Experiences and opinions of current and past marihuana users." Br. J. Addict. 1974, 69, 75-84.

2682. Fisher,G. "Milieu of marihuana use." Internat'l. J. Soc. Psychiat. 1974, 20, 44-55.

2683. Fisher,G. "Personality characteristics ascribed to marihuana users by users and nonusers." Behav. Neuropsychiat. 1972, 4, 5-12.

2684. Fisher,G. and Steckler,A. "Multiple drug use of marihuana users." Dis. Nerv. Syst. 1973, 34, 40-43.

2685. Fisher,G. and Steckler,A. "Psychological effects, personality and behavioral changes attributed to marihuana use." Internat'l. J. Addict. 1974, 9, 101-126.

2686. Fisher,G., Steckler,A., Strantz,I., and Nabholz,E. "The legalization of marihuana: views of several American populations of users and non-users." J. Psychedel. Drug. 1974, 6, 333-349.

2687. Fisher,G. and Strantz,I. "An ecosystems approach to the study of dangerous drug use and abuse with special reference to the marihuana issue." Am. J. Pub. Hlth. 1972, 62, 1407-1414.

2688. Fisher,H. "Case of cannabis indica poisoning." Cincinnati Lancet-Clinic 1896, 37, 405.

2689. Fisher,H.C. "Drug addiction." Br. Med. J. 1957, 1, 413.

2690. Fisher,J. "Cannabis in Nepal: An overview." In Rubin,V.(ed.). Cannabis and Culture. Mouton, The Hague, 1975, 247-257.

2691. Fisher,R. "Marihuana." Science 1969, 163, 1144-1145.

2692. Fisher,S., Pillard,R.C., and Botto,R.W. "Hypnotic susceptibility during cannabis intoxication." In Ban,T.A., Boissier,J.R., Gessa,G.J., Heimann,H., and Hollister,L.(eds.). Psychopharmacology, Sexual Disorders and Drug Abuse. North-Holland Pub. Co., Amsterdam, 1973, 699-700.

2693. Flaccomio,E. "The use of marihuana is increasing in Europe."(It.). Riv. It. Eppos. 1968, 50, 289-290.

2694. Flader,C. "Cultivation of hemp."(Ger.). Mitteil. Deut. Landwirtschaft. 1934, 49, 87.

2695. Flander,C. "The treatment of hemp."(It.). Klepzig. Textil. 1939, 42, 107-110, 174-178.

2696. Flannery,R.B. "Use of covert conditioning on the behavioral treatment of a drug-dependent college drop-out." J. Counsel. Psychol. 1972, 19, 547-550.

2697. Flatermayer,E.K. "What we know about marihuana." Fortune 1971, 96-98, 128-132.

2698. Fleischhauer,W. "The old man of the mountain: The growth of a legend." Symposium 1955, 9, 79-90.

2699. Fleischman,R.W., Hayden,D.W., Braude,M.C., and Rosenkrantz,H. "Chronic marihuana inhalation toxicity in rats." Toxicol. Appl. Pharmacol. 1975, 34, 467-478.

2700. Fleischman,R.W., Hayden,D.W., Rosenkrantz,H., and Braude,M.C. "Teratologic evaluation of delta-9-tetrahydrocannabinol in mice, including a review of the literature." Teratology 1975, 12, 47-50.

2701. Fleming,D. The Complete Guide to Growing Marihuana. Sundance Press, San Diego, 1970.

2702. Fleming,W.A.J. "A case of cannabis indica intoxication." Lancet 1935, 1, 1301-1302.

2703. Flom,M.C., Adams,A.J., and Jones,R.T. "Marihuana smoking and reduced pressure in human eyes: Drug action or epiphenomenon?" Invest. Ophthamol. 1975, 14, 52-55.

2704. Flom,M.C., Brown,B., Adams,A.J., and Jones, R.T. "Alcohol and ocular tracking." Am. J. Optom. Physiol. Optics 1976, 53, 764-773.

2705. Flores Marco,R. "Diagnosis and classification of cannabism in its legal aspect."(Sp.). Rev. Espan. Tuber. 1945, 14, 755-762.

2706. Florvault,M. "Rhino-conjuctival hashish allergy."(Nor.). Tid. Norsk. Laeg. 1976, 97, 563.

2707. Fluckiger,F.A. and Hanburty,D. Pharmacography or History of Drugs of Vegetable Origin.(Fr.). O. Doin, Paris, 1878.

2708. Fochtman,F.W. "The identification of marihuana." Toxicol. Ann. 1975, 1, 275-280.

2709. Fochtman,F.W. and Winek,C.L. "A note on the Duquenois-Levine test for marihuana." Clin. Toxicol. 1971, 4, 287-289.

2710. Fofonov,V. "Chemical composition of wild hemp seeds(cannabis ruderalis)."(Rus.). Ber Sarat. Naturforsh. 1925, 1, 33-36.

2711. Folk,L. "On 'dust-fever' in hemp spinning-mill workers."(Swed.). Nord. Hyg. Tid. 1936, 17, 113-116.

2712. Foltz,R.L., Fentiman,A.F., Leighty,E.G., Walter,J.L., Drewes,H.R., Schwartz,W.E., Page,T.F., and Truitt,E.B. "Metabolite of (-)-trans-delta-8-tetrahydrocannabinol: Identification and synthesis." Science 1970, 168, 344-345.

2713. Fonseka,K., Widman,M., and Agurell,S. "Chromatographic separation of cannabinoids and their mono-oxygenated derivatives." J. Chromatog. 1976, 120, 343-348.

2714. Fontoynont,M. "Cannabis intoxication of an inhabitant of Madagascar."(Fr.). Bull. Soc. Pathol. Exot. 1938, 31, 446-448.

2715. Font Quer,P. Medicinal Plants.(Sp.). Editorial Labor, Barcelona, 1962.

2716. Foote,R.S. and Jones,L.A. "An analysis of two varieties of cannabis." J. Agric. Food Chem. 1974, 22, 534-535.

2717. Ford,B.I. "Illegal drug use in a student population." Med. J. Aust. 1971, 2, 309-313.

2718. Ford,R.D., Balster,R.L., Dewey,W.L., and Beckner,J.S. "Delta-9-THC and 11-OH-delta-9-THC: Behavioral effects and relationship to plasma and brain levels." Life Sci. 1977, 20, 1993-2004.

2719. Ford,R.D. and McMillan,D.E. "Behavioral tolerance and cross tolerance to 1-delta-8-tetrahydrocannabinol and 1-delta-9-tetrahyrocannabinol in pigeons and rats." Fed. Proc. 1971, 30, 279.

2720. Ford,R.D., Witt,P.N., and Scarboro,M.B. "Effects of single and repeated administration of water soluble 1-delta-9-tetrahydrocannabinol on web-building of spiders." Pharmacologist 1973, 32, 725.

2721. Forgas,P. Study of Hemp from a Botanical, Chemical and Pharmacological View.(Fr.). Univ. France, Dept. of Pharmacy, Montpellier, 1880.

2722. Forney,R.B. "Toxicology of marihuana." Pharmacol. Rev. 1971, 23, 279-284.

2723. Forney,R.B. and Kiplinger,G.F. "Toxicology and pharmacology of marihuana." Ann. N. Y. Acad. Sci. 1971, 191, 74-83.

2724. Forney,R.B., Martz,R., Lemberger,L., Rodda,B., and Evans,M. "The combined effect of marihuana and dextroamphetamine." Ann. N. Y. Acad. Sci. 1976, 281, 162-170.

2725. Forrer,S.E. "Environmental perceptions of college student drug users." J. Coll. Stud. Person. 1975, 16, 64-68.

2726. Forrest,D.V. "Marihuana to heroin...a missing link?" Am. J. Psychiat. 1970, 127, 704-705.

2727. Forrest,I.S., Green,D.E., Rose,S.D., Skinner,G.C., Torres,D.M. "Fluorescent-labeled cannabinoids." Res. Comm. Chem. Pathol. Pharmacol. 1971, 2, 787-792.

2728. Forrest,I.S., Otis,L.S., Serra,M.T., and Skinner,G.C. "Passage of ^{3}H-delta-9-tetrahydrocannabinol into the hair(fur) of various mammals." Proc. West. Pharmacol. Soc. 1972, 15, 83-86.

2729. Forrest,I.S., Rose,S.D., Brookes,L.G., Halpern,B., Bacon,V.A., and Silberg,I.A. "Fluorescent labeling of psychoactive drugs." Aggressologie 1970, 11, 127-133.

2730. Forrest,J.E. and Heacock,R.A. "Chromatographic comparison of the constituents of nutmeg and mace (myristica fragrans) with those of marihuana and hashish(cannabis sativa L.)." J. Chromatog. 1974, 89, 113-117.

2731. Forest,S., Tennant,F.S., and Groesbeck,C.J. "Psychiatric effects of hashish." Arch. Gen. Psychiat. 1972, 27, 133-136.

2732. Forslund,M.A. "Drug use and delinquent behavior of small town and rural youth." J. Drug Educat. 1977, 7, 219-224.

2733. Fort,J. "A world view of marihuana. (Has the world gone to pot?)" J. Psychedel. Drugs 1968, 11, 1-14.

2734. Fort,J. "Drug use and the law; a case for legalizaing marihuana." Current 1969, 113, 4-13.

2735. Fort,J. "Giver of delight or liberator of sin: Drug use and 'addiction' in Asia." Bull. Narc. 1965, 17, 1-11, 13-19.

2736. Fort,J. "Marihuana: The real problems and the responsibilities of the professions in solving them." Psychiat. Opin. 1968, 5, 9-15.

2737. Fort,J. "Perspective on marihuana." In Brill,L. and Harms,E.(eds.). Yearbook of Drug Abuse. Behavioral publications, N.Y., 1973, 333-365.

2738. Fort,J. "Pot--a rational approach." Playboy 1969, 131, 154, 216.

2739. Fort,J. "Pot or not." Internat'l. J. Addict. 1970, 9, 517-521.

2740. Fort,J. "Social problems of drug use and drug policies." Calif. Law Rev. 1968, 56, 17-28.

2741. Fort,J. "Social values, American youth, and drug use." In Hollander,C.(ed.). Background Papers on Student Drug Involvement. U.S. National Student Assoc., Washington,D.C., 1967, 131-146.

2742. Fort,J. "The A.M.A. lies about pot." Ramparts 1968, 12-13.

2743. Fort,J. "The marihuana abuser and the abuser of psychedelic-hallucinogens." In Cull,J.G. and Hardy, R.E.(eds.). Types of Drug Abusers and Their Abuses. C.C. Thomas, Springfield, Ill., 1974, 135-145.

2744. Fort,J. "The semantics and logic of the drug scene." In Hollander,C.(ed.). Background Papers on Student Drug Use. U.S. National Student Assoc., Washington, D.C., 1967, 87-94.

2745. Fort,J. "Comparison chart of major substances used for mind alteration." Am. J. Nurs. 1971, 71, 1738-1739.

2746. Fossier,A.E. "The marihuana menace." New Orleans Med. Surg. J. 1931, 44, 247-252.

2747. Foster,L. "Lowland weed compagnie." High Times 1974, 4, 42-43.

2748. Foucaud,A. "Contribution to the study of medicinal plants of North Vietnam."(Fr.). Trav. Lab. Mat. Med. Pharm. Galen. 1953, 38, 1-36.

2749. Foulger,J.H. "The marihuana problem." Delaware State Med. J. 1944, 16, 24-28.

2750. Foulis,J. "Two cases of poisoning by cannabis indica." Edinburgh Med. J. 1900, 2, 201-210.

2751. Foulks,E.F. "Social psychiatric aspects of marihuana use." Sem. Drug Treat. 1971, 1, 224-228.

2752. Foulks,E.F. and Eisenman,R. "An analysis of a peer network using psychedelic drugs." Psychiat. Quart. 1969, 43, 389-395.

2753. Fournier,E., Rosenberg,E., Hardy,N., and Nahas,G. "Teratologic effects of cannabis extracts in rabbits: A preliminary study." In Nahas,G.G., Paton, W.D.M., and Idanpaan-Heikkila,J.E.(eds.). Marihuana. Springer Verlag, N.Y., 1976, 457-469.

2754. Fournier,P. Medicinal and Poisonous Plants of France.(Fr.). P. Lechevalier, Paris, 1947.

2755. Fournier Ruiz,I.G. "Acute cannabism and alcoholism. Differential diagnosis, medico-legal significance."(Sp.). Med. Lat. 1954, 13, 27-29.

2756. Fournier Ruiz,I.G. "Palpebral adjustment in acute cannabism."(Sp.). Rev. Criminal. 1954, 1, 29-30.

2757. Fowler,W.C. "Cannabis indica." Lancet 1943, 2, 368.

2758. Fox,M.N. "Cannabis and reverse tolerance: Pharmacological entity or psychological phenomenon?" Med. J. Aust. 1973, 2, 863-865.

2759. Fox,R.H. "Headaches: A study of some common forms, with special reference to arterial tension and and to treatment." Lancet 1897, 2, 307-309.

2760. Foy,F. "Note on hashish."(Fr.). J. Pharm. Chim. 1848, 13, 350-353.

2761. Foy,F. "Note on hashish."(Fr.). Rep. Pharm. 1848, 1, 92-95.

2762. Fraenkel,A. "Cannabinol." Pharmaceut. Era 1903, 30, 450.

2763. Fraenkel,F. and Joel,E. "Contribution to an experimental psychopathology of hashish intoxication." (Ger.). Zeit. Ges. Neurol. Psychiat. 1927, 111, 84-106.

2764. Fraenkel,L.D. "Use of the Rorschach test in hashish intoxication."(Fr.). Hyg. Ment. 1935, 30, 66-68.

2765. Fraenkel,S. "Chemistry and pharmacology of hashish."(Ger.). Arch. Exper. Pathol. Pharmakol. 1903, 49, 266-284.

2766. Francis,J.B. and Patch,D.J. Student Attitudes Toward Drug Programs at the University of Michigan. Univ. Committee on Drug Education, Ann Arbor, Mich., 1969.

2767. Frank,A. and Frank,S. "Marihuana." Mademoiselle, 1975, 81, 22.

2768. Frank,I.M., Hepler,R.S., Epps,L., Ungerleider, J.T., and Szara,S. "Marihuana and delta-9-tetrahydrocannabinol: Effects on intraocular pressure in young adults." Proc. 5th Internat'l. Cong. Pharmacol. 1972, 1, 71.

2769. Frank,I.M., Lessin,P.J., Tyrrell,E.D., Hahn,P.M., and Szara,S. "Acute and cumulative effects of marihuana smoking in hospitalized subjects: A 36-day study." In Braude,M.C. and Szara,S.(eds.). Pharmacology of Marihuana. Raven Press, N.Y., 1976, 2, 673-681.

2770. Frank,M. and Rosenthal,E. "Spring homegrowers planting guide." High Times 1976, 9, 48-49, 96.

2771. Frank,M. and Rosenthal,E. The Indoor Outdoor Highest Quality Marihuana Grower's Guide. And/or Press, Berkeley, Cal., 1976.

2772. Frank,T. An Economic Survey of Ancient Rome. Pageant Books, Patterson, N.J., 1959.

2773. Frankel,P.W. "Marihuana effects on sleeping states." J.A.M.A. 1972, 221, 1166.

2774. Frankenheim,J.M. "Effects of repeated doses of l-delta-8-trans-tetrahydrocannabinol on schedule-controlled temporally-spaced responding in rats." Psychopharmacol. 1974, 38, 125-144.

2775. Frankenheim,J.M., McMillan,D.E., and Harris,L.S. "Effects of l-delta-9- and l-delta-8-trans-tetrahydrocannabinol and cannabinol on schedule-controlled behavior of pigeons and rats." J. Pharmacol. Exper. Ther. 1971, 178, 241-251.

2776. Frankenheim,J.M., McMillan,D.E., and Harris,L.S. "Effects of l-delta-9- and delta-8-trans-tetrahydrocannabinol on schedule-controlled behavior in the pigeon." Fed. Proc. 1970, 29, 619.

2777. Franks,H.M., Starmer,G.A., Chesher,G.B., Jackson,D.M., Hensley,V.R., and Hensley,W.J. "The interaction of alcohol and delta-9-tetrahydrocannabinol in man: Effects on psychomotor skills related to driving." In Israelstam,S. and Lamberg,S.(eds.). Proceedings of the Sixth International Conference on Alcohol, Drugs, and Traffic Safety. Addiction Research Found., Toronto, 1975, 461-466.

2778. Franzini,L.R. and McDonald,R.D. "Marihuana usage and hypnotic susceptibility." J. Consult. Clin. Psychol. 1973, 40, 176-180.

2779. Fraser,H.A. "Law and cannabis in the West Indies." Soc. Econ. Stud. 1974, 23, 361-385.

2780. Fraser,H.F. "Problems resulting from the use of habituating drugs in industry." Am. J. Pub. Hlth. 1958, 48, 561-570.

2781. Fraser,J.D. "Withdrawl symptoms in cannabis-indica addicts." Lancet 1949, 2, 747-748.

2782. Frazier,J. "Hemp paper reconsidered." High Times 1974, 1, 17-21.

2783. Frazier,J. "Jazz, and Boo." High Times 1977, 18, 64, 97.

2784. Frazier,J. The Marihuana Farmers. Solar Age Press, New Orleans, 1975.

2785. Freedman,A.M. "Drugs and sexual behavior." Med. Aspects Human Sex. 1967, 1, 25-31.

2786. Freedman,A.M. and Brotman,R.E. "Multiple drug use among teenagers: plans for action--research." In Wittenborn,J.R., Brill,H., Smith,J.P., and Wittenborn, S.A.(eds.). Drugs and Youth. C.C. Thomas, Springfield, Ill., 1969, 335-344.

2787. Freedman,A.M. and Fink,M. "Cannabis psychosis." In Praag,H.M.(ed.). Biochemical and Pharmacological Aspects of Dependence and Reports on Marihuana Research. Interdisciplinary Society of Biological Psychiat. Amsterdam, 1971, 194-205.

2788. Freedman,D.X. "Drug-abuse--Comments on the current scene." In Wittenborn,J.R., Brill,H., Smith,J.P., and Wittenborn,S.A.(eds.). Drugs and Youth. C.C. Thomas, Springfield,Ill., 1969, 345-361.

2789. Freedman,D.X. "Drug dependence and its treatment. First of two parts." Postgrad. Med. 1970, 47, 110-114.

2790. Freedman,D.X. "Drug dependence and its treatment. Second of two parts." Postgrad. Med. 1970, 47, 150-154.

2791. Freedman,D.X. "Implications for research." J.A.M.A. 1968, 206, 1280-1284.

2792. Freedman,D.X. "Statement of the National Coordinating Council on Drug Education (for the National Commission on Marihuana and Drug Abuse)." J. Am. Osteopath. Assoc. 1971, 71, 302-306.

2793. Freedman,H. "Hempseed oil." Am. Point J. 1936, 20, 48-50.

2794. Freedman,H.L. and Rockmore,M.J. "Marihuana; a factor in personality evaluation and army maladjustment. Part 1." J. Clin. Psychopathol. 1946, 7, 765-782.

2795. Freedman,H.L. and Rockmore,M.J. "Marihuana; a factor in personality evaluation and army maladjustment. Part 2." J. Clin. Psychopathol. 1946, 8, 221-236.

2796. Freedman,W. and Sklaren,C.S. "'Seven days to life': Legal penalties for the first-time possession of marihuana in the United States." In Levin,P.(ed.). Contemporary Social Problems. C.C. Thomas, Springfield, Ill., 1972, 261-281.

2797. Freeland,J.B. and Campbell,R.S. "The social context of first marihuana use." Internat'l. J. Addict. 1973, 8, 317-324.

2798. Freedman,H.R. "The generation gap: attitudes of students and of their parents." J. Counsel. Psychol. 1972, 19, 441-447.

2799. Freemon,F.R. and Al-Marashi,M.S.H. "Long-term changes in the sleep of normal volunteers administered multiple doses of delta-9-tetrahydrocannabinol." J. Drug Alcohol Depend. 1977, 2, 39-44.

2800. Freemon,F.R., Rosenblatt,J.E., and Khaled El-Yousef,M. "Interaction of physostigmine and delta-9-tetrahydrocannabinol in man." Clin. Pharmacol. Ther. 1975, 17, 121-126.

2801. Freese,A.S. "A new look at marihuana: for new reasons, marihuana is seen as a danger by experts who scoffed at the old reasons to fear it." Am. Legion 1971, 91, 14-18.

2802. French,J.M. "Cannabis indica." Am. J. Clin. Med. 1907, 14, 1334-1336.

2803. Frenczy,L. "Antibacterial substances in seeds of cannabis." Nature 1958, 178, 639.

2804. Frenkel,F.E. "Some aspects of the use of marihuana." In Psychiatric Juridical Society. The Drug Issue of the Psychiatric Juridical Society.(Dut.). F. van Rossen,, Amsterdam, 1970, 9-30.

2805. Freudenthal,R.I., Martin,J., and Wall,M.E. "Distribution of delta-9-tetrahydrocannabinol in the mouse." Br. J. Pharmacol. 1972, 44, 244-249.

2806. Freusberg,A. "On sensory illusions in hashish intoxication."(Ger.). Allgem. Zeit. Psychiat. 1877, 34, 216-230.

2807. Frew,J.L. "Cannabis indica poisoning." Roy. Melbourne Hosp. Clin. Rep. 1939, 10, 93-94.

2808. Freyre,G. New Afro-Brazilian Studies.(Port.). Biblioteca de Divulgacao Cientifica, Rio de Janeiro, 1937.

2809. Frideres,J.S. "Impact of social restraints on the relationship between attitudes and behavior." Soc. Forces 1971, 50, 102-112.

2810. Frideres,J.S. "Situational and personality variables as influencing the relationship between attitudes and overt behavior." Can. Rev. Sociol. Anthropol. 1971, 8, 91-105.

2811. Fried,P.A. "Cross-tolerance between inhaled cannabis and intraperitoneal injections of delta-9-THC." Pharmacol. Biochem. Behav. 1976, 4, 635-638.

2812. Fried,P.A. "Parameters influencing the effect of delta-9-THC on activity wheel behavior." Pharmacol. Biochem. Behav. 1974, 2, 435-438.

2813. Fried,P.A. "Short- and long-term effects of pre-natal cannabis inhalation upon rat offspring." Psychopharmacol. 1976, 50, 285-291.

2814. Fried,P.A. and Husband,C.A. "Depth perception in rats following acute or chronic injections of delta-9-tetrahydrocannabinol." Life Sci. 1973, 12, 289-295.

2815. Fried,P.A. and McIntyre,D.C. "Electrical and behavioral attenuation of the anti-convulsant properties of delta-9-THC following chronic administrations." Psychopharmacol. 1973, 31, 215-227.

2816. Fried,P.A. and Nieman,G.W. "Inhalation of cannabis smoke in rats." Pharmacol. Biochem. Behav. 1973, 1, 371-378.

2817. Friedman,C.J. and Friedman,A.S. "Drug abuse and delinquency." In National Commission on Marihuana and Drug Abuse. Drug Use in America: Problem in Perspective. Gov't. Print. Office, Washington, D.C., 1973, I, 398-484.

2818. Friedman,E. and Gershon,S. "Effect of delta-8-THC on alcohol-induced sleeping time in the rat." Psychopharmacol. 1974, 39, 193-198.

2819. Friedman,E., Gershon,S., Hine,B., Torrelio,M., and Immanuela,R. "Cardiovascular effects of delta-9-tetrahydrocannabinol in conscious and anaesthetized dogs." Br. J. Pharmacol. 1977, 59, 561-563.

2820. Friedman,E., Hanin,I., and Gershon,S. "Effect of tetrahydrocannabinols on ^{3}H-acetylcholine biosynthesis in various rat brain slices." J. Pharmacol. Exper. Ther. 1976, 196, 339-345.

2821. Friedman,J.G. "Marihuana and testosterone levels." N. Eng. J. Med. 1975, 289, 484.

2822. Friedman,M.A. "Inhibition of arylhydrocarbon hydroxylase induction in BALB/C mouse liver by delta-9-tetrahydrocannabinol." Res. Commun. Chem. Pathol. Pharmacol. 1976, 15, 541-552.

2823. Friedman,M.A. and Wrenn,J.M. "Suppression by delta-9-THC of induction of hepatic tyrosine aminotransferase and tryptophan oxygenase." Toxicol. Appl. Pharmacol. 1977, 41, 345-352.

2824. Friedman,R. "No big deal." Nation 1973, 217, 710.

2825. Friedemann,A. "Drug addiction in children and adolescents."(Ger.). Act. Paedopsychiat. 1969, 36, 274-278.

2826. Friedrich,O. Pharmacological Study of Cannabis Sativa.(Ger.). Univ. Switzerland, Bern, 1929.

2827. Friedrich-Fiechtl,J., Spiteller,G., Just, W.W., Werner,G., and Wiechmann,M. "Detection and identification of tetrahydrocannabinol in biological fluids."(Ger.). Naturwissen. 1973, 4, 207-208.

2828. Fronmuller,F. Clinical Studies of Narcotic Remedies.(Ger.). Erlangen, Germany, 1869.

2829. Fronmuller,F. Indian Hemp, With Particular Regard to its Narcotic Properties.(Ger.). Prague, 1860.

2830. Fronmuller,F. "Tannic acid of cannabis."(Ger.). Allgem. Med. Cent.-Zeit. 1882, 51, 833-834.

2831. Frosch,W.A. "Irrational responses." Internat'l. J. Psychiat. 1970, 9, 521-525.

2832. Frosch,W.A. "Psychoanalytic evaluation of addiction and habituation." J. Am. Psychoanal. Assoc. 1970, 18, 209-218.

2833. Fruhwirth,C. "On hemp cultivation."(Ger.). Zeit. Hanf. 1922, 8, 340-401.

2834. Frumkin,R.M., Cowan,R.A., Davis,J.R. "Drug use in a midwest sample of metropolitan hinterland high school students." Correct. Psychiat. J. Soc. Ther. 1969, 15, 8-13.

2835. Frye,F.L. "Acute cannabis intoxication in a pup." J. Am. Vet. Med. Assoc. 1969, 9, 37-40.

2836. Fujimori,M. and Himwich,H.E. "Delta-9-tetrahydrocannabinol and the sleep-wakefulness cycle in rabbits." Physiol. Behav. 1973, 11, 291-295.

2837. Fujimoto,J.M. "Modification of the effects of delta-9-tetrahydrocannabinol by phenobarbital pretreatment in mice." Toxicol. Appl. Pharmacol. 1972, 23, 623-634.

2838. Fujita,S., Kawatani,T., and Kurihara,K. "Destructive effects of vapor heating and gamma-ray radiation on the germination of papever somniferum L. and cannabis sativa L."(Jap.). Bull. Nat'l. Inst. Hyg. Sci. 1968, 58, 60-71.

2839. Fujita,S., Kawatani,T., and Kurihara,K. "Destructive effects of vapor heating and gamma-ray radiation on the germination of papaver somniferum L. and cannabis sativa L. II."(Jap.). Bull. Nat'l. Inst. Hyg. Sci. 1968, 86, 68-73.

2840. Fujita,S., Kawatani,T., and Kurihara,K. "Destructive effects of vapor heating and gamma-ray radiation on the germination of papaver somniferum L. and cannabis sativa L. III."(Jap.). Bull. Nat'l. Inst. Hyg. Sci. 1968, 86, 74-77.

2841. Fujita,S., Shimomura,H., Kuriyana,E., Shighiro,M., and Akasu,M. "Studies on cannabis. Examination of the narcotic and its related components in hemp, crude drug, and plant, by gas-liquid chromatography and thin-layer chromatography."(Jap.). Jap. J. Pharmacog. 1967, 21, 57-64.

2842. Fuller,H.C. "The possibility of substituting cannabis for opium." J.A.P.A. 1918, 7, 431-432.

2843. Fullerton,D.S. and Kurzman,M.G. "Identification and misidentification of marihuana." Contemp. Drug 1974, 3, 291-344.

2844. Fulton,C.C. "Analytical classes of cannabinol compounds in marihuana resin." Indust. Engin. Chem. 1942, 14, 407-412.

2845. Fulton,C.C. "The furfural test for cannabis resin." Bull. Narc. 1970, 22, 33.

2846. Fulton,G.B. "Current assessment of marihuana: a rebuttal." J. Sch. Hlth. 1973, 43, 60-62.

2847. Furst,E.J. and Fricke,B.G. "Development and applications of structured tests of personality." Rev. Educat. Res. 1956, 26, 26-55.

2848. Fusco,A.J. and Pepe,S.A. "Drug law revision--the New Jersey approach." Seton Hall Law Rev. 1971, 2, 396-397.

2849. Fuxe,K. and Jonsson,G. "The effect of tetrahydrocannabinols on central monoamine neurons." Act. Pharmaceut. Suec. 1971, 8, 695.

G

2850. Gabfittichka,T. "On cannabis indica--obtaining high grade cannabis indica cultivated in Germany."(Ger.). Sudeten. Apot. 1925, 1, 288-296.

2851. Gaforova,K.M. "Cultivation of Indian hemp as a medicinal plant."(It.). Trud. Zoovet. 1957, 10, 145-157.

2852. Gafurof,I. "Refinement of cannabis oil." (It.). Oil Fat Indust. 1926, 6, 9-13.

2853. Gagliardi,L., Bonifazi,A., and Chiavarelli,S. "Study of the colorimetric reaction of cannbis indica." (It.). Farmaco 1976, 31, 18-22.

2854. Gagnon,M.A. and Elie,R. "Effects of marihuana and d-amphetamine on appetite, food consumption and various cardio-respiratory variables in man."(Fr.). Un. Med. Can. 1975, 104, 914-921.

2855. Gaisbauer,G. "Hashish use and fitness to drive."(Ger.). Illust. Rund. Gendarm. 1974, 27, 45.

2856. Gal,I.E. and Vajda,O. "Influence of cannabidiolic acid on microorganisms." Elelmis. Ip. 1970, 23, 336.

2857. Gal,I.E., Vajda,O., and Bekes,I. "Investigation of particular properties of cannabidioloic acid as a food preservative." Elelmis. Kozlem. 1969, 4, 208-216.

2858. Gal,I.E., Vajda,O., and Bekes,I. "Properties of cannabidiolic acid with particular regard to its use as a food preservative." Nahrung 1969, 13, 515-522.

2859. Galanter,M., Stillman,R., Wyatt,R.J., Vaughan,T. B., Weingartner,H., and Nurnberg,F.L. "Marihuana and social behavior." Arch. Gen. Psychiat. 1974, 30, 518-521.

2860. Galanter,M., Weingartner,H., Vaughan,T.B., Roth, W.T., and Wyatt,R.J. "Delta-9-tetrahydrocannabinol and natural marihuana." Arch. Gen. Psychiat. 1973, 28, 278-281.

2861. Galanter,M., Wyatt,R.J., Lemberger,L., Weingartner,H., Vaughan,T.B., and Roth,W.T. "Effects on humans of delta-9-THC adminstered by smoking." Science 1972, 176, 934-936.

2862. Galbis,R. "Pot and booze." N. Eng. J. Med 1969, 280, 1077.

2863. Galbis,R. "The free clinics: Approach to alienated youth." In Smith,D.E., Bentel,D.J., and Schwartz,J.L.(eds.). The Free Clinic: A Community Approach to Health Care and Drug Abuse. Stash Press, Beloit,Wis., 1971, 120-126.

2864. Gale,E.N. and Guenther,G. "Motivational factors associated with the use of cannabis(marihuana)." Br. J. Addict. 1971, 66, 188-194.

2865. Galen. Properties of Food Stuffs.(Lat.).(Kuhn, C.G. ed.). Hildesheim, London, 1964.

2866. Gallager,D.W., Sanders-Bush,E., and Sulser,F. "Dissociation between behavioral effects and changes in metabolism of cerebral serotonin(5 HT) following delta-9-tetrahydrocannabinol(THC)." Pharmacologist 1971, 13, 296.

2867. Galliher,J.F. and Walker,A. "The puzzle of the social origins of the Marihuana Tax Act of 1937." Soc. Prob. 1977, 24, 367-376.

2868. Galliher,J.F., McCartney,J.L., and Baum,B.A. "Nebraska's marihuana law: a case of unexpected legislative innovation." Law and Soc. Rev. 1974, 8, 441-455.

2869. Gallup,G. Gallup Poll: Public Opinion. 1935-1971. Random House, N.Y., 1972.

2870. Gallup Opinion Index. Marihuana Use By U.S. Adults. Gallup Internat'l., Princeton, N.J., 1972.

2871. Gallup Opinion Index. Marihuana Use Among Adults No Longer On The Increase. Am. Inst. Public Opinion, Princeton, N.J., 1973.

2872. Gallup Opinion Index. Public Opinion on the Controversial Issue of Legalizing Marihuana. Am. Inst. Public Opinion, Princeton, N.J., 1969.

2873. Galvin,K. and Taylor,R. "Drug education in Massachusetts." In National Commission on Marihuana and Drug Abuse. Drug Use in America: Problem in Perspective. Gov't. Print. Office, Washington, D.C., 1973, II, 411-452.

2874. Gamage,J.R. and Zerkin,E.L. A Comprehensive Guide to the English-Language Literature on Cannabis (Marihuana). Stash Press, Beloit, Wis., 1969.

2875. Gamble,K.R. "Radical notion." Schiz. Bull. 1974, 11, 16.

2876. Ganatra,J.P., Satakopan,S., Patel,M.A., and Shastri,M.R. "Identification of cannabis in seizure samples." Ind. J. Pharm. 1969, 31, 101-103.

2877. Ganz,V.P. and Volkmar,F. "Adverse reactions to marihuana use among college students." J. Am. Coll. Hlth. Assoc. 1976, 15, 93-96.

2878. Gaoni,Y. and Mechoulam,R. "Cannabichromene, a new active principle in hashish." Chem. Commun. 1966, 1, 20-22.

2879. Gaoni,Y. and Mechoulam,R. "Concerning the isomerization of delta-1- to delta-1(6)-tetrahydrocannabinol." J. Am. Chem. Soc. 1966, 88, 5673-5675.

2880. Gaoni,Y. and Mechoulam,R. "Hashish. 1: The isolation and constitution of a new component, cannabigerol." Proc. 33rd. Meet. Isr. Chem. Soc. 1963, 1, 229-230.

2881. Gaoni,Y. and Mechoulam,R. "Hashish. 3: Isolation structure, and partial synthesis of an active constituent of hashish." J. Am. Chem. Soc. 1964, 86, 1646-1647.

2882. Gaoni,Y. and Mechoulam,R. "Hashish. 7: The isomerization of cannabidiol to tetrahydrocannabinols." Tetrahedron 1966, 22, 1481-1488.

2883. Gaoni,Y. and Mechoulam,R. "Hashish. 14: The isotetrahydrocannabinols." Isr. J. Chem. 1968, 6, 679-680.

2884. Gaoni,Y. and Mechoulam,R. "The isolation and structure of delta-1-tetrahydrocannabinol and other neutral cannabinoids from hashish. J. Am. Chem. Soc. 1971, 93, 217-224.

2885. Gaoni,Y. and Mechoulam,R. "The structure and synthesis of cannabigerol, a new hashish constituent." Proc. Chem. Soc. 1964, 1, 82-83.

2886. Garattini,S. "Effects of a cannabis extract on gross behavior." In Wolstenholme,G. and Knight,J (eds.). Hashish: Its Chemistry and Pharmacology. Ciba Foundation Study Group, J. and A. Churchill, London, 1965, 70-82.

2887. Garcia,B.M. "Drug dependency in Colombia." Addict. Dis. 1977, 3, 25-26.

2888. Garcin,F., Radouco-Thomas,S. and Radouco-Thomas,C. "Contribution to the pharmacology and toxicology of cannabis derivatives."(Fr.). Toxicomanies 1970, 3, 253-303.

2889. Gard,W. "Youth gone loco." Christ. Cent. 1938, 55, 812-813.

2890. Gardikas,C.G. "Hashish and crime." Enkephalos 1950, 2, 201-210.

2891. Gardner,J. "Poisoning by cannabis indica." Month. J. Med. Sci. 1852, 14, 270-271.

2892. Garfield,E. and Garfield,M.D. "Marihuana use on campus." Internat'l. J. Addict. 1971, 6, 487-491.

2893. Garfield,M.D. and Garfield,E. "A longitudinal study of drugs on a campus." Internat'l. J. Addict. 1973, 8, 599-611.

2894. Garland,J.H. "Hemp, a minor American fiber crop." Econ. Geog. 1946, 22, 126-132.

2895. Garneau,N. "Judicial aspects and clinical work with respect to drug problems."(Fr.). Laval Med. 1969, 40, 122.

2896. Garner,J. "Penalties for possession lighter under new law on cannabis." Can. Med. Assoc. J. 1974, 111, 1283.

2897. Garnier,G., Bezanger-Beauquesne,L., and Debraux,G. Medicinal Resources of French Flora.(Fr.). Vigot, Paris, 1961.

2898. Garrett,E.R. and Hunt,C.A. "Analysis for picogram amounts of tetrahydrocannabinol and its application to biological fluids." J. Pharmaceut. Sci. 1973, 62, 1211-1214.

2899. Garrett,E.R. and Hunt,C.A. "Pharmacokinetics of delta-9-tetrahydrocannabinol in dogs." J. Pharmaceut. Sci. 1977, 66, 395-407.

2900. Garrett,E.R. and Hunt,C.A. "Physiochemical properties, solubility, and protein binding of delta-9-tetrahydrocannabinol." J. Pharmaceut. Sci. 1974, 63, 1056-1064.

2901. Garrett,E.R. and Hunt,C.A. "Picogram analysis of tetrahydrocannabinol and application to biological fluids." J. Pharmaceut. Sci. 1973, 62, 1211-1214.

2902. Garrett,E.R. and Hunt,C.A. "Separation and analysis of delta-9-tetrahydrocannabinol in biological fluids by high-pressure liquid chromatography and GLC." J. Pharmaceut. Sci. 1977, 66, 20-26.

2903. Garrett,E.R. and Hunt,C.A. "Separation and sensitive analysis of tetrahydrocannabinol in biological fluids by HPLC and GLC." In Willette,P.(ed.). Cannabinoids Assays in Humans. Nat'l. Inst. Drug Abuse Res. Monog. 7, Dept. H.E.W., Washington,D.C., 1976, 33-41.

2904. Garrett,E.R. and Tsau,J. "Stability of tetrahydrocannabinols." J. Pharmaceut. Sci. 1974, 63, 1563-1574.

2905. Garriott,J.C. "Cannabis, nicotine and alcohol compared." N. Eng. J. Med. 1971, 285, 806-807.

2906. Garriott,J.C., Forney,R.B., Hughes,F.W., and Richards,A.B. "Pharmacologic properties of some cannabis-related compounds." Arch. Internat'l. Pharmacodyn. Ther. 1969, 171, 425-434.

2907. Garriott,J.C., King,L.J., Forney,R.B., and Hughes,F.W. "Effects of some tetrahydrocannabinols on hexobarbital sleeping time and amphetamine-induced hyperactivity in mice." Life Sci. 1967, 6, 2119-2128.

2908. Garrod,I. "Indian hemp." Br. Med. J. 1864, 1, 178-181.

2909. Gary,N.E. and Keylon,V. "Intravenous administration of marihuana." J.A.M.A. 1970, 211, 501.

2910. Gascon,A.L. and Peres,M.T. "Effect of delta-9- and delta-8-tetrahydrocannabinol on the peripheral autonomic nervous system in vitro." Can. J. Physiol. Pharmacol. 1973, 51, 12-21.

2911. Gaskill,H.S. "Marihuana, an intoxicant." Am. J. Psychiat. 1945, 102, 202-204.

2912. Gasparrini,G. Research on the Embryology of Cannabis.(It.). Naples, 1862.

2913. Gastinel,J.B. "Memoir on hashish and its therapeutic applications.(Fr.). Rep. Pharm. 1849, 6, 129-142.

2914. Gastinel,J.B. "New preparation of hashish." (Fr.). Bull. Acad. Roy. Nat'l. Med. 1848, 13, 675-678, 827-829, 1386-1387.

2915. Gastinel,J.B. "Note relating to the preparation of cannabis resin."(Fr.). Rep. Pharm. 1856, 13, 78-79.

2916. Gatchell,C. Hashisch. Brentano's, N.Y., 1888.

2917. Gates,P.W. Agriculture and the Civil War. A.A. Knopf, N. Y., 1965.

2918. Gau,W., Bieniek,D., Coulston,F., and Korte,F. "Contribution to ecological chemistry. LXXIV. Metabolism of ^{14}C(-)-delta-8a-10a-THC in rhesus monkeys."(Ger.). Chemosphere 1974, 2, 71-76.

2919. Gau,W., Bieniek,D. and Korte,F. "Hashish. XXII. Synthesis of ^{14}C(-)-delta-8-6a,10a,tetrahydrocannabinol." (Ger.). Tetrahed. Let. 1972, 25, 2507-2508.

2920. Gaul,C.C. and Mellors,A. "Delta-9-THC and decreased macrophage migration and inhibition." Res. Commun. Chem. Pathol. Pharmacol. 1975, 10, 559-564.

2921. Gautier,T. "The hashish club."(Fr.). Rev. Deux-Mondes 1846, 13, 520-535.

2922. Gaukler,R.J. "Present day view of marihuana." Phil. Med. 1972, 68, 329-330.

2923. Gaver,K.D. "Man and marihuana(cannabis)." Oregon Ment. Hlth. Div. 1967, 2, 1-23.

2924. Gay,G.R. and Sheppard,C.W. "Sex-crazed dope fiends! Myth or reality?" In Harms,E.(ed.). Drugs and Youth. The Challenge of Today. Pergamon Press, N.Y., 1973, 149-163.

2925. Gayer,H. "Pharmacological standardization of Oriental hashish and cannabis indica."(Ger.). Arch. Exper. Pathol. Pharmakol. 1928, 129, 312-318.

2926. G.C. "The Fitz-Hugh Ludlow Memorial Library." High Times 1974, 4, 44-45.

2927. Geber,B. "Non-dependent drug use: some psychological aspects." In Steinberg,H.(ed.). Scientific Basis of Drug Dependence. J. and H. Churchill, London, 1969, 15-24.

2928. Geber,B., Pearson,J.F., and Tutton,C.B. Students, Apprentices and Drugs. London Sch. Econ. Drug Project, London, 1969.

2929. Geber,B., Sharpe,S., and Burski,D. The Drug Squad at New Scotland Yard, A Study of Role and Attitude to Illegal Drug Use. London Sch. Econ. Drug Project, London, 1969.

2930. Geber,B., Tutton,C., and Pearson,J. Drug Users and Peer Attitudes Amongst University Students and Industrial Apprentices. London Sch. Econ. Drug Project, London, 1969.

2931. Geber,W.F. and Schramm,L.C. "Congenital malformations in the fetal hamster and rabbit induced by marihuana extract." Lloydia 1969, 31, 428.

2932. Geber,W.F. and Schramm,L.C. "Effects of marihuana extract on fetal hamsters and rabbits." Toxicol. Appl. Pharmacol. 1969, 14, 276-282.

2933 Geber,W.F. and Schramm,L.C. "Teratogenicity of marihuana extract as influenced by plant origin and seasonal variation." Arch. Internat'l. Pharmacodyn. Ther. 1969, 177, 224-230.

2934. Geerlings,P.J. "Marihuana."(Dut.). Ned. Tijd. Geneesk. 1968, 112, 1739-1742.

2935. Geerlings,P.J. "Marihuana."(Dut.). Tijd. Ziek. 1969, 22, 68-72.

2936. Geerlings,P.J., Silbermann,R.M., and Schalken,H.F.A. "Acute adverse reactions to drug-taking." Act. Psychiat. Scand. 1972, 48, 22-29.

2937. Geiger,L.H. "Age, reported marihuana use, and belief in some assumed negative effects of the drug." Paper presented at 26th Annual Conf. of Am. Assoc. Pub. Opinion Res. Pasedena, Calif., 1971.

2938. Geis,G. "Social and epidemiological aspects of marihuana use." J. Psychedel. Drugs 1968, 2, 67-77.

2939. Geis,G. "Social and epidemiological aspects of marihuana use." Paper presented at Illinois State Med. Soc. Nat'l. Sympos. on Psychedel. Drugs and Marihuana. Chicago, 1968.

2940. Geiser,M.L. "Poisoning by cannabis indica." Med. Rec. 1896, 50, 519.

2941. Geller,A. and Boas,M. The Drug Beat. Cowles Book Co., N.Y., 1969.

2942. Gellert,V.F. and Sparber,S.B. "Delta-9-tetrahydrocannabinol(THC) interactions with amphetamine stereotypy and open field exploratory activity." Proc. 5th Internat'l. Cong. Pharmacol. 1972, 1, 79.

2943. George,C. "Ustilago maidis, viburnum prunifolium, normal liquid cannabis indica." Ther. Gaz. 1884, 8, 353-354.

2944. George,H.R. "Two psychotic episodes associated with cannabis." Br. J. Addict. 1970, 65, 119-121.

2945. George,H.R. and Glatt,M.M. "A brief survey of a drug dependency unit in a psychiatric hospital." Br. J. Addict. 1967, 62, 147-153.

2946. G.E.P. "Sentences for marihuana offences." Crim. Law Quart. 1969, 11, 263-266.

2947. Gerber,D. "Cannabis; a critical review." Western Univ. Law Rev. 1974, 13, 47-49.

2948. Gergen,M.K., Gergen,K.J., and Morse,S.J. "Correlates of marihuana use among college students." J. Appl. Soc. Psychol. 1972, 2, 1-16.

2948a. Germandt,H. "Training and use of track hounds."(Ger.). Neue Pol. 1975, 29, 42-45.

2949. Geroczy,M. "Indian hemp(cannabis sativa)--illegal use and social problems." Gyogyszereszet 1965, 9, 457-461.

2950. Gershon,S. "Marihuana--now let's get the facts." Med. Wld. News 1968, 9, G11-G12.

2951. Gershon,S. "On the pharmacology of marihuana." Behav. Neuropsychiat. 1970, 1, 9-18.

2952. Getmanov,P.I. "Effects of different amounts of KCl on production of hemp."(It.). Khim. Sel'sk. Khoz. 1966, 4, 412-413.

2953. Getmanov,P.I. "Effects of different doses and forms of potassium on the quality of cannabis fiber."(It.). Khim. Sel'sk. Khoz. 1965, 3, 8-11.

2954. Getmanov,P.I. "Effects of traces of fertilizer during the cultivation of cannabis."(It.). Khim. Sel'sk. Khoz. 1967, 5, 412-413.

2955. Ghamrawy,M. "The detection of cannabis indica. A new test." J. Egypt. Med. Assoc. 1937, 20, 193-208.

2955a. Ghamrawy,M.A. "The detection of cannabis indica."(Dut.). Pharm. Weekbl. 1938, 39, 1086.

2956. Ghani,A. "Marihuana-Some facts about it." Bangladesh Pharm. J. 1973, 2, 7-9.

2957. Gholst,S. "Notes on the use of hashish." In Solomon,D.(ed.). The Marihuana Papers. Bobbs-Merrill, Indianapolis, 1966, 216-223.

2958. Ghose,M.N. and Bhattacharjee,S.N. "Determination of physiological activity of hemp resin by a polarimetric method." Analyst 1935, 60, 313-316.

2959. Ghosh,J.J., Mitra,G., Poddar,M.K., and Chatterjee,D.K. "Effect of delta-9-tetrahydrocannabinol administration on hepatic functions." Biochem. Pharmacol. 1977, 26, 1797-1801.

2960. Ghosh,J.J., Pal,B., Datta,R.K., Antopol,W, Poddar,M.K., Biswas,B., and Chakravarty,I. "Delta-9-tetrahydrocannabinol action and 5-hydroxytryptamine metabolism in rats." Hormones 1972, 3, 267-268.

2961. Ghosh,J.J., Pal,B., and Poddar,M.K. "Delta-9-tetrahydrocannabinol action and neuronal membrane-bound enzymes." Prog. Brain Res. 1975, 42, 375.

2962. Ghosh,R., Pascall,D.C.S., and Todd,A.R. "Cannabis indica. Part III. The synthesis of dibenzopyran derivatives, including an isomer of cannabinol." J. Chem. Soc. 1940, 1, 1118-1121.

2963. Ghosh,R., Todd,A.R., and Wilkinson,S. "Cannabis indica. Part IV. The synthesis of some tetrahydrododibenzopyran derivatives." J. Chem. Soc. 1, 1123-1125.

2964. Ghosh,R., Todd,A.R., and Wilkinson,S. "Cannabis indica. Part V. The synthesis of cannabinol." J. Chem. Soc. 1940, 1, 1393-1396.

2965. Ghosh,R., Todd,A.R., and Wright,D.C. "Cannabis indica. Part VI. The condensation of pulegone with alkyl resorcinols. A new synthesis of cannabinol and a product with hashish activity." J. Chem. Soc. 1, 137-140.

2966. Gianutsos,G. and Abbatiello,E.R. "The effect of pre-natal cannabis sativa on maze learning ability in the rat." Psychopharmacol. 1972, 27, 117-122.

2967. Giantusos,R. and Litwak,A.R. "Chronic marihuana smokers show reduced coding into long term storage." Psychon. Sci. 1976, 7, 277-279.

2968. Gibbins,R.J. "Tolerance to marihuana-induced tachycardia in man." Act. Pharmacol. Toxicol. 1976, 39, 65-76.

2969. Gibelli,G. and Giacosa,P. Medicinal Plants--Manual of Botanical Medicine.(It.). E. Vallardi, Milan n.d.

2970. Gibermann,E., Chari-Bitron,A., Millo,S., and Gothilf,S. "Effect of delta-1-tetrahydrocannabinol on K^+ influx in rat erythrocytes." Exper. 1974, 30, 68-69 .

2971. Gibermann,E., Gothilf,S., Shahar,A., and Bino,T. "Effect of delta-9-tetrahydrocannabinol on the membrane permeability of bull spermatozoa to potassium." J. Reprod. Fert. 1975, 42, 389-390.

2972. Gilbert,E. "Hashish. Historical, medical, pharmacological and botanical study."(Fr.). Cent. Med. Pharm. 1912, 17, 240-242.

2973. Gilbert,E. Magical Plants and Sorcery.(Fr.). Moulin, Paris, 1899.

2974. Gilbert,J.C., Pertwee,R.G., and Wyllie,M.G. "Effects of delta-9-tetrahydrocannabinol and cannabidiol on a Mg^{++}-ATPase of synaptic vesicles prepared from rat cerebral cortex." Br. J. Pharmacol. 1977, 59, 599-601.

2975. Gil Carballo,A. "Marihuana as a factor in crime."(Sp.). First Cong. Panam Legal-med. Crim. 1946, 1, 346-348.

2976. Gil Carballo,A. Traffickers and Addicts.(Sp.). Havana, 1937.

2977. Gilder,S.S. "Marihuana, the unromantic." Can. Med. Assoc. J. 1967, 97, 132.

2978. Gill,E.W. "Propyl homologue of tetrahydrocannabinol: Its isolation from cannabis, properties, and synthesis." J. Chem. Soc. 1971, 3, 579-182.

2979. Gill,E.W. "The effects of cannabinoids and other CNS depressants on cell membrane models." Ann. N. Y. Acad. Sci. 1976, 281, 151-161.

2980. Gill,E.W. and Jones,G. "A non-exchange synthesis of tritium-labelled tetrahydrocannabinols." J. Label. Comp. 1972, 8, 237-248.

2981. Gill,E.W. and Jones,G. "Brain levels of delta-1-tetrahyrocannabinol and its metabolites in mice--correlation with behavior, and the effect of the metabolic inhibitors SKF 525A and piperonyl butoxide." Biochem. Pharmacol. 1972, 21, 2237-2248.

2982. Gill,E.W. and Jones,G. "Distribution and metabolism of tritium labelled tetrahydrocannabinol." Act. Pharmaceut. Suec. 1971, 8, 700-701.

2983. Gill,E.W. and Jones,G. "The chemical pharmacology of the active constituents of cannabis." In Praag,H.M.(ed.). Biochemical and Pharmacological Aspects of Dependence and Reports on Marihuana Research. Erven F.W. Bohn. Haarlem, The Netherlands, 1972, 103-123.

2984. Gill,E.W., Jones,G., and Lawrence,D.K. "Chemical mechanisms of action of THC." In Paton, W.D.M. and Crown,J.(eds.). Cannabis and its Derivatives. Oxford Univ. Press, London, 1972, 76-88.

2985. Gill,E.W., Jones,G., and Lawrence,D.K. "Contribution of the metabolite 7-hydroxy-delta-1-tetrahydrocannabinol towards the pharmacological activity of delta-1-tetrahydrocannabinol in mice." Biochem. Pharmacol. 1973, 22, 175-184.

2986. Gill,E.W. and Lawrence,D.K. "Blood and brain levels of delta-1-tetrahydrocannabinol in mice--the effect of 7-hydroxy-delta-1-tetrahydrocannabinol." Biochem. Pharmacol. 1974, 23, 1140-1143.

2987. Gill,E.W. and Lawrence,D.K. "The distribution of delta-1-tetrahydrocannabinol and 7-hydroxy-delta-1-tetrahydrocannabinol in the mouse brain after intraventricular injection." J. Pharm. Pharmacol. 1973, 25, 948-952.

2988. Gill,E.W. and Lawrence,D.K. "The physicochemical mode of action of THC on cell membranes." In Braude,M.C. and Szara,S.(eds.). Pharmacology of Marihuana. Raven Press, N.Y., 1976, 1, 147-157.

2989. Gill,E.W. and Paton,W.D.M. "Pharmacological experiments in vitro on the active principles of cannabis." In Joyce,C.R.B. and Curry,S.H.(eds.). The Botany and Chemistry of Cannabis. J. and A. Churchill, London, 1970, 165-175.

2990. Gill,E.W., Paton,W.D.M., and Pertwee,R.G. "Preliminary experiments on the chemistry and pharmacology of cannabis." Nature 1971, 228, 134-136.

2991. Gilmour,D.G., Bloom,A.D., Lele,K.P., Robbins,E.S., and Maximilian,C. "Chromosomal aberrations in users of psychoactive drugs." Arch. Gen. Psychiat. 1971, 24, 268-272.

2992. Gimlin,J.S. "Legalization of marihuana." Ed. Res. Rep. 1967, 1, 579-596.

2993. Ginsberg,A. "Fact sheet: small anthology of footnotes on marihuana." In Hollander,C.(ed.). Background Papers on Student Drug Involvement. U.S. Nat'l. Student Assoc., Washington, D.C., 1967, 9-14.

2994. Ginsberg,A. "First manifesto to end the bringdown." In Solomon,D.(ed.). The Marihuana Papers. Bobbs-Merrill, Indianapolis, 1966, 183-200.

2995. Ginsberg,A. "The great marihuana hoax." Atlantic Mon. 1966, 104, 107-112.

2996. Ginsberg,A. and Fox,J.H. "Seminar on marihuana and LSD controls." In Hollander,C.(ed.). Background Papers on Student Drug Involvement. U.S. Nat'l. Student Assoc., Washington, D.C., 1967, 15-36.

2997. Giono-Barber,P., Bertuletti,G., and Giono-Barber,H. "Action of cannabis on experiments with the cynocephale ape."(Fr.). Comp. Rend. Sean. Soc. Biol. 1975, 169, 264-269.

2998. Giono-Barber,P., Paris,M., Bertuletti,G., and Giono-Barber,H. "Cannabis effects on dominance in the cynocephale ape."(Fr.). J. Pharmacol. 1974, 5, 591-602.

2999. Giordano,H.L. "Marihuana--a calling card to narcotic addiction." F.B.I. Law Enforce. Bull. 1968, 37, 2-5.

3000. Giordano,H.L. "The dangers of marihuana... Facts you should know." Bull. Narc. Danger. Drugs 1968, 1, 16.

3001. Giordano,H.L. "The prevention of drug abuse." Humanist 1968, 28, 20-23.

3002. Giraud,J. "For or against the use of hashish."(Fr.). J. Magnet. 1916, 1, 30.

3003. Giraud,J. "Hashish."(Fr.). J. Magnet. 1912, 1, 28.

3004. Giraud,J. Testament of a Hashish User.(Fr.). Durville, Paris, 1913.

3005. Giraud,J. "The art of changing the effects of hashish."(Fr.). Encephale 1881, 1, 418-425.

3006. Giraud,R. and Reynier,M. "On the resin of different samples of cannabis indica. Remarks relative to its identification in the pharmacopoea." (Fr.). Chim. 1958, 21, 342-343.

3007. Giraud,R. and Reynier,M. "Research on the resin of different samples of Indian hemp. Critique of the legal definition."(Fr.). Bull. Soc. Pharm. Bord. 1956, 95, 181-184.

3008. Girdano,D.A. and Girdano,D.D. "Drug usage trends among college students." Coll. Stud. J. 1974, 8, 94-96.

3009. Girdano,D.D. and Girdano,D.A. "College drug use--a five year survey." J. Am. Coll. Hlth. Assoc. 1976, 25, 117-119.

3010. Girdano,D.D. and Girdano,D.A. Drugs--A Factual Account. Addison Wesley, Reading, Mass., 1976.

3011. Girou de Buzareingues,C. "Experiments on the generation of plants."(Fr.). Ann. Sc. Nat. 1831, 1, 148.

3012. Gisel,A. "Intensification of effects of true narcotics by cannabis indica."(Ger.). Zeit. Exper. Pathol. Ther. 1916, 18, 39-51.

3013. Gitchoff,G.T. Kids, Cop, Kilos: A Study of Contemporary Urban Youth. Malter-Westerfield, San Diego, 1969.

3014. Githens,T.S. Drug Plants of Africa. Univ. Penn. Press, Phil., 1949.

3015. Gittelson,N. "Legalized marihuana." McCalls, 1975, 102, 36-37.

3016. Gittelson,N. "Marihuana dilemma." McCalls 1975, 102, 56-57.

3017. Giulla,L. "Intoxication by maconha in Porto Alegre."(Port.). Fol. Med. 1950, 21, 173-175.

3018. Giusti,G.V. "A simple technique for the quantitative determination of THC in samples of hashish." (Ger.). Arch. Kriminol. 1973, 152, 86-90.

3019. Giusti,G.V. and Carnevale,A. "Effects of cannabinoids on bone marrow activity in adult mice." Drug Alcohol Depend. 1977, 2, 31-38.

3020. Giusti,G.V. and Carvevale,A. "Myeloid hyperplasia in growing rats after chronic treatment with delta-9-THC at behavioral doses." Arch. Toxicol. 1975, 34, 169-172.

3021. Giusti,G.V., Chiarotti,M., and Passatore,M "Muscular dystrophy in adult mice chronically treated with delta-9-THC at behavioral doses." Exper. 1977, 33, 257.

3022. Giusti,G.V. and D'Agostino,P. "Quantitative research on the THC content in domestic hemp."(It.). Zacchia 1974, 10, 69-74.

3023. Gjerstad,G. "Naturally occurring hallucinogens. I." Quart. J. Crude Drug Res. 1971, 11, 1774-1787.

3024. Gjerstad,G. "Naturally occurring hallucinogens. II." Quart. J. Crude Drug Res. 1971, 11, 1797-1805.

3025. Glaser,D., Inciardi,J.T., and Babst,D.V. "Later heroin use by marihuana-using, heroin using, and non-drug using adolescent offenders in the New York City." Internat'l. J. Addict. 1969, 4, 145-155.

3026. Glaser,D., Lander,B., and Abbott,W. "Opiate addicted and non-addicted siblings in a slum area." Soc. Prob. 1971, 18, 510-521.

3027. Glaser,D. and Snow,M. Public Knowledge and Attitudes on Drug Abuse in New York State. New York State Narcotic Addiction Control Commission, N.Y., 1969.

3028. Glaser,S. The Health of the Hemp Industry. (Fr.). Rodstein, Paris, 1935.

3029. Glatt,M.M. "From soft to hard drugs." Br. Med. J. 1970, 1, 756.

3030. Glatt,M.M. "Historical note--hashish and alcohol 'scenes' in France and Great Britain 120 years ago." Br. J. Addict. 1969, 64, 99-108.

3031. Glatt,M.M. "Is it all right to smoke pot?" Br. J. Addict. 1969, 64, 109-114.

3032. Glatt,M.M., PIttman,D.J., Gillespie,D.G., and Hills,D.R. The Drug Scene in Britain. Edward Arnold, London, 1967.

3033. Gleason,C.H. "The pediatrician and the marihuana question." Pediatrics 1970, 45, 1037.

3034. Gley,E., Heymans,J.F., and Heymans,C. "Teratogenicity of marihuana extract as influenced by plant origin and seasonal variation." Arch. Internat'l. Pharmacodyn. Ther. 1969, 177, 224-230.

3035. Gley,E., Richet,C. and Rondeau,P. "Notes on hashish."(Fr.). Rev. Phil. France 1885, 1, 105-109.

3036. Glick,S.D. and Milloy,S. "Increased and decreased eating following THC administration." Psychon. Sci. 1972, 29, 6.

3037. Glick,S.D. and Milloy,S. "Tolerance, state-dependency and long-term behavioral effects of delta-9-THC." In Lewis,M.F.(ed.). Current Research in Marihuana. Academic Press, N.Y., 1972, 1-24.

3038. Glickman,D. Marihuana: The non-narcotic Dangerous Drug; Four Papers Examining The Need For Reclassification And For Changes In Penalties. Community Service Society of New York, Dept. of Public Affairs, Committee on Youth and Correction, N.Y., 1970.

3.039. Gluck,J.P. and Ferraro,D.P. "Effects of delta-9-THC on food and water intake of deprivation experienced rats." Behav. Biol. 1974, 11, 395-401.

3.040. Gluck,J.P., Ferraro,D.P., and Marriott,R.G. "Retardation of discrimination reversal by delta-9-tetrahydrocannabinol in monkeys." Pharmacol. Biochem. Behav. 1973, 1, 605-608.

3041. Glucksmann,C. "On the identification of cannabis resin extract."(Ger.). Pharmazeut. Prax. 1913, 12, 465-471.

3042. Gobar,A.H. "Drug abuse in Afganistan." Bull. Narc. 1976, 28, 1-11.

3043. Goben,R.D. "How to handle a dope scandal." Sch. Mgt. 1966, 10, 106-107.

3.044. Gobert,E. "Customs of cannabis smokers."(Fr.). Arch. Inst. Past. 1925, 14, 422-433.

3045. Godard,E. Hashish in Egypt and Palestine.(Fr.). Paris, 1867.

3046. Goddard,J.L. "How dangerous is marihuana? A top official sparks new debate." U.S. News 1967, 63, 20.

3047. Goddard,J.L. and Barnard,A. "The high school drug problem." In Goode,E.(ed.). Marihuana. Atherton Press, N.Y., 1969, 121-127.

3048. Godefroy,W. "Investigation of hashish from Cairo."(Ger.). Zeit. Ost. Apoth. Vereins. 1874, 1, 399-400.

3049. Godwin,H. "Pollen-analytic evidence for the cultivation of cannabis in England." Rev. Palaeobot. Palynol. 1967, 4, 71-80.

3050. Godwin,H. "The ancient cultivation of hemp." Antiquity 1967, 41, 42-49.

3051. Goenechea,S. and Dieckhofer,K. "Intoxication from cannabis. 2."(Ger.). Med. Welt 1972, 23, 1148-1151.

3052. Gold,S. "Marihuana studies." Med. J. Aust. 1972, 1, 338.

3053. Goldberg,L. "Drug abuse in Sweden. I." Bull. Narc. 1968, 20, 1-31.

3054. Goldberg,L. "Drug abuse in Sweden. II." Bull. Narc. 1968, 20, 9-36.

3055. Goldberg,L. "Epidemiology of drug abuse in Sweden." In Zarafonetis,C.J.D.(ed.). Drug Abuse. Lea and Febiger, Phil., 1972, 27-66.

3056. Goldberg,M.E., Hefner,M.A., Robichaud,R.C., and Dubinsky,B. "Dissociation of shuttle-box learning in mice between delta-9-tetrahydrocannabinol and chlordiazepoxide." Proc. 5th Internat'l. Cong. Pharmacol. 1972, 1, 84.

3057. Goldberg,M.E., Hefner,M.A., Robichaud,R.C., and Dubinsky,B. "Effects of delta-9-tetrahydrocannabinol (THC) and chlordiazepoxide(CDP) on state-dependent learning: evidence for asymmetrical dissociation." Psychopharmacol. 1973, 30, 173-184.

3058. Goldberg,M.J. "Fathers talk about marihuana." Good House. 1968, 167, 10.

3059. Goldman,A. "Confessions of a hashish eater." High Times 1977, 11, 66-68, 96.

3060. Goldman,A. "The mighty Mezz." High Times 1977, 27, 47-50.

3061. Goldman,H., Dagirmanjian,R., Drew,W.G., and Murphy,S. "Delta-9-tetrahydrocannabinol alters flow of blood to subcortical areas of the conscious rat brain." Life Sci. 1975, 17, 477-482.

3062. Goldner,R.L. "Marihuana: History, effect." (Sp.). Fich. Med. Ther. 1965, 27, 29-32.

3063. Goldstein,F.J. "Marihuana--a pharmacological profile." Am. J. Pharm. 1971, 143, 59-64.

3064. Goldstein,H. "Effects of chronic administration of delta-9-tetrahydrocannabinol and cannabidiol on rat testicular esterase isozymes." Life Sci. 1977, 20, 951-954.

3065. Goldstein,H.W. "Motivations for psychoactive drug use among students." Paper presented at East. Psychol. Assoc., N.Y., 1971.

3066. Goldstein,J.W. Students' Evaluation of Their Psychoactive Drug Use. Unpub. Ms., Carnegie Mellon Univ., Pittsburgh, n.d.

3067. Goldstein,J.W. and Gleason,T.C. "Significance of increasing student marihuana use for intended use of other drugs." Proc. Am. Psychol. Assoc. 1973, 4, 305-306.

3068. Goldstein,J.W., Gleason,T.C., and Korn,J.H. _Whether the Epidemic? Psychoactive Drug Use Carreer Patterns of College Students_. Carnegie Mellon Univ., Dept. of Psychol. Res. Report, Pittsurgh, 1974.

3069. Goldstein,J.W., and Korn,J.H. "Judging the shape of things to come: Lessons learned from comparisons of student drug users in 1968 and 1970." Paper presented at East. Psychol. Assoc., N.Y., 1971.

3070. Goldstein,J.W., Korn,J., Abel,W.H., and Morgan,R.M. _The Social Psychology and Epidemiology of Student Drug Use. Report on Phase One_. Unpub. ms. Carnegie Mellon Univ. Drug Res. Report, Pittsburgh, 1970.

3071. Goldstein,J.W. and Sappington,J.T. "Personality characteristics of students who became heavy drug users: An MMPI study of an avant-garde." Paper presented at Southwest. Psychol. Assoc., New Orleans, 1976.

3072. Goldstein,R. _1 in 7--Drugs on Campus_. Walker and Co., N.Y., 1966.

3073. Goldstein,R. "The college scene in the USA." In Andrews,G. and Vinkenoog,S.(eds.). _The Book of Grass_. Grove Press, N.Y., 1967, 214-218.

3074. Goldstein,R. "The question of pot." _Moderator_ 1965, _4_, 9-10.

3075. Gollan,A. "The great marihuana problem." _Nat'l. Rev._ 1968, _20_, 74-80.

3076. Gomalez,A.F. "Vietcong's secret weapon: marihuana." _Sci. Dig._ 1969, _65_, 14-18.

3077. Gomberoff,M., Florenzano,R., and Pualuan,L "Motivations for marihuana use by teenagers."(Sp.) _Rev. Med. Chile_ 1972, _100_, 286-292.

3078. Gomberoff,M., Florenzano,R., and Thomas,J. "A study of the conscious motivations and the effects of marihuana smoking on a group of adolescents in Chile." _Bull. Narc._ 1972, _24_, 27-33.

3079. Gomberoff,M., Thomas,J., and Florenzano,R. "Use of marihuana by adolescents."(Sp.). _Rev. Med. Chile_ 1971, _99_, 75-80.

3080. Gonzales Mas,R. "Introduction to the study of addiciton to Indian hemp."(Sp.). _Medecina_ 1953, _21_, 130-136.

3081. Gonzalez,S.C. and Carlini,E.A. "Extinction of operant responses by rats under the effects of cannabis sativa extract." Psychon. Sci. 1971, 24, 203-204.

3082. Gonzalez,S.C., Gobbi,E.J., and Marenco,E. "Thin-layer chromatographic study of marihuana." Rev. Farm. 1971, 113, 58-60.

3083. Gonzalez,S.C., Karniol,I.G., and Carlini,E.A. "Effects of cannabis sativa extract on conditioned fear." Behav. Biol. 1972, 7, 83-94.

3084. Gonzalez,S.C., Matsudo,V.K.R., and Carlini,E.A. "Effects of marihuana compounds on the fighting behavior of Siamese fighting fish(Betta splendens)." Pharmacol. 1971, 6, 186-190.

3085. Gooberman,L.A. Operation Intercept. Pergamon Press, N.Y., 1974.

3086. Gooberman,L.A. Operation Intercept: A Sociological Analysis of the Multiple Consequences of Public Policy. Univ. Michigan, Ann Arbor, Mich., 1973.

3087. Goodall,A. "The physiological standarization of drugs." Pharmaceut. J. Pharmacist 1910, 30, 112-114.

3088. Goode,E. Drugs in American Society. A.A. Knopf, N.Y., 1972.

3089. Goode,E. "Drug use and grades in college." Nature 1971, 234, 225-227.

3090. Goode,E. "Drug use and sexual activity of a college campus." Am. J. Psychiat. 1972, 128, 1272-1276.

3091. Goode,E. "Effects of cannabis in another culture." Science 1975, 189, 41-43.

3092. Goode,E. "How the American marihuana market works." New Soc. 1970, 15, 992-994.

3093. Goode,E. "Ideological factors in the marihuana controversy." Ann. N. Y. Acad. Sci. 1971, 191, 246-261.

3094. Goode,E.(ed.). Marihuana. Atherton Press, N.Y., 1969.

3095. Goode,E. "Marihuana and sex." Evergreen Rev. 1969, 66, 19-21.

3096. Goode,E. "Marihuana and the politics of reality." J. Hlth. Soc. Behav. 1969, 10, 83-94.

3097. Goode,E. "Marihuana. Pseudo-scientific debate." Univ. Rev. 1970, 1, 24-28.

3098. Goode,E. "Marihuana use and the progression to dangerous drugs." In Miller,L.L.(ed.). Marihuana Effects on Human Behavior. Academic Press, N.Y., 1974, 303-338.

3099. Goode,E. "Multiple drug use among marihuana smokers." Soc. Prob. 1969, 17, 48-64.

3100. Goode,E. "Sex and marihuana." Sex. Behav. 1972, 2, 45-51.

3101. Goode,E. "Sociological aspects of marihuana use." Contemp. Drug Prob. 1976, 4, 397-446.

3102. Goode,E. "The criminogenics of marihuana." Addict. Dis. 1974, 1, 297-322.

3103. Goode,E.(ed.). The Drug Phenomenon: Social Aspects of Drug Taking. Bobbs-Merrill, Indianapolis, 1973.

3104. Goode,E. "The major drugs of use among adolescents and young adults." In Harms,E.(ed.). Drugs and Youth: The Challenge of Today. Pergamon Press, N.Y., 1973, 33-72.

3105. Goode,E. "The marihuana market." Columb. For. 1969, 12, 4-8.

3106. Goode,E. The Marihuana Smokers. Basic Books, N.Y., 1970.

3107. Goode,E. "The use of marihuana and other illegal drugs on a college campus." Br. J. Addict. 1971, 66, 335-336.

3108. Goodenday,L.S. and Perloff,D. "Research on marihuana." New Eng. J. Med. 1972, 287, 995.

3109. Goodrich,L.M. "New trends in narcotic control." Internat'l. Concil. 1960, 530, 214.

3110. Goodwin,D.W. "Marihuana." J.A.M.A. 1970, 212, 325.

3111. Goodwin,D.W. "Marihuana and amphetamine; the question of interaction." Am. J. Psychiat. 1973, 130, 707-708.

3112. Goodwin,D.W. "To the editor." Scientif. Amer. 1970, 222, 6.

3113. Godwin,D.W., Fischer,R., Keup,W., Joubert,L., and Weil,A.T. "Marihuana." Science 1969, 163, 1144-1145.

3114. Goodwin,L.R. "Psychosocial motivations for the initial, continuing, and discontinuing of marihuana and the psychedelic drugs." Diss. Abs. 1975, 35, 4625.

3115. Gordon,G. "Marihuana in adolescence." J.A.M.A. 1971, 216, 1202.

3116. Gordon,M. Narcotic Status of and Clinical Experience with Synthesis of Tetrahydrocannabinol Analogs. Smith, Kline and French, Phil., 1960.

3116a. Gordon,P.D. "Toward the resolution of the controversy surrounding the effects and social health implications of marihuana use." J. Drug Educat. 1974, 4, 13-25.

3117. Gordon,R., Gordon,R.J., and Sofia,R.D. "Antitussive activity of some naturally occurring cannabinoids in anesthetized cats." Eur. J. Pharmacol. 1976, 35, 309-313.

3118. Gordon,R., Spector,S., Sjoerdsma,A., and Udenfriend,S. "Increased synthesis of norepinephrine and epinephrine in the intact rat during exercise and exposure to cold." J. Pharmacol. Exper. Ther. 1966, 153, 440-447.

3119. Gorodetzky,C.W. "Marihuana, LSD, and amphetamines." Drug Depend. 1970, 5, 18-23.

3120. Gorodni,N.G. "Effect of fertilizers on hemp."(It.). Agrokhimiya 1964, 8, 49-56.

3121. Gorshkov,P.A. "Influence of nutritional substances on the formation of fibrous material in hemp." (It.). Dok. Vses. Acad. Sel'sk. Nauk Lenin. 1957, 22, 10-14.

3122. Gorshkov,P.A. "Nutrition of hemp."(It.). Zemledelie 1955, 3, 78-84.

3123. Gorshkov,P.A. "Peculiarities of the influence of ammonia and nitrates on hemp."(It.). Visnik Sil'sk. Nauk. 1960, 3, 31-34.

3124. Gossett,J.T., Lewis,J.M., and Phillips,V.A. "Extent and prevalence of illicit drug use as reported by 56,745 students." J.A.M.A. 1971, 213, 1464-1470.

3125. Gostomzyk,J.G., Gewecke,G., and Eisele,G. "Comparative studies of driving ability following hashish consumption and brief narcosis."(Ger.). Med. Welt 1971, 22, 1785-1789.

3126. Gostomzyk,J.G., Parade,P., and Geweeke,H. "Drug use and performance. Studies of performance under hashish."(Ger.). Zeit. Rechtsmed. 1973, 73, 131-136.

3127. Gottheil,E., Rieger,J.A., Farwell,B., and Lieberman,D.L. "An outpatient drug program for adolescent students: preliminary evaluation." Am. J. Drug Alcohol Abuse 1977, 4, 31-41.

3128. Gottschalk,L.A., Aronow,W.S., and Prakash,R. "Effect of marihuana and placebo-marihuana smoking on psychological state and on psychophysiological cardiovascular functioning in anginal patients." Biol. Psychiat. 1977, 12, 255-266.

3129. Gottschalk,L.A., Bates,D.E., Fox,R.A., and James,J.M. "Psychoactive drug use." Arch. Gen. Psychiat. 1971, 25, 395-398.

3130. Gough,A.L. and Olley,J.E. "Cannabis and amphetamine-induced stereotypy in rats." J. Pharm. Pharmacol. 1975, 27, 62-63.

3131. Gough,A.L. and Olley,J.E. "Delta-9-tetrahydrocannabinol and the extrapyramidal system." Psychopharmacol. 1977, 54, 87-99.

3132. Gould,L.C. and Kleber,H.D. "Changing patterns of multiple drug use among applicants to a multimodality drug treatment program." Arch. Gen. Psychiat. 1974, 31, 408-413.

3133. Goulding,R. "Statistics of drug addiction." Med. Sci. Law 1968, 8, 266-270.

3134. Gourves,J., Viallard,C., Lelauan,D., Girard, J.P., and Aury,R. "A case of coma from cannabis sativa." (Fr.). Toxicol. Clin. 1971, 19, 1389-1390.

3135. Government of Cyprus. "Annual report of the government analyst for the year 1935." Analyst 1936, 61, 697-698.

3136. Government of Madras. "Annual report of the chemical examiner for the year 1934." Analyst 1935, 60, 759.

3137. Government of Palestine. Annual report of the government analyst for the year 1934." Analyst 1936, 61, 118.

3138. Governor's Task Force on Narcotics, Dangerous Drugs and Alcohol Abuse. Drug Abuse in Florida. Governor's Task Force on Narcotics, Tallahassee, Fla., 1970.

3139. Gowers,H.E. "Haschisch hallucinations." Am. Phys. 1906, 32, 72-76.

3140. Goyos,A.C. and Alves,C.N. "Aggressiveness induced by marihuana and other psychotropic drugs in REM sleep deprived rats." First Lat. Amer. Cong. Psychobiol. 1973, 1, 97.

3141. Gracza,L. and Ferenczy,L. "Presence of hashish in hemp fiber."(Ger.). Pharmazie 1958, 2, 267-268.

3142. Graeffner,W. "Experiments with the balsam of cannabis indica."(Ger.). Klin. Woch. 1887, 24, 416-417.

3143. Graff,H. "Marihuana and scopolamine 'high'." Am. J. Psychiat. 1969, 125, 1258-1259.

3144. Grafton,S., Grafton,E.K., and Tierney,S. "Research news on marihuana is getting worse." In Grafton,S., Grafton,E.K., and Tierney,S.(eds.). Addiction and Drug Abuse Report. Grafton Publications Incorp., N.Y., 1974, 1-4.

3145. Graham,J.D. "Potted dreams." Br. Med. J. 1969, 1, 376.

3146. Graham,J.D.P. "Cannabinoids as therapeutic agents." In Graham,J.D.P.(ed.). Cannabis and Health. Academic Press, N.Y., 1976, 417-439.

3147. Graham,J.D.P.(ed.). Cannabis and Health. Academic Press, N.Y., 1976.

3148. Graham,J.D.P. "The effect on cannabis on A: The mind of man; B: Animal behavior." In Graham, J.D.P.(ed.). Cannabis and Health. Academic Press, N.Y., 1976, 121-143.

3149. Graham,J.D.P., Davies,B.H., Seaton,A., and Weatherstone,R.M. "Bronchodilator action of extract of cannabis and delta-1-tetrahydrocannabinol." In Braude, M.C. and Szara,S.(eds.). Pharmacology of Marihuana. Raven Press, N.Y., 1976, 1, 269-277.

3150. Graham,J.D.P., Lewis,M.J., and Li, D.M.F. "The effect of delta-1-tetrahydrocannabinol on the uptake of ^{3}H-(-)-noradrenaline by the isolated perfused heart of the rat." Br. J. Pharmacol. 1974, 51, 464-466.

3151. Graham,J.D.P., Lewis,M.J., and Li,D.M.F. "The effect of delta-1-tetrahydrocannabinol on the release of ^{3}H-(-)-nordadrenaline from the isolated vas deferens of the rat. Br. J. Pharmacol. 1974, 52, 233-236.

3151a. Graham,J.D.P. and Li,D.M.F. "Cardiovascular and respiratory effects of cannabis in cat and rat." Br. J. Pharmacol. 1973, 49, 1-10.

3151b. Graham,J.D.P. and Li,D.M.F. "The pharmacology of cannabis and cannabinoids." In Graham,J.D.P.(ed.). Cannabis and Health. Academic Press, N.Y., 1976, 143-271.

3152. Granier-Doyeaux,M. "Historical data on Indian hemp." Rev. Cent. Med. 1962, 3, 68-74.

3153. Grant,I., Adams,K.M., Carlin,A.S., and Rennick,P.M. "Neuropsychological deficit in polydrug users." Drug Alcohol Depend. 1977, 2, 91-108.

3154. Grant,I., Rochford,J., Fleming,T., and Stunkard,A. "A neuropsychological assessment of the effects of moderate marihuana use." J. Nerv. Ment. Dis. 1973, 156, 278-280.

3155. Grant,J., Gross,S.J., Lomax,P., and Wong,R. "Antibody detection of marihuana." Nature 1972, 236, 216-217.

3156. Grant-Whyte,H. "The present status of drug dependence in South Africa." Addict. Dis. 1977, 3, 61-64.

3157. Grassberger,R. "Criminological aspects of juvenile drug use in Austria."(Ger.). Kriminalistik 1971, 25, 173-176.

3158. Greb,W., Bieniek,D., and Korte,F. "Hashish XXI. Synthesis of azacannabinols."(Ger.). Tetrahed. Let. 1972, 6, 545-546.

3159. Green,C.W. Hasheesh. Hodder and Stoughton, London, 1926.

3160. Green,D.E. "Automated analysis of marihuana metabolites in biological fluids using a new, ultra-sensitive analytical technique." Paper presented at Am. Chem. Soc., N.Y., 1972.

3161. Green,D.E. "Automated detection of abused drugs by direct mass fragmentography." Proc. West. Pharmacol. Soc. 1972, 15, 74-77.

3162. Green,D.E. "Quantitation of cannabinoids in biological specimens using probability based matching gas chromatography/mass spectometry." In Willette,P.(ed.). Cannabinoid Assays in Humans. N.I.D.A. Res. Monog. 7, Gov't. Print. Office, Washington, D.C., 1976, 70-87.

3163. Green,J.R. "Does marihuana damage the brain?" Ariz. Med. 1974, 31, 835.

3164. Green,K. "Marihuana and the eye." Invest. Ophthalmol. 1972, 4, 261-263.

3165. Green,K., Bigger,J.F., Kim,K., and Boman,K. "Cannabinoid actions on the eye as mediated through the central nervous system and local adrenergic activity." Expt'l. Eye Res. 1977, 24, 189-196.

3166. Green,K. and Bowman,K. "Effect of marihuana and derivatives on aqueous humor dynamics inthe rabbit." In Braude,M.C. and Szara,S.(eds.). Pharmacology of Marihuana. Raven Press, N.Y., 1976, 2, 803-815.

3167. Green,K. and Kim,K. "Acute dose response of intraocular pressure to topical and oral cannabinoids." Proc. Soc. Expt'l. Biol. Med. 1977, 154, 228-231.

3168. Green,K. and Kim,K. "Interaction of adrenergic antagonists with prostaglandin E_2 and tetrahydrocannabinol in the eye." Invest. Ophthalmol. 1976, 15, 102-111.

3169. Green,K. and Kim,K. "Interaction of adrenergic blocking agents with prostaglandin E_2 and tetrahydrocannabinol in the eye." Expt'l. Eye Res. 1973, 15, 499-507.

3170. Green,K. and Kim,K. "Papaverine and verapamil interaction with prostaglandin E_2 and delta-9-tetrahydrocannabinol in the eye." Expt'l. Eye Res. 1977, 24, 207-214.

3171. Green,K., Kim,K., and Bowman,K. "Ocular effects of delta-9-tetrahydrocannabinol." In Cohen,S. and Stillman,R.(eds.). Therapeutic Potential of Marihuana. Plenum Press, N.Y., 1976, 49-62.

3172. Green,K. and Pederson,J.E. "Effect of delta-1-tetrahydrocannabinol on aqueous dynamics and ciliary body permeability in the rabbit." Expt'l. Eye Res. 1973, 15, 499-507.

3173. Green,K., Podos,S.M., and Kellogg,W.K. "Antagonism of arachidonic acid-induced ocular effects by delta-1-tetrahydrocannabinol." Invest. Ophthalmol. 1974, 13, 422-429.

3174. Green,L.L. and Haymes,M. "Value orientation and psychosocial adjustment at various levels of marihuana use." J. Youth Adolesc. 1973, 2, 213-231.

3175. Green,M. and Miller,R.D. "Cannabis use in Canada." In Rubin,V.(ed.). Cannabis and Culture. Mouton, The Hague, 1975, 497-520

3176. Greenberg,D.S. "Hash in Holland: The Dutch find it easier to let traffic flourish." Science 1969, 165, 476-478.

3177. Greenberg,D.S. "'Pot' and politics: How they 'busted' Stony Brook." Science 1968, 159, 607-611.

3178. Greenberg,E., Kuehnle,J., Mendelson,J.H., and Bernstein,J.G. "Effects of marihuana use on body weight and caloric intake in humans." Pasychopharmacol. 1976, 49, 79-84.

3179. Greenberg,I. "The effects of 1-delta-9-tetrahydrocannabinol on low and high response rates generated under two similar conditions." Diss. Abs. 1973, 34, 1772-1773.

3180. Greengerg,I. "Effects of marihuana use on body weight and caloric intake in humans." Psychopharmacol. Bull. 1976, 12, 79-84.

3181. Greenberg,I., Kuhn,D., and Appel,J.B. "Comparison of the discriminative stimulus properties of delta-9-THC and psilocybin in rats." Pharmacol. Biochem. Behav. 1975, 3, 931-934.

3182. Greenberg,I., Mendelson,J.H., Kuehnle,J.C., Mello,N., and Babor,T.F. "Psychiatric and behavioral observations of casual and heavy marihuana users in a controlled research setting." Ann. N. Y. Acad. Sci. 1976, 282, 72-84.

3183. Greenberg,J. "A study of male homosexuals (predominantly college students)." J. Am. Coll. Hlth. Assoc. 1973, 11, 56-60.

3184. Greenberg,J.H., Saunders,M.E., and Mellors,A. "Inhibition of a lymphocyte membrane enzyme by delta-9-tetrahydrocannabinol in vitro." Science 1977, 290, 475-477.

3185. Greenberg,J.H., Saunders,M.E., and Mellors,A. "Modification of acyltransferase activity in lymphocyte membranes by cannabinoids and other lipids." Biochem. Soc. Trans. 1977, 5, 108-110.

3186. Greenberg,S.S., Antopol,W., Baden,M.M., Chinn, M.E., Denson-Gerber,J., Faison,J.B., Louria,D.B., Mayer, H.D., Patton,E.C., and Gordon,E. "The dangerous drug problem--II." N.Y. Med. J. 1968, 24, 3-8.

3187. Greenberger,J.S. "Research on marihuana." N.Eng. J. Med. 1975, 285, 994.

3188. Greene,M.L. and Saunders,D.R. "Metabolism of tetrahydrocannabinol by the small intestine." Gastroenterology 1974, 66, 365-372.

3189. Greene,M.L., Saunders,D.R., and Smith,K. "Marihuana metabolism by small intestinal mucosa." Gastroenterology 1972, 62, 757.

3190. Greene,R. "The treatment of migraine with Indian hemp." Practitioner 1888, 41, 35-58, 143.

3191. Greenfield,H. "A forty-year's chronicle of international narcotics control: The work of the permanent central narcotics board 1928-1968, and of the drug supervisory body 1933-1968." Bull. Narc. 1968, 20, 1-4.

3192. Greenish,H.G. and Collin,E. "Vegetable powders and their diagnostic characters. IV. Flowers and flowering tops--Indian hemp." Pharmaceut. J. 1902, 14, 492-493.

3193. Greenleigh Associates. "A report on the roles and programs of social service agencies in the prevention and treatment of drug abuse and addiction." In National Commission on Marihuana and Drug Abuse. Drug Use in America: Problem in Perspective. Gov't. Print. Office, Washington, D.C., 1973, II, 126-200.

3194. Greenstein,H.M. and Diblanco,P.E. "Marihuana laws--a crime against humanity." Notre Dame Law Rev. 1972, 48, 314.

3195. Gregg,J.M., Campbell,R.L., Levin,K.J., Ghia,J., and Elliott,R.A. "Cardiovascular effects of cannabinol during oral surgery." Anesth. Analges. 1976, 55, 203-213.

3196. Gregg,J.M. and Small,E.W. "The control of anxiety in oral surgery patients with delta-9-tetrahydrocannabinol and diazepam." Nat'l. Inst. Hlth. Rec. 1974, 26, 8.

3197. Gregg,J.M., Small,E.W., Moore,R., Raft,D. and Toomey,T.C. "Emotional response to intravenous delta-9-tetrahydrocannabinol during oral surgery." J. Oral Surg. 1976, 34, 301-314.

3198. Grenn,K., Bigger,J.F., Kim,K., and Bowman,K. "Cannabinoid penetration and chronic effects in the eye." Expt'l. Eye Res. 1977, 24, 197-205.

3199. Griebel,C. "Marihuana."(Ger.). Pharmazeut. Zeit. 1923, 86, 424-428.

3200. Grierson,G.A. "On references to the hemp plant occurring in Sanskrit and Hindi literature." In Indian Hemp Drug Commission. Report. Gov't. Print. Office, London, 1892-1893, III, 246-249.

3201. Griffenhagen,G.B. "A brief history of drug abuse." In Fisher,M.T.(ed.). Teaching About Drugs. Am. Sch. Hlth. Assoc., Kent, Ohio, 1970, 117-135.

3202. Griffenhagen,G.B. "A history of drug abuse." J.A.P.A. 1968, NS8, 16-21, 36-37.

3203. Griffenhagen,G.B. "Sources of drug abuse information." In Wittenborn,J.R., Smith,J.P., and Wittenborn,S.A.(eds.). Communication and Drug Abuse. C.C. Thomas, Springfield, Ill., 1970, 295-302.

3204. Griffith,E. "The problem of cannabis dependence." Practitioner 1968, 200, 226.

3205. Griffiths,R.V. "Pharmaceutical science refresher courses for pharmacists. Psychopharmacological agents." J. Pharm. Pharmaceut. Sci. 1971, 1, 89-

3206. Griffiths-Jones,E. "Cannabis indica in smoking tobacco." Br. Med. J. 1923, 2, 841.

3207. Griffon,M.H., Paris,R., Le Breton,R., and Janvier,M. "The traffick relative to hemp(cannabis sativa L.. Identification and physiological activity." (Fr.). Ann. Pharmaceut. Fran. 1947, 5, 605-617.

3208. Grigor,J. "Hashish in childbirth."(Fr.). J. Pharm. Chim. 1853, 3, 386.

3209. Grigor,J. "Indian hemp as an oxytocic." Month. J. Med. Sci. 1852, 15, 124-125.

3210. Grilly,D.M. and Ferraro,D.P. "Effects of delta-9-tetrahydrocannabinol on delayed matching-to-sample choice speeds in chimpanzees." Psychon. Sci. 1973, 2, 413-415.

3211. Grilly,D.M., Ferraro,D.P., and Braude,M.C. "Observations on the reproductive activity of chimpanzees following long-term exposure to marihuana." Pharmacol. 1974, 11, 304-307.

3212. Grilly,D.M., Ferraro,D.P., and Marriott,R.G. "Long-term interactions of marihuana and behavior in chimpanzees." Nature 1973, 242, 119-120.

3213. Grimaux,E. On Hashish or Indian Hemp.(Fr.). Univ. Paris, Dept. of Medicine, Paris, 1865.

3214. Grimm,K. Recognition of the Narcotic Materials in Hemp Fiber.(Ger.). Ludwig-Maximillian Univ., Dept. of Natural Sciences, Munich, 1953.

3215. Grinspoon,L. "Half a loaf: a reaction to the marihuana report." Sat. Rev. 1972, 55, 21-22.

3216. Grinspoon,L. "Letters." Scientif. Amer. 1970, 222, 6-7.

3217. Grinspoon,L. "Marihuana." Internat'l. J. Psychiat. 1970, 9, 488-516.

3218. Grinspoon,L. "Marihuana." Scientif. Amer. 1969, 221, 17-26.

3219. Grinspoon,L. Marihuana Reconsidered. Harvard Univ. Press, Cambridge, Mass., 1971.

3220. Grinspoon,L. "Marihuana: Yesterday and today." In Levin,P.A.(ed.). Contemporary Problems of Drug Abuse. Publishing Science Group Inc., Acton, Mass., 1974, 134-151.

3221. Grinspoon,L. "Reply to discussants." Internat'l. J. Psychiat. 1970, 9, 535-537.

3222. Grinspoon,L. "The campaign against marihuana." Paper presented at Am. Psychiat. Assoc., Washington, D.C., 1971.

3223. Grinspoon,L. and Hedblom,P. "Marihuana and amphetamine: a mirror image." Contemp. Drug. 1973, 2, 665-682.

3224. Grisham,M.G. and Ferraro,D.P. "Biphasic effects of delta-9-tetrahydrocannabinol on variable interval schedule performance in rats." Psychopharmacol. 1972, 27, 163-169.

3225. Grizzle,G.A. The Effect of a Drug Education Program Upon Study Drug Knowledge, Drug Usage, and Psychological States. Univ. of North Carolina, Inst. of Gov't., Chapel Hill, N.C., 1974.

3226. Grlic,L. "A combined spectrophotometric differentiation of samples of cannabis." Bull. Narc. 1968, 20, 25-29.

3227. Grlic,L. "A comparative study on some chemical and biological characteristics of various samples of cannabis resin." Bull. Narc. 1962, 14, 37-46.

3228. Grlic,L. "A highly sensitive chromatographic detection of cannabis constituents by means of silica sheets treated with silver nitrate." Act. Pharmaceut. Jugo. 1970, 20, 19-22.

3229. Grlic,L. "A simple thin-layer chromatography of cannabinoids by means of silica gel sheets treated with amines." J. Chromatog. 1970, 48, 562-564.

3230. Grlic,L. "A study of infra-red spectra of cannabis resin." Plant. Med. 1965, 13, 291-295.

3231. Grlic,L. "A study of infra-red spectra of cannabis resin." U.N. Doc. ST/SOA/SER.S/14, Nov. 24, 1965.

3232. Grlic,L. "A study of some chemical characteristics of the resin from experimentally grown cannabis of various origins." U.N. Doc. ST/SOA/SER.S/10, Feb. 10, 1964.

3234. Grlic,L. "Constituents of cannabis."(It.). Farm. Glasnik, 1968, 24, 455-458.

3235. Grlic,L. "Determination of the ripening and disintegration values of cannabis resin in reacting with 2,6,-dichloroquinone-chlorimdie." Act. Pharmaceut. Jugo. 1961, 9, 123-133.

3236. Grlic,L. "Differentiation of different types of cannabis resin by ultraviolet spectrophotometry." Farm. Glasnik. 1961, 17, 424-427.

3237. Grlic,L. "Highly sensitive chromatographic detection of cannabis constituents by means of silica gel sheets treated with silver nitrate." J. Eur. Toxicol. 1971, 4, 43-45.

3238. Grlic,L. "Identification of cannabis users by detecting cannabinoids in biological media." Act. Pharmaceut. Jugo. 1974, 24, 63-72.

3239. Grlic,L. "Marihuana by N.G. Verdejo Vivas. Book review." Act. Pharmaceut. Jugo. 1971, 21, 146-147.

3240. Grlic,L. "Peroxide-sulphuric acid test as an indication of the ripeness and physiological activity of cannabis resin." J. Pharm. Pharmacol. 1961, 13, 637-638.

3241. Grlic,L. "Recent advances in the chemical research of cannabis." Bull. Narc. 1964, 16, 29-38.

3242. Grlic,L. "Recently discovered constituents of cannabis." Farm. Glasnik. 1968, 24, 455-458.

3243. Grlic,L. "Some new possibilities of separation of cannabinoids by means of thin layer chromatography on silica gel precoated plastic sheets." Act. Pharmaceut. Jugo 1970, 20, 35-39.

3244. Grlic,L. "Yugloslavian contribution to the international research program on drug addiction." Farm. Glasnik. 1962, 18, 293-300.

3245. Grlic,L. and Andrec,A. "The content of the acid fraction in cannabis resin of various ages and provenance." Exper. 1961, 17, 325-326.

3246. Grlic,L. and Tomic,N. "Examination of cannabis resin by means of ferric chloride test." Exper. 1963, 19, 267-268.

3247. Groce,J.W. and Jones,L.A. "Carbohydrate and cyclitol content of cannabis." Agric. Food Chem. 1973, 21, 211-214.

3248. Gross,L. "Marihuana: a fresh perspective." Seventeen 1972, 31, 122-123.

3249. Gross,S.J. and Soares,J.R. "Separate radio-immune measurements of body fluid delta-9-THC and 11-Nor-9-carboxy-delta-9-THC." In Willette,P.(ed.). Cannabinoid Assays in Humans. N.I.D.A. Res. Monog. 7, Dept. H.E.W., Gov't. Print. Office, Washington, D.C., 1976, 10-14.

3250. Gross,S.J., Soares, J.R., Wong,S.L.R., and Schuster,R.E. "Marihuana metabolites measured by a radioimmune technique." Science 1974, 252, 581-582.

3251. Grossman,J.C., Goldstein,R., and Eisenman,R. "Openness to experience and marihuana use: An initial investigation." Proc. Am. Psychol. Assoc. 1971, 3, 335-336.

3252. Grossman,J.C., Goldstein,R., and Eisenman,R. "Undergraduate marihuana and drug use as related to openness to experience." Psychiat. Quart. 1974, 48, 86-92.

3253. Grossman,W. "Adverse reactions associated with cannabis products in India." Ann. Intern. Med. 1969, 70, 529-533.

3254. Grotheer,M.H. "The use of marihuana by medical students." J. Kansas Med. Soc. 1973, 74, 142-144.

3255. Grouev,T. "Hemp manuring with mineral fertilizers and irrigiation on leached chernozems in the Brushylan-Sandrovo Irrigation region."(Rus.). Prochvozn Agrokim 1968, 3, 49-57.

3256. Groves,W.E., Rossi,P.H., and Grafstein,D. Study of Life Styles and Campus Communities, Preliminary Report. Johns Hopkins Univ., Baltimore, 1970.

3257. Grunfeld,Y. and Edery,H. "Psychopharmacological activity of some substances extracted from cannabis sativa L.(hashish). EEG Clin. Neurophysiol. 1969, 27, 219-220.

3258. Grunfeld,Y. and Edery,H. "Psychopharmacological activity of the active constituents of hashish and some related cannabinoids." Psychopharmacol. 1969, 14, 200-210.

3259. Grupp,S.E. "Black and white experienced marihuana smokers." In Grupp,S.E.(ed.). The Marihuana Muddle. Lexington Books, Lexington, Mass., 1973, 69-78.

3260. Grupp,S.E. "Experiences with marihuana in a sample of drug users." Sociol. Forces 1967, 1, 39-51.

3261. Grupp,S.E. "Multiple drug use in a sample of experienced marihuana smokers." Internat'l. J. Addict. 1972, 7, 481-491.

3262. Grupp,S.E. "Observations on experienced and exclusive marihuana smokers." J. Drug Iss. 1972, 2, 32-36.

3263. Grupp,S.E. "Prior criminal record and adult marihuana arrest dispositions." J. Crim. Law. Criminol. 1971, 62, 74-79.

3264. Grupp,S.E.(ed.). The Marihuana Muddle. Lexington Books, Lexington, Mass., 1973.

3265. Grupp,S.E. and Bridges,C.K. "Clinical record characteristics of California and Illinois adult marihuana arrestees." Aust. N. Z. J. Criminol. 1975, 8, 25-35.

3266. Grupp,S.E. and Bridges,C.K. "Criminal record characteristics of 1960 and 1969 California adult marihuana arrestees." In Grupp,S.E.(ed.). The Marihuana Muddle. Lexington Books, Lexington, Mass., 1973, 145-154.

3267. Grupp,S.E. and Bridges,C.K. "Marihuana use in a small college: A midwest example." Internat'l. J. Addict. 1971, 6, 463-485.

3268. Grupp,S.E. and Lucas,W.C. "The 'Marihuana Muddle' as reflected in California arrest statistics and dispositions." In Grupp,S.E.(ed.). The Marihuana Muddle. Lexington Books, Lexington, Mass., 1973, 127-143.

3269. Gubar,G. "Drug addiction: Myth and misconceptions." Penn. Psychiat. Quart. 1968, 8, 24-32.

3270. Gueche,M. "Hashish and its danger in Algeria."(Fr.). Rev. Med. Hyg. Trop. 1933, 25, 55-58.

3271. Guerra,F. "Sex and drugs in the 16th century." Br. J. Addict. 1974, 69, 269-290.

3272. Guerrero Losada,P.A. and Lasprillas,J.A. "Tentative method to determine the presence of residual marihuana on the hands of addicts, peddlers and pushers."(Sp.). Rev. Ecuat. Hig. Med. Trop. 1969, 26, 21-24.

3273. Guha,D. and Pradhan,S.N. "Effects of mescaline, delta-9-tetrahyrocannabinol and pentobarbital on the auditory evoked responses in the cat." Neuropharmacol. 1974, 13, 755-762.

3274. Guichard,M. "Study of cannabis from Marrakech."(Fr.). France-Maroc 1919, 3, 101-104.

3275. Guilly,P. "The club of hashish addicts."(Fr.). Encephale 1950, 39, 175-185.

3276. Gujral,M.L. and Saxena,P.N. "A preliminary experimental study on indigenous spasmolytics." J. Indian Med. Assoc. 1955, 25, 247.

3277. Gulas,I. and King,F.W. "On the question of pre-existing personality differences between users and nonusers of drugs." J. Psychol. 1976, 92, 65-69.

3278. Gunderson,E.R., Nail,R.L., and Kolb,D. "Health status of drug abusers as measured by the Cornell Medical Index." J. Commun. Psychol. 1975, 3, 58-67.

3279. Gunn,J.W. "Report on drugs, narcotic and dangerous." J. Assoc. Offic. Anal. Chem. 1971, 54, 287-288.

3280. Gupta,S., Grieco,M.H., and Cushman,P. "Impairment of rosette-forming T lymphocytes in chronic marihuana smokers." N. Eng. J. Med. 1974, 291, 874-877.

3281. Gurny,O., Maynard,D.E., Pitcher,R.G., and Kierstead,R.W. "Metabolism of (-)-delta-9- and (-)-delta-8-tetrahydrocannabinol by monkey liver." J. Am. Chem. Soc. 1972, 94, 7928-7929.

3282. Gurny,O., Maynard,D.E., Pitcher,R.G., and Kierstead,R.W. "Novel in vitro metabolites of (-)-delta-8- and (-)-delta-9-tetrahydrocannabinol(THC)." Proc. 5th Internat'l. Cong. Pharmacol. 1972, 1, 92.

3283. Guthrie,D. "Marihuana and the driver." Traffic Safe. 1976, 76, 14-15, 34.

3284. Gutierrez-Colomar,L. "Indian and Mexican hashish."(Sp.). Mon. Farm. Tera Peut. 1946, 52, 49-59.

3285. Guttman,H.A. "The first trip: life crisis and the first experience with hallucinogenic drugs." J. Nerv. Ment. Dis. 1972, 154, 453-456.

3286. Guyatt,A.R., Douglas,J.S., Zuskin,E., and Bouhuys,A. "Lung static recoil and airway obstruction in hemp workers with byssinosis." Am. Rev. Resp. Dis. 1973, 108, 1111-1115.

3287. Guyon,M. "Note accompanying presentation of paper on hashish."(Fr.). C. R. Acad. Sci. 1861, 52, 714-715.

H

3288. Haag,T.P. "Detection of narcotics, particularly hashish." Deut. Apoth-Ztg. 1970, 110, 1874-1877.

3289. Haagen,C.H. Social and Psychological Characteristics Associated with the Use of Marihuana by College Men. Wesleyan Univ., Middletown, Conn., 1970.

3290. Haagen-Smit,A.J., Wawra,C.Z., Koepfli,J.B., Alles,C.A., Feigen,G.A., and Prater,A.N. "A physiologically active principle from cannabis sativa(marihuana)." Science 1940, 91, 602-603.

3291. Haar,J. "In pursuit of happiness: an evaluation of the constitutional private use of marihuana." Contemp. Drug Prob. 1976, 5, 161-185.

3292. Haavik,C.O. "Modification of the hypothermic response to delta-9-tetrahydrocannabinol in the mouse." Fed. Proc. 1974, 33, 539.

3293. Haavik,C.O., Arora,S., and Collins,F. "Effect of cannabis on temperature regulation." In Braude,M.C. and Szara,S.(eds.). Pharmacology of Marihuana. Raven Press, N.Y., 1976, 1, 255-269.

3294. Haavik,C.O. and Hardman,H.F. "Effect of delta-9-tetrahydrocannabinol on tail and rectal temperature in the mouse." Pharmacologist 1976, 18, 299.

3295. Haavik,C.O. and Hardman,H.F. "Evaluation of the hypothermic action of tetrahydrocannabinols in mice and squirrel monkeys." J. Pharmacol. Exper. Ther. 1973, 187, 568-574.

3296. Haavik,C.O. and Hardman,H.F. "Hypothermic action of delta-9-tetrahydrocannabinol, 11-hydroxy-delta-9-tetrahydrocannabinol, and 11-hydroxy-delta-8-tetrahydrocannabinol in mice." Life Sci. 1973, 13, 1771-1778.

3297. Haavik,C.O. and Hardman,H.F. "The effect of tetrahydrocannabinols on body temperature." In Schonbaum,E. and Lomax,P.(eds.). The Pharmacology of Thermoregulation. S. Karger, Basel, Switzerland, 1973, 410-416.

3298. Habelson,P. "LSD and marihuana." Science 1968, 159, 1189.

3299. Haccius,B. and Engel,I. "Plasmodesma-like structures between cells of in vitro cultivated loose calli of cannabis sativa L."(Ger.). Naturwissen. 1968, 55, 45-46.

3300. Hackel,R. "Detection of cannabinoids in saliva following hashish intoxication."(Ger.). Arch. Toxicol. 1972, 29, 341-344.

3301. Hackleman,J.C. and Domingo,W.E. Hemp an Illinois War Crop. Agricultural Experimental Station, Univ. of Illinois, Urbana, Ill., 1943.

3302. Haden-Guest,A. "The garden. Inside the government pot farm." High Times 1976, 15, 59-63, 108.

3303. Hadka,A.A. "Forty years of the campaign against narcotic drugs in the United Arab Republic." Bull. Narc. 1965, 17, 1-12.

3304. Haenel,T.H. "Cultural history and current problems of hashish."(Ger.). Pharmakopsychiat. Neuro-psychopharmakol. 1970, 3, 89-115.

3305. Haertzen,C.A. "Addiction research center inventory: Development of a general drug estimation scale." J. Nerv. Ment. Dis. 1965, 141, 300-307.

3306. Haertzen,C.A. "Development of scales based on patterns of drug effects, using the Addiction Research Center Inventory(ARCI)." Psychol. Rep. 1966, 18, 163-194.

3307. Haertzen,C.A. "Subjective drug effects: A factorial representation of subjective drug effects on the Addiction Research Center Inventory." J. Nerv. Ment. Dis. 1965, 140, 280-289.

3308. Haertzen,C.A. and Hooks,T.N. "Dictionary of drug associations to heroin, benzedrine, alcohol, barbiturates and marihuana." J. Clin. Psychol. 1973, 29, 115-164.

3309. Haertzen,C.A., Hooks,N.T., and Hill,H.E. "Prediction of subjective responses to drugs." Paper presented to Am. Coll. Neuropsychopharmacol., San Juan, 1966.

3310. Hahn,E. "Nepenthe, what was its composition?" (Fr.). Chron. Med. 1898, 6, 550-552.

3311. Hahn,P.H. The Juvenile Offender and the Law. W.H. Anderson, Cincinatti, 1971.

3312. Haier,R.J. "Moral reasoning and moral character: relationship between the Kuhlberg and the Hogan models." Psychol. Rep. 1977, 40, 215-226.

3313. Haines,L. and Green,W. "Marihuana use patterns." Br. J. Addict. 1970, 65, 347-362.

3314. Haislip,G. "Current issues in the prevention and control of marihuana abuse." Paper presented at 1st Nat'l. Conference on Student Drug Involvement, Washington, D.C., 1967.

3315. Halbach,H. "Current problems posed by the abuse of psychotropic drugs.(Fr.). Actual. Pharmacol. 1968, 21, 213-224.

3316. Haley,J. "The amiable hippie: A new form of dissent." Voices 1968, 4, 102-110.

3317. Haley,S.L., Wright,P.L., Plank,J.B., Keplinger,M.L., Braude,M.C., and Calandra,J.C. "The effect of natural and synthetic delta-9-tetrahydrocannabinol on fetal development." Toxicol. Appl. Pharmacol. 1975, 25, 450.

3318. Halikas,J.A. "Marihuana use and psychiatric illness." In Miller,L.L.(ed.). Marihuana, Effects on Human Behavior. Academic Press, N.Y., 1974, 265-299.

3319. Halikas,J.A. "Predictors of multiple drug abuse." Arch. Gen. Psychiat. 1974, 31, 414-418.

3320. Halikas,J.A., Goodwin,D.A., and Guze,S.B. "Marihuana effects, a survey of regular users." J.A.M.A. 1971, 217, 692-694.

3321. Halikas,J.A., Goodwin,D.W., and Guze,S.B. "Pattern of marihuana use: A survey of one hundred regular users." Comp. Psychiat. 1972, 13, 161-163.

3322. Halki,J.J. "The effects of dextroamphetamine, dimethyltryptamine, lysergic acid diethylamide and tetrahydrocannabinol upon pregnancy and the offspring." Diss. Abs. 1974, 34, 6137-6138.

3323. Hall,F.B., Klein,A.L., and Waters,J.E. "Long term effects of marihuana smoking." J. Alter. States Conscious. 1975, 2, 161-170.

3324. Hall,J.A.S. "Preliminary studies on ganja smoking in Jamaica." Practitioner 1972, 209, 346-351.

3325. Hall,M.C. "Illicit drug abuse in Australia--a brief statistical picture." J. Drug Iss. 1977, 7, 311-318.

3326. Hall,P. Fitch,J.W., Riegel,V.J., and Best,J.B. "Effects of altitude and psychological stress on the response of the rat to cannabinoid compounds." In Lewis,M.F.(ed.). Current Research in Marihuana. Academic Press, N.Y., 1972, 151-162.

3327. Halleck,S.L. "Psychiatric treatment of the alienated college student." Am. J. Psychiat. 1967, 124, 642-650.

3328. Halpern,F. "Emotional reactions and general personality structure." In Solomon,D.(ed.). The Marihuana Papers. Bobbs-Merrill, Indianapolis, 1966, 313-335.

3329. Halpern,F. "Intellectual functioning." In Solomon,D.(ed.). The Marihuana Papers. Bobbs-Merrill, Indianapolis, 1966, 290-312.

3330. Hamaker,W.D. "A case of overdose of cannabis indica." Ther. Gaz. 1891, 7, 808.

3331. Hamarneh,S. "Pharmacy in medieval Islam and the history of drug addiction." Med. Hist. 1972, 16, 226-237.

3332. Hamburg,A. "Experiments with hashish."(Ger.). Hyg. Med. Pharmaceut. Manad. 1855, 15, 626.

3333. Hamburger,E. "Contrasting the hippie and the junkie." Internat'l. J. Addict. 1969, 4, 121-135.

3334. Hamilton,H.C. "Biological standardization." Am. J. Pharmacol. 1917, 89, 61-70.

3335. Hamilton,H.C. "Cannabis sativa: Is the medicinal value found only in the Indian grown drug?" J.A.P.A. 1915, 4, 448-451.

3336. Hamilton,H.C. "The pharmacopoeial requirements for cannabis sativa." J.A.P.A. 1912, 1, 200-203.

3337. Hamilton,H.C. "The requirements for cannabis indica of the U.S. Pharmacopoea." Bull. Am. Pharmaceut. Assoc. 1911, 6, 27-28.

3338. Hamilton,H.C. "The stability of cannabis sativa and its extracts." J.A.P.A. 1918, 7, 333-336.

3339. Hamilton,H.C., Lescohier,A.W., and Perkins,R.A. "The physiological activity of cannabis sativa." J.A.P.A. 1913, 2, 22-30.

3340. Hamilton,P. "Culture of hemp." In U.S. Congress. Documents, Legislative and Executive. Gales and Seaton, Washington, D.C., 1834, 1, 245-247.

3341. Hammer,R.H. "Commonly misused drugs--the facts." J. Drug Iss. 1971, 1, 27-46.

3342. Hammond,C.T. and Mahlberg,P.G. "Morphogenesis of capitate glandular hairs of cannabis sativa(cannabaceae)." Am. J. Bot. 1977, 64, 1023-1031.

3343. Hammond,C.T. and Mahlberg,P.G. "Morphology of glandular hairs of cannabis sativa from scanning electron microscopy." Am. J. Bot. 1973, 60, 524-528.

3344. Hammond,R.C. "Drug abuse in Canada." Appl. Ther. 1970, 12, 7-10.

3345. Handrick,G.R., Razdan,R.K., Uliss,D.B., Dalzell,H.C., and Boger,E. "Hashish. Synthesis of (±) and delta-1- and delta-6-3,4,cis-cannabidiols and their isomerization by acid catalysis." J. Org. Chem. 1977, 42, 2563-2568.

3346. Hanevald,G.T. "Hashish in Lebanon." (Dut.). Ned. Tid. Geneesk. 1959, 103, 686-688.

3347. Haney,A. and Bazzar,F.A. "Some ecological implications of the distribution of hemp(cannabis sativa L.) in the United States of America. In Joyce,C.R.B. and Curry,S.H.(eds.). The Botany and Chemistry of Cannabis. J. and A. Churchill, London, 1970, 39-49.

3348. Haney,A., Kutscheid,B.B., and Scigliano,J.A. "Quantitative variations in isomers in marihuana and hashish." Bull. Narc. 1968, 20, 52-54.

3349. Hanley,J. "Exposing the marihuana drug evil in swing bands." Radio Stars 1938, 1, 37.

3350. Hanley,J., Tyrrell,E., and Hahn,P. "The therapeutic aspects of marihuana: Computer analyses of electroencephalographic data from human users of cannabis sativa." In Cohen,S. and Stillman,R.(eds.). Therapeutic Potential of Marihuana. Plenum Press, N.Y., 1976, 187-204.

3351. Hann,J.M., Strauss,R.H., Itagaki,B., Kwon,W.J., Stanyon,R., Bindon,J., and Hong,S.K. "Marihuana smoking and cold tolerance in man." Aviat. Space Environ. 1976, 47, 634-639.

3352. Hanneman,G.J. "Communicating drug-use information among college students." Pub. Opin. Quart. 1973, 37, 171-191.

3353. Hanneman,G.J. Dissemination of Drug Related Information. Univ. Commecticut Communications Research Program, Storrs, Conn., 1972.

3354. Hanrath,B. "Increased drug use in schools." (Ger.). Jugen. 1971, 16, 120-124.

3355. Hanson,A. "Drugs of addiction. Micro-methods for their identifications." Sven. Kem. Tid. 1946, 58, 10-23.

3356. Hansson,A. "Hashish."(Ger.). Nord. Kriminal. Tid. 1950, 20, 61.

3357. Hansteen,R.W., Miller,R.D., Lonero,L., Reid,L.D., and Jones,B. "Effects of cannabis and alcohol on automobile driving and psychomotor tracking." Ann. N. Y. Acad. Sci. 1976, 282, 240-256.

3358. Hanus,L. and Krejci,A. "The present state of knowledge in the chemistry of cannabis sativa. I. Substances of cannabinoid Type." Act. Univ. Pal. Olomuc. Fac. Med. 1974, 71, 239-251.

3359. Hanus,L. and Krejci,A. "The present state of knowledge in the chemistry of cannabis sativa. II. Metabolites of cannabinoid substances." Act. Univ. Pal. Olomuc. Fac. Med. 1974, 71, 253-264.

3360. Haq,M.Z., Rose,S.J., Deidrich,L.R., and Patel,A.R. "Identification and quantitative measurement of some N-heterocyclics in marihuana smoke condensate." Anal. Chem. 1974, 46, 1781-1784.

3361. Harbison,R.D. "Maternal distribution and placental transfer to ^{14}C-delta-9-tetrahydrocannabinol in pregnant mice." Toxicol. Appl. Pharmacol. 1971, 19, 413-414.

3362. Harbison,R.D. and Mantilla-Plata,B. "Prenatal toxicity, maternal distribution and placental transfer of tetrahydrocannabinol." J. Pharmacol. Exper. Ther. 1972, 180, 446-453.

3363. Harbison,R.D., Mantilla-Plata,B., and Lubin, D.J. "Alteration of delta-9-tetrahydrocannabinol-induced teratogenicity by stimulation and inhibition of its metabolism." J. Pharmacol. Exper. Ther. 1977, 202, 455-465.

3364. Hardeman,N.P. "Portrait of a western farmer: John Locke Hardeman of Missouri 1809-1858." Missouri Hist. Rev. 1972, 66, 319-341.

3365. Harding,E. "The psychological significance of the soma ritual." In Andrews,G. and Vinkenoog,S.(eds.). The Book of Grass. Grove Press, N.Y., 1967, 155-160.

3366. Harding,G.T. "Neurosine poisoning." J.A.M.A. 1931, 96, 2054.

3367. Harding,T. and Knight,F. "Marihuana-modified mania." Arch. Gen. Psychiat. 1973, 29, 635-637.

3368. Harding,W.M. and Zinberg,N.E. "The effectiveness of the subculture in developing rituals and social sanctions for controlling drug use." In Du Toit,B.M.(ed.). Drugs, Rituals and Altered States of Consciousness. A.A. Balkema, Rotterdam, 1977, 111-133.

3369. Hardman,A.C. "Legal aspects of hallucinogens." (Fr.). Laval Med. 1969, 40, 114.

3370. Hardman,H.F., Domino,E.F., and Seevers,M.H. "General pharmacological actions of some synthetic tetrahydrocannabinol derivatives." Pharmacol. Rev. 1971, 23, 295-306.

3371. Hardman,H.F., Domino,E.F., and Seevers,M.H. "Structure activity relationships of delta-3-tetrahydrocannabinols." Proc. West. Pharmacol. Soc. 1971, 14, 14-20.

3372. Hardman,H.F., Domino,E.F., Woods,L.A., and Seevers,M.H. "Pharmacological actions of delta-3-tetrahydrocannabinol derivatives." Pharmacologist 1970, 12, 258.

3373. Hardman,H.F., Domino,E.F., Woods,L.A., and Seevers,M.H. "Pharmacological profile of delta-3-tetrahydrocannabinol derivatives." Univ. Mich. Med. Ctr. J. 1970, 36, 238.

3374. Hardman,H.F. and Hosko,M.J. "An overview of the cardiovascular-autonomic actions of cannabis." In Braude,M.C. and Szara,S.(eds.). Pharmacology of Marihuana. Raven Press, N.Y., 1976, 1, 231-239.

3375. Hardman,R. and Abu-Al-Futuh,I.M. "The occurrence of 4-hydroxyisoleucine in steroidal sapogenin-yielding plants." Phytochemistry 1976, 15, 325-326.

3376. Hardy,C.A. "Student attitudes: a study of social class." Improv. Coll. Univ. Teach. 1976, 24, 155.

3377. Hardy,R.E. and Cull,J.G.(eds.). Problems of Adolescents. C.C. Thomas, Springfield, Ill., 1974.

3378. Hare,H.A. "Clinical and physiological notes on the action of cannabis indica." Ther. Gaz. 1887, 11, 225-228.

3379. Harfenist,M. New Analogs of Tetrahydrocannabinol. Univ. of Illinois, Urbana, Ill., 1948.

3380. Harley-Mason,R.J. "The confessions of a bhang smoker." East Af. Med. J. 1938, 14, 396-397.

3381. Harmatz,J.S., Shader,R.I., and Salzman,C. "Marihuana users and nonusers." Arch. Gen. Psychiat. 1972, 26, 108-112.

3382. Harmon,J. and Aliapoulios,M.A. "Gynecomastia in marihuana users." N. Eng. J. Med. 1975, 287, 936.

3383. Harmon,J. and Aliapoulios,M.A. "Marihuana-induced gynecomastia: clinical and laboratory experience." Surg. Forum 1974, 25, 423-425.

3384. Harmon,J., Locke,D., Aliapoulios,M.A., and MacIndoe,J.H. "Interference with testicular development by delta-9-tetrahydrocannabinol." Surg. Forum 1976, 26, 350-352.

3385. Harms,E.(ed.). Drug Addiction in Youth. Pergamon Press, N.Y., 1965.

3386. Harms,E. "The heroin-marihuana relationship: A basic aspect of drug management." Br. J. Addict. 1973, 68, 31-34.

3387. Harms,E. "The three types of marihuana dependencies." Br. J. Addict. 1973, 68, 25-30.

3388. Harney,M.L. "Discussion on marihuana: Moderator's remarks." Internat'l. Narcotic Enforcement Officers Assoc. 1967, 8, 50.

3389. Harney,M.L. "Marihuana." Lancet 1964, 1, 384-385.

3390. Harr,J. "In pursuit of happiness: an evaluation of the constitutional right to private use of marihuana." Contemp. Drug Prob. 1976, 5, 161-185.

3391. Harris,B. "The art of breeding pot." High Times 1977, 26, 54-57.

3392. Harris,B.T. "Pot laws smashing our colleges!" Marihuana Rev. 1968, 1, 8-9.

3393. Harris,E.M. "A measurement of alienation in college student marihuana users and non-users." J. Sch. Hlth. 1971, 41, 130-133.

3394. Harris,L.S. "Analgesic and antitumor potential of the cannabinoids." In Cohen,S. and Stillman,R. (eds.). _Therapeutic Potential of Marihuana_. Plenum Press, N.Y., 1976, 299-312.

3395. Harris,L.S., Munson,A.E., and Carchman,R.A. "Antitumor properties of cannabinoids." In Braude,M.C. and Szara,S.(eds.). _Pharmacology of Marihuana_. Raven Press, N.Y., 1976, 749-762.

3396. Harris,L.S. "General and behavioral pharmacology." _Pharmacol. Rev._ 1971, _23_, 285-294.

3397. Harris,L.S. "Pharmacology of marihuana and constituents." Paper presented at Am. Pharmaceut. Assoc., San Francisco, 1971.

3398. Harris,L.S., Munson,A.E., Friedman,M.A., and Dewey,W.L. "Retardation of tumor growth by delta-9-tetrahydrocannabinol." _Pharmacologist_ 1974, _16_, 259.

3399. Harris,L.S., Razdan,R.K., Dewey,W.L., and Pars,H.G. "The pharmacology of some new tetrahydrocannabinol analogs." _Chem. Ther._ 1967, _2_, 167.

3400. Harris,M.L. "Pot is good for business." _Marihuana Rev._ 1968, _1_, 12.

3401. Harris,R.T., Waters,W., and McLendon,D. "Behavioral effects in rhesus monkeys of repeated intravenous doses of delta-9-tetrahydrocannabinol." _Comm. Prob. Drug Depend._ 1972, _1_, 831-843.

3402. Harris,R.T., Waters,W., and McLendon,D. "Behavioral effects in rhesus monkeys of repeated intravenous doses of delta-9-tetrahydrocannabinol." _Psychopharmacol._ 1972, _26_, 297-306.

3403. Harris,R.T., Waters,W., and McLendon,D. "Evaluation of reinforcing capability of delta-9-tetrahydrocannabinol in rhesus monkeys." _Comm. Prob. Drug Depend._ 1973, _1_, 806-812.

3404. Harris,R.T., Waters,W., and McLendon,D. "Evaluation of reinforcing capability of delta-9-tetrahydrocannabinol in rhesus monkeys." _Psychopharmacol._ 1974, _37_, 23-29.

3405. Harrison,J. "Illegal drug use by Israeli youth." _Br. J. Addict._ 1975, _70_, 335-337.

3406. Harshman,R.A., Crawford,H., and Hecht,E. "Marihuana, cognitive style, and lateralized hemispheric functions." In Cohen,S. and Stillman,R.(eds.). _Therapeutic Potential of Marihuana_. Plenum Press, N.Y., 1976, 205-254.

3407. Hart,H.(ed.). Drugs: For and Against. Hart Pub. Co., N.Y., 1970.

3408. Hart,J.B., McChesney,J.D., Greif,M., Schulz,G. "Composition of illicit drugs and the use of drug analysis in the abuse abatement." J. Psyched. Drugs 1972, 5, 83-88.

3409. Hart,R.H. "A psychiatric classification of cannabis intoxication." J. Am. Acad. Psychiat. Neurol. 1976, 1, 83-97.

3410. Hart,R.H. "Chronic effects of cannabis." J. Am. Acad. Psychiat. Neurol. 1976, 1, 25-26.

3411. Hartelius,J. "Cannabis-narcotic conventions, legislation and legislative debate."(Swed.). J. Lakartid. 1976, 73, 3879-3881.

3412. Hartelius,J. "Cannabis-subcultures and psychedelic philosophy."(Swed.). J. Lakartid. 1976, 73, 3882-3884.

3413. Hartmann,D. "A study of drug-taking adolescents." Psychoanal. Study Child 1969, 24, 384-398.

3414. Hartwich,C. Pleasures of Humanity.(Ger.). Tauchnitz, Leipzig, 1911.

3415. Harvey,D.J. "Characterization of the butyl homologues of delta-1-tetrahydrocannabinol, cannabinol and cannabidiol in samples of cannabis by combined gas chromatorgraphy and mass spectrometry." J. Pharm. Pharmacol. 1976, 28, 280-285.

3416. Harvey,D.J. "Cyclic alkylboronates as derivatives for the characterization of cannabinolic acids by combined gas chromatography and mass spectrometry." Biomed. Mass Spectrom. 1977, 4, 88-93.

3417. Harvey,D.J., Martin,B.R., and Paton,W.D.M. "Identification of glucuronides as in vivo liver conjugates of seven cannabinoids and some of their hydroxy and acid metabolites." Res. Commun. Chem. Pathol. Pharmacol. 1977, 16, 265-279.

3418. Harvey,D.J., Martin,B.R., and Paton,W.D.M. "Identification of the glucuronides of cannabidiol and hydroxycannabinoids in mouse liver." Biochem. Pharmacol. 1976, 25, 2217-2219.

3419. Harvey,D.J. and Paton,W.D.M. "Characterization of three monohydroxyacid and two dihydroxyacid metabolites of delta-1-tetrahydrocannabinol in mouse liver." Res. Commun. Chem. Pathol. Pharmacol. 1976, 13, 585-599.

3420. Harvey,D.J. and Paton,W.D.M. "Examination of the metabolites of delta-1-tetrahydrocannabinol in mouse liver, heart, and lung by combined gas chromatography and mass spectrometry." In Nahas,G.G., Paton,W.D.M., and Idanpaan-Heikkila,J.E.(eds.). Marihuana. Springer Verlag, N.Y., 1976, 93-111.

3421. Hasan,K.A. "Social aspects of the use of cannabis in India." In Rubin,V.(ed.). Cannabis and Culture. Mouton, The Hague, 1975, 235-247.

3422. Haskell,C.C. and Eckler,C.R. "Tentative standards for some biologically standardized drugs." J.A.P.A. 1913, 2, 146-151.

3422a. Hasle,A.K. "Who are the young drug abusers?" (Nor.). Tid. Nor Laege. 1973, 93, 1760-1761.

3423. Hasleton,S. "Cannabis, 'permissivism' and social response in Australia." In Connell,P.H. and Dorn,N. Cannabis and Man. Churchill Livingstone, Edinburgh, 1975, 189-203.

3424. Hasleton,S. "Marihuana: A brief review." Aust. N. Z. J. Psychiat. 1972, 6, 41-45.

3425. Hasleton,S. "Marihuana studies." Med. J. Aust. 1972, 1, 197.

3426. Hasleton,S. "Science, society and marihuana." Search 1975, 6, 70-72.

3427. Hasleton,S. "The incidence and correlates of marihuana use in an Australian undergraduate population." Med. J. Aust. 1971, 2, 302-308.

3428. Hasleton,S. and Simmonds,D. "Is Australia going to pot: Some trends relating to marihuana." Br. J. Addict. 1975, 70, 325-334.

3429. Haslip,G.R. "Current issues in the prevention and control of the marihuana abuse." Paper presented at 1st Nat'l. Conference on Student Drug Involvement, Washington,D.C., 1967.

3430. Hasnalov,K. "Detection and quantitative determination of diethylamine of lysergic acid in the presence of morphine and hashish by UV-spectroscopy." (Bulg.). Farmatsiya 1974, 24, 9-15.

3431. Hasselmann,J. and Ribeiro,O. Toxic Action of Maconha Cultivated in Brazil.(Port.). Serv. Nacional Educacao Sanitaria, Rio de Janeiro, 1958.

3432. Hattendorf,C., Hattendorf,N., Coper,H., and Fernandes,M. "Interaction between delta-9-tetrahydrocannabinol and d-amphetamine." Psychopharmacol. 1977, 54, 177-182.

3433. Hattori,T., Jakubovic,A., and McGeer,P.L. "Reduction in number of nuclear membrane-attached ribosomes in infant rat brain following acute delta-9-tetrahydrocannabinol administration." Expt'l. Neurol. 1972, 36, 207-211.

3434. Hattori,T., Jakubovic,A., and McGeer,P.L. "The effect of cannabinoids on the number of nuclear membrane-attached ribosomes in infant rat brain." Neuropharmacol. 1973, 12, 995-999.

3435. Hauck,G. "Attempts to demonstrate cannabis constituents in exhaled air."(Ger.). Beit. Gericht. Med. 1974, 32, 221--26.

3436. Hauschild,T.B. "Effects of marihuana and hashish: Further comments." Med. Bull. U.S. Army 1971, 28, 250-251.

3437. Hauschild,T.B. "Marihuana." Med. Bull. U. S. Army 1971, 28, 243-249.

3438. Hauschild,T.B. "Marihuana." Mil. Med. 1971, 136, 105-109.

3439. Hausmann,W. "Tolerance to poisons."(Ger.). Ergeb. Physiol. Biol. Chem. Exper. Pharmakol. 1907, 6, 58-104.

3440. Haustveit,G. and Wold,J.K. "Some carbohydrates of low molecular weight present in cannabis sativa L." Carbohyd. Res. 1973, 29, 325-329.

3441. Hawkins,B.L. and Roberts,J.D. "Nuclear magnetic resonance spectroscopy. ^{13}C Fourier transform spectra of delta-8- and delta-9- tetrahydrocannabinol." Proc. Nat'l. Acad. Sci. 1973, 70, 1027-1029.

3442. Hawks,D.V. "The dimensions of drug dependence in the U.K." Internat'l. J. Addict. 1971, 6, 135-160.

3443. Hawks,D. "The law relating to cannabis use 1964-1973: How subtle an ass?" In Graham,J.D.P.(ed.). Cannabis and Health. Academic Press, N.Y., 1976, 379-417.

3444. Hay,M. "A new alkaloid in cannabis indica." Pharmaceut. J. Trans. 1883, 13, 996-997.

3445. Hayes,M.H. and Bowery,L.E. "Marihuana." J. Criminol. 1933, 23, 1086-1097.

3446. Hays,R.J., Winburn,M.G., and Bloom,R. "Marihuana and the law: What young people say." J. Drug Educat. 1975, 5, 37-43.

3447. Hayward,H.E. The Structure of Economic Plants. Macmillan Co., N.Y., 1938.

3448. Hazard,S.W., Allen,V.R., Eisner,V., Garell,D. C., Hammar,S.L., Shaffer,T.E., Shen,J.T.Y., Tanner,N.M., and Welty,J.A. "Committee on youth. Statement on marihuana." Pediatrics 1972, 49, 461-462.

3449. Heachock,R.A. and Forrest,J.E. "The use of electron-acceptor reagents for the detection of some hallucinogens." J. Chromatog. 1973, 78, 241-250.

3450. Heath,R.G. "Cannabis sativa derivatives: Effects on brain function of monkeys." In Nahas,G.G., Paton,W.D.M., and Idanpaan-Heikkila,J.E.(eds.). Marihuana. Springer Verlag, N.Y., 1976, 507-521.

3451. Heath,R.G. "Effects on deep and surface electroencephalograms of man." Arch. Gen. Psychiat. 1972, 26, 577-584.

3452. Heath,R.G. "Marihuana and delta-9-THC: acute and chronic effects on brain function of monkeys." In Braude,M.C. and Szara,S.(eds.). Pharmacology of Marihuana. Raven Press, N.Y., 1976, 1, 345-357.

3453. Heath,R.G. "Marihuana: Effects on deep and surface electroencephalograms of rhesus monkeys." Neuropharmacol. 1973, 12, 1-14.

3454. Heaysman,L.T., Walker,E.A., and Lewis,D.T. "The application of gas chromatography to the examination of the constituents of cannabis sativa L." Analyst 1967, 92, 450-455.

3455. Hecht,F., Beals,R., Lees,M., Jolly,H., and Roberts,P. "Lysergic-acid diethylamide and cannabis as possible teratogens in man." Lancet 1968, 2, 1087.

3456. Heczko,P. and Krejci,Z. "On the treatment of the papilla regadae in suckling mothers and on the prevention of mastitis caused by staphylococci."(Czech.). Act. Univ. Palac. Olomuc. 1958, 14, 277-282.

3457. Hedrick,N.P. Sturtevant's Notes on Edible Plants. J.B. Lyon, Albany, N.Y., 1919.

3458. Hegi,G. Illustrated Flora of Middle Europe. (Ger.). Verlag, Munich, 1957.

3459. Heiman,E.M. "Marihuana precipitated psychoses in patients evacuated to Conus." U.S. Army Viet. Med. Bull. 1968, 9, 75-77.

3460. Heinemann,C. "Decreasing effect of initial intoxicating experiences and increasing dosage in hashish users."(Ger.). Med. Klin. 1973, 68, 826-830.

3461. Heinemann,C. "Symptoms observed following hashish use."(Ger.). Med. Klin. 1971, 66, 1648-1653.

3462. Heinemann,S. "Marihuana: Should it be controlled?" Southwest. Med. 1970, 51, 267-268.

3463. Hekimian,L.J. and Gerson,S. "Characteristics of drug abusers admitted to a psychiatric hospital." J.A.M.A. 1968, 205, 75-80.

3464. Hell,D., Baumann,U., and Angst,J. "Drug consumption and personality."(Ger.). Deut. Med. J. 1971, 20, 511-514.

3465. Helldorfer,H. "Marihuana."(Ger.). Neue Pliz. 1952, 6, 12.

3466. Heller,J.D. "The attempt to prevent illicit drug supply." In National Commission on Marihuana and Drug Abuse. Drug Use in America: Problem in Perspective. Gov't. Print. Office, Washington, D.C., 1973, III, 383-407.

3467. Hellman,A.D. Laws Against Marihuana. The Price We Pay. Univ. of Illinois Press, Chicago, Ill., 1975.

3468. Hellpach,W. "Functional differentiation of psychological stimulants."(Ger.). Deut. Med. Woch. 1941, 67, 1358-1361.

3469. Helmer,J. Drugs and Minority Oppression. Seabury Press, N.Y., 1975.

3470. Helmer,J. and Vietorisz,T. Drug Use, The Labor Market, and Class Conflict. Drug Abuse Council, Washington, D.C., 1974.

3471. Helpern,M. "Deaths resulting from narcotic addiction--a major health problem." In Keup,W.(ed.). Drug Abuse, Current Concepts and Research. C.C. Thomas, Springfield, Ill., 1972, 51.

3472. Helou,C., Banna,M., Touma,E., and Basbous,E. "The 'green plan'." Internat'l. Crim. Pol. Rev. 1968, 23, 146-151.

3473. Hembree,W.C., Nahas,G.G., Zeidenberg,P., and Dyrenfurth,I. "Marihuana effects upon the human testis." Clin. Res. 1976, 24, 272.

3474. Hembree,W.C., Zeidenberg,P., and Nahas,G. "Marihuana's effects on human gonadal functions." In Nahas,G.G., Paton,W.D.M., and Idanpaan-Heikkila,J.E. (eds.). Marihuana. Springer Verlag, N.Y., 1976, 521-538.

3475. Hemenway,S. "Poisoning by strychnia, successfully treated by cannabis." Pacif. Med. Surg. J. 1867, 10, 113-114.

3476. Henckley,R. "Nonmedical drug use and the college student." J. Am. Coll. Hlth. Assoc. 1968, 17, 35-42.

3477. Henderson,A.H., Pubsley,D.J., Robinson,A.E., Page,M.P., and Camps,F.E. "Collapse after intravenous injection of hashish." Br. Med. J. 1968, 3, 229-230.

3478. Henderson,R.L., Tennant,F.S., and Guerry,R. "Respiratory manifestations of hashish smoking." Arch. Otolaryng. 1972, 95, 248-251.

3479. Hendin,H. "Marihuana abuse among college students." J. Nerv. Ment. Dis. 1973, 156, 259-270.

3480. Hendriks,H., Malingre,T.M., Batterman,S., and Bos,R. "Alkanes of the essential oil of cannabis sativa." Phytochemistry 1977, 16, 719-721.

3481. Henley,J. and Adams,L.P. "Marihuana use in post-collegiate cohorts: Correlates of use, prevalence patterns and factors associated with cessation." Soc. Prob. 1973, 20, 514-520.

3482. Henninger,J.M. "Marihuana intoxication." J. Crim. Psychopathol. 1941, 2, 360.

3483. Henriksson,B.G. and Jarbe,T. "Cannabis-induced vocalization in the rat." J. Pharm. Pharmacol. 1971, 23, 457-458.

3484. Henriksson,B.G. and Jarbe,T. "Delta-9-tetrahydrocannabinol used as discriminative stimulus for rats in position learning in a T-shaped water maze." Psychon. Sci. 1972, 27, 25-26.

3485. Henriksson,B.G. and Jarbe,T. "Tetrahydrocannabinols and state-dependent learning in rats." Act. Pharmaceut. Suec. 1971, 8, 688-689.

3486. Henriksson,B.G. and Jarbe,T. "The effect of two tetrahydrocannabinols on conditioned avoidance learning in rats and its transfer to normal state conditions." Psychopharmacol. 1971, 22, 23-30.

3487. Henriksson,B.G., Jahan son,J.O., and Jarbe, Jarbe,T. "Delta-9-tetrahydrocannabinol produced discrimination in pigeons." Pharmacol. Biochem. Behav. 1975, 3, 771-774.

3488. Henry,G.M. "The epidemiology of psychoactive and hallucinogenic drug use." In Gibbins,R.J., Israel,Y., Kalant,H., Popham,R.E., Schmidt,W., and Smart,R.G.(eds.). Recent Advances in Alcohol and Drug Problems. J. Wiley and Sons, N.Y., 1975, 303-354.

3489. Henry,G.W. and De Jong,H. "A comparative study of the action of bulbocapnine and some other drugs in producing catatonic states." Act. Psychiat. Neurol. 1930, 5, 463-471.

3490. Henslin,J.M. "Changes in perceptions of sexual experiences of college students while under the influence." Comm. Prob. Drug Depend. 1970, 3, 6523-6534.

3491. Henslow,G. Poisonous Plants in Field and Garden. S.P.C.K., London, 1901.

3492. Henstock,H. "Cannabis indica in smoking tobacco." Pharmaceut. J. Pharmacist 1923, 57, 525.

3493. Hepler,R.S. and Frank,I.R. "Marihuana smoking and intraocular pressure." J.A.M.A. 1971, 217, 1392.

3494. Hepler,R.S., Frank,I.M., and Petrus,R. "Ocular effects of marihuana smoking." In Braude,M.C. and Szara,S.(eds.). Pharmacology of Marihuana. Raven Press, N.Y., 1976, 115-125.

3495. Hepler,R.S., Frank,I.M., and Ungerleider,J.T. "Pupillary constriction after marihuana smoking." Am. J. Opthalmol. 1972, 74, 1185-1190.

3496. Hepler,R.S. and Petrus,R. "Experiences with administration of marihuana to glaucoma patients." In Cohen,S. and Stillman,R.(eds.). Therapeutic Potential of Marihuana. Pleun Press, N.Y., 1976, 63-76.

3497. Herha,J. "Hashish and Marihuana--a review." (Ger.). Naturwissen. 1974, 61, 70-74.

3498. Herha,J. and Obe,G. "Chromosomal damage in chronic users of cannabis in vivo investigation with two-day leukocyte cultures." Pharmakopsychiat. Neuropsychopharmacol. 1974, 7, 328-337.

3499. Herich,R. "Action of 2,4-dichlorophenoxyacetic acid on the differentiation of sex in hemp."(Ger.). Biologia 1955, 10, 760-764.

3500. Herich,R. "Does a nucleolar membrane exist?" Act. Fac. Rerum. Nat. Univ. Comen. Bot. 1965, 10, 41-42.

3501. Herich,R. "Histological reactions of hemp plant(cannabis sativa) to gibberellic acid." Phyton. Ann. Bot. 1960, 9, 126-134.

3502. Herich,R. "Influence of colchicine on nucleolar structures." Act. Fac. Rerum. Nat. Univ. Comen. Bot. 1965, 10, 25-28.

3503. Herich,R. "Sexual expression and cell and pollen nuclear size in different forms of monoecious hemp."(Ger.). Zuchter 1961, 31, 48-51.

3504. Herich,R. "Significance of the nucleolar structure for cell division." Act. Fac. Rerum. Nat. Univ. Comen. Bot. 1965, 10, 29-35.

3505. Herisset,A., Besson,P., and Autin,C. "Toxicological note on the varieties of hemp cultivated in Anjou."(Fr.). Ann. Pharmaceut. Franc. 1965, 23, 631-635.

3506. Hermann,D. "Drug use among school children of a small town in northern Germany. Report on a pilot study."(Ger.). Munch. Med. Woch. 1972, 114, 393-397.

3507. Hermon,H.C. "Preliminary observations on the use of marihuana in psychotherapy." Marihuana Rev. 1968, 1, 14-17.

3508. Hermon,H.C. "Psychedelicoanalysis." J. Travis County Med. Soc. 1968, 13, 5.

3509. Herodotus. Histories. E.P. Dutton, N.Y., 1910.

3510. Herr,P. and Morley,J.E. "Drug use patterns among South African undergraduates." S. Af. Med. J. 1972, 46, 1404-1406.

3511. Herring,B. "The effect of 1-delta-1-trans-tetrahydrocannabinol on learning and retention of avoidance performance in rats." Psychopharmacol. 1972, 26, 401-406.

3512. Hershkowitz,M., Goldman,R., and Raz,A. "Effect of cannabinoids on neurotransmitter uptake, ATPase activity and morphology of mouse brain synaptosomes." Biochem. Pharmacol. 1977, 26, 1327-1331.

3513. Herz,S. "Research study on behavioral patterns in sex and drug use on college campus." Adolescence 1970, 5, 1-16.

3514. Heslop-Harrison,J. "Auxin and sexuality in cannabis sativa." Physiol. Plant. 1956, 9, 588-597.

3515. Heslop-Harrison,J. "Effect of 2-thiouracil on cell differentiation and leaf morphogenesis in cannabis sativa." Ann. Bot. 1962, 26, 375-387.

3516. Heslop-Harrison,J. "Suppressive effects of 2-thiouricil on differentiation and flowering in cannabis sativa." Science 1960, 132, 1943-1944.

3517. Heslop-Harrison,J. "The experimental modification of sex expression in flowering plants." Biol. Rev. 1957, 32, 1-51.

3518. Heslop-Harrison,J. "The ultrastructure of some chemically induced somatic chloroplast mutants in cannabis sativa L." Port. Act. Biol. Morfol. Fisiol. 1963, 8, 13-40.

3519. Heslop-Harrison,J. "Ultrastructural aspects of differentiation in sporogenous tissue." Sympos. Soc. Exp. Biol. 1963, 17, 315-340.

3520. Heslop-Harrison,J. and Heslop-Harrison,Y. "Cannabis sativa L." In Evans,L.T.(ed.). The Induction of Flowering, Some Case Histories. Cornell Univ. Press, Ithaca, N.Y., 1969, 205-226.

3521. Heslop-Harrison,J. and Heslop-Harrison,Y. "Studies on flowering-plant growth and organogenesis. I. Morphogenetic effects of 2,3,5-triiodobenzoic acid on cannabis sativa." Proc. Roy. Soc. Edin. 1956, 66B, 409-423.

3522. Heslop-Harrison,J. and Heslop-Harrison,Y. "Studies of flowering-plant growth and organogenesis. II. The modification of sex expression in cannabis sativa by carbon monoxide." Proc. Roy. Soc. Edin. 1956, 66B, 424-432.

3523. Heslop-Harrison,Y. and Woods,I. "Temperature-induced meristic and other variation in cannabis sativa." J. Linn. Soc. Lond. Bot. 1959, 56, 290-293.

3524. Hesnard,A. "Note on hemp smokers in Eastern countries."(Fr.). Encephale 1912, 2, 40-46.

3525. Hesse,E. "Indian hemp(hashish)." In Hesse,E.(ed.). Narcotics and Drug Addiction. Philosophical Lib., N.Y., 1946, 88-94.

3.526. Hesse,E. Indian Hemp(Hashish) and Other Types of Hemp.(Ger.). Verlag, Stuttgart, 1966.

3.527. Hesse,E. Narcotics and Pleasure Drugs.(Ger.). Verlag, Stuttgart, 1938.

3.528. Heuser,O. The German Hemp.(Ger.). S. Hirzel, Leipzig, 1924.

3.529. Heuyer,G. "Medical considerations concerning the free sale of hashish."(Fr.). Bull. Acad. Nat'l. Med. 1969, 153, 531-534.

3.530. Hewat,M.L. Bantu Folklore, Medical and General. Maskew Miller, Capetown, 1906.

3.531. Heyman,I.A., Bunnell,P.R., Rosenkrantz,H., and Braude,M.C. "Comprehensive behavioral assessment of the effects of delta-9-tetrahydrocannabinol." Pharmacologist 1974, 16, 260.

3.532. Heyndrickx,A. "Cannabis, nicotine and alcohol compared." N. Eng. J. Med. 1971, 285, 1437.

3.533. Heyndrickx,A., Scheiris,C., and Schepens,P. "Toxicological study of a fatal intoxication in man due to cannabis smoking." J. Pharm. 1969, 24, 371-375.

3.534. H.G.M. "Indian hemp poisoning." Br. Med. J. 1896, 2, 1619.

3.535. Hickey,J.L. "Seiden queried." Am. J. Pub. Hlth. 1975, 65, 1114-1115.

3.536. Hicks,J.T. "Cannabis." Hosp. Formul. Mgt. 1967, 1, 42-45.

3.537. Higbee,K.L. "What is the 'fear' in a fear-arousing appeal?" Psychol. Rep. 1974, 35, 1161-1162.

3.538. Hildebrand,J.E. "Marihuana-induced 'social high'." J.A.M.A. 1970, 214, 1565.

3.539. Hill,H. "The ganja problem in Singapore." Internat'l. Crim. Pol. Rev. 1968, 23, 210-220.

3.540. Hill,H.E., Haertzen,C.A., Wolbach,A.B., and Miner,E.J. "The Addiction Research Center Inventory: standardization of scales which evaluate subjective effects of morphine, amphetamine, pentobarbital, alcohol, LSD-25, pyrahexyl, and chlorpromazine." Psychopharmacol. 1963, 4, 167-183.

3.541. Hill,N.(ed.). Marihuana: Teenage Killer. Popular Lib., N.Y., 1971.

3542. Hills,S.L. Crime, Power and Morality: The Criminal Law Process in the United States. Chandler Pub. Co., Scranton, Pa., 1971.

3543. Hill,S.Y. and Goodman,D. "Stimulant effects of marihuana on three neuropsychological systems." In Cohen,S. and Stillman,R.(eds.). Therapeutic Potential of Marihuana. Plenum Press, N.Y., 1976, 139-152.

3544. Hill,S.Y., Goodwin,D.W., Schwin,R., and Powell,B. "Marihuana: CNS depressant or excitant?" Am. J. Psychiat. 1974, 131, 313-315.

3545. Hill,S.Y., Schwin,R., Goodwin,D.W., and Powell,B.J. "Marihuana and pain." J. Pharmacol. Exper. Ther. 1974, 188, 415-418.

3546. Hill,S.Y., Schwin,R., Powell,B., and Goodwin,D.W. "State-dependent effects of marihuana on human memory." Nature 1973, 243, 241-243.

3547. Hill,W.T. "High and low culture of marihuana and alcohol in the youth culture." Sound 1968, 51, 290-307.

3548. Hillenbrand,F.K.M. "Hashish." Lancet 1952, 2, 338.

3549. Hiller,A. "Experiences concerning the use and effect of some new drugs. III. Cannabine tannate." (Ger.). Deut. Med. Woch. 1883, 8, 125.

3550. Hillestad,A. and Wold,J.K. "Water soluble glycoproteins from cannabis sativa(South Africa). Phytochemistry 1977, 16, 1947-1952.

3551. Hillestad,A., Wold,J.K., and Engen,J. "Water soluble glycoproteins from cannabis sativa(Thailand)." Phytochemistry 1977, 16, 1953-1956.

3552. Hillestad,A., Wold,J.K., and Paulsen,B.S. "Water soluble glycoproteins from cannabis sativa. Structural studies." Carbohyd. Res. 1977, 57, 135-144.

3553. Hillman,F.J. "Marihuana--a smoke screen." Alaska Med. 1972, 14, 4-8.

3554. Hilner,R., Wunder,R., Zellmann,K., and Haesen, D. "Experimental research on driving ability after smoking hashish."(Ger.). Blutalkohol 1972, 9, 213-220.

3555. Himmelsbach,C.K. "Treatment of the morphine abstinence syndrome with a synthetic cannabis-like compound." South. Med. J. 1944, 37, 26-29.

3556. Himwick,H.E. "Psychopharmacologic drugs." Science 1958, 127, 59-72.

3557. Hinckley,R.G. "Nonmedical drug use and the college student." J. Am. Coll. Hlth. Assoc. 1968, 17, 35-42.

3558. Hindmarch,I. "The psychology of cannabis--techniques for investigating the frequency and patterns of use of cannabis in groups of drug users." In Connell, P.H. and Dorn,N.(eds.). Cannabis and Man. Churchill Livingstone, Edinburgh, 1975, 116-145.

3559. Hindmarch,I., Hughes,I., and Einstein,R. "Attitudes to drug users and to the use of alcohol, tobacco and cannabis on the campus of a provincial university." Bull. Narc. 1975, 27, 27-36.

3560. Hine,B., Friedman,E., Torrelio,M., and Gershon,S. "Morphine-dependent rats: Blockade of precipitated abstinence by tetrahydrocannabinol." Science 1975, 187, 443-445.

3561. Hine,B., Friedman,E., Torrelio,M., and Gershon,S. "Tetrahydrocannabinol-attenuated abstinence and induced rotation in morphine-dependent rats: Possible involvement of dopamine." Neuropharmacol. 1975, 14, 607-610.

3562. Hine,B., Torrelio,M., and Gershon,S. "Analgesic, heart rate, and temperature effects of delta-9-THC during acute and chronic administration to conscious rats." Pharmacol. 1977, 15, 65-72.

3563. Hine,B., Torrelio,M., and Gershon,S. "Attenuation of precipitated abstinence in methadone-dependent rats by delta-9-THC." Psychopharmacol. Commun. 1975, 1, 275-283.

3564. Hine,B., Torrelio,M. and Gershon,S. "Differential effect of cannabinol and cannabidiol on THC-induced responses during abstinence in morphine-dependent rats." Res. Commun. Chem. Pathol. Pharmacol. 1975, 12, 185-188.

3565. Hine,B., Torrelio,M., and Gershon,S. "Interactions between cannabidiol and delta-9-THC during abstinence in morphine-dependent rats." Life Sci. 1975, 17, 851-858.

3566. Hines,G.H. "Attitudes and practices of university students related to tobacco, alcohol, and marihuana use." N. Z. Med. J. 1974, 80, 1-5.

3567. Hing Yin Kwan,V., Rajeswaran,P., and Crim,M. "Recent additions to a bibliography on cannabis." J. Forens. Sci. 1968, 13, 279-289.

3568. Hirata,K. "Cytological basis of the sex determination in cannabis sativa L." Jap. J. Genet. 1929, 4, 198-201.

3569. Hirata,K. "Sex determination in hemp (cannabis sativa L.)." Jap. J. Genet. 1927, 19, 65-79.

3570. Hirata,K. "Sex reversal in hemp. Preliminary report."(Jap.). J. Soc. Agric. Forest. 1924, 16, 145-168.

3571. Hirschhorn,I.D. and Rosecrans,J.A. "Morphine and delta-9-tetrahydrocannabinol: Tolerance to the stimulus effects." Pscyhopharmacol. 1974, 36, 243-253.

3572. Hisar,R. and Edesen,S. "Contribution to the study of hashish."(Fr.). Chim. Indust. 1938, 42, 561.

3573. Hitzemann,W. "Tests for hashish in different species of hemp grown in Germany."(Ger.). Arch. Pharm. 1941, 279, 353-387.

3574. Hively,R.L. "A study of the chemistry of marihuana." Diss. Abs. 1967, 28, 1421.

3575. Hively,R.L. and Hoffmann,F.W. U.S. Army Technical Report EATR-4002 on Isomers of Tetrahydrocannabinol. U.S. Chemical/Biological War-weapons Plant and Arsenal, Edgewood, Md., 1966.

3576. Hively,R.L., Mosher,W.A., and Hoffman,F.W. "Isolation of trans-delta-6-tetrahydrocannabinol from marihuana." J. Am. Chem. Soc. 1966, 88, 1832-1833.

3577. H.L.S. "Cannabis indica in corn mixtures." Pharmaceut. Era 1902, 28, 528.

3578. Ho,B.T., An,R., Fritchie,G.E., Englert,L.F., McIsaac,W.M., MacKay,B., and Ho,D.H.W. "Marihuana: Some pharmacological studies." J. Pharmaceut. Sci. 1971, 60, 1761.

3579. Ho,B.T., Estevez,V.S., and Englert,L.F. "Effect of repeated administration on the metabolism of (-)-delta-9-tetrahydrocannabinols in rats." Res. Commun. Chem. Path. Pharmacol. 1973, 5, 215-218.

3580. Ho,B.T., Estevez,V.S., and Englert,L.F. "Effect of SKF-525A on the metabolism of (-)-delta-9-tetrahydrocannabinol in the rat brain and liver." Comm. Prob. Drug Depend. 1974, 1, 925-930.

3581. Ho,B.T., Estevez,V.S., and Englert,L.F. "The uptake and metabolic fate of cannabinoids in rat brains." J. Pharm. Pharmacol. 1973, 25, 488-490.

3582. Ho,B.T., Estevez,V., Englert,L.F., and McIsaac,W.M. "Delta-9-tetrahydrocannabinol and its metabolites in monkey brains." J. Pharm. Pharmacol. 1972, 24, 414-416.

3583. Ho,B.T., Fritchie,G.E., Englert,L.F., McIsaac, W.M., and Idanpaan-Heikkila,J.E. "Marihuana: Importance of the route of administration." J. Pharm. Pharmacol. 1971, 23, 309-310.

3584. Ho,B.T., Fritchie,G.E., Kralik,P.M., Englert, L.F., McIsaac,W.M., and Idanpaan-Heikkila,J. "Distribution of tritiated 1-delta-9-tetrahydrocannabinol in rat tissues after inhalation." J. Pharm. Pharmacol. 1970, 22, 538-539.

3585. Ho,B.T. and Johnson,K.M. "Sites of neurochemical action of delta-9-tetrahydrocannabinol interaction with reserpine." In Nahas,G.G., Paton,W.D.M., and Idanpaan-Heikkila,J.E.(eds.). Marihuana. Springer Verlag, N.Y., 1976, 367-383.

3586. Ho,B.T., Taylor,D., and Engler,L.F. "Effects of delta-9-tetrahydrocannnabinol on the metabolism of ^{3}H-5-hydroxytryptamine and ^{3}H-norepinephrine in the rat brain." Res. Commun. Chem. Pathol. Pharmacol. 1974, 7, 645-650.

3587. Ho,B.T., Taylor,D., Englert,L.F., and McIsaac,W.M. "Neurochemical effects of 1-delta-9-tetrahydrocannabinol in rats following repeated inhalation." Brain. Res. 1971, 31, 233-236.

3588. Ho,B.T., Taylor,D., Fritchie,G.E., Englert, L.F., and McIsaac,W.M. "Neuropharmacological study of delta-9- and delta-8-tetrahydrocannabinols in monkeys and mice." Brain Res. 1972, 38, 163-170.

3589. Ho,I.K., Loh,H.H., and Way,E.L. "Mini thin layer chromatography in the detection of narcotics in the urine." Proc. West. Pharmacol. Soc. 1971, 14, 183-186.

3590. Hoare,M. Congo Mercenary. Robert Hale, London, 1969.

3591. Hochhauser,M. "Alcohol and marihuana consumption among undergraduate polydrug users." Am. J. Drug Alcohol Abuse 1977, 4, 65-76.

3592. Hochman,J.S. Marihuana and Social Evolution. Prentice-Hall, Englewood Cliffs, N.J, 1972.

3593. Hochman,J.S. and Brill,N.Q. "Chronic marihuana usage and liver function." Lancet 1971, 2, 818-819.

3594. Hochman,J.S. and Brill,N.Q. "Chronic marihuana use and psychosocial adaptation." Am. J. Psychiat. 1973, 130, 132-140.

3595. Hochman,J.S. and Brill,N.Q. "Marihuana intoxication: Pharmacological and psychological factors." Dis. Nerv. Syst. 1971, 32, 676-679.

3596. Hockman,C.H., Duffin,J., and Kalant,H. "An assessment of physiological and behavioral variables in humans smoking marihuana cigarettes." Proc. 5th Internat'l. Cong. Pharmacol. 1972, 1, 71.

3597. Hockman,C.H., Perrin,R.G., and Kalant,H. "Electroencephalographic and behavioral alterations produced by delta-1-tetrahydrocannabinol." Science 1971, 172, 968-970.

3598. Hodapp,A.E. Marihuana, A Review of the Literure. U.S. Customs Laboratory, New Orleans, La., 1959.

3599. Hodgson,J.R., Woodhours,E.J., and Castles,T.R. "Brain chromatin template activity of rats treated with delta-9-tetrahydrocannabnol." Can. J. Physiol. Pharmacol. 1973, 51, 401-403.

3600. Hoechstetter,S.S. "Effects of alcohol and cannabis during labor." J.A.M.A. 1930, 94, 1165.

3601. Hoekman,T.B., Dettbarn,W.D., and Klausner,H.A. "Action of delta-9-tetrahydrocannabinol on neuromuscular transmission in the rat diaphram." Neuropharmacol. 1976, 15, 315-319.

3602. Hoellinger,H., Nguyen-Hoang,N., Decauchereux, J.F., and Pichat,L. "Synthesis of delta-8- and delta-9-tetrahydrocannabinol deuteriated and tritiated."(Fr.). J. Label. Comp. 1977, 13, 401-412.

3603. Hoffer,A. and Osmond,H. The Hallucinogens. Academic Press, N.Y., 1967.

3604. Hoffmann,A.M., Hudson,G.R., and Warner,R.W. "Alienation and drug use among college students." J. Coll. Stud. Person. 1975, 16, 277-281.

3605. Hoffmann,N.E. and Yang,R.K.H. "Gas chromatography of delta-1-tetrahydrocannabinol." Anal. Let. 1972, 5, 7-11.

3606. Hoffmann,P. "The great grass trials." High Times 1977, 24, 67-71, 82.

3607. Hoffmann,W. "Hemp, cannabis sativa L."(Ger.). Handbook Pflanzenzuchtung 1961, 4, 204-208.

3608. Hofling,C.K. Textbook of Psychiatry for Medical Practice. J.P. Lippincott, Phil., 1963.

3609. Hofmann,A. "Structure and synthesis of hallucinogens."(Ger.). J. Mond. Pharm. 1970, 3, 187-205.

3610. Hofman,A. and Waster,P.G. "Identification of (-)-delta-9-6a,10a-trans-tetrahydrocannabinol and two of its metabolites in rats by use of combination gas chromatography-mass spectrometry and mass fragmentography." Biochem. Pharmacol. 1971, 20, 2469-2476.

3611. Hogan,R., Mankin,D., Conway,J., and Fox,S. "Personality correlates of undergraduate marihuana use." J. Consult. Clin. Psychol. 1970, 35, 58-63.

3612. Hogan,R., Mankin,D., Conway,J., and Fox,S. "Personality correlates of undergraduate marihuana use." Paper presented at East. Psychol. Assoc., Phil., 1969.

3613. Holden,C. "House chops sex-pot probe." Science 1976, 192, 450.

3613. Hollander,C.(ed.). Background Papers on Student Drug Involvement. U.S. Nat'l. Student Assoc., Washington, D.C., 1967.

3615. Hollander,C. "Drugs and campus policy." In Hollander,C.(ed.). Background Papers on Student Drug Involvement. U.S. Nat'l. Student Assoc., Washington, D.C., 1967, 41-56.

3616. Hollander,C. "NSA and student drug involvement: A history." In Hollander,C.(ed.). Background Papers on Student Drug Involvement. U.S. Nat'l. Student Drug Assoc., Washington, D.C., 1967, 5-8.

3617. Hollander,C. "Recent research on drug involvement among college students." Paper presented at Am. Person. Guidance Assoc., Detroit, 1968.

3618. Hollander,C. "Selected bibliography." In Hollander,C.(ed.). Background Papers on Student Drug Involvement. U.S. Nat'l. Student Assoc., Washington, D.C., 1967, 159-162.

3619. Holley,J.H., Hadley,K.W., and Turner,C.E. "Constituents of cannabis sativa L. XI: Cannabidiol and cannabichromene in samples of known geographical origin." J. Pharmaceut. Sci. 1975, 64, 892-894.

3620. Hollister,C.A. "Searches and seizures." Coll Mgt. 1972, 7, 22.

3621. Hollister,L.E. "Actions of various marihuana derivatives in man." Pharmacol. Rev. 1971, 23, 349-357.

3622. Hollister,L.E. "Cannabidiol and cannabinol in man." Exper. 1973, 29, 825-826.

3623. Hollister,L.E. "Chemical psychoses." Ann. Rev. Med. 1964, 15, 203-214.

3624. Hollister,L.E. Chemical Psychoses: LSD and Related Drugs. C.C. Thomas, Springfield, Ill., 1968.

3625. Hollister,L.E. "Clinical pharmacology and human behavioral responses to marihuana." Paper presented to Am. Pharmaceut. Assoc., San Francisco, 1971.

3626. Hollister,L.E. "Clinical pharmacology of cannabis in relation to its social use." In Goldberg, L. and Hoffmeister,F.(eds.). Psychic Dependence, Definition, Assessment in Animals and Man, Theoretical and Clinical Implications. Springer Verlag, N.Y., 1973, 177-185.

3627. Hollister,L.E. "Clinical pharmacology of hallucinogens and marihuana." In Zarafonetis,C.J.D.(ed.). Drug Abuse Proceedings of the International Conference. Lea and Febiger, Phil., 1972, 321-332.

3628. Hollister,L.E. "Clinical pharmacology of marihuana." In Gibbins,R.J., Israel,Y., Kalant,H., Popham,R.E., Schmidt,W., and Smart,R.G.(eds.). Research Advances in Alcohol and Drug Problems. J. Wiley and Sons, N.Y., 1973, 243-266.

3629. Hollister,L.E. "Criminal laws and the control of drugs of abuse." J. Clin. Pharmacol. 1969, 9, 345-348.

3630. Hollister,L.E. "Current research on marihuana." J. Soc. Iss. 1971, 27, 23-34.

3631. Hollister,L.E. "Dimensions of marihuana experience." Drug Alcohol Depend. 1975, 1, 155-164.

3632. Hollister,L.E. "Human pharmacological studies of cannabis." Act. Pharmaceut. Suec. 1971, 8, 673.

3633. Hollister,L.E. "Human pharmacology of marihuana(cannabis)." In Harris,R.T., McIsaac,W.M., and Schuster,C.R.(eds.). Drug Dependence. Univ. Texas Press, Austin, 1970, 67-79.

3634. Hollister,L.E. "Human pharmacology of marihuana and heroin." Clin. Res. 1971, 19, 606-611.

3635. Hollister,L.E. "Human pharmacology of marihuana: What next?" Psychopharmacol. 1972, 26, 128.

3636. Hollister,L.E. "Hunger and appetite after single doses of marihuana, alcohol, and dextroamphetamine." Clin. Pharmacol. Ther. 1971, 12, 44-49.

3637. Hollister,L.E. "Interactions of delta-9-tetrahydrocannabinol with other pharmacological agents." Ann. N. Y. Acad. Sci. 1976, 281, 212-218.

3638. Hollister,L.E. "Interactions in man of delta-9-tetrahydrocannabinol. 1. Alphamethylparatyrosine." Clin. Pharmacol. Ther. 1974, 15, 18-21.

3639. Hollister,L.E. "Marihuana, ethanol, and dextro-amphetamine." Arch. Gen. Psychiat. 1970, 23, 199-203.

3640. Hollister,L.E. "Marihuana in man: Three years later." Science 1971, 172, 21-28.

3641. Hollister,L.E. "Reflections on marihuana research." In Braude,M.C. and Szara,S.(eds.). Pharmacology of Marihuana. Raven Press, N.Y., 1976, 1, 35-37.

3642. Hollister,L.E. "Status report on clinical pharmacology of marihuana." Ann. N. Y. Acad. Sci. 1971, 191, 132-142.

3643. Hollister,L.E. "Steroids and moods: Correlations in schizophrenics and subjects treated with lysergic acid diethylamide(LSD), mescaline, tetrahydrocannabinol, and synhexyl." J. Clin. Pharmacol. 1969, 9, 24-29.

3644. Hollister,L.E. "Structure-activity relationships in man of cannabis constituents, and homologs and metabolites of delta-9-tetrahydrocannabinol." Pharmacol. 1974, 11, 3-11.

3645. Hollister,L.E. "Tetrahydrocannabinol isomers and homologues: Contrasted effects of smoking." Nature 1970, 227, 968-969.

3646. Hollister,L.E. and Gillespie,H.K. "Action of delta-9-tetrahydrocannabinol. An approach to the active metabolite hypothesis." Clin. Pharmacol. Ther. 1975, 18, 714-719.

3647. Hollister,L.E. and Gillespie,H.K. "Delta-8- and delta-9-tetrahydrocannabinol. Comparison in man by oral and intravenous administration." Clin. Pharmacol. Ther. 1972, 14, 353-357.

3648. Hollister,L.E. and Gillespie,H.K. "Interactions in man of delta-9-tetrahydrocannabinol. II. Cannabinol and cannabidiol. Clin. Pharmacol. Ther. 1975, 18, 80-83.

3649. Hollister,L.E. and Gillespie,H.K. "Similarities and differences between the effects of lysergic acid diethylamide and tetrahyrocannabinol in man." In Wittenborn,J.R., Brill,H., Smith,J.P., and Wittenborn, S.A.(eds.). Drugs and Youth. C.C. Thomas, Springfield, Ill., 1969, 208-211.

3650. Hollister,L.E., Kanter,S.L., Board,R.D., and Green,D.E. "Marihuana metabolites in urine of man. III. Unchanged delta-9-tetrahydrocannabinol." Res. Commun. Chem. Pathol. Pharmacol. 1974, 8, 579-584.

3651. Hollister,L.E., Moore,F., Kanter,S., and Noble,E. "Delta-1-tetrahydrocannabinol, synhexyl and marihuana extract administered orally in man: Catecholamine excretion, plasma cortisol levels and platelet serotonin content." Psychopharmacol. 1970, 17, 354-360.

3652. Hollister,L.E. and Overall,J.E. "Dimensions of marihuana experience." Drug Alcohol Depend. 1975, 1, 155-164.

3653. Hollister,L.E., Overall,J.E., and Gerber,M.L. "Marihuana and setting." Arch. Gen. Psychiat. 1975, 32, 798-801.

3654. Hollister,L.E. and Reaven,G.M. "Delta-9-tetrahydrocannabinol and glucose tolerance." Clin. Pharmacol. Ther. 1974, 16, 297-302.

3655. Hollister,L.E., Richards,R.K., and Gillespie, H.K. "Comparison of tetrahydrocannabinol and synhexyl in man." Clin. Pharmacol. Ther. 1968, 9, 783-791.

3656. Hollister,L.E., Sherwood,S.L., and Cavasino,A. "Marihuana and the human electroencephalogram." Pharmacol. Res. Commun. 1970, 2, 305-308.

3657. Hollister,L.E. and Tinklenberg,J.R. "Subchronic oral doses of marihuana extract." Psychopharmacol. 1973, 29, 247-252.

3658. Holm,V.M. "Marihuana and the naval aviator." In Lewis,M.F.(ed.). Current Research in Marihuana. Academic Press, N.Y., 1972, 195-203.

3659. Holmberg,M.B. and Jansson,B. "Experiences from an out-patient department for drug addicts in Goteborg." Act. Psychiat. Scand. 1968, 44, 172-189.

3660. Holmes,E.M. "Cannabis indica." Pharmaceut. J. 1900, 13, 522-523.

3661. Holmes,E.M. "Cannabis indica." Pharmaceut. J. 1902, 15, 129-131.

3662. Holmes,E.M. "Cannabis indica--relative value of different sorts." Proc. Am. Pharmaceut. Assoc. 1905, 53, 682-684.

3663. Holmes,E.M. "Notes on cannabis indica." Pharmaceut. J. 1902, 14, 342.

3664. Holmes,E.M. "Note on cannabis indica." Pharmaceut. J. 1905, 20, 550-551.

3665. Holmes,E.M. "Note on cannabis indica." Pharmaceut. J. 1909, 29, 132.

3666. Holmes,E.M. "Some of the drug exhibits at the colonial and Indian exhibition." Pharmaceut. J. Trans. 1886, 17, 405-406, 415-416.

3667. Holmstedt,B. "Cannabis--history of its culture and scientific development."(Swed.). Lakartidningen 1976, 73, 3853-3856.

3668. Holmstedt,B. and Linnardson,H. "Chemistry and means of determination of hallucinogens and marihuana." In Zarafonetis,C.J.D.(ed.). Drug Abuse. Lea and Febiger, Phil., 1972, 291-305.

3669. Holroyd,K. and Kahn,M. "Personality factors in student drug use." J. Consult. Clin. Psychol. 1974, 42, 236-243.

3670. Holroyd,K. and Kahn,M. "Statistically derived groups of drug users." Paper presented at Southeast. Psychol. Assoc., Atlanta, 1972.

3671. Holsten,F. "Flashbacks. Clinical and social significance 1½-4 years after the 1st administration." (Nor.). Tid. Nor. Laegefor. 1976, 96, 875-878.

3672. Holtzman,D., Lovell,R.A., Jaffe,J.H., and Freedman,D.X. "L-delta-9-tetrahydrocannabinol: Neurochemical and behavioral effects in the mouse." Science 1969, 163, 1464-1468.

3673. Homedes,J. "Histomorphological data on cannabis sativa cells."(Sp.). Bol. Inst. Catal. Hist. Nat. 1929, 9, 137-140.

3674. Honecker,H.C. and Coper,H. "Thin layer chromatographic demonstration of presence of opium in hashish." Deut. Med. Woch. 1970, 95, 2129-2131.

3675. Honma,S., Kaneshima,H., Mori,M., and Kitsutaka,T. "Cannabis grown in Hokkaido. II. Content of cannabinol, tetrahydrocannabinol, and cannabidiol in wild cannabis."(Jap.). Hokkaid. Eisei Kenkyush. 1971, 21, 180-185.

3676. Honma,S., Kaneshima,H., Mori,M., and Kitsutaka,T. "Cannabis grown in Hokkaido. III. Variation in amount of narcotic substances in cannabis with growth."(Jap.). Hokkaid. Eisei Kenkyush. 1971, 21, 186-190.

3677. Hood,L.V.S., Dames,M.E., and Barry,G.T. "Headspace volatiles of marihuana." Nature 1973, 242, 402-403.

3678. Hooper,D. "Charas of Indian hemp." Pharmaceut. J. 1908, 28, 347-349.

3679. Hooper,D. "Charas of Indian hemp." Yearbook Pharm. 1908, 1, 435-444.

3680. Hooper,D. "Extract of Indian hemp." Yearbook Pharm. 1894, 1, 484-489.

3681. Hooper,D. "The valuation of Indian hemp." Pharmaceut. J. 1908, 27, 80.

3682. Hoops,J.F., Bader,H., and Biel,J.H. "A 5-aza analog of delta-6a(10a)-tetrahydrocannabinol." J. Org. Chem. 1968, 33, 2995-2996.

3683. Horan,J.J., D'Amico,M.M., and Williams,J.M. "Assertiveness and patterns of drug use. A pilot study." J. Drug Ed. 1975, 5, 217-222.

3684. Horan,J.J., D'Amico,M.M., and Williams,J.M. "Drug usage: an experimental comparison of 3 assessment conditions." Psychol. Rep. 1974, 35, 211-215.

3685. Horan,J.J. and Swisher,D. "Effecting drug attitude change in college students via induced cognitive dissonance." Paper presented at Educational Res. Assoc., Chicago, 1972.

3686. Hordern,A. "Psychopharmacology: Some historical considerations." In Joyce,C.R.B.(ed.). Psychopharmacology: Dimensions and Perspectives. Tavistock, London, 1968, 95-148.

3687. Horman,R. and Foxwell,A.(eds.). Drug Awareness: Key Documents on LSD, Marihuana and the Drug Culture. Avon, N.Y., 1970.

3688. Hornung,R. "Fear arousal, communicator credibility, and attitude to hashish."(Ger.). Soz. Praeventivmed. 1976, 21, 221-222.

3689. Horowitz,M. "Herbicidal treatments for control of cannabis sativa L." Bull. Narc. 1977, 29, 75-84.

3690. Horrowitz,J.L. and Sedlacek,W.E. University Student Attitudes and Behavior Toward Drugs. Counseling Center, Univ. Maryland, College Park, Md., 1972.

3691. Horwitz,J. "The rise and fall of marihuana luftwaffe." High Times 1976, 12, 37-39, 59-60, 65.

3692. Hoskin,H.F. "A Canadian programme of voluntary treatment of drug dependence: The work of the Narcotic Addiction Foundation of British Columbia." Bull. Narc. 1968, 20, 45-48.

3693. Hoskin,H.F., Hickey,R.F., and Pearson,K.M. Marihuana--The Questions People Ask. Narcotic Addiction Foundation of British Columbia, Vancouver, B.C., 1969.

3694. Hosko,M.J. and Hardman,H.F. "Effects of delta-9-THC on cardiovascular responses to stimulation or vasopressor loci in the neuraxis of anesthetized cats." Pharmacologist 1971, 13, 296.

3695. Hosko,M.J. and Hardman,H.F. "Evidence for a dual mechanism of action of cannabis on central cardiovascular control." In Braude,M.C. and Szara,S.(eds.). Pharmacology of Marihuana. Raven Press, N.Y., 1976, 1, 239-255.

3696. Hosko,M.J., Kochar,M.S., and Wang,R.I.H. "Effects of orally administered delta-9-tetrahydrocannabinol in man." Clin. Pharmacol. Ther. 1973, 14, 344-352.

3697. Hosko,M.J., Wang,R.I.H., and Kochar,M.S. "Behavioral and neuropharmacological effects of oral delta-9-THC in the young adult male." Comm. Prob. Drug Depend. 1972, 1, 748-757.

3698. Hoton-Dorge,M. "Isolation of the principal phenolic constituents of Indian cannabis by column chromatography and preparative chromatography."(Fr.). J. Pharm. 1974, 29, 415-422.

3699. Houghton,E. "A pharmacological study of cannabis americana." Ther. Gaz. 1908, 32, 26-28.

3700. Houghton,E. and Hamilton,H.C. "A pharmacological study of cannabis americana." Am. J. Pharmacol. 1908, 80, 16-20.

3701. Houry,S., Mechoulam,R., Fowler,P.J., Macko,E., and Loev,B. "Benzoxocin and benzoxonin derivatives. Novel groups of terpenophenols with central nervous system activity." J. Med. Chem. 1974, 17, 287-293.

3702. Houser,V.P. "The effects of delta-9-tetrahydrocannabinol upon fear-motivated behavior in squirrel monkeys." Physiol. Psychol. 1975, 3, 157-161.

3703. Howard,B.R. and Sedlacek,W.E. Trends in Freshmen Attitudes and Use of Drugs. Counselling Center, Univ. Maryland, College Park, Md., 1974.

3704. Howard,J. and Goddard,J. "Marihuana paradox." Life 1969, 67, 26B-35.

3705. Howe,J. "Early attempts to introduce the cultivation of hemp, in Eastern British America." Paper presented to New Brunswick Historical Society, St. Johns, N.B., 1897.

3706. Howes,J.F. "A study of two water soluble derivatives of delta-9-tetrahydrocannabinol." Pharmacol. 1970, 12, 322.

3707. Howes,J.F. "Antagonism of the effects of delta-9-tetrahydrocannabinol by pemoline(Cylert[R])." Res. Commun. Chem. Path. Pharmacol. 1973, 6, 901-908.

3708. Howes,J.F. "The effect of delta-9-tetrahydrocannabinol on amphetamine induced lethality in aggregated mice." Res. Commun. Chem. Pathol. Pharmacol. 1973, 6, 895-900.

3709. Howes,J.F. and Osgood,P.F. "Cannabinoids and the inhibition of prostaglandin synthesis." In Nahas, G.G., Paton,W.D.M., and Idanpaan-Heikkila,J.E.(eds.). Marihuana. Springer Verlag, N.Y., 1976, 415-425.

3710. Howes,J. and Osgood,P. "The effect of delta-9-tetrahydrocannabinol on the uptake and release of ^{14}C-dopamine from crude striatal synaptosomal preparations." Neuropharmacol. 1974, 13, 1109-1114.

3711. Howes,J.F. and Osgood,P.F. "The effects of delta-9-THC and a water soluble derivative on PGE_1 synthesis in the corpus striatum." Pharmacologist 1974, 16, 259.

3712. Hoye,D.(ed.). Hasheesh: The Herb Dangerous. And/Or Press, Berkeley, Cal., 1975.

3713. Hrbek,J., Komenda,S., Krejci,A., Siroka,A., Navratil,J., Skala,J., and Vedlich,L. "On the acute effect of some drugs on the higher nervous activity in man. Tetrahydrocannabinol(4, 8, 16 mg). Part XXXI."(Czech." Act. Univ. Palack. Olomuc. Fac. Med. 1973, 67, 233-273.

3714. Hrbek,J., Komenda,S., Siroka,A., Krejci,Z., and Navratil,J. "Acute effects of smoking tetrahydrocannabinol with tobacco on higher nervous activity in man." Activ. Nerv. Super. 1973, 15, 139-140.

3715. Hrbek,J., Komenda,S., Siroka,A., Krejci,Z., Navratil,J., and Medek,A. "Acute effects of tetrahydrocannabinol(4, 8, 16 mg) on verbal associations." Activ. Nerv. Super. 1972, 14, 107-108.

3716. Hrbek,J., Krejci,Z., Komenda,S., Siroka,A., and Navratil,J. "Influence of smoking hashish on higher nervous activity in man." Act. Pharmaceut. Suec. 1971, 8, 689-690.

3717. Huba,G.J., Segal,B., and Singer,J. L. "Organization of needs in male and female drug and alcohol users." J. Consult. Clin. Psychol. 1977, 45, 34-44.

3718. Hubacek,J. "Contribution to the treatment of sinusitis maxillaris with cannabis."(Czech.). Act. Univ. Palack. Olumuc. Fac. Med. 1961, 23, 207-212.

3719. Hubacek,J. "Study of the effect of cannabis indica in otorhinolaryngology."(Czech.). Act. Univ. Palack. Olumuc. Fac. Med. 1955, 6, 83-86.

3720. Hubacek,J. "The use of the antibacterial substances of cannabis by the country doctor."(Czech.). Lekarsky Obzor 1960, 9, 646.

3721. Huber,E. "History of medicine--hashish and opium."(Ger.). Deut. Med. Woch. 1927, 53, 1145-1146.

3722. Huber,G.L., McCarthy,C.R., Simmons,G.A., Cutting,M.B., Laguarda,R., and Pereira,W. "Depressant effect of marihuana smoke on antibactericidal activity of pulmonary alveolar macrophages." Chest 1975, 68, 769-773.

3723. Huber,G.L., O'Connell,D., McCarthy,C., Pereira,W., Mahajan,V., and Mullane,J. "Toxicologic pharmacology of tetrahydrocannabinol(THC) and marihuana (MJ) smoke components." Clin. Res. 1976, 24, 255A.

3724. Hug,C.C. "Characteristics and theories related to acute and chronic tolerance development." In Mule,S.J.(ed.). Chemical and Biological Aspects of Drug Dependence. CRC Press, Cleveland, Oh., 1972, 307-320.

3725. Hughes,G. "Drug of choice? The case for marihuana." Juris Doctor 1975, 5, 46-50.

3726. Hughes,G.A., Jen,T.Y., and Smith,H. "Oxaphenanthrenes and their intermedicates." Chem. Abs. 1971, 75, 48910x.

3727. Hughes,J.E., Steahly,L.P., and Bier,M.M. "Marihuana and the diabetic coma." J.A.M.A. 1970, 214, 1113-1114.

3728. Humphrey,J. "Cannabis indica." Pharmaceut. J. 1902, 15, 284.

3729. Humphrey,J. "The chemistry of cannabis indica." Pharmaceut. J. 1902, 14, 363-364.

3730. Humphrey,J.R. Marketing Hemp. Kentucky Agricultural Experimental Station. Univ. Kentucky, Lexington, Ky., 1919.

3731. Hungerford,M.C. "An overdose of hasheesh." Pop. Sci. Month. 1883, 24, 508-515.

3732. Hunneman,D.H. "Mass spectrometical characterization of common narcotics."(Ger.). Chem.-Ztg. 1974, 98, 28-35.

3733. Hunt,B.J. and Rigby,W. "Degradation products of gambogic acid(preparation of cannabivolactonic acid)." Chem. Indust. 1967, 42, 1790-1791.

3734. Hunt,D.G. "Parental permissiveness as perceived by the offspring and the degree of marihuana usage among offspring." Human Relat. 1974, 27, 267-285.

3735. Huot,J. "Cellular alterations induced in vitro by delta-1-tetrahydrocannabinol."(Fr.). Vie Med. Can. Fran. 1974, 3, 13-23.

3736. Huot,J. "Cellular and biochemical alternations induced in vitro by delta-1-tetrahydrocannabinol: effects on cell proliferation nucleic acids, plasma cell membrane ATPase and adenyl cyclase." In Nahas,G.G., Paton,W.D.M., and Idanpaan-Heikkila,J.(eds.). Marihuana. Springer Verlag, N.Y., 1975, 312-327.

3737. Huot,J. "Effects of delta-9-tetrahydrocannabinol on cell proliferation nucleic acids and the plasma membrane ATPase of cells cultivated in vitro."(Fr.). In Radouco-Thomas,S.(ed.). Pharmacology, Toxicology and Abuse of Psychotomimetics(Hallucinogens).(Fr.). Univ. Laval, Quebec, 1973, 347-366.

3738. Hurst,P., Cook,R.F., and Ramsay,D.A. Assessing the Prevalence of Illicit Drug Use in the Army. U.S. Army Res. Inst. Behav. Social Sci., Washington, D.C., 1975.

3739. Hussain,M.Z. and Harinath,M. "Helping alcoholics abstain: an implantable substance." Am. J. Psychiat. 1972, 129, 363.

3740. Hussey,H.H. "Marihuana use by adolescents." *J.A.M.A.* 1973, *226*, 661-662.

3741. Hutchinson,H.W. "Patterns of marihuana use in Brazil." In Rubin,V.(ed.). *Cannabis and Culture*. Mouton, The Hague, 1975, 173-185.

3742. Huto,J. "Cellular alterations induced in vitro by delta-1-tetrahydrocannabinol: Effects on cell proliferation, nucleic acids, plasma cell membrane ATPase, and adenylate cyclase." In Nahas,G.G., Paton,W.D.M., and Idanpaan-Heikkila,J.E.(eds.). *Marihuana*. Springer Verlag, N.Y., 1976, 313-329.

3742a. Hutton,G.W. "Marihuana cases: A legal problem." *Police Chief* 1975, *42*, 58-59.

3743. Huxley,A. "Culture and the individual." In Andrews,G. and Vinkenoog,S.(eds.). *The Book of Grass*. Grove Press, N.Y., 1967, 192-201.

3744. Huxley,A. "Drugs that shape men's minds." *Sat. Even. Post* 1958, *231*, 28-29.

3745. Huxley,J. "Psychometabolism." *J. Neuropsychiat.* 1962, *3*, 1.

3746. Huy,N.D., Belleau,R., and Roy,P.E. "Toxicity of marihuana and tobacco smoking in the beagle." *Internat'l. J. Clin. Pharmacol.* 1975, *12*, 267-276.

3747. Huy,N.D., Gailis,L., Cote,G., and Roy,P.E. "Effects of chronic administration of delta-9-tetrahydrocannabinol in guinea pigs." *Internat'l. J. Clin. Pharmacol.* 1975, *12*, 284-289.

3748. Huy,N.D., Gailis,L., and Roy,P.E. "Effect after three months of inhalation of marihuana and tobacco in the dog."(Fr.). *Un. Med. Can.* 1974, *10*, 65-71.

3749. Huy,N.D. and Roy,P.E. "Inhalation of tobacco and marihuana in dog over a period of 30 months: Effect on body weight, food intake and organ weight." *Res. Commun. Chem. Path. Pharmacol.* 1976, *13*, 465-472.

3750. Huy,N.D., Roy,P.E., and Belleau,R. "Toxicity of marihuana and tobacco smoking in the 'beagle'." *Internat'l. J. Clin. Pharmacol.* 1974, *10*, 155.

3751. Hyde,M.E.(ed.). *Mind Drugs*. McGraw Hill, N.Y., 1972.

I

3752. Idanpaan-Heikkila,J. "Cannabis--recent studies." Duodecim. 1972, 88, 191-198.

3753. Idanpaan-Heikkila,J., Fritchie,G.E., Englert, L.F., Ho,B.T., and McIsaac,W.M. "Placental transfer of tritiated 1-delta-9-tetrahydrocannabinol." N. Eng. J. Med. 1969, 281, 330.

3754. Idanpaan-Heikkila,P. and Schoolar,J.C. "Characteristics in a young drug-user turning from hallucinogen-usage to heroin." Scand. J. Clin. Lab. Invest. 1971, 27, 80.

3755. Iglesias,F. "Hashish smoking in Brazil."(Port.). An. Paul Med. Ciurg. 1918, 9, 274-281.

3756. Imbesi,A. "On the pharmacological action of cannabis indica. II."(It.). At. Soc. Pelo. Sci. Fis. Mat. Nat. 1958, 5, 313.

3757. Imbesi,A. "Pharmacognosic research on Indian hemp."(It.). At. Soc. Pelo. Sci. Fis. Mat. Nat. 1957, 4, 373-384.

3758. Imbesi,A. "Pharmacological action of Indian hemp. I. Influence of reserpine, chlorpromazine and 5-hydroxytryptamine."(It.). Arch. It. Sci. Farmacol. 1959, 9, 166-167.

3759. Imlah,N. Drugs in Modern Society. G. Chapman, London, 1970.

3760. Imperi,L.L., Kleber,H.D., and Davie,J.S. "Use of hallucinogenic drugs on campus." J.A.M.A. 1968, 204, 1021-1024.

3761. Inayama,S., Sawa,A., and Hosaya,E. "The oxidation of delta-1- and delta-6-tetrahydrocannabinol with selenium dioxide." Chem. Pharmaceut. Bull. 1974, 22, 1519-1525.

3762. Incekara,F. Ontogenic Anatomic and Technological Studies of Hemp Stem Fibers Cultivated in Turkey."(Turk.). Univ. Ankara, Ankara, Turkey, 1956.

3763. India. Report of the Prohibition Enquiry Commission. Planning Commission, Manager, Gov't. India Press, New Delhi, 1955.

3764. Indian Hemp Drugs Commission. Report. Gov't. Print. Office, London, 1893-1894.

3765. Ingersoll,J.E. "Effect of legalizing marihuana and heroin." Vital Speech. 1972, 39, 24-27.

3766. Ingersoll,J.E. "Narcotics and dangerous drugs: news briefing." Week. Compil. President. Doc. 1969, 5, 1479.

3767. Inglis,B. The Forbidden Game. Charles Scribner's Sons, N.Y., 1975.

3768. Inglis,R. "Solubility of the extract of cannabis indica." Med. Time. 1845, 12, 104, 144.

3769. Inglis,R. "Traumatic tetanus and Indian hemp." Med. Time. 1845, 12, 454.

3770. Interdisciplinary Society of Biological Psychiatry. "The use of cannabis: East and West." In van Praag,H.M.(ed.). Biochemical and Pharmacological Aspects of Dependence and Reports on Marihuana Research. De Erven F. Bohn, Haarlem, Netherlands, 1972.

3771. International Narcotic Education Association and World Narcotics Defense Association. Marihuana or Indian Hemp and its Preparations. Internat'l. Narc. Educat. Assoc. Wld. Narc. Defens. Assoc., Los Angeles, 1936.

3772. International Narcotic Enforcement Officers Assocation. Non-narcotic Drug Abuse. Smith, Kline, and French, Phil., 1964.

3773. Ireland,T. "Indian hemp as a cause of insanity." Br. Med. J. 1893, 2, 813-814.

3774. Ireland,T. "Insanity from the abuse of Indian hemp." Alien. Neurol. 1893, 14, 622-630.

3775. Irish,W. Marihuana. Dell, N.Y., 1972.

3776. Irudayasamy,A. and Natarajan,A.R. "An improved and rapid test for detection of marihuana with diazotized p-nitroaniline." Ind. J. Chem. 1965, 3, 327-328.

3777. Irvin,J.E. and Mellors,A. "Delta-9-tetrahydrocannabinol uptake by rat liver lysosomes." Biochem. Pharmacol. 1975, 24, 305-307.

3778. Irwin,S. "Drugs and abuse: An introduction to their actions and potential hazards." J. Psyched. Drug. 1971, 3, 5-15.

3779. Irwin,S. "Effect of marihuana and d,l-delta-6-tetrahydrocannabinol on the mouse, cat and squirrel monkey." Comm. Prob. Drug Depend. 1969, 2, 6142-6153.

3780. Irwin,S. "Pros and cons of marihuana legalization." In Blachly,P.H.(ed.). Drug Abuse: Data and Debate. C.C. Thomas, Springfield, Ill., 1970, 296-313.

3781. Isbell,H. "Clinical aspects of the various forms of nonmedical use of drugs. Part II." Anesth. Analges. 1971, 50, 897-905.

3782. Isbell,H. "Clinical pharmacology of marihuana." Pharmacol. Rev. 1971, 23, 337-338.

3783. Isbell,H. "Comparison of (-)-delta-9-trans-tetrahydrocannabinol and LSD-25." Drug Depend. 1970, 4, 36-38.

3784. Isbell,H. "Drug dependence of the LSD(hallucinogen) and cannabis(marihuana) types." Cienc. Cult. 1973, 25, 758-764.

3785. Isbell,H. "Effects on infant brestfed by marihuana-smoking mother." J.A.M.A. 1970, 213, 135.

3786. Isbell,H. "Research in cannabis(marihuana)." Bull. Narc. 1973, 25, 37-48.

3787. Isbell,H. "Substances occurring naturally in marihuana(cannabis sativa) and identical or related semisynthetic materials." Comm. Prob. Drug Depend. 1968, 1, 35.

3788. Isbell,H. "The marihuana problem." Comm. Prob. Drug Depend. 1968, 2, 5227-5233.

3789. Isbell,H. "The question of control of synthetic substances with marihuana-like effect." Comm. Prob. Drug Depend. 1968, 1, 6.

3790. Isbell,H. and Chrusciel,T.L. "Dependence liability of 'non-narcotic- drugs. Tetrahydrocannabinols." Bull. W.H.O. 1970, 43, 95-98.

3791. Isbell,H. and Gattozzi,A.A. "Marihuana; the familiar compound poses many challenges." U.S. Pub. Hlth. Serv. 1968, 1743, 163-165.

3792. Isbell,H., Gorodetzky,C.W., Jasinski,D., Claussen,U., Spulak,F., and Korte,F. "Effects of (-)-delta-9-trans-tetrahydrocannabinol in man." *Ment. Hlth. Dig.* 1967, *1*, 11-12.

3793. Isbell,H., Gorodetzky,C.W., Jasinski,D., Claussen,U., Spulak,F., and Korte,F. "Effects of (-)-delta-9-trans-tetrahydrocannabinol in man." *Psychopharmacol.* 1967, *11*, 184-188.

3794. Isbell,H. and Jasinski,D.R. "A comparison of LSD-25 with (-)-delta-9-tetrahydrocannabinol(THC) and attempted cross tolerance between LSD and THC." *Psychopharmacol.* 1969, *14*, 115-123.

3795. Isbell,H., Jasinski,D.J., Gorodetzky,C.W., Korte,F., Claussen,U., Haage,M., Sieper,H., and Spulak,F. "Studies on tetrahydrocannabinol." *Comm. Prob. Drug Depend.* 1967, *2*, 4832-4845.

3796. Isbell,H., Keeler,M.H., Bloomquist,E.R. "The marihuana problem." *Ment. Hlth. Dig.* 1967, *1*, 10-15.

3797. Isbell,H., Korte,F., Claussen,U., Haage,M., Sieper,H., and Spulak,F. "Studies on tetrahydrocannabinol. I. Method of assay in human subjects and results with crude extracts, purified tetrahydrocannabinols and synthetic compounds." *Comm. Prob. Drug Depend.* 1967, *2*, 4832-4846.

3798. Ishii,A. and Motohashi,N. "Drug abuse in Japan." *Addict. Dis.* 1977, *3*, 105-114.

3799. Isley,D. "Nocious weed seeds." *Iowa State Coll. J. Sci.* 1954, *28*, 521-586.

3800. Israelstam,D.M. "Selected bibliography on marihuana and LSD-type drugs." *Calif. Law Rev.* 1968, *56*, 160-166.

3801. Isyurhash,M. and Rusoff,G. *The Gourmet Guide to Grass*. Pinnacle Books, N.Y., 1973.

3802. Itokawa,H., Takeya,K., and Mihashi,S. "Biotransformation of cannabinoid precursors and related alcohols by suspension cultures of callous induced from cannabis sativa L." *Chem. Pharm. Bull.* 1977, *25*, 1941-1946.

3803. Itokawa,H., Takeya,K., and Akasu,M. "Stereochemistry in oxidation of primary allylic alcohols by cell-free system of callus induced from cannabis sativa L." *Chem. Pharm. Bull.* 1976, *24*, 1681-1683.

3804. Izquierdo,I. "Effect of anticonvulsant drugs on the number of afferent stimuli needed to cause a hippocampal seizure discharge." Pharmacol. 1974, 11, 146-150.

3805. Izquierdo,I. and Berardi,A.C. "Effect of various cannabis sativa compounds on the seizure threshold of rat hippocampus." Cienc. Cult. 1973, 25, 747-749.

3806. Izquierdo,I. and Nasello,A.G. "Effects of cannabidiol and of diphylhydantoin on the hippocampus and on learning." Psychopharmacol. 1973, 31, 167-175.

3807. Izquierdo,I., Orsingher,O.A., and Berardi,A.C. "Effect of cannabidiol and other cannabis sativa compounds on hippocampal seizure discharges." Psychopharmacol. 1973, 28, 95-102.

3808. Izquierdo,I. and Tannhauser,M. "The effect of cannabidiol on maximal electroschock seizures in rats." J. Pharm. Pharmacol. 1973, 25, 916-917.

3809. Izquierdo,I. and Tannhauser,M. "Effect of cannabidiol on maximal electroshock seizures in rats." Paper presented at 1st Lat. Amer. Cong. Psychobiol., Sao Paulo, 1973.

J

3810. Jackson,B. and Reed,A. "Catnip and alteration of consciousness." J.A.M.A. 1969, 207, 1349-1350.

3811. Jackson,D.M., Malor,R., Chesher,G.B., Starmer,G.A., Welburn,P.J., and Bailey,R. "The interaction between protaglandin E_1 and delta-9-tetrahydrocannabinol on intestinal motility and on the abdominal constriction response in the mouse." Psychopharmacol. 1976, 47, 187-193.

3812. Jackson,J.R. "Churus." Pharmaceut. J. Trans. 1873, 3, 764.

3813. Jackson,J.W. "Marihuana." J. Indiana Med. Assoc. 1939, 32, 24-25.

3814. Jacob,A. and Todd,A.R. "Cannabidiol and cannabinol, constituents of cannabis indica resin." Nature 1940, 145, 350.

3815. Jacob,A. and Todd,A.R. "Cannabis indica. Part II. Isolation of cannabidiol from Egyptian hashish. Observations on the structure of cannabinol." J. Chem. Soc. 1940, 1, 649-653.

3816. Jacobs,M. "Observations on a case of poisoning by hashish."(Fr.). Rep. Pharm. 1848, 1, 242-244.

3817. Jacobsen,E. "An analysis of the gross action of drugs on the central nervous system." In Walaas,O.(ed.). Molecular Basis of Some Aspects of Mental Activity. Academic Press, N.Y., 1967, 3-18.

3818. Jacobsen,E. "Simulants and mentality."(Swed.). Farmaceut. Tid. 1964, 74, 939-951.

3819. Jacobsen,E. "The hallucinogens." In Joyce, C.R.B.(ed.). Psychopharmacology: Dimensions and Perspectives. Tavistock, London, 1968, 175-213.

3820. Jacoby,J.E., Weiner,N.A., Thornberry,T.P., and Wolfgang,M.E. "Drug use and criminality in a birth cohort." In National Commission on Marihuana and Drug Abuse. Drug Use in America: Problem in Perspective. Gov't. Print. Office, Washington, D.C., 1973, I, 300-372.

3821. Jaenicke,A. "Cannabis--side effects."(Ger.). Schweiz. Med. Woch. 1970, 100, 1089-1090.

3822. Jaffe,D.T. "Drug laws: Perceptions of illegal users." Drug Forum 1974, 3, 321-329.

3823. Jaffe,J.H. "Drug addiction and drug abuse." In Goodman,L. and Gilman,A.(eds.). The Pharmacological Basis of Therapeutics. MacMillan, N.Y., 1965, 299-301.

3824. Jaffe,J.H. "Drug addiction and drug abuse." In Goodman,L. and Gilman,A.(eds.). The Pharmacological Basis of Therapeutics. MacMillan, N.Y., 1970, 298-300.

3825. Jaffe,H.H. "Drug addiction and drug abuse." In Goodman,L. and Gilman,A.(eds.). The Pharmacological Basis of Therapeutics. MacMillan, N.Y., 1975, 306-309.

3826. Jaffe,J.H. "Psychiatric consequences of marihuana." In Tinklenberg,J.R.(ed.). Marihuana and Health Hazards. Academic Press, N.Y., 1975, 153-159.

3827. Jaffe,P.J. and Baum,M. "Increased resistance-to-extinction of an avoidance response in rats following the administration of hashish resin." Psychopharmacol. 1971, 20, 97-102.

3828. Jahr,G.H.G. New Homeopathic Pharmacopoeia and Posology. J. Dobson, Phil., 1842.

3829. Jain,M.L., Curtis,B.M., and Bakutis,E.V. "In vivo effect of LSD, morphine, ethanol and delta-9-tetrahydrocannabinol on mouse brain adenosine triphosphatase activity." Res. Commun. Chem. Pathol. Pharmacol. 1974, 7, 229-232.

3830. Jacob-Stang,H. "Use and abuse of euphoric substances by conscripts at the Oslo sessions of 1969." (Nor.). Tid. Norsk. Laeg. 1970, 90, 1549-1546, 1572.

3831. Jakubovic,A., Hattori,T., and McGeer,P.L. "Radioactivity in suckled rats after giving ^{14}C-tetrahydrocannabinol to the mother." Pharmacol. 1973, 22, 221-223.

3832. Jakubovic,A. and McGeer,P.L. "Biochemical changes in rat testicular cells in vitro produced by cannabinoids and alcohol: metabolism and incorporation of labeled glucose, amino acids, and nucleic acid precursors." Toxicol. Appl. Pharmacol. 1977, 41, 473-486.

3833. Jakubovic,A. and McGeer,P.L. "Inhibition of rat brain protein and nucleic acid synthesis by cannabinoids in vitro." Can. J. Biochem. 1972, 50, 654-662.

3834. Jakubovic,A. and McGeer,P.L. "Intracellular distribution of ^{3}H-delta-8-tetrahydrocannabinol in rat organs after i.v. administration." Res. Commun. Chem. Pathol. Pharmacol. 1974, 9, 197-200.

3835. Jakubovic,A. and McGeer,P.L. "In vitro inhibition of protein and nucleic acid synthesis in rat testicular tissue by cannabinoids." In Nahas,G.G., Paton,W.D.M., and Idanpaan-Heikkila,J.E.(eds.). Marihuana. Springer Verlag, N.Y., 1976, 223-243.

3836. Jakubovic,A., McGeer,P.L., and Fitzsimmons,R.C. "Effects of delta-9-tetrahydrocannabinol and ethanol on body weight protein and nucleic acid synthesis in chick embryos." J. Toxicol. Environ. Hlth. 1976, 1, 441-447.

3837. Jakubovic,A., Tait,R.M., and McGeer,P.L. "Excretion of THC and its metabolites in ewe's milk." Toxicol. Appl. Pharmacol. 1974, 28, 38-43.

3838. James,T. "Dagga: A review of fact and fancy." S. Af. Med. J. 1970, 44, 575-580.

3839. James,T. "Dagga and driving." S. Af. Med. J. 1970, 44, 580-581.

3840. James,W. The Principles of Psychology. Henry Holt, N.Y., 1890.

3841. Jamison,K. and McGlothlin,W.H. "Drug usage, personality, and behavioral correlates of drug behavior." J. Psychol. 1973, 83, 123-130.

3842. Jandhyala,B.S. and Buckley,J.P. "Autonomic and cardiovascular effects of chronic delta-9-tetrahydrocannabinol administration in mongrel dogs." Res. Commun. Chem. Pathol. Pharmacol. 1977, 16, 593-607.

3843. Jandhyala,B.S. and Buckley,J.P. "Influence of several anesthetic agents on the effects of delta-9-tetrahydrocannabinol on the heart rate and blood pressure of the mongrel dog." Eur. J. Pharmacol. 1977, 44, 9-16.

3844. Jandhyala,B.S., Cavero,I., and Buckley,J.P. "Parasympatholytic activity of (-)-delta-9-tetrahydrocannabinol(THC) in mongrel dogs." Proc. 5th Internat'l. Cong. Pharmacol. 1972, 1, 115.

3845. Jandhyala,B.S., Malloy,K.P., and Buckley,J.P. "Effects of acute administration of delta-9-tetrahydrocannabinol on pulmonary hemodynamics of anesthetized dogs." Eur. J. Pharmacol. 1976, 38, 183-187.

3846. Jandhyala,B.S., Malloy,K.P., and Buckley,J.P. "Effects of chronic administration of delta-9-tetrahydrocannabinol on the heart rate of mongrel dogs." Res. Commun. Chem. Pathol. Pharmacol. 1976, 14, 201-202.

3847. Janiger,O. "The use of hallucinogenic agents in psychiatry." Calif. Clin. 1949, 55, 221-224, 251-259.

3848. Janowitz,J.F. "There's no hiding place down there." Am. J. Orthopsychiat. 1967, 37, 296.

3849. Janowsky,D.S., Meacham,M.P., Blaine,J.D., Schoor,M., and Bozzetti,L.P. "Simulated flying performance after marihuana intoxication." Aviat. Space Environ. Med. 1976, 47, 124-128.

3850. Janowsky,D.S., Meacham,M.P., Blaine,J.D., Schoor,M., and Bozzetti,L.P. "Marihuana effects on simulated flying ability." Am. J. Psychiat. 1976, 133, 384-388.

3851. Janowitz,J.F. "On prolonged marihuana reactions." J. Am. Coll. Hlth. Assoc. 1967, 16, 106-107.

3852. Jansen,T.T. "A physician's opinion on marihuana problems." J. Jap. Med. Assoc. 1971, 65, 785-792.

3853. Jaques,M.E. "Marihuana and the counselor: It's not so simple." Person. Guid. J. 1973, 52, 17-21.

3854. Jarbe,T.U.C. "Alcohol discrimination in gerbils: Interactions with bemegride, DH-524, amphetamine, and delta-9-THC." Arch. Internat'l. Pharmacodyn. Ther. 1977, 227, 118-129.

3855. Jarbe,T.U.C. and Henriksson,B.G. "Acute effects of two tetrahydrocannabinols on water intake in water deprived rats: Implications for behavioral studies on marihuana compounds." Psychopharmacol. 1973, 30, 315-322.

3856. Jarbe,T.U.C. and Henriksson,B.B. "Discriminative response control produced with hashish, tetrahydrocannabinols, and other drugs." Psychopharmacol. 1974, 40, 1-16.

3857. Jarbe,T.U.C. and Henriksson,B.G. "Effects of delta-8- and delta-9-THC on the acquisition of a discriminative positional habit in rats." Psychopharmacol. 1973, 31, 321-332.

3858. Jarbe,T.U.C. and Henriksson,B.G. "Effects of long-term administration and withdrawal of tetrahydrocannabinols(delta-8- and delta-9-THC) on open-field behavior in rats." Pharmacol. Biochem. Behav. 1973, 1, 243-249.

3859. Jarbe,T.U.C. and Henriksson,B.G. "Open-field behavior and acquisition of discriminative response control in delta-9-THC tolerant rats." Exper. 1973, 29, 1251-1253.

3860. Jarbe,T.U.C. and Henriksson,B.G. "State dependent learning with tetrahydrocannabinols and other drugs." Cienc. Cult. 1973, 25, 752.

3861. Jarbe,T.U.C. and Henriksson,B.G. "The transitions between normal and tetrahydrocannabinol-induced states on reversal learning." Psychopharmacol. 1973, 31, 321-332.

3862. Jarbe,T.U.C. and Henriksson,B.G. "Vocalization: A characteristic cannabis-induced behavior in the rat?" Physiol. Psychol. 1973, 1, 351-353.

3863. Jarbe,T.U.C., Henriksson,B.G., and Ohlin,G.C. "Delta-9-THC as a discriminative cue in pigeons: Effects of delta-8-THC, CBD, and CBN." Arch. Internat'l. Pharmacodyn. Ther. 1977, 228, 68-72.

3864. Jarbe,T.U.C., Johansson,J.O., and Henriksson,B.G. "Delta-9-tetrahydrocananbinol and pentobarbital as discriminative cues in the mongolian gerbil(Meriones Unguiculatus)." Pharmacol. Biochem. Behav. 1975, 3, 403-410.

3865. Jarbe,T.U.C. and Ohlin,G.C. "Stimulus effects of delta-9-THC and its interaction with naltrexone and catecholamine blockers in rats." Psychopharmacol. 1977, 54, 193-195.

3866. Jarines Carrion,H. "Marihuana in America." (Sp.). Rev. Farm. Cuba 1951, 29, 34-44.

3867. Jarvik,L.F., Bishun,N.P., Bleiweiss,H., Kato,T., and Moralishvili,E. "Chromosome examinations in patients on lithium carbonate." Arch. Gen. Psychiat. 1971, 24, 166.

3868. Jarvik,M.E. "The psychopharmacological revolution." Psychol. Today 1967, 1, 51-59.

3869. Jarvis,C.S. "The drug smugglers of Egypt." Cornhill 1937, 156, 588-605.

3870. Jarvis,C.S. "Hashish smugglers of Egypt." Asia 1930, 30, 440-444.

3871. Jarvis,C.S. "Hashish smuggling in Egypt." Living Age 1938, 353, 442-447.

3872. Jasinski,D.R., Haertzen,C.A., and Isbell,H. "Review of the effects in man of marihuana and tetrahydrocannabinols on subjective state and physiologic functioning." Ann. N. Y. Acad. Sci. 1971, 191, 196-206.

3873. Jeffery,W.H. "Drug-induced pulmonary disease." Ann. Intern. Med. 1973, 78, 617-618.

3874. Jelinek,C.F. "Marihuana structure." Chem. Engin. News 1970, 48, 6.

3875. Jen,T.Y., Gughes,G.A., and Smith,H. "Total synthesis of delta-8-(delta-1(6))-tetrahydrocannabinol, a biologically active constituent of hashish." J. Am. Chem. Soc. 1967, 89, 4551-4552.

3876. Jenison,L.M. and Markie,D.J. "Parents' views on selected issues facing higher education." Coll. Stud. J. 1974, 8, 90-93.

3877. Jenkins,J.W. and Patterson,D.A. "The relationship between chemical composition and geographical origin of cannabis." Forens. Sci. 1973, 2, 59-66.

3878. Jeri,F.R. "Use of drugs and hallucinogens by adolescents and schoolchildren."(Sp.). Rev. Neuro-psiquiat. 1971, 34, 243-273.

3879. Jersild,J. "The abuse of narcotics in Denmark." Internat'l. Crim. Pol. Rev. 1968, 23, 124.

3880. Jersild,T., Ott,C., and Thiede,J. "Innoculation hepatitis in narcomaniacs and after tattooing."(Dan.). Ugeskr. Laeg. 1967, 129, 1664-1665.

3881. Jessor,R. "Predicting time of onset of marihuana use: a developmental study of high school youth." J. Consult. Clin. Psychol. 1976, 44, 125-134.

3882. Jessor,R., Jessor,S.L., and Finney,J. "A social psychology of marihuana use: longitudinal studies of high school and college youth." J. Person. Soc. Psychol. 1973, 26, 1-15.

3883. Jimenez Diaz,C. and Lahoz,C. "Asthma and fibrosis. (Considerations on hemp and feather grass patients.)."(Sp.). Rev. Clin. Esp. 1966, 103, 182-188.

3884. Jimenez Diaz,C. and Lahoz,C. "Cannabism." (Sp.). Rev. Clin. Esp. 1944, 14, 366-376.

3885. J.M.P. "The marihuana bugaboo." Milit. Surg. 1943, 93, 94-95.

3886. Joachimoglu,G. "Cannabis(hashish)."(Ger.). Hefter's Hdbh. Exper't. Pharmakol. 1924, 2, 1114-1119.

3887. Joachimoglu,G. "Natural and smoked hashish." In Wolstenholme,G.E.W. and Knight,J.(eds.). Hashish. Its Chemistry and Pharmacology. Ciba Foundation Study Group No. 21, Little Brown, Boston, 1965, 2-14.

3888. Joachimoglu,G. "Some remarks on the problem of cannabis." Biological evaluation of cannabis preparations." Bull. Narc. 1959, 11, 5-6.

3889. Joachimoglu,G., Kiburis,J., and Miras,C.J. "Distribution and excretion of tetrahydrocannabinol-^{14}C in rats."(Gr.). Prakt. Akad. Athenon 1967, 42, 161-167.

3890. Joachimoglu,G., Kiburis,J., and Miras,C.J. "Studies on the distribution and excretion of ^{14}C-tetrahydrocannabinol in rats." U.N. Doc. ST/SOA/SER.S/15, Sept. 25, 1967.

3891. Joachimoglu,G., Kiburis,J., and Miras,C.J. "Studies with the U.N. cannabis reference sample." Bull. Narc. 1967, 19, 21-22.

3892. Joachimoglu,G. and Miras, C.J. "Study of the pharmacology of hashish." Bull. Narc. 1963, 15, 7-8.

3893. Jochle,W. "Cannabis sativa and geniture." N. Eng. J. Med. 1974, 291, 535.

3894. Joel,B. "Hashish the exotic elixir." Marihuana Month. 1976, 2, 42.

3895. Joel,E. "Is it necessary to cultivate Indian hemp in Germany?"(Ger.). Klin. Woch. 1926, 5, 364-365.

3896. Joel,E. "Is the cultivation of Indian hemp possible?" Klin. Woch. 1926, 5, 1280.

3897. Joel,E. "Pharmacology of the body position and labyrinthine reflexes. XIII. Hashish."(Ger.). Pflug. Arch. Gesamt. Physiol. Mensch. Tier. 1925, 209, 526-536.

3898. Joel,E. "The culture of Indian hemp."(Fr.). J. Suisse Pharm. 1926, 1 214.

3899. Joel,E. and Frankel,F. "Hashish intoxication. Contribution to experimental psychopathology."(Ger.). Klin. Woch. 1926, 5, 1707-1709.

3900. Johansson,J.O., Henriksson,B.G., and Jarbe, T.U.C. "Effects of delta-9-THC on dissociation of conditioned avoidance responding in tolerant and nontolerant rats." Phsyiol. Psychol. 1974, 2, 431-432.

3901. Johansson,J.O., Jarbe,T.U.C., and Henriksson, B.G. "Acute and subchronic influences of tetrahydrocannabinols on water and food intake, body weight, and temperature in rats." Life Sci. 1975, 5, 17-28.

3902. Johansson,J.O., Jarbe,T.U.C., and Henriksson, B.G. "Physostigmine attenuation of delta-9-tetrahydrocannabinol induced hyperthermia in rats." Exper. 1974, 30, 779-780.

3903. John Howard Society. "Brief on marihuana." Correct. Process 1968, 9, 5.

3904. John Howard Society. "Sanctions on marihuana." Can. J. Correct. 1968, 11, 62.

3905. John Howard Society. "The use of marihuana: a brief." Can. Welfare 1969, 45, 14.

3906. Johnson,B.B. "A junior high school seminar on dangerous drugs and narcotics." J. Sch. Hlth. 1968, 38, 84-87.

3907. Johnson,B.C. "Sense and nonsense in the scientific study of drugs: an acute-commission report." Society 1973, 10, 53-58.

3908. Johnson,B.D. Marihuana Users and Drug Subcultures. J. Wiley and Sons, N.Y., 1973.

3909. Johnson,B.D. Social Determinants of the Use of 'Dangerous Drugs' by College Students. Univ. Michigan, Ann Arbor, Mich., 1971.

3910. Johnson,D.D., McNeill,J.R., Crawford,R.D., and Wilcox,W.C. "Epileptiform seizures in domestic fowl. V. The anticonvulsant activity of delta-9-tetrahydrocannabinol." Can. J. Physiol. Pharmacol. 1975, 53, 1007-1013.

3911. Johnson,D.M. Indian Hemp; A Social Menace. C. Johnson, London, 1952.

3912. Johnson,D.M. The Hallucinogenic Drugs. C. Johnson, London, 1953.

3913. Johnson,F.K. and Westman,J.C. "The teenager and drug abuse." J. Sch. Hlth. 1968, 38, 646-654.

3914. Johnson,G. and Newmeyer,J. "Pleasure, punishment and moral indignation." Sociol. Soc. Res. 1975, 59, 82-95.

3915. Johnson,G.E. "Marihuana--a product of controversy." Appl. Ther. 1968, 10, 458.

3916. Johnson,H.D. "'Potted dreams'." Br. Med. J. 1969, 1, 376.

3917. Johnson,K.G., Donnelly,J.H., Scheble,R., Wine,R.L., and Weitman,M. "Survey of adolescent drug use. I. Sex and grade distribution." J. Pub. Hlth. 1971, 61, 2418-2432.

3918. Johnson,K.M. "Some structural requirements for inhibition of high-affinity synaptosomal serotonin uptake by cannabinoids." Mol. Pharmacol. 1976, 12, 345-352.

3919. Johnson,K.M., and Dewey,W.L. "In vitro alteration of the subcellular distribution of ^{3}H-reserpine in the rat forebrain by delta-9-tetrahydrocannabinol." Res. Commun. Chem. Pathol. Pharmacol. 1976, 15, 655-671.

3920. Johnson,K.M., Dewey,W.L., and Harris,L.S. "Delta-9-THC induced elevations of mouse brain tryptophan and consequent increased serotonin production." Pharmacologist 1976, 18, 296.

3921. Johnson,K.M., Dewey,W.L., and Harris,L.S. "Some structural requirements for inhibition of high affinity synaptosomal serotonin uptake by cannabinoids." Mol. Pharmacol. 1976, 12, 345-352.

3922. Johnson,K.M., Ho,B.T., and Dewey,W.L. "Effects of delta-9-tetrahydrocannabinol on neurotransmitter accumulation and release mechanisms in rat forebrain synaptosomes." Life Sci. 1976, 19, 347-356.

3923. Johnson,L. Drugs and American Youth. Univ. Michigan Inst. for Social Res., Ann Arbor, Mich., 1973.

3924. Johnson,M.H. "Marihuana--a political drug." J. Med. Soc. N.J. 1975, 72, 866-868.

3925. Johnson,R.D. "Medico-social aspects of marihuana." Rhode Is. Med. J. 1968, 51, 171-178.

3926. Johnson,R.D. "The pediatrician and the marihuana question." Pediatrics 1970, 45, 1037.

3927. Johnson,R.D. "Why so many teenagers fall for marihuana: with group discussion program." Parents Mag. 1969, 44, 58-61.

3928. Johnson,R.J. and Wiersema,V. "Effects of delta-9-tetrahydrocannabinol metabolite on bone marrow myelopoiesis." Res. Commun. Chem. Pathol. Pharmacol. 1974, 8, 393-396.

3929. Johnson,R.J. and Wiersema,V. "Repression of bone marrow leukopoiesis by delta-9-tetrahydrocannabinol." Res. Commun. Chem. Pathol. Pharmacol. 1974, 7, 613-616.

3930. Johnson,S. and Domino,E.F. "Some cardiovascular effects of marihuana smoking in normal volunteers." Clin. Pharmacol. Ther. 1971, 12, 762-768.

3931. Johnson,W.T. and Bogomolony,R. "Selective justice: Drug law enforcement in six American cities." In National Commission on Marihuana and Drug Abuse." Drug Use in America: Problem in Perspective. Gov't. Print. Office, Washington, D.C., 1973, III, 498-650.

3932. Johnson-Romuald,F. "Narcotics control in the republic of Togo." Bull. Narc. 1969, 21, 41-45.

3933. Johnston,L.D. "Drug use during and after high school: Results of a national longitudinal study." Am. J. Pub. Hlth. 1974, 64, 29-37.

3934. Johnstone,R.E., Lief,P.L., Kulp,R.A., and Smith,T.C. "Combination of delta-9-tetrahydrocannabinol with oxymorphone or pentobarbital: Effects on ventilatory control and cardiovascular dynamics." Anesthesiology 1975, 42, 674-684.

3935. Jolles,K. "Danger! Drivers at risk--2." Nurs. Times 1969, 65, 1652-1654.

3936. Jolley,J.C. "Clergy attitudes about drug abuse and drug education: a case study." Rocky Mt. Soc. Sci. J. 1972, 9, 75-82.

3937. Jonckheere,P. "Psychodynamics and psychotherapy in a case of hashish intoxication."(Fr.). Brux. Med. 1971, 51, 911.

3938. Joneja,M.G. "A study of teratological effects of intravenous, subcutaneous, and intragastric administration of delta-9-tetrahydrocannabinol in mice." Toxicol. Appl. Pharmacol. 1976, 36, 151-162.

3939. Joneja,M.G. "Effects of delta-9-tetrahydrocannabinol on hamster fetuses." J. Toxicol. Environ. Hlth. 1977, 2, 1031-1040.

3940. Jones,A.D. "Cannabis and alcohol usage among the Tonga: an observational report of the effects of cultural expectations." Psychol. Rec. 1975, 25, 329-332.

3941. Jones,B.C., Clark,D.L., Consroe,P.F., and Smith,H.J. "Effects of (-)-delta-9-tetrahydrocannabinol on social behavior of squirrel monkey dyads in a water competition situation." Psychopharmacol. 1974, 37, 37-43.

3942. Jones,B.C., Consroe,P.F., and Laird,H.E. "The interaction of delta-9-tetrahydrocannabinol with cholinomimetic drugs in an agonist-antagonist paradigm." Eur. J. Pharmacol. 1976, 38, 253-259.

3943. Jones,G. and Pertwee,R.G. "A metabolic interaction in vivo between cannabidiol and delta-1-tetrahydrocannabinol." Br. J. Pharmacol. 1972, 45, 375-377.

3944. Jones,G., Pertwee,R.G., Gill,E.W., Paton, W.D.M., Nilsson,I.M., Widman,M., and Agurell,S. "Relative pharmacological potency in mice of optical isomers of delta-1-tetrahydrocannabinol." Biochem. Pharmacol. 1974, 23, 439-446.

3945. Jones,G., Widman,M., Agurell,S., and Lindgren,J. "Monohydroxylated metabolites of delta-1-tetrahydrocannabinol in mouse brain." Act. Pharmaceut. Suec. 1974, 11, 283-294.

3946. Jones,H.B. "The deception of drugs." Clin. Toxicol. 1971, 4, 129-136.

3947. Jones,H.B. "The effects of sensual drugs on behavior: clues to the function of the brain." Adv. Psychobiol. 1974, 2, 297-312.

3948. Jones,H.B. "What the practicing physician should know about marihuana." Priv. Pract. 1976, 1, 35-38.

3949. Jones,H.B. and Jones,H.C. Sensual Drugs. Cambridge Univ. Press, N.Y., 1977.

3950. Jones,H.L. "Cannabis indica as a narcotic." Can. Lancet 1884, 17, 148.

3951. Jones,H.L. "Note on cannabis indica as a narcotic." Practitioner 1885, 35, 251.

3952. Jones,K.L., Shainberg,L.W., and Byer,C.O. Drugs, Alcohol and Tobacco. Canfield Press, San Francisco, 1970.

3953. Jones,K.L., Shainberg,L.W., and Byer,C.O. Drugs and Alcohol. Harper and Row, N.Y., 1969.

3954. Jones,L.A. and Foote,R.S. "Cannabis smoke condensate. Identification of some acids, bases, and phenols." Agricult. Food Chem. 1975, 23, 1129-1131.

3955. Jones,R.T. "Biological effects of cannabis: 1972 literature." In National Commission on Marihuana and Drug Abuse. Drug Use in America: Problem in Perspective. Gov't. Print. Office., Washington, D.C., 1973, I, 168-180.

3956. Jones,R.T. "Cannabis." In Mule,S.H.(ed.). Chemical and Biological Aspects of Drug Dependence. CRC Press, Cleveland, Oh., 1972, 65-81.

3957. Jones,R.T. "Drug models of schizophrenia." In Cole,J.O., Freeman,A.M., and Friedhoff,A.J.(eds.). Psychopathology and Psychopharmacology. Johns Hopkins Univ. Press, Baltimore, 1973, 71-86.

3958. Jones,R.T. "Effects of marihuana on the mind." In Tinklenberg,J.R.(ed.). Marihuana and Health Hazards. Academic Press, N.Y., 1975, 115-121.

3959. Jones,R.T. "Human effects." In Petersen,R.C. (ed.). Marihuana Research Findings: 1976." N.I.D.A. Res. Monog. Ser 14., Dept. H.E.W., Rockville, Md., 1971, 128-178.

3960. Jones,R.T. "Marihuana-induced 'high': Influence of expectation, setting and previous drug experience." Pharmacol. Rev. 1971, 23, 359-369.

3961. Jones,R.T. "Mental illness and drugs: Pre-existing psychopathology and response to psychoactive drugs." In National Commission on Marihuana and Drug Abuse. Drug Use in America: Problem in Perspective. Gov't. Print. Office, Washington D.C., 1973, I, 373-397.

3962. Jones,R.T. "Tetrahydrocannabinol and the marihuana-induced social 'high' or the effects of the mind on marihuana." Ann. N. Y. Acad. Sci. 1971, 191, 155-166.

3963. Jones,R.T. "The marihuana induced 'social high': A note of caution." Proc. West. Pharmacol. Soc. 1971, 14, 21-25.

3964. Jones,R.T. and Benowitz,N. "The 30-day trip: Clinical studies of cannabis tolerance and dependence." In Braude,M.C. and Szara,S.(eds.). Pharmacology of Marihuana. Raven Press, N.Y., 1976, 2, 627-643.

3965. Jones,R.T., Benowitz,N., and Bachman,J. "Clinical studies of cannabis tolerance and dependence." Ann. N. Y. Acad. Sci. 1976, 282, 221-239.

3966. Jones,R.T. and Stone,G.C. "Psychological studies of marihuana and alcohol in man." Psychopharmacol. 1970, 18, 108-117.

3967. Jonsson,G. and Fuxe,K. "Effect of tetrahydrocannabinols on central monoamine neurons." Act. Pharmacol. Toxicol. 1972, 31, 6.

3968. Jordon,H.V., Lang,A.L., and Enfield,G.H. "Effects of fertilizers on yields and breaking strengths of American hemp, cannabis sativa." J. Am. Soc. Agron. 1946, 38, 551-563.

3969. Jorgensen,F. "Abuse of psychotomimetics." Act. Psychiat. Scand. 1968, 203, 205-216.

3970. Jorgensen,F. "Abuse of psychotomimetics." (Dan.). Ugeskr. Laeg. 1968, 203, 205.

3971. Jorgensen,F. "Control organizations for the restriction of narcotic and drug abuse."(Dan.). Ugeskr. Laeg. 1970, 132, 2192-2194.

3972. Jorgensen,F. "Psychoses in connection with cannabis."(Dan.). Ugeskr. Laeg. 1967, 129, 1648-1656.

3973. Jorgensen,F. "Treatment of young female addicts in a general psychiatric department."(Dan.). Ugeskr. Laeg. 1970, 132, 1242-1251.

3974. Jornander,O. and Person,C. "The drug problem in Sweden." Internat'l. Crim. Pol. Rev. 1969, 24, 235-241.

3975. Joseph,R. "Economic significance of cannabis sativa in the Moroccan rif." In Rubin,V.(ed.). Cannabis and Culture. Mouton, The Hague, 1975, 185-195.

3976. Joseph,R. "The economic significance of cannabis sativa in the Moroccan rif." Econ. Bot. 1973, 27, 235-240.

3977. Josephson,E. "Adolescent marihuana use, 1971-1972: Findings from two national surveys." Addict. Dis. 1974, 1, 55-72.

3978. Josephson,E. and Carroll,E.(eds.). Drug Use: Epidemiological and Sociological Approaches. Hemisphere Pub. Corp., N.Y., 1974.

3979. Josie,G.H. A Report on Drug Addiction in Canada. King's Printer and Controller of Statistics, Ottawa, 1948.

3980. Joubert,L. "Marihuana." Science 1969, 163, 1144-1145.

3981. Joyce,C.R.B. "A critical approach to experiments on cannabis and the interpretation of their results." In Graham,J.D.P.(ed.). Cannabis and Health. Academic Press, N.Y., 1976, 109-121.

3982. Joyce,C.R.B. "Cannabis." Br. J. Psychiat. 1975, 9, 278-283.

3983. Joyce,C.R.B. and Curry,S.H.(eds.). The Botany and Chemistry of Cannabis. J. and H. Churchill, London, 1970.

3984. Judd,L.L., Gunderson,E., Alexander,G.R., Attewell,P., Buckingham,B., Blau,E., Crichton,J., Mandell,A.J., and Schuckit,J. "Youth drug survey." In National Commission on Marihuana and Drug Abuse. Drug Use in America: Problem in Perspective. Gov't. Print. Office, Washington, D.C., 1973, I, 942-974.

3985. Judee,C. "On the hallucinations produced by hashish."(Fr.). Gaz. Hop. Civil. Milit. 1855, 28, 279.

3986. Juel-Jensen,B.E. "Cannabis and recurrent herpes simplex." Br. Med. J. 1972, 4, 296.

3987. Julien,M.S. "Chinese surgery--anesthetic substance used in China in the 3rd century B.C. for paralysing movement and sensibility."(Fr.). C. R. Acad. Sci. 1849, 28, 192-198.

3988. Junger-Tas,J. "School youth and drugs in Belgium."(Dut.). Ned. T. Criminol. 1972, 14, 111-128.

3989. Junod,H.A. The Life of a South African Tribe. Attinger Feres, Neuchatel, Switzerland, 1912.

3990. Just,W.W., Erdmann,G., Thel,S., Werner,G., and Wiechmann,M. "Metabolism and autoradiographic distribution of delta-8- and delta-9-tetrahydrocannabinol in some organs of the monkey Callithrix Jacchus." Arch. Pharmacol. 1975, 287, 219-225.

3991. Just,W.W., Erdmann,G., Werner,G., Wiechmann,M., and Thel,E. "Forensic, metabolic, and autoradiographic studies of delta-8- and delta-9-tetrahydrocannabinol." In Nahas,G.G., Paton,W.D.M., and Idanpaan-Heikkila,J.E. (eds.). Marihuana. Springer Verlag, N.Y., 1976, 123-141.

3992. Just,W.W., Filipovic,N., and Werner,G. "Detection of delta-9-tetrahydrocanabinol in saliva of men by means of thin-layer chromatography and mass spectrometry." J. Chromatog. 1974, 96, 189-194.

3993. Just,W.W., Werner,G., and Wiechmann,M. "Determination of delta-1- and delta-1(6)-tetrahydrocannabinol in blood, urine, and saliva of hashish smokers."(Ger.). Naturwissen. 1972, 59, 222.

3994. Just,W.W., Werner,G., Wiechmann,M., and Erdmann,G. "Detection and identification of delta-8- and delta-9-tetrahydrocannabinol in the saliva of man and autoradiographic investigation of their distribution in the salivary glands of the monkey." Jugoslav. Physiol. Pharmacol. 1973, 9, 263-268.

3995. Just,W.W., Werner,G., Wiechmann,M. and Erdmann,G. "Detection and identification of delta-8- and delta-9-tetrahydrocannabinol in saliva of man and autoradiographic investigation of their distribution in different organs of the monkey." Strahlentherapie 1975, 74, 90-97.

3996. Just,W.W. and Wiechmann,M. "Detection of tetrahyrocannabinol in saliva of man and studies on its metabolism in the monkey." Arch. Pharmacol. 1974, 282, 22.

K

3997. Kabelik,J. "Hemp(cannabis sativa) an antibiotic drug. 1. Report: hemp in old and folk medicine."(Ger.). *Pharm*. 1957, *12*, 439-443.

3998. Kabelik,J. "Hemp--history, traditional, and popular uses."(Czech.). *Act*. *Univ*. *Palack*. *Olom*. 1955, *6*, 31-41.

3999. Kabelik,J., Krejci,Z., and Santavy,F. "Cannabis as a medicament." *Bull*. *Narc*. 1960, *12*, 5-23.

4000. Kahn,M. and Holroyd,K. "Comparability of drug abuse rating scales." *Psychol*. *Rep*. 1973, *33*, 699-702.

4001. Kaistha,K.K. "Drug abuse screening programs: Detection procedures, development costs, street-sample analysis and field test." *J*. *Pharm*. *Sci*. 1972, *61*, 655-678.

4002. Kalant,H. "Marihuana and simulated driving." *Science* 1969, *166*, 640.

4003. Kalant,H. and Kalant,O.J. "Cannabis--some new answers to old questions." *Addictions* 1974, 21, 48-61.

4004. Kalant,H. and LeBlanc,A.E. "Effect of acute and chronic pretreatment with delta-1-tetrahydrocannabinol on motor impairment by ethanol in the rat." *Can*. *J*. *Physiol*. *Pharmacol*. 1974, *52*, 291-297.

4005. Kalant,O. J. *An Interim Guide to the Cannabis (Marihuana)Literature*. Addiction Research Foundation, Toronto, 1968.

4006. Kalant, O.J. "Ludlow on cannabis: A modern look at a nineteenth century drug experience." *Internat'l*. *J*. *Addict*. 1971, *6*, 309-322.

4007. Kalant,O.J. "Marihuana, the experts and the public." _Addictions_ 1971, _18_, 20-27.

4008. Kalant,O.J. "Moreau, hashish, and hallucinations." _Internat'l. J. Addict._ 1971, _6_, 553-560.

4009. Kalant,O.J. "Report of the Indian Hemp Drugs Commission, 1893-1894: A critical review." _Internat'l. J. Addict._ 1972, _7_, 77-96.

4010. Kales,A., Hanley,J., Rickles,W., Kanas,N., Baker,M., and Goring,P. "Effects of marihuana administration and withdrawal in chronic users and naive subjects." _Psychophysiology_ 1972, _9_, 92.

4011. Kales,A., Heuser,G., Kales,J.D., Rickles,W.H., Rubin,R.T., Sharf,M.B., Ungerleider,J.T., and Winters,W.D. "Drug dependency. Investigations of stimulants and depressants." _Ann. Intern. Med._ 1969, _70_, 591-614.

4012. Kalter,H. "Teratogenicity, embryolethality, and mutagenicity of drugs of dependence." In Mule,S.J.(ed.). _Chemical and Biological Aspects of Drug Dependence_. CRC Press, Cleveland, Oh., 1972, 413.

4013. Kamstra,J. "A portrait of the artist as a young dope smuggler." _High Times_ 1974, _6_, 45-49, 68.

4014. Kamstra,J. "Highway 15 revisited. A smuggler remembers when it was easy." _High Times_ 1976, _16_, 76-79, 122.

4015. Kamstra,J. _Weed: Adventures of a Dope Smuggler_. And/or Press, Berkeley, Cal., 1975.

4016. Kanakis,C., Pouget,M., and Rosen,K. "Effects of delta-9-tetrahydrocannabinol(cannabis)on cardiac performance as measured by echocardiography." _Clin. Res._ 1976, _24_, 255A.

4017. Kanakis,C., Pouget,M., and Rosen,K. "The effects of delta-9-tetrahydrocannabinol(cannabis) on cardiac performance with and without beta blockade." _Circulation_ 1976, _53_, 703-707.

4018. Kanakis,C. and Rosen,K. "The cardiovascular effects of marihuana in man." _Chest_ 1977, _72_, 2-3.

4019. Kandel,D. "Adolescent marihuana use: Role of parents and peers." _Science_ 1973, _181_, 1067-1070.

4020. Kandel,D. "Inter- and intragenerational influences on adolescent marihuana use." _J. Soc. Iss._ 1974, _30_, 107-135.

4021. Kandel,D. "States in adolescent involve in drug use." _Science_ 1975, _190_, 912-914.

4022. Kandel,D., Kessler,R., and Margulies,R. "Adolescent initiation into stages of drug use: A sequential analysis." Paper presented at Conference on Strategies of Longitudinal Research in Drug Use, Puerto Rico, 1976.

4023. Kandel,D., Treisman,D., Faust,R., and Single,E. "Adolescent involvement in legal and illegal drug use: a multiple classification analysis." Soc. Forces 1976, 55, 438-458.

4024. Kane,F.J. "Severe emotional disturbance accompanying marihuana use." J. Louisiana State Med. Soc. 1972, 124, 287-291.

4025. Kane,H.H. Drugs That Enslave. P. Blakiston's Sons, Phil., 1881.

4026. Kane,J. "Dope in the cinema." High Times 1977, 19, 69-74; 20, 61-66, 70; 22, 72-75, 80.

4027. Kane,V.V. "Structure of cannabicyclol, a detailed NMR study of a synthetic analog." Tetrahed. Let. 1971, 14, 4101-4104.

4028. Kane,V.V. and Razdan,R.K. "Constituents of hashish. A novel reaction of olivetol with citral in the presence of pyridine. Total synthesis of dl-cannabicyclol and dl-cannabichromene." J. Am. Chem. Soc. 1968, 90, 6551-6553.

4029. Kane,V.V. and Razdan,R.K. "Hashish II: Reaction of substituted resorcinols with citral in the presence of pyridine--A proposed mechanism." Tetrahed. Let. 1969, 7, 591-594.

4030. Kaneshima,H., Mori,M., Honma,S., Kinoshita,Y., and Kitsutaka,T. "Studies on cannabis in Hokkaido. V. Relation between the variation of cannabis constituents and growth environment."(Jap.). Hokkaid. Eisei Kenkyush.

4031. Kaneshima,H., Mori,M., and Mizuno,N. "Studies on cannabis in Hokkaido. VI. Dependence of cannabis on iron nutrition."(Jap.). Hokkaid. Eisei Kenkyush. 1973, 23, 3-5.

4032. Kang,S. and Green,J.P. "Hallucinogenic compounds: electronic and steric correlates of the activity of indolealkylamines, amphetamines, LSD, and tetrahydrocannabinol." Fed. Proc. 1970, 29, 650.

4033. Kannenberg,H. "How to grow hemp successfully." (Ger.). Mitteil. Landwirt. 1942, 57, 25.

4034. Kanner,L. and Schilder,P. "Movements in optic images and the optic imagination of movements." J. Nerv. Ment. Dis. 1930, 72, 489-517.

4035. Kant,F. "Forms of reaction of psychotic individuals to hashish intoxication."(Ger.). Arch. Psychiat. Nerven. 1930, 91, 694-721.

4036. Kant,F. and Krapf,E. "Delusions during hashish intoxication."(Ger.). Zeit. Gesamte Neurol. Psychiat. 1927, 48, 107-108.

4037. Kant,F. and Krapf,E. "Psychic phenomena produced by use of hashish."(Ger.). Arch. Exper'tl. Pathol. Pharmakol. 1928, 129, 319-338.

4038. Kant,F. and Krapf,E. "Question of intact function during hashish intoxication."(Ger.). Zeit. Gesamte Neurol. Psychiat. 1928, 112, 302-305.

4039. Kanter,S.L., Hollister,L.E., Moore,F., and Green,D. "Cannabinoids in the urine of man after single and subchronic oral doses of marihuana." Internat'l. Pharmacopsychiat. 1972, 7, 205-213.

4040. Kanter,S.L., Hollister,L.E., Moore,F., and Green,D. "Detection of cannabinols in the urine of man after oral ingestion of marihuana." Clin. Chem. 1971, 17, 636.

4041. Kanter,S.L., Hollister,L.E., Moore,F., and Green,D.E. "Marihuana metabolites in urine of man. II. Undescribed metabolite following oral ingestion of delta-9-tetrahydrocannabinol." Res. Commun. Chem. Pathol. Pharmacol. 1974, 7, 79-84.

4042. Kanter,S.L., Hollister,L.E., Moore,F., and Green,D.E. "Marihuana(M) metabolites in urine of man. III. Detection and temporary excretion of delta-9-tetrahydrocannabinol(THC) and metabolites after oral ingestion of THC." Clin. Chem. 1974, 20, 860.

4043. Kanter,S.L., Hollister,L.E., Moore,F., and Green,D.E. "Marihuana metabolites in urine of man. IV. Extraction procedures using diethyl ether." Res. Commun. Chem. Pathol. Pharmacol. 1974, 9, 205-213.

4044. Kanter,S.L., Hollister,L.E., Moore,F., and Green,D.E. "Marihuana metabolites in urine of man." V. Characterization and separation of polar metabolites of delta-9-tetrahydrocannabinol." Res. Commun. Chem. Pathol. Pharmacol. 1975, 10, 215-219.

4045. Kanter,S.L., Hollister,L.E., Moore,F., and Green,D.E. "Marihuana metabolites in urine of man. VII. Excretion patterns of acidic metabolites detected by sequential thin layer chromatography." Res. Commun. Chem. Pathol. Pharmacol. 1977, 17, 421-431.

4046. Kapadia,G.J., Mosby,J.R., Kapadia,G.G., and Zalucky,T.B. "Structure-chromogenic activity relationship of phenolic compounds with Ehrlich reagent." J. Pharmaceut. Sci. 1965, 54, 41-48.

4047. Kaplan,H.S. "Psychosis associated with marihuana." N.Y. State J. Med. 1971, 71, 433-435.

4048. Kaplan,J. "Criminal laws and the control of drugs of abuse. The special case of marihuana(or, it's the doctor's fault)." J. Clin. Pharmacol. 1969, 9, 349-351.

4049. Kaplan,J. "Drug laws handicapping control and education." J. Clin. Toxicol. 1971, 4, 141-146.

4050. Kaplan,J. "Intersections of anthropology and law in the cannabis area." In Rubin,V.(ed.). Cannabis and Culture. Mouton, The Hague, 1975, 549-559.

4051. Kaplan,J. "Introduction." In Report of the Indian Hemp Drugs Commission 1893-1894. Jefferson Pub. Co., Silver Spring, Md., 1969, v-xvi.

4052. Kaplan,J. "Marihuana: A Signal of Misunderstanding. First Report of the National Commission on Marihuana and Drug Abuse. Cannabis. A Report of the Commission of Inquiry into the Non-Medical Use of Drugs." Science 1973, 179, 167-169.

4053. Kaplan,J. "Marihuana and drug abuse in Vietnam." Ann. N. Y. Acad. Sci. 1971, 191, 261-269.

4054 Kaplan,J. "Marihuana and the law." J. Drug Iss. 1971, 1, 199-204.

4055. Kaplan,J. "Marihuana laws: an empirical study of enforcement and administration in Los Angeles county." U.C.L.A. Law Rev. 1968, 15, 1499.

4056. Kaplan,J. Marihuana--The New Prohibition. World Pub., Co., Cleveland, Oh., 1970.

4057. Kaplan,J. "Prohibition of marihuana." New Repub. 1970, 163, 11-12.

4058. Kaplan,J. "Prohibition of marihuana." New Repub. 1971, 164, 42-43.

4059. Kaplan,J. "Statement of John Kaplan to the National Commission on Marihuana and Drug Abuse." Alaska Med. 1972, 14, 17-19.

4060. Kaplan,J. "The cost of marihuana laws." In Radouco-Thomas,S.(ed.). Pharmacology, Toxicology, and Abuse of Psychototmimetics(Hallucinogens).(Fr.). Univ. Laval Press, Quebec, 1974, 461-473.

4061. Kaplan,J. "What legal status for marihuana?" Current 1970, 123, 44-47.

4062. Kaplan,J. "What the legislator should consider." In Wittenborn,J.R., Brill,H., Smith,J.P., and Wittenborn, S.A.(eds.). Drugs and Youth. C.C. Thomas, Springfield, Ill., 1969, 250-259.

4063. Karacan,I., Fernandez-Salas,A., Coggins,W.J., Coggins,W.J., Carter,W.E., Williams,R.L., Thornby,J.I., Salis,P.J., Okawa,M., and Villaume,J.P. "Sleep electroencephalographic-electrooculographic characteristics of chronic marihuana users." Ann. N. Y. Acad. Sci. 1976, 282, 348-376.

4064. Karasek,F.W., Karasek,D.E., and Kim,S.H. "Detection of lysergic acid diethylamide, delta-9-tetrahydrocannabinol and related compounds by plasma chromatography." J. Chromatog. 1975, 105, 345-352.

4065. Karbe,H. "Hashish."(Ger.). Arzneimittelforshung 1951, 1, 37-48.

4066. Karczmar,A.G. and Koella,W.P.(eds.). Neurophysiological and Behavioral Aspects of Psychotropic Drugs. C.C. Thomas, Springfield, Ill., 1969.

4067. Karler,R. "Anticonvulsant activity of delta-9-tetrahydrocannabinol." Fed. Proc. 1973, 32, 756.

4068. Karler,R. "Chemistry and metabolism." In Petersen,R.C.(ed.). Marihuana Research Findings: 1976. N.I.D.A. Res. Monog. Ser. 14, Dept. H.E.W., Rockville, Md., 1977, 55-66.

4069. Karler,R. "Toxicological and pharmacological effects." In Petersen,R.C.(ed.). Marihuana Research Findings: 1976. N.I.D.A. Res. Monog. Ser. 14, Dept. H.E.W., Rockville, Md., 1977, 67-85.

4070. Karler,R., Cely,W., and Turkanis,S.A. "A study of the development of tolerance to an anticonvulsant effect of delta-9-tetrahydrocannabinol and cannabidiol." Res. Commun. Chem. Pathol. Pharmacol. 1974, 9, 23-29.

4071. Karler,R., Cely,W., and Turkanis,S.A. "A study of the relative anticonvulsant and toxic activities of delta-9-tetrahydrocannabinol and its congeners." Res. Commun. Chem. Pathol. Pharmacol. 1974, 7, 353-358.

4072. Karler,R., Cely,W., and Turkanis,S.A. "Anticonvulsant activity of delta-9-tetrahydrocannabinol and its 11-hydroxy and 8a, 11,dihydroxy metabolites in the frog." Res. Commun. Chem. Pathol. Pharmacol. 1974, 9, 441-452.

4073. Karler,R., Cely,W., and Turkanis,S.A. "Anticonvulsant properties of delta-9-tetrahydrocannabinol and other cannabinoids." Life Sci. 1974, 15, 931-947.

4074. Karler,R., Cely,W., and Turkanis,S.A. "The anticonvulsant activity of cannabidiol and cannabinol." Life Sci. 1973, 13, 1527-1531.

4075. Karler,R. and Turkanis,S. "The antiepileptic potential of the cannabinoids." In Cohen,S. and Stillman, R.(eds.). Therapeutic Potential of Marihuana. Plenum Press, N.Y., 1976, 383-398.

4076. Karler,R. and Turkanis,S. "The development of tolerance and 'reverse tolerance' to the anticonvulsant activity of delta-9-tetrahyrocannabinol and cannabidiol." In Braude,M.C. and Szara,S.(eds.). Pharmacology of Marihuana. Raven Press, N.Y., 1976, 1, 299-313.

4077. Karlsen,J., Exler,T.H.H., and Svendsen,A.B. "Rapid detection and identification of cannabis by means of micro slide thin-layer chromatography. Studies on terpenes and related compounds." Pharmaceut. Weekbl. 1969, 104, 583-587.

4078. Karlsen,J., Exler,T.J.H. and Svendsen,A.B. "Thin-layer chromatographic analysis of cannabis." U.N. Doc. ST/SOA/SER.S/20, Aug. 18, 1969.

4079. Karniol,I.G. "Pharmacological interactions between cannabidiol and delta-9-tetrahydrocannabinol." Paper presented at 1st Lat. Am. Cong. Psychobiol., Sao Paulo, 1973.

4080. Karniol,I.G. and Carlini,E.A. "Comparative studies in man and in laboratory animals on delta-8- and delta-9-trans-tetrahydrocannabinol." J. Pharm. 1973, 9, 115-126.

4081. Karniol,I.G. and Carlini,E.A. "Comparative study between semipurified extracts of marihuana obtained in Germany and Brazil. Possible interference of cannabidiol and/or cannabinol on the effect of delta-9-trans-tetrahydrocannabinol." Cienc. Cult. 1973, 25, 749-751.

4082. Karniol,I.G. and Carlini,E.A. "Pharmacological activity of cannabis sativa and some of its constituents." (Port.). Cienc. Cult. 1974, 26, 686-690.

4083. Karniol,I.G. and Carlini,E.A. "Pharmacological interaction between cannabidiol and delta-9-tetrahydrocannabinol." Psychopharmacol. 1973, 33, 53-70.

4084. Karniol,I.G. and Carlini,E.A. "The content of (-)-delta-9-trans-tetrahydrocannabinol does not explain all biological activity of some Brazilian marihuana samples." J. Pharm. Pharmacol. 1972, 24, 833-835.

4085. Karniol,I.G. and Carlini,E.A. "The possibility of predicting the effects of marihuana in man by means of pharmacological tests in laboratory animals."(Port.). Rev. Assoc. Med. Brasil 1972, 18, 3-10.

4086. Karniol,I.G., Mincis,M., Pfeferman,A., Guimaraes,R.Y., Ramos,O.L., and Zukerman,E. "Prolonged administration of cannabidiol on human beings. A pilot study." Paper presented at 1st Lat. Am. Cong. Psychobiol., Sao Paulo, 1973.

4087. Karniol,I.G., Shirakawa,I., Kasinski,R.N., Pfeferman,A., and Carlini,E.A. "Cannabidiol interferes with the effects of delta-9-tetrahydrocannabinol in man." Eur. J. Pharmacol. 1974, 28, 172-177.

4088. Karniol,I.G., Shirakawa,I., Takahashi,R.N., Knobel,E., and Musty,R.E. "Effects of delta-9-tetrahydrocannabinol and cannabinol in man." Pharmacol. 1975, 13, 502-512.

4089. Karniol,I.G., Takahashi,R.N., and Musty,R.E. "Effects of delta-9-tetrahydrocannabinol and cannabinol on operant performance in rats." Arch. Internat'l. Pharmacodyn. Ther. 1974, 212, 230-237.

4090. Katemir,I. "The durability of oily extracts of opium and cannabis."(Turk.). Turk. Ig. Tec. Biyol. Derg. 1951, 11, 341-344.

4091. Kaufamn,J., Allen,J.R., and West,L.J. "Runaways, hippies, and marihuana." Am. J. Psychiat. 1969, 126, 717-720.

4092. Kaufamn,P.R. "Marihuana--the watched pot." N.Y. State J. Med. 1970, 70, 1793-1799.

4093. Kay,E.J. "Aversive effects of repeated injections of THC in rats." Psychol. Rep. 1975, 37, 1051-1054.

4094. Kayaalp,S.O., Kaymakcalan,S., Verimer,T., Ilhan, M., and Onur,R. "In vitro neuromuscular effects of delta-9-tetrahydrocannabinol(THC). Arch. Internat'l. Pharmacodyn. Ther. 1974, 212, 67-75.

4095. Kaye,S. "Marihuana." Virginia Trooper 1951, 4, 12.

4096. Kaymakcalan,S. "Physiological and psychological dependence on THC in rhesus monkeys." In Paton,W.D.M. and Crown,J.(eds.). Cannabis and its Derivatives. Oxford Univ. Press, London, 1972, 142-150.

4097. Kaymakcalan,S. "Potential dangers of cannabis." Internat'l. J. Addict. 1975, 10, 721-735.

4098. Kaymakcalan,S. "Tolerance and dependence to cannabis." Pahlavi Med. J. 1973, 4, 366-376.

4099. Kaymakcalan,S. "Tolerance to and dependence on cannabis." Bull. Narc. 1973, 25, 39-47.

4100. Kaymakcalan,S. and Deneau,G.A. "Some pharmacologic properties of synthetic delta-9-tetrahydro-cannabinol(THC)." Act. Med. Turc. 1972, 1, 5-27.

4101. Kaymakcalan,S. and Deneau,G.A. "Some pharmacological effects of synthetic delta-9-tetrahydro-cannabinol(THC)." Pharmacol. 1971, 13, 247.

4102. Kaymakcalan,S., Ercan,Z.S., and Turker,R.K. "The evidence of the release of prostaglandin-like material from rabbit kidney and guinea-pig lung by (-)-trans-delta-9-tetrahydrocannabinol." J. Pharm. Pharmacol. 1975, 27, 564-568.

4103. Kaymakcalan,S. and Sivil,S. "Lack of tolerance to the bradycardic effect of delta-9-trans-tetrahydrocananbinol in rats." Pharmacol. 1974, 12, 290-295.

4104. Kaymakcalan,S., Turker,R.K., and Turker,M.N. "Analgesic effect of delta-9-tetrahydrocannabinol in the dog." Psychopharmacol. 1974, 35, 123-128.

4105. Kazan,I. "In dopest Africa." High Times 1976, 9, 37-39, 96.

4106. Kazieva,D.K. "A clinical characterization of personality degradation from hashish addiction." (Rus.). Uch. Zap. Azerb. Med. Inst. 1966, 23, 216-221.

4107. Kazieva,D.K. "Clinical structure of acute psychoses resulting from intoxication(cannabis sativa)."(Rus.). Vop. Psikhonevrol. 1966, 3, 71-78.

4108. Kazieva,D.K. "Study of experimental models of acute and chronic hashish intoxication in animals." (Rus.). Zh. Otd. Vyp. Farmakol. Khimioter. Sred. Toksikol. 1967, 4.54.934.

4109. Keats,J. "Appraising marihuana--the new American pastime." Holiday 1970, 47, 52-53.

4110. Kechatov,E.A. "Chemical and biological evaluation of the resin of hemp grown for seed in the central districts of the European part of the U.S.S.R." Bull. Narc. 1959, 11, 5-9.

4111. Keeler,M.H. "Adverse reactions to marihuana." Am. J. Psychiat. 1967, 124, 674-677.

4112. Keeler,M.H. "Marihuana induced hallucinations." Dis. Nerv. Syst. 1968, 29, 314-315.

4113. Keeler,M.H. "Motivation for marihuana use: A correlate of adverse reaction." Am. J. Psychiat. 1968, 125, 142-146.

4114. Keeler,M.H. "What are the questions concerning marihuana?" N. Carolina Med. J. 1969, 30, 41-43.

4115. Keeler,M.H., Ewing,J.A., and Rouse,B.A. "Hallucinogenic effects of marihuana as currently used." Am. J. Psychiat. 1971, 128, 213-216.

4116. Keeler,M.H. and Moore,E. "Paranoid reactions while using marihuana." Dis. Nerv. Syst. 1974, 35, 533-536.

4117. Keeler,M.H. and Reifler,C.B. "Grand mal convulsions subsequent to marihuana use." Dis. Nerv. Syst. 1967, 28, 474-475.

4118. Keeler,M.H., Reifler,C.B., and Liptzin,M.B. "Spontaneous recurrence of marihuana effect." Am. J. Psychiat. 1968, 125, 384-386.

4119. Keen,R. "Poisonous symptoms from cannabis indica." Med. Times Gaz. 1863, 2, 572.

4120. Keipperstem,L.R. "Assessing the nature and dimensions of the drug problem." Ann. Am. Acad. 1975, 417, 76-85.

4121. Keiser,M. "A new name of the spice,(riq) (gannapu): hemp oil, hashish(?)."(Fr.). Rev. Assyr. Archeol. Mid. East 1921, 18, 97.

4122. Keiser,M. "Letters and contracts, no. 162." (Fr.). Rev. Assyr. Archeol. Mid. East 1921, 18, 97.

4123. Keith,E., Fetterman,P., Doorenbos,N.J., Quimby,M.W., and Waller,C.W. "Mississippi grown cannabis sativa L..Chemical definition of a genotype--a preliminary observation." Paper presented at Am. Pharmaceut. Assoc., Washington, D.C., 1970.

4124. Kelley,J.A. and Arnold,K.P. "Detection of urinary cannabis metabolites: a preliminary investigation." J. Forens. Sci. 1976, 21, 252-262.

4125. Kelly,L.A. and Butcher,R.W. "The effects of delta-1-tetrahydrocannabinol on cyclic AMP levels in WI-38 fibroblasts." Biochim. Biophys. 320, 540-544.

4126. Kelly,W.M. "Cannabis indica." Br. Med. J. 1883, 1, 1281.

4127. Kender,A. Cannabis Sativa L.(Hung.). Magyaroszag Kulturfloraja, Adakemiai Kiado, Budapest, 1962.

4128. Keng,H. "Economic plants of ancient North China as mentioned in Shih Ching(Book of Poetry)." Econ. Bot. 1974, 28, 391-410.

4129. Keniston,K. "Drug use and student values." In Hollander,C.(ed.). Background Papers on Student Drug Involvement. U.S. Nat'l. Student Assoc., Washington, D.C., 1967, 121-130.

4130. Keniston,K. "Heads and seekers. Drugs on campus, counter-cultures and American society." Ment. Hlth. Dig. 1968, 1, 9-12.

4131. Keniston,K. The Uncommitted: Alienated Youth in American Society. Harcourt, Brace and World, N.Y., 1965.

4132. Kennedy,G.W. "Does cannabis indica contain nicotine?" Pharmaceut. J. Trans. 1886, 16, 453-454.

4133. Kennedy,G.W. "The asserted presence of nicotine in cannabis." Proc. Am. Pharmaceut. Assoc. 1886, 34, 119-121.

4134. Kennedy,J.S. "Some aspects of the pharmacology of delta-9-tetrahydrocannabinol and delta-8-tetrahydrocannabinol in dogs and rodents." Diss. Abs. 1972, 32, 7207-7208.

4135. Kennedy,J.S. and Waddell,W.J. "Whole body autoradiography of the pregnant mouse after administration of ^{14}C-delta-9-tetrahydrocannabinol." Fed. Proc. 1971, 30, 279.

4136. Kennedy,J.S. and Waddell,W.J. "Whole-body autoradiography of the pregnant mouse after administration of ^{14}C-delta-9-THC." Toxicol. Appl. Pharmacol. 1972, 22, 252-258.

4137. Kentfield,C. "Turning of the Tijuana grass: Operation intercept." Esquire 1970, 73, 8.

4138. Kephalas,T.A., Kiburis,J., Michael,C.M., Miras,C.J., and Papadakis,D.P. "Some aspects of cannabis smoke chemistry." In Nahas,G.G., Paton,W.D.M., and Idanpaan-Heikkila,J.E.(eds.). Marihuana. Springer Verlag, N.Y., 1976, 39-51.

4139. Kephalas,T.A., Michael,C.M., Papadakis,D.P., Livanou,T.H., and Miras,C.J. "Effects of cannabis resin on diabetic rats." U.N. Doc. ST/SOA/SER.S/42.4, June 4, 1973.

4140. Keplinger,M.L., Wright,P.L., Haley,S.L., Plank,J.B., Braude,M.C., and Calandra,J.C. "The effect of natural and synthetic delta-9-tetrahydrocannabinol on reproductive and lactation performance in albino rats." Toxicol. Appl. Pharmacol. 1973, 25, 499.

4141. Kerim,G.F. "Development of mental diseases in Turkey due to misure of heroin and hashish."(Ger.). Zent. Neurol. Psychiat. 1937, 158, 428-436.

4142. Kerim,G.F. "Psychiatric difficulties resulting from hashish."(Fr.). Hyg. Ment. 1930, 25, 93-106.

4143. Kerr,M.H. "Marihuana and the American military." Abs. Criminol. Penol. 1971, 11, 143-157.

4144. Kerswell,R.G. "Dagga(cannabis sativa) in Southern Rhodesia." Outpost 1956, 34, 3.

4145. Kettenes-van den Bosch,J.J. and Salemink,C.A. "XVI. Constituents of marihuana smoke condensate." J. Chromatog. 1977, 131, 422-424.

4146. Kettle,M. and Kettle,P. "Big Sur hophead harvest." High Times 1976, 13, 49-53.

4147. Keup,W. "Marihuana." Science 1969, 163, 1144.

4148. Keup,W. "Psychotic symptoms due to cannabis abuse. A survey of newly admitted mental patients." Dis. Nerv. Syst. 1970, 31, 119-126.

4149. Keup,W. "The legal status of marihuana." Dis. Nerv. Syst. 1969, 30, 517-523.

4150. Kew,M.C., Bersohn,I., and Siew,S. "Possible hepatotoxicity of cannabis." Lancet 1969, 1, 578-579.

4151. Khaled El-Yousef,M., Janowsky,D.S., Davis,J.M., and Rosenblatt,J.E. "Induction of severe depression by physostigmine in marihuana intoxicated individuals." Br. J. Addict. 1973, 68, 321-325.

4152. Khalifa,A.M. "Traditional patterns of hashish use in Egypt. In Rubin,V.(ed.). Cannabis and Culture. Mouton, The Hague, 1975, 195-207.

4153. Khan,M.A., Abbas,A., and Jensen,K. "Cannabis usage in Pakistan: A pilot study of long-term effects on social status and physical health." In Rubin,V.(ed.). Cannabis and Culture. Mouton, The Hague, 1975, 345-355.

4154. Khouri,J. "Application of filtered ultra-violet radiation in the examination of hashish in a pure state or mixed with other drugs."(Fr.). Ann. Falsif. Fraude. 1935, 28, 582-584.

4155. Khouri,J. "Qualitative test for presence of small amounts of hashish in various drugs by means of Wood's filtered ultra-violet light."(Fr.). Ann. Med. Leg. 1936, 16, 249-252.

4156. Kieffer,E. "Trial of Elaine Murphy." Good House. 1969, 168, 12.

4157. Kieffer,S.N. "Marihuana--general statement; research supported by various National Institute of Mental Health programs." Drug Depend. 1970, 4, 27-28.

4158. Kieffer,S.N. and Moritz,T.B. "Psychedelic drugs." Penn. Med. 1968, 71, 57-67.

4159. Kielholz,P. "Addiction dangers."(Ger.). Bull. Schweiz. Akad. Med. Wissen. 1971, 26, 366-373.

4160. Kielholz,P. "Drug addiction among juveniles especially involving hashish smoking."(Ger.). Deut. Med. Woch. 1970, 95, 101-105.

4161. Kielholz,P. "Present problems of drug addiction in Switzerland." Bull. Narc. 1970, 22, 1-6.

4162. Kielholz,P. "Symptomatology of hashish intoxication."(Ger.). Deut. Med. Woch. 1970, 95, 2586.

4163. Kielholz,P., Goldberg,L., Hobi,V., Ladewig,D., Reggiani,G., and Richter,R. "Cannabis and driving ability. An experimental study." Ger. Med. 1973, 3, 38-48.

4164. Kielholz,P., Goldberg,L., Hobi,V., Ladewig,D., and Reggiani,G. "Quantitative measurement of change in psychic experience under delta-9-tetrahydrocannabinol." (Ger.). Pharmakopsychiat. 1972, 5, 301-312.

4165. Kielholz,P., Goldberg,L., Hobi,V., Ladewig,D., Reggiani,G., and Richter,R. "Hashish and driving behavior. An experimental study."(Ger.). Deut. Med. Woch. 1972, 97, 789-794.

4166. Kielholz,P., Hobi,V., Ladewig,D., Richter,R., and Miest,P. "An experimental investigation of the effect of cannabis on car driving." Pharmakopsychiat. Neuro-psychopharmakol. 1973, 6, 91-103.

4167. Kier,L.C. "A simple method for the determination of the smoking of marihuana." In Israelstam,S. and Lamberg, S.(eds.). Drugs and Traffic Safety. Addiction Res. Found., Toronto, 1975, 623-626.

4168. Kihlbom,M. "Cannabis abuse."(Swed.). Lakartidningen 1969, 66, 5006-5020.

4169. Kilbey,M.M., Fritchie,G.E., and McLendon,D.M. "Attack behavior in mice inhibited by delta-9-tetrahydrocannabinol." Nature 1972, 238, 463-465.

4170. Kilbey,M.M., Forbes,W.B., and Olivetti,C.C. "Delta-9-tetrahydrocannabinol: Inhibition of deprivation and carbacol-induced water consumption in the rat after central and peripheral administration." Behav. Biol. 1973, 8, 679-685.

4171. Kilbey,M.M., Harris,R.T., and Moore,J.W. "Increased latency of frog-killing behavior in the rat following administration of delta-9-tetrahydrocannabinol." Comm. Prob. Drug Depend. 1971, 11, 1832-1840.

4172. Kilbey,M.M., Johnson,K.M., McLendon,D.M. "Time course of delta-9-tetrahydrocannabinol inhibition of predatory aggression." Pharmacol. Biochem. Behav. 1977, 7, 117-120.

4173. Kilbey,M.M., Moore,J.W., and Hall,M. "Delta-9-tetrahydrocannabinol induced inhibition of predatory aggression in the rat." Psychopharmacol. 1973, 31, 157-166.

4174. Kilbey,M.M., Moore,J.W., and Harris,R.T. "Effects of delta-9-tetrahydrocananbinol on appetitive- and aggressive-rewarded maze performance in the rat." Physiol. Psychol. 1973, 1, 174-176.

4175. Killam,K.K. and Killam,E.K. "The action of tetrahydrocannabinol on EEG and photomyoclonic seizures in the baboon." Proc. 5th Internat'l. Cong. Pharmacol. 1972, 1, 124.

4176. Kim,K., Won,H., and Shin,T. "Marihuana smokers in the Seoul area." J. Korean Med. Assoc. 1973, 16, 42-50.

4177. Kimball,G. "The green grass harvest in River City(Kan.)." Scanlan's Month. 1970, 1, 21-26.

4178. Kimura,M. and Okamoto,K. "Distribution of tetrahydrocannabinolic acid in fresh wild cannabis." Exper. 1970, 26, 819-820.

4179. King,A.B. and Cowen,D.L. "Effect of intravenous injection of marihuana." J.A.M.A. 1969, 210, 724-725.

4180. King,A.B., Pechet,G.S., and Pechet,L. "Intravenous injection of crude marihuana." J.A.M.A. 1970, 214, 1711.

4181. King,F.A. "The origin of hemp 'the assuager of grief'." East Af. Med. J. 1953, 30, 345-347.

4182. King,F.W. "Marihuana and LSD usage among male college students: Prevalence rate, frequency, and self-estimates of future use." Psychiat. 1969, 32, 265-276.

4183. King,F.W. "Personal factors and drug use." Paper presented to Am. Coll. Hlth. Assoc., Chicago, 1973.

4184. King,F.W. "Users and nonusers of marihuana: Some attitudinal and behavioral correlates." J. Am. Coll. Hlth. Assoc. 1970, 18, 213-215.

4185. King,L.J. and Forney,R.B. "The absorption and excretion of the marihuana constituents, cannabinol and tetrahydrocannabinol." Fed. Proc. 1967, 26, 540.

4186. King,L.J., Teale,J.D., and Marks,V. "Biochemical aspects of cannabis." In Graham,J.D.P.(ed.). Cannabis and Health. Academic Press, N.Y., 1976, 77-109.

4187. King,M. "Wild hemp of India." Nation 1970, 211, 402-403.

4188. King,M.R. and Manaster,G.J. "Time perspective, attitudinal and demographic correlates of collegiate marihuana users." Paper presented at Southwest. Psychol. Assoc., Dallas, 1973.

4189. King,M.R. and Manaster,G.J. "Time perspective correlates of collegiate marihuana use." J. Consult. Clin. Psychol. 1975, 43, 99.

4190. King,R. The Drug Hang Up. C.C. Thomas, Springfield, Ill., 1972.

4191. Kingman,R. "The green goddess; A study in dreams, drugs and dementia." Med. J. Rec. 1927, 126, 470-475.

4192. Kingston,C.R. and Kirk,P.L. "Separation of components of marihuana by gas-liquid chromatography." Anal. Chem. 1961, 33, 1794-1795.

4193. Kinzer,G.W., Foltz,R.L., Mitchell,R.I., and Truitt,E.B. "The fate of the cannabinoid components of marihuana during smoking." Bull. Narc. 1974, 26, 41-54.

4194. Kipfer,H. "Hashish and society."(Ger.). Praxis 1971, 60, 491-494.

4195. Kiplinger,G.F. "The effects of cannabis derivatives on cognitive function." In Paton,W.D.M. and Crown,J.(eds.). Cannabis and Its Derivatives. Oxford Univ. Press, London, 1972, 176-184.

4196. Kiplinger,G.F. and Manno,J.E. "Dose-response relations to cannabis in human subjects." Pharmacol. Rev. 1971, 23, 339-347.

4197. Kiplinger,G.F., Manno,J., and Forney,R.B. "Cannabis research--three years experience." Comm. Prob. Drug Depend. 1971, 2, 1712-1726.

4198. Kiplinger,G.F., Manno,J.E., Rodda,B.E., and Forney,R.B. "Dose-response analysis of the effects of tetrahydrocannabinol in man." Clin. Pharmacol. Ther. 1971, 12, 650-657.

4199. Kiplinger,M.L., Wright,P.L., Haley,S.L., Plank,J.B., Braude,M.C., and Calandra,J.C. "The effect of natural and synthetic delta-9-tetrahydrocannabinol on reproductive and lactation performance in albino rats." Toxicol. Appl. Pharmacol. 1975, 25, 449.

4200. Kirby,D. "A counter-culture explanation of student activism." Soc. Prob. 1971, 19, 203-216.

4201. Kirtany,J.K. and Paknikar,S.K. "A synthetic cannabinoid with a camphane moiety." Chem. Indust. 1976, 3, 324-325.

4202. Kirtikar,K.R. and Basu,B.D. "Indian medicinal plants." Allahabad. 1918, 2, 1181-1182.

4203. Kisser,W. "Detection of hashish components in urine."(Ger.). Arch. Toxikol. 1972, 29, 331-334.

4204. Kissin,B. "On marihuana." Downstate Med. Ctr. Rep. 1967, 7, 2.

4205. Kitagawa,H. and Kamataki,T. "Effect of NADPH-linked lipid peroxidation on the activity of drug metabolizing enzymes in microsomes of rat liver." Proc. 5th Internat'l. Cong. Pharmacol. 1972, 1, 126.

4206 Kitsutaka,T., Honma,S., Kaneshima,H., and Mori,M. "Studies on cannabis in Hokkaido. IV. Soil and microelements of wild cannabis."(Jap.). Hokkaid. Inst. Pub. Hlth. 1971, 21, 191-193.

4207. Kitsutaka,T., Honma,S., Kaneshima,H., Mori,M., Koga,Y., Kihoioka,S., and Suda,K. "Cannabis in Hokkaido. I. Distribution and narcotic constituents of cannabis in Hokkaido."(Jap.). Hokkaid. Eisei Kenk. 1969, 19, 140-143.

4208. Kittrie,N.N. "Marihuana--the right to truth." S.C. Law Rev. 1971, 23, 361.

4209. Kittrie,N.N., Weaver,J., Trencher,W.M., Wofgang,J., Dalhlke,A., and Tro.J.A. "The juvenile drug offender and the justice system." In National Commission on Marihuana and Drug Abuse. Drug Use in America: Problem in Perspective. Gov't. Print. Office, Washington, D.C., 1973, III, 686-797.

4210. Kitzinger,A. and Hill,P.J. Drug Abuse: A Source Book and Guide for Teachers. .Kitzinger, Sacramento, 1967.

4211. Klabusay,L. and Lenfeld,J. "Pharmacodynamic effect of substances isolated from cannabis indica." (Czech.). Act. Univ. Palack. Olomuc. 1955, 6, 67-72.

4212. Klapper,J.A., McColloch,M.A., and Sidell,F.R. "The effect on personality of reactivity to 1,2-dimethylheptyl tetrahydrocannabinol." Arch. Gen. Psychiat. 1972, 26, 483-485.

4213. Kalusner,H.A. and Dingell,J.V. "Studies on the metabolism and distribution of delta-9-tetrahydrocannabinol." Pharmacologist 1970, 12, 259.

4214. Klausner,H.A. and Dingell,J.V. "The metabolism and excretion of delta-9-tetrahydrocannabinol in the rat." Life Sci. 1971, 10, 49-59.

4215. Klausner,H.A., Wilcox,H.G., and Dingell,J.V. "Investigation of the plasma binding of tetrahydrocannabinol and other drugs by zonal ultracentrifugation." Proc. 5th Internat'l. Cong. Pharmacol. 1972, 1, 126.

4216. Klausner,H.A., Wilcox,H.G., and Dingell,J.V. "Studies on the interaction of delta-9-tetrahydrocannabinol with plasma lipoproteins." Act. Pharmaceut. Suec. 1971, 8, 705-706.

4217. Klausner,H.A., Wilcox,H.G., and Dingell,J.V. "The use of zonal ultracentrifugation in the investigation of the binding of delta-9-tetrahydrocannabinol by plasma lipoproteins." Drug Metabol. Disposit. 1975, 3, 314-319.

4218. Kleber,H.D. "Student use of hallucinogens." J. Am. Coll. Hlth. Assoc. 1965, 14, 109-117.

4219. Klee,G.D. "Drugs and American youth. A psychiatrist looks at the psychedelic generation." Med. Times 1969, 97, 165-171.

4220. Klee,G.D. "Marihuana psychosis." Psychiat. Quart. 1969, 43, 719-733.

4221. Klein,A.W., Davis,J.H., and Blackbourne,B.D. "Marihuana and automobile crashes." J. Drug Iss. 1971, 1, 18-26.

4222. Klein,D. Everything You Always Wanted to Know About Marihuana. Belmont-Tower, N.Y., 1972.

4223. Klein,D. The Marihuana Question and the Answer. Belmont-Tower, N.Y., 1972.

4224. Klein,F.K., Rapoport,H., and Elliott,H.W. "Cannabis alkaloids." Nature 1971, 232, 258-259.

4225. Klein,J. and Phillips,D.L. "From hard to soft drugs: temporal and substantive changes in drug usage among gangs in a working-class community." J. Hlth. Soc. Behav. 1968, 9, 139-145.

4226. Kleiner,D. "Hashish and alcohol. Similarities and differences."(Ger.). Jugend 1971, 23, 463-470.

4227. Klerman,G.L. "Drugs and American social values." In Wittenborn,J.R., Smith,J.P., and Wittenborn,S.A. (eds.). Communication and Drug Abuse. C.C. Thomas, Springfield, Ill., 1970, 149-156.

4228. Kline,C.M. "The thirty-seventh convention of the National Wholesale Druggists' Association." Am. J. Pharm. 1912, 84, 30-32.

4229. Klonoff,H. "Effects of marihuana on driving in a restricted area and on city streets: Driving performance and physiological changes." In Miller,L.L.(ed.). Marihuana, Effects on Human Behavior. Academic Press, N.Y., 1974, 359-399.

4230. Klonoff,H. "Marihuana and driving in real-life situations." Science 1974, 186, 317-324.

4231. Klonoff,H. "Strategy and tactics of marihuana research." Can. Med. Assoc. J. 1973, 108, 145-149.

4232. Klonoff,H. "The logics of marihuana research: Methodological, legal and societal." In Miller,L.L.(ed.). Marihuana, Effects on Human Behavior. Academic Press, N.Y., 1974, 1-23.

4233. Klonoff,H. "The phenomenology of the marihuana user." Can. J. Pub. Hlth. 1973, 64, 552-561.

4234. Klonoff,H. and Clark,C. "Drug patterns in the chronic marihuana user." Internat'l. J. Addict. 1976, 11, 71-80.

4235. Klonoff,H. and Low,M.D. "Psychological and neurophysiological effects of marihuana in man: An interaction model." In Miller,L.L.(ed.). Marihuana, Effects on Human Behavior. Academic Press, N.Y., 1974, 121-153.

4236. Klonoff,H., Low,M.D., and Marcus,A. "Neuropsychological effects of marihuana." Can. Med. Assoc. J. 1973, 108, 150-157.

4237. Klug,E. "Drug tracing."(Ger.). Zeit. Rechtsmed. 1971, 68, 171-179.

4238. Knaffl-Lenz,E. "Causes of the chronic abuse of narcotic drugs." Bull. Narc. 1952, 4, 1-8.

4239. Knaus,E.E., Coutts,R.T., and Kazakoff,C.W. "The separation, identification, and quantitation of cannabinoids and their t-butyldimethylsiyl, trimethylsiylacetate, and diethylphosphate derivaties using high-pressure liquid chromatography, gas-liquid chromatography, and mass-spectrometry." J. Chromatog. Sci. 1976, 14, 525-530.

4240. Knecht,S.D. "The prediction of marihuana use from personality scales." Educat. Psychol. Measure. 1972, 32, 1111-1117.

4241. Knight,F. "Role of cannabis in psychiatric disturbance." Ann. N. Y. Acad. Sci. 1976, 282, 64-71.

4242. Knight,R.C. "College student marihuana use and social alienation." J. Hlth. Soc. Behav. 1974, 15, 28-35.

4243. Knights,R.M. and Grenier,M.L. "Problems in studying the effects of chronic cannabis use on intellectual abilities." Ann. N. Y. Acad. Sci. 1976, 282, 307-312.

4244. Knowles,L.W. "Pot smoking students not easy to discipline." Nation's Sch. 1972, 89, 58.

4245. Knudten,R.D. and Meade,A.C. "Marihuana and social policy." Addict. Dis. 1974, 1, 323-351.

4246. Ko,C. "Account of the excavation of an early Chou tomb at Kao-chia-pao, Chin-yang."(Chin.). Wen-wu 1972, 7, 5-7.

4247. Koberbeck,S. "Marihuana reconsidered; L. Grinspoon." Nat'l. Rev. 1971, 23, 597.

4248. Kobert,E.R. Historical Studies.(Ger.). Tauch and Grosse, Halle, Germany, 1889.

4249. Kobert,R. "On cannabindon."(Ger.). Chem.-Zeit. 1894, 18, 741-742.

4250. Kochar,M.S. and Hosko,M.J. "Electrocardiographic effects of marihuana." J.A.M.A. 1973, 225, 25-27.

4251. Kochi,H. and Matsui,M. "Chemical studies on hashish. A synthesis of dl-cannabidiol dimethylether." Agricult. Biol. Chem. 1967, 31, 625-627.

4252. Kodilinye,A.G. "Proof of guilt under the Indian hemp decree." Nigerian Bar J. 1974, 12, 69-75.

4253. Koehler,B. "Hemp seed treatments in relation to different dosages and conditions of storage." Phytopath. 1946, 36, 937-942.

4254. Koff,W.C. "Marihuana and sexual activity." J. Sex Res. 1974, 10, 194-204.

4255. Kohler,D.P. "Homozygous males in hemp." Nature 1962, 195, 625-626.

4256. Kohler,D. "Influence of day's length on the development of cannabis sativa." Physiol. Plant. 1958, 11, 249-259.

4257. Kohler,D. "Sex change in cannabis sativa induced by gibberellic acid."(Ger.). Deut. Bot. Ges. 1964, 77, 275.

4258. Kohler,D. "The long day and induction of flowering in cannabis sativa."(Ger.). Naturwissen. 1963, 50, 158.

4259. Kohn,P.M. and Mercer,G.W. "Drug use, drug-use attitudes and the authoritarian-rebellion dimension." J. Hlth. Soc. Behav. 1971, 12, 125-131.

4260. Kohn-Abrest,E. and Truffert,L. "Indian hemp--hashish O kif and Table B."(Fr.). Ann. Med. Leg. 1946, 26, 61-65.

4261. Kok,J.C.F. "The Amersterdam program. What now?" In Marshamn,J.A.(ed.). Street Drug Analysis and its Social and Clinical Implications. Addict. Res. Found., Toronto, 1974, 15-17.

4262. Kokka,N. and Garcia,J.F. "Effects of delta-9-THC on growth hormone and ACTH secretion in rats." Life Sci. 1974, 15, 329-338.

4263. Klansky,H. and Moore,W.T. "Clinical effects of marihuana on young." Internat'l. J. Psychiat. 1972, 10, 55-67.

4264. Kolansky,H. and Moore,W.T. "Effects of marihuana on adolescents and young adults." J.A.M.A. 1971, 216, 486-492.

4265. Kolansky,H. and Moore,W.T. "Marihuana. Can it hurt you?" J.A.M.A. 1975, 232, 923-924.

4265a. Kolansky,H. and Moore,W.T. "Toxic effects of chronic marihuana use." J.A.M.A. 1972, 222, 35-41.

4266. Kolb,L. "Marihuana." Fed. Prob. 1938, 2, 22-25.

4267. Kolodny,R.C. "Research issues in the study of marihuana and male reproductive physiology in humans." In Tinklenberg,J.R.(ed.). Marihuana and Health Hazards. Academic Press, N.Y., 1975, 71-83.

4268. Kolodny,R.C., Lessin,P.J., Toro,G., Masters, W.H., and Cohen,S. "Depression of plasma testosterone with acute marihuana administration." In Braude,M.C. and Szara,S.(eds.). Pharmacology of Marihuana. Raven Press, N.Y., 1976, 1, 217-226.

4269. Kolodny,R.C., Masters,W.H., Kolodner,R.M., and Toro,G. "Depression of plasma testosterone levels after chronic intensive marihuana use." N. Eng. J. Med. 1974, 290, 872-874.

4270. Kolodny,R.C., Masters,W.H., and Toro,G. "Marihuana and sex." N. Eng. J. Med. 1974, 291, 310.

4271. Kolsek,J., Maticic,M., and Repic,R. "Paper chromatography of hemp constituents(cannabis sativa)." (Ger.). Arch. Pharm. 1962, 295, 151-157.

4272. Komenda,S. and Hrbek,J. "An analysis of the acute effect of tetrahydrocannabinol(THC) and tobacco on verbal associations." Activ. Nerv. Super. 1972, 14, 199-206.

4273. Konkle,R.A. "A program to deter marihuana sales." Law Order 1969, 17, 28-33.

4274. Koon,L.H. "Patterns of drug abuse in South East Asia." In Btesh,S.(ed.). Drug Abuse. Plenum Press, N.Y., 1972, 128-132.

4275. Kooyman,M. "Marihuana, alcohol and their sequela in Uganda."(Dut.). *Tid. Ziekenver*. 1968, *21*, 664.

4276. Kooyman,M. "Soft drugs--a matter of definition." (Dut.). *Ned. Tij. Geneesk*. 1971, *115*, 267-276.

4277. Kopell,B.S., Tinklenberg,J.R., and Hollister, L.E. "Contingent negative variation amplitudes." *Arch. Gen. Psychiat*. 1972, *27*, 809-811.

4278. Kopp,R. "Baudelaire and hashish. Experience and documentation."(Fr.). *Rev. Sci. Humain*. 1967, *125*, 467-476.

4279. Koppikar,G.S. "Drug addiction in Bombay: Opium, bhang, ganja." *Ind. J. Med. Sci*. 1948, *2*, 131-137.

4280. Kopplin,D.A., Greenfield,T.K., and Wong, H.Z. "Changing patterns of substance use on campus: A four-year follow-up study." *Internat'l. J. Addict*. 1977, *12*, 73-94.

4281. Koran,L.M. "American responses to heroin addiction and marihuana use." In Coelho,G.V. and Rubenstein,E.A.(eds.). *Social Change and Human Behavior*. Dept. H.E.W., Gov't. Print. Office, Washington, D.C., 1972, 72-91.

4282. Kornhaber,A. "Clinical effects of marihuana on the young. Clinical corroboration." *Internat'l. J. Psychiat*. 1972, *10*, 79-81.

4283. Kornhaber,A. "Marihuana in an adolescent psychiatric outpatient population." *J.A.M.A*. 1971, *215*, 1988.

4284. Korte,F. "Recent results in hashish chemistry." In Joyce,C.R.B. and Curry,S.H.(eds.). *The Botany and Chemistry of Cannabis*. J. and A. Churchill, London, 1970, 119-135.

4285. Korte,F. and Bieniek,D. "Chemical and biological attempts to elucidate physiological action of cannabis." *Cienc. Cult*. 1973, *25*, 634-643.

4286. Korte,F. and Bieniek,D. "Hashish(cannabis sativa)."(Ger.). *Mater. Med. Nordmark* 1968, *20*, 607-612.

4287. Korte,F., Dlugosch,E., and Claussen,U. "On the chemical classification of plants. XXIX. Hashish. Synthesis of dl-cannabidiol and its methylhomologs."(Ger.). *Lieb. Ann. Chem*. 1966, *693*, 165-170.

4288. Korte,F., Haag,M., and Claussen,U. "Tetrahydrocannabinolcarboxylic acid, a component of hashish." (Ger.). Ang. Chem. 1965, 4, 872.

4289. Korte,F., Hackel,E., and Sieper,H. "Hashish V. Synthesis of the cannabidiol-dimethyl-ether."(Ger.). Lieb. Ann. Chem. 1965, 685, 122-128.

4290. Korte,F. and Sieper,H. "Chemical classification of plants. XX. Separation of hashish constituents from cannabis sativa."(Ger.). Lieb. Ann. Chem. 1960, 630, 71-83.

4291. Korte,F. and Sieper,H. "Determination of hashish containing substances by paper chromatography." (Ger.). Tetrahedron 1960, 10, 153-159.

4292. Korte,F. and Sieper,H. "New results on hashish-specific constituents." Bull. Narc. 1965, 17, 35-43.

4293. Korte,F. and Sieper,H. "On the chemical classification of plants. XXIV. Investigation of hashish constituents by means of thin-layer chromatography."(Ger.). J. Chromatog. 1964, 13, 90-98.

4294. Korte,F. and Sieper,H. "On the chemical classification of plants. XXV. Quantitative investigation of hashish constituents after thin-layer chromatography." (Ger.). J. Chromatog. 1964, 14, 178-183.

4295. Korte,F. and Sieper,H. "Paper chromatographic identification of hashish constituents."(Ger.). Ang. Chem. 1960, 72, 210.

4296. Korte,F. and Sieper,H. "Recent results of hashish analysis." In Wolstenholme,G.E.W. and Knight, J.(eds.). Hashish: Its Chemistry and Pharmacology. Ciba Found. Study No. 21, J. and A. Churchill, London, 1965, 15-30.

4297. Korte,F. and Sieper,H. "R_f values of some hashish constituents." J. Chromatog. 1961, 6, 1.

4298. Kosersky,D.S., Dewey,W.L., and Harris,L.S. "Antipyretic, analgesic and anti-inflammatory effects of delta-9-tetrahydrocannabinol in the rat." Eur. J. Pharmacol. 1973, 24, 1-7.

4299. Kosersky,D.S., McMillan,D.E., and Harris,L.S. "Delta-9-tetrahydrocannabinol and 11-hydroxy-delta-9-tetrahydrocannabinol: Behavioral effects and tolerance development." J. Pharmacol. Exper. Ther. 1974, 189, 61-81.

4300. Kossobudzki,S. "Three cases of poisoning by Indian hemp tincture and fluid extract."(Pol.). Medycyna 1901, 29, 211-214.

4301. Kosviner,A. "Prevalence, characteristics and correlates of cannabis use in the U.K. student population." In Connell,P.H. and Dorn,N.(eds.). Cannabis and Man. Churchill Livingstone, Edinburgh, 1975, 156-180.

4302. Kosviner,A. "Social science and cannabis use." In Graham,J.D.P.(ed.). Cannabis and Health. Academic Press, N.Y., 1976, 343-379.

4303. Kosviner,A. and Hawks,D. "Cannabis use amongst British university students: patterns of use and attitudes to use." Br. J. Addict. 1977, 72, 41-57.

4304. Kosviner,A. and Hawks,D. "Seven attitudinal scales used in assessing cannabis use amongst students." Drug Alcohol Depend. 1976, 1, 339-348.

4305. Kosviner,A., Hawks,D., and Webb,M.G.T. "Cannabis use amongst British university students." Br. J. Addict. 1973, 69, 35-60.

4306. Kotin,J., Post,R.M., and Goodwin,F.K. "Delta-9-tetrahydrocannabinol in depressed patients." Arch. Gen. Psychiat. 1973, 28, 345-348.

4307. Koukkou,M. and Lehmann,D. "Human EEG spectra before and during cannabis hallucinations." Biol. Psychiat. 1976, 11, 663-677.

4308. Kouretas,D. and Skouras,P. "The poisonous plants of Greece."(Fr.). Prog. Med. 1932, 29, 1257.

4309. Kovatsis,A. "Identification of cannabis by thin layer chromatography."(Ger.). Ellen. K. Teniat. 1968, 1, 208-212.

4310. Kraatz,U. and Korte,F. "Oxygen analogs of delta-8- delta-9-tetrahydrocannabinol."(Ger.). Zeit. Naturforsch 1976, 31B, 1382-1386.

4311. Kralik,P.M., Ho,B.T., and Matthews,H.R. "Effect of delta-9-THC on ethanol withdrawl in mice." Exper. 1976, 32, 723-725.

4312. Kramer,J. and Ben-David,M. "Suppression of prolactin secretion by acute administration of delta-9-THC in rats." Proc. Soc. Expt'l. Biol. Med. 1974, 147, 482-484.

4313. Kramer,L. "The grass and hash business at Syracuse University." Fortune 1971, 84, 102-103.

4314. Krantz,J.C., Berger,H.J., and Welch,B.L. "Blockade of (-)-trans-delta-9-tetrahydrocannabinol depressant effect by cannabinol in mice." Am. J. Pharm. 1971, 143, 149-152.

4315. Krantz,S. "Deterents to drug abuse: The role of law." J.A.M.A. 1968, 206, 1276-1279.

4316. Krapf,E.E. and Kranik,R. "Experiments with intoxicating drugs: Their usefulness in psychopathology and clinical psychiatry."(Sp.). Neurobiologia 1951, 14, 99.

4317. Krauth,W.T. and Tuttle,A. "I was a smuggler in the Merchant Marine." High Times 1976, 10, 37-39, 48, 95.

4318. Krebs,A. "Hashish, avant garde and rearguard." Streets 1965, 1, 17-22.

4319. Krejci,Z. "Antibacterical action of cannabis indica."(Czech.). Lekarske Listy 1952, 7, 500-503.

4320. Krejci,Z. "Antibacterial effects of cannabis indica."(Czech.). Act. Univ. Palack. Olomuc. 1955, 6, 43-57.

4321. Krejci,Z. "Changes with maturation in the amounts of biologically interesting substances of cannabis." In Joyce,C.R.B. and Curry,S.H.(eds.). The Botany and Chemistry of Cannabis. J. and A. Churchill, London, 1970, 49-55.

4322. Krejci,Z. "Hemp(cannabis sativa)--antibiotic drug. II. Methodology and results of bacteriological experiments and tentative clinical observations."(Ger.). Pharmazie 1958, 13, 155-166.

4323. Krejci,Z. "Micro-method of thin-layer chromatography adapted for the analysis of cannabis." U.N. Doc. ST/SOA/SER.S./16, Nov. 30, 1967.

4324. Krejci,Z. "On the problem of materials with antibacterial and hashish action in hemp."(Czech.). Cas. Lek, Cesk. 1961, 100, 1351-1353.

4325. Krejci,Z. "Thin layer chromatographic analysis of hashish and Indian hemp."(Fr.). Act. Univ. Palack. Olomuc. 1966, 43, 111-124.

4326. Krejci,Z., Horak,M., and Santavy,F. "Constitution of the cannabidiolic acid and of an acid of the m.p. 133 isolated from cannabis sativa."(Czech.). Act. Univ. Palack. Olomuc. 1958, 16, 9-17.

4327. Krejci,Z., Horak,M., and Santavy,F. "Hemp (cannabis sativa) antibiotic drug. III. Isolation and constitution of two acids obtained from cannabis sativa." (Ger.). Pharmazie 1959, 14, 349-355.

4328. Krejci,Z. and Santavy,F. "Isolation of other substances from the leaves of Indian hemp(cannabis sativa L. var. indica)."(Czech.). Act. Univ. Palack. Olomuc. 1955, 6, 59-66.

4329. Krejci,Z. and Vybiral,L. "Chromatographic isolation of biologically active materials in cannabis sativa."(Czech.). Scripta Med. 1962, 35, 71-72.

4330. Kreuz,D.S. and Axelrod,J. "Delta-9-tetrahydrocannabinol: Localization in Body Fat." Science 1973, 179, 391-392.

4331. Krimmer,E.E. and Barry,H. "Discriminable stimuli produced by marihuana constituents." Psychopharmacol. Commun. 1976, 2, 319-322.

4332. Krippner,S. "Illicit drug usage: Hazards for learning disability students." Orthomol. Psychiat. 1972, 1, 67-78.

4333. Krippner,S. "Marihuana and Viet Nam. Twin dilemmas for American youth." In Parker,R.S.(ed.). The Emotional Stress of War, Violence, Peace. Stanwix House, Pittsburgh, 1972, 37-45.

4334. Krishnamurty,H.G. and Kaushal,R. "Analysis of Indian marihuana." Ind. J. Pharm. 1974, 36, 152-154.

4335. Krishnamurty,H.G. and Kaushal,R. "Free sugars and cyclitols of Indian marihuana." Ind. J. Chem. 1976, 14B, 639-640.

4336. Kroll,P. "Psychoses associated with marihuana use in Thailand." J. Nerv. Ment. Dis. 1975, 161, 149-156.

4337. Krumsick,L. "Hashish oil."(Ger.). Kriminalistik 1975, 29, 124-125.

4338. Krupinski,J., Stoller,A., and Graves,G.D. "Drug use among the young population of the State of Victoria, Australia: A metropolitan and rural city survey." J. Drug Iss. 1977, 7, 365-376.

4339. Kubena,R.K. "Behavioral and physiological effects of delta-1-tetrahydrocannabinol." Diss. Abs. 1971, 32, 1741.

4340. Kubena,R.K. and Barry,H. "Delta-1-tetrahydrocannabinol potentiation of central barbiturate poisoning." Pharmacologist 1969, 11, 237.

4341. Kubena,R.K. and Barry,H. "Interactions of delta-1-tetrahydrocannabinol with barbiturates and methamphetamine." J. Pharmacol. Exper. Ther. 1970, 173, 94-100.

4342. Kubena,R.K. and Barry,H. "Stimulus characteristics of marihuana components." Nature 1972, 235, 397-398.

4343. Kubena,R.K., Barry,H., Segelman,A.B., Theiner,M., and Farnsworth,N.R. "Biological and chemical evaluation of a 43 year old sample of cannabis fluid extract." J. Pharmaceut. Sci. 1972, 61, 144-145.

4344. Kubena,R.K., Cavero,I., Jandhvala,B.S., and Buckley,J.P. "Certain respiratory and cardiovascular effects of delta-9-THC in dogs." Pharmacologist 1971, 13, 247.

4345. Kubena,R.K., Perhach,J.L., and Barry,H. "Corticosterone elevation mediated centrally by delta-1-tetrahydrocannabinol in rats." Eur. J. Pharmacol. 1971, 14, 89-92.

4346. Kudrin,A.N. "Search for antagonists of hashish and LSD." Paper presented to International Congress of Neuro-psychopharmacology, Prague, 1970.

4347. Kudrin,A.N. and Davydova,O.N. "Elimination of hashish effect with phenitrone in dogs."(Rus.). Farmakol. Toksikol. 1968, 5, 549-552.

4348. Kuehn,J.L. "Counseling the college student drug user." Bull. Menninger Clin. 1970, 34, 205-214.

4349. Kuehn,J.L. "The turkey in the straw: A brief review of the known effects of marihuana usage in man." J. Louisiana State Med. Soc. 1971, 123, 197-200.

4350. Kuehnle,J., Mendelson,J.H., Davis,K.R., and New,P.F.J. "Computed topographic examination of heavy marihuana smokers." J.A.M.A. 1977, 237, 1231-1232.

4351. Kuhn,P.H. "Marihuana." J.A.M.A. 1972, 222, 1423.

4352. Kuhne,S.L. "All the evidence on pot isn't in." Seventeen 1977, 36, 32.

4353. Kuiper,P.C. "Soft drugs and the question of individual freedom."(Ger.). Deut. Med. J. 1971, 22, 525-528.

4354. Kulich,F. and Kahn,M. "A profile of regular marihuana users." Paper presented at Souteast. Psychol. Assoc., Atlanta, 1972.

4354. Kumar,S. "Chromosome abnormalities in cannabis addicts." Assoc. Physicians Ind. J. 1971, 19, 193-195.

4355. Kumar,R. "Psychopharmacology." Ann. Rev. Pharmacol. 1970, 21, 595-628.

4356. Kung,C.T. Archeology in China. Univ. Toronto Press, Toronto, 1959.

4357. Kupfer,D.J., Detre,T., Koral,J., and Fajans,P. "A comment on the 'amotivational syndrome' in marihuana smokers." Am. J. Psychiat. 1973, 130, 1319-1322.

4358. Kupfer,D., Jansson,I., and Orrenius,S. "Spectral interactions of marihuana constituents (cannabinoids) with rat liver microsomal monooxygenase system." Chem.-Biol. Interact. 1972, 5, 201-206.

4359. Kupfer,D., Levin,E., and Burstein,S.H. "Studies on the effects of delta-1-tetrahydrocannabinol and DDT on the hepatic microsomal metabolism of delta-1-THC and other compounds in the rat." Chem.-Biol. Interact. 1973, 6, 59-66.

4360. Kuppers,F.J.E.M., Bercht,C.A.L., Salemink,C.A., Lousberg,R.J.J.C., Terlouw,J.K., and Heerma,W. "Cannabis XIV. Pyrolysis of cannabidiol--analysis of the volatile constituents." J. Chromatog. 1975, 108, 375-379.

4361. Kuppers,F.J.E.M., Bercht,C.A.L., Salemink,C.A., Lousberg,R.J.J.C., Terlouw,J.K., and Heerma,W. "Cannabis XV. Pyrolysis of cannabidiol. Structure elucidation of four pyrolytic products." Tetrahedron 1975, 31, 1513-1516.

4362. Kuppers,F.J.E.M., Lousberg,R.J.J.C., Bercht, C.A.L., Salemink,C.A., Terlouw,J.K., Heerma,W., and Laven,A. "Cannabis VII. Pyrolysis of cannabidiol. Structure elucidation of the main pyrolytic product." Tetrahedron 1973, 29, 2797-2802.

4363. Kurilopa,A.V. "The transpiration coefficient and the influence of soil humidity on the growth and production of hemp."(Ger.). J. Bot. URSS 1935, 20, 46.

4364. Kurland,A.A., Rech,R.H., Moore,K., Shepherd, M.L., Malcolm,R., and Rodnight,R. "Hashish and mental illness." J. Nerv. Ment. Dis. 1975, 160, 375-377.

4365. Kurth,H.J., Kraata,U., and Korte,F. "Synthesis of 1-mercaptocannabinoids."(Ger.). Lieb. Ann. Chem. 1976, 791, 1313-1318.

4366. Kurtines,W., Hogan,R., and Weiss,D. "Personality dynamics of heroin use." J. Abn. Psychol. 1975, 84, 87-89.

4367. Kurtz,R.S. "The use of marihuana and LSD on the college campus." J. Nat'l. Assoc. Women's Deans Counsel. 1967, 30, 124-128.

4368. Kurzman,M.G. "The decriminalization of marihuana." Proc. Nat'l. Sympos. Marihuana 1974, 1, 59-63.

4369. Kuykendall,G.B. "Personal experience of the effects of cannabis indica." Med. Surg. Report. 1875, 32, 421-423.

4370. Kuznik,A. "The effect of lowered age of majority and relaxed dormitory policies on drug use by dormitory students." J. Minnesota Coll. Person. Assoc. 1974, 6, 18-19.

4371. Kwan,V.H.Y. and Rajeswaran,P. "Recent additions to a bibliography on cannabis." J. Forens. Sci. 1968, 13, 279-289.

4372. Kwang-iel,K., Ho-taek,W., and Tae-song,S. "Marihuana smokers in the Seoul area." J. Korean Med. Assoc. 1973, 16, 458-466.

L

4373 Laage,R.J. "Louis Lewin and his opinions of cannabis indica."(Dut.). Pharm. Weekbl. 1969, 104, 839-846.

4374. La Barre,J.E. "Harms resulting from use of marihuana." Prosecutor 1970, 6, 90-93.

4375. Labhardt,F. "Modern drugs and schizophrenia." (Fr.). Arch. Neurol. Neurochir. Psychiat. 1973, 113, 398-400.

4376. Labin,S. "Goa, end of the line; hashish trail at Kalengute." Nat'l. Rev. 1971, 23, 750-753.

4377. Labin,S. Hippies, Drugs and Promiscuity. Arlington House, N.Y., 1972.

4378. Lacine,E.E., Zohdy,A.M., and Tawab,S.A. "Effect of a combination of the alcoholic extract of cannabis sativa and hyoscine hydrobromide(scopolamine HBr) on the EEG patterns in rabbits." Drug Res. J. 1968, 1, 94-116.

4379. Ladewig,D. "Clinical pharmacodynamic effects of delta-9-tetrahydrocannabinol."(Ger.). Lebensversicherungsmedizin 1973, 25, 37-40.

4380. Ladewig,D. and Hobi,V. "The effects of delta-9-THC on simulated driving performance." In Ban,T.A., Bossier,J.R., Gessa,G.J., Heinmann,H., and Hollister,L.(eds). Psychopharmacology, Sexual Disorders and Drug Abuse. North-Holland Pub. Co., Amsterdam, 1973, 693-698.

4381. LaDriere,M.L., Odell,R.E., and Pseys,E. "Marihuana: Its meaning to a high school population." J. Psychol. 1975, 91, 297-307.

4382. Ladriere,M.L. and Szczepkowski,T.R. "Marihuana: Its meaning to a college population." J. Psychol. 1972, 81, 173-180.

4383. Laforest,L. The Incidence of Drug Use Among High School Students of the Montreal Island Area. Office of Prevention and Treatment of Alcohol and Other Drugs, Quebec, Quebec, Can., 1969.

4384. Lage,G. "Clinical study of marihuana intoxication; review of 23 cases."(Sp.). Pol. Sec. Nac. 1943, 12, 246-263.

4385. Lage,G. "Clinical study of marihuana intoxication. Review of 23 cases."(Sp.). Rev. Med. Cirug. Habana 1943, 48, 441-469.

4386. Lahiri,P.K. and Hardman,H.F. "Effects of delta-9-tetrahydrocannabinol on the cardiovascular system of anesthetized dogs." Proc. 5th Internat'l. Cong. Pharmacol. 1972, 1, 133.

4387. Lahiri,P.K., Laddu,A.R., and Hardman,H.F. "Effect of delta-9-tetrahydrocannabinol(THC) on the heart rate(HR) of the dog." Fed. Proc. 1972, 31, 505.

4388. Laidler,P.W. "Pipes and smoking in South Africa." Trans. Roy. Soc. S. Afr. 1938, 26, 1-23.

4389. Lailler,A. "On Indian hemp."(Fr.). Ann. Med.-Psychol. 1890, 12, 78-83.

4390. Laird-Clowes,W. "An amateur assassin." Belgravia 1877, 31, 353-359.

4391. Lallemand,F. Hashish.(Fr.). Vigot, Paris, 1843.

4392. Lamarck,J.B. Encyclopedia of Botany.(Fr.). Panckoucke, Paris, 1783.

4393. Lambo,T.A. "Further neuropsychiatric observations in Nigeria, with comments on the need for epidemiological study in Africa." Br. Med. J. 1960, 2, 1696.

4394. Lambo,T.A. "Malignant anxiety in Africans." J. Ment. Sci. 1962, 108, 256.

4395. Lambo,T.A. "Medical and social problems of drug addiction in West Africa, with special emphasis on psychiatric aspects." Bull. Narc. 1965, 17, 3-13.

4396. Lamontagne,Y. and Bordeleau,J.M. "Marihuana: Review of the literature."(Fr.). Un. Med. Can. 1971, 100, 2413-2419.

4397. Lamontagne,Y., Hand,I., Annable,L., and Gagnon,M. "Physiological and psychological effects of alpha and EMG feedback training with college drug users." Can. Psychol. Assoc. J. 1975, 26, 337-349.

4398. Lamprecht,F., Kvetnansky,R., Ng,L.K.Y., Williams,R.B., and Kopin,I.J. "Effect of delta-9-tetrahydrocannabinol on immobilization-induced changes in rat adrenal medullary enzymes." Eur. J. Pharmacol. 1973, 21, 249-251.

4399. Land,H.W. "How a parent can reach his child about drugs." Today's Hlth. 1971, 49, 425.

4400. Landau,S.F. and Drapkin,I. "Drug offenders in Israel."(Heb.). Delinquency Soc. 1967, 2, 7-17.

4401. Lande,A. "The international drug control system." In National Commission on Marihuana and Drug Abuse. Drug Use in America: Problem in Perspective. Gov't. Print. Office, Washington, D.C., 1973, III, 6-132.

4402. Lander,N., Ben-Zvi,Z., Mechoulam,R., Martin, B., Nordquist,M., and Agurell,S. "Total synthesis of cannabidiol and delta-1-tetrahydrocannabinol metabolites." J. Chem. Soc. 1976, 1, 8-16.

4403. Landerer,X. "Further contribution to the knowledge of hashish, through letters from Cairo." (Ger.). Rep. Pharm. 1842, 30, 359-362.

4404. Landerer,X. "Hemp wine, Contribution to the knowledge of Greek and Oriental remedies."(Ger.). Rep. Pharm. 1846, 34, 240-252.

4405. Landerer,X. "Hemp intoxication."(Ger.). Rep. Pharm. 1840, 28, 356-358.

4406. Landerer,X. "On narcotics used in the East." (Ger.). Rep. Pharm. 1843, 31, 289-295.

4407. Landry,L.P. "Concerning the increase in abuse of hallucinatory drugs in Montreal."(Fr.). Toxicomanies 1968, 1, 199-204.

4408. Lane,F.C. "The rope factory and hemp trade in the fifteenth and sixteenth centuries." J. Econ. Bus. Hist. 1932, 4, 17-30.

4409. Laneau,J. "Remarks on hashish and its pharmacological uses."(Fr.). Rep. Pharm. 1856, 12, 311-314.

4410. Lang,E. Contribution to the Study of Cannabis.(Ger.). Dept. of Med., Univ. of Bern, Bern, 1941.

4411. Lang,E. "Hallucinogenic substances. Legal aspects and control problems." J. Mond. Pharm. 1970, 3, 258-269.

4412. Lang,S.C. "Treatment of acute appendicitis with a mixture of ma jen. Preliminary report."(Chin.). Zhonghua Waike Zazhi 1961, 8, 64-65.

4413. Langeluddeke,A. "Drug addicts and the law." (Ger.). Zeit. Ges. Neurol. Psychiat. 1937, 158, 436-439.

4414. Langrod,J. "Secondary drug use among heroin users." Internat'l. J. Addict. 1970, 5, 6-1-635.

4415. Lapa,A.J. and Abreu,L.C. "Thin-layer chromatography of cannabis and biological assays of strip eluates." Paper presented at Internat'l. Pharmacol. Conference, Sao Paulo, 1966.

4416. Lapa,A.J., Sampaio,C.A.M., Timo-laria,C., and Valle,J.R. "Blocking action of tetrahydrocannabinol upon transmission in the trigeminal system of the cat." J. Pharm. Pharmacol. 1968, 20, 373-376.

4417. Larue-Dubarry,F. "On hashish."(Fr.). Rep. Pharm. 1848, 4, 357-358.

4418. La Rue,F.A.H. "Medical jurisprudence and toxicology." N.Y. Med. J. 1867, 4, 142-144.

4419. Laskowska,R. "Influence of the age of pollen and stigmas on sex determination in hemp." Nature 1961, 192, 147-148.

4420. Lastuvka,Z., Minar,J., and Navatil,O. "Mutual influence of rye(secale cereale L) and hemp (cannabis sativa L) in water culture with supplementary feedings."(Ger.). Biol. Plant. Acad. Sci. Bohemoslov 1965, 7, 349.

4421. Latta,R.P. and Eaton,B.J. "Seasonal fluctuations in cannabinoid content of Kansas marihuana." Econ. Bot. 1975, 29, 153-163.

4422. Lau,R.J., Tubergen,D.G., Barr,M., Domino,E.F., Benowitz,N., and Jones.R.T. "Phytohemagglutinin-induced lymphocyte transformation in humans receiving delta-9-tetrahydrocannabinol." Science 1976, 192, 805-807.

4423. Laurance,J. "From the ill effects of the use of bhang." Madras Quart. Med. J. 1844, 6, 274-278.

4424. Laurent,B. and Roy,P.E. "Alterations of membrane integrity by delta-1-tetrahydrocannabinol." Internat'l. J. Clin. Pharmacol. 1975, 12, 261-266.

4425. Laurent,B., Roy,P.E., and Gailis,L. "Inhibition by delta-1-tetrahydrocannabinol of a Na^+-K^+ transport ATPase from rat ileum. Preliminary report." Can. J. Physiol. Pharmacol. 1974, 52, 1110-1113.

4426. Laurie,P. Drugs: Medical, Psychological, and Social Facts. Penguin Books, Baltimore, 1967.

4427. Lavenhar,M.A. Survey of Drug Abuse in Six New Jersey High Schools. II. Characteristics of Drug Users and Nonusers. Baywood Pub. Co., N.J., 1972.

4428. Law,F.C.P. "Metabolism of delta-1-tetrahydrocannabinol by the isolated perfused rabbit lung(IPL): Comparison with lung(LUM) and liver(LIM) microsomal incubations." Pharmacologist 1976, 18, 292.

4429. Lawrence,D.K. and Gill,E.W. "The effects of delta-1-tetrahydrocannabinol and other cannabinoids on spin-labeled liposomes and their relationship to mechanisms of general anesthesia." Mol. Pharmacol. 1975, 11, 595-602.

4430. Lawrence,D.K. and Pertwee,R.G. "Brain levels of delta-1-tetrahydrocannabinol and its metabolites in mice tolerant to the hypothermic effect of delta-1-tetrahydrocannabinol." Br. J. Pharmacol. 1973, 49, 373-375.

4431. Lawrence,D.K., Pertwee,R.G., Gill,E.W., and Piper,J.M. "Brain levels and relative potency of the 1,2-dimethylheptyl analogue of delta-1-tetrahydrocannabinol in mice." Biochem. Pharmacol. 1974, 23, 3017-3027.

4432. Lawrence,H.C. "Cannabis indica." Br. Med. J. 1883, 1, 1177.

4433. Lawrence,H.C. "Toxic effects of cannabis indica." Lancet 1890, 1, 824.

4434. Lawrence,S. "The Davis two-by-four conspiracy." Marihuana Mon. 1976, 2, 44-45.

4435. Lawrence,T.S. and Velleman,J.P. "Correlates of student drug use in a suburban high school." Psychiatry 1974, 2, 129-136.

4436. Layman,J.M. and Milton,A.S. "Distribution of tritium labelled delta-1-tetrahydrocannabinol in the rat brain following intraperitoneal administration." Br. J. Pharmacol. 1971, 42, 308-310.

4437. Layman,J.M. and Milton,A.S. "Some actions of delta-1-tetrahydrocannabinol and cannabidiol at cholinergic junctions." Br. J. Pharmacol. 1971, 41, 379P-380P.

4438. Leach,H.C. "One more peril for youth." Forum 1939, 101, 1-2.

4439. Leaf,G., Todd,A.R., and Wilkinson,S. "Cannabis indica. IX. The isolation of 3':4':5':6'-tetrahydrodibenzopyran derivatives from pulegone-olivetol condensation products. Synthesis of d-tetrahydrocannabinol." J. Chem. Soc. 1942, 1, 185-188.

4440. League of Nations Advisory Committee on Traffic on Opium and Other Dangerous Drugs. Position in Regard to Hemp. Doc. O.C. 1542(a), July 4, 1934.

4441. Leary,T. "The politics, ethics, and meaning of marihuana." In Solomon,D.(ed). The Marihuana Papers. Bobbs-Merrill, Indianapolis, 1966, 82-89.

4442. Lebbe,J., Lafarge,J.P., and Laplace,M. "Utilization of gas phase chromatography in toxicological inquiry. I. Characterizations of cannabis sativa. Application to resin traces in tobacco."(Fr.). Ann. Fals. Expert. Chim. 1972, 65, 410-417.

4443. LeBlanc,M. "Delinquency in the middle class: A group culture of committed drug users."(Fr.). Act. Criminol. 1972, 5, 167-181.

4444. LeClerc,H. "Indian hemp."(Fr.). Presse Med. 1902, 30, 1928-1930.

4445. Lederer,F.I. and Lederer,C.M. "Admisibility of evidence found by marihuana detection dogs." Mil. Pol. J. 1973, 22, 22-25.

4446. Lee,M.L., Novotny,M., and Bartle,K.D. "Gas chromatography/mass spectrometric and nuclear magnetic resonance spectrometric studies of carcinogenic polynuclear aromatic hydrocarbons in tobacco and marihuana smoke condensates." Anal. Chem. 1976, 48, 405-416.

4447. Leech,K. and Jordan,B. Drugs For Young People: Their Use and Misure. Religious Education Press, Oxford, 1967.

4448. Lees,R.C. "Cannabis sativa see indica: Indian hemp." Br. Med. J. 1895, 1, 300-301.

4449. Lefkowitz,S.S. and Chiang,C.Y. "Effects of delta-9-tetrahydrocannabinol on mouse spleens." Res. Commun. Chem. Pathol. Pharmacol. 1975, 11, 659-662.

4450. Lefkowitz,S.S., Hung,C.Y., and Geber,W.F. "The effect of psychotomimetic drugs on interferon production." Res. Commun. Chem. Pathol. Pharmacol. 1973, 5, 885-888.

4451. Legator,M.S., Weber,E., Connor,T., and Stoeckel,M. "Failure to detect mutagenic effects of delta-9-tetrahydrocannabinol in the dominant lethal test, host-mediated assay, blood-urine studies, and cytogenetic evaluation with mice." In Braude,M.C. and Szara,S.(eds.). Pharmacology of Marihuana. Raven Press, N.Y., 1976, 699-711.

4452. Legewie,H. and Simonova,O. "Subjective and physiological correlations of cannabis smoking." Paper presented at Internat'l. Cong. on Neuro-psychopharmacology, Prague, 1970.

4453. Legowada,Z. "Thin-layer chromatographic detection of hashish and strychnine."(Pol.). Farmacja 1975, 31, 315-317.

4454. Lehmann,W.X. "Doctor, what about marihuana?" Reader's Dig. 1971, 98, 169-170.

4455. Lehr,D. "Grass, acid, and speed. A pharmacologist views the contemporary drug scene of the Hippie subculture." Proc. Rud. Virchow Med. Soc. N.Y. 1968, 27, 285-307.

4456. Leighty,E.G. "Metabolism and distribution of cannabinoids in rats after different methods of administration." Biochem. Pharmacol. 1973, 22, 1613-1621.

4457. Leighty,E.G., Fentiman,A.F., and Foltz,R.L. "Delta-9- and delta-9-tetrahydrocannabinols long-retained metabolites identified as novel fatty acid conjugates." Pharmacologist 1976, 18, 293.

4458. Leighty,E.G., Fentiman,A.F., and Foltz,R.L. "Long-retained metabolites of delta-9- and delta-8-tetrahydrocannabinol identified as novel fatty acid conjugates." Res. Commun. Chem. Pathol. Pharmacol. 1976, 14, 13-28.

4459. Leinwald,M.A. "International law of treaties and the U.S. legalization of marihuana." Columbia J. Transnat'l. Law 1971, 10, 413.

4460. Leite,J.R. "Failure to obtain cannabis-directed behavior and abstinence syndrome in rats chronically treated with cannabis sativa extracts." Paper presented at 1st Lat. Amer. Cong. Psychobiol., Sao Paulo, 1973.

4461. Leite,J.R. and Carlini,E.A. "Failure to obtain cannabis-directed behavior and abstinence syndrome in rats chronically treated with cannabis sativa extracts." Psychopharmacol. 1974, 36, 133-145.

4462. Lelord,G. and Stephant,J.L. "Of grass that one holds in his hands and rolls...or from timidity to schizophrenia through hashish."(Fr.). Ann. Med.-Psychol. 1972, 2, 17-32.

4463. Lemar-Detroit. The Case For the Re-Legalization of Marihuana. Lemar, Detroit, 1966.

4464. Lemar-SUNYAB. Lemar-SUNYAB Information Kit. Lemar, State University of New York at Buffalo, 1967.

4465. Le May,M.L. and Penn,J.R. "Drug usage trends in college living units during a 3-year period." Drug For. 1973, 2, 309-315.

4466. Lemberger,L. "Clinical pharmacology of natural and synthetic cannabinoids." In Cohen,S. and Stillman,R.(eds.). Therapeutic Potential of Marihuana. Plenum Press, N.Y., 1976, 405-418.

4467. Lemberger,L. "Tetrahydrocannabinol metabolism in man." Drug Metab. Disposit. 1973, 1, 461-468.

4468. Lemberger,L. "The metabolism of the tetrahydrocannabinols." Adv. Pharmacol. 1972, 10, 221-254.

4469. Lemberger,L. "The pharmacokinetics of delta-9-tetrahydrocannabinol and its metabolites: Importance and relationship in developing methods for detecting cannabis in biologic fluids." In Nahas,G.G., Paton,W.D.M., and Idanpaan-Heikkila,J.E.(eds.). Marihuana. Springer Verlag, N.Y., 1976, 169-179.

4470. Lemberger,L., Axelrod,J., and Kopin,I.J. "Clinical studies on the disposition and metabolism of delta-9-THC and their correlates with its pharmacologic effects." Act. Pharmaceut. Suec. 1971, 8, 692.

4471. Lemberger,L., Axelrod,J., and Kopin,I.J. "Metabolism and disposition of delta-9-tetrahydrocannabinol in man." Pharmacol. Rev. 1971, 23, 371-380.

4472. Lemberger,L., Axelrod,J., and Kopin,I.J. "Metabolism and disposition of tetrahydrocannabinols in naive subjects and chronic marihuana users." Ann. N.Y. Acad. Sci. 1971, 191, 142-155.

4473. Lemberger,L., Crabtree,R.E., and Rowe,H.M. "11-hydroxy-delta-9-tetrahydrocannabinol: Pharmacology, disposition, and metabolism of a major metabolite of marihuana in man." Science 1972, 177, 62-64.

4474. Lemberger,L., Crabtree,R., Rowe,H., and Clemens,J. "Tetrahydrocannabinols and serum prolactin in man." Life Sci. 1973, 16, 1339-1343.

4475. Lemberger,L., Dalton,B., Martz,R., Rodda,B., and Forney,R. "Clinical studies on the interaction of psychopharmacologic agents with marihuana." Ann. N.Y. Acad. Sci. 1976, 281, 219-228.

4476. Lemberger,L., Martz,R., Rodda,B., Forney,R., and Rowe,H. "Comparative pharmacology of delta-9-tetrahydrocannabinol and its metabolite 11-OH-delta-9-tetrahydrocannabinol." J. Clin. Invest. 1973, 52, 2411-2417.

4477. Lemberger,L., McMahon,R., and Archer,R. "The role of metabolic conversion on the mechanism of action of cannabinoids." In Braude,M.C. and Szara,S. (eds.). Pharmacology of Marihuana. Raven Press, N.Y., 1976, 125-133.

4478. Lemberger,L., McMahon,R., Archer,R., Matsumoto,K., and Rowe,H. "DMHP(delta-6a,10a dimethylheptyl tetrahydrocannabinol): Pharmacology and physiologic disposition in man." Pharmacologist 1973, 15, 201.

4479. Lemberger,L., McMahon,R., Archer,R., Matsumoto,K., and Rowe,H. "Metabolism of DMHP(delta-6a,10a dimethyl heptyl tetrahydrocannabinol)." Proc. 5th Internat'l. Cong. Pharmacol. 1972, 1, 137.

4480. Lemberger,L., McMahon,R., Archer,R., Matsumoto,K., and Rowe,H. "Pharmacologic effects and physiologic disposition of delta-6a,10 dimethyl heptyl tetrahydrocannabinol(DMHP) in man." Clin. Pharmacol. Ther. 1974, 15, 380-386.

4481. Lemberger,L., McMahon,R.E., Archer,R., Matsumoto,K., and Rowe,H. "The in vitro and in vivo metabolism of delta-6a,10a dimethyl heptyl tetrahydrocannabinol(DMHP)." J. Pharmacol. Exper. Ther. 1973, 187, 169-175.

4482. Lemberger,L. and Rowe,H. "Clinical pharmacology of nabilone, a cannabinol derivative." Clin. Pharmacol. Ther. 1975, 18, 720-726.

4483. Lemberger,L. and Rubin,A. "The physiological disposition of marihuana in man." Life Sci. 1974, 17, 1637-1642.

4484. Lemberger,L., Silberstein,S.D., Axelrod,J., and Kopin,I.J. "Marihuana: Studies on the disposition and metabolism of delta-9-tetrahydrocannabinol in man." Science 1970, 170, 1320-1322.

4485. Lemberger,L., Tamarkin,N.R., Axelrod,J., and Kopin,I.J. "Delta-9-tetrahydrocannabinol: Metabolism and disposition in long-term marihuana smokers." Science 1971, 173, 72-74.

4486. Lemberger,L., Weiss,J.L., Watanabe,A.M., Galanter,I.M., Wyatt,R.J., and Cardon,P.V. "Delta-9-tetrahydrocannabinol. Temporal correlation of the psychologic effects and blood levels after various routes of administration." N. Eng. J. Med. 1972, 286, 685-688.

4487. Lemmo,R. "Pot, peasants and Pancho Villa." High Times 1974, 1, 32-33, 36-37.

4488. Lendon,N.C. "Drugs causing dependence." Br. J. Addict. 1965, 61, 115-124.

4489. Lenicque,P.M., Paris,M.R., and Poulot,M. "Effects of some components of cannabis sativa on the regenerating planarian worm Dugesia Tigrina." Exper. 1972, 20, 1399-1400.

4490. Lennertz,E. "The question of antisocial personality in young hashish smokers."(Ger.). Zeit. Sozialpsychol. 1970, 1, 48-56.

4491. Lentz,P.L., Turner,C.E., Robertson,L.W., and Gentner,W.A. "First North American record for cercospora cannabina, with notes on the identification of c. cannabina and c. cannabis." Plant Dis. Rep. 1974, 58, 165-168.

4492. Leonard,B.E. "Cannabis: A short review of its effects and the possible dangers of its use." Br. J. Addict. 1969, 64, 121-130.

4493. Leonard,B.E. "The effect of delta-1-6-tetrahydrocannabinol on biogenic amines and their amino acid precursors in the rat brain." Pharmacol. Res. Commun. 1971, 3, 139-145.

4494. Leong,J.H.K. "The present status of drug dependence treatment in Singapore." Addict. Dis. 1977, 3, 93-98.

4495. Leonhardt,R.W. Hashish Report.(Ger.). Piper, Munich, 1970.

4496. Lepinois,M.E. "A little known preparation of Indian hemp."(Fr.). J. Pharm. Chim. 1896, 3, 65-68.

4497. Lepinois,E. "A little known preparation of Indian hemp."(Fr.). Rep. Pharm. 1896, 8, 241-244.

4498. Lepinske,H.C. Jamaican Ganja. Exposition Press, N.Y., 1955.

4499. Lerner,M. "Marihuana: Tetrahydrocannabinol and related compounds." Science 1963, 140, 175-176.

4500. Lerner,M., Mills,A.B., Mount,S.F. "Narcotic analysis: A simple approach." J. Forens. Sci. 1963, 8, 126-131.

4501. Lerner,M. and Zeffert,J.T. "Determination of tetrahydrocannabinol isomers in marihuana and hashish." Bull. Narc. 1968, 20, 53-54.

4502. Lerner,P. "The precise determination of tetrahydrocannabinol in marihuana and hashish." Bull. Narc. 1969, 21, 39-42.

4503. Lerner,S.E. and Lindar,R.L. "Drugs in the elementary school." J. Drug Educat. 1974, 4, 317-322.

4504. Lerner,S.E., Linder,R.L., and Burke,E.M. "Drugs in junior high school. II." J. Psyched. Drugs. 1974, 6, 51-56.

4505. Lesik,B.V. "Quality of hemp fibers and the use of different forms of nitric fertilizers."(Rus.). Vest. Selskokhoz. Nauk. 1959, 4, 125-128.

4506. Lessin,P.J. and Thomas,S.A. "Assessment of the chronic effects of marihuana on motivation and achievement: A preliminary report." In Braude,M.C. and Szara,S. (eds.). Pharmacology of Marihuana. Raven Press, N.Y., 1976, 681-685.

4507. Lester,L.F., Perea,P., and Zohner, D. "An empirical investigation of value systems among college students." Paper presented to East. Psychol. Assoc., Washington, D.C., 1973.

4508. Leszczynski,J.R. "Synergism of narcotic poisons."(Pol.). Poznan. Tow. Przyjac. Nauk. 1934, 4, 1-6.

4509. Lett,S. "The opium habit and its treatment." Can. Practitioner 1884, 9, 301-307.

4510. Leuchtenberger,C. and Leuchtenberger,R. "Abnormalities of mitosis, DNA metabolism and growth in human lung cultures exposed to smoke from marihuana cigarettes, and their similarity with alterations evoked by tobacco cigarette smoke." U.N. Doc. ST/SOA/SER.S/37, Nov. 17, 1972.

4511. Leuchtenberger,C. and Leuchtenberger,R. "Cytological and cytochemical studies of the effects of fresh marihuana cigarette smoke on growth and DNA metabolism of animal and human lung cultures." In Braude,M.C. and Szara,S.(eds.). Pharmacology of Marihuana. Raven Press, N.Y., 1976, 2, 595-613.

4512. Leuchtenberger,C. and Leuchtenberger,R. "Enhancement of abnormal cell proliferation in lung explants after marihuana cigarette smoke." Exper. 1971, 27, 737-738.

4513. Leuchtenberger,C. and Leuchtenberger,R. "Morphological and cytochemical effects of marihuana cigarette smoke on epitheloid cells of lung explants from mice." Nature 1971, 234, 227-229.

4514. Leuchtenberger,C., Leuchtenberger,R., and Ritter,U. "Effect of marihuana and tobacco smoke on DNA and chromosomal complement in human lung explants." Nature 1973, 242, 403-404.

4515. Leuchtenberger,C., Leuchtenberger,R., and Schneider,A. "Effects of marihuana and tobacco smoke on human lung physiology." Nature 1973, 241, 137-139.

4516. Leuchtenberger,C., Leuchtenberger,R., Zbinden, J., and Schleh,E. "Cytological and cytochemical effects of whole smoke and of the gas vapor phase from marihuana cigarettes on growth and DNA metabolism of cultured mammalian cells." In Nahas,G.G., Paton,W.D.M., Idanpaan-Heikkila,J.E.(eds.). Marihuana. Springer Verlag, N.Y., 1976, 243-257.

4517. Leuw,E. Cannabis and Schoolchildren.(Dut.). Foundation Alcohol Drug Research, Amsterdam, 1972.

4518. Leuw,E. "Drug use in the Netherlands." In Connell,P.H. and Dorn,N.(eds.). Cannabis and Man. Churchill Livingstone, Edinburgh, 1975, 180-183.

4519. Leuw,E. "Use of cannabis among secondary school populations: attempt at interpretation."(Dut.). Ned. T. Criminol. 1972, 14, 241-255.

4520. Levander,S., Binder,M., Agurell,S., Bader-Bartfai,A., Gustafsson,B., Leander,K., Lindgren,J.E., Olsson,A., and Tobisson,B. "Pharmacokinetics in relation to physiological and psychological effects of delta-8-THC." Act. Pharmaceut. Suec. 1974, 11, 662-663.

4521. Levett,A. "The effects of cannabis sativa on the behavior of adult female chacma baboons(Papio ursinus) in captivity." Psychopharmacol. 1977, 53, 79-81.

4522. Levey,M. "Medieval Arabic toxicology." Trans. Am. Philosoph. Soc. 1966, 33, 5-19.

4523. Levi,A. and Brugnera,M. "Pharmacological effects of 3-(1,2,dimethylheptyl) cannabinol."(It.). At. Soc. Natural. Matemat. Modena 1948, 79, 33-42.

4524. Levi,W.M. The Pigeon. Levi, Sumpter, S. Carolina, 1957.

4525. Levin,A. "Psychiatric disorders as sequelai of cannabis abuse." Proc. 1st S. Afr. Internat'l. Conf. Alcohol. Drug Depend. 1974, 1, 145-156.

4526. Levin,L. and Lewis,A. Chronic Paranoid Symptoms and Thought Disorders in Users of Marihuana and LSD as Observed in Psychotherapy. Unpub. ms., Sinai Hospital, Baltimore, 1969.

4527. Levin,P.A.(ed.). Contemporary Problems of Drug Abuse. Pub. Sciences Group, Acton, Mass., 1974.

4528. Levine,H. Legal Dimensions of Drug Abuse in the United States. C.C. Thomas, Springfield, Ill., 1974.

4529. Levine,H. and Clark,M. "Marihuana use: Social discontent and political alienation." Am. Polit. Sci. Rev. 1971, 65, 120.

4530. Levine,J. "Origin of cannabinol." J. Am. Chem. Soc. 1944, 66, 1868-1870.

4531. Leviton,H.S. "Drug control." Pupil Person. Serv. J. 1975, 4, 29-34.

4532. Levitt,S. "The White House smoke-in." High Times 1977, 26, 51-53.

4533. Levy,J.A., Munson,A.E., Harris,L.S., and Dewey,W.L. "Effects of delta-8- and delta-9-tetrahydrocannabinol on the immune response in mice." Pharmacologist 1974, 16, 259.

4534. Levy,L. "Drug use on campus: Prevalence and social characteristics of collegiate drug users on campuses of University of Illinois." Drug For. 1973, 2, 141-171.

4535. Levy,R. and Livne,A. "Mode of action of hashish compounds in reducing blood platelet count." Biochem. Pharmacol. 1976, 25, 359-360.

4536. Levy,R. "Impairment of ADP-induced platelet aggregation by hashish components." Thromb. Haemostas. 1976, 3, 634-640.

4537. Levy,S. and McCallum,N.K. "Cannabidiol and its pharmacokinetic interaction with delta-1-tetrahydrocannabinol. Exper. 1975, 31, 1268-1269.

4538. Lewin,L. Phantastica. Kegan Paul, Trench and Co., London, 1931.

4539. Lewis,A. "Historical perspective." Br. J. Addict. 1968, 63, 241-245.

4540. Lewis,A.A. "New research on cannabis." Br. Med. J. 1971, 2, 526.

4541. Lewis,B. The Assassins. Basic Books, N.Y., 1968.

4542. Lewis,B. The Sexual Power of Marihuana: An Intimate Report on 208 Adult Middle Class Users. Wyden, N.Y., 1970.

4543. Lewis,B. "The sources for the history of the Syrian assassins." Speculum 1952, 27, 475-489.

4544. Lewis,C.R. and Slavin,R.G. "Allergy to marihuana: A clinical and skin testing study." J. Allergy Clin. Immunol. 1975, 55, 131-132.

4545. Lewis,E.G., Dustman,R.E., and Beck,E.C. "The effect of alcohol and marihuana on cerebral evoked potentials." Prog. Clin. Neurophysiol. 1977, 2, 160-174.

4546. Lewis,E.G., Dustman,R.E., Peters,B.A., and Beck,E.C. "The influence of delta-1-THC on the human visual evoked response." Res. Ment. Hlth. Behav. 1973, 15, 43-46.

4547. Lewis,E.G., Dustman,R.E., Peters,B.A., Straight,R.C., and Beck,E.C. "The effects of varying doses of delta-9-tetrahydrocannabinol on the human visual and somatosensory evoked response." EEG Clin. Neurophysiol. 1973, 35, 347-354.

4548. Lewis,H.E. "Cannabis indica. A study of its physiologic action, toxic effects and therapeutic indications." Merck's Archives 1900, 1, 247-251.

4549. Lewis,M.F.(ed.). Current Research in Marihuana. Academic Press, N.Y., 1972.

4550. Lewis,M.F., Ferraro,D.P., Mertens,H.W., and Steen,J.A. "Interaction between marihuana and altitude on a complex behavioral task in baboons." Aviat. Space Environ. Med. 1976, 1, 121-123.

4551. Lewis,M.J. "Delta-9-tetrahydrocannabinol and adrenergic mechanisms." Br. J. Pharmacol. 1975, 54, 277P.

4552. Lewis,S.C., Neel,M.A., Brown,D.J., and Forney,R.B. "Vasodepressor response to delta-9-tetrahydrocannabinol in hypertensive rats." Pharmacologist 1973, 15, 200.

4553. Lewitus,V. "Marihuana." Am. J. Nurs. 1936, 36, 677-678.

4554. Ley,W. "Observations on the cannabis indica, or Indian hemp." Prov. Med. J. Retro. Med. Sci. 1843, 5, 487-489.

4555. Li,D.M.F. "Cardiovascular and respiratory effects of cannabis extracts in delta-1-tetrahydrocannabinol." Br. J. Pharmacol. 1973, 47, 627P.

4556. Li,H.L. "An archeological and historical account of cannabis in China." Econ. Bot. 1974, 28, 437-448.

4557. Li,H.L. "Origin and use of cannabis in Eastern Asia. Linguistic-cultural implications." Econ. Bot. 1974, 28, 293-301.

4558. Li,H.L. "The origin and use of cannabis in Eastern Asia: Their linguistic-cultural implications." In Rubin,V.(ed.). Cannabis and Culture. Mouton, The Hague, 51-63.

4559. Li,H.L. "The vegetables of ancient China." Econ. Bot. 1969, 23, 253-260.

4560. Liakos,A., Boulougouris,J.C., and Stefanis,C. "Psychophysiologic effects of acute cannabis smoking in long-term users." Ann. N. Y. Acad. Sci. 1976, 282, 375-386.

4561. Liatuaud,M. "Memoir on the natural history and the medical properties of Indian hemp."(Fr.). C. R. Acad. Sci. 1844, 18, 149-150.

4562. Lichty,R. "The super lawyers." High Times 1974, 3, 22-26.

4563. Lidz,T. "Psychedelism: Dionysus reborn." Psychiat. 1968, 31, 116-125.

4564. Lieber,M. "The economics and distribution of cannabis sativa in urban Thailand." Econ. Bot. 1975, 29, 164-170.

4565. Lieberman,C.M. and Lieberman,B.W. "Marihuana--A medical review." N. Eng. J. Med. 1971, 284, 88-91.

4566. Liebert,R.S. "Drug use: symptoms, disease, or adolescent experimentation--the task of therapy." J. Am. Coll. Hlth. Assoc. 1967, 16, 25-29.

4567. Liebman,A.A., Malarek,D.H., Dorsky,A.M., and Kaegi,H.H. "Synthesis of olivetol-4,6$^{14}C_2$ and its conversion to (-)-delta-9-6a,10a, trans-tetrahydrocannabinol 2,4$^{14}C_2$ via (-)-delta-8-6a,10a-trans-tetrahydrocannabinol-2,4$^{14}C_2$. J. Label. Compds. 1971, 7, 241-246.

4568. Liedgren,S.R.C., Odkvist,L.M., Davis,E.R., and Fredrickson,J.M. "Effect of marihuana on hearing." J. Otolaryngol. 1976, 5, 233-237.

4569. Light,P.K. "Let the children speak: A psychological study of young teenagers and drugs." Diss. Abs. 1973, 34, 1278-1279.

4570. Lilly,J.R. "Marihuana on a small college campus." J. Drug Iss. 1972, 2, 56-65.

4571. Limberg,J. "The influence of photoperiodicity on the sexual index in hemp(cannabis sativa L.)." Biol. Plant. 1959, 1, 176-186.

4572. Limentani,A. "On drug dependence: Clinical appraisals of the predicaments of habituation and addiction to drugs." Internat'l. J. Psychoanal. 1968, 49, 578-590.

4573. Lincoln,L., Berryman,M., and Linn,M.W. "Drug abuse: a comparison of attitudes." Comp. Psychiat. 1973, 14, 465-471.

4574. Lind,B.B. "New major trends in the development of narcotic use among young people."(Nor.). Tid. Nor. Laegefor. 1973, 93, 1757-1760.

4575. Lind,B.B. "The use of marihuana and hashish among the young in Oslo." In Anonymous(ed.). Marihuana and Health.(Nor.). Universitetsforlaget, Oslo, 1970.

4576. Lindemann,E. "The neurophysiological effect of intoxicating drugs." Am. J. Psychiat. 1934, 90, 1007-1037.

4577. Lindemann,E. and Clarke,L.D. "Modifications in ego structure and personality reactions under the influence of the effects of drugs." Am. J. Psychiat. 1952, 108, 561-567.

4578. Lindemann,E., and Felsinger,J.M. "Drug effects and personality theory." Psychopharmacol. 1961, 2, 69-92.

4579. Lindemann,E. and Malamud,W. "Experimental analysis of the psychopathological effects of intoxicating drugs." Am. J. Psychiat. 1934, 13, 853-881.

4580. Linder,R.L., Lerner,S.E., and Burke,E.M. "Drugs in the junior high school. Part 1." J. Psyched. Drugs 1974, 6, 43-57.

4581. Lindesmith,A.R. "Assessment of the current situation by a sociologist." In Wittenborn,J.R., Brill,H., Smith,J.P., and Wittenborn,S.A.(ed.). Drugs and Youth. C.C. Thomas, Springfield, Ill., 1969, 320-331.

4582. Lindesmith,A.R. "Drug use as a divisive influence: Review of Poisoned Ivy by W. Surface." Phi Delta Kappan 1968, 50, 218-221.

4583. Lindesmith,A.R. "Introduction." In Solomon, D.(ed.). The Marihuana Papers. Bobbs-Merrill, Indianapolis, 1966, xxiii-xxvi.

4584. Lindesmith,A.R. The Addict and the Law. Indiana Univ. Press, Bloomington, 1965.

4585. Lindsey,C.J. and Carlini,E.A. "Pharmacological manipulation of brain catecholamine levels and the aggressive behavior induced by marihuana in REM-sleep deprived rats." Paper presented at 1st Lat. Am. Cong. Psychobiol., Sao Paulo, 1973.

4586. Lindskov,J. "Drug addiction--hepatitis."(Dan.). Ugeskr. Laeg. 1967, 129, 1663.

4587. Ling,G.M., Thomas,J.A., Usher,D.R., and Singhal,R.K. "Effects of chronically administered delta-1-tetrahydrocannabinol on adrenal and gonadal activity of male rats." Internat'l. J. Clin. Pharmacol. 1973, 7, 1-5.

4588. Linken,A. "A study of drug-taking among young patients attending a clinic for venereal diseases." Br. J. Ven. Dis. 1968, 44, 337-341.

4589. Linkletter,A. "Don't legalize marihuana." PTA Mag. 1971, 65, 15.

4590. Linn,L.S. "Psychopathology and experience with marihuana." Br. J. Addict. 1971, 67, 55-64.

4591. Linn,L.S. "Social identification and the use of marihuana." Internat'l. J. Addict. 1971, 6, 79-107.

4592. Linnaeus,C. Species of Plants.(Lat.). Laurenti, Sweden, 1753.

4593. Linton,P.H., Kuschenmeister,C.A., and White, H.B. "Drug preference and response to marihuana and alcohol." Res. Commun. Psychol. Psychiat. Behav. 1976, 1, 629-643.

4594. Linton,P.H., Kuechenmeister,C.A., White,H.B., and Travis,R.P. "Marihuana: Heart rate and EEG response." Res. Commun. Chem. Pathol. Pharmacol. 1975, 10, 201-214.

4595. Lipa,B. "Bromural used by hashish smokers." (Ger.). Arch. Schiffs Tropenhyg. 1908, 12, 496-497.

4596. Lipinski,E. and Lipinski,B.G. "Motivational factors in psychedelic use by male college students." J. Am. Coll. Hlth. Assoc. 1967, 16, 145-149.

4597. Lipp,M.R. "Marihuana use by nurses and nursing students(based on a 1970 survey at two nursing conventions)." Am. J. Nurs. 1971, 71, 2339-2341.

4598. Lipp,M.R. and Benson,S.G. "Physician use of marihuana, alcohol and tobacco." Am. J. Psychiat. 1972, 129, 612-616.

4599. Lipp,M.R., Benson,S.G., and Taintor,Z. "Marihuana use by medical students." Am. J. Psychiat. 1971, 128, 207-212.

4600. Lipp,M.R., Tinklenberg,J., Taintor,Z., Peterson,M., Benson,S., and Melges,F. "Marihuana and medical students: A study of four U.S. medical colleges." J. Med. Educat. 1970, 45, 821-822.

4601. Lipparini,F., De Carolis,A.S., and Longo,V.G. "A neuropharmacological investigation of some trans-tetrahydrocannabinol derivatives." Physiol. Behav. 1969, 4, 527-532.

4602. Lipscomb,W.R. "Drug use in a black ghetto." Am. J. Psychiat. 1971, 127, 1166-1169.

4603. Lipton,D.S., Stephens,R.C., Babst,D.V., Dembo, R., Diamond,S.C., Spielman,C.R., Schmeidler,J., Bergman,P.J., and Uppal.G.S. "A survey of substance use among junior and senior high school students in New York State, winter 1974-1975." Am. J. Drug Alcohol Abuse 1977, 4, 153-164.

4604. Lipton,L. "The holy barbarians." In Andrews,G. and Vinkenoog,S.(eds.). The Book of Grass. Grove Press, N.Y., 1967, 211.

4605. Liskow,B. "Marihuana deterioration." J.A.M.A. 1970, 214, 1709.

4606. Liskow,B. "Book Forum: Marihuana: Deceptive Weed." J.A.M.A. 1973, 224, 631.

4607. Liskow,B., Liss,J.L., and Parker,C.W. "Allergy to marihuana." Ann. Intern. Med. 1971, 75, 571-573.

4608. Lissenberg,E. Mothers of Adolescents on the Use of Hemp, Report of an Investigation.(Dut.). Foundation for Alcohol Drug Research, Amersterdam, 1971.

4609. List,A., Nazar,B., Nyquest,S., and Harclerode,J. "The effects of delta-9-tetrahydrocannabinol and cannabidiol on the metabolism of gonadal steroids in the rat." Drug Metab. Dispos. 1977, 5, 268-272.

4610. List,A.F., Bartram,S.F., Nazar,B.L., and Harclerod,J. "Interactions of delta-9-tetrahydrocannabinol, adrenal steroids, and ethanol." J. Pharm. Pharmacol. 1975, 27, 606-607.

4611. Lister,J. "Cannabis controversy and other sundry problems." N. Eng. J. Med. 1969, 280, 712.

4612. Littlejohn,M.J., Grupp,S.E., and Schmitt,R.L. "Marihuana use in a small college: A midwest example." Internat'l. J. Addict. 1971, 6, 57-68.

4613. Littleton,I.M. and MacLean,K.I. "The effect of delta-8-tetrahydrocannabinol on dopamine metabolism in the rat corpus striatum: the influence of environment." Br. J. Pharmacol. 1974, 51, 117P.

4614. Littleton,J.M., MacLean,K.I., and Brownlee,G. "Alterations in dopamine uptake in rat corpus striatum induced by combinations of stress and delta-9-tetrahydrocannabinol." Br. J. Pharmacol. 1976, 56, 370P.

4615. Liu,R.K. "Hypothermic effects of marihuana, marihuana derivatives and chlorpromazine in laboratory mice." Res. Commun. Chem. Pathol. Pharmacol. 1974, 9, 215-228.

4616. Livet,L. "Smokers of kif."(Fr.). Bull. Soc. Clin. Med. Ment. 1921, 14, 40-45.

4617. Livet,L. "Smokers of marihuana."(Fr.). Ann. Med.-Psychol. 1920, 12, 257-267.

4618. Livet,L., Roger,E.P., and Bonnet, L. "Pharmacological note on hashish and Indian hemp."(Fr.). Evol. Ther. Medicochiurg. 1925, 6, 13-16.

4619. L.J.P.D. "Hashish."(Fr.). Rev. Can. 1871, 8, 681-682.

4620. Lloyd,D. "Drug misuse in teenagers." Appl. Ther. 1970, 12, 19-25.

4621. Lloyd,J. "Washington report: A new look on marihuana." Sr. Scholast. 1969, 1, 2.

4622. Lobato,J.B. "Organization of an administrative organ for the control of narcotic drugs: Fortieth session of the economic and social council." Bull. Narc. 1966, 18, 63-67.

4623. Lockhart,J.G. "Effects of 'speed' and 'pot' on the juvenile diabetic." J.A.M.A. 1970, 214, 2065.

4624. Lockwood,A.H. "Marihuana and alcohol intolerance in Hodgkin's disease." N. Eng. J. Med. 1973, 288, 526.

4625. Loev,B., Bender,P.E., Sowalo,F., Macko,E., and Fowler,P.J. "Cannabinoids. Structure-activity studies related to 1,2-dimethylheptyl derivatives." J. Med. Chem. 1973, 16, 1200-1206.

4626. Loev,B., Dienel,B., Goodman,M.M., and van Hoeven,H. "Synthesis of a norcannabinoid." J. Med. Chem. 1974, 17, 1234-1235.

4627. Loewe,S. "Bioassay by direct potency estimation." Science 1947, 106, 89-91.

4628. Loewe,S. "Effective ingredients in cannabis and pharmacology of cannabis."(Ger.). Arch. Pharmakol. Expt'l. Pathol. 1950, 211, 175-193.

4629. Loewe,S. "Marihuana activity of cannabinol." Science 1945, 102, 615-616.

4630. Loewe,S. "Pharmacological study. I. The relationship between structure and activity and the significance of coordinated pharmacological and chemical investigations as applied to marihuana." In Mayor's Committee on Marihuana. The Problem of Marihuana in the City of New York. Jacques Cattell Press, Lancaster, Pa., 1944, 149-212.

4631. Loewe,S. "Studies on the pharmacology and acute toxicity of compounds with marihuana activity." J. Pharmacol. Exper. Ther. 1946, 88, 154-161.

4632. Loewe,S. "Substance from the circulating blood." J. Pharmacol. Exper. Ther. 1946, 86, 294-295.

4633. Loewe,S. "Synergism of cannabis and butylbromallyl-barbituric acid." J.A.P.A. 1940, 29, 162-163.

4634. Loewe,S. "The chemical basis of marihuana activity." J. Pharmacol. Exper. Ther. 1945, 84, 78-81.

4635. Loewe,S. "The rate of disappearance of a marihuana-active substance from the circulating blood." J. Pharmacol. Exper. Ther. 1946, 86, 294-296.

4636. Loewe,S. "Toxicity of marihuana-active principles." Fed. Proc. 1945, 4, 127-128.

4637. Loewe,S. and Adams,R. "Structure-activity relationship(SAR) and pharmacological peculiarities of new synthetic congeners of tetrahydrocannabinol." Fed. Proc. 1947, 6, 352.

4638. Loewe,S. and Goodman,L.S. "Anticonvulsant action of marihuana-active substances." Fed. Proc. 1947, 6, 52.

4639. Loewe,S. and Modell,W. "The action of chemical components of cannabis extracts." J. Pharmacol. Exper. Ther. 1941, 72, 27.

4640. Logie,P., Morley,J.E., and Bensusan,A.D. "The dagga smoker: A survey." S. Af. Med. J. 1972, 1, 1400-1403.

4641. Loisellep,R. and Whitehead,P.C. "Scaling drug use: an examination of the popular wisdom." Can. J. Behav. Sci. 1971, 3, 347-356.

4642. Lokhandwala,M.F., Pariani,H.K., Buckley,J.P., and Jandhyala,B.S. "Involvement of central a-adrenoreceptors in the hypotensive and bradycardic effects of (-)-delta-9-trans-tetrahydrocannabinol." Eur. J. Pharmacol. 1977, 42, 107-112.

4643. Lomax,P. "Acute tolerance to the hypothermic effect of marihuana in the rat." Res. Commun. Chem. Pathol. Pharmacol. 1971, 2, 159-167.

4644. Lomax,P. "Animal pharmacology of marihuana." Proc. West. Pharmacol. Soc. 1971, 14, 10-13.

4645. Lomax,P. "The effect of marihuana on pituitary-thyroid activity in the rat." Agents Actions 1970, 1, 252-257.

4646. Lomax,P. and Campbell,C. "Phenitrone and marihuana induced hypothermia." Exper. 1971, 27, 1191-1192.

4647. Lomax,P., Gross,S.J., and Campbell,C. "Immunological blockade of the hypothermic effect of delta-9-tetrahydrocannabinol in the rat." In Schoenbaum, E.(ed.). Pharmacology of Thermoregulation. E. Karger, Basel, 1973, 488-490.

4648. Lombillo,J.R. and Hain,J.D. "Patterns of drug use in a high school population." Am. J. Psychiat. 1972, 128, 834-841.

4649. Lombrozo,L., Kanter,S.L., and Hollister,L.E. "Marihuana metabolites in urine. VI. Separation of cannabinoids by sequential thin layer chromatography." Res. Commun. Chem. Pathol. Pharmacol. 1976, 15, 697-703.

4650. Lomonaco,T. "Use of drugs by flight personnel during a flight."(It.). Min. Med. 1973, 64, 940-945.

4651. Londergan,S.J., Wilson,R.A., and McGrath,J.H. "Patterns of drug use among adolescents in a rural community." Paper presented at Rural Sociol. Soc. Meet., Denver, 1971.

4652. Long,S. "Michael Stepanian. Interview." High Times 1976, 13, 23-32, 82-83.

4653. Lopes,C.O. Mental Hygiene.(Port.). Pongetti, Rio de Janeiro, 1960.

4654. Lopez,G. and Manuel,L. "Effects of marihuana on sensory function in adolescents."(Sp.). Neurol. Neurocirug. Psiquiat. 1973, 14, 33-40.

4655. Lopez,H.H., Goldman,S.M., Liberman,I.I., and Barnes,D.T. "Cannabis--accidental peroral intoxication." J.A.M.A. 1974, 227, 1041-1042.

4656. Lord,J.R. Marihuana and Personality Change. Lexington Books, Lexington, Mass., 1971.

4657. Lordi,M. The Truth About Marihuana: Stepping Stone to Destruction. Essex County Youth and Economic Rehabilitation Commission, Newark, N.J., 1967.

4658. Lorentz,R.L. "Levels of dogmatism and attitudes toward marihuana." Psychol. Rep. 1972, 30, 75-78.

4659. L'Ortije,M.J.E. "Experimental study of the toxic effect of preparations from substances in cannabis sativa L."(Dut.). *Pharm. Weekbl.* 1972, *107*, 53-64.

4660. Losada,P.A.G. and Lasprillas,J.A. "Tentative method for investigating the presence of residues of marihuana on the hands of addicts, traffickers and pushers of illegal drugs."(Sp.). *Rev. Ecuat. Hig. Med. Trop.* 1969, *26*, 21-24.

4661. Los Angeles Police Department. *Facts About Marihuana*. Narcotic Educational Foundation of America, Los Angeles, 1968.

4662. Losciuto,L.A. and Karlin,R.M. "Correlates of the generation gap." *J. Psychol.* 1972, *81*, 253-262.

4663. Loseva,Z.E. "Change in monoecism resulting from growing conditions."(Rus.). *Selekt Semenovod* 1964, *29*, 38-40.

4664. Lotter,H.L., Abraham,D.J., Turner,C.E., Knapp,J.E., Schiff,P.L., and Slatkin,D.J. "Cannabisativine, a new alkaloid from cannabis sativa L. root." *Tetrahed. Let.* 1975, *33*, 2815-2818.

4665. Lotz,F., Krantz,U., and Korte,F. "Synthesis of delta-8-tetrahydrocannabinol."(Ger.). *Liebig. Ann. Chem.* 1977, *1*, 1132-1140.

4666. Louisiana Commission on Law Enforcement and Administration of Criminal Justice. *Narcotics in Louisiana*. Louisiana Narcotics Crime Control, Baton Rouge, La., 1969.

4667. Louria,D.B. "Chronic cough and bronchial irritation in teen-age drug addict." *J.A.M.A.* 1971, *216*, 337-338.

4668. Louria,D.B. "Drug abuse: A current assessment." *Am. Fam. Phys/GP* 1970, *1*, 76.

4669. Louria,D.B. "Hallucinogens: a growing problem in indiscriminate use. Part II." *Mass. Phys.* 1967, *26*, 1070-1072.

4670. Louria,D.B. "Marihuana and the drug scene." Paper presented at Nat'l. Sympos. on Marihuana, University, Miss., 1974.

4671. Louria,D.B. *Nightmare Drugs*. Simon and Schuster, N.Y., 1966.

4672. Louria,D.B. "Some aspects of the current drug scene: With emphasis on drugs in use by adolescents." *Pediatrics* 1968, *42*, 904-911.

4673. Louria,D.B. The Drug Scene. McGraw-Hill, N.Y., 1968.

4674. Louria,D.B., Baden,M.M., Chinn,M.E., Faison,J.B., Gordon,E., Greenberg,S.S., McCarroll,J.R., and Mayer,H.D. "The dangerous drug problem." N.Y. Med. 1966, 22, 3-8.

4675. Lousberg,R.J.J.C., Bercht,C.A., van Ooyen Ludwig,R., and Spronck,H.J.W. "Cannabinodiol: Conclusive identification and synthesis of a new cannabinoid from cannabis sativa." Phytochem. 1976, 16, 595-597.

4676. Lousberg,R.J.J.C. and Salemink,C.A. "Some aspects of cannabis research." Pharm. Weebl. 1973, 108, 1-9.

4677. Love,H.D. Youth and the Drug Problem. C.C. Thomas, Springfield, Ill., 1971.

4678. Low,M.D. "The neurophysiological basis of the marihuana experience." EEG Clin. Neurophysiol. 1973, 34, 756-757.

4679. Low,M.D., Klonoff,H., and Marcus,A. "The neurophysiological basis of the marihuana experience." Can. Med. Assoc. J. 1973, 108, 157-164.

4680. Lowes,P.D. The Genesis of International Narcotics Control. Librairie Droz, Geneva, 1966.

4681. Lowinger,P. "Psychiatrists' attitudes about marihuana." Am. J. Psychiat. 1971, 127, 970-971.

4682. Lowinger,P. "Psychiatrists, marihuana and the law: A survey." Med. Trial Tech. Quart. 1974, 21, 77-87.

4683. Lowry,W.T. "The forensic taxonomy of cannabis." J. Forens. Sci. 1976, 21, 453-456.

4684. Lowry,W.T. and Garriott,J.C. "On the legality of cannabis; the responsibility of the expert witness." J. Forens. Sci. 1975, 20, 624-629.

4685. Lublinski,A. "Discussion at the medical meeting, Feb. 5, 1883."(Ger.). Deut. Med. Woch. 1883, 9, 178-181.

4686. Lucas,A. "Beam's color test for hashish." Analyst 1933, 58, 602.

4687. Lucas,A. "Some notes on hashish." Cairo Sci. J. 1911, 5, 144-159.

4688. Lucas,W.L., Grupp,S.E., and Schmitt,R.L. "Longitudinal research and marihuana smoking. A successful approach." Criminol. 1974, 5, 315-327.

4689. Lucena,J. "Cannabism and hallucination." (Port.). J. Brazil Psiquiat. 1950, 1, 218-228.

4690. Lucena,J. "Cannabism and hallucinations." (Port.). Neurobiologia 1939, 2, 110-120.

4691. Lucena,J. Chronic Use of Maconha and Psychoses. (Port.). Ministry of Health, Rio de Janeiro, 1958.

4692. Lucena,J. "Smokers of maconha in Pernambuco." (Port.). Arquiv. Assist. Psicopat. 1934, 1, 53-96.

4693. Lucena,J. "Smokers of maconha in Pernambuco." (Port.). Rev. Med. Pernambuco 1935, 5, 355-365, 391-404, 429-441, 467-484.

4694. Lucena,J. "Some new data on maconha smokers." (Port.). Arquiv. Assist. Psicopat. 1935, 1, 197-207.

4695. Lucena,J. "Symptoms of cannabis use."(Port.). Proc. 3rd World Cong. Psychiat. 1961, 1, 401-406.

4696. Lucena,J., Ataide,L., and Coelho,P. "Chronic cannabism and psychoses."(Port.). Neurobiologia 1949, 12, 235-258.

4697. Ludlow,F. "The apocalypse of hasheesh." Putnam's Month. Mag. Am. Lit. Sci. Art 1856, 8, 625-630.

4698. Ludlow,F. The Hasheesh Eater. Being Passages From the Life of a Pythagorean. Harper Bros. N.Y., 1857.

4699. Ludlow,P. "In defense of pot: Confessions of a Canadian marihuana smoker." Sat. Night 1965, 80, 28-29.

4700. Ludwig,A.M. and Levine,J. "Patterns of hallucinogenic drug abuse." J.A.M.A. 1965, 191, 92-96.

4701. Ludwig,A.M. and Pyle,R.L. "Danger potential of commonly abused drugs." Wisconsin Med. J. 1969, 68, 216.

4702. Luetgert,M.J. and Armstrong,A.H. "Methodological issues in drug surveys: anonymity, recency, and frequency." Internat'l. J. Addict. 1973, 8, 683-689.

4703. Lukas,M.C. and Temple,D.M. "Some effects of chronic cannabis treatment." Aust. J. Pharmaceut. Sci. 1974, NS3, 20-23.

4704. Lum,E.A. "Native African medicine." Pharmaceut. J. 1949, 163, 128-129.

4705. Lundberg,G.D. "Adulteration of 'street drugs'." J.A.M.A. 1973, 225, 758.

4706. Lundberg,G.D., Adelson,J., and Prosnitz,E.H. "Marihuana-induced hospitalization." J.A.M.A. 1971, 215, 121.

4707. Lundberg,G.D., Gupta,R.C., and Montgomery,S. "A street drug identification program." Lab. Med. 1974, 5, 8-10.

4708. Lussana,F. "Some effects of hashish."(It.). Gaz. Med. Lombard. 1851, 2, 441-442.

4709. Luthra,Y.K. and Rosenkrantz,H. "Cannabinoids: Neurochemical aspects after oral chronic administration to rats." Toxicol. Appl. Pharmacol. 1974, 27, 158-168.

4710. Luthra,Y.K., Rosenkrantz,H., and Braude,M.C. "Cerebral and cerebellar neurochemical changes and behavioral manifestations in rats chronically exposed to marihuana smoke." Toxicol. Appl. Pharmacol. 1976, 35, 455-456.

4711. Luthra,Y.K., Rosenkrantz,H., and Heyman,I.A. "Levels of rat brain protein, RNA and glycolytic metabolites after oral administration of delta-9-tetrahydrocannabinol." Paper presented at Am. Chem. Soc., Chicago, 1973.

4712. Luthra,Y.K., Rosenkrantz,H., Heyman,I.A., and Braude,M.C. "Differential neurochemistry and temporal pattern in rats treated orally with delta-9-tetrahydrocannabinol for periods up to six months." Toxicol. Appl. Pharmacol. 1975, 32, 418-431.

4713. Lyle,M.A. "Synthesis and characterization of glucuronides of cannabinol, cannabidiol, delta-9-tetrahydrocannabinol." Biomed. Mass Spectrom. 1977, 4, 190-196.

4714. Lyman,R. "Review of 'Marihuana, America's New Drug Problem'." Am. J. Pharmaceut. Educat. 1939, 3, 10.

4715. Lynch,J.R. "A case of accidental poisoning by seven minims and half of tincture of cannabis indica. Recovery." Lancet 1871, 2, 493.

4716. Lynch,V. "An analysis of proposed therapeutic applications of cannabis sativa." Comm. Prob. Drug Depend. 1970, 3, 6556-6563.

4717. Lynch,W.C., Ferraro,D.P., and Grilly,D.M. "Behavioral effects of minimum doses of marihuana extract distillate." Rocky Mt. Psychol. Assoc. 1971, 1, 1-6.

4718. Lyons,A.B. "Resolution standard for cannabis." J.A.P.A. 1917, 6, 877-879.

4719. Lyons,J., Ferraro,D.P., Lyons,J.E., Sullivan,J.G., and Downey,D. "Effects of delta-9-tetrahydrocannabinol on stimulus control." Psychon. Sci. 1973, 2, 302-304.

4720. Lys,P. "Indian hemp in Lebanon."(Fr.). Ann. Fac. Med. Pharm. Beyrouth 1932, 1, 333-343.

4721. Lyushinskii,W. "Comparative physiological evaluation of different ecological types of cannabis." (Rus.). Tr. Priklad. Bot. Genet. Selekt. 1963, 35, 204-210.

M

4722. Maben,T. "Cannabis indica and digitalis." Pharmaceut. J. 1902, 14, 281.

4723. Maben,T. "Note on cannabis indica." Pharmaceut. J. 1902, 15, 131.

4724. Mabileau,J.F. "The patterns of drug abuse in France." In Btesh,S.(ed.). Drug Abuse. Plenum Press, N.Y., 1972, 104-110.

4725. MacAvoy,M.G. and Marks,D.F. "Divided attention performance of cannabis users and non-users following cannabis and alcohol." Psychopharmacol. 1975, 44, 147-152.

4726. MacCannell,K.L., Clark,S.C., Karr,G.W., Milstein,S.L., and van Petten, G. "Cardiovascular responses to marihuana in man." In Sellers,E.M.(ed.). Clinical Pharmacology of Psychoactive Drugs. Addiction Res. Found., Toronto, 1975, 127-145.

4727. MacCraken,W.H. "Cannabis sativa." J. Michigan Med. Soc. 1937, 36, 848-849.

4728. MacDonald,A.D. "Chairman's concluding remarks." In Wolstenholme,G.E.W. and Knight,J.(eds.). Hashish: Its Chemistry and Pharmacology. Ciba Found. Study Group, J. and A. Churchill, London, 1965, 93.

4729. MacDonald,A.D. "Drug dependence in Britain." Current Med. Drugs 1966, 6, 23-30.

4730. MacDonald,A.D. "The actions and uses of hemp drugs." Nature 1941, 147, 167-168.

4731. MacDonald,A.D., Walls,R.T., and LeBlanc,R. "College female drug users." Adolescence 1973, 8, 189-196.

4732. MacDonald,N. "Hemp and imperial defence." Can. Hist. Rev. 1936, 17, 385-398.

4733. Machata,G. "Analytical procedure for identification and estimation of hashish(marihuana)."(Ger.). Arch. Toxikol. 1969, 25, 19-26.

4734. Machata,G. and Krypspin-Exner,K. "Detection of hashish in urine following experimental ingestion." (Ger.). Klin. Woch. 1970, 82, 849.

4735. Machbert,G. and Lukowica,A. "presence of hashish."(Ger.). Pharm. Ztg. 1971, 116, 517-523.

4736. Macintosh,M. "Drugs."(Dut.). Ons. Gezin. 1970, 36, 42-45.

4737. MacKenzie,N. Dreams and Dreaming. Aldus, London, 1965.

4738. MacKenzie,S. "On the special therapeutic value of Indian hemp in certain morbid conditions."(Fr.). Semaine Med. 1894, 14, 399-400.

4739. MacKenzie,S. "Remarks on the value of Indian hemp in the treatment of a certain type of headache." Br. Med. J. 1887, 1, 97-98.

4740. MacLagan,H. "Extract of cannabis india." Am. Drug. 1884, 13, 121-122.

4741. MacLean,K.I. and Littleton,J.M. "Environmental stress as a factor in the response of rat brain catecholamine metabolism to delta-8-tetrahydrocannabinol." Eur. J. Pharmacol. 1977, 41, 171-182.

4742. Mader,R. and Sluga,W. "Changes in the picture of drug addiction in adolescents."(Ger.). Wien. Med. 1970, 120, 330-333.

4743. Madinaveitia,A., Russell,P.B., and Todd,A.R. "Cannabis indica. Pt. XI. An examination of the alkali-soluble portion of American hemp resin." J. Chem. Soc. 1942, 1, 628-630.

4744. Madson,P.F. "Marihuana paranoia." Chem. Engin. News 1970, 48, 12.

4745. Maehly,A. "Chemical methods in criminal technology." Kem. Tidskr. 1974, 86, 38-40.

4746. Magence,D.N. and Petzel,T.P. "Evaluation of the reported effects of marihuana use." J. Alter. States Conscious. 1975, 2, 147-160.

4747. Magour,S., Coper,H., and Fahndrich,C. "An attempt to correlate the development of tolerance to delta-9-tetrahyrocannabinol and d-amphetamine with their subcellular distribution in rat brain." Pol. J. Pharmacol. 1976, 28, 589-592.

4748. Magour,S., Coper,H., and Fahndrich,C. "Is tolerance to delta-9-THC cellular or metabolic?" Psychopharmacol. 1977, 51, 141-145.

4749. Magour,S., Coper,H., Fahndrich,C., and Hill,R. "Relationship between the subcellular distribution of delta-9-tetrahydrocannabinol and its metabolites in rat brain and the duration of the effect on motor activity." Life Sci. 1976, 18, 575-584.

4750. Magre,M. The Night of Hashish and Opium.(Fr.). Flammarion, Paris, 1929.

4751. Maguire,J. "Trip or tragedy?" Hlth. News 1968, 45, 3.

4752. Magus,R.D. and Harris,L.S. "Carcinogenic potential of marihuana smoke condensate." Fed. Proc. 1971, 30, 279.

4753. Mahabir,W. "History of the psychedelic drug experience." Can. Psychiat. Assoc. J. 1968, 13, 189-190.

4754. Mahfouz,M., Makar,A.B., Ghoneim,M.T., and Mather,M.M. "Effect of hashish on brain gamma aminobutyric acid system, blood fibrinolytic activity and glucose and some serum enzymes in the rat."(Ger.). Pharmazie 1975, 30, 772-774.

4755. Mahi,T.E. "Portrait of a hashish smoker." Wld. Hlth. 1960, 1, 24-25.

4756. Mahoney,J.M. and Harris,R.A. "Effect of delta-9-tetrahydrocannabinol on mitrochondrial processes." Biochem. Pharmacol. 1972, 21, 1217-1226.

4757. Maier,R. and Maitre,L. "Steroidogenic and lipolytic effects of cannabinoids in the rat and the rabbit." Biochem. Pharmacol. 1975, 24, 1695-1699.

4758. Mair,W. "Indian hemp." Pharmaceut. Era 1898, 20, 281-282.

4759. Mair,W. "The cultivation and manufacture of the official cannabis indica." Pharmaceut. J. 1900, 11, 732-733.

4760. Maitre,L. "Effects of some cannabinols on biosynthesis of brain amines and on pituitary response in the rat." Act. Pharmaceut. Suec. 1971, 8, 693-694.

4761. Maitre,L., Baumann,P.A., and Delini-Stula,A. "Neurochemical tolerance to cannabinols." In Paton,W.D.M. and Crown,J.(eds.). Cannabis and its Derivatives. Oxford Univ. Press, London, 1972, 101-117.

4762. Maitre,L., Staehelin,M., and Bein,H.J. "Effect of an extract of cannabis and of some cannabinols on catecholamine metabolism in rat brain and heart." Agents Actions 1970, 1, 136-143.

4763. Maitre,L., Waldmeier,P.C., and Baumann,P.A. "Effects of some tetrahydrocannabinols on the biosynthesis and utilization of catecholamines in the rat brain." In Usdin,E. and Snyder,S.H.(eds.). Frontiers in Catecholamine Research. Pergamon Press, N.Y., 1973, 1015-1020.

4764. Makris,K. The History of Hashish.(Gr.). Athens, 1927.

4765. Malcolm,A.I. The Case Against the Drugged Mind. Clarke, Irwin Co., Toronto, 1973.

4766. Malcolm,A.I. "Drug abuse and social alienation." Today's Educat. 1970, 59, 28-31.

4767. Malcolm,A.I. "Marihuana research." Can. Med. Assoc. J. 1973, 108, 824-825.

4768. Malcolm,A.I. "Some behavioral aspects of drug dependence." Can. J. Pub. Hlth. 1969, 60, 159-163.

4769. Malhotra,M.K. "Cannabis experience of Wuppertal pupils."(Ger.). Psychopharmacol. 1973, 33, 349-354.

4770. Malik,O.P., Kapil,R.S., and Anand,N. "Studies on cannabinoids. Part I. Synthesis of 5-hydroxy-2,2-dimethyl-7-n-pentylchromene, trans-3-n-butyl-5-hydroxy-2,2,4-trimethyl-7-n-pentylchroman and some related compounds." Ind. J. Chem. 1976, 14B, 449-454.

4771. Malik,O.P., Kapil,R.S., and Anand,N. "Studies on cannabinoids. Part II. Synthesis of trans-6a,7,12,12a-tetrahydro-6,6-dimethyl-3-n-pentyl-6H-benzol(b)naphtho (2,3-d)pyran-1-ol and some related compounds." Ind. J. Chem. 1976, 14B, 455-458.

4772. Malik,O.P., Kapil,R.S., and Anand,N. "Studies on cannabinoids. Part III. Synthesis of 9,10,11,11a-tetrahydro-6H,8H-pyridol(1,2-c)(1,3)benzoxazine." Ind. J. Chem. 1976, 14B, 975-978.

4773. Malingre,T., Hendriks,H., Batterman,S., Bos,R., and Visser,J. "The essential oil of cannabis sativa." Plant. Med. 1975, 28, 56-61.

4774. Malinovskii,S.M. "Stimulation of hemp seed(cannabis sativa L.)."(Rus.). Mem. Inst. Agron. Lenin 1927, 4, 289-348.

4775. Malit,L.A., Johnstone,R.E., Bourke,D., Kulp,R.A., Lein,V., and Smith,T.C. "Intravenous delta-9-tetrahydrocannabinol: Effects of ventilatory control and cardiovascular dynamics." Anesthesiology 1975, 42, 666-673.

4776. Malloy,K.P., Buckley,J.P., and Jandhyala,B.S. "Influence of several anesthetic agents on the effects of delta-9-tetrahydrocannabinol on heart rate(HR) in mongrel dogs." Pharmacologist 1976, 18, 301.

4777. Malor,R., Jackson,D.M., and Chesher,G.B. "The effect of delta-9-tetrahydrocannabinol, cannabidiol and cannabinol on ether anesthesia in mice." J. Pharm. Pharmacol. 1975, 27, 610-612.

4778. Malowan,L.S. "Chemistry and pharmacology of cannabis sativa from Panama."(Ger.). Arch. Internat'l. Pharmacodyn. Ther. 1938, 276, 150-154.

4779. Mamede,E.B. "Maconha--opium of the poor."(Port.). Neurobiologia 1945, 8, 71-93.

4780. Man,D.P. and Consroe,P.F. "Anticonvulsant effect of delta-9-tetrahydrocannabinol on sound-induced seizures in audiogenic rats." Int. Res. Commun. Med. Sci. 1973, 1, 12.

4781. Manasseh,A.J. "Symptoms of poisoning from a small dose of tincture of cannabis indica." Lancet 1899, 1, 723.

4782. Mandalena,J.C. "The problem of psychotropic drug dependence and its importance to the medical and pharmaceutic authority service."(Port.). Folha Med. 1967, 54, 115.

4783. Mandel,J. "Hashish, assassins, and the love of God." Iss. Criminol. 1966, 2, 149-156.

4784. Mandel,J. "Myths and realities of marihuana pushing." In Simmons,J.(ed.). Marihuana, Myths and Realities. Brandon House, Berkeley, 1967, 58-110.

4785. Mandel,J. "Who says marihuana use leads to heroin addiction?" J. Second. Educat. 1968, 43, 211-216.

4786. Mandell,A.J. "Drugs that move the mind." Trauma 1968, 9, 73-115.

4787. Mandell,A.J. and West,L.J. "Hallucinogens." In Freedman,A.M.(ed.). Human Behavior: Biology, Psychology, Sociology. Athenum, N.Y., 1972.

4788. Mandell,S.R. "Looking at the law." Marihuana Month. 1976, 2, 14.

4789. Manheimer,D.E. and Mellinger,G.D. "Marihuana use among urban adults." Science 1969, 166, 1544-1545.

4790. Manheimer,D.I., Millinger,G.D., and Balter,M.B. "Use of marihuana in the urban cross-section of adults." In Wittenborn,J.R., Smith,J.P., and Wittenborn,S.A.(eds.). Communications and Drug Use. C.C. Thomas, Springfield, Ill., 1970, 225-243.

4791. Mann,P.E.G., Cohen,A.B., Finley,T.N., and Ladman,A.J. "Alveolar macrophages. Structural and functional differences between nonsmokers and smokers of marihuana and tobacco." Lab. Invest. 1971, 25, 111-120.

4792. Mann,P.E.G., Finley,T.N., and Ladman,A.J. "Marihuana smoking: A study of its effects on alveolar lining material and pulmonary macrophages recovered by bronchopulmonary lavage." J. Clin. Invest. 1970, 49, 60a-61a.

4793. Mann,T. "Effects of pharmacological agents on male sexual functions." J. Reprod. Fert. 1968, 4, 101-114.

4794. Mann,T. "Hashish."(Ger.). Deut. Milit. 1942, 7, 410-412.

4795. Manniche,E. and Hogh,E. "Factors in the diffusion of hashish etc. in suburban areas."(Dan.). Sociol. Med. 1967, 12, 71-84.

4796. Manniche,E. and Hogh,E. "Hashish use among Danish urban youth."(Dan.). Sociol. Med. 1967, 12, 61-67.

4797. Manniche,E. and Hogh,E. "What do you think about hashish?"(Dan.). Tid. Sygepeljersk. 1968, 68, 383-385.

4798. Manning,F.J. "Acute tolerance to the effects of delta-9-tetrahydrocannabinol on spaced responding by monkeys." Pharmacol. Biochem. Behav. 1973, 1, 665-671.

4799. Manning,F.J. "Chronic delta-9-tetrahydrocannabinol. Transient and lasting effects on avoidance behavior." Pharmacol. Biochem. Behav. 1976, 4, 17-21.

4800. Manning,F.J. "Role of experience in acquisition and loss of tolerance to the effect of delta-9-THC on spaced responding." Pharmacol. Biochem. Behav. 1976, 5, 269-273.

4801. Manning,F.J. "Tolerance to effects of delta-9-tetrahydrocannabinol on free operant shock avoidance." Fed. Proc. 1974, 33, 481.

4802. Manning,F.J., McDonough,J.H., Elsmore,T.F., Saller,C., and Sodetz,F.J. "Inhibition of normal growth by chronic administration of delta-9-tetrahydrocannabinol." Science 1971, 174, 424-426.

4803. Manning,F.J. and Elsmore,T.F. "Delta-9-tetrahydrocannabinol effects on operant responding maintained by nutritive and non-nutritive reinforcers." Proc. 5th Internat'l. Cong. Pharmacol. 1972, 1, 218.

4804. Manning,F.J. and Elsmore,T.F. "Shock-elicited fighting and delta-9-tetrahydrocannabinol." Psychopharmacol. 1972, 25, 218-228.

4805. Manno,J.E., Kiplinger,G.F., Bennett,I., and Forney,R.B. "Human motor and mental performance under the influence of alcohol and/or marihuana." Toxicol. Appl. Pharmacol. 1970, 17, 306.

4806. Manno,J.E., Kiplinger,G.F., and Forney,R.B. "The influence of alcohol and marihuana on motor and mental performance." Clin. Pharmacol. Ther. 1971, 12, 202-211.

4807. Manno,J.E., Kiplinger,G.F., Haine,S.E., Bennett,I.F., and Forney,R.B. "Comparative effects of smoking marihuana or placebo on human motor and mental performance." Clin. Pharmacol. Ther. 1970, 11, 808-815.

4808. Manno,J.E., Kiplinger,G.F., Scholz,N., and Forney,R.B. "The influence of alcohol and marihuana on motor and mental performance." Clin. Pharmacol. Ther. 1971, 12, 202-211.

4809. Manno,J.E. and Manno,B.R. "The interaction of delta-9-tetrahydrocannabinol, pentobarbital and SKF-525A with the cardiovascular system of the rat." Fed. Proc. 1973, 32, 755.

4810. Manno,J.E., Manno,B.R., Kiplinger,G.F., and Forney,R.B. "Motor and mental performance with marihuana: Relationship to administered dose of delta-9-tetrahydrocannabinol and its interaction with alcohol." In Miller,L.L.(ed.). Marihuana, Effects on Human Behavior. Academic Press, N.Y., 1974, 45-71.

4811. Manno,J.E., Turk,R.F., Kiplinger,G., Bennett,I., Richards,A., and Forney,R.B. "Effect of smoking marihuana on motor and mental performance in humans." Pharmacologist 1969, 11, 278.

4812. Mansfeld,R. Hemp Culture.(Ger.). Akademie Verlag, Berlin, 1959.

4813. Mantilla-Plata,B., Clewe,G.L., and Harbison,R.D. "Delta-9-tetrahydrocannabinol-induced changes in prenatal growth and development in mice." Toxicol. Appl. Pharmacol. 1975, 33, 333-340.

4814. Mantilla-Plata,B. and Harbison,R. "Alteration of delta-9-tetrahydrocannabinol-induced prenatal toxicity by phenobarbital and SKF-525A." In Nahas,G.G., Paton,W.D.M., and Idanpaan-Heikkila,J.E.(eds.). Marihuana. Springer-Verlag, N.Y., 1976, 469-481.

4815. Mantilla-Plata,B. and Harbison,R.D. "Distribution studies of ^{14}C-delta-9-tetrahydrocannabinol in mice: Effect of vehicle, route of administration, and duration of treatment." Toxicol. Appl. Pharmacol. 1975, 34, 292-300.

4816. Mantilla-Plata,B. and Harbison,R.D. "Effects of phenobarbital and SKF-525A pretreatment, sex, liver injury, and vehicle on delta-9-tetrahydrocannabinol toxicity." Toxicol. Appl. Pharmacol. 1974, 27, 123-130.

4817. Mantilla-Plata,B. and Harbison,R.D. "Influence of alteration of tetrahydrocannabinol metabolism on tetrahydrocannabinol-induced teratogenesis." In Braude, M.C. and Szara,S.(eds.). Pharmacology of Marihuana. Raven Press, N.Y., 1976, 2, 733-743.

4818. Mantilla-Plata,B. and Harbison,R.D. "Phenobarbital and SKF525A effect on delta-9-tetrahydrocannabinol(THC) toxicity and distribution in mice." Pharmacologist 1971, 13, 297.

4819. Mantz,H.W. "Cannabis sativa. I. Pharmaceutical studies on the fruits." Pa. Pharmacist 1937, 18, 35.

4820. Mercandier,N. Treatise on Hemp.(Fr.). Lyon, Paris, 1758.

4821. Marcotte,D.B. "Marihuana and mutism." Am. J. Psychiat. 1972, 129, 475-477.

4822. Marcotte,J., Skelton,F.S., Cote,M.G., and Witschi,H. "Induction of aryl hydrocarbon hydroxylase in rat lung by marihuana smoke." Toxicol. Appl. Pharmacol. 1975, 33, 231-245.

4823. Marcotte,J. and Witschi,H.P. "Induction of pulmonary aryl hydrocarbon hydroxylase by marihuana." Res. Commun. Chem. Pathol. Pharmacol. 1972, 4, 561-568.

4824. Marcovitz,E. "Marihuana problems." J.A.M.A. 1945, 129, 378.

4825. Marcovitz,E. and Myers,H.J. "The marihuana addict in the army." War. Med. 1944, 6, 382-391.

4826. Marcus,A.M., Klonoff,J., and Low,M. "Psychiatric status of the marihuana user." Can. Psychiat. Assoc. J. 1974, 19, 31-39.

4827. Marderosian,A. "Psychotomimetics and their abuse." Am. J. Pharmacol. 1968, 140, 83-96.

4828. Margara,J. "Variation of endogenous gibberellic activity following the reduction of photoperiod in cannabis sativa L."(Fr.). Ann. Physiol. Veget. 1965, 7, 41.

4829. Margetts,S. "Pot smoking young executives." D. Ins. 1970, 95, 42-43.

4830. Margolis,C.G. "Personality and social factors predisposing to drug abuse." Am. J. Pharmacol. 1970, 142, 146-150.

4831. Margolis,J.S. and Clorfene,R. A Child's Garden of Grass. Pocket Books, N.Y., 1972.

4832. Margolis-Kazan,H. and Blamire,J. "The effect of delta-9-tetrahydrocannabinol on cytoplasmic DNA metabolism." Biochem. Biophys. Res. Commun. 1977, 76, 674-681.

4833. Marie,A. "Hashish madness."(Fr.). Nov. Icon. Salpetr. 1907, 20, 252-257.

4834. Marin,G. "Psychosocial aspects of use of marihuana."(Sp.). Rev. InterAm. Psicol. 1974, 8, 117-124.

4835. Marino-Zucco,F. and Vignolo,G. "On the alkaloids of cannabis indica and cannabis sativa."(It.). Gaz. Chim. Ital. 1895, 25, 262-268.

4836. Marks,B.H. "Delta-1-tetrahydrocannabinol and luteinizing hormone secretion." Prog. Brain Res. 1973, 39, 331-338.

4837. Marks,V., Teale,D., and Fry,D. "Detection of cannabis products in urine by radioimmunoassay." Br. Med. J. 1975, 3, 348-349.

4838. Marks,V., Teale,J.D., and King,L.J. "Radioimmunoassay of cannabis products in blood and urine." In Nahas,G.G., Paton,W.D.M., and Idanpaan-Heikkila,J.E.(eds.). Marihuana. Springer Verlag, N.Y., 1976, 71-85.

4839. Marra,E.F. Intoxicant Drugs: Survey of Student Use, Roles and Policies of the University. University Committee on Drugs and the Campus, State Univ. of N.Y. at Buffalo, Buffalo, 1968.

4840. Marsh,R. "The Illinois hemp project at Polo in World War II." J. Ill. Hist. Soc. 1967, 60, 391-410.

4841. Marshall,C.R. "A contribution to the pharmacology of cannabis indica." J.A.M.A. 1898, 31, 882-891.

4842. Marshall,C.R. "A review of recent work on cannabis indica." Pharmaceut. J. 1902, 15, 131-132.

4843. Marshall,C.R. "Cannabis indica." Pharmaceut. J. 1902, 14, 362.

4844. Marshall,C.R. "Cannabis indica." Pharmaceut. J. 1902, 15, 263.

4845. Marshall,C.R. "Experiments on the cause of the loss of activity of Indian hemp." Pharmaceut. J. 1909, 28, 418.

4846. Marshall,C.R. "Note on the pharmacological action of cannabis resin." Proc. Cambridge Phil. Soc. 1896, 1, 149-150.

4847. Marshall,C.R. "Report on the standardization of preparations of Indian hemp." Br. Med. J. 1911, 2, 1171.

4848. Marshall,C.R. "The active principle of Indian hemp: A preliminary communication." Lancet 1897, 1, 235-238.

4849. Marshall,C.R. "The pharmacology of cannabis indica." Br. Med. J. 1899, 2, 1449-1450.

4850. Marshall,C.R. "The pharmacology of cannabis indica." Br. Med. J. 1899, 2, 1708.

4851. Marshall,C.R. and Wigner,J.H. "Standardization of preparation of Indian hemp." Pharmaceut. J. 1911, 32, 739-740.

4852. Marshall,C.R. and Wood,J.K. "On the standardization of preparations of Indian hemp. Part II. The value of 'acetyl number'." Br. Med. J. 1912, 1, 1234.

4853. Marshall,C.R. and Wood,J.K. "Uselessness of acetylization for the standardization of Indian hemp." Pharmaceut. J. 1912, 35, 201.

4854. Marshall,M.A. "Marihuana." Am. Scholar 1958, 8, 95-101.

4855. Marshman,J.A. "Chemical and biochemical methods of drug detection and measurement." In Gibbins, R.J., Israel,Y., Kalant,H., Popham,R.E., Schmidt,W., and Smart,R.G.(eds.). Research Advances in Alcohol and Drug Problems. J. Wiley and Sons, N.Y., 1974, 33-92.

4856. Marshman,J.A. and Gibbins,R.J. "A note on the composition of illicit drugs." Ont. Med. Rev. 1970, 1, 1-3.

4857. Marshman,J.A. and Gibbins,R.J. "The credibility gap in the illicit drug market." Addictions 1969, 16, 22-25.

4858. Marshman,J.A., Popham,R.E., and Yawney,C.D. "A note on the cannabinoid of Jamaican ganja." Bull. Narc. 1976, 28, 63-68.

4859. Marshman,J.A. and Walther,K. "Street drug information for health care personnel. A preliminary report." In Marshman,J.A.(ed.). Street Drug Analysis and Its Social and Clinical Implications. Addict. Res. Found., Toronto, 1974, 79-101.

4860. Marten,G.W. "Adverse reaction to the use of marihuana." J. Tennessee Med. Assoc. 1969, 62, 627-630.

4861. Martens,S. "International aspects of cannabis."(Swed.). Lakartidningen 1976, 73, 3874-3875.

4862. Martin,B., Agurell,S., Nordquist,M., and Lindgren,J.E. "Dioxygenated metabolites of cannabidiol formed by rat liver." J. Pharm. Pharmacol. 1976, 28, 603-608.

4863. Martin,B., Agurell,S, and Rieger,H. "Perfusion of the isolated rat brain with ^{14}C-delta-1-tetrahydrocannabinol." Biochem. Pharmacol. 1977, 26, 2307-2309.

4864. Martin,B., Nordquist,M., Agurell,S., Lindren, J.E., Leander,K., and Binder,M. "Identification of monohydroxylated metabolites of cannabidiol formed by rat liver." J. Pharm. Pharmacol. 1976, 28, 275-279.

4865. Martin,B.R., Dewey,W.L., Aceto,M.D., Adams,M.D., Earnhardt,J.T., and Carney,J.M. "A potent antinociceptive cannabinoid which lacks opiate substitution properties." Res. Commun. Chem. Pathol. Pharmacol. 1977, 16, 187-190.

4866. Martin,B.R., Dewey,W.L., Harris,L.S., and Beckner,J.S. "^{3}H-delta-9-tetrahydrocannabinol tissue and subcellular distribution in the central nervous system and tissue distribution in peripheral organs of tolerant and nontolerant dogs." J. Pharmacol. Exper. Ther. 1976, 196, 128-144.

4867. Martin,B.R., Dewey,W.L., Harris,L.S., and Beckner,J.S. "Subcellular localization of ^{3}H-delta-9-tetrahydrocannabinol in dog brain after acute or chronic administration." Pharmacologist 1974, 16, 260.

4868. Martin,B.R., Dewey,W.L., Harris,L.S., Beckner,J., Wilson,R.S., and May,E.L. "Marihuana-like activity of new synthetic tetrahydrocannabinols." Pharmacol. Biochem. Behav. 1975, 3, 849-853.

4869. Martin,B.R., Harvey,D.J., and Martin,B.R. "Biotransformation of cannabidiol in mice. Identification of new acid metabolites." Drug Metab. Disposit. 1977, 5, 259-267.

4870. Martin,I., Heghies,A., and Martin,I. "Some economic aspects of bundle hemp."(Ruman.). Probleme Agricole 1973, 8, 30-38.

4871. Martin,L., Smith,D.M., and Farmilo,C.G. "Essential oil from fresh cannabis sativa and its use in identification." Nature 1961, 191, 774-776.

4872. Martin,M.A. "Ethnobotanical aspects of culture in Southeast Asia." In Rubin,V.(ed.). Cannabis and Culture. Mouton, The Hague, 1975, 63-77.

4873. Martin,P. and Consroe,P. "Cannabinoid induced behavioral convulsions in rabbits." Science 1976, 194, 965-967.

4874. Martin,P.A. "Cannabis and chromosomes." Lancet 1969, 1, 370.

4875. Martin,P.A., Thorburn,J.J., and Bryant,S.A. "In vivo and in vitro studies of cytogenetic effects of cannabis sativa in rats and men." Teratology 1974, 9, 81-85.

4876. Martin,W. "Some experiences in the testing of drugs by biochemical methods with special reference to digitalis squill, and strophanthus." Pharmaceut. J. 1909, 29, 149-153.

4877. Martinec,T. and Felklova,M. "Change of the antibacterial activity in the course of the individual development of hemp(cannabis sativa L.)."(Ger.). Pharmazie 1959, 14, 279-281.

4878. Martinec,T. and Felklova,M. "Influence of various kinds of fertilizers on anti-bacterial action of hemp(cannabis sativa L.)."(Ger.). Pharmazie 1959, 14, 276-279.

4879. Martinez,J.L., Stadnicki,S.W., and Schaeppi,U.H. "Delta-9-tetrahydrocannabinol: Effect of i.v. infusion upon EEG and behavior of unrestrained rhesus monkeys." Pharmacologist 1971, 13, 246.

4880. Martinez,J.L., Stadnicki,S.W., and Schaeppi,U.H. "Delta-9-tetrahydrocannabinol: Effects on EEG and behavior of rhesus monkeys." Life Sci. 1972, 11, 643-651.

4881. Martino,E.R. "Attitudes, beliefs, and behavior: A further test of Fishbein's model for reducing discrepancies." Diss. Abs. 1974, 34, 4090.

4882. Martino,E.R. and Truss,C.V. "Drug use and attitudes toward social and legal aspects of marihuana in a large metropolitan university." J. Counsel. Psychol. 1973, 20, 120-126.

4883. Martino,E.R. and Truss,C.V. "Drug use and attitudes toward social and legal aspects of marihuana in a large metropolitan university." Paper presented at Southeast. Psychol. Assoc., Atlanta, 1972.

4884. Martz,R. "The effect of marihuana on auditory thresholds." J. Aud. Res. 1972, 12, 146-148.

4885. Martz,R., Brown,D.J., Forney,R.B., Bright,T.P., Kiplinger,G.F., and Rodda,B.E. "Propranolol antagonism of marihuana induced tachycardia." Life Sci. 1972, 2, 999-1005.

4886. Marx,G. "Marihuana and motivation." Science 1972, 176, 8.

4887. Marx,H. "Clinical study on effects of hashish. III. Disturbances of metabolism."(Ger.). Nervenzrzt 1932, 5, 346-350.

4888. Marx,H. and Eckhardt,G. "Animal experiments investigating the effects of hashish."(Ger.). Arch. Expt'l. Pharmaceut. Pharmacol. 1933, 170, 395-406.

4889. Marx,M.R. "Residual effects of recurrent use of marihuana on immediate and short-term memory processes. With special reference to LSD." Diss. Abs. 1974, 34, 3468-3469.

4890. Marx-Skliar,N. and Iwanow,R. "Anascha intoxication."(Ger.). Zeit. Psychiat. 1932, 98, 300-330.

4891. Mascherpa,P. and Bazzi,M. "Effect of cannabis indica on respiration."(It.). Boll. Soc. Ital. Biol. Speriment. 1940, 15, 856-857.

4892. Mascherpa,P. and Bazzi,M. "Respiratory effects of cannabis sativa L. var. indica Lam."(Ger.). Arch. Expt'l. Pharmaceut. Pharmacol. 1941, 197, 306-312.

4893. Maser,J.D., Gallup,G.G., Thorn,W.R., and Edson,P.H. "Relative potency of tetrahydrocannabinol derivatives on tonic immobility in chickens." Pharmacol. Biochem. Behav. 1975, 3, 1069-1072.

4894. Maskarinec,M.P., Alexander,G., and Novotny,M. "Analysis of the acidic fraction of marihuana smoke condensate by capillary gas chromatography-mass spectrometry." J. Chromatog. 1976, 126, 559-568.

4895. Maslov,E.V. and Streljuchin,A.K. "Schizophrenic clinical aspects of acute and chronic hashish intoxication." (Rus.). Nevropatol. Psikhiat. 1937, 6, 85-90.

4896. Mason,J.S. "Goa; an addendum; hashish trail at Katmandu, Nepal." Nature 1971, 223, 1255.

4897. Mason,M.M. and Thompson,G.R. "Marihuana related pathology in rats." Toxicol. Appl. Pharmacol. 1972, 22, 321.

4898. Mason,P. "Drug dependence caused by non-narcotics." Yearbook Med. Publish. 1967, 2, 383-388.

4899. Masoud,A.N. and Doorenbos,N.J. "Mississippi grown cannabis sativa L. III. Cannabinoid and cannabinoic acid content." J. Pharmaceut. Sci. 1973, 62, 313-315.

4900. Masoud,A.N., Doorenbos,N.J., Fetterman,P., and Quimby,M.W. "Mississippi grown cannabis sativa L. Effects of gibberellic acid and indoleacetic acid." Paper presented at Am. Pharmaceut. Assoc., Washington, 1970.

4901. Masoud,A.N., Doorenbos,N.J., and Quimby,M.W. "Mississippi grown cannabis sativa L. IV. Effect of gibberellic acid and indole acetic acid." J. Pharmaceut. Sci. 1973, 62, 316-318.

4902. Massett,L. "Marihuana and behavior: the unfilled gaps." Sci. News 1970, 97, 156-158.

4903. Masters,R.E.L. and Houston,J. Psychedelic Art. Grove Press, N.Y., 1968.

4904. Masters,R.E.L. and Houston,J. The Varieties of Psychedelic Experience. Holt, Rinehart and Winston, N.Y., 1966.

4905. Masur,J. "Labor division of rats under the influence of prolonged administration of (-)-delta-9-trans-tetrahydrocannabinol." Pharmacol. 1973, 9, 35-40.

4906. Masur,J. "Modification of behavior of working rats during chronic administration of (-)-delta-9-trans-tetrahydrocannabinol."(Port.). Cienc. Cult. 1973, 25, 753-754.

4907. Masur,J., Karniol,I.G., and Palermo Neto,J. "Cannabis sativa induces 'winning' behavior in previously 'loser' rats." J. Pharm. Pharmacol. 1972, 24, 262.

4908. Masur,J. and Khazan,N. "Induction by cannabis sativa(marihuana) of rhythmic spike discharges overriding REM sleep electrocorticogram in the rat." Life Sci. 1970, 9, 1275-1280.

4909. Masur,J. and Martz,R.M.W. "The behavior of worker and nonworker rats under the influence of acute and prolonged administration of delta-9-THC." Proc. 5th Internat'l. Cong. Pharmacol. 1972, 1, 152.

4910. Masur,J., Martz,R.M.W., Bieniek,D., and Korte,F. "Influence of (-)-delta-9-trans-tetrahydro-cannabinol and mescaline on the behavior or rats submitted to food competition situations." Psychopharmacol. 1971, 22, 187-194.

4911. Masur,J., Martz,R.M.W., and Carlini,E.A. "Effects of acute and chronic administration of cannabis sativa and (-)-delta-9-trans-tetrahydrocannabinol on the behavior of rats in an open field area." Psychopharmacol. 1971, 19, 388-397.

4912. Masur,J., Martz,R.M.W., and Carlini,E.A. "Effects of cannabis sativa on the social behavior of rats." Act. Pharmaceut. Suec. 1971, 8, 687-688.

4913. Masur,J., Martz,R.M.W., and Carlini,E.A. "The behavior of worker and non-worker rats under the influence of (-)-delta-9-trans-tetrahydrocannabinol, chlorpromazine and amylobarbitone." Psychopharmacol. 1972, 25, 57-68.

4914. Matchett,J.R., Levine,J.B.L., Robinson,B.B., and Pope,O.A. "Marihuana investigations. II. The effects of variety, maturity, fertilizer treatment and sex on the intensity of response to the Beam tests." J.A.P.A. 1940, 29, 399-404.

4915. Matchett,J.R. and Loewe,S. "On the preparation of an extract having 'marihuana-like' activity from the fruits of cannabis sativa." J.A.P.A. 1941, 30, 130-132.

4916. Matchett,W.F. "Who uses drugs? A study in a suburban high school." J. Sch. Hlth. 1971, 41, 90-93.

4917. Matke,D.J. "Report on the chemical composition of illicit drugs." In Marshman,J.A.(ed.). Street Drug Analysis and its Social and Clinical Implications. Addict. Res. Found., Toronto, 1974, 9-13.

4918. Matsuyama,S.S. "Cytogenetic studies of marihuana." In Tinklenberg,J.R.(ed.). Marihuana and Health Hazards. Academic Press, N.Y., 1975, 17-25.

4919. Matsuyama,S. and Jarvik,L. "Effects of marihuana on the genetic and immune systems." In Petersen,R.C.(ed.). Marihuana Research Findings: 1976. N.I.D.A. Res. Monog. Ser. 14, Dept. H.E.W., Rockville, Md., 1977, 179-193.

4920. Matsuyama,S., Jarvik,L.F., Fu,T., and Yen,F. "Chomosome studies before and after supervised marihuana smoking." In Braude,M.D. and Szara,S.(eds.). Pharmacology of Marihuana. Raven Press, N.Y., 1976, 723-730.

4921. Matsuyama,S.F., Yen,S., Jarvik,L.F., and Fu,T. "Marihuana and human chromosomes." Genetics 1973, 74, 175.

4922. Matsuyama,S.S., Yen,F., Jarvik,L.F., Sparkes, R.S., Fu,T., Fisher,H., Reccius,N., and Frank,I.M. "Marihuana exposure in vivo and human lymphocyte chromosomes." Mutation Res. 1977, 48, 255-266.

4923. Matte,A.C. "Effects of hashish on isolation induced aggression in wild mice." Psychopharmacol. 1975, 45, 125-128.

4924. Matthews,S.A. "Cannabis tannate." J.A.M.A. 1908, 51, 1780.

4925. Mattison,J.B. "A case of double narcotic addiction. Opium and alcohol--imbecility--recovery." Can. Lancet 1884, 17, 101-104.

4926. Mattison,J.B. "Cannabis indica as an anodyne and hypnotic." St. Louis Med. Surg. J. 1891, 61, 265-271.

4927. Mattison,J.B. "The treatment of opium addiction." Can. Med. Rec. 1885, 13, 73-84.

4928. Mattox,K.L. "Pneumomediastinum in heroin and marihuana users." J. Am. Coll. Emerg. Phys. 1976, 5, 26-28.

4929. Matussek,N. "Biochemical, pharmacological and clinical studies with opiates, cannabinols, stimulants, and hallucinogens."(Ger.). Oeffent. Gesundeit. 1971, 33, 534-540.

4930. Matzler,A. "Death following narcotics usage." (Ger.). Kriminalistik 1971, 25, 177-180.

4931. Mauer,D. "Marihuana addicts and their lingo." Am. Mercury 1946, 63, 571-575.

4932. Maugh,T.H. "A conversation with NIDA's Robert L. Dupont." Science 1976, 192, 647-649.

4933. Maugh,T.H. "Marihuana. Does it damage the brain?" Science 1974, 185, 775-776.

4934. Marugh,T.H. "Marihuana: New support for immune and reproductive hazards." Science 1975, 190, 865-867.

4935. Maugh,T.H. "Marihuana: The grass may no longer be greener." Science 1974, 185, 683-685.

4936. Maugh,T.H., Stefanis,C.N., and Issidorices,M.R. "Marihuana: New support for immune and reproductive natures." Science 1976, 191, 1217.

4937. Maurer,D. and Vogel,V.H. Narcotics and Narcotic Addiction. C.C.Thomas, Springfield, Ill., 1962.

4938. Mauss,A.L. "Anticipatory socialization toward college as a factor in adolescent marihuana use." Soc. Prob. 1969, 16, 357-364.

4939. Mayer,J.E. The Herbalist. Indiana Botanic Gardens, Hammond, Ind., 1934.

4940. Maynard,D.E., Gurny,O., Pitcher,R.G., and Kierstead,R.W. "(-)-delta-8-tetrahydrocannabinol: Two novel in vitro metabolites." Exper. 1971, 27, 1154-1155.

4941. Mazhar,O.B. Hashish and Dementia Praecox. (Turk.). Chichli Musamereliri, Istambul, 1916.

4942. Mazurkiewicz-Kwilecki,I.M. and Filczewski,M. "The effects of chronic treatment with delta-9-tetrahydrocannabinol on catecholamine synthesis in the rat." Psychopharmacol. 1973, 33, 71-79.

4943. McAree,C.P., Steffen-Hagen,R.A., and Zheutlin, L.S. "Personality factors and patterns of drug usage of college students." Am. J. Psychiat. 1972, 128, 890-893.

4944. McAree,C.P., Steffen-Hagen,R.A., and Zheutlin, L.S. "Personality factors of college drug users." Internat'l. J. Soc. Psychiat. 1969, 15, 102-106.

4945. McBroom,P. "Pot boils." Sci. News 1967, 92, 500.

4946. McBroom,P. "Pot penalties too severe." Sci. News 1966, 90, 270.

4947. McCallum,N.K. "The determination of cannabinol levels in the blood and interpretation of their significance." Pharmacol. 1974, 11, 33-37.

4948. McCallum,N.K. "The effect of cannabinol on delta-1-tetrahydrocannabinol clearance from the blood." Exper. 1975, 31, 957-958.

4949. McCallum,N.K. "The measurement of cannabinols in the blood by gas chromatography." J. Chromatog. Sci. 1973, 11, 509-511.

4950. McCallum,N.K. and Cairns,E.R. "Simple device for GLC separations of cannabinoids using a surface-coated open tube column without stream splitting." J. Pharmaceut. Sci. 1977, 66, 114-116.

4951. McCallum,N.K., Gugelmann,A., Brenninkmeijer, C.A.M., and Mechoulam,R. "Isotope effect studies on the dehydrogenation of delta-1-tetrahydrocannabinol in the rat." Exper. 1977, 33, 1012-1014.

4952. McCallum,N.K., Yagen,B., Levy,S., and Mechoulam, R. "Cannabinol: A rapidly formed metabolite of delta-1- and delta-6-tetrahydrocannabinol." Exper. 1975, 31, 520-521.

4953. McCarthy,C.R., Cutting,M.B., Simmons,G.A., Pereira,W., Laguarda,R., and Huber,G.L. "The effect of marihuana on the in vitro function of pulmonary alveolar macrophages." In Braude,M.C. and Szara,S.(eds.). Pharmacology of Marihuana. Raven Press, N.Y., 1976, 211-217.

4954. McCarthy,T.J. and van Zyl,J.D. "Breath analysis of cannabis smokers." J. Pharm. Pharmacol. 1972, 24, 489-490.

4955. McCaughran,J.A., Corcoran,M.E., and Wada, J.A. "Anticonvulsant activity of delta-8- and delta-9-tetrahydrocannabinol in rats." Pharmacol. Biochem. Behav. 1974, 2, 227-233.

4956. McCauley,C.R. "Marihuana effects amid great expectations." Science 1969, 165, 204.

4957. McClean,D.K. "Cell division and marcro-molecular synthesis in tetrahymena pryiformis: The action of tetrahydrocannabinol, levorphanol and levallorphan." Diss. Abs. 1974, 34, 4258-4259.

4958. McClean,D.K. and Zimmerman,A.M. "Action of delta-9-tetrahydrocannabinol on cell division and macromolecular synthesis in division-synchronized protozoa." Pharmacol. 1976, 14, 307-321.

4959. McConnell,J.F.P. "Use of cannabis indica." Practitioner 1888, 40, 95-98.

4960. McCormack,G.R. "Marihuana." Hygeia 1937, 15, 898-899.

4961. McCoy,D.J., Brown,D.J., and Forney,R.B. "The effect of cannabinoid mixtures on the response to stimulant drugs in mice." Pharmacologist 1974, 16, 281.

4962. McCoy,D.J., Brown,D.J., and Forney,R.B. "The influence of cannabinoid mixtures on drug induced sleep in mice." Toxicol. Appl. Pharmacol. 1974, 29, 76-77.

4963. McCracken,S. "Drugs of habit and the drugs of belief." Commentary 1971, 51, 43-52.

4964. McDonald,W.F. "Enforcement of narcotic and dangerous drug laws in the District of Columbia." In National Commission on Marihuana and Drug Abuse. Drug Use in America: Problem in Perspective. Gov't. Print. Office, Washington, D.C., 1973, III, 651-685.

4965. McDonough,J.H., Manning,F.J., and Elsmore,T.F. "Reduction of predatory aggression of rats following administration of delta-9-tetrahydrocannabinol." Life Sci. 1972, 11, 103-111.

4966. McGlothlin,W.H. "An approach to marihuana legislation." J. Psyched. Drugs 1968, 2, 149-156.

4967. McGlothlin,W.H. "Cannabis: A reference." In Solomon,D.(ed.). The Marihuana Papers. Bobbs-Merrill, Indianapolis, 1966, 401-416.

4968. McGlothlin,W.H. "Cannabis intoxication and its similarity to peyote and LSD." In Andrews,G. and Vinkenoog,S.(eds.). The Book of Grass. Grove Press, N.Y., 1967, 165-176.

4969. McGlothlin,W.H. "Drug use and abuse." Ann. Rev. Psychol. 1975, 26, 45-64.

4970. McGlothlin,W.H. "Epidemiology of marihuana use." In Petersen,R.D.(ed.). Marihuana Research Findings: 1976. N.I.D.A. Res. Monog. Ser. 14, Dept. H.E.W., Rockville, Md., 1977, 38-54.

4971. McGlothlin,W.H. "Hallucinogenic drugs: A perspective with special reference to peyote and cannabis." Psyched. Rev. 1965, 6, 16-57.

4972. McGlothlin,W.H. Hallucinogenic Drugs: A Perspective with Special Reference to Peyote and Cannabis. Rand Corp., Santa Monica, Cal., 1964.

4973. McGlothlin,W.H. "Hippies and early Christianity." J. Psyched. Drugs 1967, 1, 24-35.

4974. McGlothlin,W.H. "Marihuana: An analysis of use, distribution and control." Contemp. Drug Prob. 1972, 1, 467-500.

4975. McGlothlin,W.H. "Marihuana control: A perspective." J. Second. Educat. 1968, 43, 223-227.

4976. McGlothlin,W.H. "Marihuana use among adults." Psychiat. 1970, 3, 433-443.

4977. McGlothlin,W.H. "Marihuana use, distribution, and control." In Blum,R.H. and Associates(ed.). Drug Dealers--Taking Action. Jossey Bass Pub., San Francisco, 1973, 31-61.

4978. McGlothlin,W.H. "Social and para-medical aspects of hallucinogenic drugs." In Abramson,H.A.(ed.). The Use of LSD in Psychotherapy and Alcoholism. Bobbs-Merrill, Indianapolis, 1967, 3-34.

4979. McGlothlin,W.H. "Sociocultural factors in marihuana use in the United States." In Rubin,V.(ed.). Cannabis and Culture. Mouton, The Hague, 1975, 531-549.

4980. McGlothlin,W.H. "The epidemiology of hallucinogenic drug use." In Josephson,E. and Carroll, E.E.(eds.). Drug Use. Epidemiological and Sociological Approaches. Hemisphere Pub. Corp., Washington, D.C., 1974, 279-301.

4981. McGlothlin,W.H. "The use of cannabis: East and West." In van Praag,H.M.(ed.). Biochemical and Pharmacological Aspects of Dependence. De Erven F. Bohn, Haarlem, Netherlands, 1972, 167-193.

4982. McGlothlin,W.H. "Toward a rational view of hallucinogenic drugs." J. Psyched. Drugs. 1967, 1, 40--2.

4983. McGlothlin,W.H. "Toward a rational view of marihuana." In Simmons,J.L.(ed.). Marihuana, Myths and Realities. Brandon House, Berkeley, Cal., 1967, 163-214.

4984. McGlothlin,W.H., Arnold,D.O., and Rowan,P.K. "Marihuana use among adults." Psychiat. 1970, 33, 433-443.

4985. McGlothlin,W.H. and Cohen,S. "The use of hallucinogenic drugs among college students." Am. J. Psychiat. 1965, 122, 572-574.

4986. McGlothlin,W.H., Jamison,K., and Rosenblatt,S. "Marihuana and the use of other drugs." Nature 1970, 228, 1227-1228.

4987. McGlothlin,W.H.and West,L.J. "The marihuana problem: An overview." Am. J. Psychiat. 1968, 125, 370-378.

4988. McGuire,J.S. "Personality adjustment associated with different levels of marihuana use in a youthful offender population." F.C.I. Res. Rep. 1973, 5, 1-16.

4989. McGuire,J.S. and Megargee,E.I. "Personality correlates of marihuana use among youthful offenders." J. Consult. Clin. Psychol. 1974, 42, 124-133.

4990. McIntosh,J.R. Perspectives on Marginality. Understanding Deviance. Allyn and Bacon, Boston, 1974.

4991. McIsaac,W.M., Fritchie,G.E., Idanpaan-Heikkila,J.E., Ho,B.T., and Englert,L.F. "Distribution of marihuana in monkey brain and concomitant behavioral effects." Nature 1971, 230, 593-594.

4992. McIsaac,W.M., Harris,R.T., and Ho,B.T. "Behavioral correlates of brain distribution of tetrahydrocannabinol." Act. Pharmaceut. Suec. 1971, 8, 703-704.

4993. McKee,M.R. "Hashish." J.A.M.A. 1971, 217, 1706-1707.

4994. McKee,S. "Report on manufactures." In McKee,S. (ed.). Alexander Hamilton's Papers on Public Credit Commerce and Finance. Liberal Arts Press, N.Y., 1957, 229-265.

4995. McKenna-Hartung,S. "Self- and ideal self-concept in a drug-using subculture." J. Person. Assess. 1971, 35, 463-471.

4996. McKenzie,J.D. Trends in Marihuana Use Among Undergraduate Students at the University of Maryland. Counselling Center, Univ. Maryland, College Park, Md., 1969.

4997. McKillip,J., Johnson,J.E., and Petzel,T.P. "Patters and correlates of drug use among urban high school students." J. Drug Educat. 1973, 3, 1-12.

4998. McLaughlin,J.F. "Selected personality characteristics of the moderate marihuana, heavy marihuana, and poly-drug-using marihuana smoker." Diss. Abs. 1974, 34, 3881.

4999. McLendon,D.M., Harris,R.T., and Maule,W.F. "Suppression of the cardiac conditioned response by delta-9-tetrahydrocannabinol: A comparison with other drugs." Psyhcopharmacol. 1976, 50, 159-163.

5000. McMillan,D.E. "Drugs and punished responding. III. Punishment intensity as a determinant of drug effect." Psychopharmacol. 1973, 30, 61-74.

5001. McMillan,D.E. "Effects of drugs on punished and unpunished responding in pigeons." Pharmacologist 1971, 13, 628.

5002. McMillan,D.E. "On the mechanism of tolerance to delta-9-THC." In Lewis,M.C.(ed.). Current Research in Marihuana. Academic Press, N.Y., 1972, 97-114.

5003. McMillan,D.E., Dewey,W.L., and Harris,L.S. "Characteristics of tetrahydrocannabinol tolerance." Ann. N. Y. Acad. Sci. 1971, 191, 83-99.

5004. McMillan,D.E., Dewey,W.L., Turk,R.F., and Harris,L.S. "Distribution of radioactivity in brain, liver, and lung of tolerant and nontolerant pigeons treated with ^{3}H-delta-9-tetrahydrocannabinol." Proc. 5th Internat'l. Cong. Pharmacol. 1972, 1, 154.

5005. McMillan,D.E., Dewey,W.L., Turk,R.F., Harris,L.S., and McNeil,J.H. "Blood levels of ^{3}H-delta-9-tetrahydrocannabinol and its metabolites in tolerant and nontolerant pigeons." Biochem. Pharmacol. 1973, 22, 383-397.

5006. McMillan,D.E., Ford,R.D., Frankenheim,J.M., Harris,R.A., and Harris,L.S. "Tolerance to active constituents of marihuana." Arch. Internat'l. Pharmacodyn. Ther. 1972, 198, 132-144.

5007. McMillan,D.E., Harris,L.S., Frankenheim,J.M., and Kennedy,J.S. "1-delta-9-trans-tetrahydrocannabinol in pigeons: Tolerance to the behavioral effects." Science 1970, 169, 501-503.

5008. McMillan,D.E., Harris,L.S., Turk,R.F., and Kennedy,J.S. "Development of marked behavioral tolernace to 1-delta-9-tetrahydrocannabinol and cross tolerance to 1-delta-8-tetrahydrocannabinol in the pigeon." Pharmacologist 1970, 12, 258.

5009. McMorris,S.C. "What price euphoria? The case against marihana." Br. J. Addict. 1967, 62, 203-208.

5010. McMullan,J. "Suburbia in transition: Patterns of cannabis use and social control in the suburban community." In Buckner,H.T.(ed.). Observations on the Normalization of Cannabis. Sir George Williams Univ. Press, Montreal, Quebec, Can., 1972, 1-31.

5011. McPeek,R.W., and Edwards,J.D. "Expectancy, disconfirmation, and attitude change." J. Soc. Psychol. 1975, 96, 193-208.

5012. McPhee,H.C. "Meiotic cytokenesis of cannabis." Bot. Gaz. 1924, 78, 335-341.

5013. McPhee,H.C. "The genetics of sex in hemp." J. Agricult. Res. 1925, 31, 935-943.

5014. McPhee,H.C. "The influence of environment on sex in hemp, cannabis sativa L." J. Agricult. Res. 1924, 28, 1067-1080.

5015. McWalter,J.C. "Concerning cannabis indica poisoning." Pharmaceut. J. 1900, 11, 498.

5016. McWhinnie,H.J. "Chemical agents for behavior change: Creative, psychotic and ecstatic states--some implications for drug education." Br. J. Addict. 1970, 65, 123-137.

5017. Meacham,M.P., Janowsky,D.S., Blain,J.D., Bozzetti,L.P., and Schorr,M. "Effects of marihuana on flying ability." J.A.M.A. 1974, 230, 1258.

5018. Meachanick,P. "Nonmedical drug use among medical students." Arch. Gen. Psychiat. 1973, 29, 48-53.

5019. Mechoulam,R. "Cannabis."(Heb.). Harokeach Haivri 1964, 10, 96-98.

5020. Mechoulam,R. "Cannabis in the social life of monkeys."(Fr.). Recherche 1976, 73, 1018-1026.

5021. Mechoulam,R. "Cannabinoid chemistry." In Mechoulam,R.(ed.). *Marihuana, Chemistry, Pharmacology, Metabolism and Clinical Effects*. Academic Press, N.Y., 1973, 2-88.

5022. Mechoulam,R. "Chemistry and cannabis activity." *Cienc. Cult*. 1973, *25*, 742-747.

5023. Mechoulam,R. "Developments in hashish research." *Harokeach Haivri* 1970, *13*, 535-539.

5024. Mechoulam,R. "Formulas of known natural cannabinoids and metabolites and some synthetic cannabinoids." In Mechoulam,R.(ed.). *Marihuana, Chemistry, Pharmacology, Metabolism and Clinical Effects*. Academic Press, N.Y., 1973, 367-389.

5025. Mechoulam,R. "Hashish research--an overview." *Toxicon* 1970, *8*, 162.

5026. Mechoulam,R. "Medicines developed from hashish."(Heb.). *Harefoah* 1976, *90*, 378-380.

5027. Mechoulam,R. "Metabolism of cannabis." *Br. Med. J*. 1971, *2*, 332.

5028. Mechoulam,R. "Panel on marihuana(hashish) and other psychomimetics." *Lexicon* 1970, *8*, 162-163.

5029. Mechoulam,R. "Recent advances in cannabinoid chemistry." *Act. Pharmaceut. Suec*. 1971, *8*, 675-676.

5030. Mechoulam,R. "Recent advances in cannabinoid chemistry open the area to more sophisticated biological research." *Science* 1970, *168*, 1159-1166.

5031. Mechoulam,R. "Recent advances in hashish research."(Heb.). *Harokeach Haivri* 1970, *13*, 535-539.

5032. Mechoulam,R. "Structure-activity relationships in the cannabinoid series." In Mechoulam,R.(ed.). *Marihuana, Chemistry, Pharmacology, Metabolism and Clinical Effects*. Academic Press, N.Y., 1973, 101-133.

5033. Mechoulam,R. "The absolute configuration of delta-1-tetrahydrocannabinol, the major active constituent of hashish." *Tetrahed. Let*. 1967, *12*, 1109-1111.

5034. Mechoulam,R. and Ben-Zvi,Z. "Carboxylation of resorcinols with methylmagnesium carbonate. Synthesis of cannabinoid acids." *J. Chem. Soc*. 1969, *1*, 343-344.

5035. Mechoulam,R., Ben-Zvi,Z., Agurell,S., Nilsson,I.M., Nilsson,J.L.G., Edery,H., and Grunfeld,Y. "Delta-6-tetrahydrocannabinol-7-oic acid, a urinary delta-6-THC metabolite: isolation and synthesis." Exper. 1973, 29, 1193-1195.

5036. Mechoulam,R., Ben-Zvi,Z., and Gaoni,Y. "Hashish. XIII. On the nature of the Beam test." Tetrahedron 1968, 24, 5615-1624.

5037. Mechoulam,R., Ben-Zvi,Z., and Shani,A. "A new tetrahydrocannabinolic acid." Tetrahed. Let. 1969, 71, 2341-2349.

5038. Mechoulam,R., Ben-Zvi,Z., Shani,A., Zemler,H., Levy,S., Edery,H., and Grunfeld,Y. "Cannabinoids and cannabis activity." In Paton,W.D.M. and Crown,J.(eds.). Cannabis and its Derivatives. Oxford Univ. Press, London, 1972, 1-16.

5039. Mechoulam,R., Ben-Zvi,Z., Varconi,H., and Samuelov,Y. "Cannabinol arrangements. Synthesis of delta-5-tetrahydrocannabinol." Tetrahedron 1969, 25, 1615-1619.

5040. Mechoulam,R., Ben-Zvi,Z., Yagnitinski,B., and Shani,A. "Tetrahydrocannabinolic acid." Tetrahed. Let. 1969, 71, 2339-2341.

5041. Mechoulam,R., Braun,P., and Gaoni,Y. "A stereospecific synthesis of (-)-delta-1- and (-)-delta-1(6)-tetrahydrocannabinols." J. Am. Chem. Soc. 1967, 89, 4552-4554.

5042. Mechoulam,R., Braun,P., and Gaoni,Y. "Synthesis of delta-1-tetrahydrocannabinol and related cannabinoids." J. Am. Chem. Soc. 1972, 94, 6159-6165.

5043. Mechoulam,R. and Edery,H. "Structure-activity relationships in the cannabinoid series." In Mechoulam,R.(ed.). Marihuana, Chemistry, Pharmacology, Metabolism and Clinical Effects. Academic Press, N.Y., 1973, 101-136.

5044. Mechoulam,R. and Gaoni,Y. "A total synthesis of dl-delta-1-tetrahydrocannabinol, the active constituent of hashish." J. Am. Chem. Soc. 1965, 87, 3273-3275.

5045. Mechoulam,R. and Gaoni,Y. "Hashish. IV. The isolation and structure of cannabinolic and cannabigerolic acids." Tetrahedron 1965, 21, 1223-1229.

5046. Mechoulam,R. and Gaoni,Y. "Hashish: VI. A total synthesis of dl-delta-1-tetrahydrocannabinol, the active constituent of hashish." J. Am. Chem. Soc. 1965, 87, 3273-3275.

5047. Mechoulam,R. and Gaoni,Y. "Recent advances in the chemistry of hashish." Fortsch. Chem. Organ. Natur. 1967, 25, 175-213.

5048. Mechoulam,R. and Gaoni,Y. "The absolute configuration of delta-1-tetrahydrocannabinol, the major active constituent of hashish." Tetrahed. Let. 1967, 58, 1109-1111.

5049. Mechoulam,R., Lander,N., Dikstein,S., Carlini,E.A., and Blumenthal,M. "On the therapeutic possibilities of some cannabinoids." In Cohen,S. and Stillman,R.(eds.). Therapeutic Potential of Marihuana. Plenum Press, N.Y., 1976, 35-48.

5050. Mechoulam,R., McCallum,N.K., and Burstein,S. "Recent advances in the chemistry and biochemistry of cannabis." Chem. Rev. 1976, 76, 75-112.

5051. Mechoulam,R., McCallum,N.K., Lander,N., Yagen,B., Ben-Zvi,Z., and Levy,S. "Aspects of cannabis chemistry and metabolism." In Braude,M.C. and Szara,S. (eds.). Pharmacology of Marihuana. Raven Press, N.Y., 1976, 39-47.

5052. Mechoulam,R., McCallum,N., Levy,S., and Lander,N. "Cannabinoid chemistry: An overview." In Nahas,G.G., Paton,W.D.M., and Idanpaan-Heikkila,J.E. (eds.). Marihuana. Springer Verlag, N.Y., 1976, 3-13.

5053. Mechoulam,R., Shani,A., Edery,H., and Grunfeld,Y. "Chemical basis of hashish activity." Science 1970, 169, 611-612.

5054. Mechoulam,R., Shani,A., Yagnitinsky,B., Ben-Zvi,Z., Braun,P., and Gaoni,Y. "Some aspects of cannabinoid chemistry." In Joyce,C.R.B. and Curry,S.H. (eds.). The Botany and Chemistry of Cannabis. J. and H. Churchill, London, 1970, 93-117.

5055. Mechoulam,R. and Shvo,Y. "Hashish. I. The structure of cannabidiol." Tetrahedron 1963, 19, 2073-2078.

5056. Mechoulam,R., Varconi,H., Ben-Zvi,Z., Edery,H., and Grunfeld,Y. "Synthesis and biological activity of five tetrahydrocannabinol metabolites." J. Am. Chem. Soc. 1972, 94, 7930-7931.

5057. Mechoulam,R. and Yagen,B. "Stereoselective cyclizations of cannabinoid 1,5 dienes." Tetrahed. Let. 1969, 60, 5349-5352.

5058. Mechoulam,R., Yagnitinsky,B., and Gaoni,Y. "Stereoelectronic factor in the chloranil dehydrogenation of cannabinoids. Total synthesis of dl-cannabichromene." J. Am. Chem. Soc. 1968, 90, 2418-2420.

5059. Medek,A., Navratil,J., Hřbek,J., Macakova,J., Siroka,A., and Krejci,Z. "Comparison of the effect of atropine and cannabis upon the fixed conditioned alimentary motor reflexes in cats affected by nicotine." Activ. Nerv. Sup. 1974, 16, 215.

5060. Medical Staff, Pretoria Mental Hospital. "Mental symptoms associated with the smoking of dagga." S. Af. Med. J. 1930, 12, 85-88.

5061. Medlicott,R.W., Sutherland,D.C. and Medlicott,P.A.W. "A study of patients with a record of drug dependence of drug abuse admitted to a private psychiatric hospital 1882-1969." N. Zealand M. J. 1970, 72, 92-95.

5062. Medlin,K.C. "Search and seizure in the public schools." Louisiana Law Rev. 1976, 36, 1067-1074.

5063. Medwedewa,G.B. "The cytology of hemp. The pollen development in Italian hemp."(Ger.). Genet. Ned. Tijd. Afstammings. 1934, 15, 353-391.

5064. Mehndiratta,S.S. and Wig,N.N. "Psychosocial effects of longterm cannabis use in India. A study of fifty heavy users and controls." Drug Alcohol Depend. 1975, 1, 71-81.

5065. Mehra,N. "Socio-psychological correlates of non-medical use of drugs among university students." Alberta J. Educat. Res. 1973, 19, 259-269.

5066. Meier,R.F. and Jonson,W.T. "Deterrence as social control: The legal and extra legal production of conformity." Am. Sociol. Rev. 1977, 42, 292-304.

5067. Meldrum,B.S., Fariello,R.G., Puil,E.A., Derouaus,M., and Naquet,R. "Delta-9-tetrahydrocannabinol and epilepsy in the photosensitive baboon, Papio papio." Epilepsia 1974, 15, 255-264.

5068. Melges,F.T. "Tracking difficulties and paranoid ideation during hashish and alcohol intoxication." Am. J. Psychiat. 1976, 133, 1024-1028.

5069. Melges,F.T., Tinklenberg,J.R., Deardorff,C.M., Davies,N.H., Anderson,R.E., and Owen,C.A. "Temporal disorganization and delusional-like ideation." Arch. Gen. Psychiat. 1974, 30, 855-861.

5070. Melges,F.T., Tinklenberg,J.R., Hollister,L.E., and Gillespie,H.K. "Marihuana and temporal disintegration." Science 1970, 168, 1118-1120.

5071. Melges,F.T., Tinklenberg,J.R., Hollister,L.E., and Gillespie,H.K. "Marihuana and the temporal span of awareness." Arch. Gen. Psychiat. 1971, 24, 564-567.

5072. Melges,F.T., Tinklenberg,J.R., Hollister,L.E., and Gillespie,H.K. "Temporal disintegration and depersonalization d ing marihuana intoxication." Arch. Gen. Psychiat. 1970, 23, 204-210.

5073. Melikian,A.P. and Forrest,I.S. "Dansyl derivatives of delta-9- and delta-8-tetrahydrocannabinols." J. Pharmaceut. Sci. 1973, 62, 1025-1026.

5074. Melikian,L.H., Nassar,N.T., and DerKarabetian, A. "Studies in the non medical use of drugs in Lebanon. II. Some personality correlates of marihuana users at A.U.B." Lebanon Med. J. 1973, 26, 233-240.

5075. Mellinger,G.D. "Psychotherapeutic drug use among adults: A model for young drug users?" J. Drug Iss. 1971, 1, 274-285.

5076. Mellinger,G.D., Somers,R.H., Davidson,S.T., and Manheimer,D.I. "The amotivational syndrome and the college student." Ann. N. Y. Acad. Sci. 1976, 282, 37-55.

5077. Mellors,A. "Cannabinoids: Effects of lysosomes and lymphocytes." In Nahas,G.G., Paton,W.D.M., and Idan-paan-Heikkila,J.E.(eds.). Marihuana. Springer Verlag, N.Y., 1976, 283-299.

5078. Mendelson,J.H. "Marihuana use. Biologic and behavioral aspects. Postgrad. Med. 1976, 60, 111-115.

5079. Mendelson,J.H., Babor,T.F., Kuehnle,J.C., Rossi,A.M., Bernstein,J.G., Mello,N.K., and Greenberg,I. "Behavioral and biological aspects of marihuana use." Ann. N. Y. Acad. Sci. 1976, 282, 186-210.

5080. Mendelson,J.H., Kuehnle,J., Ellingboe,J., and Babor,T.F. "Effects of marihuana on plasma testosterone." In Tinklenberg,J.R.(ed.). Marihuana and Health Hazards. Academic Press, N.Y., 1975, 83-95.

5081. Mendelson,J.H., Kuehnle,J., Ellingboe,J., and Babor,T.F. "Plasma testosterone levels before, during and after chronic marihuana smoking." N. Eng. J. Med. 1974, 291, 1051-1055.

5082. Mendelson,J.H., Kuehnle,J.C., Greenberg,I., and Mello,N.K. "Operant acquisition of marihuana in man." J. Pharmacol. Exper. Ther. 1976, 198, 42-52.

5083. Mendelson,J.H., Kuehnle,J.C., Greenberg,I., and Mello,N.K. "The effects of marihuana use on human operant behavior: Individual data." In Braude,M.C. and Szara,S.(eds.). Pharmacology of Marihuana. Raven Press, N.Y., 1976, 2, 643-654.

5084. Mendelson,J.H., Meyer,R.E. and Rossi,A.M. "Conclusions and implications." In Mendelson,J.H., Rossi,A.M., and Meyer,R.E.(eds.). The Use of Marihuana. Plenum Press, N.Y., 1974, 175-199.

5085. Mendelson,J.H., Rossi,A.M., and Meyer,R.E. "Background and experimental design." In Mendelson,J.H., Rossi,A.M., and Meyer,R.E.(eds.). The Use of Marihuana. Plenum Press, N.Y., 1974, 1-4.

5086. Mendes,J.F. "Medicinal intoxication."(Port.). J. Med. 1964, 54, 625-632.

5087. Menzel,M.Y. "Meiotic chromosomes of monoecious Kentucky hemp(cannabis sativa). Bull. Torrey Bot. Club 1964, 91, 193.

5088. Merari,A., Barak,A., and Plaves,M. "Effects of delta-1(2)-tetrahydrocannabinol on copulation in the male rat." Psychopharmacol. 1973, 28, 243-246.

5089. Mercer,B.W. "Cannabis indica." Chicago Med. Times 1901, 34, 165-167.

5090. Mercer,G.W. and Kohn,P.M. "Values associated with marihuana use among college students." Br. J. Addict. 1977, 72, 151-158.

5091. Merck,E. "Cannabin." Pharmaceut. J. 1883, 13, 1052.

5092. Mering,V. "Study of the action of hashish." (Ger.). Arch. Psychiat. Nervenk. 1884, 15, 275-276.

5093. Merino,V.L., Lombart,R.L., Marco,R.F., Carnicero,A.B., and Bouhuys,A. "Arterial blood gas tensions and lung function during acute responses to hemp dust." Am. Rev. Respirat. Dis. 1973, 107, 809-815.

5094. Meriwether,W.F. "Acute marihuana toxicity in a dog. A case report." Vet. Med. 1969, 64, 577-578.

5095. Merkus,F.W.H.M. "Cannabivarin, a new constituent of hashish."(Ger.). Pharm. Weekbl. 1971, 106, 69-71.

5096. Merkus,F.W.H.M. "Cannabivarin and tetrahydrocannabivarin, two new constituents of hashish." Nature 1971, 232, 579-580.

5097. Merkus,F.W.M.H. "Marihuana and hashish: Chemical and pharmacological problem and social problem." (Dut.). Chem. Weekbl. 1970, 66, 23-25.

5098. Merkus,F.W.H.M. "Thin-layer chromatography of cannabis constituents." Pharmacol. Weekbl. 1971, 106, 49-55.

5099. Merkus,F.W.H.M., van Wouw Jaspers,M.G.L., and Roovers-Bollen,JF.C. "Discovery of cannabivarin, a new constituent in hashish."(Ger.). Beitr. Gericht. Med. 1972, 29, 154-156.

5100. Merkus,F.W.H.M., van Wouw Jaspers,M.G.L., and Roovers-Bollen,J.F.C. "Introduction to the analysis of cannabis constituents especially in smoke and body fluids." Pharmaceut. Weekbl. 1972, 107, 79-82.

5101. Merkus,F.W.H.M., van Wouw Jaspers,M.G.L., and Roovers-Bollen,J.F.C. "TLC, GLC and MS of cannabidivarin, tetrahydrocannabivarin and cannabivarin." Act. Pharmaceut. Suec. 1971, 8, 681-683.

5102. Merkus,F.W.H.M. and Roovers-Bollen,J.F.C. "Thin-layer chromatographic separation of constituents of hashish and marihuana." Internat'l. Sympos. Chromatog. Electrophor. Brussels, 1970, 1, 355-363.

5103. Merlin,M.D. Man and Marihuana. Farleigh Dickenson Univ. Press, Rutherford, N.J., 1968.

5104. Merrill,F.T. "Marihuana: Hashish in modern dress." Am. Foreign Service 1939, 1, 265.

5105. Merrill,F.T. "Marihuana: Increasing use and terrifying effects." J. Home Econ. 1938, 30, 477-479.

5106. Merrill,F.T. Marihuana--The New Dangerous Drug. Opium Research Committee Foreign Policy Association, N.Y., 1938.

5107. Merson,G.F. "Cannabis indica." Pharmaceut. J. 1902, 14, 301.

5108. Merson,G.F. "Extract and tincture of Indian hemp." Pharmaceut. J. 1902, 14, 234-236, 246-247.

5109. Merz,K.W. and Bergner,K.G. "Chemical investigation of the medicinally valuable substances in Indian hemp."(Ger.). Arch. Expt'l. Pathol. Pharmacol. 1940, 278, 49-70, 97-109.

5110. Messer,M. "Running out of an era: Some nonpharmacological notes on the psychedelic revolution." J. Psyched. Drugs 1968, 2, 157-166.

5111. Messer,M. "Predictive value of marihuana use: A note to researchers of student culture." Sociol. Educat. 1969, 42, 91-97.

5112. Messiha,F.S. and Soskin,R.A. "Effect of cannabis sativa administered by smoking on biogenic amine excretion in man." Res. Commun. Chem. Pathol. Pharmacol. 1973, 8, 325-328.

5113. Metzger,M.H. "Notes on marihuana identification in criminal cases." Clin. Toxicol. 1975, 8, 465-473.

5114. Metzner,R. "Two new laws relating to psychedelics: 1. Federal law. 2. New York State law." Psychedel. Rev. 1966, 7, 3-10.

5115. Meunier,R. Hashish. An Essay on the Epemeral Paradise. (Fr.). Bloud and Cie, Paris, 1909.

5116. Meutisse,G. Hashish. (Fr.). Univ. Paris, Dept. Med., Paris, 1891.

5117. Meyer,J.C. "Marihuana use by white college students." Crime Delinquen. 1973, 19, 79.

5118. Meyer,R. "The acute effects of marihuana." In van Praag,H.M.(ed.). Biochemical and Pharmacological Aspects of Dependence and Reports on Marihuana Research. De Erven F. Bohn, Haarlem, Netherlands, 1972, 144-159.

5119. Meyer,R. "The progression hypothesis: Myth or reality?" In van Praag,H.M.(ed.). Biochemical and Pharmacological Aspects of Dependence and Reports on Marihuana Research. De Erven F. Bohn, Haarlem, Netherlands, 1972, 205-213.

5120. Meyer,R.E. "Psychiatric consequences of marihuana use: The state of the evidence." In Tinklenberg, J.R.(ed.). Marihuana and Health Hazards. Academic Press, N.Y., 1975, 133-153.

5121. Meyer,R.E., Patch,V.D., Bernstein,J.G., and Rossi,A.M. "The subjects." In Mendelson,J.H., Rossi,A.M., and Meyer,R.E.(eds.). The Use of Marihuana. Plenum Press, N.Y., 1974, 9-12.

5122. Meyer,R.E., Pillard,R.C., Shapiro,L.M., and Mirin,S.M. "Administration of marihuana to heavy and casual marihuana users." Am. J. Psychiat. 1971, 128, 90-96.

5123. Meyerhof,M. "Hemp, a stimulant of the Orient." (Ger.). Oesterreich. Monat. Orient. 1916, 42, 240-249.

5124. Meyers,F.H. "Pharmacological effects of marihuana." J. Psyched. Drugs 1968, 2, 31-36.

5125. Meyers,S.A. and Caldwell,D.R. "The drug scene in perspective." Metro. Detroit Sci. Rev. 1970, 31, 57-60.

5126. Meyerstein,A.N. "Drug addiction: A review." J. Sch. Hlth. 1964, 34, 77-87.

5127. Meyerstein,A.N. "Glossary of slang terms related to drug usage." J. Sch. Hlth. 1970, 40, 184-192.

5128. Mezzrow,M. Really the Blues. Random House, N.Y., 1946.

5129. Michaux,H. "Light through darkness." In Andrews,G. and Vinkenoog,S.(eds.). The Book of Grass. Grove Press, N.Y., 1967, 94-107.

5130. Michel,L. "Medical properties of the Indian hemp or cannabis indica."(Fr.). Montpel. Med. 1880, 45, 103-116.

5131. Mickel,E.J. The Artificial Paradises in French Literature. Univ. N. Carolina Press, Chapel Hill, N.C., 1969.

5132. Miczek,K.A. "Does THC induce aggression? Suppression and induction of aggressive reactions by chronic and acute delta-9-THC treatment in laboratory rats." In Braude,M.C. and Szara,S.(eds.). Pharmacology of Marihuana. Raven Press, N.Y., 1976, 499-515.

5133. Miczek,K.A. "Mouse-killing and motor activity: Effects of chronic delta-9-tetrahydrocannabinol and pilocarpine." Psychopharmacol. 1976, 47, 59-64.

5134. Miczek,R.A. "Delta-9-tetrahydrocannabinol and aggressive behavior in rats." Behav. Biol. 1974, 11, 261-267.

5135. Miczek,K.A. and Barry,H. "Effects of delta-9-tetrahydrocannbinol on aggressive behavior in laboratory rats." Clin. Toxicol. 1974, 7, 281-282.

5136. Miczek,K.A. and Barry,H. "Effects of delta-9-tetrahydrocannabinol on aggressive behavior in laboratory rats." In Singh,J.M. and Lal,H.(eds.). Neurobiology and Influences on Behavior. Intercontinental Med. Book Corp., N.Y., 1974, 19-38.

5137. Miczek,K.A. and Barry,H. "Delta-9-tetrahydrocannabinol and defense behavior in rats." Toxicol. Appl. Pharmacol. 1973, 25, 450.

5138. Miczek,K.A., Gibbons,J.L., and Barry,H. "Effects of delta-9-tetrahydorcannabinol and methysergide on defensive behavior in rats." Fed. Proc. 1973, 32, 725.

5139. Mieses-Reif,M. "A case of hypersensitivity to cannabis."(Ger.). Zeit. Augenheil. 1936, 89, 226-227.

5140. Migdail,C. "Mexico's war on marihuana." U.S. News 1969, 67, 21-23.

5141. Mikes,F., Hofmann,A., and Waser,P.G. "Identification of (-)-delta-9-6a,10a-trans-tetrahydrocannabinol and two of its metabolites in rats by use of combination gas chromatography-mass spectrometry and mass fragmentography." Biochem. Pharmacol. 1971, 20, 2469-2476.

5142. Mikes,F. and Waser,P.G. "Marihuana components: Effects of smoking on delta-9-tetrahydrocannabinol and cannabidiol." Science 1971, 172, 1158-1159.

5143. Mikuriya,T.H. "Historical aspects of cannabis sativa in western medicine." Comm. Prob. Drug Depend. 1969, 3, 6121-6134.

5144. Mikuriya,T.H. "Historical aspects of cannabis sativa in western medicine." New Phys. 1969, 1, 902-908.

5145. Mikuriya,T.H. "Kif cultivation in the Rif mountains." Econ. Bot. 1967, 21, 230-234.

5146. Mikuriya,T.H. "Marihuana in medicine: Past, present and future." Cal. Med. 1969, 110, 34-40.

5147. Mikuryia,T.(ed.). Marihuana: Medical Papers. Medi-Comp. Press, Oakland, Cal., 1973.

5148. Mikuriya,T.H. "Marihuana: Medical, social and moral aspects." Clin. Toxicol. 1975, 8, 233-237.

5149. Mikuriya,T.H. "Medical facts about marihuana." Marihuana Rev. 1973, 1, 6.

5150. Mikuriya,T.H. "Need for just marihuana laws." Am. J. Psychiat. 1968, 125, 852-853.

5151. Mikuriya,T.H. "Physical, mental, and moral effects of marihuana: The Indian Hemp Drugs Commission Report." Internat'l. J. Addict. 1968, 3, 253-270.

5152. Mikuriya,T.H. "Psychopathological aspects of the cannabis situation in Morocco: Statistical data for 1956 revisited." Internat'l. J. Addict. 1968, 3, 397-398.

5153. Mikuriya,T.H. "Cannabis substitution: An adjunctive therapeutic tool in the treatment of alcoholism." Med. Times 1970, 98, 187-191.

5154. Mikuriya,T.H. and Weil,A.J. "Thinking about using pot." San Francisco Psychiat. Med. Clin. 1969, 1, 30.

5155. Mildner,T. "Hashish and its evaluation for 100 years."(Ger.). Deut. Med. Woch. 1972, 23, 26-32.

5156. Milenkov,K.R., Kirin,I., Agopian,K., and Zakharieva,Z. "Effect of hemp dust on certain functions of the organism."(Rus). Gigiena Sanitar. 1961, 26, 25-32.

5157. Miles,C.G. "A selective review of studies of long term use of cannabis on behaviour, personality and cognitive functioning." In Connell,P.H. and Dorn, N.(eds.). Cannabis and Man. Churchill Livingstone, Edinburgh, 1975, 66-90.

5158. Miles,C.G., Congreve,G.R.S., Gibbins,R.J., Marshman,J., Devenyi,P., and Hicks,R.C. "An experimental study of the effects of daily cannabis smoking on behaviour patterns." Act. Pharmacol. Toxicol. 1974, 34, 9-43.

5159. Miles,V.L. "Constitutional law--state statute prohibiting use of marihuana in the home is violation of the right of privacy--Ravin vs. State of Alaska." Howard Law J. 1976, 19, 190-204.

5160. Milford,E.L. A Statistical Study of a Marihuana Subculture. Social Relations Dept., Harvard Univ., Cambridge, Mass., 1967.

5161. Millant,R. "Narcotic drugs used by Turks." (Fr.). Rev. Med. Hyg. Tropic. 1912, 9, 43-61.

5162. Miller,D.E. "Marihuana: The law and its enforcement." Suffolk Univ. Law Rev. 1968, 3, 81-96.

5163. Miller,D.E. "Narcotic drug and marihuana controls." J. Psyched. Drugs 1967, 1, 28-39.

5164. Miller,D.E. "Narcotic drug and marihuana controls." Internat'l. J. Addict. 1969, 4, 276.

5165. Miller,D.E. "What policemen should know about the marihuana controversy." Paper presented at Internat'l. Narcotic Enforcement Officer's Assoc., Louisville, Ky., 1967.

5166. Miller,G. "Narcotics: A study in black and white." City 1969, 3, 2-9.

5167. Miller,H. "Utopian speculations." In Andrews,G. and Vinkenoog,S.(eds.). The Book of Grass. Grove Press, N.Y., 1967, 206-207.

5168. Miller,L. "Drug abuse in Israel." Addict. Dis. 1977, 3, 65-66.

5169. Miller,L.L. "Marihuana and behavior: Human and infrahuman comparisons." In Miller,L.L. Marihuana, Effects on Human Behavior. Academic Press, N.Y., 1974, 189-217.

5170. Miller,L.L. "Marihuana and human cognition: A review of laboratory investigations." In Cohen,S. and Stillman,R.(eds.). Therapeutic Potential of Marihuana. Plenum Press, N.Y., 1976, 271-292.

5171. Miller,L.L.(ed.). Marihuana, Effects on Human Behavior. Academic Press, N.Y., 1974.

5172. Miller,L.L., Cornett,T., Brightwell,D., McFarland,D., Drew,W.G., and Wiler,A. "Marihuana and memory impairment: The effect of retrieval cues on free recall." Pharmacol. Biochem. Behav. 1976, 5, 639-643.

5173. Miller,L.L., Cornett,T., Brightwell,D., McFarland,D., Drew,W.G., and Wikler,A. "Marihuana: Effects on storage and retrieval of prose material." Psychopharmacol. 1977, 51, 311-316.

5174. Miller,L.L., Cornett,T., Drew,W.G., McFarland,D., Brightwell,D., and Wikler,A. "Marihuana: Dose-response effects on pulse rate, subjective estimates of potency, pleasantness, and recognition memory." Pharmacol. 1977, 15, 268-275.

5175. Miller,L.L. and Drew,W.G. "Cannabis: Neural mechanisms and behavior." In Miller,L.L.(ed.). Marihuana, Effects on Human Behavior. Academic Press, N.Y., 1974, 158-182.

5176. Miller,L.L. and Drew,W.G. "Cannabis: Review of behavioral effects in animals." Psychol. Bull. 1974, 81, 401-417.

5177. Miller,L.L. and Drew,W.G. "Impairment of latent learning in the rat by a marihuana component." Nature 1973, 243, 473-474.

5178. Miller,L.L. and Drew,W.G. "Marihuana(M)-induced impairment of recent memory(RM) and mental set shifting(MSS). Fed. Proc. 1972, 31, 515.

5179. Miller,L.L., Drew,W.G., and Joyce,P. "Delta-9-THC: Effect on acquisition and retention of a one-trial passive avoidance response." Behav. Biol. 1973, 8, 421-426.

5180. Miller,L.L., Drew,D.G., and Kiplinger,G.F. "Effects of marihuana on recall of narrative material and stroop colour-word performance." Nature 1972, 237, 172-173.

5181. Miller,L.L., Drew,W.G., and Wikler,A. "Comparison of delta-9-THC, LSD-25 and scopolamine on nonspatial single alternation performance in the runway." Psychopharmacol. 1973, 28, 1-11.

5182. Miller,M.G. "The problem of drug abuse: alienation and the 'alienist'." Milit. Med. 1969, 134, 577-584.

5183. Miller,M.G. "The genera of the cannabaceae in the Southeastern United States." J. Arnold Arbor. 1970, 51, 185-203.

5184. Miller,M.G. "The National Institute of Mental Health marihuana research program." Comm. Prob. Drug Depend. 1970, 3, 6386-6393.

5185. Miller,R.D. "Is street drug analysis necessary in Canada?" In Marshman,J.A.(ed.). Street Drug Analysis and Its Social and Clinical Implications. Addict. Res. Found, Toronto, 1974, 41-66.

5186. Miller,R.D. "Some suggested research priorities." In Connell,P.H. and Dorn,N.(eds.). Cannabis and Man. Churchill Livingstone, Edinburgh, 1975, 204-228.

5187. Miller,R.D., Hansteen,R.W., Lehmann,H.E., Reid,L., Lonero,L., Adamec,C., Theodore,L., and Jones,B. "The Commission's experimental studies of acute effects of marihuana, delta-9-THC and alcohol in humans." In Ban,T.A., Boissier,J.R., Gessa,G.J., Heimann,H., and Hollister,L.E.(eds.). Psychopharmacology, Sexual Disorders and Drug Abuse. North-Holland Pub. Co., Amsterdam, 1973, 685-688.

5188. Miller,R.E. and Deets,A.C. "Delta-9-THC and nonverbal communication in monkeys." Psychopharmacol. 1976, 48, 53-58.

5189. Miller,W.E., Spiekermann,R.E., and Hepper,N.G. "Pneumodiastinum resulting from performing valsalva maneuvers during marihuana smoking." Chest 1972, 62, 233-234.

5190. Mills,L. and Brawley,P. "The psychopharmacology of 'cannabis sativa': A review." Agents Actions 1972, 2, 201-215.

5191. Milman,D.H. "A cannabis registry?" Pediatrics 1976, 58, 916.

5192. Milman,D.H. "Adverse effects of cannabis." N.Y. State J. Med. 1971, 71, 1675.

5193. Milman,D.H. "Approach to the study of the effects of marihuana." J. Pediat. 1969, 75, 342-343.

5194. Milman,D.H. "Marihuana in adolescents." J.A.M.A. 1971, 216, 2145.

5195. Milman,D.H. "Marihuana psychosis." J.A.M.A. 1969, 210, 2397-2398.

5196. Milman,D.H. "The clinician's role in the problem of drug usage by young people." Am. J. Psychiat. 1970, 126, 1040.

5197. Milman,D.H. "The pediatrician and the marihuana question." Pediatrics 1970, 45, 1038-1039.

5198. Milman,D.H. "The role of marihuana in patterns of drug abuse by adolescents." J. Pediat. 1969, 74, 283-290.

5199. Milman,D.H. "Toxic effects of marihuana." J.A.M.A. 1973, 223, 799.

5200. Milman,D.H. and Anker,J.L. "Patterns of drug usage among university students, multiple drug usage." In Keup,W.(ed.). Drug Abuse, Current Concepts and Research. C.C. Thomas, Springfield, Ill., 1972, 190-201.

5201. Milman,D.H. and Anker,J.L. "Patterns of drug usage among university students. IV. Use of marihuana, amphetamines, opium, and LSD by undergraduates." J. Am. Coll. Hlth. Assoc. 1971, 20, 96-105.

5202. Milman,D.H. and Su,W.H. "Patterns of drug usage among university students. V. Heavy use of marihuana and alcohol by undergraduates." J. Am. Coll. Hlth. Assoc. 1973, 21, 181-187.

5203. Milner,G. "Drug abuse, alcohol and marihuana problems, errors, costs and concepts." Med. J. Aust. 1973, 2, 285-290.

5204. Milner,G. Drugs and Driving. S. Karger, Basel, 1972.

5205. Milner,G. "Marihuana and driving hazards." Med. J. Aust. 1977, 1, 208-211.

5206. Milowska,J. "Medicinal plants in the Lublin province."(Pol.). Ann. Univ. Mariae Curie-Skold. 1959, 14, 321-354.

5207. Milstein,S.L., MacCannell,K.L., Karr,G.W., and Clark,S. "Marihuana produced changes in cutaneous sensitivity and affect: Users and non-users." Pharmacol. Biochem. Behav. 1974, 2, 367-374.

5208. Milstein,S.L., MacCannell,K.L., Karr,G.W., and Clark,S. "Marihuana-produced impairments in coordination." J. Nerv. Ment. Dis. 1975, 161, 26-31.

5209. Milstein,S.L., MacCannell,K.L., Karr,G.W., and Clark,S. "Marihuana-produced changes in pain tolerance. Experienced and non-experienced subjects." Internat'l. Pharmacopsychiat. 1975, 10, 177-182.

5210. Milzoff,J.R. "Cardiovascular pharmacology of delta-9-tetrahydrocannabinol." Diss. Abs. 1973, 33, 3835-3836.

5211. Milzoff,J.R., Brown,D.J., and Stone,C.J. "The respiratory and cardiovascular effects of delta-9-tetrahydrocannabinol in the rat." Fed. Proc. 1971, 30, 443.

5212. Mims,R.B. "Adverse effects of intravenous cannabis tea." J. Nat'l. Med. Assoc. 1977, 69, 491-495.

5213. Minar,J., Lastuvka,Z., and Navratil,O. "Mutual influence of rye(Secale cereale L.) and hemp (cannabis sativa L.) in an aqueous culture without additional feeding."(Ger.). Biol. Plant. Acad. Sci. Bohemoslov 1965, 7, 357.

5214. Mincis,M., Pfeferman,A., Guimares,R.X., Ramos,O.L., Zukerman,E., Karniol,I.G., and Carlini,E.A. "Chronic administration of cannabidiol in man." Rev. Assoc. Med. Brazil. 1973, 19, 185-190.

5215. Minckler,L.S. "Drug habits and immaturity." Science 1968, 161, 419.

5216. Mingoia,T. Chemical Components of Cannabis. (Port.). Biol. Soc. Sao Paulo, Sao Paulo, 1960.

5217. Minnesota Corrections Department. Survey of Drug Use Among Institutionalized Juvenile Boys at Red Wing. Research Information and Data Systems Division, Corrections Dept., Minneapolis, Minn., 1972.

5218. Minter,L.J. "Indian hemp poisoning." Br. Med. J. 1896, 2, 1773-1774.

5219. Miraglea,P.J. "Selected correlates of self-reported alcohol use among Catholic college women." Paper presented to Eastern Psychol. Assoc., N.Y., 1976.

5220. Miras,C.J. "Clinical not annecdotal evidence." Internat'l. J. Psychiat. 1970, 9, 533-535.

5221. Miras,C.J. "Experience with chronic hashish smokers." In Wittenborn,J.R., Brill,H., Smith,J.P., and Wittenborn,S.A.(eds.). Drugs and Youth. C.C. Thomas, Springfield, Ill., 1969, 191-198.

5222. Miras,C.J. "Some aspects of cannabis action." In Wolstenhome,G.E.W. and Knight,J.(eds.). Hashish, Its Chemistry and Pharmacology. Ciba Found. Study Group 21, J. and A. Churchill, London, 1965, 37-53.

5223. Miras,C.J. "Studies on the effects of chronic administration to man." In Patcn,W.D.M. and Crown,J. (eds.). Cannabis and Its Derivatives. Oxford Univ. Press, London, 1972, 150-154.

5224. Miras,C.J. "The effect of hashish on nor-adrenaline concentration and uptake in the brain." Act. Pharmaceut. Suec. 1971, 8, 694-695.

5225. Miras,C. and Coutselinis,A. "The distribution and excretion of tetrahydrocannabinol-C^{14} in humans." Med. Sci. Law 1971, 11, 197-199.

5226. Miras,C.J. and Coutselinis,A. "The distribution of tetrahydrocannabinol-C^{14} in humans." U.N. Doc. ST/SOA/SER.S/24, Nov. 2, 1970.

5227. Miras,C.J. and Coutselinis,A. "The presence of cannabinols in the urine of hashish smokers." U.N. Doc. ST/SOA/SER.S/25, Nov. 4, 1970.

5228. Miras,C.J., Kephalas,T.A., and Papadakis,D.P. "The effect of hashish extract on the norepinephrine in rabbit brain." Bull. Narc. 1971, 23, 33-34.

5229. Miras,C.J., Simos,S., and Kiburis,J. "Comparative assay of the constituents from the sublimate of smoked cannabis with that from ordinary cannabis." Bull. Narc. 1964, 16, 13-15.

5230. Mirin,S. "Dr. Mirin replies." Am. J. Psychiat. 1970, 127, 705-706.

5231. Mirin,S.M. and McKenna,G.J. "Combat zone adjustment: The role of marihuana use." Milit. Med. 1975, 140, 482-485.

5232. Mirin,S.M., Shapiro,L.M., Meyer,R.E., Pillard,R.C., and Fisher,S. "Casual versus heavy use of marihuana: A redefinition of the marihuana problem." Am. J. Psychiat. 1971, 127, 54-60.

5233. Mitchell,E. "Folklore of marihuana smoking." Sol. Folk. Quart. 1970, 34, 127-130.

5234. Mitchell,J. "Dagga." Nongqai 1960, 51, 17.

5235. Mitchell,J. "Marihuana: is it time for a change in our laws." Newsweek 1970, 76, 20-22.

5236. Mitchell,K. "The drug-dependence dilemma: Problems in rehabilitation." Aust. J. Soc. Iss. 1969, 4, 24-39.

5237. Mitchell,K.R., Kirby,R.J., and Mitchell,D.M. "Drug use by university freshmen." J. Coll. Stud. Person. 1970, 11, 332-336.

5238. Mitchell,R.E. "Personality correlates of frequent alcohol and marihuana use in a college male population." Diss. Abs. 1972, 32, 6655.

5239. Mitra,G., Poddar,M.K., and Ghosh,J.J. "Effect of delta-9-tetrahydrocannabinol on rat liver microsomal lipid peroxidation." Toxicol. Appl. Pharmacol. 1975, 34, 525-528.

5240. Mitra,G., Poddar,M.K., and Ghosh,J.J. "Interaction of cannabis extract with reserpine, phenobarbital, amphetamine and LSD-525A on activities of hepatic enzymes." Ind. J. Biochem. Biophys. 1975, 12, 279-282.

5241. Mitra,G., Poddar,M.K., and Ghosh,J.J. "In vivo and in vitro effects of delta-9-tetrahydrocannabinol on rat liver microsomal drug-metabolizing enzymes." Toxicol. Appl. Pharmacol. 1976, 35, 523-530.

5242. Mitosinka,G.T., Thornton,J.I., and Hayes,T.L. "The examination of cystolithic hairs of cannabis and other plants by means of the scanning electron microscope." J. Forens. Sci. Soc. 1972, 12, 521-529.

5243. Mizner,G.L., Barter,J.T., and Werme,P.H. "Patterns of drug use among college students: A preliminary report." Am. J. Psychiat. 1970, 127, 15-24.

5244. Mobarak,Z. "Some chromatographic aspects of hashish analysis." J. Forens. Sci. 1974, 19, 161-169.

5245. Mobarak,Z., Bieniek,D., and Korte,F. "Studies on non-cannabinoids of hashish. Isolation and identification of some hydrocarbons." Chemosphere 1974, 3, 5-8.

5246. Mobarak,Z., Bieniek,D., and Korte,F. "Studies on non-cannabinoids of hashish. II." Chemosphere 1974, 3, 265-270.

5247. Modell,W. "Mass drug catastrophes and the roles of science and technology." Science 1967, 156, 346-351.

5248. Mohan,H. and Sood,G.C. "Conjugate deviation of the eyes after cannabis indica intoxication." Br. J. Opthalmol. 1964, 48, 160-161.

5249. Mohan Ram,H.Y. and Jaiswal,V.S. "Feminization of male flowers of cannabis sativa L. by a morphactin." Naturwissen. 1971, 58, 149-150.

5250. Mohan Ram,H.Y. and Jaiswal,V.S. "Induction of female flowers on male plants of cannbis sativa L. by 2-chloroethanephosephonic acid." Exper. 1970, 26, 214-216.

5251. Mohan Ram,H.Y. and Nath,R. "The morphology and embryology of cannabis sativa L." Phytomorphology 1964, 14, 414-429.

5252. Moise,L.C. "Marihuana. Sex-crazing drug menace." Phys. Cult. 1937, 77, 18-19.

5253. Moldenke,H.N. and Moldenke,A.L. Plants of the Bible. Chronica Botanica Co., Waltham, Mass., 1952.

5254. Mole,M.L., Buelke,J., and Turner,C.E. "Preliminary observations on cardiac activities of cannabis sativa L. root extracts." J. Pharmaceut. Sci. 1974, 63, 1169-1170.

5255. Mole,M.L. and Turner,C.E. "Phytochemical screening of cannabis sativa L. II. Choline and neurine in the roots of a mexican variant." Act. Pharmaceut. Jugoslav. 1973, 23, 203-205.

5256. Mole,M.L. and Turner,C.E. "Propyl homologues of THC and sterols from cannabis sativa." Lloydia 1973, 36, 436.

5257. Mole,M.L. and Turner,C.E. "Phytochemical screening of cannabis sativa L. I. Constituents of an Indian variant." J. Pharmaceut. Sci. 1974, 63, 154-156.

5258. Mole,M.L., Turner,C.E., and Henry,J.T. "Delta-9-tetrahydrocannabinolic acid 'B' from an Indian variant of cannabis sativa." U.N. Doc. ST/SOA/SER.S./48, Aug. 9, 1974.

5259. Moll,J.W., Janssonius,H.H., and van Eck-de-Wiljes,M. "Herba cannabis indicae." In Moll,J.W. and Janssonius,H.H.(eds.). Botanical Pen-portraits. Nijhoff, The Hague, 1974, 278-290.

5260. Moller,K.O. "Hashish(charas, marihuana)." (Ger.). In Moller,K.O.(ed.). Exotic Intoxicants.(Ger.). Benno Schwabe, Basel, 1951, 360-370.

5261. Molotkovskii,G.K. and Butnitskii,I.N. "Morphological and biochemical characteristics of sex in hemp." Ukran. Bot. Zh. 1971, 28, 23-29.

5262. Monforte,J., Weber,K., and Grlic,L. "Effect of major cannabinoids on the chemiluminescence of luminol." Act. Pharmaceut. Jugoslav. 1972, 22, 27-29.

5263. Mongeri,C. "On hashish, cannabis and erar." (Fr.). Ann. Therapeut. Mat. Med. 1865, 25, 59-81.

5264. Monroe,J. "Canvass, cables, and cordage, made from American and foreign flax and hemp, contrasted." In Dickins,A. and Forney,J.W.(eds.). American State Papers. Documents, Legislative and Executive, of the Congress of the United States. Gales and Seaton, Washington, D.C., 1834, 1, 27-33.

5265. Monroe,J.J. and English,C.P. "Ascription of favorable and unfavorable attitudes to substance abuse by college age males." Psychol. Rep. 1973, 32, 875-882.

5266. Monteiro,D.B. "Toxic drugs and toxicomania." (Port.). Rev. Brasil Farmacol. 1972, 53, 179-188.

5267. Montemartini,L. "Effects of treatment of pollen by the Pirovan method on the proportion of sex in cannabis sativa L."(It.). Rend. R. Ist. Lombardo 1926, 59, 748-752.

5268. Montgomery County, Maryland. Joint Committee on Drug Abuse. A Survey of Secondary Schools Students' Perceptions of and Attitudes Toward Use of Drugs by Teenagers. Joint Comm. Drug Abuse, Montgomery Co., Md., 1970.

5269. Monti,J.M. and Carlini,E.A. "Spontaneous behavior and sleep-wakefulness cycle in isolated and paired REM sleep deprived marihuana treated rats." Pharmacol. Biochem. Behav. 1975, 3, 1025-1029.

5270. Mookerjee,H.C. "Hemp drug-addiction and physical damage." Calcutta Rev. 1948, 109, 84-96.

5271. Mookerjee,H.C. "Hemp drug addiction and mental derangement." Calcutta Rev. 1948, 109, 147-160.

5272. Mookerjee,H.C. "Hemp drug addiction and moral damage." Calcutta Rev. 1949, 110, 1-12.

5273. Mookerjee,H.C. "India's hemp drug policy under British rule." Modern Rev. 1948, 84, 446-454.

5274. Mookerjee,H.C. "Two major objections to ganja prohibition." Calcutta Rev. 1949, 110, 1-16.

5275. Mookerjee,H.C. "The problem of hemp drugs addiction in India." New Rev. 1948, 28, 401-414.

5276. Mookerjee,H.C. "The problem of hemp drugs addiction in India." New Rev. 1949, 29, 48-60.

5277. Moore,L.A. Marihuana Bibliography 1960-1968. Bruin Humanist Forum, Los Angeles, 1969.

5278. Moore,M.D. "The marihuana merry-go-round." J. Pol. Sci. Administ. 1975, 3, 387-393.

5279. Moore,W.P. and Kolansky,H. "Marihuana experts; findings of a study." New Repub. 1971, 164, 7-8.

5280. Moreau,B. "Note on Indian hemp."(Fr.). Bull. Sci. Pharmacol. 1912, 19, 599-601.

5281. Moreau,H. Study of Hashish.(Fr.). Univ. Paris, Dept. Med., Paris, 1904.

5282. Moreau,J.J. On Hashish and Mental Alientation. (Fr.). Masson, Paris, 1845.

5283. Moreau,J.J. "Depression with stupor; tendence to dementia. Treatment with a resinous extract of cannabis indica--cure."(Fr.). Gaz. Hop. Civil. Milit. 1857, 30, 391.

5284. Moreno,G. Aspects of Maconhism in Sergipe. (Port.). Serv. Nacion. Educac. Sanit., Rio de Janeiro, 1958.

5285. Moreton,J.E. "Effects of marihuana on sleep and wakefulness: An electroencephalographic study in the rat and cat." Diss. Abs. 1972, 32, 4118.

5286. Moreton,J.E. and Davis,W.M. "A simple method for the preparation of injectables of tetrahydrocannabinol and cannabis extracts." J. Pharm. Pharmacol. 1972, 24, 176.

5287. Moreton,J.E. and Davis,W.M. "Effects of delta-9-tetrahydrocannabinol on locomotor activity and on phase of sleep." Pharmacologist 1970, 12, 258.

5288. Moreton,J.E. and Davis,W.M. "Electroencephalographic study of effects of delta-9- and delta-8-tetrahydrocannabinol and cannabis extract on sleep in the rat." Pharmacologist 1971, 13, 246.

5289. Moreton,J.E. and Davis,W.M. "Electroencephalographic study of the effects of tetrahydrocannabinols on sleep in the rat." Neuropharmacol. 1973, 12, 897-907.

5290. Morgenstern,J.J. "Observations on teenage drug abuse." Clin. Med. 1970, 77, 15-18.

5291. Morier,M.W. Home Grown Happiness. Merkus, N.Y., 1967.

5292. Morishima,A., Henrich,R., Jou,S., and Nahas,G.G. "Errors of chromosome segregation induced by olivetol, a compound with the structure of C-ring common to cannabinoids: Formation of bridges and multipolar divisions." In Nahas,G.G., Paton,W.D.M., and Idanpaan-Heikkila,J.E.(eds.). Marihuana. Springer Verlag, N.Y., 1976, 265-271.

5293. Morishima,A., Milstein,M., Henrich,R., and Nahas,G.G. "Effects of marihuana smoking, cannabinoids, and olivetol on replication of human lymphocytes: Formation of micronuclei." In Braude,M.C. and Szara,S. (eds.). Pharmacology of Marihuana. Raven Press, N.Y., 1976, 711-723.

5294. Morkholdt,A.J., Nielsen,E., Schou,J., Steentoft,A., and Worm,K. "A specific method for the demonstration of cannabis intake by TLC of urine." Act. Pharmacol. Toxicol. 1971, 29, 111-112.

5295. Morley,J.E. and Bensusan,A.D. "Dagga: Tribal uses and customs." Med. Proc. 1971, 17, 409-412.

5296. Morley,J.E., Logie,P., and Bensusan,A.D. "The subjective effects of dagga: including comparative studies with Britain and America." S. Af. Med. J. 1973, 47, 1145-1149.

5297. Morris,A. "Some reflections on dealing." Drugs Soc. 1972, 1, 6-8.

5298. Morris,F.S. and Houghton,H.C. "Should narcotics education be extended to juveniles?" Congress. Dig. 1954, 33, 3-12, 314.

5299. Morrisey,L. "I was JFL's dealer." High Times 1974, 2, 27-29.

5300. Morrisey,L. "The night they raided Crosby's." High Times 1974, 3, 42-45.

5301. Morrison,D.E. "The legality of university-conducted dormitory searches for internal disciplinary purposes." Duke Law Rev. 1976, 4, 770-778.

5302. Morrison,L. "Dana Beal interview." High Times 1977, 22, 34-45.

5303. Morrison,R.L. Preliminary Report on the Incidence of the Use of Drugs at Sacramento College. Unpub. ms., Sacramento College, Sacramento, 1969.

5304. Morrow,R.S. "Pscyhological aspects. Psycho-physical and other functions." In Mayor's Committee on Marihuana. The Marihuana Problem in the City of New York. Jacques Cattell Press, Lancaster, Pa., 1944,

5305. Morton,D.M. "The identification and analysis of hallucinogenic substances." J. Mond. Pharm. 1970, 3, 221-230.

5306. Moscou,P.J. "A survey of drug use at Ithica college." J. Coll. Hlth. Assoc. 1968, 17, 43-51.

5307. Mosk,S.A. "Subsidized hemp production in Spanish California." Agricult. Hist. 1939, 13, 171-175.

5308. Moskowitz,H. "Marihuana and driving." Accid. Anal. Prevent. 1976, 8, 21-26.

5309. Moskowitz,H. "Marihuana: effects on simulated driving performance." Accid. Anal. Prevent. 1976, 8, 45-50.

5310. Moskowitz,H. "Psychological tests and drugs." Pharmakopsychiat. Neuropsychopharmakol. 1973, 6, 114-126.

5311. Moskowitz,H. and McGlothlin,W. "Effects of marihuana on auditory signal detection." Psychopharmacol. 1974, 40, 137-145.

5312. Moskowitz,H., McGlothlin,W., and Hulbert,S. The Effects of Marihuana Dosage on Driver Performance. Inst. Transportation Traffic Engineering, Univ. Cal., Los Angeles, 1973.

5313. Moskowitz,H., Shea,R., and Burns,M. "Effect of marihuana on the psychosocial refractory period." Percept. Motor Skills 1974, 38, 959-962.

5314. Moskowitz,H., Sharma,S., and McGlothlin,W. "Effect of marihuana upon peripheral vision as a function of the information processing demands in central vision." Percept. Motor Skills 1972, 35, 875-882.

5315. Moskowitz,H., Sharma,S., and Schapero,M. "A comparison of the effects of marihuana and alcohol on visual functions." In Lewis,M.F.(ed.). Current Research in Marihuana. Academic Press, N.Y., 1972, 129-150.

5316. Moskowitz,H., Ziedman,K., and Sharma,S. "Visual search behavior while viewing driving scenes under the influence of alcohol and marihuana." Human Fact. 1976, 18, 417-432.

5317. Mosnaim,A.D., Inwang,E.E., and Sabelli,H.C. "The influence of psychotropic drugs on the levels of endogenous 2-phenylethylamine in rabbit brain." Biol. Psychiat. 1974, 8, 227-234.

5318. Moss,G.C. "Legalize marihuana?" Med. J. Aust. 1970, 2, 252.

5319. Moss,I.R. and Friedman,E. "Delta-9-tetrahydrocannabinol: Depression of ventilatory regulation; other respiratory and cardiovascular effects." Life Sci. 1976, 19, 99-104.

5320. Mothes,K. and Engelbrecht,L. "Sexually differentiated metabolism of dioecious annual plants. I. Investigation of the changes of the nitrogenous compounds in hemp(cannbis sativa L.)."(Ger.). Flora 1952, 139, 1-27.

5321. Mount,F. "Wild grass chase." Nat'l. Rep. 1968, 20, 81-84.

5322. Mouren,P., Tatossian,A., Giudicelli,S., Fresco,R., Scarone,M., and Rosello,P. "Notes on drug addicts in a medical environment."(Fr.). Marseille Med. 1970, 107, 463-466.

5323. Moutschen,J. and Govaerts,J. "Action of gamma-rays on seeds of cannabis sativa L." Nature 1953, 172, 350-351.

5324. Mouza,A. "A symposium on drug dependence." Internat'l. Crim. Pol. Rev. 1972, 27, 230-231.

5325. Muggia,A. "New legislative regulations for possession and use of marihuana."(It.). Minerv. Med. 1972, 63, 20-21.

5326. Mukhopadhyay,B.K., Subramanian,K.S., and Dunnicliff,H.B. "A colorimetric method for estimating the narcotic power of hemp drugs." Analyst 1943, 68, 70-74.

5327. Muller,A. "Preparations of extracts from cannabis sativa."(Fr.). J. Pharm. Chim. 1855, 27, 296-298.

5328. Muller,K.H.G. and Heuck,F. "The chest X-ray in advanced cannabiosis."(Ger.). Deut. Med. Woch. 1974, 99, 952-954.

5329. Muller-Oswald,U. "Personality aspects of 19-year-old male drug abusers."(Ger.). Arch. Psychiat. Nervenk. 1973, 217, 207-222.

5330. Mullins,C.J., Vitola,B.M., and Abellera,J.W. "Users of cannabis only." Cat. Select. Doc. Psychol. 1975, 5, 240.

5331. Mullins,C.J., Vitola,B.M., and Michelson,A.E. "Variables related to cannabis use." Internat'l. J. Addict. 1975, 10, 481-502.

5332. Mullins,C.J., Vitola,B.M., and Michelson,A.E. "Variables related pre-service cannabis use in a sample of Air Force enlistees." Cat. Select. Doc. Psychol. 1974, 4, 134.

5333. Munch,J.C. "Marihuana and crime." Bull. Narc. 1966, 18, 15-22.

5334. Munch,J.C. "The toxicity of cannabis sativa (marihuana)." Cur. Med. Dig. 1968, 35, 692-697.

5335. Munch,J.C. "The toxicity of cannabis sativa (marihuana). Toxicol. Appl. Pharmacol. 1968, 12, 293.

5336. Munch,J.C. and Mantz,H.W. "Cannabis sativa. III. Pharmacology and pharmacy of 'hemp seed'." Pa. Pharmacist 1937, 17, 18-19.

5337. Munch,J.C., Mantz,H.W., Dietrich,W.C., and Pratt,H.J. "Cannabis sativa. II. Qualitative identity tests." Pa. Pharmacist 1937, 17, 17-18.

5338. Muniz-Angulo,L. "Marihuana intoxication."(Sp.). Rev. Sanidad Milit. 1944, 8, 115-129.

5339. Munroe,J. and Harris,R.A. "Effects of delta-9-tetrahydrocannabinol on mitochrondrial processes." Fed. Proc. 1971, 30, 1199.

5340. Munsen,A.E. "Marihuana and immunity." In Tinklenberg,J.R.(ed.). Marihuana and Health Hazards. Academic Press, N.Y., 1975, 39-47.

5341. Munson,A.E., Levy,J.A., Harris,L.S., and Dewey,W.L. "Effects of delta-9-tetrahydrocannabinol on the immune system." In Braude,M.C. and Szara,S.(eds.). Pharmacology of Marihuana. Raven Press, N.Y. 1976, 187-199.

5342. Munson,A.E., Harris,L.S., Friedman,M.A., Dewey,W.L., and Carchman,R.A. "Antineoplastic activity of cannabinoids." J. Nat'l. Cancer Inst. 1975, 55, 597-602.

5343. Murphree,H.B. "Clinical effects of hemp preparations." Sem. Drug Treat. 1971, 1, 195-206.

5344. Murphree,H.B. "Neuropharmacology of psychotomimetic drugs." N.J. Med. Soc. J. 1968, 65, 537-542.

5345. Murphy,B.M. "The cannabis habit. A review of recent psychiatric literature." Bull. Narc. 1963, 15, 15-23.

5346. Murphy,B.W., Leventhal,A.M., and Balter,M.D. "Drug use on the campus: A survey of university health services and counselling centers." J. Am. Coll. Hlth. Assoc. 1969, 17, 389-402.

5347. Murphy,E.F. The Black Candle. Thomas Allen, Toronto, 1926.

5348. Murphy,P.A. "Marihuana." Maryland State Med. J. 1974, 23, 58-62.

5349. Murray,T.F. and Craigmill,A.L. "Interactions between delta-9-tetrahydrocannabinol and phencyclidine in rats and mice." Proc. West. Pharmacol. Soc. 1976, 19, 362-368.

5350. Musto,D.F. The American Disease; Origins of Narcotic Control. Yale Univ. Press, New Haven, 1973.

5351. Musto,D.F. "Evolution of American Narcotic Controls." In National Commission on Marihuana and Drug Abuse. Drug Use in America: Problem in Perspective. Gov't. Print. Office, Washington,D.C., 1973, III, 335-351.

5352. Musto,D.F. "The Marihuana Tax Act of 1937." Arch. Gen. Psychiat. 1972, 26, 101-108.

5353. Musty,R.E., Karniol,I.G., Shirakawa,I., Takahashi,R.N., and Knobel,E. "Interactions of delta-9-THC and cannabinol in man." In Braude,M.C. and Szara,S.(eds.). Pharmacology of Marihuana. Raven Press, N.Y., 1976, 559-565.

5354. Musty,R.E., Lindsey,C.J., and Carlini,E.A. "6-hydroxydopamine and the aggressive behavior induced by marihuana in REM sleep-deprived rats." Psychopharmacol. 1976, 48, 175-179.

5355. My,D. "Which reports are to be published on the differences between the effects of German and Indian hemp?"(Ger.). Pharm. 1950, 3, 136.

5356. Myers,H.B. "Cross tolerance. Altered susceptibility to codein, heroin, cannabis indica and chloral hydrate in dogs having an acquired tolerance for morphine." J. Pharmacol. 1916, 8, 417-437.

5357. Myers,S.A. and Caldwell,D.F. "Effects of marihuana on auditory and visual sensation." Mich. Ment. Hlth. Res. Bull. 1969, 3, 60-62.

5358. Myers,S.A. and Caldwell,D.F. "The effects of marihuana on auditory and visual sensation: A preliminary report." New Phys. 1969, 18, 212-215.

5359. Myers,S.A., Craves,F.B., Caldwell,D.F., and Loh,H.H. "Inhalation induced tolerance and physical dependence: The hazard of opiate suffused marihuana." Milit. Med. 1972, 137, 431-433.

5360. Myers,W.A. "LSD and marihuana: Where are the answers?" Science 1968, 160, 1062.

5361. Myttenaere,F. "Seventh study on cannabis. Cannabinol."(Fr.). Bull. Acad. Roy. Med. Belg. 1941, 6, 326-344.

N

5362. Nader,P. and Haggerty,R. "The pediatrician and the marihuana question." Pediatrics 1970, 45, 1040.

5363. Nader,P.R. and Haggerty,R.J. "The pot hot spot. Where does the pediatrician stand on marihuana?" Pediatrics 1970, 45, 1-3.

5364. Naditch,M.P. "Acute adverse reactions to psychoactive drugs, drug usage, and psychopathology." J. Abnorm. Psychol. 1974, 83, 394-403.

5365. Naditch,M.P. "Ego functioning and acute adverse reactions to psychoactive drugs." J. Personal. 1957, 43, 305-320.

5366. Naditch,M.P. "Ego mechanisms and marihuana usage." In Lettieri,D.J.(ed.). Predicting Adolescent Drug Abuse: A Review of Issues, Methods and Correlates. N.I.D.A. Res. Iss. Ser. 11, Gov't. Print. Office, Washington, D.C., 1975, 207-222.

5367. Naditch,M.P., Alker,P.C., and Joffe,P. "Individual differences and setting as determinants of acute adverse reactions to psychoactive drugs." J. Nerv. Ment. Dis. 1975, 161, 326-335.

5368. Nahas,G.G. "Biomedical aspects of cannabis usage." Bull. Narc. 1977, 29, 13-27.

5369. Nahas,G.G. "Cannabis arteritis." N. Eng. J. Med. 1971, 284, 113.

5370. Nahas,G.G. "Cannabis sativa. The deceptive weed." N.Y. State J. Med. 1972, 72, 856-868.

5371. Nahas,G.G. "Clinical pharmacology of cannabis sativa with special reference to delta-9-THC." Bull. Narc. 1973, 25, 9-39.

5372. Nahas,G.G. "Effects of hashish consumption in Egypt." N. Eng. J. Med. 1972, 207, 310.

5373. Nahas,G.G. "Effects of marihuana smoking and natural cannabinoids on the replication of human lymphocytes and the formation of hypodiploid cells." In Tinklenberg,J.R.(ed.). Marihuana and Health Hazards. Academic Press, N.Y., 1975, 47-55.

5374. Nahas,G.G. Keep Off The Grass. Reader's Digest Press, N.Y., 1976.

5375. Nahas,G.G. "Lethal cannabis intoxication." N. Eng. J. Med. 1971, 284, 792.

5376. Nahas,G.G. "Marihuana." J.A.M.A. 1975, 233, 79-80.

5377. Nahas,G.G. "Marihuana: Deceptive weed." Nat'l. Rep. 1973, 25, 1312.

5378. Nahas,G.G. Marihuana--Deceptive Weed. Raven Press, N.Y., 1973.

5379. Nahas,G.G. "Toxicology and pharmacology of cannabis sativa with special reference to delta-9-THC." Bull. Narc. 1972, 24, 11-27.

5380. Nahas,G.G., Armand,J.P., and Hsu,J. "In vitro inhibition of blastogenesis of T lymphocytes by delta-9-tetrahydrocannabinol."(Fr.). C. R. Acad. Sci. 1974, 278, 679-680.

5381. Nahas,G.G., Desoize,B., Hsu,J., and Morishima,A. "Inhibitiory effects of delta-9-tetrahydrocannabinol on nucleic acid synthesis and proteins in cultured lymphocytes." In Nahas,G.G., Paton,W.D.M., and Idanpaan-Heikkila,J.E.(eds.). Marihuana. Springer Verlag, N.Y., 1976, 299-312.

5382. Nahas,G.G. and Greenwood,H. "A critique of the First Report of the National Commission on Marihuana and Drug Abuse(1972)." Psychiat. Ann. 1973, 3, 94-106.

5384. Nahas,G.G. and Greenwood,A. "The First Report of the National Commission of Marihuana (1972): Signal of misunderstanding or exercise in ambiguity." Bull. Narc. 1974, 40, 55-75.

5385. Nahas,G.G., Morishima,A., and Dosoize,B. "Effects of cannabinoids on macromolecular synthesis and replication of cultured lymphocytes." Fed. Proc. 1977, 36, 1748-1752.

5386. Nahas,G.G., Schwartz,I.W., Adamec,J., and Manger,W.M. "Tolerance to delta-9-tetrahydrocannabinol in the spontaneously hyptertensive rat." Proc. Soc. Expt'l. Biol. Med. 1973, 142, 58-60.

5387. Nahas,G.G., Schwartz,I., Palacek,I., and Tannieres,M.L. "Delta-9-tetrahydrocannabinol tolerance in the hypertensive rat."(Fr.). J. Physiol. 1972, 65, 461A.

5388. Nahas,G.G., Schwartz,I., Palacek,J., and Zagury,D. "Effect of an inhibitor of the immunogenic response on the development of tolerance to delta-9-tetrahydrocannabinol."(Fr.). C. R. Acad. Sci. 1973, 276, 667-668.

5389. Nahas,G.G., Schwartz,I., Palacek,J., and Zagury,D. "Tolerance to delta-9-tetrahydrocannabinol in the hypertensive rat."(Fr.). C. R. Acad. Sci. 1972, 275, 1931-1932.

5390. Nahas,G.G., Sesoiz,B., Armand,J.P., Hsu,J., and Morishima,A. "Natural cannabinoids: Apparent depression of nucleic acids and protein synthesis in cultured human lymphocytes." In Braude,M.C. and Szara,S.(eds.). Pharmacology of Marihuana. Raven Press, 1976, 1, 177-187.

5391. Nahas,G.G., Suciu-Foca,N., and Armand,J.P. "Decrease of cellular immunity in hashish(marihuana) smokers."(Fr.). C. R. Acad. Med. 1973, 227, 979-980.

5392. Nahas,G.G., Suciu-Foca,N., Armand,J.P., and Morishima,A. "Inhibition of cellular mediated immunity in marihuana smokers." Science 1974, 183, 419-420.

5393. Nahas,G.G. and Vourc'h,G. "Toxic derivatives of cannabis sativa."(Sp.). Rev. Med. Legal Colombia 1969, 24, 193-202.

5394. Nahas,G.G. and Vourc'h,G. "Toxic derivatives of the cannabis sativa."(Fr.). Presse Med. 1970, 78, 1679-1684.

5395. Nahas,G.G. and Vourc'h,G. "Toxicity of Indian hemp." Presse Med. 1973, 2, 167-173.

5396. Nahas,G.G., Zagury,D., Schwartz,I.W., and Nagel,M.D. "Evidence for the possible immunogenicity of delta-9-tetrahydrocannabinol(THC) in rodents." Nature 1973, 243, 407-408.

5397. Nahas,G.G., Zeidenberg,P., and Lefebure,C. "Kif in Morocco." Internat'l. J. Addict. 1975, 10, 977-993.

5398. Nail,R.L. and Dean,L.M. "Drug abuse: a manifestation of the cyclic nature of human behavior." Drug Alcohol Depend. 1975, 1, 429-434.

5399. Nail,R.L., Gunderson,E.K.E., and Kolb,D. "Motives for drug use among light and heavy users. J. Nerv. Ment. Dis. 1974, 159, 131-136.

5400. Nail,R.L., Gunderson,E.K.E., Kolb,D., and Butler,M. "Drug histories of navy amnesty cases." Milit. Med. 1975, 11, 172-178.

5401. Nakamura,G.R. "Drug abuse control. Forensic aspects of cystolith hairs of cannabis and other plants." J. Assoc. Offic. Anal. Chem. 1969, 52, 5-16.

5402. Nakamura,G.R. and Thornton,J.L. "The forensic identification of marihuana: some questions and answers." J. Pol. Sci. Admin. 1973, 1, 102-112.

5403. Nakazawa,K. and Costa,E. "Metabolism of delta-9-tetrahydrocannabinol by lung and liver homogenates of rats treated with methylcholanthrene." Nature 1971, 234, 48-49.

5404. Nakazawa,K. and Costa,E. "The pharmacological implications of delta-9-tetrahydrocannabinol metabolism by lung: Effects of 3-methylcholanthrene." Ann. N. Y. Acad. Sci. 1971, 191, 216-222.

5405. Naliboff,B.D., Rickles,W.H., Cohen,M.J., and Naimark,R.S. "Interactions of marihuana and induced stress: forearm blood flow, heart rate, and skin conductance." Psychophysiol. 1976, 13, 517-522.

5406. Nassar,N.T. "Studies in the nonmedical use of drugs in Lebanon. I. The nonmedical use of marihuana, LSD, and amphetamine by students at the American University of Beirut." J. Med. Liban. 1973, 26, 215-232.

5407. Nassonov,V.A. "Anatomical characteristics of geographical races of cannabis."(Rus.). Vest. Sotsial. Rastenievost. 1940, 4, 107-120.

5408. National Council for Civil Liberties. Drugs and Civil Liberties. Nat'l. Council Civil Liberties, London, 1967.

5409. National Organization for the Reform of Marihuana Laws. A Compilation of State Citation Laws for Minor Marihuana Offences. N.O.R.M.L., Washington, D.C., 1975.

5410. National Organization for the Reform of Marihuana Laws. Position Paper. N.O.R.M.L., Washington, D.C., 1971.

5411. National Student Association. "NSA's resolution concerning drugs on campus: Codification of NSA policy." In Hollander,C.(ed.). Background Papers on Student Drug Involvement. Nat'l. Stud. Assoc., Washington,D.C., 1967, 37-40.

5412. Navratil,J. "Effects of cannabis indica on chronic otitis medica."(Czech.). Act. Univ. Palack. Olomuc. 1955, 6, 87-89.

5413. Navratil,J., Medek,A., Hrbek,J., Krejci,Z., Komenda,S., and Dvorak,M. "The effect of cannabis on the conditioned alimentary motor reflex in cats." Act. Nerv. Sup. 1972, 14, 109-110.

5414. Navratil,J., Medek,A., Hrbek,J., Krejci,Z., Komenda,S., and Dvorak,M. "The effect of interaction of syntostigmine and cannabis upon alimentary motor reflexes in cats." Act. Nerv. Sup. 1975, 17, 66-67.

5415. Nazar,B.L., Harclerode,J., Roth,R.I., and Butler,R.C. "Acquisition of tolerance to delta-9-THC as measured by the response of a cellular function." Life Sci. 1974, 14, 2513-2520.

5416. Negm,M. Contribution to the Toxicological Study of Hashish and Its Prohibition in Egypt.(Fr.). Ehesis, Strassburg, 1938.

5417. Negrete Cordova,R.E. "Cannabis sativa cultivated in Chile."(Sp.). An. Fac. Quim. Far. Univ. 1962, 14, 49-56.

5418. Negrete Cordova,R.E. "Psychological adverse effects of cannabis smoking. A tentative classification." Can. Med. Assoc. J. 1973, 108, 195-202.

5419. Negrete Cordova,R.E. and Kwan,M.W. "Relative value of various etiological factors in short lasting, adverse psychological reactions to cannabis smoking." Internat'l. Pharmacopsychiat. 1972, 7, 249-259.

5420. Negrete Cordova,R.E. and Kwan,M.W. "Symptoms of cannabis intoxication among a group of users and nonusers."(Fr.). Toxicomanies 1974, 7, 7-18.

5421. Neier,A. "Public boozers and private smokers. Law enforcement involving victimless crimes, particularly public drunkeness and marihuana smoking." Civil Lib. Rev. 1975, 2, 41-56.

5422. Nel,E. "Opinion change in the advocate as a function of the persuasibility of his audience: a clarification of the meaning of dissonance." J. Personal. Soc. Psychol. 1969, 12, 17-24.

5423. Neligan,J.M. Medicines, Their Uses and Mode of Administration. Harper and Bros., 1844.

5424. Nelson,E. and Panzacella,J. "Drug use in the military service." In Hardy,R.E. and Cull,J.G. (eds.). Drug Dependence And Rehabilitation Approaches. C.C. Thomas, Springfield, Ill., 1971, 88-112.

5425. Nesbitt,M. "Psychosis due to exogenous toxins--marihuana." Ill. Med. J. 1940, 77, 278-282.

5426. Nesi,W. "Oral effects resulting from smoking cannabis sativa(marihuana)."(Port.). Rev. Brazil Odont. 1970, 27, 81-92.

5427. Neto,J.P. "The effects of chronic cannabis treatment upon brain 5-hydroxytryptamine, plasma corticosterone and aggressive behavior in female rats with different hormonal status." Psychopharmacol. 1975, 42, 195-200.

5428. Nettels,C.P. The Emergence of a National Economy. Holt, Rinehart and Winston, N.Y., 1962.

5429. Neu,C., DiMascio,A., and Zwilling,G. "Hypnotic properties of THC: Experimental comparison of THC, chloral hydrate and placebo." In Cohen,S. and Stillman,R.(eds.). Therapeutic Potential of Marihuana. Plenum Press, N.Y., 1976, 153-160.

5430. Neu,R., Powers,H.O., King,S., and Gardner,L.I. "Cannabis and chromosomes." Lancet 1969, 1, 675.

5431. Neu,R., Powers,H.O., King,S., and Gardner,L.I. "Delta-8- and delta-9-tetrahydrocannabinol: Effects on cultured human leucocytes." J. Clin. Pharmacol. 1970, 10, 228-230.

5432. Neuberg,R. "Drug dependence and pregnancy. A review of the problems and their management." J. Obstet. Gynecol. 1970, 77, 1117-1122.

5433. Neumeyer,J.L. and Shagoury,R.A. "Chemistry and pharmacology of marihuana." J. Pharmaceut. Sci. 1971, 60, 1433-1457.

5434. Nevinnykh,V.A. "Hybridization of southern dioecious varieties of cannabis sativa with monoecious varieties."(Rus.). Agrobiologiya 1962, 2, 205-212.

5435. New Jersey. Commission to Study and Review the Penalties Imposed on Individuals Convicted of Using Certain Substances. First Report to the Legislature. State House, Trenton, 1974.

5436. New Jersey. Commission to Study and Review the Penalties Imposed on Individuals Convicted of Using Certain Substances. Second Report to the Legislature. State House, Trenton, 1975.

5437. New Jersey. General Assembly. Judiciary Committee. Public Hearings on Assembly No. 2312 (Decriminalization of Marihuana), Held Trenton, N.J., Mar. 3, 1975. State House, Trenton, 1975.

5438. New Jersey. State Police Uniform Crime Reporting Unit. Drug Abuse and Crime in New Jersey. State Law Enforcement Planning Agency, Trenton, 1971.

5439. New York. Department of Health. "Violence direct result of marihuana, says Bellizzi: State Health official cites 27 murders by drug users." N.Y. Dept. Hlth. Week. Bull. 1967, 20, 101.

5440. New York. Nassau County Probation Department. Drug Abuse in Suburbia. Probation Dept., Minneola, 1972.

5441. New York. Parole Division. Lawbreaking and Drug Dependency. Parole Div., Albany, 1969.

5442. Newby,J.H. "Small group dynamics and drug abuse in an army setting: A case study." Internat'l. J. Addict. 1977, 12, 287-300.

5443. Newcomb,E.L., Smyithe,C.E., and Hodel,E.R. "Notes on the ash yield of cannabis." J.A.P.A. 1921, 10, 695-687.

5444. Newitt,J. and Kahn,H. "Some speculations on U.S. drug use." J. Soc. Iss. 1971, 27, 107-122.

5445. Newman,L.M., Lutz,M.P., Gould,M.H., and Domino,E.F. "Delta-9-tetrahydrocannabinol and ethyl alcohol: Evidence for cross-tolerance in the rat." Science 1971, 175, 1022-1023.

5446. Newman,L.M., Lutz,M.P., and Domino,E.F. "Delta-9-tetrahydrocannabinol and some CNS depressants: Evidence for cross-tolerance in the rat." Arch. Internat'l. Pharmacodyn. Ther. 1974, 207, 254-259.

5447. Newmeyer,J.A. "Addicts' attitudes toward drugs: a semantic-differential study." Drug Alcohol Depend. 1976, 1, 255-262.

5448. Newton,J.E. "The potential drug problem on Norfolk Island." J. Drug Iss. 1977, 7, 427-437.

5449. Ng,L.K.Y., Lamprecht,F., Williams,R.B., and Kopin,I.J. "Delta-9-tetrahydrocannabinol and ethanol: Differential effects of sympathetic activity in different environmental setting." Science 1973, 180, 1368-1369.

5450. Nicholas,J.L. Drug Use and Highway Saftey: A Review of the Literature. Univ. Wisconsin, Stevens Point, Wis., 1971.

5451. Nichols,M. "Adolescent marihuana use and deviance: A sociopsychological approach." Diss. Abs. 1975, 35, 5648.

5452. Nochols,W.W., Miller,R.C., Heneen,W., Bradt,C., Hollister,L.E., and Kanter,S. "Cytogenetic studies on human subjects receiving marihuana and delta-9-tetrahydrocannabinol." Mut. Res. 1974, 26, 413-417.

5453. Nocholson,M.T., Pace,H.B., and Davis,W.M. "Effects of marihuana and lysergic acid diethylamide on leukocyte chromosomes of the golden hamster." Res. Commun. Chem. Pathol. Pharmacol. 1973, 6, 427-434.

5454. Nickolls,L.C. "Note on Beam's test for hashish(Indian hemp)." Analyst 1936, 61, 604.

5455. Nidorf,J.F. "The social-psychological context of cannabis use in Denmark: A study of compatability and contrast in attitudes and beliefs." Diss. Abs. 1974, 34, 6748.

5456. Nielsen,E. "Thin-layer chromatographic analysis of cannabis from Danish and other sources." Dan. Tid. Farm. 1970, 44, 359-364.

5457. Nigam,M.C., Handa,K.L., Nigam,I.C., and Levi,L. "Essential oils and their constituents. XXIX. The essential oil of marihuana: Composition of genuine Indian cannabis sativa L." Can. J. Chem. 1965, 43, 3372-3376.

5458. Nightingale,S.L. "Treatment for drug abusers in the United States." Addict. Dis. 1977, 3, 11-20.

5459. Nigrete,J.C. "Psychological adverse effects of cannabis smoking: a tentative classification." Can. Med. Assoc. J. 1973, 108, 195-196.

5460. Nikiforov,I.D. "The taxonomy of widespread forms of wild hemp seed in Azerbijan SSR."(Rus.). Trud. Priklad. Bot. Genet. Selek. 1963, 35, 201-203.

5461. Nilsson,I.M., Agurell,S., Leander,K., Nilsson,J.L.G., and Widman,M. "Cannabidiol: Structure of three metabolites formed in rat liver." *Act. Pharmaceut. Suec.* 1971, *8*, 700-701.

5462. Nilsson,I.M., Agurell,S., and Nilsson,J.L.G. "Synthesis of cannabinoid metabolites." *Act. Pharmaceut. Suec.* 1971, *8*, 676-677.

5463. Nilsson,I.M., Agurell,S., and Nilsson,J.L.G. Ohlsson,A., Lindgren,J.E., and Mechoulam,R. "Metabolism of 7-hydroxy-1(6)-tetrahydrocannabinol in the rabbit." *Act. Pharmaceut. Suec.* 1973, *10*, 97-106.

5464. Nilsson,I.M., Agurell,S., Nilsson,J.L.G., Ohlsson,A., Sandberg,F., and Wahlquist,M. "Delta-1-tetrahydrocannabinol: Structure of a major metabolite." *Science* 1970, *168*, 1228-1229.

5465. Nilsson,I.M., Agurell,S., Nilsson,J.L.G., Widman,M., and Leander,K. "Two cannabinoid metabolites formed by rat liver." *J. Pharm. Pharmacol.* 1973, *25*, 486-487.

5466. Nilsson,J.L.G., Lars,G., Nilsson,I.M., and Agurell,S. "Synthesis of isotope-labelled tetrahydrocannabinol, active material of cannabis."(Swed.). *Kemisk Tidskrift* 1970, *82*, 30-31.

5467. Nilsson,J.L.G., Lars,G., Nilsson,I.M., and Agurell,S. "Synthesis of ^{3}H- and ^{14}C-labelled tetrahydrocannabinols." *Act. Chem. Scand.* 1969, *23*, 2209-2211.

5468. Nilsson,J.L.G., Nilsson,I.M., and Agurell,S. "Metabolism of cannabis. XI. Synthesis of tetrahydrocannabinol and 7-hydroxy-tetrahydrocannabinol." *Act. Chem. Scand.* 1971, *25*, 768-769.

5469. Nilsson,J.L.G., Nilsson,I.M., Agurell,S., Ben-Zvi,Z., and Mechoulam,R. "Metabolism of cannabis. XII. Synthesis of a potential urinary tetrahydrocannabinol metabolite." *Act. Chem. Suec.* 1972, *9*, 215-220.

5470. Nimb,M. "The danger of drugs to society. Rational and irrational considerations." In Wittenborn, J.R., Smith,J.P., and Wittenborn,S.A.(eds.). *Communication and Drug Abuse*. C.C. Thomas, Springfield, Ill., 1970, 217-222.

5471. Nimb,M. "Transcultural contrasts in patterns of drug abuse in light of Scandinavian experience." In Wittenborn,J.R., Brill,H., Smith,J.P., and Wittenborn, S.A.(eds.). *Drugs and Youth*. C.C. Thomas, Springfield, Ill., 1969, 447-451.

5472. Nir,I., Ayalon,D., Tsafrivi,A., Cordova,T., and Lindner,H.R. "Suppression of the cyclic surge of luteinizing hormone secretion and of ovulation in the rat by delta-1-tetrahydrocannabinol." Nature 1973, 243, 470-471.

5473. Nisbet,C.T. and Vakil,R. "Some estimates of price and expenditure elasticities of demand for marihuana among UCLA students." Rev. Econ. Stat. 1972, 54, 473-475.

5474. Nisbet,C.T. and Vakil,R. "Some social and economic characteristics of UCLA student marihuana users." Soc. Sci. Quart. 1971, 52, 179-189.

5475. Nishioka,I. "Cannabis."(Jap.). Fol. Pharmacol. Jap. 1971, 46, 115P-120P.

5476. Noble,P.J. "Drug-taking in delinquent boys." Br. Med. J. 1970, 1, 102-105.

5477. Noirfalise,A. "Considerations on cannabis sativa." Arch. Belg. Med. Soc. 1965, 23, 373-386.

5478. Nordal,A. "Microscopic detection of cannabis in the pure state and in semi-combusted residues." In Joyce,C.R.B. and Curry,S.H.(eds.). The Botany and Chemistry of Cannabis. J. and A. Churchill, London, 1970, 61-69.

5479. Nordal,A. and Braenden,O. "Variations in the cannabinoid content of cannabis plants grown from the same seeds under different ecological conditions." (Swed.). Med. Norsk Farmaceut. Selskap 1973, 35, 8-15.

5480. Nordquist,M., Agurell,S., Binder,M., and Nilsson,I.M. "Structure of an acidic metabolite of delta-1-tetrahydrocannabinol isolated from rabbit urine." J. Pharm. Pharmacol. 1974, 26, 471-473.

5481. Nordquist,M., Lindren,J.E., and Agurell,S. "A method for the identification of acid metabolites of tetrahydrocannabinol(THC) by mass fragmentography." In Willette,P.(ed.). Cannabinoid Assays in Humans. N.I.D.A. Res. Monog. Ser. 7, Dept. H.E.W., Gov't. Print. Office, Washington,D.C., 1976, 64-69.

5482. Norman,C. "New state laws on marihuana." Drugs Soc. 1973, 3, 18-20.

5483. Norton,W.A. "The marihuana habit: Some observations of a small group of users." Can. Psychiat. Assoc. J. 1968, 13, 163-173.

5484. Norris,A.S. "The physician, marihuana, and reason." J. Iowa Med. Soc. 1970, 60, 623-630.

5485. Norris,A.S. "We know too little on marihuana." Sci. Dig. 1971, 69, 78-81.

5486. Norwich,I. "A chapter of early medical Africana." S. Af. Med. J. 1971, 8, 501-504.

5487. Novak,I., Buzas,G., and Toth,L. "Comparative qualitative examinations of Hungarian and Indian hemp varieties. 2nd communication."(Ger.). Pharmazie 1962, 17, 166-173.

5488. Novak,I., Buzas,G., Toth,L., and Simon,L. "Comparative investigation of Hungarian and Indian hemp."(Ger.). Pharmazie 1962, 17, 95-98.

5489. Novak,I., Haznagy,A., and Szendrei,K. "UV spectrophotometric research and 'Beam chloride values' of Hungarian and Indian hemp."(Ger.). Pharmazie 1962, 17, 294-297.

5490. Novelli,A. "Active substances in cannabis." (Port.). Rev. Cent. Estud. Farm. Bioquim. 1944, 33, 281-285.

5491. Novotny,M. and Lee,M.L. "Detection of marihuana smoke in the atomosphere of a room." Exper. 1973, 29, 1038-1039.

5492. Novotny,M., Lee,M.L. and Low,C.E. "A possible chemical basis for the higher mutagenicity of marihuana smoke as compared to tobacco smoke." Exper. 1976, 32, 280-282.

5493. Novotny,M., Lee,M.L., Low,C.E., and Maskarinec,M.P. "High resolution gas chromatography/ mass spectrometric analysis of tobacco and marihuana sterols." Steroids 1976, 27, -65-673.

5494. Novotny,M., Lee,M.L., Low,C.E., and Raymond,A. "Analysis of marihuana samples from different origins by high-resolution gas-liquid chromatography for forensic application." Anal. Chem. 1976, 48, 24-29.

5495. Nowell,C.E. "The Old Man of the Mountain." Speculum 1947, 22, 497-519.

5496. Nowlan,R. and Cohen,S. "Tolerance to marihuana." Clin. Pharmacol. Ther. 1977, 22, 550-556.

5497. Nowlis,H.H. "Student drug use. What to do?" In Harris,R.T.(ed.). Drug Dependence. Univ. Texas Press, Austin, 1970, 251-259.

5498. Nowlis,H.H. "Will-o'-the-wisp." Internat'l. J. Psychiat. 1970, 9, 525-532.

5499. Noyes,R. and Baran,D. "Cannabis analgesia." Comp. Psychiat. 1974, 15, 531-535.

5500. Noyes,R., Brunk,S.F., Avery,D.H., and Canter,A. "The analgesic properties of delta-9-tetrahydrocannabinol and codeine." Clin. Pharmacol. Ther. 1975, 18, 84-89.

5501. Noyes,R., Brunk,S.F., Baram,D.A., and Canter,A. "Analgesic effects of delta-9-tetrahydro-cannabinol." J. Clin. Pharmacol. 1975, 15, 139-143.

5502. Noyes,R., Brunk,S.F., Baram,D.A., and Canter, A. "Analgesic effects of delta-9-tetrahydrocannabinol." In Braude,M.C. and Szara,S.(eds.). Pharmacology of Marihuana. Raven Press, N.Y., 1976, 833-837.

5503. Nurco,D. and Mitchell,B. Drug Abuse Study. Maryland State Department of Mental Hygiene, Baltimore, 1969.

5504. Nykamen,M.W. "Death in the desert." High Times 1974, 2, 24-26.

O

5505. Oakum.P. Growing Marihuana in New England (and Other Cold Climates). Cobblesmith, Ashville, Maine, 1971.

5506. Obata,Y. and Ishikawa,Y. "Studies on the constituents of hemp plant(cannabis sativa L.). Part I. Volatile phenol fraction." Bull. Agricult. Chem. Soc. Jap. 1960, 24, 667-669.

5507. Obata,Y. and Ishikawa,Y. "Studies on the constituents of hemp plant(cannabis sativa L.). Part III. Isolation of a Gibbs-positive compound from Japanese hemp." Bull. Agricult. Chem. Soc. Jap. 1966, 30, 619-620.

5508. Obata,Y., Ishikawa,Y., and Kitazawa,R. "Studies on the components of the hemp plant(cannabis sativa L.). Part II. Isolation and identification of piperidine and several amino acids in the hemp plant." Bull. Agricult. Chem. Soc. Jap. 1960, 24, 670-672.

5509. Oberman,J.W. "Marihuana and delinquency." Gen. Practition. 1969, 39, 135.

5510. O'Callaghan,S. The Drug Traffic. A. Bland, London, 1967.

5511. O'Donnell,J.A. "On education to prevent marihuana use." In Wittenborn,J.R., Smith,J.P., and Wittenborn,S.A.(eds.). Communication and Drug Abuse. C.C. Thomas, Springfield, Ill., 1970, 395-403.

5512. Ohlsson,A., Abou-Chaar,C.I., Agurell,S., Nilsson,I.M., Olofsson,K., and Sandberg,F. "Cannabinoid constituents of male and female cannabis sativa." Bull. Narc. 1971, 23, 29-32.

5513. Ohlsson,A., Lindgren,J.E., Leander,K., and Agurell,S. "Detection and quantification of tetrahydrocannabinol in blood plasma." In Willette,P.(ed.). Cannabinoid Assays in Humans. N.I.D.A. Res. Monog. 14, Gov't. Print. Office, Washington, D.C., 1976, 48-63.

5514. Okamoto,T., Chan,P.C., and So,B.T. "Effect of tobacco, marihuana and benzo(a)pyrene on aryl hydrocarbon hydroxylase in hamster lung." Life Sci. 1972, 11, 733-741.

5515. Okamoto,T. and Watanbe,K. "Rapid identification of cannabis by means of infrared spectroscopy." J. Pharmaceut. Soc. Jap. 1970, 90, 15-19.

5516. Okey,A.B. and Truant,G.S. "Cannabis demasculinizes rats but is not estrogenic." Life Sci. 1975, 17, 1113-1118.

5517. Okuyama,T., Kitada,A., and Fueno,T. "Catalysis and mechanism of the isomerization of a delta-5-3-keto steroid." Bull. Chem. Soc. Jap. 1977, 50, 2358-2361.

5518. Oliver,J. "On the action of cannabis indica." Br. Med. J. 1883, 1, 905-906.

5519. Ollivier,H. and Quicke,J. "Note about the identification of Indian hemp cultivated in France."(Fr.). Ann. Med. Leg. 1961, 41, 592-595.

5520. Olmsted,C.A. "Effects of cannabinoids on synaptic membrane enzymes. I. In vitro studies on synaptic membranes isolated from rat brain." Am. J. Drug Alcohol Abuse 1976, 3, 485-505.

5521. Olson,J. and Carder,B. "Behavioral tolerance to marihuana as a function of amount of prior training." Pharmacol. Biochem. Behav. 1974, 2, 243-247.

5522. Olsen,J.L., Lodge,J.W., Shapiro,B.J.,and Tashkin,D.P. "An inhalation aerosol of delta-9-tetrahydrocannabinol." J. Pharm. Pharmacol. 1976, 28, 86.

5523. Olsen,J.L., Makhani,M., Davis,K.H., and Wall,M.E. "Preparation of delta-9-tetrahydrocannabinol for intravenous injection." J. Pharm. Pharmacol. 1973, 25, 344.

5524. Onion,D.K. "Adverse reactions to cannabis." Ann. Intern. Med. 1969, 71, 430.

5525. Ono,M., Shimamine,M., and Takahashi,K. "Studies on cannabis. III. Distribution of tetrahydrocannabinol in the cannabis plant."(Jap.). Bull. Nat'l. Hygien. Sci. 1972, 90, 1-4.

5526. Ono,M., Shimamine,M., Takahashi,K., and Inoue,T. "Studies on hallucinogens. VI. Synthesis of delta-6a, 10a-tetrahydrocannabinol." Bull. Nat'l. Hygien. Sci. 1974, 92, 44-46.

5527. Opinion Research Corporation. Use of Marihuana and Views on Related Penalties Among Teens and the General Public. Drug Abuse Council, Washington, 1974.

5528. Orcutt,J.D. "A theoretical and empirical analysis of the social determinants of recreational drug effects." Diss. Abs. 1973, 34, 863.

5529. Orcutt,J.D. "Social determinants of alcohol and marihuana effects: a systematic theory." Internat'l. J. Addict. 1975, 10, 1021-1033.

5530. Orcutt,J.D. "Toward a sociological theory of drug effects: a comparison of marihuana and alcohol." Sociol. Soc. Res. 1972, 56, 242-253.

5531. Orcutt,J.D. and Biggs,D.A. "A formalization and empirical test of a sociological theory of recreational drug effects." Paper presented at South. Sociol. Soc., Atlanta, 1973.

5532. Orcutt,J.D. and Biggs,D.A. "Perceived risks of marihuana and alcohol use: Comparisons of non-users and regular users." J. Drug Iss. 1973, 3, 355-360.

5533. Orcutt,J.D. and Biggs,D.A. "Recreational effects of marihuana and alcohol: Some descriptive dimensions." Internat'l. J. Addict. 1975, 10, 229-239.

5534. Orcutt,J.D. and Biggs,D.A. "Testing a sociological theory of recreational drug effects." Sociol. Soc. Res. 1975, 59, 136-149.

5535. Oregon. Legislative Research Branch. Effect of the Oregon Decriminalization Possession and Use of Small Quantities of Marihuana. State Capital, Salem, Oregon, 1974.

5536. Orsingher,O.A. and Fulginiti,S. "Effects of cannabis sativa on learning in rats." Pharmacol. 1970, 3, 337-344.

5537. Ortega-Corona,B.G. "Certain enzymes induced by cannabis."(Sp.). Arcg. Ubvest. Med. 1974, 5, 195-204.

5538. Ortiz Velasquez,J. "Marihuana effects."(Sp.). An. Acad. Med. Medel. 1948, 3, 498-510.

5539. Ortiz Velasquez,J. "Effects of acute and chronic hashish intoxication. A case of rape. The club of addicts. The experience of T. Gautier. Conclusions." (Sp.). Rev. Psiquiat. Criminol. 1948, 13, 127-136.

5540. Orzechowski,G. "Will opium or hashish become the religion of the masses."(Ger.). Deut. Apoth. 1970, 22, 89-94.

5541. Os, F.H. "Legalized flight from reality?" (Dut.). Pharmaceut. Weekbl. 1970, 105, 1054-1058.

5542. Osgood,P. and Howes,J. "Cannabinoid induced changes in mouse striatal homovanillic acid and dihydroxyphenylacetic acid: The effects of amphetamine and L-dopa." Res. Commun. Chem. Pathol. Pharmacol. 1974, 9, 621-631.

5543. O'Shaughnessy,R. "Case of tetanus, cured by preparation of hemp." Trans. Med. Physical Soc. Calcutta 1842, 8, 462-469.

5544. O'Shaughnessy,R. "Indian hemp." Prov. Med. J. Retrospect Med. Sci. 1843, 5, 397-398.

5545. O'Shaughnessy,R. "On the cannabis indica, or Indian hemp." Pharmaceut. J. Trans. 1843, 2, 594-595.

5546. O'Shaughnessy,R. "On the preparation of the Indian hemp, or gunjah. Their effects on the animal system in health, and their utility in the treatment of tetanus and other convulsive diseases." Prov. Med. J. Retrospect Med. Sci. 1843, 5, 343-347.

5547. O'Shaughnessy,R. "On the preparation of the Indian hemp or gunjah(cannabis indica): The effects on the animal system in health, and their utility in the treatment of tetanus and other convulsive diseases." Trans. Med. Physical Soc. Bombay 1842, 8, 421-461.

5548. Oskoui,M. "Effects of delta-1-tetrahydrocannabinol on cardiovascular and respiratory systems, vasomotor center(VC), sympathetic and vagus nerve discharge activ es and myocardial function." Fed. Proc. 1972, 31, 505.

5549. Oskoui,M. "Effects of delta-1-tetrahydrocannabinol on neuromuscular and autonomic nervous activity." Fed. Proc. 1971, 30, 443.

5550. Oskoui,M. and Hofmann,S. "Mechanism of cardiovascular action of delta-1-tetrahydrocannabinol." Pharmacologist 1976, 18, 302.

5551. Osmond,H. "A review of the clinical effects of psychotomimetic agents." Ann. N. Y. Acad. Sci. 1957, 66, 418-434.

5552. Osterhammel,D. and Jensen,H.A. "Somatic complications from abuse of euphoric substances. A brief review and account of 13 hepatitis cases."(Dan.). Ugesk. Laeger 1967, 129, 1660-1662.

5553. Oswalt,R. and Sexton,D. "Marihuana and LSD usage among female college students." J. Am. Coll. Hlth. Assoc. 1972, 20, 265-268.

5554. Oteri,J. "Marihuana is still illegal; Mass. ruling." Time 1967, 90, 38.

5555. Oteri,J.S. and Norris,J. "The use of expert and documentary evidence in a constitutional attack in a state criminal statute: the marihuana test case." Calif. Law Rev. 1968, 56, 29-36.

5556. Oteri,J.S. and Silverglate,H.A. "In the marketplace of free ideas: A look at the passage of the Marihuana Tax Act." In Simmons,J.L.(ed.). Marihuana; Myths and Realities. Brandon House, Berkeley, Cal., 1967, 137-162.

5557. Oteri,J.S. and Silverglate,H.A. "The pursuit of pleasure: Constitutional dimensions of the marihuana problem." Suffolk Univ. Law Rev. 1968, 3, 55-80.

5558. Oteri,J.S., Weinberg,M.G., and Pinales,M.S. "Cross-examination of chemists in narcotic and marihuana cases." Contemp. Drug Prob. 1973, 2, 225-238.

5559. Ottersen,T. and Aasen,A. "X-ray structure of cannabispiran: A novel cannabis constituent." J. Chem. Soc. 1976, 1, 580-581.

5560. Ouellet,J., Palaic,D., Albert,J.M., and Tetreault,L. "Effect of delta-9-THC on serotonin, MAO and tryptophan hydroxylase in rat brain." Rev. Can. Biol. 1973, 32, 213-217.

5561. Oursler,W. Marihuana, The Facts the Truth. Paul S. Ersksson, N.Y., 1968.

5562. Owen,P.H. "A description of the peculiar properties of cannabis indica, with an account of experiments in its use." N.Y. Med. Press 1860, 3, 280-283.

5563. Ozen,C. and Sozen,H. "The problem of marihuana in Turkey and the Oriental countries. A case of poisoning resulting in death."(Turk.). Tip. Fac. Mec. 1969, 32, 543-562.

P

5564. Pace,H.B., Davis,W.M., and Borgen,L.A. "Teratogenesis and marihuana." Ann. N. Y. Acad. Sci. 1971, 191, 123-132.

5565. Pack,A.T., Brill, N.Q., and Christie,R.L. "Quitting marihuana." Dis. Nerv. Syst. 1976, 25, 205-209.

5566. Page,J.B. "The study of San Jose, Costa Rica, street culture: Codes and communication in lower class society." In Du Toit,B.M.(ed.). Drugs, Rituals and Altered States of Consciousness. A.A. Balkema, Rotterdam, 1977, 207-216.

5567. Pal,B. and Ghosh,J.J. "Delta-9-tetrahydrocannabinol: Effects on the urinary excretion of 5-hydroxyindoleacetic acid." U.N. Doc ST/SOA/SER.S/30, Aug. 16, 1971.

5568. Pal,B. and Ghosh,J.J. "Delta-9-tetrahydrocannabinol: Effects on the urinary excretion of 5-hydroxyindoleacetic acid after tryptophan, 5-hydroxytryptamine load." U.N. Doc. ST/SOA/SER.S/31, Apr. 17, 1972.

5569. Pal,B. and Ghosh,J.J. "L-delta-9-tetrahydrocannabinol--effects on the urinary excretion of 5-hydroxyindole acetic acid." Biochem. Pharmacol 1972, 21, 263-264.

5570. Palermo Neto,J. and Carlini,E.A. "Aggressive behavior elicited in rats by cannabis sativa: Effects of p-chlorophenylalanine and dopa." Eur. J. Pharmacol. 1972, 17, 215-220.

5571. Palermo Neto,J. and Carvalho,F.V. "The effects of chronic cannabis treatment on the aggressive behavior and brain 5-hydroxytryptamine levels of rats with different temperaments." Psychopharmacol. 1973, 32, 383-392.

5572. Palermo Neto,J. and Nunes,J.F. "Effect of stress and chronic cannabis treatment upon brain 5-HT, blood ACTH and aggressive behavior in female rats with different hormonal status." Paper presented at 1st Lat. Am. Cong. Psychobiol., Sao Paulo, 1973.

5573. Palgi,P. "The traditional role and symbolism of hashish among Moroccan Jews in Israel and the effect of acculturation." In Rubin,V.(ed.). Cannabis and Culture. Mouton, The Hague, 1975, 207-217.

5574. Palgrave,E.F. "A case of poisoning by cannabis indica." St. Barthol. Hosp. J. 1900, 7, 76.

5575. Palmer,D.L., Reed,W.P., and Kisch,A.L. "Health in a rural hippie commune." J.A.M.A. 1970, 213, 1307-1310.

5576. Pamplona,M. and Ramos,A.C. "Specificity of some chemical reactions for cannabis."(Sp.). An. Fac. Farm. Univ. Recife 1968, 8, 65-76.

5577. Panama Rose. The Hashish Cookbook. Gnaoua Press, N.Y., 1966.

5578. Pandina,R.J. and Musty,R.E. "Effects of delta-9-tetrahydrocannabinol on active avoidance acquisition and passive avoidance retention in rats with amygdaloid lesions." Pharmacol. 1975, 13, 297-308.

5579. Panzica,N. "Legal grass: a caseworker's view." Crim. Law Quart. 1971, 13, 445-452.

5580. Panzica,N. "Prohibition and marihuana." Chitty's Law J. 1972, 20, 269-272.

5581. Paolillo,D.J. "The structure of grana in flowering plants." Am. J. Bot. 1969, 56, 344-347.

5582. Paolillo,D.J., Falk,R.H., and Reighard,J.A. "The effect of chemical fixation on the fretwork of chloroplasts of edodea cannadense, nicotiana rustica, spimacid oleracea, cannabis sativa, pisum sativum, phaseolus vulgaris and zeamays." Trans-Am. Microscop. Soc. 1967, 86, 225.

5583. Papadakis,D.P., Michael,C.M., Kephalas,T.A., and Miras,C.J. "Effects of cannabis smoking in blood lactic acid and glucose in humans." Exper. 1974, 30, 1183-1184.

5584. Papavasiliou,M.J. and Liberato,S.N. "The Beam reaction by the experts."(Fr.). J. Pharm. Chim. 1938, 27, 19-32.

5585. Parfrey,P.S. "Factors associated with undergraduate marihuana use in Cork." Br. J. Addict. 1977, 72, 59-65.

5586. Parfrey,P.S. "The effect of religious factors on intoxicant use." Scand. J. Soc. Med. 1976, 4, 135-140.

5587. Paris,M.R. "Resin-content and physiological reactivity of cannabis cultivated in the Paris area."(Fr.). Ann. Pharmaceut. Fran. 1949, 7, 47-51.

5588. Paris,M.R., Boucher,F., and Cosson,L. "The constituents of cannabis sativa pollen." Econ. Bot. 1975, 29, 245-253.

5589. Paris,M.R., Dempsey,D. "New methods for the identification and evaluation of cannabis activity."(Fr.). Plant. Med. Phytother. 1971, 5, 28-38.

5590. Paris,M.R., Ghirlanda,C., Chaigneau,M., Giry,L. "Delta-1-tetrahydrocannabidivaric acid, a new constituent of cannabis sativa L."(Fr.). C. R. Acad. Sci. 1973, 276, 205-207.

5591. Paris,M.R. and Lenicque,P.M. "Effects of tetrahydrocannabinol and cannabidiol on the healing and regeneration of the planarium Dugesia tigrina."(Fr.). Therapie 1975, 30, 97-102.

5592. Paris,M.R. and Mounajjed,D.E. "Isolation of two constituents(cannabidiolic and tetrahydrocannabinolic acids) from cannabis sativa L. by preparative thin layer TLC."(Fr.). Ann. Pharmaceut. Fran. 1973, 31, 181-188.

5593. Paris,M.R. and Paris,R.R. "Importance of chromatography for the study of cannabis sativa L. constituents."(Fr.). Bull. Soc. Chim. Fran. 1973, 1, 118-122.

5594. Paris,R.R. and Paris,M.R. "On the flavonoids of hemp(cannabis sativa L.)."(Fr.). C. R. Acad. Sci. 1973, 277, 2369-2371.

5595. Park,Y.Y. and Tilton,B.E. "Effects of marihuana smoke on avoidance response in rats." Proc. West. Pharmacol. Assoc. 1970, 13, 151-155.

5596. Parker,C.S. "Synthetic cannabis preparations in psychiatry: Synhexyl." J. Ment. Sci. 1950, 96, 276-279.

5597. Parker,J.M., Borke,M.L., Block,L.H., and Cochran,T.G. "Decomposition of cannabidiol in chloroform solution." J. Pharmaceut. Sci. 1974, 63, 970-971.

5598. Parker,J.M. and Dubas,T.C. "Automatic determination of the pain threshold to electroshock and the effects of delta-9-THC." Internat'l. J. Clin. Pharmacol. 1973, 7, 75-81.

5599. Parker,J.M. and Dubas,T. "Information sought on analgesic properties of cannabis." Can. Med. Assoc. J. 1972, 107, 493-496.

5600. Parker,J.M. and Fiske,H.L. "Thin layer chromatography of marihuana." J. Assoc. Off. Anal. Chem. 1972, 55, 876-879.

5601. Parker,J.M. and Stembal,B.L. "Review of gas-liquid chromatography of marihuana." J. Assoc. Off. Anal. Chem. 1974, 57, 888-892.

5602. Parker,K.D., Wright,J.A., Halpern,A.F., and Hine,C.H. "Preliminary report on the separation and quantitative determination of cannabis constituents present in plant material, and when added to urine, by thin-layer and gas chromatography." Bull. Narc. 1968, 20, 9-14.

5603. Parreiras,D. "Cannabism or maconhism."(Port.). Impren. Med. 1949, 430, 34-64.

5604. Parreiras,D. "Census of drug addicts in Brazil: Incidence and nature of drug addiction."(Port.). Bull. Narc. 1965, 17, 21-23.

5605. Parreiras,D. Maconha Prophylaxis in Sao Paulo: Police and Vigilance at the Borders; Interception of Maconha Trasport."(Port.). Soc. Biol., Sao Paulo, 1960.

5606. Parreiras,D. The International Problem of Cannabism. Serv. Nac. Educac. Sanit., Rio de Janeiro, 1958.

5607. Parreiras,D. "The meeting of the Interamerican Consultive Group on narcotics control: Rio de Janeiro, 27 November-7 December, 1961." Bull. Narc. 1963, 15, 47-53.

5608. Parry,A. "The menace of marihuana." Am. Mercury 1935, 36, 487-490.

5609. Parry,E.J. "American-grown cannabis indica not distinguished from the drug of commerce." Oil Paint Drug Report. 1917, 92, 56.

5610. Parry,H.J. "Primary levels of under-reporting psychotropic drug use." Pub. Opin. Quart. 1970, 34, 582-592.

5611. Pars,H.G. "The other side of marihuana research." J. Anesthesiol. 1973, 38, 519-520.

5612. Pars,H.G., Granchelli,F.E., Keller,J.K., and Razdan,R.K. "Physiologically active nitrogen analogs of tetrahydrocannabinols. Tetrahydrobenzopyrano(3,4,-d) pyridines." J. Am. Chem. Soc. 1966, 88, 3664-3665.

5613. Pars,H.G., Granchelli,F.E., Keller,J.K., Razdan,R.K., Shoer,L., and Thompson,W.R. "New pharmacologically active tetrahydrocannabinol analogs." Chem. Ther. 1967, 2, 167.

5614. Pars,H.G., Granchelli,F.E., Razdan,R.K., Keller,J.K., Teiger,D.G., Rosenberg,F.J., and Harris,L.S. "Drugs derived from cannabinoids. I. Nitrogen analogs, benzopyranopyridines and benzopyranopyrroles." J. Med. Chem. 1976, 19, 445-454.

5615. Pars,H.G. and Razdan,R.K. "Heterocyclic analogs of the cannabinoids." In Cohen,S. and Stillman,R.(eds.). Therapeutic Potential of Marihuana. Plenum Press, N.Y., 1976, 419-438.

5616. Pars,H.G. and Razdan,R.K. "Tetrahydrocannabinols and synthetic analogs." Ann. N. Y. Acad. Sci. 1971, 191, 15-23.

5617. Partridge,W.L. The Hippie Ghetto: The Natural History of a Subculture. Holt Rinehardt and Winston, N.Y., 1973.

5618. Pascal,E. "A revealer of the subconscious: hashish."(Fr.). Rev. Metapsychique 1930, 1, 53-70.

5619. Pascal,H. The Marihuana Maze. Alba Books, Canfield, Oh., n.d.

5620. Patch,V.D. "Marihuana use in man: An experimental inquiry--clinical psychiatric impressions." Psychopharmacol. Bull. 1973, 9, 52-54.

5621. Patch,V.D. "Public health aspects of adolescent drug use." In National Commission on Marihuana and Drug Abuse. Drug Use in America: Problem in Perspective. Gov't. Print. Office, Washington, D.C., 1973, I, 975-1077.

5622. Patel,A.R. and Gori,G.B. "Preparation and monitoring of marihuana smoke condensate samples." Bull. Narc. 1975, 27, 47-54.

5623. Patino,V.M. Cultivated Plants and Domesticated Animals in South America. Imprensa Dept., Cali, Colombia, 1967-1969.

5624. Pato,M. "The kif harvest." High Times 1976, 8, 59-53.

5625. Paton,W.D.M. "Additional remarks on the chronic toxicity of cannabis." In Braude,M.C. and Szara,S. (eds.). Pharmacology of Marihuana. Raven Press, N.Y., 1976, 617-619.

5626. Paton,W.D.M. "Cannabis and its problems." Proc. Roy. Soc. Med. 1973, 66, 718-721.

5627. Paton,W.D.M. "Cannabis. Pharmacological aspects." Pharm. J. 1972, 209, 347-348.

5628. Paton,W.D.M. "Concluding summary." In Nahas,G.G., Paton,W.D.M., and Idanpaan-Heikkila,J.E. (eds.). Marihuana. Springer Verlag, N.Y., 1976, 551.

5629. Paton,W.D.M. "Pharmacology of marihuana." Ann. Rev. Pharmacol. 1975, 15, 191-220.

5630. Paton,W.D.M. "The uses and implications of the log-normal distribution of drug use." In Connell,P.H. and Dorn,N.(eds.). Cannabis and Man. Churchill Livingstone, Edinburgh, 1975, 108-116.

5631. Paton,W.D.M. "Unconventional anaesthetic molecules." In Halsey,M.J., Millar,R.A., and Sutton,J.A. (eds.). Molecular Mechanisms in General Anaesthesia. Churchill Livingstone, Edinburgh, 1974, 48-64.

5632. Paton,W.D.M. and Crown,J.(eds.). Cannabis and Its Derivatives. Oxford Univ. Press, London, 1972.

5633. Paton,W.D.M. and Pertwee,R.G. "Effect of cannabis and certain of its constituents on pentobarbitone sleeping time and phenazone metabolism" Br. J. Pharmacol. 1972, 44, 250-261.

5634. Paton,W.D.M. and Pertwee,R.G. "The actions of cannabis in man." In Mechoulam,R.(ed.). Marihuana, Chemistry, Pharmacology, Metabolism and Clinical Effects. Academic Press, N.Y., 1973, 288-330.

5635. Paton,W.D.M. and Pertwee,R.G. "The general pharmacology of cannabis." Act. Pharmaceut. Suec. 1971, 8, 691-692.

5636. Paton,W.D.M. and Pertwee,R.G. "The pharmacology of cannabis in animals." In Mechoulam,R.(ed.). Marihuana, Chemistry, Pharmacology, Metabolism and Clinical Effects. Academic Press, N.Y., 1973, 192-265.

5637. Paton,W.D.M., Pertwee,R.G., and Temple,D. 'The general pharmacology of the cannabinols." In Paton,W.D.M. and Crown,J.(eds.). Cannabis and Its Derivatives. Oxford Univ. Press, London, 1972, 50-73.

5638. Paton,W.D.M., Pertwee,R.G., and Tylden,E. "Clinical aspects of cannabis action." In Mechoulam,R. (ed.). Marihuana, Chemistry, Pharmacology, Metabolism and Clinical Effects. Academic Press, N.Y., 1973, 335-362.

5639. Paton,W.D.M. and Temple,D.M. "Effects of chronic and acute cannabis treatment upon thiopentone anaesthesia in rabbits." Br. J. Pharmacol. 1972, 44, 346P-347P.

5640. Partridge,W.L. "Cannabis and cultural groups in a Colombian municipio." In Rubin,V.(ed.). Cannabis and Culture. Mouton, The Hague, 1975, 147-173.

5641. Patterson,C.D. "Self-reported unpleasant effects from illicit use of fourteen substances." Br. J. Addict. 1974, 69, 249-256.

5642. Patterson,D.A. and Stevens,H.M. "Identification of cannabis." J. Pharm. Pharmacol. 1970, 22, 391-392.

5643. Patwardhan,G.M. "Thin-layer chromatography demonstration of hashish substances in cannabis seeds." (Ger.). Arch. Kriminol. 1977, 159, 36-39.

5644. Patzsch,H. "Marihuana."(Ger.). Med. Welt 1939, 13, 1440-1441.

5645. Paul,M.I. and Carson,I.M. "Marihuana and communication." Lancet 1973, 3, 270-271.

5646. Paulson,P. "Behavioral aspects of marihuana use." J. Am. Coll. Hlth. Assoc. 1973, 21, 465-469.

5647. Paulus,I. "Psychedelic drug use on the Canadian Pacific coast. Notes on the new drug scene." Internat'l. J. Addict. 1969, 4, 77-88.

5648. Paulus,I. and Williams,H.R. "LSD-25 and young adults." Br. Columb. Med. J. 1967, 9, 88-91.

5649. Paulus,I. and Williams,H.R. "Marihuana and young adults." Br. Columb. Med. J. 1966, 8, 240-244.

5650. Paulus,I. and Williams,H.R. "Marihuana and young adults. A preliminary report." Addictions 1966, 13, 26-33.

5651. Pausanias. Description of Greece. Loeb Classical Lib., London, 1966.

5652. Payne,R.J. and Brand,S.N. "The toxicity of intravenously used marihuana." J.A.M.A. 1975, 233, 351-354.

5653. Pe,U.W. "A rapid method for testing marihuana." Forens. Sci. 1976, 8, 203.

5654. Pearl,J.H. "The effects of marihuana on human cognition." Diss. Abs. 1972, 33, 2329.

5655. Pearl,J.H., Domino,E.F., and Rennick,P. "Short-term effects of marihuana smoking on cognitive behavior in experienced male users." Psychopharmacol. 1973, 31, 13-24.

5656. Pearlman,S. "A select bibliography on drug usage in colleges and universities." J. Attitude Res. 1968, 2, 5-7.

5657. Pearlman,S. "Drug use and experience in an urban college population." Am. J. Orthopsychiat. 1968, 38, 503-514.

5657a. Pearlman,S.(ed.). Drugs on Campus: An Annotated Guide to the Literature. Brooklyn College, N.Y., 1968.

5647b. Pearlman,S. "The college drug scene." Paper presented at Am. Educat. Res. Assoc, N.Y., 1971.

5657c. Pearson,W.A. "Standard cannabis." J.A.P.A. 1917, 6, 876.

5657d. Pearson,W.A. "The physiological standardization of cannabis." J.A.P.A. 1916, 5, 1194-1195.

5657e. Pearson,W.A. "The requirements for cannabis indica of the United States Pharmacopoeia." Am. Drug. Pharmaceut. Rec. 1910, 57, 235.

5657f. Pearson,W.A. "The U.S.P. requirements of cannabis indica." Bull. Am. Pharmaceut. Assoc. 1910, 5, 559-562.

5657g. Pechet,L., King,A.B., and Pechet,G.S. "The effect of intravenous marihuana on coagulation, and on platelet and white cell count." Fed. Proc. 1970, 29, 441.

5657h. Pechmeja,A. "Hashish."(Fr.). J. Magnet. 1869, 1, 15-26, 252-257.

5657i. Peebles,A.S.M. and Mann,H.V. "Ganja as a cause of insanity and crime in Bengal." Ind. Med. Gaz. 1914, 49, 395-396.

5657j. Peeke,S.C., Jones,R.T., and Stone,G.C. "Effects of practice on marihuana-induced changes in reaction time." Psychopharmacol. 1976, 48, 159-163.

5658. Pelicier,Y. "Drugs and the permissive society."(Fr.). Rev. Psychol. Peuples 1969, 24, 419-428.

5659. Pelner,L. "Long road to Nirvana; dissertation on marihuana." N.Y. State J. Med. 1967, 67, 952-956.

5660. Peltz,A. "About Indian hemp and its active ingredients."(Ger.). Pharmazeut. Zeit. Russland 1876, 15, 705-714.

5661. Peon del Valle,J. "Some aspects of the present struggle against drug addiction in Mexico."(Sp.). Bol. Of. Sanit. PanAm. 1933, 12, 347-355.

5662. Peralta,F. "How hashish is obtained, prepared and used."(Sp.). Actas Ciba 1942, 1, 9-17.

5663. Peralta,F. "On the history of hashish use." (Sp.). Actas Ciba 1942, 1, 2-8.

5664. Peralta,F. "The effects of hashish."(Sp.). Actas Ciba 1942, 1, 18-21.

5665. Peralta,F. "Two famous hashish eaters."(Sp.). Actas Ciba 1942, 1, 22-25.

5666. Pereira,A. Cannabis or 'Diamba'; Its Power of Intoxication.(Port.). Serv. Nac. Educac. Sanit., de Janeiro, 1958.

5667. Pereira,J. The Elements of Materia Medica and Therapeutics. Lea and Blanchard, Phil., 1843.

5668. Perera,V. "Rap on grass." Sat. Rev. Educat. 1973, 55, 14.

5669. Peres,H. 'Diambism.'(Port.). Serv. Nac. Educac. Sanit., Rio de Janeiro, 1958.

5670. Perez-Reyes,M., Brine,D., and Wall,M.E. "Clinical study of frequency of marihuana use: Adrenal cortical reserve metabolism of a contraceptive agent and development of tolerance." Ann. N. Y. Acad. Sci. 1976, 282, 172-179.

5671. Perez-Reyes,M., Lipton,M.A., Timmons,M.C., Wall,M.E., Brine,D.R., and Davis,K.H. "Pharmacology of orally administered delta-9-tetrahydrocannabinol." Clin. Pharmacol. Ther. 1973, 14, 48-55.

5672. Perez-Reyes,M., Lipton,M.A., Wall,M.E., Brine, D.E. and Timmons,M.C. "Absorption, excretion, and metabolic degradation of orally administered delta-9-tetrahydrocannabinol to human subjects." Proc. 5th Internat'l. Cong. Pharmacol. 1972, 1, 180.

5673. Perez-Reyes,M., Simmons,J., Brine,D., Kimmel,G.L., Davis,K.H., and Wall,M.E. "Rate of penetration of delta-9-tetrahydrocannabinol and 11-hydroxy-delta-9-tetrahydrocannabinol to the brain of mice." In Nahas,G.G., Paton, W.D.M., Idanpaan-Heikkila,J.E.(eds.). Marihuana. Springer Verlag, N.Y., 1976, 179-187.

5674. Perez-Reyes,M., Timmons,M.C., Davis,K.H., and Wall,E.M. "A comparison of the pharmacological activity in man of intravenously administered delta-9-tetrahydrocannabinol, cannabinol, and cannabidiol." Exper. 1973, 29, 1368-1369.

5675. Perez-Reyes,M., Timmons,M.C., and Lipton,M.A. "Intravenous injection in man of delta-9-tetrahydrocannabinol and 11-OH-delta-9-tetrahydrocannabinol." Science 1972, 177, 633-635.

5676. Perez-Reyes,M., Timmons,M.C., and Wall,M.E. "Long-term use of marihuana and the development of tolerance or sensitivity to delta-9-tetrahydrocannabinol." Arch. Gen. Psychiat. 1974, 31, 89-91.

5677. Perez-Reyes,M., Wagner,D., Brine,D.R., Christensen,D.H., Davis,K.H., and Wall,M.E. "Tetrahydrocannabinols: Plasma disappearance in man and rate of penetration to mouse brain." In Braude,M.C. and Szara, S.(eds.). Pharmacology of Marihuana. Raven Press, N.Y., 1976, I, 117-125.

5678. Perez-Reyes,M., Wagner,D., Wall,M.E., and Davis,K.H. "Intravenous administration of cannabinoids and intraocular pressure." In Braude,M.C. and Szara,S. (eds.). Pharmacology of Marihuana. Raven Press, N.Y., 1976, II, 829-833.

5679. Perez-Reyes,M. and Wingfield,M. "Cannabidiol and electroencephalographic epileptic activity." J.A.M.A. 1974, 230, 1935.

5680. Perez-Victoria,C. "Gynecomastia and marihuana." (Sp.). Rev. Iber. Endocrinol. 1976, 23, 437-444.

5681. Permutt,M.A., Goodwin,D.W., Schwin,R., and Hill,S.Y. "The effect of marihuana on carbohydrate metabolism." Am. J. Psychiat. 1976, 133, 220-224.

5682. Perna,D. "Marihuana." J.A.M.A. 1970, 214, 760.

5683. Perna,D. "Psychotogenic effect of marihuana." J.A.M.A. 1969, 209, 1085-1086.

5684. Pernambucano,J. Maconha in Pernambuco.(Port.). Nov. Estud. Afro-Brasil, Rio de Janeiro, 1937.

5685. Pernambuco Filho,P. Survey of the Conclusions Approved by the 'Convention on Maconha' Adopted in San Salvador in Dec. 1946.(Port.). Serv. Nac. Educac. Sanit., Rio de Janeiro, 1958.

5686. Perrot,E. and Weitz,R. "Indian hemp."(Fr.). Bull. Gen. Ther. 1924, 175, 217-218.

5687. Perrussel,G. "Preliminary notes on the psychopathology of cannabis smokers in Tunisia."(Fr.). Arch. Inst. Past. Tunis 1925, 14, 434-440.

5688. Persaud,T.V.N. and Ellington,A.C. "Cannabis in early pregnancy." Lancet 1967, 2, 1306.

5689. Persaud,T.V.N. and Ellington,A.C. "Teratogenic activity of cannabis resin." Lancet 1968, 2, 406-407.

5690. Persaud,T.V.N. and Ellington,A.C. "The effects of cannabis sativa L.(ganja) on developing rat embryos--preliminary observations." West. Ind. Med. J. 1968, 17, 232-234.

5691. Persyko,I. "Marihuana psychosis." Am. J. Psychiat. 1970, 126, 1675-1676.

5692. Persyko,I. "Marihuana psychosis." J.A.M.A. 1970, 212, 1527.

5693. Persyko,I. "Marihuana psychosis revisited." J.A.M.A. 1971, 216, 144.

5694. Pertwee,R.G. "The ring test: a quantitative method for assessing the 'cataleptic' effect of cannabis in mice." Br. J. Pharmacol. 1972, 46, 753-763.

5695. Pertwee,R.G. "Tolerance to the effect of delta-1-tetrahydrocannabinol on corticosterone levels in mouse plasma produced by repeated administration of cannabis extract of delta-1-tetrahydrocannabinol." Br. J. Pharmacol. 1974, 51, 391-397.

5696. Pertwee,R.G. and Tavendale,R. "Effects of delta-9-THC on the rates of oxygen consumption in mice." Br. J. Pharmacol. 1977, 60, 559-568.

5697. Pestel,M. "Psychotropic agents in the generation of revolutionaries."(Fr.). Presse Med. 1970, 78, 510.

5698. Pet,D. "Marihuana: current and recurrent issues in Connecticut." Conn. Med. 1977, 41, 91-94.

5699. Pet,D. and Ball,J.C. "Marihuana smoking in the United States." Fed. Prob. 1968, 32, 8-15.

5700. Petcoff,D.G., Strain,M., and Bibi,E. "Centrifugal chromatography of cannabinoids in marihuana." Fed. Proc. 1971, 30, 443.

5701. Petcoff,D.G., Strain,S.M., Brown,W.R., and Ribi,E. "Marihuana: Identification of cannabinoids by centrifugal chromatography." Science 1971, 173, 824-826.

5702. Peters,B.A. "Acute effects of delta-9-THC on sensory, perceptual, motor and cognitive functioning and on subjective experiences." Diss. Abs. 1973, 33, 5523-5524.

5703. Peters,B.A., Lewis,E.G., Dustman,R.E., Straight,R.C., and Beck,E.C. "Sensory, perceptual, motor and cognitive functioning and subjective reports following oral administration of delta-9-tetrahydrocannabinol." Psychopharmacol. 1976, 47, 141-148.

5704. Petersen,B.H., Graham,J., and Lemberger,L. "Marihuana, tetrahydrocannabinol and T-cell function." Life Sci. 1976, 19, 395-400.

5705. Petersen,B.H., Graham,J., Lemberger,L., and Dalton,B. "Studies of the immune response in chronic marihuana smokers." Pharmacologist 1974, 16, 259.

5706. Petersen,B.H., Lemberger,L., Graham,J., and Dalton,B. "Alterations in the cellular-mediated immune responsiveness of chronic marihuana smokers." Psychopharmacol. Commun. 1975, 1, 67-74.

5707. Petersen,D.M., Schwirian,K.P., and Bleda,S.E. "The drug arrest." Criminology 1975, 13, 106-110.

5708. Petersen,R.C. "Marihuana and health." In van Praag,H.M.(ed.). Biochemical and Pharmacological Aspects of Dependence and Reports on Marihuana Research. De Erven F. Bohn, Haarlem, Netherlands, 1972, 123-143.

5709. Petersen,R.C.(ed.). Marihuana Research Findings: 1976. N.I.D.A. Res. Monog. Ser. 14, Dept. H.E.W., Rockville, Md., 1977.

5710. Petersen,R.C. "The psychosocial context of cannabis research." In Braude,M.C. and Szara,S.(eds.). Pharmacology of Marihuana. Raven Press, N.Y., 1976, 1, 13-19.

5711. Petersen,R.C. "Toward a rationally based social policy on marihuana usage." Ann. N. Y. Acad. Sci. 1976, 282, 422-426.

5712. Petersik,J.T., Poundstone,J.E., Worth,J., Cohen,S., King,D.M., Seitner,P.G., Tanton,J.H., Whitehouse,J.D., Jarod,S.H., Ellerbroek,W.C., and Hanael,H.M. "Of cats, catnip, and cannabis." J.A.M.A. 1969, 208, 360.

5713. Peterson,D.W., Cohen,G.M., and Sparber,S.B. "The delay of the behavioral effects of delta-9-tetrahydrocannabinol in rats by 2-diethylaminoethyl 2,2-diphenylvalerate HCl(SKF-525-A). Life Sci. 1971, 10, 1381-1386.

5714. Peterseon,F.T. "Marihuana smokers and non-smokers: A self-concept study." Diss. Abs. 1972, 32, 5619.

5715. Peterson,R.C. "Expectations make a profound difference." Sex. Behav. 1972, 2, 47.

5716. Petit,L. and Pichon,J. "A novel synthesis of delta-9-tetrahydrocannabinol."(Fr.). Eur. J. Toxicol. 1976, 9, 442-445.

5717. Petri,H. "Hashish and the development of addiction in a 17 year old girl."(Ger.). Prax. Kinderpsychol. Kinderpsychiat. 1970, 19, 242-245.

5718. Petrzilka,T. "Chemistry of synthetic cannabis derivative."(Ger.). Bull. Schweiz. Akad. Med. Wissen. 1971, 27, 22-30.

5719. Petrzilka,T. "Synthesis of (-)-tetrahydrocannabinol and analogous compounds." In Joyce,C.R.B. and Curry,S.H.(eds.). The Botany and Chemistry of Cannabis. J. and A. Churchill, London, 1970, 79-93.

5720. Petrzilka,T., Demuth,M., and Lusuardi,W. "Synthesis of (-)-delta-8-11-hydroxytetrahydrocannabinol." Act. Pharmaceut. Suec. 1971, 8, 679.

5721. Petrzilka,T., Haefliger,W., and Sikemeier,C. "Synthesis of hashish constituents."(Ger.). Helv. Chim. Act. 1969, 52, 1102-1134.

5722. Petrzilka,T., Haefliger,W., Sikemeier,C., Ohloff,G., and Eschenmoser,A. "Synthesis and chirality of (-)-cannabidiols."(Ger.). Helv. Chim. Act. 1967, 50, 719-723.

5723. Petrzilka,T., Haefliger,W., Sikemeier,C., Ohloff,G., and Eschenmoser,A. "Synthesis of (-)-11-hydroxy-delta-8-6a,10a, trans-tetrahydrocannabinol." (Ger.). Helv. Chim. Act. 1974, 57, 121-150.

5724. Petrzilka,T. and Lusuard,W. "Synthesis of hashish constituents."(Ger.). Helv. Chim. Act. 1973, 56, 510-518.

5725. Petrzilka,T. and Sikemeier,C. "Components of hashish. II. Synthesis of (-)-delta-6-1-3,4-trans-tetrahydrocannabinol and (±)-delta-6,1-3,4-trans-tetrahydrocannabinol."(Ger.). Helv. Chim. Act. 1967, 50, 1416-1419.

5726. Petrzilka,T. and Silemeier,C. "Components of hashish. III. Conversion of (-)-delta-6,1-3,4-trans-tetrahydrocannabinol to (-)-delta-1,2-3,4-trans-tetrahydrocannabinol."(Ger.). Helv. Chim. Act. 1967, 50, 2111-2113.

5727. Pfeiffer,W.M. "Transcultural aspects of cannabis consumption." Paper presented at Internat'l. Cong. of Neuro-psychopharmacology, Prague, 1970.

5728. Phalen,J.M. "Sanity concerning marihuana." Milit. Surg. 1945, 96, 532-533.

5729. Philip,A.F. "Preventitive and therapeutic approaches to illicit drug use." Paper presented at Am. Orthopsychiat. Assoc., Washington, D.C., 1967.

5730. Philip,P.F. "The 'personality' of the drug user." Internat'l. J. Clin. Pharmacol. 1971, 4, 442-445.

5731. Phillips,G.F. "Controlling drugs of abuse." Chem. Brit. 1972, 8, 123-130.

5732. Phillips,G.F. "The legal description of cannabis and related substances." Med. Sci. Law 1973, 13, 139-142.

5733. Phillips,J.R. "Free exercises. Religion goes to 'pot'." Calif. Law Rev. 1968, 56, 100-115.

5734. Phillips,R.N. "Toxicology of delta-9-tetrahydrocannabinol." Diss. Abs. 1973, 33, 3836.

5735. Phillips,R.N., Brown,D.J., and Forney,R.B. "Enhancement of depressant properties of alcohol and barbiturate in combination with aqueous suspended delta-9-tetrahydrocannabinol in rats." J. Forens. Sci. 1971, 16, 152-161.

5736. Phillips,R.N., Brown,D.J., Martz,R., Hubbard, J.D., and Forney,R.B. "Subacute toxicity of aqueous-suspended delta-9-tetrahydrocannabinol in rats." Toxicol. Appl. Pharmacol. 1972, 22, 45-49.

5737. Phillips,R.N., Turk,R.F., and Forney,R.B. "Acute toxicity of delta-9-tetrahydrocannabinol in rats and mice." Proc. Soc. Expt'l. Biol. Med. 1971, 136, 260-263.

5738. Phillips,R., Turk,R., Manno,J., Jain,N., and Forney,R. "Seasonal variation in cannabinolic content of Indiana marihuana." J. Forens. Sci. 1970, 15, 191-200.

5739. Phokas,G. "Thin-layer chromatography of Indian hemp and hashish." Arch. Pharmacol. 1968, 24, 75-82.

5740. Pickens,R., Thompson,T., and Muchow,D.C. "Cannabis and phencyclidine self-administration by animals." In Goldberg,L. and Hoffmeister,F.(eds.). Psychic Dependence. Springer Verlag, N.Y., 1973, 78-87.

5741. Pickering,M. "Memoires of a kif smoker." In Andrews,G. and Vinkenoog,S.(eds.). The Book of Grass. Grove Press, N.Y., 1967, 218-220.

5742. Piedelievre,R. and Derobert,L. "A rare instance of profession intoxication; a case of cannabism." (Fr.). Ann. Med. Leg. 1953, 33, 23-25.

5743. Piemme,T.E. "Hashishectomy." N. Eng. J. Med. 1971, 285, 124.

5744. Pieper,W.A. "Great apes and rhesus monkeys as subjects for psychopharmacological studies of stimulants and depressants." Fed. Proc. 1976, 35, 2254-2257.

5745. Pletzcker,A. "Psychotic episodes following smoking of hashish."(Ger.). Nervenarzt 1975, 46, 378-383.

5746. Pihl,R.O., Hickcox,P., and Costa,L. "The discrimination of marihuana intoxication." J. Clin. Psychol. 1977, 33, 908-911.

5747. Pihl,R.O., Spiers,P. and Shea,D. "The disruption of marihuana intoxication." Paper presented at Can. Psychol. Assoc., Toronto, 1976.

5748. Pihl,R.O., Spiers,P., and Shea,D. "The disruption of marihuana intoxication." Psychopharmacol. 1977, 52, 227-230.

5749. Pike,A. and Goldstein,E. "History of drug use in the military." In National Commission on Marihuana and Drug Abuse. Drug Use in America: Problem in Perspective. Gov't. Print. Office, Washington, D.C., 1973, I, 1115-1135.

5750. Pillard,R.C. "Cannabis arteritis." N. Eng. J. Med. 1971, 284, 113.

5751. Pillard,R.C. "Marihuana." N. Eng. J. Med. 1974, 283, 294-303.

5752. Pillard,R.C. "Marihuana is not a public health menace: It is time to relax our social policy." In Ingelfinger,F.J., Finland,M., Relman,A., and Elbert, R.(eds.). Controversy in Internal Medicine. W.B. Saunders Co, 1974, 762-768.

5753. Pillard,R.C. "Medical progress--marihuana." N. Eng. J. Med. 1970, 283, 294-303.

5754. Pillard,R.C. "Reply to Dr. G.G. Nahas." N. Eng. J. Med. 1971, 284, 113.

5755. Pillard,R.C., McNair,D.M., and Fisher,S. "Does marihuana enhance experimentally induced anxiety?" Psychopharmacol. 1974, 40, 205-210.

5756. Pil'nik,V. and Tarasov,A.V. "Experiment on chemical weeding of cannabis."(Rus.). Konoplya 1964, 8, 30-32.

5757. Pimentel,M.P. Penal Aspect of Marihuana. (Port.). Soc. Biol. Sao Paulo, Sao Paulo, 1960.

5758. Pinto,P.A. "Medical terminology. Monoecious liamba."(Port.). Brasil-Med. 1951, 65, 245-247.

5759. Pirch,J.H. "Enhancement of shuttle-box performance of rats by marihuana and pentobarbital." Pharmacologist 1973, 15, 201.

5760. Pirch,J.H., Barnes,P.R., and Barratt,E. "Tolerance to EEG effects of marihuana in rats." Pharmacologist 1971, 13, 246.

5761. Pirch,J.H., Cohn,R.A., Barnes,P.R., and Barratt,E.S. "Effects of acute and chronic administration of marihuana extract on the rat electrocorticogram." Neuropharmacol. 1972, 11, 231-240.

5762. Pirch,J.H., Cohn,R.A., Barnes,P.R., and Barratt,E.S. "Tolerance to EEG and behavior effects of marihuana in rats." In Singh,J.M., Miller,L., and Lal,H. (eds.). Drug Addiction: Experimental Pharmacology. Futura Pub. Co., Mount Kisco, N.Y., 1974, 133-144.

5763. Pirch,J.H., Cohn,R.A., Osterholm,K.C., and Barratt,E.S. "Antagonism of amphetamine locomotor stimulation in rats by single doses of marihuana extract admihistered orally." Neuropharmacol. 1973, 12, 485-493.

5764. Pirch,J.H., Cohn,R.A., Osterholm,K.C. and Barratt,E.S. "Tolerance to the effects of marihuana on behavior and body weight of rats." Proc. 5th Internat'l. Cong. Pharmacol. 1972, 1, 183.

5765. Pirch,J.H. and Osterholm,K.C. "Influence of a-methyltryrosine on enhancement of shuttle-box avoidance by marihuana and pentobarbital." Res. Commun. Chem. Pathol. Pharmacol. 1974, 8, 203-211.

5766. Pirch,J.H., Osterholm,K.C., Barratt,E.S., and Cohn,R.A. "Marihuana enhancement of shuttle-box performance in rats." Proc. Soc. Expt'l. Biol. Med. 1972, 141, 590-592.

5767. Pirch,J.H., Osterholm,K.C., Cohn,R.A., and Barratt,E.S. "Studies on EEG tolerance to marihuana in the rat." Arch. Internat'l. Pharmacodyn. Ther. 1973, 203, 213-220.

5768. Pires Da Veiga,E. and De Pinho,A.R. "Contribution to the study of maconha in Bahia."(Port.). Neurobiologia 1962, 25, 38-68.

5769. Pitt,C.G., Hauser,F., Hawks,R.L., Sathe,S., and Wall,M.E. "Synthesis of 11-hydroxy-delta-9-tetrahydrocannabinol and other physiologically active metabolites of delta-8- and delta-9-tetrahydrocannabinol." J. Am. Chem. Soc. 1972, 94, 8578-8579.

5770. Pitt,C.G., Hendron,R.W., and Hsia,R.S. "The specificity of the Duquenois color test for marihuana and hashish." J. Forens. Sci. 1972, 17, 693-700.

5771. Pitt,C.G., Hobbs,D.T., Schran,H., Twine,C.E., and Williams,D.L. "The synthesis of deuterium, carbon-14, and carrier-free tritium labeled cannabinoids." J. Label. Compds. 1975, 11, 551-575.

5772. Pitt,C.G., Wildes,J.W., Martin,N.H., and Wall,M.E. "Synthesis of (-)-delta-9(11)-trans-tetrahydrocannabinol." J. Org. Chem. 1971, 36, 721-723.

5773. Pittel,S.N. "Developmental factors in adolescent drug use. A study of psychedelic drug users." J. Am. Acad. Child Psychiat. 1971, 10, 640-660

5774. Pittel,S.M. "The etiology of youthful drug involvement." In National Commission on Marihuana and Drug Use. Drug Use in America: Problem in Perspective. Gov't. Print. Office, Washington,D.C., 1973, I, 879-913.

5775. Pivik,R.T., Zarcone,V., Dement,W.C., and Hollister,L.E. "Delta-9-tetrahydrocannabinol and synhexyl: Effects on human sleep patterns." Clin. Pharmacol. Ther. 1972, 13, 426-435.

5776. Pivik,R.T., Zarcone,V., Hollister,L.E., and Dement,W. "The effects of hallucinogenic agents on sleep." *Psychophysiol*. 1969, *6*, 261.

5777. Plant,M.A. "Assessing drug taking as a problem: An English observational study." *Br. J. Psychol*. 1974, *124*, 125-130.

5778. Plant,M.A. "Drug takers in an English town." *Br. J. Criminol*. 1975, *15*, 181-186.

5779. Plant,M.A. *Drug Takers in an English Town*. Tavistock Pub., London, 1975.

5780. Plant,M.A. "The escalation theory reconsidered: Drug takers in an English town." *Br. J. Addict*. 1973, *68*, 309-313.

5781. Plichet,A. "Hashish."(Fr.). *Presse Med*. 1952, *60*, 1523-1524.

5782. Pilner,P. and Cappell,H. "Cognitive moderators of marihuana intoxication: The effect of motivating instructions." In Singh,J.M. and Lal,H. (eds.). *Drug Addiction*. Stratton, N.Y., 1974, 97-104.

5783. Pilner,P. and Cappell,H. "Volitional control of marihuana intoxication in man." *Clin. Toxicol*. 1974, *7*, 308-309.

5784. Pliny,G.C. *Natural History*. Loeb Class. Lib., Heinemann, London, 1928.

5785. Plotnikoff,N.P. "New benzopyrans: Anticonvulsant activities." In Cohen,S. and Stillman,R.(eds.). *Therapeutic Potential of Marihuana*. Plenum Press, N.Y., 1976, 475-494.

5786. Plutarch. *On Rivers' and Moutains' Names*. In *Essays and Miscellanies*. Simplin, Marshall, Hamilton Kent, London, n.d.

5787. Poddar,M.K. and Ghosh,J.J. "Cannabidiol: Effect on delta-9-tetrahydrocannabinol-induced heapatic enzyme activity." *U.N. Doc*. ST/SOA/SER.S/43, July 20, 1973.

5788. Poddar,M.K. and Ghosh,J.J. "Effect of cannabis extract and delta-9-tetrahydrocannabinol administration on liver enzymes." *Sci. Cult*. 1972, *38*, 377-378.

5789. Poddar,M.K. and Ghosh,J.J. "Effects of cannabis extract and delta-9-tetrahydrocannabinol on adrenocortical activity." *U.N. Doc*. ST/SOA/SER.S/36, Nov. 10, 1972.

5790. Poddar,M.K. and Ghosh,J.J. "Effect of cannabis extract and delta-9-tetrahydrocannabinol on brain adenosine triphosphatase activity." Ind. J. Biochem. Biophys. 1976, 13, 267-272.

5791. Poddar,M.K. and Ghosh,J.J. "Effect of cannabis extract, delta-9-tetrahydrocannabinol and lysergic acid diethylamide on rat liver enzymes." Biochem. Pharmacol. 1972, 21, 3301-3303.

5792. Poddar,M.K. and Ghosh,J.J. "Neuronal membrane as the site of action of delta-9-tetrahydrocannabinol." In Braude, M.C. and Szara,S.(eds.). Pharmacology of Marihuana. Raven Press, N.Y., 1976, 157-174.

5793. Poddar,M.K. and Ghosh, J.J. "Potentiating effect of cannabidiol on delta-9-tetrahydrocannabinol induced changes in hepatic enzymes." Biochem. Pharmacol. 1974, 23, 758-759.

5794. Poddar,M.K., Ghosh,J.J., and Dutta,J. "A study of cannabinol composition of Indian cannabis." J. Ind. Acad. Forens. Sci. 1973, 12, 1-4.

5795. Podolsky,S., Pattavina,C.G., and Amaral,M.A. "Effect of marihuana on the glucose-tolerance test." Ann. N. Y. Acad. Sci. 1971, 191, 54-60.

5796. Pohl,K.D. "Forensic-toxicological aspects of the detection and identification of natural narcotic agents, especially cannabis preparations."(Ger.). Chem. Ztg. 1974, 98, 35-40.

5797. Pohl,K.D. "Methodological contributions to the detection of synthethic (-)-delta-9-tetrahydrocannabinol."(Ger.). Arch. Kriminol. 1972, 150, 93-101.

5798. Pohl,K.D. "Methodological contributions to the detection of hashish consumption."(Ger.). Arch. Kriminol. 1971, 147, 141-157.

5799. Poirier,J. "The problems of cannabis indica usage in Madagascar."(Fr.). Toxicomanies 1970, 3, 65-88.

5800. Polakoff,P.L. and Lowinger,P. "Do medical students 'turn on'?" Comp. Psychiat. 1972, 13, 185-188.

5801. Polakow,R.L. and Doctor,R.M. "Treatment of marihuana and barbiturate dependency by contingency contracting." J. Behav. Ther. Psychiat. 1973, 4, 375-377.

5802. Polderman,R. "The medical use of cannabis sativa." In Andrews,G. and Vinkenoog,S.(eds.). The Book of Grass. Grove Press, N.Y., 1967, 153-155.

5803. Pollard,J.C. "Teen-agers and the use of drugs: Reflections on the emotional setting." Clin. Pediat. 1967, 6, 613-620.

5804. Polli,G. "Further observations on haschish in medicine." St. Andrew's Med. Grad. Assoc. Trans. 1870, 3L, 98-101.

5805. Polli,G. "Haschish in melancholia." Med. Times 1972, 100, 236-238.

5806. Polli,G. and Kuykendall,D. "On the effect and therapeutical use of hashish."(Ger.). Schmidt's Jahrbuch. 1875, 168, 8-11.

5807. Pollock,M.B. "The drug abuse problem: some implications for health education." J. Am. Coll. Hlth. Assoc. 1969, 17, 403-411.

5808. Pollock,S.H. "Attitudes of medical students toward marihuana." J. Psyched. Drugs 1972, 5, 56-61.

5809. Pomazal,R.J. and Brown,J.D. "Understanding drug use motivation: a new look at a current problem. J. Hlth. Soc. Behav. 1977, 18, 212-222.

5810. Pond,D.A. "Psychological effects in depressive patients of the marihuana homologue synhexyl." J. Neurol. Neuropsychiat. 1940, 11, 271-279.

5811. Ponting,L.I. and Nicol,C.S. "Drug dependency among patients attending a department of venerology." Br. J. Vener. Dis. 1970, 46, 111-113.

5812. Popoff,D. "Feedback on drugs. Our readers turn on, turn in, and tell." Psychol. Today 1970, 3, 51-52.

5813.. Porot,A. "Cannabism(hashish--kif--chira--marihuana)."(Fr.). Ann. Med.-Psychol. 1942, 1, 1-24.

5814. Porter,C.D., Burbridge,T.N., and Scott,K.G. "A comparison of ethanol and cannabis sativa(THC) extract upon the inhibition of active transport by erythrocytes." Proc. West. Pharamcol. Soc. 1970, 13, 144-146.

5815. Porter,C.D. and Scott,K.G. "Action of tetrahydrocannabinol on active cation transport of the rat and human erythrocytes." Res. Commun. Chem. Pathol. 1970, 1, 733-739.

5816. Porter,M.R., Vieira,T.A., Kaplan,G.J., Hersch,J.R., and Colyar,A.B. "Drug use in Anchorage, Alaska. A survey of 15,634 students in grades 6 through 12--1971." J.A.M.A. 1973, 223, 657-664.

5817. Post,P. "Joint effort: decriminalizing marihuana." Seventeen 1976, 35, 30.

5818. Postel,W.B. "Marihuana use in Vietnam: A preliminary report." U.S. Army Vietnam Med. Bull. 1968, 11, 56-59.

5819. Postma,W.P. Mitosis, Meiosis in Cannabis Sativa."(Dut.). H.D. Tjeenk and N.V. Zoon, Haarlem, Netherlands, 1946.

5820. Potvin,R.J. and Fried,P.A. "Acute and chronic effects on rats of (-)-delta-1-trans-tetrahydrocannabinol on unlearned motor tasks." Psychopharmacol. 1972, 26, 369-378.

5821. Pouchet,G. "Indian hemp."(Fr.). Prec. Pharmacol. Mat. Med. 1907, 1, 207-210.

5822. Powell,G. and Bembry,T.H. "Synthesis of cannabinol." J. Am. Chem. Soc. 1940, 62, 2568-2569.

5823. Powell,G., Salmon,M., Bembry,T.H., and Walton,R.P. "The active principle of marihuana." Science 1941, 93, 522-523.

5824. Powelson,D.H. "Marihuana: more dangerous than you know." Readers Dig. 1974, 105, 95-99.

5825. Power,D.J. "Illicit drug taking." Med. Sci. Law 1974, 14, 260-267.

5826. Pradhan,S.N. and Bailey,P.T. "Behavioral effects of marihuana and its derivatives." In Singh,J.M. (ed.). Drug Addiction. Futura Pub. Co., Mt. Kisco, N.Y., 1972, 1, 17-29.

5827. Pradhan,S.N., Bailey,P.T., and Ghosh,B. "Some behavioral effects of delta-9-tetrahydrocannabinol in rats." Res. Commun. Chem. Pathol. Pharmacol. 1972, 3, 197-204.

5828. Pradhan,S.N. and Ghosh,B. "Effects of delta-9-THC on timing behavior in rats." Psychon. Sci. 1972, 27, 179-181.

5829. Prain,D. On the Morphology Teratology, and Diclinism of the Flowers of Cannabis. Superintendant of Gov't. Printing, Calcutta, 1904.

5830. Prakash,R., Aronow,W.S., Warren,M., Laverty,W., and Gottschlak,L.A. "Effects of marihuana and placebo marihuana smoking on hemodynamics in coronary disease." Clin. Pharmacol. Ther. 1975, 18, 90-95.

5831. Pranikoff,K., Karacan,I., Larson,E.A., Williams,R.L., Thornby,J.I., and Hursch,C.J. "Effects of marihuana smoking on the sleep EEG. Preliminary studies. J. Florida Med. Assoc. 1973, 60, 28-31.

5832. Pratt,F. "Marihuana." Cath. Sch. J. 1969, 69, 4.

5833. Prendergast,T.J. "Family characteristics associated with marihuana use." Internat'l. J. Addict. 1974, 9, 827-839.

5834. Prentiss,D.W. "Case of intoxication from a comparatively small dose of cannabis indica." Ther. Gaz. 1892, 16, 104-105.

5835. Preston,J.D. A Survey of Drug Use among High School Students in Houston, Texas. Dept. Agricultural Economics and Rural Sociol., Houston, 1970.

5836. Preston,J.D. "On student marihuana use and societal alienation." J. Hlth. Soc. Behav. 1976, 17, 314-316.

5837. Pretoria Mental Hospital. "Mental symptoms associated with the smoking of dagga. Report of an investigation conducted by the medical staff of the hospital." S. Af. Med. J. 1938, 12, 85-88.

5838. Price,P.J., Suk,W.A., Spahn,G.J., and Freeman, A.E. "Transformation of Fischer rat embryo cells by the combined action of murine leukemia birus and (-)-trans-delta-9-tetrahydrocannabinol." Proc. Soc. Expt'l. Biol. Med. 1972, 140, 454-456.

5839. Priest,T.B. and McGrath,J.H. "Techniques of neutralization: young adult marihuana smokers." Criminology 1970, 8, 185-194.

5840. Prince,R., Greenfield,R., and Marriott,J. "Cannabis or alcohol?" Bull. Narc. 1972, 24, 1-9.

5841. Princton University Student Committee on Mental Health. Psychedelics and the College Student. Princeton Univ. Press, Princton, N.J., 1967.

5842. Prior,J. "On new cannabis preparations."(Ger.). Munch. Med. Woch. 1888, 35, 547-551.

5843. Pritchard,F.J. "Change of sex in hemp." J. Hered. 1916, 7, 325-329.

5844. Procek,J. "Preliminary investigation of the localized effects of cannabis indica--a cure for specific fistulas."(Czech.). Act. Univ. Palack. Olomunc. 1955, 6, 91-92.

5845. Procter,B.G., Dussault,P., Rona,G., and Chappel,C.I. "Studies of the carcinogenicity of an acetone extract of hashish." Toxicol. Appl. Pharmacol. 1974, 29, 76.

5846. Procter,W. "On a test for the resin of cannabis indica." Proc. Am. Pharmaceut. Assoc. 1864, 12, 244-248.

5847. Protiva,M. "News in chemistry of psychotropic drugs in the year 1969." Act. Nerv. Sup. 1970, 12, 193-214.

5848. Prue,T.E. and Hargraves,R. "Decriminalization of marihuana: dealing with the reality, not the symbol." Christ. Cent. 1974, 91, 822-823.

5849. Pryor,G.T. "Acute and subacute behavioral and pharmacological interactions of delta-9-THC with other drugs." In Braude,M.C. and Szara,S.(eds.) Pharmacology of Marihuana. Raven Press, N.Y., 1976, 2, 543-555.

5850. Pryor,G.T. and Braude,M.C. "Interactions between delta-9-tetrahydrocannabinol(THC) and phencyclidine (PC). Pharmacologist 1975, 17, 182.

5851. Pryor,G.T., Husain,S., Larsen,F., McKenzie,C.E., Carr,J.D., and Braude, M.C. "Interactions between delta-9-tetrahydrocannabinol and phencyclidine hydrochloride in rats." Pharmacol. Biochem. Behav. 1977, 6, 123-136.

5852. Pryor,G.T., Husain,S., and Mitoma,C. "Influence of fasting on the absorption and effects of delta-9-tetrahydrocannabinol after oral administration in sesame oil." Pharmacol. Biochem. Behav. 1977, 6, 331-341.

5853. Pryor,G.T., Husain,S., Mitoma,C., and Braude, M.C. "Acute and subacute interactions between delta-9-tetrahydrocannabinol and other drugs in the rat." Ann. N. Y. Acad. Sci. 1976, 281, 171-189.

5854. Pryor,G.T., Husain,S., and Siemens,A.J. "A comparison of the disposition of ^{14}C-delta-9-tetrahydrocannabinol and ^{3}H-delta-9-tetrahydrocannabinol." Life Sci. 1977, 21, 441-450.

5855. Pryor,G.T., Mills,P.J., and Lydell,K.W. "Interaction of delta-9-tetrahydrocannabinol, caffeine(C), nicotine(N), phenobarbital(P): Effects on conditioned avoidance(CAR)." Fed. Proc. 1973, 32, 725.

5856. Pulewka,P. "Unresolved questions concerning hashish."(Ger.). Med. Welt. 1971, 45, 1779-1784.

5857. Pulewka,P. "Pharmacological assay of intoxicating hemp and its preparations(esrar, hashish, etc.)."(Ger.). Act. Med. Turc. 1951, 3, 77-94.

5858. Pulewka,P. "The relative effectiveness of Turkish hashish plants."(Ger.). Arch. Expt'l. Pathol. Pharmakol. 1950, 211, 278-286.

5859. Pulewka,P. and Yeginsoy,A.T. "Effects of cannabis extracts on the central nervous system of mice."(Turk.). Turk. Ijiyen Tecrub. Biyol. Derg. 1940, 2, 103-116.

5860. Pulewka,P. and Yeginsoy,A.T. "Pharmacological studies of cannabis(esar, hashish). I. Experiments on the effects of cannabis extracts on the central nervous system of the mouse."(Turk.). Turk. Ijiyen Tecrub. Biyol. Derg. 1940, 2, 117-121.

5861. Pullen,J.R. "Marihuana laws." Southwest. Med. 1970, 51, 179-180.

5862. Purdue Opinion Panel. Incidence of Drug Use and Issues of Prevention. Measurement and Res. Ctr., Purdue Univ., West Lafayette, Ind., 1973.

5863. Purnell,W.D. and Gregg,J.M. "Delta-9-THC, euphoria and intraocular pressure in man." Ann. Ophthalmol. 1975, 7, 921-923.

5864. Pusinelli,A. "Tannate of cannabis as an hypnotic."(Ger.). Berlin Klin. Woch. 1884, 21, 7-9.

5865. Pyle,R.L. "Effects of the Grossmont District drug policy on attitudinal and overt response of secondary students." Diss. Abs. 1970, 31, 2115-2116.

Q

5866. Quarles,W., Ellman,G., and Jones,R. "Toxicology of marihuana: conditions for conversion of cannabidiol to THC upon smoking." Clin. Toxicol. 1973, 6, 211-216.

5867. Quer,P.F. "Marihuana(cannabis sativa L.)."(Sp.). In Quer,P.F.(ed.). Medicinal Plants, Dioscorides Renewed.(Sp.). Editorial Labor, Barcelona, 1962, 127-129.

5868. Quimby,M.W. "Botany of cannabis sativa." Arch. Invest. Med. 1974, 5, 127-134.

5869. Quimby,M.W. and Doorenbos,N.J. "The botany of cannabis sativa." Lloydia 1973, 36, 437.

5870. Quimby,M.W., Doorenbos,N.J., Turner,C.E., and Masoud,A. "Mississippi-grown-marihuana--cannabis sativa cultivation and observed morphological variations." Econ. Bot. 1973, 27, 117-127.

5871. Quin,W.F. "Marihuana, LSD, and other dangerous substances." Bull. Los Angeles County Med. Assoc. 1967, 97, 20-21.

5872. Quinn,W.F. "Narcotics and the dangerous drug problems. Current status of legislation, control and rehabilitation." Calif. Med. 1967, 106, 108-111.

R

5873. R. "A dope taster." High Times 1974, 4, 12-14.

5874. Rabelais,F. "The herb Pantagruelion." In Solomon,D.(ed.). The Marihuana Papers. Bobbs-Merrill, Indiana, 1966, 105-120.

5875. Rabinovich,A.S., Aizenman,B.E., and Zelepukha, S.I. "Antimicrobial materials isolated from cannabis cultivated in the Ukraine."(Rus.). Antibiotiki 1961, 6, 74-76.

5876. Rabinovich,A.S., Aizenman,B.E., and Zelepukha, S.I. "Isolation and study of antibacterial properties of preparations from wild hemp(cannabis ruderatis) growing in the Ukraine."(Rus.). Mikrobiol. Zhurn. 1959, 21, 40-48.

5877. Rachelefsky,G.S. and Opelz,G. "Normal lymphocyte function in the presence of delta-9-tetrahydrocannabinol." Clin. Pharmacol. Ther. 1977, 21, 44-46.

5878. Rachelefsky,G.S., Opelz,G., Mickey,R., Lessin,P., Kiuchi,M., Silverstein,M.J., and Stiehm,E.R. "Intact humoral and cell-mediated immunity in chronic marihuana smoking." J. Allerg. Clin. Immunol. 1976, 58, 483-490.

5879. Rachin,R.L. "Florida's drug dilemma." J. Drug Iss. 1971, 1, 56-73.

5880. Racime,H. "Hashish or Indian hemp/"(Fr.). Montpel. Med. 1876, 36, 432-449.

5881. Radosevic,A., Kupinic,M., and Grlic,L.J. "Antibiotic activity of various types of cannabis resin." Nature 1962, 195, 1007-1009.

5882. Radouco-Thomas,S., Bordage,G., Lambert,M., Langlois,D., Grenon,R., and Radouco-Thomas,C. "Student drug abuse survey in the Province of Quebec: Comparative study 1968-1971." Proc. 5th Internat'l. Cong. Pharmacol. 1972, 1, 187.

5883. Radouco-Thomas,S and Garcin,F. "Classification and nomenclature of psychodysleptics(hallucinogens)."(Fr.). Toxicomanies 1969, 2, 315-340.

5884. Radouco-Thomas,S., Magnan,F., Grove,R.N., Singh,P., Garcin,F., and Radouco-Thomas,C. "Effect of chronic administration of delta-1-THC on learning and memory in developing mice." In Braude,M.C. and Szara,S. (eds.). Pharmacology of Marihuana. Raven Press, N.Y., 1976, 487-499.

5885. Radouco-Thomas,S., Magnan,F., and Radouco-Thomas,C. "Pharmacogenetic studies on cannabis and narcotics: Effects of delta-1-tetrahydrocannabinol and morphine in developing mice." In Nahas,G.G., Paton,W.D.M., and Idanpaan-Heikkila,J.E.(eds.). Marihuana. Springer Verlag, N.Y., 1876, 481-495.

5886. Radouco-Thomas,S., Villeneuve,A., Hudon,M., Monnier,M., Tanguay,C., Tessier,L., Lajeunesse,N., Gendron,C., and Radouco-Thomas,C. "Inquiry into the use of psychodysleptics(hallucinogens) in the colleges and universities of the Province of Quebec. 1. Questionaire used."(Fr.). Laval Med. 1968, 39, 817-833.

5887. Radovsky,E.S. "Marihuana foolishness." N. Eng. J. Med. 1969, 280, 620.

5888. Rafaelsen,L., Christrup,H., Bech,P., and Rafaelsen,O. "Effects of cannabis and alcohol on psychological tests." Nature 1973, 242, 117-118.

5889. Rafaelsen,O.J. "Cannabis and alcohol: Effects on simulated car driving and psychological tests." In Paton,W.D.M. and Crown,J.(eds.). Cannabis and Its Derivatives. Oxford Univ. Press, London, 1972, 184-193.

5890. Rafaelsen,O.J., Bech,P., Christiansen,J., Christrup,H., Nyboe,J., and Rafaelsen,L. "Cannabis and alcohol: Effects on simulated car driving." Science 1973, 173, 920-923.

5891. Rafaelsen,O.J., Bech,P., Christiansen,J., and Rafaelsen,L. "Cannabis and alcohol: Effects on simulated car driving and psychological tests. Correlation with urinary metabolites." Psychopharmacol. 1972, 26, 125.

5892. Rafaelsen,O.J., Bech,P., Christiansen,J., and Rafaelsen,L. "Cannabis and alcohol: Effects on simulated car driving and psychological tests. Correlation with urinary metabolites." In Ban,T.A., Boissier,J.R., Gessa,G.J., Heimann,H., and Hollister,L.(eds.). Psychopharmacology, Sexual Disorders and Drug Abuse. North-Holland Pub. Co., Amsterdam, 1973, 689-691.

5893. Rafaelsen,O.J., Bech,P., and Rafaelsen,L. "Simulated car driving influenced by cannabis and alcohol." Pharmakopsychiat. Neuro-psychopharmakol. 1973, 6, 71-83.

5894. Rafaelsen,O.J. and Christiansen,J. "Cannabis metabolites in urine after oral administration." U.N. Doc. ST/SOA/SER.S/17, Mar. 25, 1969.

5895. Ragsky,M. "Observations on hashish, Dutch liquid and ethyl iodide."(Ger.). Zeit. Gesell. Aerzte Wien 1852, 8, 94.

5896. Ram,H.M. "Occurrence of endosperm haustorium in cannabis sativa L." Ann. Bot. 1960, 24, 79 32.

5897. Ram,H.M. and Jaiswal,V.S. "Feminization of male flowers of cannabis sativa L. by a morphactin." Naturwissen. 1971, 58, 149-150.

5898. Ram,H.M. and Jaiswal,V.S. "Induction of female flowers on male plants of cannabis sativa by 2-chloroethanephosphonic acid." Exper. 1970, 26, 214-216.

5898a. Ram,H.M. and Jaiswal,V.S. "Induction of male flowers on female plants of cannabis sativa by gibberellins and its inhibition by abscisic acid." Planta 1972, 105, 263-266.

5899. Ram,H.M. and Jaiswal,V.S. "Sex reversal in the male plants of cannabis sativa L by ethyl hydrogen-1-propylphosphonate." Zeit. Planzenphysiol. 1972, 68, 181-183.

5900. Ram,H.M. and Nath,P. "The morphology and embryology of cannabis sativa Linn." Phytomorphol. 1964, 14, 414-429.

5901. Ramirez Moreno,N. "Mental difficulties produced by marihuana intoxication."(Fr.). Ann. Med.-Psychol. 1936, 1, 278.

5902. Ramsbotham,F.H. "Clinical midwifery." Med. Times Gaz. 1863, 2, 245-246.

5903. Rand,M.E. "A survey of drug use at Ithica College." Paper presented to Am. Coll. Hlth. Assoc., N.Y., 1968.

5904. Rand,M.E., Graf,W., and Thurdow,C. "Alcohol and marihuana: A follow up survey of Ithica College." J. Am. Coll. Hlth. Assoc. 1970, 18, 366-367.

5905. Rand.M.E., Hammond,J.D., and Moscou,P.J. "A survey of drug use at Ithica College." J. Am. Coll. Hlth. Assoc. 1968, 17, 43-51.

5906. Rao,S.M., Swonger,A.K., and Smith,N. "The effects of delta-8- and delta-9-tetrahydrocannabinol (THC) on the performance of rat shuttle-box avoidance behavior." Res. Commun. Psychol. Psychiat. Behav. 1976, 1, 381-390.

5907. Raquini,S. "Histomorphological data on cannabis sativa cells."(Fr.). Bol. Inst. Catal. Hist. Nat. 1929, 9, 1937.

5908. Rasmussen,K.E. "Analysis of cannabinoids in cannabis by means of gas-liquid chromatography and solid injection. Improvements to the method." J. Chromatog. 1975, 109, 175-176.

5909. Rasmussen,K.E. "On-column silylation of cannabinoids after injection of solid plant material and cold trapping." J. Chromatog. 1975, 114, 250-254.

5910. Rasmussen,K.E. "Quantitative determination of heptacosane and nonacosane in Norwegian-grown cannabis plants." Med. Nersk. Farmaceut. Selskäp 1975, 37, 128-135.

5911. Rasmussen,K.E., Rasmussen,S., and Baerheim-Svendsen,A.B. "Gas-liquid chromatography of cannabinoids in micro quantities of cannabis by solid injection." J. Chromatog. 1972, 69, 381-384.

5912. Rasmussen,K.E., Rasmussen,S., and Baerheim-Svendsen,A.B. "Quantitative determination of cannabinoids in cannabis by means of gas-liquid chromatography with solid injection." Act. Pharmaceut. Suec. 1972, 9, 457-462.

5913. Rasmussen,K.E., Rasmussen,S., and Baerheim-Svendsen,A.B. "A new technique for the detection of cannabinoids in micro quantities of cannabis by means of gas-liquid chromatography and solid sample injection." U.N. Doc. ST/SOA/SER.S/33, Apr. 24, 1972.

5914. Rasmussen,K.E., Rasmussen,S., and Baerheim-Svendsen,A.B. "Quantitative determination of cannabinoids in micro quantities of cannabis by means of gas liquid chromatography and solid sample injection." U.N. Doc. ST/SOA/SER.S/35, July 21, 1972.

5915. Rasmussen,K.E. and Baerheim-Svendsen,A.B. "The ratio of CBD/THC in various leaves of a cannabis plant containing CBD and THC as the main cannabinoids." *U.N. Doc*. ST/SOA/SER.S/40, Mar. 23, 1973.

5916. Rathenasinkam,E. "A modified 'Acid Beam' test for cannabis sativa resin." *Analyst* 1948, *73*, 509.

5917. Rathod,N.H. "Cannabis psychosis." In Connell, P.H. and Dorn,N.(eds.). *Cannabis and Man*. Churchill Livingstone, Edinburgh, 1975, 90-107.

5918. Rathod,N.H. "Effects of cannabis in man." *Proc. Roy. Soc. Med*. 1973, *66*, 722.

5919. Rathore,P. "A case report of a patient addicted both to opium and cannabis indica." *Antiseptic* 1944, *41*, 610-612.

5920. Rathing,D., Broermann,I., Honecker,H., Kluwe,S., and Coper,H. "Effect of subchronic treatment with (-)-delta-9-trans-tetrahydrocannabinol on food intake, body temperature, hexobarbital sleeping time and hexobarbital elimination in rats." *Psychopharmacol*. 1972, *27*, 349-357.

5921. Ratnam,E.V. "Cannabis indica." *J. Ceylon Branch Br. Med. Assoc*. 1916, *13*, 30-34.

5922. Ratnam,E.V. "Cannabis indica." *J. Ceylon Branch Br. Med. Assoc*. 1920, *17*, 36-42, 361.

5923. Ratsifandrihananana,B. "Cannabism or hemp intoxication."(Fr.). *Ann. Univ. Madagascar* 1964, *2*, 69-76.

5923 a. Rawitch,A.B., Schultz,G.S., Ebner,K.E., and Vardaris,R.M. "Competition of delta-9-tetrahydrocannabinol with estrogen in rat uterine estrogen receptor binding." *Science* 1977, *197*, 1189-1191.

5924. Rawlins,D.C. "Drug-taking by patients with venereal disease." *Br. J. Vener. Dis*. 1969, *45*, 238-240.

5925. Raz,A. and Goldman,R. "Effect of hashish compounds on mouse peritoneal macrophages." *Isr. J. Med. Sci*. 1975, *11*, 1177.

5926. Raz,A. and Goldman,R. "Effect of hashish compounds on mouse peritoneal macrophages." *Lab. Invest*. 1976, *34*, 69-76.

5927. Raz,A., Schurr,A., and Livne,A. "The interaction of hashish components with human erythrocytes." Biochim. Biophys. Act. 1972, 274, 269-271.

5928. Raz,A., Schurr,A., Livne,A., and Goldman,R. "Effect of hashish compounds on rat liver lysosomes in vitro." Biochem. Pharmacol. 1973, 22, 3129-3131.

5929. Razani,J. "Status of drug abuse and its treatment in Iran." Addict. Dis. 1977, 3, 69-74.

5930. Razdan,R.K. "Recent advances in the chemistry of cannabinoids." Prog. Org. Chem. 1973, 8, 78-101.

5931. Razdan,R.K. and Dalzell,H.C. "Drugs derived from cannabinoids. 6. Synthesis of cyclic analogues of dimethylheptylpyran." J. Med. Chem. 1976, 19, 719-721.

5932. Razdan,R.K., Dalzell,H.C., and Handrick,G.R. "Hashish. A simple one-step synthesis of (-)-delta-1-tetrahydrocannabinol(THC) from p-mentha-2,8-dien-1-ol and olivetol." J. Am. Chem. Soc. 1974, 96, 5860-5865.

5933. Razdan,R.K., Dalzell,H.C., Herlihy,P., and Howes,J.F. "Hashish. Unsaturated side-chain analogues of delta-8-tetrahyrocannabinol with potent biological activity." J. Med. Chem. 1976, 19, 1328-1330.

5934. Razdan,R.K. and Handrick,G.R. "Direct synthesis of (-)-trans-delta-9-tetrahydrocannabinol from olivetol and (+)-trans-delta-2-carene oxide." Chem. Abs. 1973, 79, 78615e.

5935. Razdan,R.K. and Handrick,G.R. "Hashish. A stereospecific synthesis of (-)-delta-1- and (-)-delta-1(6)-tetrahydrocannabinols." J. Am. Chem. Soc. 1970, 92, 6061-6062.

5936. Razdan,R.K., Handrick,G.R., and Dalzell,H.C. "A one-step synthesis of (-)-delta-1-tetrahydrocannabinol from chrysanthenol." Exper. 1975, 31, 16-17.

5937. Razdan,R.K., Handrick,G.R., Dalzell,H.C., Howes,J.F., Winn,M., Plotnikoff,N.P., Dodge,P.W., and Dren,A.T. "Drugs derived from cannabinoids. 4. Effect of alkyl substitution in sulfur and carbocyclic analogs." J. Med. Chem. 1976, 19, 5-2-554.

5938. Razdan,R.K., Handrick,G.R., Pars,H.G., Puttick, A.J., Weinhardt,K.K., Howes,J.F., Harris,L.S., and Dewey,W.L. "Cannabis: Studies on delta-8- and delta-9-tetrahydrocannabinols: Their preparation, stability and water-soluble derivatives." Comm. Prob. Drug Depend. 1970, 3, 6860-6867.

5939. Razdan,R.K., Howes,J.F., Uliss,D.B., Dalzell, H.C., Handrick,G.R., and Dewey,W.L. "(-)-8b-hydroxymethyl-delta-1-tetrahydrocannabinol: A novel physiologically active analog of delta-1-tetrahydrocannabinol." Exper. 1976, 32, 416-417.

5940. Razdan,R.K. and Kane,V.V. "Hashish, a novel cannabinoid containing a cyclic peroxide." J. Am. Chem. Soc. 1969, 91, 5190-5191.

5941. Razdan,R.K., Kane,V.V., Pars,H.G., Kucera,J.L., Reid,D.H., Harris,L.S., Dewey,W.L., and Howes,J.F. "Studies on cannabis constituents and synthetic analogs." Comm. Prob. Drug Depend. 1969, 3, 6135-6141.

5942. Razdan,R.K. and Pars,H.G. "Studies on cannabis constituents and synthetic analogues." In Joyce,C.R.B. and Curry,S.H.(eds.). The Botany and Chemistry of Cannabis. J. and A. Churchill, London, 1970, 137-150.

5943. Razdan,R.K., Pars,H.G., Granchelli,F.E., and Harris,L.S. "A steroidal analog of a tetrahydrocannabinol." J. Med. Chem. 1968, 11, 377-378.

5944. Razdan,R.K., Pars,H.G., Thompson,W.R., and Granchelli,F.E. "Lithium-ammonia reduction of tetrahydrocannabinols." Tetrahed. Let. 1974, 60, 4315-4318.

5945. Razdan,R.K., Puttick,A.J., Zitko,.B.A., and Handrick,G.R. "Hashish. VI. Conversion of (-)-delta-1(6)-tetrahydrocannabinol to (-)-delta-1-(7)-tetrahydrocannabinol. Stability of (-)-delta-1- and (-)-delta-1(6)-tetrahydrocannabinols." Exper. 1972, 28, 121-122.

5946. Razdan,R.K., Terris,B.Z., Pars,H.G., Plotnikoff,N.P., Dodge,P.W., Dren,A.T., Kynel,J., and Somani,P. "Drugs derived from cannabinoids. 2, Basic esters of nitrogen and carbocyclic analogs." J. Med. Chem. 1976, 19, 454-461.

5947. Razdan,R.K., Thompson,W.R., Pars,H.G., and Granchelli,F.E. "Pyridyl benzopyrans related to tetrahydrocannabinols." Chim. Ther. 1967, 2, 167.

5948. Razdan,R.K., Uliss,D.B., and Dalzell,H.C. "Hashish. IX. Synthesis of 7-hydroxy-delta-1-tetrahydrocannabinol(THC). An important active metabolite of delta-1-THC in man." J. Am. Chem. Soc. 1973, 95, 2361-2362.

5949. Razdan,R.K. and Zitko,B.A. "Hashish. IV. Some acid catalyzed tranf mations in cannabinoids." Tetrahed. Let. 1969, 56, 4947-4950.

5950. Razdan,R.K. and Zitko,B.A. "Hashish. IV. Some acid catalyzed transformations in cannabinoids." Tetrahed. Let. 1969, 56, 4947-4950.

5951. Razdan,R.K., Zitko,B.A., Terris,B., and Pars,H.G. "Drugs derived from cannabinoids. 2. Basic esters of nitrogen and carbocyclic analogs." J. Med. Chem. 1976, 19, 454-461.

5952. Razdan,R.K., Zitko,B.A., Terris,B., Handrick,G.R., Dalzell,H.C., Pars,H.G., and Howes,J.F. "Drugs derived from cannabinoids. 3. Sulfur analogs, thiopyranobenzopyrans and thienobenzopyrans." J. Med. Chem. 1976, 19, 549-551.

5953. Razdan,R.K., Zitko,B.A., Weinhardt,K.K., Howes,J.F., Dalzell,B.C., Dalzell,H.C., Sheehan,J.C. Pars,H.G., Dewey,W.L., and Harris,L.S. "Water-soluble derivatives of delta-1-and delta-1(6)-THC's and the synthesis of the metabolite of delta-1(6)-THC." Act. Pharmaceut. Suec. 1971, 8, 677-679.

5954. Reading,D.K. The Anglo-Russian Commercial Treaty of 1734. Yale Univ. Press, New Haven, 1938.

5955. Reales,O. "General aspects of poisoning by marihuana and its psychiatric manifestation in Barranquilla." (Sp.). Rev. Med. Leg. Colombia 1953, 13, 142-148.

5956. Reasons,C.E. "The addict as criminal. Perpetuation of a legend." Crime Delinquency 1975, 1, 19-27.

5957. Reasons,C.E. The Criminologist: Crime and the Criminal. Goodyear, Pacific Palisades, 1974.

5958. Rech,M. "Effects of hashish on the normal man and the lunatic."(Fr.). Ann. Med.-Psychol. 1848, 12, 1-37.

5959. Rector,M.G. "Drinking and pot parties." Educat. Dig. 1967, 33, 45-47.

5960. Rector,M.G. "Drinking and pot parties; with study discussion program by Smollenberg,C. and Smollenberg,H." PTA Mag. 1967, 61, 4-7, 35-36.

5961. Redhardt,R. "The psychopathology of ideological and sociocultural motivational aspects of hashish abuse." (Ger.). Nachrichtendienst 1971, 51, 302-307.

5962. Redhardt,R. "On the pathology of the ideological and sociocultural motivation of hashish abuse."(Ger.). Zeit. Rechtsmed. 1971, 68, 57-72.

5963. Reed,H.B.C. "Cognitive effects of marihuana." In Mendelson,J.H., Rossi,A.M., and Meyer,R.E.(eds.). The Use of Marihuana. Plenum Press, N.Y., 1974, 107-114.

5964. Reed,H.B.C. "Marihuana and brain dysfunction: Selected research issues." In Tinklenberg,J.R.(ed.). Marihuana and Health Hazards. Academic Press, N.Y., 1975, 121-125.

5965. Reenie,S.J. "On the therapeutic value of tinctura cannabis indica in the treatment of dysentery more particularly in its subacute and chronic forms." Ind. Med. Gaz. 1886, 21, 353-354.

5966. Rees,W.L. "Modern developments in psychopharmacology." Chem. Brit. 1972, 8, 109-114.

5967. Reese,K.M. "Reefers bad for health?" Chem. Engin. News 1970, 48, 68.

5968. Regallo Pereira,J. "Contribution to the study of hallucinatory plants, particularly marihuana." (Port.). Rev. Flor. Med. 1945, 12, 81-210.

5969. Regallo Pereira,J. "Maconha and other social poisons."(Port.). Arquiv. Pol. Sao Paulo 1951, 21, 65-104.

5970. Regardie,I.(ed.). Roll Away the Stone: An Introduction to Aleister Crowley's Essays on the Psychology of Hashish. Llewellyn Pub., St. Paul, Minn., 1968.

5971. Regelson,W., Butler,J.R., Schulz,J., Kirk,T., Peek,L., Green,M.L., and Zalis,M.O. "Delta-9-tetrahydrocannabinol as an effective antidepressant and appetite stimulating agent in advanced cancer patients." In Braude,M.C. and Szara,S.(eds.). Pharmacology of Marihuana. Raven Press, N.Y., 1976, 2, 763-777.

5972. Regla,P. "Hashish."(Fr.). Rev. Hypnotisme 1892, 11, 229.

5973. Rehert,G.M. "Pot-smoking blood donors out." N. Eng. J. Med. 1971, 284, 856.

5974. Reich,C.A. The Greening of America. Random House, N.Y., 1970.

5975. Reichard,J.D. "Marihuana problem." J.A.M.A. 1944, 125, 594-595.

5976. Reichard,J.D. "Some myths about marihuana." Fed. Prob. 1946, 10, 15-22.

5977. Reid,L. and Ibraham,M.F. "The application of human operator-describing functions to studies on the effects of alcohol and marihuana on human performance." Trans. Systems Man Cybernetics 1975, 5, 506-519.

5978. Reigler,A. "Contribution to the pharmacological knowledge of Indian hemp and the poppy."(Ger.). Rep. Pharm. 1847, 1, 356-366.

5979. Reimann,B.E.F. "Marihuana, the plant." Southwest. Med. 1970, 8, 164-166.

5980. Reininger,W. "Hashish."(Ger.). Ciba Zeit. 1941, 7, 2765-2788.

5981. Reininger,W. "Remnants of hemp dating from prehistoric times." Ciba Sympos. 1946, 8, 401.

5982. Reininger,W. "The herb Pantagruelion." Ciba Sympos. 1946, 8, 402-403.

5983. Reininger,W. "The use of hashish in a cult." Ciba Sympos. 1946, 8, 401.

5984. Reininger,W. "The use of hemp in the manufacture of ropes and fabrics." Ciba Sympos. 1946, 8, 403.

5985. Reininger,W. "Two celebrated hashish eaters." Ciba Sympos. 1946, 8, 397-400.

5986. Reinstein,M. "Drugs and the military physician." Milit. Med. 1972, 137, 122-125.

5987. Reisner,H. "The forensic psychiatric significance of psychotropic substances."(Ger.). Ost. Arztezt. 1966, 21, 1955-1966.

5988. Reiss,J. "Thin layer chromatographic separation of the constituents of hashish on pre-coated silica gel sheet."(Ger.). Arch. Toxicol. 1972, 29, 265-266.

5989. Reissner,M. "On the subcutaneous administration of medicines to the mentally ill."(Ger.). Allgem. Zeit. Psychiat. Med. 1867, 24, 74-151.

5990. Reiter,P.J. "On symptomatic therapy for depressive illnesses, especially with respect to experiments with Indian hemp and electrolytic therapy."(Dan.). Ugeskrift Laeg. 1929, 91, 840-843.

5991. Reko,V.A. Magical Gifts, Narcotics and Anesthetics of the New World.(Ger.). Ferdinand Enke Verlag, Stuttgart, 1936.

5992. Remschmidt,H. "Hashish and LSD. Part I."(Ger.). Med. Klin. 1972, 67, 706-716.

5993. Remschmidt,H. "Hashish and LSD. Part II." (Ger.). Med. Klin. 1972, 67, 781-786.

5994. Renault,P.F., Schuster,C.R., Freedman,D.X., Sikic,B., de Mello,D.N., and Halaris,A. "Repeat administration of marihuana smoke to humans." Arch. Gen. Psychiat. 1974, 31, 95-102.

5995. Renault,P.F., Schuster,C.R., Heinrich,R., and Freedman,D.X. "Marihuana: Standardization of smoke administration and dose effect curves on heart rate in humans." Comm. Prob. Drug Depend. 1971, 2, 1745-1755.

5996. Renault,P.F., Schuster,C.R., Heinrich,R., and Freedman,D.X. "Marihuana: Standardized smoke administration and dose effect curves on heart rate in humans." Science 1971, 174, 589-592.

5997. Renborg,B.A. "Limitation and control of natural narcotics raw materials: Scheme of the League of Nations and the United Nations." Bull. Narc. 1963, 15, 13-26.

5998. Renborg,B.A. "Should cannabis derivatives be regarded as narcotics?"(Ger.). Alkoholfragan 1971, 65, 152-154.

5999. Rende,G. "A psuedo-specific reaction for hashish."(Fr.). Ann. Falsif. Fraudes 1932, 25, 332-336.

6000. Renfrew County School Board, Pembroke Police Department and Pembroke R.C.M.P. Detachment. Secondary School Drug Survey. Pembroke Police Dept., Pembroke, Ontario, 1969.

6001. Renz,G.A. "My experiment with cannabis indica." Northwest. Lancet 1885, 5, 203-204.

6002. Repetto,M. and Lopez-Artiguez,M. "Identification of cannabinoids in viscera." J. Eur. Toxicol. 1973, 6, 218-223.

6003. Repetto,M., Lopez-Artiguez,M., and Martinez,D. "Separation of cannabinoids." Bull. Narc. 1976, 28, 69-74.

6004. Repetto,M. and Menendez,M. "Identification of cannabis products from the fingertips and blood of smokers."(Fr.). J. Eur. Toxicol. 1972, 4, 502-504.

6005. Repetto,M. and Menendez,M. "Study of cannabis. Research on the plant, smoke and urine."(Fr.). J. Eur. Toxicol. 1970, 3, 392-396.

6006. Republic of South Africa. The Dagga Problem. Dept. Soc. Welfare and Pensions, Pretoria, 1966.

6007. Republic of South Africa. Research and Information Department of Social Welfare and Pension. Drug Dependence and Some of Its Concomitant Aspects in the Republic of South Africa. Dept. Soc. Welfare and Pensions, Pretoria, 1970.

6008. Research Concepts, Inc. "Treatment and rehabilitation programs for drug-induced offenders in state correction systems." In National Commission on Marihuana and Drug Abuse. Drug Use in America: Problem in Perspective. Gov't. Print. Office, Washington, D.C., 1973, III, 810-852.

6009. Retterstol,N. "Abuse of drugs, particularly with respect to causes and preventions."(Nor.). Tid. Norsk. Laegeforen. 1966, 86, 1465-1472.

6010. Retterstol,N. "Are cannabis materials hazardous?"(Nor.). Tid. Norsk. Laegeforen. 1973, 93, 1754-1757.

6011. Retterstol,N. "Can cannabis produce long-lasting psychoses in a 'well-balanced' individual?" (Nor.). Tid. Norsk. Laegeforen. 1970, 90, 715.

6012. Retterstol,N. "Cannabis again."(Nor.). Tid. Norsk. Laegeforen. 1971, 91, 1841-1842.

6013. Retterstol,N. "Cannabis and driving."(Nor.). Tid. Norsk. Laegeforen. 1973, 93, 2121-2122.

6014. Retterstol,N. "Cannabis drugs--personality characteristics."(Nor.). Tid. Norsk. Laegeforen. 1974, 94, 48.

6015. Retterstol,N. "Cannabis psychoses. 46 cases reported from Sweden."(Nor.). Tid. Norsk. Laegeforen. 1973, 93, 1410.

6016. Retterstol,N. "Cannabis reports."(Nor.). Tid. Norsk. Laegeforen. 1973, 93, 2123-2124.

6017. Retterstol,N. "Cannabis--new research."(Nor.). Tid. Norsk. Laegeforen. 1971, 91, 2272.

6018. Retterstol,N. "Cannabis research."(Nor.) Tid. Norsk. Laegeforen. 1973, 93, 2185-2186.

6019. Retterstol,N. "Cannabis--clinical pharmacology." (Nor.). Tid. Norsk. Laegeforen. 1973, 93, 2125-2126.

6020. Retterstol,N. "Chronic use of marihuana--psychological function."(Nor.). Tid. Nor. Laegeforen. 1973, 93, 2332.

6021. Retterstol,N. "Clinical and social aspects of marihuana intoxication."(Nor.). Tid. Norsk. Laegeforen. 1971, 91, 1438.

6022. Retterstol,N. "Drug dependence in adolescents." (Nor.). Tid. Norsk. Laegeforen. 1968, 88, 2093-2098.

6023. Retterstol,N. "Experimental data on marihuana." (Nor.). Tid. Norsk. Laegeforen. 1971, 91, 2037.

6024. Retterstol,N. "Hospitalization after marihuana abuse."(Nor.). Tid. Norsk. Laegeforen. 1971, 91, 1482.

6025. Retterstol,N. "More on cannabis."(Nor.). Tid. Norsk. Laegeforen. 1971, 91, 1839-1840.

6026. Retterstol,N. "New data on cannabis."(Nor.). Tid. Norsk. Laegeforen. 1973, 93, 2122-2123.

6027. Retterstol,N. "News on cannabis metabolites--psychopharmacology."(Nor.). Tid. Norsk. Laegeforen. 1971, 91, 2340.

6028. Retterstol,N. "Present status of the cannabis problem."(Nor.). Tid. Norsk. Laegeforen. 1968, 88, 985-988.

6029. Retterstol,N. "Psychoses induced by cannabis." (Nor.). Tid. Norsk. Laegeforen. 1971, 91, 1839.

6030. Retterstol,N. "The effects of marihuana on adolescents and young people."(Nor.). Tid. Norsk. Laegeforen. 1971, 91, 2274-2275.

6031. Retterstol,N. "The pattern of marihuana usage." (Nor.). Tid. Norsk. Laegeforen. 1971, 91, 2425.

6032. Retterstol,N. "The psychiatric effects of hashish--dependence on the dosage."(Nor.). Tid. Norsk. Laegeforen. 1972, 92, 2460.

6033. Retterstol,N. "Toxic effects of chronic cannabis abuse."(Nor.). Tid. Norsk. Laegeforen. 1973, 93, 2124-2124.

6034. Reuben,D.R. "Marihuana and alcohol." J.A.M.A. 1968, 204, 407.

6035. Reuter,P. "The obligations of states under the single convention on narcotic drugs, 1961." Bull. Narc. 1968, 20, 3-7.

6036. Reutter de Rosement,L. "Indian hemp as a sensorial drug."(Fr.). Chron. Pharmaceut. 1921, 1, 323-324.

6037. Reynolds,J.R. "Therapeutic uses and toxic effects of cannabis indica." Lancet 1890, 1, 637-638.

6038. Reznick,S.P. "Marihuana addiction." Soc. Work Technique 1937, 2, 173-177.

6039. Ribeiro do Valle,J. "Considerations on cannabis."(Sp.). Rev. Inst. Adolfo Lutz 1961, 21, 83-98.

6040. Ribeiro do Valle,J. "Pharmacological approaches to the study of the cannabis problem." Internat'l. J. Addict. 1969, 4, 623-647.

6041. Ribi,E., Smith,R., Strain,M., Petcoff,D., and Filz,C. "Purification of delta-9-tetrahydrocannabinol, an active constituent of marihuana, by accelerated microparticulate GEL chromatography." Fed. Proc. 1972, 31, 506.

6042. Ribi,E., Smith,R., Strain,M., Petcoff,D., Parker,R., and Geede,G. "Purification of delta-9-tetrahydrocannabinol, an active constituent of marihuana, by accelerated microparticulate GEL chromatography." Prep. Biochem. 1973, 3, 209-220.

6043. Ribush,N. "Doctors and cannabis." Med. J. Aust. 1971, 2, 1202.

6044. Richards,L. and Carroll,E.E. "Illicit drug use and addiction in the United States." Ment. Hlth. Dig. 1971, 3, 45-48.

6045. Richards,W.A. "Marihuana: Our present knowledge." Engage 1971, 3, 408.

6046. Richardson,B.E. "On hashish." St. Andrew's Med. Grad. Assoc. Trans. 1872, 3, 90-97.

6047. Richardson,J. Sinsemilla. Marihuana Flowers. And/Or Press, Berkeley, Cal., 1976.

6048. Richet,C. Man and Intelligence.(Fr.). Alcan, Paris, 1887.

6049. Richet,C. "Poisons of the intelligence--hasheesh." Pop. Sci. Month. 1878, 13, 482-487.

6050. Richek,H.G. "'Traditional' religious values and the mental health characteristics of college freshmen and high school juniors and seniors." Paper presented at Rocky Mt. Psychol. Assoc., Phoenix, 1976.

6051. Richek,H.G., Angle,J.F., McAdams,W.S., and D'Angelo,J. "Personality/mental health correlates of drug use by high school students." J. Nerv. Ment. Dis. 1975, 160, 435-442.

6052. Richmon,J., Murawski,B., Matsumiya,Y., Duffy,F.H., and Lombroso,C.T. "Long term effects of chronic marihuana smoking." E.E.G. Clin. Neurophysiol. 1974, 36, 223-224.

6053. Richter,N. "On cannabinon."(Ger.). Deut. Med. Woch. 1884, 10, 834.

6054. Rickards,B.R. "New York City's campaign against marihuana." Hlth. News 1935, 12, 135-136.

6055. Rickles,W.H., Chatoff,B., and Whitaker,C. Marihuana; a Selective Bibliography 1924-1970. U.C.L.A. Brain Inform. Serv., Los Angeles, 1970.

6056. Rickles,W.H., Cohen,M.J., Whitaker,C.A., and McIntyre,K.E. "Marihuana induced state-dependent verbal learning." Psychopharmacol. 1973, 30, 349-354.

6057. Rickles,W.H. and Whitaker,C. "Effects of marihuana on evoked heart rate and skin conductance." Psychophysiol. 1971, 8, 259-260.

6058. Riedel,M. "A modern hashish eater."(Ger.). Deut. Klin. 1867, 18, 175-177.

6059. Riedmann,M. "Analytical methods in detection of drugs and poisons."(Ger.). Naturwissen. 1972, 59, 306-310.

6060. Riegler,A. "Contribution to the pharmacological knowledge of Indian hemp and the poppy." Rep. Pharm. 1847, 87, 356-366.

6061. Riley,D.N., Jamieson,B.D., and Russell,P.N. 'A survey of drug use at the university of Canterbury." N. Z. Med. J. 1971, 74, 365-368.

6062. Rippetoe,J.R. "The chemistry of the pharmacopeia." J.A.P.A. 1917, 6, 463-465.

6063. Rist,R.C. "Marihuana: a signal of misunderstanding by the National Commission on Marihuana and Drug ABuse." Society 1975, 12, 94.

6064. Rist,R.C. "Marihuana and the young: problem or protest?" Intellect 1972, 101, 154-156.

6065. Ritson,E.B. "Drug use in the provinces." Drugs Soc. 1971, 2, 19-24.

6066. Ritson,E.B., Toller,P., and Harding,F. "Drug abuse in the East Midlands. A study of 139 patients referred to an addiction unit." Br. J. Addict. 1973, 68, 65-71.

6067. Ritter,D.R. "Governmental response to widespread marihuana use as determined by a comparison of 1969 and 1971 statutes." J. Drug Educat. 1972, 2, 57-62.

6068. Ritti,M. "In praise of J. Moreau (de Tours)." (Fr.). Ann. Med.-Psychol. 1887, 60, 112-145.

6069. Robbins,E., Robbins,L., Frosch,W.A., and Stern,M. "Implications of untoward reactions to hallucinogens." Bull. N. Y. Acad. Med. 1967, 43, 985-999.

6070. Robbins,E.S. "College student drug use." Am. J. Psychiat. 1970, 126, 1743-1751.

6071. Robbins,L., Robbins,E., Pearlman,S., Philip,A., Robinson,E., and Schmitter,B. "College students' opinion of various aspects of drug use: A comparison of users and nonusers." Proc. Am. Psychol. Assoc. 1970, 1, 319-320.

6072. Robbins,L., Robbins,E., Pearlman,S., Philip,A., and Schmitter,B. "College students' perceptions of their parents' attitudes and practices toward drug use." Paper presented at Am. Educat. Res. Assoc., N.Y., 1971.

6073. Robbins,P.R. "Heroin addicts' views of commonly abused drugs: A semantic differential approach." J. Personal. Assess. 1972, 36, 366-370.

6074. Robbins,P.R. and Tanck,R.H. "Psychological correlates of marihuana use: An exploratory study." Psychol. Rep. 1973, 33, 703-706.

6075. Robbins,W.W. and Ramalay,F. Plants Useful to Man. P. Blakiston's Sons, Phil., 1933.

6076. Roberge,M. and Witschi,H. "Incorporation of uridine into ribonucleic acid in rat brain slices after delta-9-tetrahydrocannabinol and cannabis." Toxicol. Appl. Pharmacol. 1972, 23, 455-458.

6077. Robertson,A. "On extract of Indian hemp." Pharmaceut. J. Trans. 1847, 6, 70-72.

6078. Robertson,J. "Limited legislation of marihuana." Trial Mag. 1970, 52, 38-39.

6079. Robertson,M. "The poison ship." Harper's Month. Mag. 1915, 30, 952-957.

6080. Robertson,R. "Toxic symptoms from tincture of Indian hemp in official doses." Med. Times Gaz. 1885, 1, 817-819.

6081. Robertson-Milne,C.J. "Notes on insanity with illustrative cases." Ind. Med. Gaz. 1906, 41, 129-132.

6082. Robichaud,R.C., Hefner,M.A., Anderson,J.E., and Goldberg,M.E. "Effects of delta-9-tetrahydrocannabinol (THC) on several rodent learning paradigms." Pharmacol. 1973, 10, 1-11.

6083. Robins,L.N. The Vietnam Drug User Returns. U.S. Special Office for Drug Abuse Prevention, Washington, D.C., 1974.

6084. Robins,L.N. Veterens' Drug Use Three Years After Vietnam. Washington Univ. Sch. Med., St. Louis, n.d.

6085. Robins,L.N., Darvish,H.S., and Murphy,G.E. "The long-term outcome for adolescent drug users: A follow-up study of 76 users and 146 nonusers." Proc. Am. Psychopathol. Assoc., 1970, 59, 159-180.

6086. Robins,L.N., and Murphy,G.E. "Drug use in a normal population of young negro men." Am. J. Pub. Hlth. 1967, 57, 1580-1596.

6087. Robins,L.N. and Taibleson,M. "An actuarial method for assessing the direction of influence between two life events." Sociol. Methods Res. 1972, 1, 243-270.

6088. Robinson,A.E. "Recovery of cannabis constituents from the hands at autopsy." Bull. Narc. 1971, 23, 37-39.

6089. Robinson,B.B. "A study of marihuana toxicity on goldfish applied to hemp breeding." J.A.P.A. 1941, 30, 616-619.

6090. Robinson,B.B. "Greenhouse seed treatment studies on hemp." J. Am. Soc. Agron. 1943, 35, 910.

6091. Robinson,B.B. Hemp Farmers Bulletin. U.S.D.A., Washington, D.C. 1935.

6092. Robinson,B.B. and Matche-t,J.R. "Marihuana investigations. III. The effect of region of growth of hemp on response to the acid and alkaline Beam tests." J.A.P.A. 1940, 29, 448-453.

6093. Robinson,G.L. and Miller,S.T. "Drug abuse and the college campus." Ann. Am. Acad. Polit. Soc. Sci. 1975, 417, 101-109.

6094. Robonson,G.L., Young,L.R., and Duffy,M.E. "Review of college and university policies concerning illegal and unprescribed drugs and narcotics." In Natonal Commission on Marihuana and Drug Abuse. Drug Use in America: Problem in Perspective. Gov't. Print. Office, Washington, D.C., 1973, II, 548-581.

6095. Robinson,J.F. "An early effort in street drug analysis." J.A.P.A. 1973, 13, 677.

6096. Robinson,L. "Marihuana use in high-school girls: A psycho-social study." Diss. Abs. 1970, 31, 2196.

6097. Robinson,V. "An essay on hasheesh; including observations and experiments." Med. Rev. Rev. 1912, 18, 159-169.

6098. Robinson,V. "An essay on hasheesh. Part II." Med. Rev. Rev. 1912, 18, 300-313.

6099. Robinson,V. An Essay on Hasheesh--Historical and Experimental. E.H. Ringer, N.Y., 1925.

6100. Robinson,V. "Concerning cannabis indica." Ciba Sympos. 1946, 8, 378-386.

6101. Robinson,V. "Experiments with hashish." Ciba Sympos. 1946, 8, 387-396.

6102. Robinson,V. "Hashish: A drug and a dream." Ciba Sympos. 1946, 8, 374-377.

6103. Robiquet,E. "Report on the contest on the analysis of cannabis."(Fr.). J. Pharm. Chim. 1855, 28, 461-463.

6104. Robiquet,E. "Report on the meeting regarding the analysis of cannabis, presented in the name of the Society of Pharmacy."(Fr.). J. Pharm. Chim. 1857, 31, 46-51.

6105. Robitscher,J. "Morality, marihuana, and the law." Med. Opin. Rev. 1969, 1, 22-29.

6106. Robitscher,J. "The right of society to protect its members." In Wittenborn,J.R., Brill,H., Smith,J.P., and Wittenborn,S.A.(eds.). Drugs and Youth. C.C. Thomas, Springfield, Ill., 1969, 299-306.

6107. Rockwell,D.A. "Alcohol and marihuana--social problem perspective." Br. J. Addict. 1973, 68, 209-214.

6108. Rockwell,D.A. "Social problems--alcohol and marihuana." J. Psyched. Drugs 1972, 5, 49-55.

6109. Rodger,J.R. "Cannabis roots." J.A.M.A. 1971, 217, 1705-1706.

6110. Rodgers,R.C. "Chronic marihuana use and psychosocial adaptation." Am. J. Psychiat. 1973, 130, 139-140.

6111. Rodin,E.A. and Domino,E.F. "Effects of acute marihuana smoking on EEG." EEG Clin. Neurophysiol. 1970, 29, 321.

6112. Rodin,E.A., Domino,E.F., and Porzak,J.P. "The marihuana-induced 'social high'." J.A.M.A. 1970, 213, 1300-1302.

6113. Rodman,M.J. "Marihuana in Review." RN 1971, 34, 69-74, 76.

6114. Rodriguez-Morini,A. "Notes on the therapeutic action of hashish."(Sp.). Rev. Frenopat. Espan. 1909, 7, 142-146.

6115. Roemer,B. "On tetanus and tetanoid affections, with cases." St. Louis Med. Surg. J. 1873, 10, 363-378.

6116. Roffman,R.A. and Sapol,E. "Marihuana in Vietnam." Internat'l. J. Addict. 1970, 5, 1-42.

6117. Roger, B.L. "Pharmacological note on hashish and Indian hemp."(Fr.). Evol. Ther. Medicochiurg. 1925, 6, 13-16.

6118. Rohm,E. "Study on marihuana."(Ger.). Arch. Kriminol. 1961, 128, 5-6, 164.

6119. Rojas Hernanadez Simon,R. "Marihuana addiction."(Sp.). Enquiridion 1954, 2, 7.

6120. Roland,J.L. and Teste,M. "Cannabism in Morocco."(Fr.). Maroc Med. 1958, 37, 694-703.

6121. Roletto,G.B. "The cultivation of hemp in Italy."(Fr.). Ann. Geog. 1923, 32, 339-348.

6122. Rollings,E.J. Marihuana--The Weed of Woe. Defender Club Tract, Widhita, Kansas, 1938.

6123. Rollins,J.H. and Holden,R.H. "Dynamics of drug use." J. Drug Educat. 1977, 7, 231-235.

6124. Rolls,E.J. and Stafford-Clark,D. "Depersonalization treated by cannabis indica and psychotherapy." Guy's Hosp. Rep. 1954, 102, 330-336.

6125. Rootman,I. "Drug use among rural students in Alberta." Can. Ment. Hlth. 1972, 20, 9-14.

6126. Rosado,P.N.G.S. Study of Nervous Disorders Caused by Maconha.(Port.). Serv. Nac. Educ. Sanit., Rio de Janeiro, 1958.

6127. Rosado,P. Abuse of Liama in Para, a Toxic Reaction which Reappears in Our Country.(Port.). Serv. Nac. Educ. Sanit., Rio de Janeiro, 1958.

6128. Rose,P. The Hashish Cookbook. And/Or Press, Berkeley, Cal., 1973.

6129. Rose,R.M. "Background paper on testosterone and marihuana." In Tinklenberg,J.R.(ed.). Marihuana and Health Hazards. Academic Press, N.Y., 1975, 63-101.

6130. Rosell,S. "Cannabis in our society."(Swed.). Lakartidningen 1976, 73, 3852.

6131. Rosell,S. and Agurell,S. "Effects of 7-hydroxy-delta-6-tetrahydrocannabinol and some related cannabinoids on the guinea pig isolated ileum." Act. Physiol. Scand. 1975, 94, 142-144.

6132. Rosell,S., Agurell,S., and Martin,B. "Effects of cannabinoids on isolated smooth muscle preparations." In Nahas,G.G., Paton,W.D.M., and Idanpaan-Heikkila,J.E.(eds.). Marihuana. Springer Verlag, N.Y., 1976, 397-407.

6133. Rosenberg,C.M. "Marihuana reinforcement of disulfiram use in the treatment of alcoholism." Psychopharmacol. Bull. 1973, 9, 25.

6134. Rosenberg,C.M. "The use of marihuana in the treatment of alcoholism." In Cohen,S. and Stillman,R. (eds.). Therapeutic Potential of Marihuana. Plenum Press, N.Y., 1976, 173-182.

6135. Rosenberg,C.M. "Young drug addicts: Addiction and its consequences." Med. J. Aust. 1970, 1, 1031-1033.

6136. Rosenberg,C.M. "Young drug addicts: Background and personality." J. Nerv. Ment. Dis. 1969, 148, 65-73.

6137. Rosenberg,P. "The effects of mood altering drugs: Pleasures and pitfalls." In Hardy,R.E. and Cull,J.G. (eds.). Drug Dependence and Rehabilitation Approaches. C.C. Thomas, Springfield, Ill., 1973, 3-31.

6138. Rosenberg,R. "Pharmacological aspects of cannabis research."(Nor.). Nord. Med. 1971, 85, 357-361.

6139. Rosenblatt,J.E., Janowsky,D.S., Davis,J.M., and Khaled El-Yousef,M. "The augmentation of physostigmine toxicity in the rat by delta-9-tetrahydrocannabinol." Res. Commun. Chem. Pathol. Pharmacol. 1972, 3, 479-482.

6140. Rosenblum,I., Coulston,F., Gau,W., Greb,W., and Korte,F. "Role of 11-hydroxylation in the cardiovascular activity of delta-8-tetrahydrocannabinol." Comm. Prob. Drug Depend. 1973, 1, 178-181.

6141. Rosenfeld,A. "Marihuana: millions of turned-on users." Life 1967, 63, 16-23.

6142. Rosenfeld,A. "Marihuana: millions of turned-on users." In Guthrie,R.V.(ed.). Psychology in the World Today. Addison-Wesley, Reading, Mass., 1968, 224-229.

6143. Rosenfeld,J. "Mass fragmentographic assays for the cannabinoids and their metabolites." In Nahas, G.G., Paton,W.D.M., and Idanpaan-Heikila,J.E.(eds.). Marihuana. Springer Verlag, N.Y., 1976, 87-93.

6144. Rosenfeld,J.J., Bowins,B., Roberts,J., Perkins,J., and Macpherson,A.S. "Mass fragmentographic assay for delta-9-tetrahydrocannabinol in plasma." Anal. Chem. 1974, 46, 2232-2234.

6145. Rosenfeld,J.M. and Traguchi,V.Y. "Mass-fragmentation assay for 11-hydroxy-delta-9-tetrahydrocannabinol from plasma." Anal. Chem. 1976, 48, 726-728.

6146. Rosenkrantz,H. "The immune response and marihuana." In Nahas,G.G., Paton,W.D.M., and Idanpaan-Heikkila,J.E.(eds.). Marihuana. Springer Verlag, N.Y., 1976, 441-457.

6147. Rosenkrantz,H. and Braude,M.C. "Acute, subacute and 23-day chronic marihuana inhalation toxicities in the rat." Toxicol. Appl. Pharmacol. 1974, 28, 428-441.

6148. Rosenkrantz,H. and Braude,M.C. "Comparative chronic toxicities of delta-9-THC administered orally or by inhalation in rat." In Braude,M.C. and Szara,S.(eds.). Pharmacology of Marihuana. Raven Press, N.Y., 1976, 2, 571-585.

6149. Rosenkrantz,H., Hayden,D., and Braude,M.C. "Inhalation toxicity of Turkish marihuana, cannabichromene (CBCH) and cannabidiol(CBD) in rats." Fed. Proc. 1976, 35, 643.

6150. Rosenkrantz,H. and Braude,M.C. "Rat inhalation toxicity of Turkish marihuana." Pharmacologist 1975, 17, 181.

6151. Rosenkrantz,H., Heyman,I.A., Braude,M.C. "Inhalation, parenteral and oral LD_{50} values of delta-9-tetrahydrocannabinol in Fischer rats." Toxicol. Appl. Pharmacol. 1974, 28, 18-27.

6152. Rosenkrantz,H., Luthra,Y., Sprague,R., Thompson,G., and Braude,M.C. "Lipid and biopolymer levels in monkey brain after 28-day i.v. treatment with delta-9-tetrahydrocannabinol." Fed. Proc. 1972, 31, 506.

6153. Rosenkrantz,H., Miller,A.J., and Esber,H.J. "Delta-9-tetrahydrocannabinol suppression of the primary immune response in rats." J. Toxicol. Environ. Hlth. 1975, 1, 119-125.

6154. Rosenkrantz,H., Sprague,R.A., Fleischman,R.W., and Braude,M.C. "Oral delta-9-tetrahydrocannabinol toxicity in rats treated for periods up to six months." Toxicol. Appl. Pharmacol. 1975, 32, 399-399-417.

6155. Rosenkrantz,H., Thompson,G.R. and Braude,M.C. "Oral and parenteral formulations of marihuana constituents." J. Pharmaceut. Sci. 1972, 61, 1106-1112.

6156. Rosenquist,E. and Ottersen,T. "The crystal and molecular structure of delta-9-tetrahydrocannabinolic acid B." Act. Chem. Scand. 1975, 29B, 379-384.

6157. Rosenthal,F. The Herb, Hashish Versus Medieval Muslim Society. E.J. Brill, Leiden, Netherlands, 1971.

6158. Rosenthal,M.P. "Amelioration of the marihuana laws." In Harris,R.T., McIsaac,W.M.,, and Schuster,C.R. (eds.). Drug Dependence. Univ. Texas Press, Austin, 1970, 294-304.

6159. Rosenthal,M.P. "Drug crimes and the revision of the federal criminal code." In Wittenborn,J.R., Smith, J.P., and Wittenborn,S.A.(eds.). Communication and Drug Abuse. C.C. Thomas, Springfield, Ill., 1970, 431-470.

6160. Rosenthal,M.P. "Legal controls on mind- and mood-altering drugs." J. Soc. Iss. 1971, 27, 53-72.

6161. Rosenthal,M.P. "Marihuana: Some alternatives." In Wittenborn,J.R., Brill,H., Smith,J.P., and Wittenborn, S.A.(eds.). Drugs and Youth. C.C. Thomas, Springfield, Ill., 1969, 260-279.

6162. Rosenthal,M.P. "Plea for amelioration of the marihuana laws." Texas Law Rev. 1969, 47, 1359.

6162a. Rosenthal,M.P. "The legislative response to marihuana: when the shoe pinches enough." J. Drug Iss. 1977, 7, 61-77.

6163. Rosenthal,M.S. "Clinical effects of marihuana on the young. A call for more systematic clinical inquiry." Internat'l. J. Psychiat. 1972, 10, 75-77.

6164. Rosenthal,S.H. "Persistent hallucinosis following repeated administration of hallucinogenic drugs." Am. J. Psychiat. 1964, 121, 238.

6165. Rosenthaler,L. "On Greek hemp."(Ger.). J. Pharm. Elsass-Loth. 1910, 37, 232-234.

6166. Rosenwasser,H.M. "Marihuana as an etiology for contact lens problems." Opt. J. Rev. Optholmol. 1973, 110, 27.

6167. Rosevear,J. Pot, A Handbook of Marihuana. Lancer, N.Y., 1967.

6168. Rossberg,R.H. "Jumping over the paper moon." J. Assoc. Deans Admin. Student Affairs 1967, 4, 119-120.

6169. Rossaro,E.A. "Spontaneous tetraploidy in hemp."(It.). Ric. Sci. 1968, 38, 147-150.

6170. Rossi,A.M. "Marihuana effects on short term memory and time estimation." Proc. Am. Psychol. Assoc. 1973, 8, 1035-1036.

6171. Rossi,A.M., Babor,T.F., Meyer,R.E., and Mendelson,J.H. "Mood states." In Mendelson,J.H., Rossi,A.M., and Meyer,R.E.(eds.). The Use of Marihuana. Plenum Press, N.Y., 1974, 115-126.

6172. Rossi,A.M., Bernstein,J.G., and Mendelson,J.H. "Sleep-wakefullness behavior." In Mendelson,J.H., Rossi,A.M., and Meyer,R.E.(eds.). The Use of Marihuana. Plenum Press, N.Y., 1974, 161-171.

6173. Rossi,A.M., Mendelson,J.H., and Meyer,R.E. "Experimental analysis of marihuana acquisition and use." In Mendelson,J.H., Rossi,A.M., and Meyer,R.E.(eds.). The Use of Marihuana. Plenum Press, N.Y., 1974, 27-43.

6174. Rossi,A.M., Kuehnle,J.C., and Mendelson,J.H. "Effects of marihuana on reaction time and short-term memory in human volunteers." Pharmacol. Biochem. Behav. 1977, 6, 73-77.

6175. Rossi,A.M. and O'Brien,J. "Memory and time estimation." In Mendelson,J.H., Rossi,A.M., and Meyer,R.E. (eds.). The Use of Marihuana. Plenum Press, N.Y., 1974, 89-102.

6176. Rossi,G.V. "Mischievous drugs." Am. J. Pharmacol. 1968, 140, 38-43.

6177. Rossi,G.V. "Pharmacologic effects of drugs which are abused." Am. J. Pharmacol. 1970, 142, 161-170.

6178. Rossman,M. "Cannabis calculations." Marihuana Rev. 1968, 1, 3-6.

6179. Rost,E. "A new Mexican narcotic drug."(Ger.). Deut. Med. Woch. 1940, 66, 552-553.

6180. Rotenberg,D.L. "Marihuana in the Houston high schools--a first report." Houston Law Rev. 1969, 6, 759.

6181. Roth,W.T., Galanter,M., Weingartner,H., Vaughan,T.B., and Wyatt,R.J. "Marihuana and synthetic delta-9-trans-tetrahydrocannabinol: Some effects on the auditory evoked response and background EEG in humans." Biol. Psychiat. 1973, 6, 221-233.

6182. Roth,W.T., Rosenbloom,M.J., Darley,C.F., Tinklenberg,J.R., and Kopell,B.S. "Marihuana effects on TAT form and content." Psychopharmacol. 1975, 43, 261-266.

6183. Roth,W.T., Tinklenberg,J.R., and Kopell,B.S. "Ethanol and marihuana effects of event-related potentials in a memory retrieval paradigm." EEG Clin. Neurophysiol. 1977, 42, 381-388.

6184. Roth,W.T., Tinklenberg,J., and Kopell,B.S. "Subjective benefits and drawbacks of marihuana and alcohol." In Cohen,S. and Stillman,R.(eds.). Therapeutic Potential of Marihuana. Plen Press, N.Y., 1976, 255-270.

6185. Roth,W.T., Tinklenberg,J.R., Kopell,B.S., and Hollister,L.E. "Continuous electrocardiographic monitoring during marihuana intoxication." Clin. Pharmacol. Ther. 1973, 14, 533-540.

6186. Roth,W.T., Tinklenberg,J.R., Whitaker,C.A., Darley,C.F., Kopell,B.S., and Hollister,L.W. "The effect of marihuana on tracking task performance." Psychopharmacol. 1973, 33, 259-265.

6187. Rothlin,E. The Central Nervous Effects of Drugs.(Ger.). Thieme, Stuttgart, 1954.

6188. Rothschild,B. "Marihuana(cannabis)."(Ger.). Schweiz. Med. Woch. 1969, 99, 1003-1004.

6189. Rothschild,M. "Storage of cannabinoids by Arctia caja and zonocerus elegans fed on chemically distinct strains of cannabis sativa." Nature 1977, 266, 650-651.

6190. Roubinovitch,J. Hashish; Mental Pathology. (Fr.). Gilbert Ballet, Paris, 1903.

6191. Rouse,B.A. and Ewing,J.A. "Marihuana and other drug use by graduate and professional students." Am. J. Psyhciat. 1972, 129, 415-420.

6192. Rouse,B.A. and Ewing,J.A. "Marihuana and other drug use by women college students: Associated risk taking and coping activities." Am. J. Psychiat. 1973, 130, 486-490.

6193. Rouse,B.A. and Ewing,J.A. "Student drug use, risk-taking and alienation." J. Am. Coll. Hlth. Assoc. 1974, 22, 226-230.

6194. Rousinov,K.S. and Anthanasova-Shopova,S. "Experimental testing of anticonvulsive effects of certain plants used in popular medicine in Bulgaria." (Bulg.). Doklady. Bolg. Akad. Nauk. 1966, 19, 334-336.

6195. Roux,F. "Study on cannabis."(Fr.). Bull. Gen. Ther. Med. Chirurg. 1886, 111, 492-514.

6196. Rouyer,P.C. Description of Egypt.(Fr.). Paris, 1809.

6197. Rouyer,P.C. "On the typical medicines of the Egyptians."(Fr.). Bull. Pharm. 1810, 2, 385-415.

6198. Rowan,M.G. and Fairbairn,J.W. "Cannabinoid patterns in seedlings of cannabis sativa L. and their use in the determination of chemical race." J. Pharm. Pharmacol. 1977, 29, 491-494.

6199. Rowell,E.A. The Adventures of David Dare. Nashville, 1937.

6200. Rowell,E.A. and Rowell,R. On The Trail Of Marihuana, The Weed Of Madness. Pacific Press, Mountain View, Cal., 1939.

6201. Rowles,A. "Marihuana and the narcotic control act." Univ. Brit. Columbia Law Rev. 1967, 3, 250.

6202. Rowley,G.L., Armstrong,T.A., Crowl,C.P., Eimstad,W.H., Kam,J.K., Rodgers,R., Ronald,R.C., Rubenstein,K.E., Sheldon,B.G., and Ullman,E.F. "Determination of THC and its metabolites by EMIT homogenous enzyme immunoassay: A summary report." In Willette,P.(ed.). Cannabinoid Assays in Humans. N.I.D.A. Res. Monog. 7, Gov't. Print. Office, Washington, D.C., 1976, 28-32.

6203. Roy,J.C. "The soma plant." Ind. Hist. Quart. 1939, 15, 197-207.

6204. Roy,P.E., Magnan-Lapointe,F., Huy,N.D., and Boutet,M. "Chronic inhalation of marihuana and tobacco in dogs: pulmonary pathology." Res. Commun. Chem. Pathol. Pharmacol. 1976, 14, 305-317.

6205. Royfe,E.H. "An exploratory examination of the social and psychological characteristics of 100 Pennsylvania drug addicts." Pa. Psychiat. Quart. 1965, 5, 38-47.

6206. Royle,J.F. Fibrous Plants of India. Smith, Elder, and Co., London, 1855.

6207. Rozett,O. "Marihuana and alcohol: Harmful effects." Am. J. Psychiat. 1971, 128, 240-242.

6208. Rubin,P.E. and Cluff,L.E. "Differential diagnosis of emergency drug reactions." In Bourne,P.G. (ed.). Acute Drug Abuse Emergencies. Academic Press, N.Y., 1976, 15-20.

6209. Rubin,R.T. "Clinical aspects of marihuana and amphetamine use." Ann. Int. Med. 1969, 70, 596-598.

6210. Rubin,V. "Cross-cultural perspectives on therapeutic uses of cannabis." In Cohen,S. and Stillman, R.(eds.). Therapeutic Potential of Marihuana. Plenum Press, N.Y., 1976, 1-18.

6211. Rubin,V. "The 'ganja vision' in Jamaica." In Rubin,V.(ed.). Cannabis and Culture. Mouton, The Hague, 1975, 257-269.

6212. Rubin,V. "Variations and patterns in the cultural response to cannabis use." Ment. Hlth. Res. News. 1971, 131, 5-11.

6213. Rubin,V. and Comitas,L. "Effect of chronic smoking of cannabis in Jamaica." Report submitted to Center for Studies of Narcotic and Drug Abuse, N.I.M.H., Rockville, Md., 1972.

6214. Rubin,V. and Comitas,L. Ganja in Jamaica, A Medical Anthropological Study of Chronic Marihuana Use. Mouton, The Hague, 1975.

6215. Rubin,V. and Comitas, L. Ganja in Jamaica: The Effects of Marihuana. Anchor, N.Y., 1976.

6216. Rubins,J.L. "The role of the psychoanalyst in the marihuana problem." Am. J. Psychoanal. 1973, 33, 193-205.

6217. Rublowsky,J. The Stoned Age: A History of Drugs in America. Putnam's Sons, N.Y., 1973.

6218. Rudenko,F.E. "The conversion of male hemp plants into females."(Rus.). Dokl. Soob. Uzhgor. Gosud. 1962, 5, 20-22.

6219. Ruelle,F. "Accidental intoxication resulting from fatty extract of Indian hemp."(Fr.). Cent. Med. Pharmaceut. 1897, 1, 154-155.

6220. Ruhl,D. "Suicide while intoxicated with hashish."(Ger.). Kriminalistik 1971, 25, 406-407.

6221. Ruiz Ogara,C. "Experimental psychoses. A comparative study of LSD, mescaline and cannabis indica, with remarks on the psychiatric problems of each."(Sp). Med. Clin. 1961, 36, 278-290.

6222. Runge,M., Arnold,W., and Schreiber,D. "Actual forms of drug addiction with particular attention to hashish and LSD."(Ger.). Med. Welt. 1971, 35, 1301-1308.

6223. Runk,B. and Zinn,U. "Hashish--constituents, synthesis, effects."(Ger.). Med. Monat. 1965, 19, 165-168.

6224. Rushin,W.B. "Two cases of acute poisoning from solid extract of cannabis indica." South. Med. Rec. 1890, 20, 363-364.

6225. Russell,G.K. Marihuana Today. Myrin Inst. for Adult Education, N.Y., 1975.

6226. Russell,J. Survey of Drug Use in Selected British Columbia Schools. Narcotic Addiction Found. of B.C., Vancouver, 1970.

6227. Russell,P.B., Todd,A.R., Wilkinson,S., Macdonald,A.D., and Woolfe,G. "Cannabis indica. Pt. VII. The relation between chemical constitution and hashish activity." J. Chem. Soc. 1941, 1, 169-172.

6228. Russell,P.B., Todd,A.R., Wilkinson,S., Macdonald,A.D., and Woolfe,G. "Cannabis indica. Pt. VIII. Further analogues of tetrahydrocannabinol." J. Chem. Soc. 1941, 1, 826-829.

6229. Russell,R.P. "Alcohol and other mood-modifying substances in ecological perspective: a framework for communicating and educating." Quart. J. Stud. Alcohol 1974, 35, 606-619.

6230. Russell,W.R. "Cerebral atrophy in young cannabis smokers." Lancet 1971, 2, 1314.

6231. Russell Pasha,T.W. "Drug addiction in Egypt." Br. J. Ineb. 1931, 29, 60-65.

6232. Ryan,G.W. "Marihuana in Indiana." Indiana State Brd. Hlth. Bull. 1939, 42, 222, 227-228.

6233. Rybicka,H. and Engelbrecht,L. "Zeatin in cannabis fruit." Phytochem. 1974, 13, 282-283.

6234. Ryland,K. "Experiments with hemp." Iowa Med. J. 1854, 2, 103-107.

6235. Ryrfeldt,A., Ramsay,C.H., Agurell,S., Nilsson,I.M., and Widman,M. "Whole-body autoradiographic studies on the distribution of delta-1(6)-tetrahydrocannabinol(THC) in mice after intravenous administration." Act. Pharmaceut. Suec. 1971, 8, 704-705.

6236. Ryrfeldt,A., Ramsay,C.H., Nilsson,I.M., Widman,M., and Agurell,S. "Whole-body autoradiography of delta-1-tetrahydrocannabinol and delta-1(6)-tetrahydrocannabinol in mouse." Act. Pharmaceut. Suec. 1973, 10, 13-28.

S

6237. Sabalitschka,T. "On cannabis indica, particularly the cultivation of high-grade cannabis indica fiber grown in Germany."(Ger.). Heil. Gewurz. 1925, 8, 73-81.

6238. Sabalitschka,T. "Is cultivation of Indian hemp in Germany feasible?"(Ger.). Klin. Woch. 1926, 5, 1279-1280.

6239. Sabalitschka,T. "On cannabis indica, especially concerning its cultivation in Germany."(Ger.). Arbeit. Pharmazeut. Inst. Univ. Berlin 1927, 13, 157-159.

6240. Sabelli,H.C., Mosnaim,A.D., Vazquez,A.J., and Pedemonte,L.M. "(-)-trans-delta-9-tetrahydrocannabinol-induced increase in brain 2-phenylethylamine: Its possible role in the behavioral effects of marihuana." In Singh,J.M. and Lal,H.(eds.). Drug Addiction. Stratton Intercontinental Med. Book Corp., N.Y., 1974, 271-283.

6241. Sabelli,H.C., Pedemonte,W.A., Whalley,C., Mosnaim,A.D., and Vazquez,A.J. "Further evidence for a role of 2-phenylethylamine in the mode of action of delta-9-tetrahydrocannabinol." Life Sci. 1974, 14, 149-156.

6242. Sabelli,H.C., Vazquez,A.J., Mosnaim,A.D., and Pedemonte,L.M. "2-phenylethylamine as a possible mediator for delta-9-tetrahydrocannabinol-induced stimulation." Nature 1974, 248, 144-145.

6243. Sachs-Benedict,B. "North to Alaska." High Times 1974, 5, 29-30, 63, 66.

6244. Sadava,S.W. "A field-theoretical study of college student drug use." Can. J. Behav. Sci. 1971, 3, 337-346.

6245. Sadava,S.W. "Becoming a marihuana user: a longitudinal social learning study." Paper presented to Can. Psychol. Assoc., Montreal, 1972.

6246. Sadava,S.W. "Initiation to cannabis use: A longitudinal social psychological study of college freshmen." Can. J. Behav. 1973, 5, 371-384.

6247. Sadava,S.W. "Patterns of college students drug use: A longitudinal social learning study." Psychol. Rep. 1973, 33, 75-86.

6248. Sadava,S.W. "Research approaches in illicit drug use: A critical review." Genet. Psychol. Monog. 1975, 91, 3-59.

6249. Sadava,S.W. "Stages of college student drug use: A methodological contribution to cross-sectional study." J. Consult. Clin. Psychol. 1972, 38, 298.

6250. Sadava,S.W. and Forsyth,R. "Decisions about drug use: an application of the choice shifts paradigm." Psychol. Rep. 1976, 38, 1119-1133.

6251. Sadava,S.W. and Forsyth,R. "Turning on, turning off and relapse: Social psychological determinants of status change in cannabis use." Internat'l. J. Addict. 1977, 12, 509-528.

6252. Safi,E. "Contribution to the study of Indian hemp in Lebanon."(Fr.). Ann. Fac. Med. Pharm. Beyrouth 1935, 4, 204-247.

6253. Sagoe,T.E.C. "Narcotic control in Ghana." Bull. Narc. 1966, 18, 5-13.

6254. Saha,R. Narcotic Drugs.(Turk.). Univ. Istanbul, Istanbul, 1948.

6255. Sainte-Lager,J.B. "Historical remarks on the words, 'male plants' and female plants'."(Fr.). Ann. Soc. Bot. Lyon 1884, 11, 1-48.

6256. Sainte-Marie,C. "Notes on some experiences with hashish."(Fr.). J. Med. Bordeaux 1850, 8, 565-571.

6257. Saito,M. "Possibility of simplifying the phytochrome test method by using young shoots of hemp." Res. Rep. Fac. Text. Sericult. Shinshu Univ. 1953, 3, 27-29.

6258. Salaschek,M., Matte,A., and Seifert,A. "Investigation of the problems of detection of hashish components in urine by thin-layer chromatography."(Ger.). J. Chromatog. 1973, 78, 393-400.

259. SalazarViniegra,L. "Present status of marihuana research."(Sp.). Gac. Med. Mex. 1940, 70, 383-396.

6260. SalazarViniegra,L. The Myth of Marihuana.(Sp.). Acad. Nacional Med., Mexico, 1938.

6261. SalazarViniegra,L. "Drug addiction."(Sp.). Gac. Med. Mex. 1945, 75, 65-70.

6262. Salemink,C.A. "Pyrolysis of cannabinoids." In Nahas,G.G., Paton,W.D.M., and Idanpaan-Heikkila,J.E. (eds.). Marihuana. Springer Verlag, N.Y., 1976, 31-39.

6263. Salemink,C.A., Veen,E., and de Kloet,W.A. "On the basic constituents in cannabis sativa."(Ger.). Plant. Med. 1965, 13, 211-217.

6264. Sallan,S.E., Zinberg,N.E., and Frei,E. "Antiemetic effect of delta-9-tetrahydrocannabinol in patients receiving cancer chemotherapy." N. Eng. J. Med. 1975, 293, 795-797.

6265. Sallan,S.E., Zinberg,N.E., and Frei,E. "Antiemetic effect of delta-9-tetrahydrocannabinol in patients receiving cancer chemotherapy." In Cohen,S. and Stillman,R.(eds.). Therapeutic Potential of Marihuana. Plenum Press, N.Y., 1976, 329-336.

6266. Salmon,R. "An analysis of public marihuana policy." Soc. Casework 1972, 53, 19-29.

6267. Salmon,T. A Pilot Study Among East Village 'Hippies'. Associated Y.M.-Y.W.H.A.s of Greater New York, N.Y., 1968.

6268. Saltman,J. Marihuana and Your Child. Grosset and Dunlap, N.Y., 1970.

6269. Saltman,J. What About Marihuana? Univ. Texas, Austin, 1969.

6270. Salustiano,J., Hoshino,K., and Carlini,E.A. "Effects of cannabis sativa and chlorpromazine on mice as measured by two methods used for evaluation of tranquilizing agents." Med. Pharmacol. Exp. 1966, 15, 153-162.

6271. Salvendy,G. and McCabe,G.P. "Marihuana and human performance." Human Fact. 1975, 17, 229-235.

6272. Salzman,C., Kochansky,G.E., and Porrino,L.J. "Group behavior: Hostility and aggression." In Mendelson, J.H., Rossi,A.M., and Meyer,R.E.(eds.). The Use of Marihuana. Plenum Press, N.Y., 1974, 73-79.

6273. Salzman,C., Kochansky,G.E., and Porrino,L.J. "The effect of marihuana on hostility in an experimental group setting: Preliminary observations." Psychopharmacol. Bull. 1973, 9, 54-55.

6274. Salzman,C., van der Kolk,B.A., and Shader,R.I. "Marihuana and hostility in a small group setting." Am. J. Psychiat. 1976, 133, 1029-1033.

6275. Salzman,C., van der Kolk,B.A., and Shader,R.I. "Marihuana and hostility in a small group setting." Paper presented at Am. Psychiat. Assoc., Chicago, 1975.

6276. Sampaio,C.A., Lapa,A.J., and Valle,J.R. "Influence of cannabis, tetrahydrocannabinol and pyrahexyl on the linguomandibular reflex of the dog." J. Pharm. Pharmacol. 1967, 19, 552-554.

6277. Samrah,H. "A preliminary investigation of the possible presence of alkaloidal substances in cannabis." U.N. Doc. ST/SOA/SER.S/27, Dec. 11, 1970.

6278. Samrah,H. "A preliminary study of the occurrence of cannabis component in the various parts of the plant." U.N. Doc. ST/SOA/SER.S/26, Dec. 1, 1970.

6279. Samrah,H., Lousberg,R.J., Bercht,C.A.L., Salemink,C.A., Ham,M.T., and van Noordwijk,J. "On the presence of basic indole components in cannabis sativa L." U.N. Doc. ST/SOA/SER.S/34, May 5, 1972.

6280. Samuelson,L.H. Some Zulu Customs. Churchill Print. Co., London, n.d.

6281. Sanchez,E., Tampier,L., Nunez,L., and Mardones, J. "Chilean marihuana. Chemical analysis and pharmacological aspects."(Sp.). Rev. Med. Chile 1972, 100, 236-243.

6282. Sanders,C.R. "Caught in the con-game: The young, white drug-users contact with the legal system." Law. Soc. Rev. 1975, 9, 197-217.

6283. Sanders,C. "Remarks on the contributions of R. Meyer and P. Bech." In van Praag,H.M.(ed.). Biochemical and Pharmacological Aspects of Dependence and Reports on Marihuana Research. De Erven F. Bohn, Haarlem, Netherlands, 1972, 211.

6284. Sandison,R.A. "Hallucinogens." Practitioner 1964, 192, 30-36.

6285. Sanford,D. "Grass and the brass." New Repub. 1970, 162, 11-12.

6286. Sanford,D. "Pot bust at Cornell." New Repub. 1967, 156, 17-20.

6287. Sanford,D. "Risks of marihuana." New Repub. 1967, 156, 11-12.

6288. San Mateo Department of Public Health and Welfare. Five Mind Altering Drugs. San Mateo, Cal., 1969.

6289. Santavi,F. "Notes on the structure of cannabidiol compounds." Act. Univ. Palack. Olomuc. Fac. Med. 1964, 35, 5-8.

6290. Santos,M., Sampaio,M.R.P., Fernandes,N.S., and Carlini,E.A. "Effect of cannabis sativa(marihuana) on the fighting behavior of mice." Psychopharmacol. 1966, 8, 437-444.

6291. Sapol,E. and Roffman,R.A. "Marihuana in Vietnam." J.A.P.A. 1969, NS9, 615-618, 630.

6292. Sargent,M. "A cross-cultural study of attitudes and behavior towards alcohol and drugs." Br. J. Sociol. 1971, 22, 83-96.

6293. Sarguine,K.D.. and Vassilyeva,V.V. "Biological study of cannabis preparations." Pharmacol. Toxicol. 1939, 2, 63-66.

6294. Sarkar,C. and Ghosh,J.J. "Effect of delta-9-tetrahydrocannabinol on gangliosides and sialoglycoproteins in subcellular fractions of rat brain." J. Neurochem. 1976, 26, 721-733.

6295. Sasman,M. "Cannabis indica in pharmaceuticals." J. Med. Soc. New Jersey 1938, 34, 51-52.

6296. Sassenrath,E.N. and Chapman,L.F. "Primate social behavior as a method of analysis of drug action: Studies with THC in monkeys." Fed. Proc. 1976, 35, 2238-2244.

6297. Sassenrath,E.N. and Chapman,L.F. "Tetrahydrocannabinol-induced manifestations of the 'marihuana syndrome' in group-living macaques." Fed. Proc. 1975, 34, 1666-1670.

6298. Sassenrath,E.N., Cowen,J.D., and Goo,G.P. "Effects of delta-9-tetrahydrocannabinol(THC) on social behavior of group caged macaques." Paper presnted and Soc. for Neuroscience, San Diego, 1973.

6299. Sattes,H. "How dangerous is hashish?"(Ger.). Schwest. Rev. 1970, 8, 15-16.

6300. Sattin,A. "Persistence of biochemical effect." Am. J. Psychiat. 1969, 125, 1129-1130.

6301. Satz,P., Fletcher,J.M., and Stucker,L.S. "Neuropsychologic, intellectural, and personality correlates of chronic marihuana use in native Costa Ricans." Ann. N. Y. Acad. Sci. 1976, 282, 266-306.

6302. Sauer,L.W. "Your adolescent's health: Drug abuse among teenagers." P.T.A. Mag. 1969, 63, 25-26.

6303. Saulle,R.D. "Psychopharmacology of the cannabinoids." Psychosomatics 1973, 14, 352-354.

6304. Saulnier,V.L. "The enigma of Pantagruelion." (Fr.). Etud. Rabelais. 1956, 1, 48-72.

6305. Savage,J. "The marihuana bugs." High Times 1976, 9, 64-65.

6306. Savary,P., Laurenceau,J.L., de Lean,A., Roy,P., and Marquis,Y. "Acute cardiovascular effects of inhaled cannabis sativa smoke in man." Internat'l. J. Clin. Pharmacol. 1974, 10, 136-158.

6307. Savelli,R. "Poliembrionia in cannabis sativa L." Arch. Bot. 1928, 4, 128-137.

6308. Savignac,D. "Obstetrical medicines."(Fr.). Bull. Gen. Ther. Med. Chirurg. 1871, 81, 293-294.

6309. Savory,M. "Extractum cannabis indicae." Pharmaceut. J. Trans. 1843, 3, 80.

6310. Sawtelle,H.W. "Notes relating to the effects of cannabis indica with an illustrative case." New Orleans Med. Surg. J. 1896, 49, 670-675.

6311. Sayre,L.E. "The cultivation of medicinal plants with observation concerning cannabis." J.A.P.A. 1915, 4, 1303-1307.

6312. Sayer,J.W. and Rotenberg,D.L. "Marihuana in the Houston high schools--a first report." Houston Law Rev. 1969, 6, 759.

6313. Sayer,J.W. and Rotenberg,D.L. "Marihuana in Houston: a second report and a proposal." Houston Law Rev. 1970, 8, 209.

6314. Scaringelli,F. "Spectrophotometric identification of marihuana." J. Assoc. Off. Agricult. Chem. 1961, 44, 296-303.

6315. Schacter,S. "Cognition and response to marihuana." In Berkowitz,L.(ed.). Advances in Experimental Psychology. Academic Press, N.Y., 1964, 1, 76-79.

6316. Schaefer,C.F., Gunn,C.G., and Dubowski,K.M. "Dose-related heart-rate, perceptual, and decisional changes in man following marihuana smoking." Percept. Motor Skills 1977, 44, 3-16.

6317. Schaefer,C.F., Gunn,C.G., and Dubowski,K.M. "Marihuana dosage control through heart rate." N. Eng. J. Med. 1975, 393, 101.

6318. Schaefer,C.F., Gunn,C.G., and Dubowski,K.M. "Normal plasma testosterone concentrations after marihuana smoking." N. Eng. J. Med. 1975, 292, 867-868.

6319. Schaefer,G. "Hard, sticky yarns are of no use to the knitting trade." Ciba Rev. 1945, 49, 93.

6320. Schaefer,J. "The significance of marihuana in a small agricultural community in Jamaica." In Rubin,V.(ed.). Cannabis and Culture. Mouton, The Hague, 1975, 355-389.

6321. Schaefer,J.F., Loetzer,R., and Sofia,R.D." "Effect of delta-1-tetrahydrocannabinol and propranolol on oubain induced arrythmias." Arch. Internat'l. Pharmacodyn. Ther. 1973, 205, 5-10.

6322. Schafer,E.H. The Golden Peaches of Samarkand. Univ. of Cal. Press, Berkeley, Cal., 1963.

6323. Schafer,R.J. The Economic Societies in the Spanish World (1763-1821). Syracuse Univ. Press, Syracuse, 1958.

6324. Schaffer,H. "Contemporary drug addiction." J. Indiv. Psychol. 1970, 26, 224.

6325. Schaffer,H. and Merdinger,R.P. "Cannabis toxicomania." Trans. Illinois State Acad. Sci. 1970, 63, 386-391.

6326. Schaffner,J.H. "Further experiments in repeated rejuvenations in hemp and their bearing on the general problem of sex." Am. J. Bot. 1928, 15, 77-85.

6327. Schaffner,J.H. "Influence of environment on sexual expression in hemp." Bot. Gaz. 1921, 71, 197-219.

6328. Schaffner,J.H. "The fluctuation curve of sex reversal in staminate hemp plants induced by photoperiodicity." Am. J. Bot. 1931, 18, 424-430.

6329. Schaffner,J.H. "The influence of relative length of daylight on the reversal of sex in hemp." Ecology 1923, 4, 323-334.

6330. Schaflander,G.M. "Passion, pot and politics." In Lipset,S.M. and Schaflander,G.M.(eds.). Passion and Politics: Student Activism in America. Little Brown, Boston, 1971, 265-286.

6331. Schainfeldt,L.F. and Strimbou,J.L. "College student drug usage in a state system as a function of type of institution." Res. High. Educat. 1975, 3, 275-284.

6332. Schaller,M. "The federal prohibition of marihuana." J. Soc. Hist. 1970, 1, 61-73.

6333. Schaps,E. and Sanders,C.R. "Purposes, patterns and protection in a campus drug using community." J. Hlth. Soc. Behav. 1970, 11, 135-145.

6334. Scharer,K. "Diuretic effect of cannabis sativa." (Ger.). Pharmakol. Inst. Univ. Bern 1944, 1, 27.

6335. Scheckel,C.L., Boff,E., Dahlen,P., and Smart,T. "Behavioral effects in monkeys of racemates of two biologically active marihuana constituents." Science 1968, 160, 1467-1469.

6336. Schenk,J. "The neurotic personality of hashish users."(Ger.). Zeit. Klin. Psychol. Psychother. 1974, 22, 340-351.

6337. Schenk,J. "Structure of drug use and drug definition among youth. Internat'l. J. Addict. 1977, 12, 459-469.

6338. Scher,J. "Marihuana as an agent in rehabilitating alcoholics." Am. J. Psychiat. 1971, 127, 971-972.

6339. Scher,J. "Patterns and profiles of addiction and drug abuse." Internat'l. J. Addict. 1967, 2, 171-190.

6340. Scher,J. "The marihuana habit." J.A.M.A. 1970, 214, 1120.

6341. Scherer,S.E. "Hard and soft hallucinogenic drug users: their drug taking patterns and objectives." Internat'l. J. Addict. 1973, 8, 755-766.

6342. Scherer,S.E., Ettinger,R.F., and Mandrick,N.J. "Need for social approval and drug use." J. Consult. Clin. Psychol. 1972, 38, 118-121.

6343. Scherrmann,J.M., Howllinger,H., Hoang-Nam,N., Bourdon,R., and Fournier,E. "Methodology for the detection and quantitation of delta-9-tetrahydrocannabinol in plasma by dansylation and double labelling." Clin. Chim. Act. 1977, 79, 401-409.

6344. Schicks,G.C. "Marihuana: Depraver of youth." *Drug*. *Circ*. 1938, *82*, 12.

6345. Schiel,V. and Kesier,G. "Short notes (LXI, hemp oil, hashish)."(Fr.). *Rev*. *Assyriol*. *Orient*. 1921, *18*, 97.

6346. Schieser,D.W. and Cohen,S. "Drugs and their effects." *Cal*. *Hlth*. 1968, *25*, 2-6, 21.

6347. Shildkraut,J.J. and Efron,D.H. "The effects of delta-9-tetrahydrocannabinol on the metabolism of norepinephrine in rat brain." *Psychopharmacol*. 1971, *20*, 191-196.

6348. Schilling,E. "Morphology, physiology and diagnostic evaluation of cannabis sativa stem fibers." (Ger.). *Bericht* *Deut*. *Bot*. *Gesell*. 1923, *41*, 121.

6349. Schlegal,R.P. "Multidimensional measurement of attitude towards smoking marihuana." *Can*. *J*. *Behav*. *Sci*. 1975, *7*, 387-396.

6350. Schlegal,R.P. "Multidimensional measurement and structure of attitudes toward smoking marihuana with prediction of marihuana use." *Diss*. *Abs*. 1973, *34*, 2769-2770.

6351. Schlesinger,L. "Effect of Indian hemp on labor."(Fr.). *Sem*. *Hop*. *Paris* 1848, *24*, 2929-2931.

6352. Schlesinger,S. "Research on cannabis sativa."(Ger.) *Rep*. *Pharm*. 1840, *71*, 190-208.

6353. Schmalzbach,O.R. "Sociological and rehabilitative aspects of drug dependence. Drug hysteria." *Aust*. *J*. *Forens*. *Sci*. 1970, *3*, 53-56.

6354. Schmeling,W.T. and Hosko,M.J. "Blockade of delta-9-THC induced hypothermia in rats." *Arch*. *Internat'l*. *Pharmacodyn*. *Ther*. 1977, *227*, 302-308.

6355. Schmeling,W.T. and Hosko,M.J. "Hypothermia induced by delta-9-tetrahydrocannabinol in rats with electrolytic lesions of preoptic region." *Pharmacol*. *Biochem*. *Behav*. 1976, *5*, 79-83.

6356. Schmevelyn,E. *Cooking with Marihuana*. And/Or Press, Berkeley, Cal., 1974.

6357. Schmidt,L. "Magical gifts: Stimulants and hallucinogenic drugs."(Ger.). *Arch*. *Pharm*. 1964, *293*, 181-182.

6358. Schmidt,W.K., Burchiel,S.W., and Myers,F.H. "The pharmacology of drug abuse--A novel approach to drug education at San Quentin." Drug Alcohol Depend. 1977, 2, 175-183.

6359. Schmirz-Scherzer,R. "An analysis of lives of drug consumers."(Ger.). Arch. Psychol. 1971, 123, 244-250.

6360. Schmitt,R.L. and Grupp,S.E. "Marihuana as a social object." In Grupp,S.E.(ed.). The Marihuana Muddle, Lexington Books, Lexington, Mass., 1973, 11-31.

6361. Schneider,A. Microanalysis of Powdered Vegetal Drugs. P. Blakiston's Sons, Phil., 1921.

6362. Schneider,A. "The effects of large doses of cannabis indica." J.A.P.A. 1923, 12, 208-214.

6363. Schnoll,S.H. and Vogel,W.H. "Analysis of 'street drugs'." N. Eng. J. Med. 1971, 284, 791.

6364. Schoeneman,A.L. "Some effects of marihuana on the functional integerity of the central nervous system." Diss. Abs. 1974, 34, 4675.

6365. Schofield,M. The Strange Case of Pot. Penguin, London, 1971.

6366. Scholtens,J. "Reports on the use of 'ganja' (Indian hemp) in Surinam and on the insanity (cannabism) resulting from it."(Dut.). Psychiat. Neurol. Blad. Ned. 1905, 9, 244-253.

6367. Schonhofer,P. "New methods in the case of drug endangered youth in the U.S.A. and the German Federal Republic."(Ger.). Nachrichtendienst 1971, 51, 294-298.

6368. Schonhofer,P.S. "Pharmacology of the active principle of cannabis."(Ger.). Arzneim-Forsch. 1973, 23, 50-56.

6369. Schoolar,J.C., Ho,B.T., and Estevez,V.S. "Comparison of various solvent extractions for the chromatographic analysis of delta-9-tetrahydrocannabinol and its metabolites." In Nahas,G.G., Paton,W.D.M., and Idanpaan-Heikkila,J.E.(eds.). Marihuana. Springer Verlag, N.Y., 1976, 63-71.

6370. Schou,J. and Nielsen,E. "Cannabinols in various United Nations samples and in cannabis sativa grown in Denmark under varying conditions. Experiments with Korte and Sieper's thin-layer chromatography." U.N. Doc. ST/SOA/SER.S/22, Oct. 19, 1970.

6371. Schou,J., Prockop,L.D., Dahlstrom,G., and Rohde,C. "Penetration of delta-9-tetrahydrocannabinol and 11-OH-delta-9-tetrahydrocannabinol through the blood-brain barrier." Act. Pharmacol. Toxicol. 1977, 41, 33-38.

6372. Schou,J., Steentoft,A., Work,K., Morkholdt,J.M., and Nielsen,E. "Highly sensitive method for gas chromatographic measurement of tetrahydrocannabinol(THC) and cannabinol(CBN). Act. Pharmacol. Toxicol. 1971, 30, 480-482.

6373. Schou,J., Worm,K., Morkoldt,A.J., Nielsen,E., and Steentoft,A. "Studies on the metabolism and disposition of delta-9-tetrahydrocannabinol(Delta-9-THC) in Danish pigs before and after prolonged intravenous administration of delta-9-THC." Proc. 5th Internat'l. Cong. Pharmacol. 1972, 1, 205.

6374. Schrenck-Notzing,F. "Importance of narcotics in hypnotism with special emphasis on Indian hemp."(Ger.). Schrift. Gesel. Psychol. Forsch. 1891, 1, 1-73.

6375. Schroeder,R.C. "Marihuana and the law." Ed. Res. Rep. 1975, 1, 123-140.

6376. Schroth,R.A. "Marihuana and its effects." Cath. Sch. J. 1969, 69, 44-47.

6377. Schuckit,M.A. "Drug use and psychiatric problems on campus. I. Methods and drug use at outset." In Ricks,D.F., Thomas,A., and Roff,M.(eds.). Life History Research in Psychopathology. Univ. Minn. Press, Minneapolis, 1974, 163-176.

6378. Schuch,J.H. and Francis,R.L. "A comparison of student and parental attitudes." J. Coll. Stud. Person. 1976, 17, 376-379.

6379. Schultz,J.D. "The campus is restless." In Kroespsch,R.H. and Buck, D.P.(eds.). Covering the Restless Campus. Estern Interstate Commission for Higher Education, Boulder, 1970, 48-52.

6380. Schultz,J.P. "The campus is restless: The use and abuse of drugs." Paper presented at Western Interstate Commission for Higher Education Legislative Workshop on Higher Education, Phoenix, 1969.

6381. Schultes,R.E. "Hallucinogens of plant origin." Science 1969, 163, 245-254.

6382. Schultes,R.E. "Man and marihuana." Nat. Hist. 1973, 82, 59-65.

6383. Schultes,R.E. "Random thoughts and queries on the botany of cannabis." In Joyce, C.R.B. and Curry, S.H.(eds.). The Botany and Chemistry of Cannabis. J. and A. Churchill, London, 1970, 11-39.

6384. Schultes,R.E. "The botanical and chemical distribution of hallucinogens." Ann. Rev. Plant Physiol. 1970, 21, 571-598.

6385. Schultes,R.E. "The plant kingdom and hallucinogens. Part II." Bull. Narc. 1969, 21, 15-27.

6386. Schultes,R.E., Klein,W.M., Plowman,T., and Lockwood,T.E. "Cannabis: An example of taxonomic neglect." Bot. Mus. Leaf. 1974, 23, 337-367.

6387. Schultes,R.E., Klein,W.M., Plowman,T., and Lockwood,T.E. "Cannabis: An example of taxonomic neglect." In Rubin,V.(ed.). Cannabis and Culture. Mouton, The Hague, 1975, 21-39.

6388. Schultz,O.E. "Current status of cannabis research."(Ger.). Plant. Med. 1964, 12, 371-383.

6389. Schultz,O.E. and Haffner,G. "A sedative and antibacterial principle from common German hemp(cannabis sativa)."(Ger.). Zeit. Naturforsch. 1959, 14b, 98-100.

6390. Schultz,O.E. and Haffner,G. "On the question of the biosynthesis of cannabinol. Part III."(Ger.). Arch. Pharmakol. 1960, 293, 1-8.

6391. Schultz,O.E. and Haffner,G. "Study of a sedative active principle for common German hemp(cannabis sativa.)."(Ger.). Arch. Pharmakol. 1958, 291, 391-403.

6392. Schultz,O.E. and Mohrmann,H.L. "Contribution to the paper chromatography of the constituents of German fibrous hemp--cannabis sativa L."(Ger.). Arch. Pharmakol. 1962, 295, 66-67.

6393. Schulz,D.A. and Wilson,R.A. "Some traditional family variables and their correlates with drug use among high school students." J. Marriage Fam. 1973, 4, 628-631.

6394. Schuman,S.H. and Polkowski,J. "Drug and risk perceptions of ninth-grade students: Sex differences and similarities." Comm. Ment. Hlth. J. 1975, 11, 184-194.

6395. Schurr,A. and Livne,A. "Differential inhibition of mitochrondrial monoamine oxidase from brain by hashish components." Biochem. Pharmacol. 1976, 25, 1201-1203.

6396. Schurr,A., Sheffer,N., Graziani,Y., and Livne,A. "Inhibition of glucose efflux from human erythrocytes by hashish components." Biochem. Pharmacol. 1974, 23, 2005-2009.

6397. Schuschny,H. "Instability of cannabis preparations."(Ger.). Ther. Monat. 1887, 1, 204-205.

6398. Schuster,E. "Hallucinogens and psychotropic drugs, their dangers and distribution."(Ger.). Oeffent. Gesundheit. 1970, 32, 330-338.

6399. Schwartz,E.S. "Changes in attitude toward legalization of marihuana as a function of fear arousal, felt competence and source credibility." Diss. Abs. 1973, 33, 5501-5502.

6400. Schwartz,E.S., Feinglass,S.J., and Drucker,C. "Popular music and drug lyrics: Analysis of a scapegoat." In National Commission on Marihuana and Drug Abuse. Drug Use in America. Problem in Perspective. Gov't. Print. Office, Washington, D.C., 1973, II, 718-746.

6401. Schwartz,G., Turner,P., and Peluso,E. "Neither heads nor freaks: Working class drug subculture." Urban Life Cult. 1973, 2, 288-313.

6402. Schwartfarb,L., Needle,M., and Chavez-Chase,M. "Dose-related inhibition of leukocyte migration by marihuana and delta-9-tetrahydrocannabinol(THC) in vitro." J. Clin. Pharmacol. 1974, 14, 35-41.

6403. Schwarz,C.J. "Effects of marihuana use." Science 1973, 180, 1121.

6404. Schwarz,C.J. "LSD, marihuana and the law." Br. Columbia Med. J. 1967, 9, 274.

6405. Schwarz,C.J. "Marihuana: an attempt at perspective." In Blachly,P.H.(ed.). Drug Abuse. Data and Debate. C.C. Thomas, Springfield, Ill., 1970, 205-216.

6406. Schwarz,C.J. "The marihuana debate." Br. Columbia Med. J. 1969, 11, 273-276.

6407. Schwarz,C.J. "Toward a medical understanding of marihuana." Can. Psychiat. Assoc. J. 1969, 14, 591-600.

6408. Schweitzer,G. and Levin,A. "Cannabis-related acute brain syndrome following major trauma." S. Af. Med. J. 1976, 50, 639-640.

6409. Schwin,R., Goodwin,D.W., and Hill,S.Y. "Marihuana and tidal volume." J.A.M.A. 1973, 223, 269.

6410. Schwin,R., Hill,S.Y., Goodwin,D.W., and Powell,B. "Marihuana and critical flicker fusion." J. Nerv. Ment. Dis. 1974, 158, 142-144.

6411. Scigliano,J.A. and Waller,C.W. "The marihuana programme of the Center for Studies of Narcotic and Drug Abuse. N.I.M.H." In Joyce,C.R.B. and Curry,S.H.(eds.). The Botany and Chemistry of Cannabis. J. and A. Churchill, London, 1970, 193.

6412. Sciolino,E. "Picking off pot-pickers; Palaski county inc. patrols." Newsweek 1976, 88, 13.

6413. Scott,D.R. "Rash claims re marihuana." N. Eng. J. Med. 1973, 288, 585.

6414. Scott,N.R., Orzen,W., Musillo,C. and Cole,P.T. "Methadone in the southwest: A three-year follow-up of Chicano heroin addicts." Am. J. Orthopsychiat. 1973, 48, 355-361.

6415. Scouras,P. "Baudelaire drug addiction."(Fr.). Hyg. Ment. 1930, 25, 231-241.

6416. Scouras,P. "Catatonic syndrome of acute psychosis due to cannabis."(Fr.). Encephale 1939, 34, 78-85.

6417. Scouras,P. Medico-psychological Essay on Charles Baudelaire.(Fr.). Univ. of Lyon, Lyon, 1929.

6418. Seaberg,G.P. "The drug abuse problem and some proposals." J. Crim. Law. Criminol. Pol. Sci. 1967, 58, 349-377.

6419. Seal,E. "Keep off the grass?" Aust. N. Z. J. Psychiat. 1972, 6, 3-6.

6420. Seale,C.C., Joyner,J.F., and Pati,J.B. Agronomic Studies of Fiber Plants: Jute, Sisal, Henequen, Hemp and Other Miscellaneous Types. Univ. Florida Agricultural Station, Gainesville, 1952.

6421. Sebrell,W.H. "Chemistry in chronic disease research." Chem. Engin. News 1955, 33, 1856-1860.

6422. Sedir,R. Magical Plants.(Fr.). Chacornac, Paris, 1907.

6423. See,G. "Cannabis indica." Lancet 1890, 2, 261-262.

6424. See,G. "Cannabis indica in diseases of the stomach." Ther. Gaz. 1890, 14, 684-685.

6425. See,G. "The action of cannabis indica on dyspepsia." Lancet 1890, 2, 592.

6426. See,G. "Cannabis indica in gastic disorders." J.A.M.A. 1890, 15, 540.

6427. See,G. "Cannabis indica in gastric disorders." Lancet 1890, 2, 631-632.

6428. See,G. "The use of cannabis indica in treatment of neurosis and gastric dyspepsia."(Fr.). Deut. Med. Woch. 1890, 60, 679-682, 727-730, 748, 754, 771-774.

6429. See,G. "The use of cannabis indica in treatment of neurosis and gastric dyspepsia."(Fr.). Bull. Acad. Nat'l. Med. 1890, 24, 158-193.

6430. See,G. "Use of cannabis indica in treatment of neurosis and gastric dyspepsia."(Fr.). Med. Mod. 1890, 32, 609-618.

6431. Seed,A. Caretaking the Wild Sinsemilla. Adam Seed Pub., Healdsburg, Cal., 1977.

6432. Seeman,P., Chau-Wong,M., and Moyyen,S. "The membrane binding of morphine, diphenylhydantoin, and tetrahydrocannabinol." Can. J. Physiol. Pharmacol. 1972, 50, 1193-1200.

6433. Seevers,M.H. "Marihuana in perspective." Mich. Quart. Rev. 1966, 5, 247-251.

6434. Seevers,J.H. "Psychopharmacological elements of drug dependence." J.A.M.A. 1968, 206, 1263-1266.

6435. Segal,B. "Drug use and fantasy processes: Criterion for prediction of potential users." Internat'l. J. Addict. 1974, 9, 475-480.

6436. Segal,B. "Fantasy correlates of college drug users." Paper presented at Southwest. Psychol. Assoc., New Orleans, 1973.

6437. Segal,B. "Locus of control and drug and alcohol use in college students." J. Alcohol Drug Educat. 1974, 19, 1-5.

6438. Segal,B. "Personality factors related to drug and alcohol use." In Lettieri,D.J.(ed.). Predicting Adolescent Drug Abuse: A Review of Issues, Methods and Correlates. Gov't. Print. Office, Washington,D.C., 1975, 165-191.

6439. Segal,B. and Feger,G. "Drug use and fantasy processes in college students." J. Alt. States Conscious. 1973, 1, 5-14.

6440. Segal,M. "Central implantation of cannabinoids: Induction of epileptiform discharges." Eur. J. Pharmacol. 1974, 27, 40-45.

6441. SEgal,M. and Cochin,J. "Delta-9-tetrahydrocannabinol-imipramine interaction on mouse body temperature." Pharmacologist 1974, 16, 282.

6442. Segal,M. and Kenney,A.F. "Delta-1- and delta-1-6-tetrahydrocannabinol: Preliminary observations on similarities and differences in central pharmacological effects in the cat." Exper. 1972, 28, 816-819.

6443. Segal,M. and Kenney,A.F. "Preliminary observations on a cannabis constituent's effects on central nervous system excitability." Comm. Prob. Drug Depend. 1971, 2, 1671-1691.

6444. Segawa,T., Bando,S., and Hosokawa,M. "Brain serotonin metabolism and delta-9-tetrahydrocannabinol-induced muricide behavior in rats." Jap. J. Pharmacol. 1977, 27, 581-582.

6445. Segawa,T., Takeuchi,S., and Nakano,M. "Mechanisms for the increase of brain 5-hydroxytryptamine and 5-hydroxyindoleacetic acid following delta-9-tetrahydrocannabinol administration to rats." Jap. J. Pharmacol. 1976, 26, 430-431.

6446. Segelman,A.B. "Cannabis sativa L.(marihuana). III. The RIM test: A reliable and useful procedure for the detection and identification of marihuana utilizing combined microscopy and thin-layer chromatography." J. Chromatog. 1973, 82, 151-157.

6447. Segelman,A.B., Babcock,P.A., Braun,B.L., and Segelman,F.H. "Cannabis sativa L.(marihuana). II. Standardized and reliable microscopic method for detection and indentification of marihuana." J. Pharmaceut. Sci. 1973, 62, 515-516.

6448. Segelman,A.B., Pettler,F.H., and Farnsworth,N.R. "Cannabis sativa L.(marihuana). A correction on reported thin-layer chromatography data." Pharm. Weekbl. 1970, 105, 1360-1362.

6449. Segelman,A.B. and Segelman,F.P. "Cannabis sativa L.(marihuana). VII. The relative specificity of the RIM test." J. Chromatog. 1976, 123, 79-100.

6450. Segelman,A.B. and Segelman,F.P. "Possible non-inhibition of cellular-mediated immunity in marihuana smokers." Science 1974, 185, 543-544.

6451. Segelman,A.B. and Sofia,R.D. "Cannabis sativa L.(marihuana). IV. Chemical basis for increased potency related to novel method of preparation." J.A.P.A. 1973, 62, 2044-2046.

6452. Segelman,A.B., Sofia,R.D., Segelman,F.P., Harakal,J.J., and Knobloch,L.C. "Cannabis sativa L. (marihuana). V. Pharmacological evaluation of marihuana aqueous extract and volatile oil." J. Pharmaceut. Sci. 1974, 63, 962-964.

6453. Segelman,A.B., Sofia,R.D., and Segelman,F.H. "Cannabis sativa L.(marihuana). VI. Variations in marihuana preparations and usage--chemical and pharmacological consequences." In Rubin,V.(ed.). Cannabis and Culture. Mouton, The Hague, 1975, 269-293.

6454. Segura Millan,J.R. Marihuana, Socio-medical Study.(Sp.). Univ. Mexico, Mexico, 1939.

6455. Seidel,G. "Drug dependence."(Ger.). Deut. Med. J. 1967, 92, 980.

6456. Seidel,G. "Hashish."(Ger.). Deut. Med. Woch. 1969, 94, 1257.

6457. Seiden,R.H., Tomlinson,K.R., and O'Carroll,M. "Patterns of marihuana use among public health students." Am. J. Pub. Hlth. 1975, 65, 613-621.

6458. Seifert,O. "A case of poisoning by balsam cannabis indica."(Ger.). Munch. Med. Woch. 1886, 33, 347-348.

6459. Selby,J.B. "Pot and booze." N. Eng. J. Med. 1969, 280, 1077.

6460. Selegman,J. and Howard,L. "Easing the pot laws." Newsweek 1977, 89, 76.

6461. Sells,H.F. A Bibliography on Drug Dependence. Texas Christian Univ. Press, Fort Worth, Texas, 1967.

6462. Semon,W. and Gagnon,J.H. "Children of the drug age; high school students." Sat. Rev. 1968, 51, 60-63.

6463. Semuels,M. "From the Committee for a Sane Drug Policy." Drugs Soc. 1972, 2, 37.

6464. Sengupta,D., Bhattacharyya,P., Chakravarty,I., and Ghosh,J.J. "Effects of cannabis extract administration on intestinal disaccharidases of the rat." U.N. Doc. ST/SOA/SER.S/39, Mar. 14, 1973.

6465. Sennett,E.F. "Temporal patterns of drug use: a pilot study." Percept. Motor Skills 1976, 43, 793-794.

6466. Sennett,E.R., Wampler,K.S., and Harvey,W.M. "Consistency of patterns of drug use." Psychol. Rep. 1972, 31, 143-152.

6467. Seratoni,E.F., Merlini,L., Mongiorgi,R., and DiSanseverino,L.R. "The crystal and molecular structure of a synthetic cannabinoid derivative, 8,5a-trans-5a,9a-cis-1,8-dimethyl-5a-isopropyl-5a,6,7,8,9a-hexahydrodibenzofuran-3-ol."(It.). Gaz. Chim. Ital. 1974, 104, 1153-1159.

6468. Serebriakova,T.I. and Sizov,I.A. Cannabinaceae. (Rus.). Kulturnaia Flora SSR, Moscow, 1940.

6469. Sermak,E.R., Miller,A.J., and Tormey,H.J. "Physical and chemical similarities of oils isolated from components of the ethnolic extract of cannabis sativa." Sci. Stud. St. Bonavent. Coll. 1940, 9, 3-5.

6470. Sernec-Avsic,T. "Quantitative gas-chromatographic analysis of extracts of Slovenia samples of cannabis sativa."(Rus.). Farm-Vestn. 1970, 21, 27-39.

6471. Serrera Contreras,R.M. Cultivation and Manufacture of Linen and Cannabis in New Spain(1777-1800). (Sp.). School for Spanish American Studies, Seveille, 1974.

6472. Seyfeddininpur,N. "Clinical and electroencephalographic observations during the acute action of hashish."(Ger.). Munch. Med. Woch. 1975, 117, 477-482.

6473. Shaffer,J.H., Hill,R.M., and Fischer,R. "Delta-9-THC and psilocybin induced changes in sensory magnitude estimations." Proc. 5th Internat'l. Cong. Pharmacol. 1972, 1, 209.

6474. Shaffer,J.H., Hill,R.M., and Fischer,R. "Psychophysics of psilocybin and delta-9-tetrahydrocannabinol." Agents and Actions 1973, 3, 48-51.

6475. Shafii,M., Lavely,R., and Jaffe,R. "Meditation and marihuana." Am. J. Psychiat. 1974, 131, 60-63.

6476. Shahar,A. and Bino,T. "Effect of delta-9-tetrahydrocannabinol(THC) on the kinetic morphology of spermatozoa." In Afzelius,B.A.(ed.). The Functional Anatomy of Spermatozoon. Pergamon Press, N.Y., 1973, 189-193.

6477. Shahar,A. and Bino,T. "In vitro effects of delta-9-tetrahydrocannabinol(THC) on bull sperm."

Biochem. Pharmacol. 1974, 23, 1341-1342.

6478. Shain,M., Riddell,W., and Kilty,H.L. Influence, Choice, and Drugs. Lexington Books, Lexington, Mass., 1977.

6479. Shane,J. "Marihuana law." New Repub. 1968, 158, 910.

6480. Shani,A. and Mechoulam,R. "A new type of cannabinoid. Synthesis of cannabielsoic acid A by a novel photooxidative cyclisation." J. Chem. Soc. 1970, 5, 273-274.

6481. Shani,A. and Mechoulam,R. "Cannabielsoic acids, isolation and synthesis by a novel oxidative cyclization." Tetrahedron 1974, 30, 2437-2446.

6482. Shani,A. and Mechoulam,R. "Photochemical reactions of cannabidiol. Cyclization to delta-1-tetrahydrocannabinol and other transformations." Tetrahedron 1971, 27, 601-606.

6483. Shanks,L.P. Baudelaire. Little Brown, Boston, 1930.

6484. Shannon,M.E. and Fried,P.A. "The macro- and microdistribution and polymorphic electroencephalographic effects of delta-9-tetrahydrocannabinol in the rat." Psychopharmacol. 1972, 27, 141-156.

6485. Shapiro,B.J. and Tashkin,D.P. "Effects of beta-adrenergic blockade and muscarinic stimulation on cannabis bronchodilation." In Braude,M.C. and Szara,S. (eds.). Pharmacology of Marihuana. Raven Press, N.Y., 1976, 1, 277-287.

6486. Shapiro,B.J., Tashkin,D.P., and Frank,I.M. "Mechanism of increased specific airway conductance with marihuana smoking in healthy young men." Ann. Intern. Med. 1973, 78, 832-833.

6487. Shapiro,B.J., Tashkin,D.P., McLatchie,C.C., and Rosenthal,D.L. "Sputum cytology following subacute marihuana smoking in healthy males." In Braude,M.C. and Szara,S.(eds.). Pharmacology of Marihuana. Raven Press, N.Y., 1976, 2, 685-689.

6488. Shapiro,B.J., Tashkin,D.P., and Vachon,L. "Tetrahydrocannabinol as a bronchodilator." Chest 1977, 71, 558-559.

6489. Shapiro,C.M., Orlina,A.R., Unger,P., and Billings,A.A. "Antibody response to cannabis." J.A.M.A. 1974, 230, 81-82.

6490. Shapiro,C.M., Orlina,A.R., Unger,P.J., Telfer,M., and Billings,A.A. "Marihuana-induced antibody response." J. Lab. Clin. Med. 1976, 88, 194-201.

6491. Shapiro,C.M., Orlina,A.R., Unger,P.J., Telfer,M., and Billings,A.A. "Marihuana induced antibody response and laboratory correlates." Clin. Res. 1975, 23, 488A.

6492. Shapiro,D. "The ocular manifestations of the cannabinols." Ophthalmologica 1974, 168, 366-369.

6493. Shapiro,R. "Adolescent drug behavior: Some problems of assessment." Proc. 7th Wrld. Cong. Sociol. Assoc. 1970, 1, 357.

6494. Sharar,A. and Bino,T. "In vitro effects of delta-9-tetrahydrocannabinol(THC) on bull sperm." Biochem. Pharmacol. 1974, 23, 1341-1342.

6495. Sharma,B.P. "Cannabis and its users in Nepal." Br. J. Psychiat. 1975, 127, 550-552.

6496. Sharma,S. and Moskowitz,H. "A marihuana dose study of vigilance performance." Proc. Am. Psychol. Assoc. 1973, 8, 1035-1036.

6497. Sharma,S. and Moskowitz,H. "Effect of marihuana on the visual autokinetic phenomenon." Percept. Motor Skills 1972, 35, 891-894.

6498. Sharma,S. and Moskowitz,H. "Effects of two levels of attention demand on vigilance performance under mairhuana." Percept. Motor Skills 1974, 38, 967-970.

6499. Sharma,T.D. "Clinical observations of patients who used tetra-hydrocannabinol(T.H.C.) intravenously." Behav. Neuropsychiat. 1972, 4, 17-19.

6500. Sharma,T. "Marihuana: Recent research findings--1972." Texas Med. 1972, 68, 109-110.

6501. Sharpe,T.G. "Pot full of discretion: comprehensive drug abuse prevention and control act." Texas Bar J. 1972, 34, 397.

6502. Shaw,J. "On the use of the cannabis indica (or Indian hemp)--1st, in tetanus; 2nd, in hydrophobia; 3rd, in cholera, with remarks on its effects." Madras Quart. Med. J. 1843, 5, 74-80.

6503. Shaw,W.S.J. "Cannabis indica: A 'dangerous drug'." Br. Med. J. 1923, 2, 586.

6504. Shea,P. "Marihuana studies." Med. J. Aust. 1972, 1, 497-498.

6505. Shean,G.D. and Fechtmann,F. "Purpose in life scores of student marihuana users." J. Clin. Psychol. 1971, 27, 112-113.

6506. Shearer,L. "The mystique of marihuana: Why students smoke pot." Parade 1967, 8, 10-11.

6507. Shearn,C.R. and Fitzgibbons,D.J. "Survey of reasons for illicit drug use in a population of youthful psychiatric inpatients." Internat'l. J. Addict. 1973, 8, 623-633.

6508. Shepherd,J. "Drugs on the campus." Look 1967, 31, 14-17.

6509. Sherpherd,J. "Wheeling and dealing with tragedy." Look 1968, 32, 56-59.

6510. Shetterley,H.T. "Self and social perceptions and personal characteristics of a group of suburban high school marihuana users." Diss. Abs. 1971, 31, 3279.

6511. Shibuya,R.R. "Categorizing drug users and nonusers on selected social and personality variables." J. Sch. Hlth. 1974, 44, 442-444.

6512. Shibuya,R.R. "Differentiating traits among LSD abusers, marihuana abusers and nonusers." Diss. Abs. 1972, 32, 5460.

6513. Shick,J.F.E., Smith,D.E., and Meyers,F.H. "Patterns of drug use in the Haight-Ashbury neighborhood." Clin. Toxicol. 1970, 3, 19-56.

6514. Shick,J.F.E., Smith,D.E., and Meyers,F.H. "Use of marihuana in the Haight-Ashbury subculture." J. Psyched. Drugs 1968, 2, 49-66.

6515. Shiedeman,F.E. "Recent advances in the pharmacology of tetrahydrocannabinols." Fol. Pharmacol. Jap. 1971, 46, 113P-115P.

6516. Shit,T.M. and Oskoui,M. "The effects of delta-1-tetrahydrocannabinol and ethanol on monosynaptic and polysynaptic transmission in the central nervous system." Fed. Proc. 1973, 32, 7-6.

6517. Shimomura,H., Shigehiro,M., Kuriyana,E., and Fujita,M. "Studies on cannabis. I. Microscopic characteristics of their internal morphology and spodogram." (Jap.). J. Pharmaceut. Soc. Jap. 1967, 87, 1334-1341.

6518. Shinkarenko,V.I. "Hashish smoking in the underworld in Krasnodar, Soviet Rusia."(Rus.). Sov. Sovet. Psikhoneurolog. 1930, 4, 269-278.

6519. Shinogi,M., Murai,Y., Mori,I., and Takeuchi,T. "Determination of phosphorus in cannabis by neutron activation analysis--measurement of 32P Cerenkov radiation by liquid scintilation spectoscopy."(Jap.). J. Pharmaceut. Soc. Jap. 1976, 96, 1282-1287.

6520. Shinogi,M., Murai,Y., Mori,I., and Takeuchi,T. "Study of trace elements in organisms by neutron activation analysis. I. Multielement instrumental neutron activation analysis of cannabis."(Jap.). Yak. Zassh. 1974, 94, 1550-1559.

6521. Shipper,J.C. "An earthquake under grass." Calif. Med. 1971, 115, 75.

6522. Shirakawa,I., Kasinski,N., Pfeferman,A., Karniol,I.G., and Carlini,E.A. "Cannabidiol interferes with the effects of delta-9-tetrahydrocannaibnol." Paper presented at 1st Lat. Am. Cong. Psychobiol., Sao Paulo, 1973.

6523. Shirkey,H.C. "Cannabis roots." J.A.M.A. 1971, 218, 1434.

6524. Shoemaker,J.V. "The therapeutic value of cannabis indica." Texas Med. News 1899, 8, 477-488.

6525. Shoham,S. "Cultural factors associated with cannabis use in Israel." In Btesh,S.(ed.). Drug Abuse. C.C. Thomas, Springfield, Ill., 1972, 48-66.

6526. Shoham,S.G., Geva,N., Klinger,D., and Chai,T. "Drug use among Israeli youth: Epidemiological pilot study." Bull. Narc. 1974, 26, 9-26.

6527. Showanasai,C.A. "Treatment report from Thailand." Addict. Dis. 1977, 3, 89-92.

6528. Shoyama,Y., Fujita,T., Yamauchi,T., and Nishioka,I. "Cannabichromene acid, a genuine substance of cannabichromene." Chem. Pharmaceut. Bull. 1968, 16, 1157-1158.

6529. Shoyama,Y., Hirano,H., Makino,H., Umekita,N., and Nishioka,I. "Cannabis. X. The isolation and structures of four new propyl cannabinoid acids, tetrahydrocannabivarinic acid, cannabidivarninic acid, cannabichromevarinic acid and cannabigerovarinic acid, from Thai cannabis." Chem. Pharmaceut. Bull. 1977, 25, 2306-2311.

6530. Shoyama,Y., Kuboe,K., Niskioka,I., and Yamauchi,T. "Cannabidiol monomethyl ether. A new neutral cannabinoid." Chem. Pharmaceut. Bull. 1972, 20, 2072.

6531. Shoyama,Y., Oku,R., Yamauchi,T., and Nishioka,I. "Cannabis. VI. Cannabicyclolic acid." Chem. Pharmaceut. Bull. 1972, 20, 1927-1930.

6532. Shoyama,Y., Yagi,M., and Nishioka,I. "Biosynthesis of cannabinoid acids." Phytochemistry 1975, 14, 2189-2192.

6533. Shoyama,Y., Yamaguchi,T., Akiko,S.T., Yamauchi,T., and Nishioka,I. "Cannabis. IV. Smoking test."(Jap.). J. Pharmaceut. Soc. Jap. 1969, 89, 842-

6534. Shoyama,Y., Yamuchi,T., and Nishioka,I. "Cannabis. V. Cannabigerolic acid monomethyl ether and cannabinolic acid." Chem. Pharmaceut. Bull. 1970, 18, 1327-1332.

6535. Shuaib,B.H. "Report on status of drug abuse treatment in Pakistan." Addict. Dis. 1977, 3, 75-78.

6536. Shukla,D.D. and Pathak,V.N. "A new species of Ascochyta on cannabis sativa L." Sydow. Ann. Mycol. 1967, 21, 277-278.

6537. Shulgin,A.T. "Hallucinogens, CNS stimulants, and cannabis." In Mule,S.J.(eds.). Chemical and Biological Aspects of Drug Dependence. CRC Press, Cleveland, 1972, 163.

6538. Shulgin,A.T. "Preliminary studies of the synthesis of nitrogen analogs of delta-1-THC." Act. Pharmaceut. Suec. 1971, 8, 680-681.

6539. Shulgin,A. "Recent developments in cannabis chemistry." J. Psyched. Drugs 1968, 2, 14-29.

6540. Sidell,F.R., Pless,J.E., Neitlich,H., Sussman,P., Copelan,H.W., and Sim,V.D. "Dimethylheptyl-delta 6a-10a-tetrahydrocannabinol: Effects after parenteral administration to man." Proc. Soc. Expt'l. Biol. Med. 1975, 142, 867-873.

6541. Siebold,L. and Bradbury,T. "Note on the alleged presence of nicotine in Indian hemp." Pharmaceut. J. Trans. 1881, 12, 326-327.

6542. Siegel,R.K. "Effects of cannabis sativa and lysergic acid diethylamide on a visual discrimination task in pigeons." Psychopharmacol. 1969, 15, 1-8.

6543. Siegel,R.K. "Effects of cannabis sativa and LSD on pigeons in three visual environments." Percept. Motor Skills 1970, 30, 510.

6544. Siegel,R.K. "Hallucinogenic-induced effects on a visual discrimination task in pigeons." Paper presented at 4th Internat'l. Cong. Pharmacol., Lausanne, Switzerland, 1969.

6545. Siegel,R.K. "Hallucinogens and perceptual changes." Drug Ther. 1971, 1, 34-44.

6546. Siegel,R.K. "Studies of hallucinogens in fish, birds, mice, and men: The behavior of "psychedelic" populations." Paper presented at 7th Internat'l. Cong. Neuro-psychopharmacol., Prague, 1970.

6547. Siegel,R.K. and Poole,J. "Psychedelic-induced social behavior in mice: A preliminary report." Psychol. Rep. 1969, 25, 704-706.

6548. Siegel,R.K. and West,L.J.(eds.). Hallucinations. J. Wiley and Sons, N.Y., 1975.

6549. Siegesmund,K.A. and Hunter,G.M. "Scanning electron microscopy of selected crime laboratory specimens." In Johari,O. and Corvin,I.(eds.). Scanning Electron Microscope Symposium. ITT Res. Inst., Chicago, 1971, 577-584.

6550. Siemens,A.J. Acute and Chronic Metabolic Interactions of Delta-1-tetrahydrocannabinol and Other Drugs. Univ. of Toronto, Dept. Pharmacol., Toronto, 1973.

6551. Siemens,A.J. "Effects of delta-9-tetrahydrocannabinol on the disposition of d-amphetamine in the rat." Life Sci. 1977, 20, 1891-1904.

6552. Siemens,A.J., deNie,L.C., Kalant,H., and Khanna,J.M. "Effects of various psychoactive drugs on the metabolism of delta-1-tetrahydrocannabinol by rats in vitro and in vivo." Eur. J. Pharmacol. 1975, 31, 136-147.

6553. Siemens,A.J. and Kalant,H. "Metabolism of delta-1-tetrahydrocannabinol by rats tolerant to cannabis." Can. J. Physiol. Pharmacol. 1974, 52, 1154-1166.

6554. Siemens,A.J. and Kalant,H. "Metabolism of delta-1-tetrahydrocannabinol by the rat in vivo and in vitro." Biochem. Pharmacol. 1975, 24, 755-762.

6555. Siemens,A.J., Kalant,H., and deNie,J.C. "Metabolic interactions between delta-9-tetrahydrocannabinol and other cannabinoids in rats." In Braude, M.C. and Szara,S.(eds.). Pharmacology of Marihuana. Raven Press, N.Y., 1976, 1, 77-93.

6556. Siemens,A.J., Kalant,H., and Khanna,J.M. "Effect of cannabis on pentobarbital-induced sleeping time and pentobarbital metabolism in the rat." Biochem. Pharmacol. 1974, 23, 477-488.

6557. Siemens,A.J., Kalant,H., Khanna,J.M., and Marshman,J. "Effect of cannabidiol in cannabis on pentobarbital metabolism." Fed. Proc. 1973, 32, 756.

6558. Siemens,A.J., Kalant,H., Khanna,J.M., Marshman, J., and Ho,G. "Effect of cannabis on pentobarbital-induced sleeping time and pentobarbital metabolism in the rat." Biochem. Pharmacol. 1974, 23, 477-488.

6559. Siemens,A.J. and Khanna,J.M. "Acute metabolic interactions between ethanol and cannabis." Alcoholism 1977, 1, 343-348.

6560. Sieper,H., Longo,R., and Korte,F. "The chemical classification of plants: 23."(Ger.). Arch. Pharmakol. 1963, 296, 403.

6561. Sievert,W.A. "The campus drug scene 1972. A milkman routine." Chron. High. Educat. 1972, 6, 1-6.

6562. Sigg,B.W. Chronic Cannabism, Fruit of Under-development and Capitalism.(Fr.). Unpub. ms., Algeria, 1963.

6563. Silberman,D. and Levy,J. "A preliminary survey of 24 Victorian marihuana users." Med. J. Aust. 1969, 2, 286-289.

6564. Siler,J.F., Sheep,W.L., Bates,L.B., Clark,G.F., Cook,G.W., and Smith,W.A. "Marihuana smoking in Panama." Milit. Surg. 1933, 73, 269-280.

6565. Silva,J.B. "Chromatographic determination of cannabinol in the blood, urine and saliva of individuals addicted to cannabis sativa."(Port.). Rev. Fac. Farmacol. Bioquim. 1967, 5, 205-214.

6566. Silva,J.B. "Comparative chromatographic analysis of 100 samples of Brazilian cannabis sativa L." (Port.). Rev. Fac. Farmacol. Bioquim. 1966, 4, 55-69.

6567. Silva,M.T.A., Carlini,E.A., Claussen,U., and Korte,F. "Lack of cross tolerance in rats among (-)-delta-9-trans-tetrahydrocannabinol, cannabis extract, mescaline and lysergic acid diethylamide(LSD-25)." Psychopharmacol. 1968, 13, 332-340.

6568. Silva,M.T.A. and Cutait,M.A. "Effect of delta-9-tetrahydrocannabinol on taste preference in rats." Paper presented at 1st Lat. Am. Cong. Psychobiol., Sao Paulo, 1973.

6569. Silver,A. "On the value of Indian hemp in menorrhagia and dysmenorrhoea." Med. Times Gaz. 1870, 2, 59-61.

6570. Silverstein,M.J. and Lessin,P.J. "DNCB skin testing in chronic marihuana users." In Braude,M.C. and Szara,S.(eds.). Pharmacology of Marihuana. Raven Press, N.Y., 1976, 1, 199-204.

6571. Silverstein,M.J. and Lessin,P.J. "Normal skin test responses in chronic marihuana users." Science 1974, 186, 740-741.

6572. Silvestre de Sacy,M. "Memoirs on the dynasty of the Assassins and on the origin of their name."(Fr.). Gaz. Nat. Moniteur Univ. 1809, 210, 828-830.

6573. Silvestre de Sacy,M. "Preparations made with hemp."(Fr.). Bull. Sci. Med. 1809, 4, 204.

6574. Simek,J. "Use of cannabis indica extract in preserving stomatology."(Czech.). Act. Univ. Palack. Olomunc. 1955, 6, 79-82.

6575. Simmonberg,L. "The budding marihuana bar." Juris Doc. 1975, 5, 37-45.

6576. Simmons,J.L. "Marihuana: A checklist of facts. Physical and mental effects of use." In Simmons, J.L.(ed.). Marihuana, Myths and Realities, Brandon House, North Hollywood, 1967, 29-42.

6577. Simmons,J.L. "Marihuana futures." In Simmons, J.L.(ed.). Marihuana, Myths and Realities. Brandon House, North Hollywood, 1967, 215-222.

6578. Simmons,J.L.(ed.). Marihuana, Myths and Realities. Brandon House, North Hollywood, 1967.

6579. Simmons,J.L. "The current marihuana scene." In Simmons,J.L.(ed.). Marihuana, Myths and Realities. Brandon House, North Hollywood, 1967, 7-14.

6580. Simmons,J.L. and Winograd,B. It's Happening. Marc-Laird Pub., Santa Barbara, 1966.

6581. Simon,C. "From opium to hasheesh; startling facts regarding the narcotic evil and its many ramifications throughout the world." Scientif. Am. 1921, 14-15.

6582. Simon,G. and Trout,G. "Hippies in college--from teenyboppers to drug freaks." Trans-action 1967, 5, 27-32.

6583. Simon,P. "The problem of pot." Southwest. Med. 1970, 51, 162-164.

6584. Simon,W.E. "Marihuana use and a measure of perceptual rigidity." Psychol. Rep. 1973, 33, 122.

6585. Simon,W.E. "Psychological needs, academic achievement and marihuana consumption." J. Clin. Psychol. 1974, 30, 496-498.

6586. Simon,W. and Gagnon,J. "Children of the drug age." Sat. Rev. 1968, 60, 75.

6587. Simon,W. and Gagnon,J.H. The End of Adolescence: The College Experience. Harper and Row, N.Y., 1970.

6588. Simon,W., Simon,M.G., Primavera,L.H., and Orndoff,R.K. "A comparison of marihuana users and nonusers on a number of personality variables." J. Consult. Clin. Psychol. 1974, 42, 917-918.

6589. Simonberg,L. "The U.N.'s secret vendetta against dope." High Times 1976, 8, 46-48.

6590. Simonsen,J.L. and Todd,A.R. "Cannabis indica. Part X. The essential oil from Egyptian hashish." J. Chem. Soc. 1942, 1, 188-191.

6591. Simpson,H.T. "AMA does its thing on pot." Marihuana Rev. 1968, 1, 13-15.

6592. Simpson,P.A. "Native poisons of India." Pharmaceut. J. Trans. 1872, 2, 604-606, 665-667.

6593. Sinclair,J. "The marihuana revolution." Marihuana Rev. 1968, 1, 8-9.

6594. Singer,H. "Primer on pot." Progressive 1969, 33, 25-28.

6595. Singer,P.R., Scibetta,J.J., and Rosen,M.G. "Simulated marihuana smoking in the maternal and fetal guinea pig." Am. J. Obstet. Gynecol. 1973, 117, 331-340.

6596. Singh,P.P. "Role of catecholamines in the hypothermic activity of cannabis in albino rats." Psychopharmacol. 1976, 50, 199-204.

6597. Singh,S.P. "Floral anatomy of cannabis sativa L." Agra Univ. J. Res. 1956, 5, 155-162.

6598. Single,E., Kandel,D., and Faust,R. "Patterns of multiple drug use in high school." J. Hlth. Soc. Behav. 1974, 15, 344-357.

6599. Sinnett,E.R., Wampler,K.S., and Harvey,W.M. "Marihuana--a psychedelic drug?" Psychol. Rep. 1974, 34, 47-53.

6600. Sirek,J. "Importance of hempseed in tuberculosis therapy."(Czech.). Act. Univ. Palack. Olomuc. 1955, 6, 93-108.

6601. Sironval,C. "On the separation of the sexes in a population of hemp cultivated in short daylight from generation to generation."(Fr.). Bull. Soc. Roy. Botan. Belg. 1959, 91, 2-5-265.

6602. Sizemore,H. "Marihuana." West Virginia Med. J. 1972, 68, 33-34.

6603. Sjoden,P.O., Jarbe,T.U.C., and Henriksson,B.G. "Effects of long term administration and withdrawl of tetrahydrocannabinols(delta-8- and delta-9-THC) on open field behavior in rats." Pharmacol. Biochem. Behav. 1973, 1, 243-249.

6604. Sjoden,P., Jarbe,T.U.C., and Henriksson,B.G. "Influence of tetrahydrocannabinols (delta-8- and delta-9-THC) on body weight, food, and water intake in rats." Pharmacol. Biochem. Behav. 1973, 1, 395-399.

6605. Skelton,F.S. and Witshi,H.P. "Aryl hydrocarbon hydroxylase activity induced by cannabis resin: Analysis for polycyclic hydrocarbons." Toxicol. Appl. Pharmacol. 1974, 27, 551-557.

6606. Skinner,N.F. "Personality characteristics of heavy smokers and abstainers, as a function of perceived predispositions toward marihuana use." Soc. Behav. Personal. 1974, 2, 157-160.

6607. Skinner,R.P. "The determination of submicrogram amounts of delta-9-tetrahydrocannabinol and its metabolites." Proc. West. Pharmacol. Soc. 1972, 15, 136-138.

6608. Skinner,R.F. "The state of the art in the analysis of marihuana." Proc. West. Pharmacol. Soc. 1971, 14, 4-9.

6609. Sklenovsky,A., Navratil,J., Hrbek,J., and Krejce,Z. "Effect of delta-9-tetrahydrocannabinol on free amino acids in brain." Activ. Nerv. Sup. 1974, 16, 216-217.

6610. Sklenovsky,A., Navratil,J., Hrbek,J., and Skrabal,J. "Effect of delta-9-tetrahydrocannabinol (THC) on the 'labilization' of phospholipoid complexes of brain tissue." Activ. Nerv. Sup. 1975, 17, 67.

6611. Skliar,N. "Psychoses due to anascha."(Ger.). Allgem. Zeit. Psychiat. Med. 1934, 102, 304-312.

6612. Skliar,N. and Iwanow,A. "Anascha intoxication." (Ger.). Allegem. Zeit. Psychiat. Med. 1932, 98, 300-330.

6613. Skousen,W. "Drug addiction: The chief takes a hard look at drub abuse." Law Order 1969, 17, 16-18.

6614. Slaby,A.E., Lieb,J., and Schwartz,A.A. "A comparative study of the psychological correlates of drug use among medical and law students." J. Med. Educat. 1972, 47, 717-723.

6615. Slatkin,D.J., Doorenbos,N.J., Harris,L.S., Masoud,An.n., Quimby,M.W., and Schiff,P.L. "Chemical constitutents of cannabis sativa L. root." J. Pharmaceut. Sci. 1971, 60, 1891-1892.

6616. Slatkin,D.J., Knapp,J.E., Schiff,P.L., Turner, C.E., and Mole,M.L. "Steroids of cannabis sativa root." Phytochemistry 1975, 14, 580-581.

6617. Slaybaugh,G., Sanford,J.F., Brown,S.C., Thompson,C.P. "Retrieval failure or selective attention." Science 1971, 173, 1040.

6618. Sledjesky,S.S. "Characteristics and attitudes of college students in relation to marihuana." Florida J. Educat. Res. 1971, 13, 14-22.

6619. Small,E. "American law and the species problem in cannabis: Science and semantics." Bull. Narc. 1975, 27, 1-20.

6620. Small,E. "Interfertility and chromosomal uniformity in cannabis." Can. J. Bot. 1972, 50, 1947-1949.

6621. Small,E. "'Legal' species of cannabis." J. Forens. Sci. 1975, 20, 739-741.

6622. Small,E. "The case of the curious 'cannabis'." Econ. Bot. 1975, 29, 254.

6623. Small,E. "The forensic taxonomic debate on cannabis: semantic hokum." J. Forens. Sci. 1976, 21, 239-251.

6624. Small,E. "The hemp problem in Canada." Greenhouse-Garden Grass, 1972, 11, 46-52.

6625. Small,E. "The systematics of cannabis." Am. J. Bot. 1974, 61, 50.

6626. Small,E. and Beckstead,H.D. "Cannabinoid types in cannabis sativa." Nature 1973, 245, 147-148.

6627. Small,E. and H.D. "Common cannabinoid phenotypes in 350 stocks of cannabinoids." Lloydia 1973, 36, 144-165.

6628. Small,E., Beckstead,H.D., and Chan,A. "The evolution of cannabinoid phenotypes in cannabis." Econ. Bot. 1975, 29, 219-232.

6629. Small,E. and Cronquist,A. "A practical and natural taxonomy for cannabis." Taxonomy 1976, 25, 435.

6630. Small,J.K. Flora of Southeastern U.S. Priv. Pub., N.Y., 1913.

6631. Smallenberg,C., Smallenberg,H., and Powelson, D.H. "Drug scene, has it changed?" PTA Mag. 1971, 66, 3-4.

6632. Smart,R.G. "Cannabis and driving risk." In Connell,P.H. and Dorn,N.(eds.). Cannabis and Man. Churchill Livingstone, London, 1975, 6-25.

6633. Smart,R.G. "Discrepancies between drug educators and students in attitudes toward marihuana: Their implications for communication." J. Alcohol Drug Educat. 1973, 19, 21-30.

6634. Smart,R.G. "Drug abuse among high school students in Metropolitan Toronto: Current studies of psychoactive and hallucinogenic drug use." In Healy,P.F. and Manak,J.P.(eds.). Drug Dependence and Abuse Resource Book. Nat'l. District Attorneys Assoc., Chicago, 1971, 295-303.

6635. Smart,R.G. "Drug abuse and its treatment in Canada." Addict. Dis. 1977, 3, 5-10.

6636. Smart,R.G. Drug Use in Canada; Its History, Current Concerns and Unsolved Problems. John Howard Soc. of Ontario, Toronto, 1970.

6637. Smart,R.G. "Marihuana and driving risk among college students." Comm. Prob. Drug Depend. 1974, 1, 1107-1112.

6638. Smart,R.G. "Marihuana and driving risk among college students." J. Safe. Res. 1974, 6, 155-157.

6639. Smart,R.G. "Rejection of the source in drug education." J. Drug Iss. 1972, 2, 55-60.

6640. Smart,R.G. "Some current studies of psychoactive and hallucinogenic drug use." Can. J. Behav. Sci. 1970, 2, 230-245.

6641. Smart,R.G. and Fejer,D. "Drug use and driving risk among high school students." Accid. Anal. Prevent. 1976, 8, 33-38.

6642. Smart,R.G. and Fejer,D. "Marihuana use among adults in Toronto." Br. J. Addict. 1973, 68, 117-128.

6643. Smart,R.G. and Fejer,D. "Relationships between parental and adolescent drug use." In Keup,W. (ed.). Drug Abuse. C.C. THomas, Springfield, Ill., 1972, 146-153.

6644. Smart,R.G. and Fejer,D. "The extent of illicit drug use in Canada: A review of current epidemiology." In Craig,L.G., Grindstaff,C.F., and Whitehead, P.C.(eds.). Critical Issues in Canadian Society. Holt Rinehart and Winston, Toronto, 1971, 508-520.

6645. Smart,P.G., Fejer,D., and Eileen,A. Drug Use Among High School Students and Their Parents in Lincoln and Welland Counties. Addiction Res. Found., Toronto, 1970.

6646. Smart,R.G., Fejer,D. and White,J. The Extent of Drug Use in Metropolitan Toronto Schools: A Study of Changes from 1968 to 1970. Addiction Res. Found, Toronto, 1970.

6647. Smart,R.G. and Jackson,D. A Preliminary Report on the Attitudes and Behavior of Toronto Students in Relation to Drugs. Addiciton Res. Found, Toronto, 1969.

6648. Smart,R.G. and Krakowski,M. "The nature and frequency of drugs content in magasines and television." J. Alcohol Drug Educat. 1973, 18, 16-23.

6649. Smart,R.G., Laforest,L., and Whitehead,P.C. "Comparative rates of drug use among adolescent students: Halifax-Montreal-Toronto." Paper presented at Atlantic Assoc. Sociol. Anthropol., Halifax, 1970.

6650. Smart,R.G., Laforest,L., and Whitehead,P.C. "The epidemiology of the use of drugs among three student populations."(Fr.). Toxicomanies 1970, 3, 212-226.

6651. Smart,R.G., and Whitehead,P.C. "The consumption of illicit drugs and their implications for prevention of abuse." Bull. Narc. 1972, 24, 39-47.

6652. Smiley,K.A., Karler,R., and Turkanis,S.A. "Effects of cannabinoids on the perfused rat heart." Res. Commun. Chem. Pathol. Pharmacol. 1976, 14, 659-675.

6653. Smith,B.C. "Drug use on a university campus." J. Am. Hlth. Assoc. 1970, 18, 360-365.

6654. Smith,D.E. "Acute and chronic toxicity of marihuana." J. Psyched. Drugs 1968, 2, 37-47.

6655. Smith,D.E. "Marihuana: Some notes, queries and answers." Med. Counterpoint 1971, 1, 29-32.

6656. Smith,D.E.(ed.). The New Social Drug. Prentice-Hall, Englewood Cliffs, N.J., 1970.

6657. Smith,D.E., Cromy,R., Downing,J., and Sutton,L. "Psychedelic drugs and religion." J. Psyched. Drugs 1967, 1, 45-71.

6658. Smith,D.E., Fort,J., and Craton,D.L. "Psychoactive drugs (a reference for the staff of the Haight-Ashbury clinic)." J. Psychedel. Drugs 1967, 1 127.

6659. Smith,D.E. and Luce,J. Love Needs Care. Little Brown Co., Boston, 1971.

6660. Smith,D.E. and Mehl,C. "An analysis of marihuana toxicity." Clin. Toxicol. 1970, 3, 101-115.

6661. Smith,D.E. and Meyers,F.M. "The new generation and the new drugs." Cal. Hlth. 1968, 25, 7-11, 15.

6662. Smith,D.E. and Rose,A.J. "Observations in the Haight-Ashbury medical clinic of San Francisco." Clin. Pediat. 1968, 7, 313-316.

6663. Smith,F.P. and Stuart,G.A. Chinese Materia Medica. Am. Presbyterian Mission, Shanghai, 1911.

6664. Smith,G.F., Coles,G.V., Schilling,R.S., and Walford,J. "A study of rope workers exposed to hemp and flax." Br. J. Indust. Med. 1969, 26, 109-114.

6665. Smith,G.M. and Fogg,C.P. "Longitudinal study of teenage drug use." Paper presented at Conference on Strategies of Longitudinal Research in Drug Use, Puerto Rico, 1976.

6666. Smith,G.M. and Fogg,C.P. "Teenage drug use: A search for causes and consequences." In Lettieri,D.J. (ed.). Predicting Adolescent Drug Abuse: A Review of Issues, Methods and Correlates. N.I.D.A. Res. Monog. Ser. 11, Gov't. Print. Office, Washington,D.C., 1975, 279-282.

6667. Smith,H.F. "Cannabis indica. Does it contain an alkaloid?" Am. J. Pharmacol. 1891, 63, 386-391.

6668. Smith,J.P. "International cooperation in cannabis research." In Braude,M.C. and Szara,S.(eds.). Pharmacology of Marihuana. Raven Press, N.Y., 1976, 1, 9-13.

6669. Smith,M.E. Report to Parents of Students in Castro Valley Unified School District. Castro Valley Unified School District, Castro Valley, Cal., 1967.

6670. Smith,M.G., Augier,R., and Nettleford,R. The Ras Tafari Movement in Kingston, Jamaica. Univ. College of West Indies, Kingston, 1960.

6671. Smith,R.C. "U.S. marihuana legislation and the creation of a social problem." J. Psyched. Drugs 1968, 2, 93-103.

6672. Smith,R.M. and Kempfert,K.D. "Delta-1-3,4-cis-tetrahydrocannabinol in cannabis sativa." Phytochemistry 1977, 16, 1088-1089

6673. Smith,R.N. "A brief note on the response of some essential oils and extracts of vegetale origin to the Duqenois-Levine test for cannabis." J. Forens. Sci. 1974, 14, 191-194.

6674. Smith,R.N. "High-pressure liquid chromatography on cannabis. Identification of separated constituents." J. Chromatog. 1975, 115, 101-106.

6675. Smith,R.N., Jones,L.V., Breknan,J.S., and Vaughan,C.G. "Identification of hexadecanamide in cannabis resin." J. Pharm. Pharmacol. 1977, 29, 126-127.

6676. Smith,R.N. and Vaughan,C.G. "High pressure liquid chromatography of cannabis quantitative analysis of acidic and neutral cannabinoids." J. Chromatog. 1976, 129, 347-354.

6677. Smith,R.N. and Vaughan,C.G. "The decomposition of acidic and neutral cannabinoids in organic solvents." J. Pharm. Pharmacol. 1977, 29, 286-290.

6678. Smith,T. "Cannabin." Pharmaceut. J. Trans. 1885, 15, 853.

6679. Smith,T. and Smith,H. "On the resin of Indian hemp." Pharmaceut. J. Trans. 1847, 6, 127-128.

6680. Smith,T. and Smith,H. "Process for preparing cannabine or hemp resin." Pharmaceut. J. Trans. 1846, 6, 171-174.

6681. Smith,T. and Smith,H. "Properties of Indian hemp." Pharmaceut. J. Trans. 1848, 8, 36-37.

6682. Smith,T.C. and Kulp,R. "Respiratory and cardiovascular effects of delta-9-tetrahydrocannabinol alone and in combination with oxymorphone, pentobarbital and diazepam." In Cohen,S. and Stillman,R.(eds.). Therapeutic Potential of Marihuana. Plenum Press, N.Y., 1976, 123-132.

6683. Smith,T.F.H. "Cannabis indica in smoking tobacco." Br. Med. J. 1923, 2, 590.

6684. Snellen,H., Doorenbos,N.J., and Quimby,M.W. "Mississippi grown cannabis sativa L. delta-9-THC content versus age in a Mexican strain." Lloydia 1970, 33, 492-493.

6685. Snider,A.J. "Drug dangers, the case gets stronger." Science Dig. 1968, 64, 62-63.

6686. Snider,A.J. "Pot smoking: less harm than feared?" Science Dig. 1972, 71, 53.

6687. Snider,A.J. "Psychiatrists comment on pot." Science Dig. 1971, 69, 72.

6688. Snider,A.J. "Who is smoking pot?" Science Dig. 1972, 71, 69.

6689. Snyder,E.W., Lewis,E.G., Dustman,R.E., and Beck,E.C. "Sustained ingestion of delta-9-tetrahydrocannabinol and the operant behavior of stump-tailed macaques." Pharmacol. Biochem. Behav. 1975, 3, 1129-1132.

6690. Synder,S.H. "Cannabis." Psychol. Today 1971, 4, 39.

6691. Snyder,S.H. "Marihuana." J. Psyched. Drugs 1971, 3, 106-107.

6692. Snyder,S.H. "Work with marihuana: I. Effects." Psychol. Today 1971, 4, 37-38, 40, 64-65.

6693. Snyder,S.J. Use of Marihuana. Oxford Univ. Press, N.Y., 1971.

6694. Sobecki,J.F. "Reactions to the marihuana articles." Person. Guid. J. 1973, 52, 214-215.

6695. Sobeloff,J. "The Marihuana Tax Act." Suffolk Univ. Law Rev. 1968, 3, 101-129.

6696. Sodetz,F.J. "Delta-9-tetrahydrocannabinol: Behavioral toxicity in laboratory animals." In Lewis, M.(ed.). Current Research in Marihuana. Academic Press, N.Y., 1972, 25-48.

6697. Sofia,R.D. "A paradoxical effect for delta-1-tetrahydrocannabinol on rectal temperature in rats." Res. Commun. Chem. Pathol. Pharmacol. 1972, 4, 281-288.

6698. Sofia,R.D. "Interactions of chronic and acute delta-1-tetrahydrocannabinol pretreatment with zoxazolamine and barbiturates." Res. Commun. Chem. Pathol. Pharmacol. 1973, 5, 91-98.

6699. Sofia,R.D. "Some effects of delta-1-tetrahydrocannabinol on the central nervous system." Diss. Abs. 1972, 32, 5361.

6700. Sofia,R.D. "The lethal effects of delta-1-tetrahydrocannabinol in aggregated and isolated mice following single dose administration." Eur. J. Pharmacol. 1972, 20, 139-142.

6701. Sofia,R.D. and Barry,H. "Acute and chronic effects of delta-9-tetrahydrocannabinol on food intake by rats." Psychopharmacol. 1974, 39, 213-222.

6702. Sofia,R.D. and Barry,H. "Depressant effect of delta-1-tetrahydrocannabinol enhanced by inhibition of its metabolism." Eur. J. Pharmacol. 1970, 13, 134-137.

6703. Sofia,R.D. and Barry,H. "Food intake by rats following acute and chronic administration of delta-1-tetrahydrocannabinol." Proc. 5th Internat'l. Cong. Pharmacol. 1972, 1, 1304.

6704. Sofia,R.D. and Barry,H. "The influence of SKF 525A on the analgesic action of delta-1-tetrahydrocannabinol." Fed. Proc. 1972, 31, 506.

6705. Sofia,R.D., Delgado,C.J., and Douglas,J.F. "The effects of various naturally occuring cannabinoids on hypotonic-hyperthermic lysis of rat erythrocytes." Eur. J. Pharmacol. 1974, 27, 155-157.

6706. Sofia,R.D. and Dixit,B.N. "The effect of delta-1-tetrahydrocannabinol on rat brain 5-hydroxytyrptamine(5-HT)." Fed. Proc. 1971, 30, 279.

6707. Sofia,R.D., Dixit,B.N., and Barry,H. "The effect of delta-1-tetrahydrocannabinol on serotonin metabolism in the rat brain." Life Sci. 1971, 10, 425-436..

6708. Sofia,R.D., Ertel,R.J., Dixit,B.N., and Barry, H. "The effect of delta-1-tetrahydrocannabinol on the uptake of serotonin by rat brain homogenates." Eur. J. Pharmacol. 1971, 16, 257-259.

6709. Sofia,R.D. and Knobloch,L.C. "Comparative effects of various naturally occurring cannabinoids on food, sucrose and water consumption by rats." Pharmacol. Biochem. Behav. 1976, 4, 591-599.

6710. Sofia,R.D. and Knobloch,L.C. "Influence of acute pretreatment with delta-9-tetrahydrocannabinol on the LD_{50} of various substances that alter neurohumoral transmission." Toxicol. Appl. Pharmacol. 1974, 28, 227-234.

6711. Sofia,R.D. and Knobloch,L.C. "The effect of delta-9-tetrahydrocannabinol pretreatment on ketamine thiopental or CT-1341-induced loss of righting reflex in mice." Arch. Internat'l. Pharmacodyn. Ther. 1974, 207, 270-281.

6712. Sofia,R.D. and Knobloch,L.C. "The interaction of delta-9-tetrahydrocannabinol pretreatment with various sedative-hypnotic drugs." Psychopharmacol. 1973, 30, 185-194.

6713. Sofia,R.D., Knobloch,L.C., and Vassar,H. "The anti-edema activity of various naturally occurring cannabinoids." Res. Commun. Chem. Pathol. Pharmacol. 1973, 6, 909-918.

6714. Sofia,R.D., Kubena,R.K., and Barry,H. "Comparison among four vehicles and four routes of administering delta-9-tetrahydrocannabinol." J. Pharmaceut. Sci. 1974, 63, 939-941.

6715. Sofia,R.D., Kubena,R.K., and Barry,H. "Comparison of four vehicles for intraperitoneal administration of delta-1-tetrahydrocannabinol." J. Pharm. Pharmacol. 1971, 23, 889-891.

6716. Sofia,R.D., Kubena,R.K., and Barry,H. "Inactivity of delta-9-tetrahydrocannabinol in antidepressant screening tests." Psychopharmacol. 1973, 31, 121-130.

6717. Sofia,R.D., Nalepa,S.D., Harakal,J.J., and Vassar,H.B. "Anti-edema and analgesic properties of delta-9-tetrahydrocananbinol(THC)." J. Pharmacol. Exper. Ther. 1973, 186, 646-665.

6718. Sofia,R.D., Nalepa,S.D., Vassar,H.B., and Knobloch,L.C. "Comparative anti-phlogistic activity of delta-9-tetrahydrocannabinol, hydrocortisone and aspirin in various rat paw edema models." Life Sci. 1974, 15, 251-260.

6719. Sofia,R.D. and Segelman,A.B. "Marihuana: Chemical basis for increased potency related to a novel method of use." Lloydia 1973, 36, 437.

6720. Sofia,R.D., Solomon,T.A., and Barry,H. "Anticonvulsant activity of delta-9-tetrahydrocananbinol compared with three other drugs." Eur. J. Pharmacol. 1976, 35, 7-16.

6721. Sofia,R.D., Solomon,T.A., and Barry,H. "The anticonvulsant activity of delta-1-tetrahydrocannabinol in mice." Pharmacologist 1971, 13, 246.

6722. Sofia,R.D., Vassar,H.B., and Knobloch,L.C. "Comparative analgesic activity of various naturally occurring cannabinoids in mice and rats." Psychopharmacol. 1975, 40, 285-295.

6723. Soldan,J. "Therapeutic effects in stomatology after cannabis indica application."(Czech.). Act. Univ. Palack. Olomuc. 1955, 6, 73-78.

6724. Soler,M. "Of cannabis and the courts: A critical examination of constitutional challenges to statutory marihuana prohibition." Conn. Law Rev. 1974, 6, 601-723.

6725. Solms,H. "Drug use among the young; successes and failures of preventative efforts."(Fr.). Paper presented at Internat'l. Inst. on Prevention and Treatment of Drug Dependence, Lausanne, Switzerland, 1970.

6726. Solms,H. "Drugs and youth."(Fr.). Reeducation 1969, 24, 61-72.

6727. Solms,H. "Drugs and youth: successful and unsuccessful preventative attempts (problems set by techniques of information."(Fr.). Praxis 1971, 60, 145-148.

6728. Solomon,D. "The marihuana myths." In Solomon,D.(ed.). The Marihuana Papers. Bobbs-Merrill, Indianapolis, 1966, xiii-xxi.

6729. Solomon,D.(ed.). The Marihuana Papers. Bobbs-Merrill, Indianapolis, 1966.

6730. Solomon,J., Cocchia,M.A., and DiMartino,R. "Effect of delta-9-tetrahydrocannabinol on uterine and vaginal cytology of ovariectomized rats." Science 1977, 195, 875-877.

6731. Solomon,J., Cocchia,M.A., Gray,R., Shattuck,D., and Vossmer,A. "Uterotrophic effect of delta-9-tetrahydrocannabinol in ovariectomized rats." Science 1976, 192, 559-561.

6732. Solomon,J. and Shattuck,D. "Marihuana and sex." N. Eng. J. Med. 1974, 291, 309.

6733. Solomon,P. "Medical management of drug dependence." J.A.M.A. 1968, 206, 1521-1526.

6734. Solomon,R. "Analysis of public marihuana policy." Soc. Casework 1972, 53, 19-29.

6735. Solursh,L.P. "Hallucinogenic drug reactions." Med. Trial Tech. Quart. 1969, 16, 1-6.

6736. Solursh,L.P. and Clement,W.R. "Hallucinogenic drug abuse: Manifestations and management." Can. Med. Assoc. J. 1968, 98, 407-410.

6737. Solursh,L.P., Weinstock,S.J., Saunders,C.S., and Ungerleider,J.T. "Attitudes of medical students toward cannabis." J.A.M.A. 1971, 217, 1371-1372.

6738. Somekh,D. "Prevalence of self-reported drug use among London undergraduates." Br. J. Addict. 1976, 71, 79-88.

6739. Somekh,D. "Use of drugs other than cannabis and attitudes to drug use in UK student populations." In Connell,P.H. and Dorn,N.(eds.). Cannabis and Man. Churchill Livingstone, Edinburgh, 1975, 145-156.

6740. Song,C.H., Kanter,S.L., and Hollister,L.E. "Extraction and gas chromatographic quantification of tetrahydrocannabinol from marihuana." Res. Commun. Chem. Pathol. Pharmacol. 1970, 1, 375-382.

6741. Sonnereich,C., and Goes,J.F. "Marihuana and mental disturbances."(Sp.). Neurobiologia 1962, 25, 69-91.

6742. Sonnenreich,M.R., Roccograndi,A.J., and Bogomolny,R.L. "Commentary on the Federal Controlled Substances Act." In National Commission on Marihuana and Drug Abuse. Drug Use in America: Problem in Perspective. Gov't. Print. Office. Washington, D.C., 1973, III, 169-239.

6743. Sorenson,D.P. "Student attitudes, judgments, usage and personal characteristics with regard to marihuana and LSD at Univ. N. Colorado." Diss. Abs. 1971, 31, 4268-4269.

6744. Sorfleet,P. "Dealing hashish: Sociological notes on trafficking and use." Can. J. Criminol. 1976, 18, 123-151.

6745. Soria,J. "Vice as a psychiatric infirmity." (Sp.). Act. Luso Espagnol. Neurol. Psiquiat. 1967, 147, 377-385.

6746. Soroka,V.P. "Female sterility in hemp (cannabis sativa L.)."(Rus.). Tsitol. Genet. 1974, 8, 448-449.

6747. Soroka,V.P. and Zhatova,O.H. "Structure of the styles in female hemp(cannabis sativa L.) flowers and growth of pollen tubules."(Ukr.). Ukran. Bot. Zh. 1971, 28, 61-65.

6748. Soueif,M.I. "Cannabis ideology: A study of opinions and beliefs centering around cannabis consumption." Bull. Narc. 1973, 25, 33-37.

6749. Soueif,M.I. "Cannabis type dependence: The psychology of chronic heavy consumption." Ann. N. Y. Acad. Sci. 1976, 282, 121-125.

6750. Soueif,M.I. "Chronic cannabis takers: Some temperamental characteristics." Drug Alcohol Depend. 1975, 1, 125-154.

6751. Soueif,M.I. "Chronic cannabis users; Further analysis of objective test results." Bull. Narc. 1975, 27, 1-25.

6752. Soueif,M.I. "Differential association between chronic cannabis use and brain function deficits." Ann. N. Y. Acad. Sci. 1976, 282, 323-343.

6753. Soueif,M.I. "Hashish consumption in Egypt, with special reference to psychosocial aspects." Bull. Narc. 1967, 19, 1-11.

6754. Soueif,M.I. "Psychomotor and cognitive deficits associated with long- and short-term cannabis consumption: Comparison of research findings and discussion of selected extrapolations." In Connell,P.H. and Dorn,N. (eds.). Cannabis and Man. Churchill Livingstone, Edinburgh, 1975, 25-45.

6755. Soueif,M.I. "Some determinants of psychological deficits associated with chronic cannabis consumption." Bull. Narc. 1976, 28, 25-42.

6756. Soueif,M.I. "The social psychology of cannabis consumption: Myth, mystery and fact." Bull. Narc. 1972, 24, 1-10.

6757. Soueif,M.I. "The use of cannabis in Egypt: A behavioral study." Bull. Narc. 1971, 23, 17-27.

6758. Southall,M. "Indian hemp from India and Greece."(Fr.). Nouv. Rem. 1912, 28, 141.

6759. Southern,T. Red-dirt Marihuana and Other Tastes. Signet, N.Y., 1968.

6760. Sapladon,E. and Laskos,J. "Effect of row space on yield of hemp seed."(Czech.). Polnohospodarstvo 1962, 9, 165-172.

6761. Spaldon,E. and Laskov,J. "Influence of hoeing on yield of hemp seed."(Czech.). Polnohospodarstvo 1959, 6, 811-822.

6762. Spandon,E. and Laskov,J. "Influence of sowing depth on quantity and quality of hemp stems and fibers."(Czech.). Polnohospodarstvo 1959, 6, 647-660.

6763. Sparber,S.B. "Marihuana. What type of problem?" Minn. Med. 1973, 56, 197-200.

6764. Sparks,W. "Narcotics and the law." Commonwealth 1971, 74, 467-469.

6765. Spaulding,T.C. "Investigation into the cannabinoid antagonistic effect and pharmacological activity of phenitrone." Diss. Abs. 1973, 34, 2212.

6766. Spaulding,T.C. and Dewey,W. L. "Interaction of the behaviorally active drug, phenitrone, a purported hashish and LSD antagonist, with several central neurochemical systems." Fed. Proc. 1973, 32, 755.

6767. Spaulding,T.C. and Dewey,W.L. "Some effects of the behaviorally active drug, phenitrone, a purported hashish and LSD antagonist, on brain noradrenergic and serotonergic systems." Res. Commun. Chem. Pathol. Pharmacol. 1975, 11, 503-506.

6768. Spaulding,T.C. and Dewey,W.L. "The effects of phenitrone, a reported hashish antagonist, on the overt behavior of cats." Res. Commun. Chem. Pathol. Pharmacol. 1974, 7, 347-352.

6769. Spaulding,T.C., Dewey,W.L., and Harris,L.S. "The pharmacological effects of and the lack of delta-9-tetrahydrocannabinol blocking activity in phenitrone." Pharmacologist 1971, 13, 296.

6770. Spaulding,T.C., Ford,R.D., Dewey,W.L., McMillan,D.E., and Harris,L.S. "Some pharmacological effects of phenitrone and its interaction with delta-9-THC. Eur. J. Pharmacol. 1972, 19, 310-317.

6771. Spector,M. "Actute vestibular effects of marihuana." J. Clin. Pharmacol. 1973, 13, 214-217.

6772. Spector,M. "Chronic vestibular and auditory effects of marihuana." Laryngoscope 1974, 84, 816-820.

6773. Speight,W.L. "Dagga." Pharmaceut. J. Pharmacist 1932, 128, 372.

6774. Spencer,D.J. "Cannabis induced psychosis." Br. J. Addict. 1970, 65, 369-372.

6775. Spencer,D.J. "Cannabis induced psychosis." Internat'l. J. Addict. 1971, 6, 323-326.

6776. Spencer,D.J. "Cannabis induced psychosis." West. Ind. Med. J. 1970, 19, 228-230.

6777. Spencer,R.R. "Marihuana." Hlth. Officer 1936, 1, 299-305.

6778. Spencer,S. "Marihuana." Br. Med. J. 1967, 2, 444.

6779. Spencer,S.M. "Marihuana: How dangerous is it?" Reader's Dig. 1970, 96, 67-71.

6780. Spengler,R. "On hashish and opium."(Ger.). Deut. Med. Woch. 1927, 53, 1357-1358.

6781. Sperling,A. "Analysis of hallucinogenic drugs." J. Chromatog. Sci. 1972, 10, 268-275.

6782. Sperling,F. and Coker,A. "Responses of isolated rat lungs to delta-9-tetrahydrocannabinol." Fed. Proc. 1972, 31, 505.

6783. Spevack,M. "Nonmedical drug use by high school students: A three-year survey study." Internat'l. J. Addict. 1976, 11, 755-792.

6784. Spille,D. and Gruski,R. "Long term use of drugs and personality traits: an empirical observation." (Ger.). Zeit. Sozialpsychol. 1975, 6, 31-42.

6785. Spin,F.P. "Marihuana." J.A.M.A. 1972, 222, 1424.

6786. Spock,B. "My view of drug use and drug abuse." Redbook 1971, 136, 29.

6787. Spock,B. "Preventing drug abuse in children." Redbook 1971, 137, 36.

6788. Sprague,G. and Craigmill,A. "Behavioral and metabolic interaction of propylene glycol vehicle and delta-9-tetrahydrocannabinol." Res. Commun. Chem. Pathol. Pharmacol. 1976, 14, 739-742.

6789. Sprague,G.L. and Craigmill,A.L. "Development of cross-tolerance between delta-9-tetrahydrocannabinol and ethanol." Pharmacologist 1975, 17, 130.

6790. Sprague,G.L. and Craigmill,A.L. "Ethanol and delta-9-tetrahydrocannabinol: Mechanism for cross-tolerance in mice." Pharmacol. Biochem. Behav. 1976, 5, 409-415.

6791. Sprague,R.A., Rosenkrantz,H., and Braude,M.C. "Cannabinoid effects on liver glycogen stores." Life. Sci. 1973, 12, 409-416.

6792. Sprague,R.A., Rosenkrantz,H., Thompson,G.R., and Braude,M.C. "Monkey brain and lung respiration after chronic i.v. treatment with delta-9-tetrahydrocannabinol." Fed. Proc. 1972, 31, 909.

6793. Spratto,G.R. "A statement concerning the use of marihuana." J. Sch. Hlth. 1972, 42, 213.

6794. Spronck,H.J.W., and Lousberg,R.J.J.C. "Pyrolysis of cannabidiol. Structure elucidation of a major pyrolytic conversion product." Exper. 1977, 33, 705-706.

6795. Squibb,E.R. "The green color of cannabis indica extract not due to the presence of copper." Ther. Gaz. 1884, 8, 576.

6796. Squibb,E.R., Squibb,E.H., and Squibb,C.F. "Copper as the cause of the green color in preparations of cannabis indica." Ephemeris 1884, 2, 647-653.

6797. St. Angelo,A.J., Conkerton,E.J., Dechary,J.M., and Altschul,A.M. "Modification of edestin(globulin of hemp seed, cannabis sativa) with N-carboxy-D,L-alanine anhydride." Biochim. Biophys. Act. 1966, 121, 181.

6798. St. Angelo,A.J., Ory,R.L., and Hansen,H.J. "Localization of an acid proteinase in hempseed." Phytochemistry 1969, 8, 1135-1138.

6799. St. Angelo,A.J., Ory,R.L., and Hansen,J.J. "Purification of acid proteinase from cannabis sativa L." Phytochemistry 1969, 8, 1873-1877.

6800. St. Angelo,A.J., Yatsu,L.Y., and Altschul,A.M. "Isolation of edestin from aleurone grains of cannabis sativa." Arch. Biochem. Biophys. 1968, 124, 199-205.

6801. St. Charles,A.J. The Narcotic Menace. Borden, Los Angeles, 1952.

6802. St. Clair,J.D. "Commonwealth v. Leis and Weiss: The case against marihuana." Suffolk Univ. Law Rev. 1968, 3, 42-54.

6803. St. John's,A.R. "Walking on air." Hearst's Internat'l. Cosmopol. 1938, 104, 36-39, 103-110.

6804. Stadnicki,S.W., Schaeppi,U., Rosenkrantz,H., and Braude,M.C. "Crude marihuana extract: EEG and behavioral effects of chronic oral administration in rhesus monkeys." Psychopharmacol. 1974, 37, 225-233.

6805. Stadnicki,S.W., Schaeppi,U., Rosenkrantz,H., and Braude,M.C. "Delta-9-tetrahydrocannabinol: Subcortical spike bursts and motor manifestations in a Fischer rat treated orally for 109 days." Life Sci. 1974, 14, 463-472.

6806. Stafford,P. and Eisner,B. "Who turned on whom." High Times 1977, 26, 41-46, 70-72.

6807. Stafford-Clark,D. "A case for cannabis." Br. Med. J. 1967, 3, 435.

6808. Stahl,E. and Kunke,R. "New constituents in the essential oil of cannabis sativa."(Ger.). Tetrahed. Lett. 1973, 30, 2841-2844.

6809. Stahl,E. and Kunke,R. "Principal substances guiding the dog in searching for hashish."(Ger.). Kriminalistik 1973, 27, 385-389.

6810. Stahl,W. "On hashish, history and effectiveness." "(Ger.). Zahnarzl. Prax. 1967, 18, 232.

6811. Stanford,E. Economic Plants. Appleton Century, N.Y., 1934.

6812. Stang,H.J. "Use and abuse of euphoric substances among conscripts at the Oslo sessions of 1969." (Nor.). Tid. Nor. Laegeforen. 1970, 90, 1549-1556.

6813. Stanley,E. "Marihuana as a developer of criminals." Am. J. Pol. Sci. 1931, 2, 252-261.

6814. Stannard,L.J., de Witt,J.R., and Vance,T.C. "The marihuana thrips, Oxythrips cannabensis, a new record for Illinois and North America." Trans. Ill. State Acad. Sci. 1970, 63, 152-156.

6815. Stanton,A.H. "Drug use among adolescents." Am. J. Psychiat. 1966, 122, 1282-1283.

6816. Stanton,M.D. "Dr. Stanton replies." Am. J. Psychiat. 1973, 130, 1400.

6817. Stanton,M.D. "Drug use in Vietnam." Arch. Gen. Psychiat. 1972, 26, 279-286.

6818. Stanton,M.D. "Drug use surveys: Method and madness." Internat'l. J. Addict. 1977, 12, 95-119.

6819. Stanton,M.D. and Bardoni,A. "Drug flashbacks: Reported frequency in a military population." Am. J. Psychiat. 1972, 129, 751-755.

6820. Stanton,M.D. and Mintz,J. "Drug flashbacks. II. Some additional findings." Internat'l. J. Addict. 1976, 11, 53-69.

6821. Stanwood,E. "Flax, hemp and jute products." Wash. Census Rep. 1902, 9, 235-242.

6822. State of California. A First Report of the Impact of California's New Marihuana Law (SB 95). State Capitol, Sacremento, 1977.

6823. Stauth,C. "Developing a new policy on campus drugs." Coll. Mgt. 1970, 5, 15-16.

6824. Steadward,R.D. "The effects of smoking marihuana on physical performance." Med. Sci. Sports 1975, 7, 309-311.

6825. Stearn,J. Drugs and the New Generation. Doubleday, Garden City, N.Y., 1969.

6826. Stearn,W.T. "The cannabis plant: Botanical characteristics." In Joyce,C.R.B. and Curry,S.H.(eds.) The Botany and Chemistry of Cannabis. J. and A. Churchill, London, 1970, 1-11.

6827. Stearn,W.T. "Typification of cannabis sativa L." Bot. Mus. Leaf. Harv. Univ. 1974, 23, 329-336.

6828. Stearn,W.T. "Typification of cannabis sativa L." In Rubin,V.(ed.). Cannabis and Culture. Mouton, The Hague, 1975, 13-21.

6829. Steckler,A. "Marihuana as a socio-political issue: Attitudes of officials in a selected community." J. Drug Educat. 1973, 3, 85-93.

6830. Steege,A. "Note on Arab hashish."(Ger.). Rep. Pharm. 1845, 87, 228-231.

6831. Stefanis,C., Ballas,C., and Madianou,D. "Sociocultural and epidemiological aspects of hashish use in Greece." In Rubin,V.(ed.). Cannabis and Culture. Mouton, The Hague, 1975, 303-327.

6832. Stefanis,C., Boulougouris,A., Kiakos,A., Panayiotopoulos,C., and Kokkevis,A. "Studies of chronic hashish users." Psychopharmacol. 1972, 26, 128.

6833. Stefanis,C., Boulougouris,J., and Liakos,A. "Clinical and psychophysiological effects of cannabis in long-term users." In Braude,M.C., and Szara,S.(eds.). Pharmacology of Marihuana. Raven Press, N.Y., 1976, 659-667.

6834. Stefanis,C.N. and Issidorides,M.R. "Cellular effects of chronic cannabis use in man." InNahas,G.G., Paton,W.D.M., Idanpaan-Heikkila,J.E.(eds.). Marihuana. Springer Verlag, N.Y., 1976, 533-551.

6835. Stefanis,C., Liakos,A., and Boulougouris,J.C. "Incidence of mental illness in hashish users and controls." Ann. N. Y. Acad. Sci. 1976, 282, 58-63.

6836. Stefanis,C., Liakos,A., Boulougouris,J., Fink,M., and Freedman,A.M. "Chronic hashish use and mental disorder." Am. J. Psychiat. 1976, 133, 255-227.

6837. Steffenhagen,R.A., McAree,C.P., and Persing, B.C. "Socio-demographic variables associated with drug use at a New England College." Internat'l. J. Soc. Psychiat. 1971, 17, 277-286.

6838. Steffhagen,R.A., McAree,C.P., and Zheutlin,L.S. "Social and academic factors associated with drug use on the University of Vermont campus." Internat'l. J. Soc. Psychiat. 1969, 15, 92-96.

6839. Steffanhagen,R.A., McAree,C.P., and Zheutlin,L.S. "Some social factors in college drug usage." Internat'l. J. Soc. Psychiat. 1969, 15, 97-101.

6840. Stein,A. and Kahn,M. "Attitudes and characteristics of non users." Paper presented at Southwest. Psychol. Assoc., Atlanta, 1972.

6841. Stein,B., Laessig,R.H., and Indriksons,A. "An evaluation of drug testing procedures used by forensic laboratories and the qualifications of their analysis." Wisconsin Law Rev. 1973, 173, 734-774.

6842. Steiner,K. "Hops and hashish."(Ger.). Schweiz. Brau- Rundsch. 1971, 82, 160-161.

6843. Steinigen,M. "Detection and quantitative determination of substances in marihuana and hashish." Pharm. Ztg. 1970, 115, 1939-1943.

6844. Steininger,M.P. "Dogmatism and attitudes." Psychol. Rep. 1972, 30, 151-157.

6845. Steininger,M. and Lesser,H. "Sex and generation differences and similarities in social attitudes." J. Counsel. Psychol. 1974, 21, 459-460.

6846. Stenchever,M.A. "Observations on the cytogenetic effects of marihuana." In Tinklenberg,J.R.(ed.). Marihuana and Health Hazards. Academic Press, N.Y., 1975, 25-31.

6847. Stenchever,M.A. and Allen,M. "The effect of delta-9-tetrahydrocannabinol on the chromosomes of human lymphocytes in vitro." Am. J. Obstet. Gynecol. 1972, 114, 819-821.

6848. Stenchever,M.A., Kunysz,T.J., and Allen,M. "Chromosome breakage in users of marihuana." Am. J. Obstet. Gynecol. 1974, 118, 106-113.

6849. Stenchever,M.A., Parks,K.J., and Stenchever,M. "Effects of delta-8-tetrahydrocannabinol, delta-9-tetrahydrocannabinol, and crude marihuana on human cells in tissue culture." In Nahas,G.G., Paton,W.D.M., and Idanpaan-Heikkila,J.E.(eds.). Marihuana. Springer Verlag, N.Y., 1976, 257-265.

6850. Stenmark,D.E. "Demographic and personality predictors of hallucinogen use among college males." Unpub. report, U. South Carolina, 1975.

6851. Stenszky,E., Kelentey,B., and Czollner,F. "The pharmacology of crystalline cannabidiols."(Ger.). Act. Physiol. Acad. Sci. Hung. 1961, 18, 76.

6852. Stepanov,G.S. "Inheritability of basic productive substances and expected yield from populations of different types of interspecies hemp hybrids."(Rus.). Tsitol. Genet. 1976, 10, 458-461.

6853. Stepanov,G.S. "Matching varieties of hemp when choosing heterosis."(Rus.). Tsitol. Genet. 1974, 8, 441-444.

6854. Stepanov,G.S. "Relationship between crossing type and character on variability and hereditability of plant height in populations of intervarietal hemp hybrids."(Rus.). Tsitol. Genet. 1975, 10, 326-330.

6855. Stepanova,I.V. "Lipid fatty acid content in new varieties of hemp."(Rus.). Biokhim. Mikrob. 1973, 9, 323-325.

6856. Stephan,J. "Stimulation attempts with cannabis sativa."(Ger.). Faser Frosch. 1928, 7, 292-298.

6857. Stephens,C.R. "Marihuana and society." Southwest. Med. 1970, 51, 177-179.

6858. Stephenson,N.L., Boudewyns,P., and Lessing,R.A. "Long-term effects of peer group confrontation therapy with polydrug abusers." J. Drug. Iss. 1977, 7, 135-150.

6859. Sterba,J. "The politics of pot." Esquire 1968, 58-61, 118-119.

6860. Sterling-Smith,R.S. "Alcohol, marihuana and other drug patterns among operators involved in fatal motor vehicle accidents." In Israelstam,S. and Lambert,S.(eds.). Alcohol, Drugs, and Traffic Safety. Addiction Res. Found., Toronto, 1975, 93-105.

6861. Stern,G. "Marihuana and the law: Will the real issues please stand up." Criminol. 1973, 11, 275-282.

6862. Stern,G. "Reforming marihuana laws." Am. Bar Assoc. J. 1972, 58, 727-730.

6863. Sterne,J. and Ducastaing,C. "Cannabis indica and arteritis."(Fr.). Arch. Mal. Coeur. 1960, 53, 143-147.

6864. Sterne,J. and Ducastaing,C. "Arteritis from cannabis indica."(Fr.). Maroc Med. 1960, 39, 819-822.

6865. Sterne,J. and Ducastaing,C. "Arteritis from cannabis indica."(Fr.). Rev. Atheroscler. 1960, 53, 143-147.

6866. Stevens,G.R. "From the outposts; the king's writ." Blackwood's Mag. 1944, 255, 423-426.

6867. Stevens,M. How to Grow Marihuana Indoors Under Lights. And/Or Press, Berkeley, Cal., 1974.

6868. Stewart,H., Gibbens,T.C.N., and Howard,A. "Drugs and delinquency." Medioleg. J. 1965, 33, 56-71.

6869. Sticker,G. "On the action of cannabinon." (Ger.). Deut. Med. Woch. 1885, 11, 825.

6870. Stillman,R., Eich,J.E., Weingartner,H., and Wyatt,R.J. "Marihuana-induced state-dependent amnesia and its reversal by cueing." In Braude,M.C. and Szara,S.(eds.). Pharmacology of Marihuana. Raven Press, N.Y., 1976, 453-457.

6871. Stillman,R., Galanter,M., Lemberger,L., Fox,S., Weingartner,H., and Wyatt,R.J. "Tetrahydrocannabinol(THC): metabolism and subjective effects." Life Sci. 1976, 19, 569-576.

6872. Stillman,R.C., Weingartner,H., Wyatt,R.J., Gillin,J.C., and Eich,J. "State-dependent (dissociative) effects of marihuana on human memory." Arch. Gen. Psychiat. 1974, 31, 81-85.

6873. Stockberger,W.W. "Drug plants under cultivation. Cannabis." Farmer's Bull. 1915, 663, 24-25.

6874. Stockings,G.T. "A new euphoriant for depressive mental states." Br. Med. J. 1947, 1, 918-922.

6875. Stockwell,D.M., Dechary,J.M., and Altschul,A.M. "Chromatography of edestin from cannabis sativa at 50 degrees." Biochim. Biophys. Act. 1964, 82, 221-

6876. Stockwell,G.A. "Indian hemp(Cannabis indica seu sativa)." Pharmaceut. Era 1898, 20, 8-10.

6877. Stoelting,R.K., Martz,R.C., Gartner,J., Creasser,C., Brown,D.J., and Forney,R.B. "Effects of delta-9-tetrahydrocannabinol on halothane MAC in dogs." Anesthesiology 1973, 38, 521-534.

6878. Stokes,J. "Marihuana." J.A.M.A. 1972, 222, 1424.

6879. Stoller,K. "Effects on visual tracking of delta-9-tetrahydrocannabinol and pentobarbital." J. Clin. Pharmacol. 1976, 16, 271-275.

6880. Stone,C.I. and Shute,R.E. "Persuader sex differences and peer pressure effects on attitudes toward drug abuse." Am. J. Drug Alcohol Abuse 1977, 4, 55-64.

6881. Stone,C.J., McCoy,D.J., and Forney,R.B. "Combined effect of methaqualone and two cannabinoids." J. Forens. Sci. 1976, 21, 108-111.

6882. Stone,H.M. "An investigation into forensic chemical problems associated with cannabis." U.N. Doc. ST/SOA/SER.S/18, Aug. 12, 1969.

6883. Stone,H.M. and Stevens,H.M. "Detection of cannabis constituents in the mouth and on the fingers of smokers." J. Forens. Sci. Soc. 1969, 9, 31-34.

6884. Stone Mountain. Pot Art: Marihuana Reading Matter. Apocrypha Books, Tucson, Ariz., 1972.

6885. Storr,A. "Marihuana and alcohol." In Andrews,G. and Vinkenoog,S.(eds.). The Book of Grass. Grove Press, N.Y., 1967, 234-235.

6886. Strahilevitz,M., Kelly,K.A., Tsui,P.T., Sehon,A.H., and Bliss,M. "Blocking of the effect of delta-1-tetrahydrocannabinol on spontaneous motor activity in the rat by immunization with a protein conjugate of delta-1-THC." Life Sci. 1975, 14, 1975-1989.

6887. Straight,R., Wayne,A.W., Lewis,E.G., and Beck, E.C. "Marihuana extraction and purification for oral administration of known amounts of delta-9-tetrahydrocannabinol." Biochem. Med. 1973, 8, 41-44.

6888. Strange,W. "Cannabis indica: As a medicine and as a poison." Br. Med. J. 1883, 2, 14.

6889. Stratman,D. "Economy of crime: a new approach to the study of marihuana and other illegal substances."(It.). Quad. Criminol. Clin. 1971, 13, 285-301.

6890. Straub,W. "Bavarian hashish."(Ger.). Munch. Med. Woch. 1928, 75, 49-51.

6891. Straub,W. "Intoxication drugs." Stanford Univ. Pub. Med. Sci. Ser. 1931, 3, 1.

6892. Street,H.V. "Identification of drugs by a combination of gas liquid, paper and thin-layer chromatography." J. Chromatog. 1970, 48, 291-294.

6893. Street,H. "Searching without a warrant." New Soc. 1967, 10, 701-702.

6894. Steit,F. and Oliver,H.G. "The child's perception of his family and its relationship to drug use." Drug Forum 1972, 1, 283-289.

6895. Steit,F., Oliver,H.G., and Boher,A.M. "The relationship between drug use and perceived ability in the schools." Drug Forum 1973, 2, 299-308.

6896. Strimbu,J.L., Schoenfeldt,L.F., and Sims,O.S. "Drug usage in college students as a function of social classification and minority group status." Res. High. Educat. 1973, 1, 263-272.

6897. Strimbu,J.L., Schoenfeldt,L.F., and Sims,O.S. "Sex differences in college student drug use." J. Coll. Stud. Person. 1973, 14, 507-510.

6898. Strimbu,J.L., Sims,O.S., and Schoenfeldt,L.E. "College student drug use as a function of place of residence." J. Coll. Univ. Hous. 1973, 3, 38-31.

6899. Stringaris,M.G. "Clinic aspects of hashish-pscyhoses. (Studies in Greece.)."(Ger.). Archiv. Psychiat. Nervenkrancheit. 1933, 100, 522-532.

6900. Stringaris,M.G. Hashish.(Ger.). Saliveros, Athens, 1937.

6901. Stringaris,M.G. Hashish.(Ger.). Springer Verlag, Berlin, 1972.

6902. Stringaris,M.G. The Hashish Habit.(Ger.). J. Springer, Berlin, 1939.

6903. Stromberg,L.E. "Minor components of cannabis resin. I. Their separation by gas chromatography, thermal stability, and protolytic properties." J. Chromatog. 1971, 63, 391-396.

6904. Stromberg,L. "Minor components of cannabis resin. II. Separation by gas chromatography, mass spectra, and molecular weights of some components with shorter retention times than cannabidiol." J. Chromatog. 1972, 68, 248-252.

6905. Stromberg,L. "Minor components of cannabis resin. III. Comparative gas-chromatographic analysis of hashish." J. Chromatog. 1972, 68, 253-258.

6906. Stromberg,L. "Minor components of cannabis resin. IV. Mass spectrometric data and gas chromatographic retention times of terpenic components with retention times shorter than that of cannabidiol." J. Chromatog. 1974, 96, 99-114.

6907. Stromberg,L. "Minor components of cannabis resin. V. Mass spectrometric data and gas chromatographic retention times of cannabinoid compnents with retention times shorter than that of cannabidiol." J. Chromatog. 1974, 96, 179-187.

6908. Stromberg,L. "Minor components of cannabis resin. VI. Mass spectrometric data and gas chromatographic retention times of components eluted after cannabinol." J. Chromatog. 1976, 96, 313-322.

6909. Stroup,R.K. "A time for change." In Levin,P.A. (ed.). Contemporary Problems of Drug Abuse. Pub. Sci. Group, Acton, Mass., 1974, 155-166.

6910. Strub,P.J. and Priest,T.B. "Two patterns of establishing trust: The marihuana user." Sociol. Focus 1976, 9, 399-411.

6911. Stuart,K.L. "Ganja(cannabis sativa) review." West Ind. Med. J. 1963, 12, 156-160.

6912. Stuart,R.B. "Penalty for marihuana possession." Contemp. Drug Prob. 1976, 5, 553-563.

6913. Stubing,G. "Hashish and marihuana."(Ger.). Oeffent. Gesundheit 1970, 32, 379-386.

6914. Stungo,E. "Marihuana." Lancet 1963, 2, 1124.

6915. Suarez Castelles,A.J. "Addiction to marihuana--causes and effects."(Sp.). Pol. Sec. Nac. 1946, 16, 118-131.

6916. Subramanian,E. "Colorimetric estimation for narcotic power of hemp drugs." Analyst 1943, 68, 70.

6917. Suchman,E.A. "The 'hang-loose' ethic and the spirit of drug use." J. Hlth. Soc. Behav. 1968, 9, 146-155.

6918. Suckling,C.W. "On the therapeutic value of Indian hemp." Br. Med. J. 1891, 2, 12.

6919. Suffet,F. and Brotman,R. "Female drug use: Some observations." Internat'l. J. Addict. 1976, 11, 19-33.

6920. Sulkowski,A. and Vachon,L. "Side effects of simultaneous alcohol and marihuana use. Clinical and research reports." Am. J. Psychiat. 1977, 134, 691-692.

6921. Sulkowski,A., Vachon,L., and Rich,E.S. "Propranolol effects of acute marihuana intoxication in man." Psychopharmacol. 1977, 52, 47-53.

6922. Sullwald,L. "Hard facts about the dangers of hashish."(Ger.). Jugendschutz 1971, 16, 1-5.

6923. Sumach,A. A Treasury of Hashish. Stoneworks Pub. Co., Toronto, 1976.

6924. Suppan,L. "Hashish." Nat'l. Drug. 1922, 1, 508-512.

6925. Suput,M. "The effect of soil moisture on germination and growth of soybeans, vetch, sunflower, flax, hemp and turnip."(Slav.). Zbornik Rad. Belgrade Univ. Poljo. Fok. 1954, 2, 68-80.

6926. Surridge,T. and Lambert,L.R. A Survey of Drug Use Among Wards Prior to Admission to Training Schools. Ontario Correction Services Dept., Res. Branch, Toronto, 1973.

6927. Susanna,V. "On the biological effects of Indian hemp grown in the experimental station for official plants next to the Botanical Garden in Naples." (It.). Bol. Orto Bot. Reale Univ. Napoli 1936, 13, 83.

6928. Susanna,V. "On the pharmacological effects of Indian hemp grown in the Botanical Garden in Naples." (It.). Bol. Soc. It. Biol. Speriment. 1936, 11, 325-326.

6929. Susanna,V. "On the pharmacological effects of the alcohol and ether extracts of Indian hemp grown in the Botanical Garden of Naples."(It.). Bol. Soc. It. Biol. Speriment. 1948, 24, 668-670.

6930. Susman,R.M. "Drug abuse, congress, and the fact-finding process." Ann. Am. Acad. Polit. Soc. Sci. 1975, 1, 16-26.

6931. Susser,M. "Cerebral atrophy in young cannabis smokers." Lancet 1972, 1, 41-42.

6932. Sustrina,V.E. "Vegetative hybridization of hemp as a means of deriving initial plants for selection." (Rus.). Agrobiologiya 1960, 3, 386-391.

6933. Sutter,J.B. "Are you growing marihuana without knowing it?" Better Homes Gardens 1971, 58, 42.

6934. Swinyard,E.A. "The Marihuana Act." In Goodman,L.S. and Gilman,A.(eds.). The Pharmacological Basis of Therapeutics. MacMillan Co., N.Y., 1970, 1718.

6935. Swisher,J.D. and Warner,R.W. "Drug education: Pushing or preventing?" Peabody J. Educat. 1971, 1, 68-75.

6936. Symons,A.M., Teale,J.D., and Marks,V. "Effect of delta-9-tetrahydrocannabinol on the hypothalamic-pituitary-gonadal system in the maturing male rat." J. Endocrinol. 1976, 68, 43P-44P.

6937. Szara,S. "Clinical pharmacology of cannabis: Scientific and nonscientific constraints." In Braude,M.C. and Szara,S.(eds.). Pharmacology of Marihuana. Raven Press, N.Y., 1976, 1, 27-35.

T

6938. Tadros,C. "The artifical paradise."(Fr.). Praxis 1964, 53, 665-668.

6939. Takeda,K.I. "Active constituents of cannabis." (Jap.). Kagaku Ryoiki 1948, 2, 170-176.

6940. Takahashi,R.N. and Karniol,I.G. "Pharmacological interaction between cannabinol(CBN) and delta-9-tetrahydrocannabinol." Paper presented at 1st Lat. Am. Cong. Psychobiol., Sao Paulo, 1973.

6941. Takahashi,R.N. and Karniol,I.G. "Pharmacological interaction between cannabinol and delta-9-tetrahydrocannabinol." Psychopharmacol. 1975, 41, 277-284.

6942. Takeya,K. and Itokawa,H. "Stereochemistry in oxidation of allylic alcohols by cell-free system of callus induced from cannabis sativa L." Chem. Pharmaceut. Bull. 1977, 25, 1947-1951.

6943. Takman,J. "An epidemiological study of narcotic use among Stockholm adolescents." In Cleghorn, R.A., Moll,R.E., and Roberts,C.A.(eds.). Proceedings of The Third World Congress of Psychiatry. Univ. Toronto Press, 1961, 1, 412-415.

6944. Talbott,J.A. "Emergency management of marihuana psychosis." In Bourne,P.G.(ed.). Actute Drug Abuse Emergencies. Academic Press, N.Y., 1976, 153-161.

6945. Talbott,J.A. "How to recognize and treat 'bad trips' on marihuana." Med. Times 1973, 101, 45-49.

6946. Talbott,J.A. "'Pot reactions'." U.S. Army Vietnam Med. Bull. 1968, 40, 40-41.

6947. Talbott,J.A. and Teague,J.W. "Marihuana psychosis: Acute toxic psychosis associated with the use of cannabis derivatives." J.A.M.A. 1969, 210, 299-302.

6948. Talley,P.J. "Carbohydrate-nitrogen ratios with respect to the sexual expression of hemp." Plant Physiol. 1934, 9, 731-748.

6949. Tamas,F. "The cannabis mania is spreading." (Swed.). Orv. Hetil. 1972, 113, 622-626.

6950. Tamerin,J.S. "Recent increase in adolescent cigarette smoking." Arch. Gen. Psychiat. 1973, 28, 116-119.

6951. Tampier,L. and Linetzky,R. "Cannabinols in smoke and ashes of marihuana."(Sp.). Arch. Biol. Med. Exp. 1973 9, 55-56.

6952. Tampier,L., Linetzky,R., and Mardones,J. "Effect of cannabinols of marihuana on smooth muscle." (Sp.). Arch. Biol. Med. Exp. 1973, 9, 16-19.

6953. Tanner,R.E. "Drug addiction in East Africa." Internat'l. J. Adddict. 1966, 1, 9.

6954. Tannhauser,M. and Izquierdo,I. "Effect of seizures and anticonvulsant agents on hippocampal RNA concentration." Pharmacol. 1974, 11, 139-145.

6955. Tao,C. and Wang,K. "The relic site of 'oath documents' of East Chou at Houma."(Chin.). Wen-wu 1972, 4, 27-71.

6956. Tapper,T.S. "Drug abuse in adolescence." Pediatrics 1969, 44, 1038-1039.

6957. Taqi,S. "A lid on pot." Vista 1971, 6, 14-17.

6958. Taqi,S. "Approbation of drug usage in rock and roll music." Bull. Narc. 1969, 21, 29-35.

6959. Taqi,S. "The drug cinema." Bull. Narc. 1972, 24, 19-28.

6960. Tart,C.T. "Marihuana intoxication: Common experiences." Nature 1970, 226, 701-704.

6961. Tart,C.T. "Marihuana intoxication: Reported effects on sleep and dreams." Paper presented at Assoc. Psychophysiol. Study of Sleep, Santa Fe, 1970.

6962. Tart,C.T. On Being Stoned. Science and Behavior Books, Palo Alto, Cal., 1971.

6963. Tart,C.T. "The effects of marihuana on consciousness." In Tart,C.T.(ed.). Altered State of Consciousness. J. Wiley and Sons, N.Y., 1969, 335-355.

6964. Tart,C.T. "Work with marihuana: II. Sensations." Psychol. Today 1971, 4, 41-44, 66-68.

6965. Tart,C.T. and Crawford,H.J. "Marihuana intoxication: Reported effects on sleep." Psychophysiol. 1970, 7, 348.

6966. Tart,C.T. and Kvstensky,E. "Marihuana intoxication: Feasibility of experiential scaling of level." J. Alt. States Conscious. 1973, 1, 15-21.

6967. Tashkin,D.P., Levisman,J.A., Abbasi,A.S., Shapiro,B.J., and Ellis,N.M. "Short-term effects of smoked marihuana on left ventricular function." Chest 1977, 72, 20-26.

6968. Tashkin,D.P., Reiss,S., Shapiro,B.J., Calvarese,B., Olsen,J.L., and Lodge,J.W. "Bronchial effects of aerosolized delta-9-tetrahydrocannabinol in healthy and asthmatic subjects." Am. Rev. Resp. Dis. 1977, 115, 57-65.

6969. Tashkin,D.P., Shapiro,B.J., and Frank,I.M. "Acute effects of marihuana on airway dynamics in spontaneous and experimentally induced bronchial asthma." In Braude, M.C. and Szara,S.(eds.). Pharmacology of Marihuana. Raven Press, N.Y., 1976, 785-803.

6970. Tashkin,D.P., Shapiro,B.J., and Frank,I.M. "Acute effects of smoked marihuana and oral delta-9-tetrahydrocannabinol: Mechanisms of increased specific airway conductance in asthmatic subjects." Am. Rev. Resp. Dis. 1974, 109, 420-428.

6971. Tashkin,D.P., Shapiro,B.J., and Frank,I.M. "Acute pulmonary physiologic effects of smoked marihuana and oral delta-9-tetrahydrocannabinol in healthy young men." N. Eng. J. Med. 1973, 289, 336-341.

6972. Tashkin,D.P., Shapiro,B.J., Lee,Y.E., and Harper,C.E. "Effects of smoked marihuana in experimentally induced asthma." Am. Rev. Resp. Dis. 1975, 112, 377-386.

6973. Tashkin,D.P., Shapiro,B.J., Lee,E.Y., and Harper,C.E. "Subacute effects of heavy marihuana smoking on pulmonary function in healthy men." N. Eng. J. Med. 1976, 294, 125-129.

6974. Tashkin,D.P., Shapiro,B.J., Ramanna,L., Taplin,G.V., Lee,Y.E., and Harper,C.E. "Chronic effects of heavy marihuana smoking on pulmonary function in healthy young males." In Braude,M.C. and Szara,S.(eds.). Pharmacology of Marihuana. Raven Press, N.Y., 1976, 1, 291-299.

6975. Tashkin,D.P., Shapiro,B., Reiss,S., Olsen,J., and Lodge,J. "Bronchial effects of aerosolized delta-9-tetrahydrocannabinol." In Cohen,S. and Stillman,R.(eds.). Therapeutic Potential of Marihuana. Plenum Press, N.Y., 1976, 97-110.

6976. Tassinari,C. "Effects of marihuana and delta-9-THC at high doses in man." EEG Clin. Neurophysiol. 1973, 34, 760.

6977. Tassinari,C., Ambrosetto,H.G., Peraita-Adrados,M.R., and Gastaut,H. "Neurophysiological effects of high doses of marihuana in man." EEG Clin. Neurol. 1973, 35, 404-405.

6978. Tassinari,C.A., Ambrosetto,G., Peraita-Adrados,M.R., and Gastaut,H. "The neuropsychiatric syndrome of delta-9-THC and cannabis intoxication in naive subjects." In Braude,M.C. and Szara,S.(eds.). Pharmacology of Marihuana. Raven Press, N.Y., 1976, 1, 357-376.

6979. Tassinari,C.A., Peraita-Adrados,M.R., Ambrosetto,G., and Gastaut,H. "Effects of marihuana and delta-9-tetrahydrocannabinol at high doses in man. A polygraphic study." EEG Clin. Neurol. 1974, 36, 94.

6980. Taube-Wun-er,R., Helmer,R., Zellmann,K., and Haesen,D. "Hashish and personality."(Ger.). Deut. Med. Woch. 1973, 98, 214-217.

6981. Tauger,H. "The self-concept as a measure of parent-child relationships among users and non-users of marihuana." Diss. Abs. 1974, 34, 4061.

6982. Tauro,G.J. "Marihuana and relevant problems." Am. Crim. Law Quart. 1969, 7, 174.

6983. Tauro,G.J. "Marihuana and relevant problems." In Healy,P.F. and Manak,J.P.(eds.). Drug Dependence and Abuse Resource Book. Nat'l. District Attorneys Assoc., Chicago, 1971, 224-231.

6984. Tauro,G.J. "Marihuana and the law." In Healy,P.F. and Manak,J.P.(eds.). Drug Dependence and Abuse Resource Book. Nat'l. District Attorneys Assoc., Chicago, 1971, 27-29.

6985. Tayal,G., Gupta,L., Agarwal,S.S., and Arora,R.B. "Effects of cannabis on conditioned avoidance response and brain monoamine oxidase activity in rats." Ind. J. Expt'l. Biol. 1974, 12, 375-376.

6986. Taylor,A. "Test for measuring students' knowledge of marihuana." Measure. Eval. Guid. 1971, 4, 116.

6987. Taylor,A.R. "Marihuana." N. Z. Med. J. 1973, 503, 460.

6988. Taylor,B. A Journey to Central Africa; Or Life and Landscapes from Egypt to the Negro Kingdoms of the White Nile. G.P. Putnam Co., N.Y., 1854.

6989. Taylor,B. "The hasheesh eater." Putnam's Month. Mag. Am. Lit. 1856, 8, 233-239.

6990. Taylor,E.C., Lenard,K., and Loev,B. "Tetrahydrocannabinol analogs. Synthesis of 2-(3-methyl-2-octyl)-3-hydroxy-6,6,9-trimethyl-7,8,9,10-tetrahydrodibenzo (b,d) pyran." Tetrahedron 1967, 23, 77-85.

6991. Taylor,E.C., Lenard,K., and Shvo,Y. "Active constituents of hashish. Synthesis of dl-delta-6-3,4-trans-tetrahydrocannabinol." J. Am. Chem. Soc. 1966, 88, 367-368.

6992. Taylor,E.C. and Strojny,E.J. "The synthesis of some model compounds related to tetrahydrocannabinol." J. Am. Chem. Soc. 1960, 82, 5198-5202.

6993. Taylor,H. "Opinions on marihuana: Sex differences at a western Canadian university." Can. Counsel. 1972, 6, 116-119.

6994. Taylor,N. Narcotics, Nature's Dangerous Gifts. Dell, N.Y., 1963.

6995. Taylor,R.L., Maurer,J.I., and Tinklenberg,J.R. "Management of 'bad trips' in an evolving drug scene." J.A.M.A. 1970, 213, 422-425.

6996. Taylor,S.P., Vardaris,R.M., Rawtich,A.B., Gammon,C.B., Cranston,J.W., and Lubetkin,A.I. "The effect of alcohol and delta-9-tetrahydrocannabinol on human physical aggression." Aggressive Behav. 1976, 2, 153-161.

6997. Taylor,W.J.R. "History and pharmacology of psychedelic drugs." Internat'l. Klin. Pharmakol. Ther. Toxikol. 1971, 5, 51-57.

6998. Teale,D. and Marks,V. "A fatal motor-car and cannabis use. Investigation by radioimmunoassay." Lancet 1976, 1, 884-885.

6999. Teale,J.D., Clough,M., Piall,E.M., King,L.J., and Marks,V. "Plasma cannabinoids measured by radioimmunoassay in rabbits after intravenous injection of tetrahydrocannabinol, 11-hydroxy-tetrahydrocannabinol, cannabinol and cannabidiol." Res. Commun. Chem. Pathol. Pharmacol. 1975, 11, 339-342.

7000. Teale,J.D., Forman,E.J., King,L.J., and Marks,V. "Production of antibodies to tetrahydrocannabinol as the basis for its radioimmunoassay." Nature 1974, 249, 154-155.

7001. Teacle,J.D., King,L.J., Forman,E.J., and Marks,V. "Radioimmunoassay of cannabinoids in blood and urine." Lancet 1974, 2, 553-555.

7002. Teale,J.D., Forman,E.J., King,L.J., and Marks,V. "The development of a radioimmunoassay for tetrahydrocannabinol in plasma." Proc. Soc. Anal. Chem. 1974, 11, 219-220.

7003. Teale,J.D., Forman,E.J., King,L.J., Piall,E.M., and Marks,V. "The development of a radioimmunoassay for cannabinoids in blood and urine." J. Pharm. Pharmacol. 1975, 27, 465-472.

7004. Tec,N. "A clarification of the relationship between alcohol and marihuana." Br. J. Addict. 1973, 68, 191-195.

7005. Tec,N. "Differential involvement with marihuana and its sociocultural context: A study of suburban youths." Internat'l. J. Addict. 1972, 7, 655-669.

7006. Tec,N. "Drugs among suburban teenagers: Basic findings." Soc. Sci. Med. 1971, 5, 77-84.

7007. Tec,N. "Family and differential involvement with marihuana: A study of suburban teenagers." J. Mar. Fam. 1970, 32, 656-664.

7008. Tec,N. Grass Is Green in Suburbia. Libra Pub., Roslyn Heights, N.Y., 1974.

7009. Tec,N. "Marihuana and other illegal drugs." Internat'l. J. Soc. Psychiat. 1975, 20, 173-179.

7010. Tec,N. "Parent-child drug abuse: Generational continuity or adolescent deviancy?" Adolescence 1974, 9, 350-364.

7011. Tec,N. "Parental educational pressure, adolescent educational conformity and marihuana use." Youth Soc. 1973, 4, 291-312.

7012. Tec,N. "Peer group and marihuana use." Crime Delinquency 1972, 18, 298-309.

7013. Tec,N. "Socio-cultural context of marihuana." In Einstein,S. and Allen,S.(eds.). Student Drug Surveys. Baywood Pub. Co., N.Y., 1972, 109-120.

7014. Tec,N. "Some aspects of high school status and differential involvement with marihuana: a study of suburban teenagers." Adolescence 1972, 6, 1-28.

7015. Tecce,R. "Hygiene in the hemp industry."(It.). Fog. Med. 1938, 1, 953-958.

7016. Tecce,R. "Hygiene in the hemp industry, research and observations."(It.). Rass. Med. Appl. Lavor. Indust. 1938, 9, 242-257.

7017. Teevan,J.J. "Deterrent effects of punishment: subjective measures continued." Can. J. Criminol. Correct. 1976, 18, 152-160.

7018. Teff,H. Drugs, Society and the Law. Lexington Books, Lexington, Mass., 1975.

7019. Teigland,J.D. "Marihuana." J. Iowa Med. Soc. 1973, 63, 103-110.

7020. Telligen,P. "Non-conformism and the use of hashish among students."(Dut.). Ned. Tijd. Criminol. 1970, 12, 162, 220.

7021. Tells,A., Asuni,T., Tinubu,K., and Sessi,J. "Indian hemp smoking." Soc. Hlth. Nigeria 1967, 1, 40-50.

7022. Ten Ham,M. "Effects of cannabis roots on the heart." J.A.M.A. 1973, 225, 525.

7023. Ten Ham,M. "Tolerance to the effects of delta-9-THC on shuttlebox performance and body temperature." Pharmacol. Biochem. Behav. 1977, 6, 183-185.

7024. Ten Ham,M. and DeJong,Y. "Absence of interaction between delta-9-tetrahydrocannabinol and cannabidiol (CBD) in aggression, muscle control and body temperature experiments in mice." Psychopharmacol. 1975, 41, 169-174.

7025. Ten Ham,M. and DeJong,Y. "Effects of delta-9-tetrahydrocannabinol and cannabidiol on blood glucose concentrations in rabbits and rats." Pharm. Weekbl. 1975, 110, 1157-1161.

7026. Ten Ham,M. and DeJong,Y. "Tolerance to the hypothermic and aggression-attenuating effect of delta-8- and delta-9-tetrahydrocannabinol in mice." Eur. J. Pharmacol. 1974, 28, 144-148.

7027. Ten Ham,M., den Tonkelaar,E.M., and Koomen,J.M. "Influence of two tetrahydrocannabinols(THCs) on the activity of biotransformation enzymes." Adv. Expt'l. Med. Biol. 1973, 35, 181-194.

7028. Ten Ham,M., den Tonkelaar,E.M., and Koomen,J.M. "Influence of two tetrahydrocannabinols(THCs) on the activity of biotransformation enzymes." In Gross,M.M.(ed.). Alcohol Intoxication and Withdrawal. Plenum Press, N.Y., 1973, 181-194.

7029. Ten Ham,M., Fokkens,J., Housberg,R.J.J., and Bercht,C.A.L. "Effects of cannabis roots on the heart." J.A.M.A. 1973, 225, 525.

7030. Ten Ham,M., Loskota,W.J., and Lomax,P. "Acute and chronic effects of delta-9-tetrahydrocannabinol on seizures in the gerbil." Eur. J. Pharmacol. 1975, 31, 148-152.

7031. Ten Ham,M. and van Noordwijk,J. "Lack of tolerance to the effect of two tetrahydrocannabinols on aggressivenness." Psychopharmacol. 1973, 29, 171-176.

7032. Tennant,F.S. "Dependency traits among parents of drug users." J. Drug Educat. 1976, 6, 83-88.

7033. Tennant,F.S. and Groesbeck,C.J. "Psychiatric effects of hashish." Arch. Gen. Psychiat. 1972, 27, 133-136.

7034. Tennant,F.S., Guerry,R.L., and Henderson,R.L. "Hashish." J.A.M.A. 1971, 217, 1707.

7035. Tennant,F.S., Preble,M., Pendergast,T.J., and Ventry,P. "Medical manifestations associated with hashish." J.A.M.A. 1971, 216, 1965-1969.

7036. Ter Laage,R.J. "Louis Lewin and his ideas of cannabis indica." Pharm. Weekbl. 1969, 104, 839.

7037. Terad,C.W. and Masur,J. "Amphetamine- and apomorphine-induced alteration of the behavior of rats submitted to a competititve situation in a straight runway." Eur. J. Pharmacol. 1973, 24, 375-380.

7038. Teresa,M., Silva,A., Carlini,E.A., Claussen,U., and Korte,F. "Lack of cross-tolerance in rats among (-)-delta-9-trans-tetrahydrocannabinol, cannabis extract, mescaline and lysergic acid diethylamide(LSD-25)." Psychopharmacol. 1968, 13, 332-340.

7039. Terlouw,J.K., Heerma,W., Burgers,P.C., Dijkstra,G., Boon,A., Kramer,H.F., and Salemink,C.A. "The use of metastable ion characteristics for the determination of ion structures of some isomeric cannabinoids." Tetrahedron 1974, 30, 424-448.

7040. Terner,M. "Marihuana: tetrahydrocannabinol and related compounds." Science 1963, 140, 175.

7041. Terrence,C. "'Grass'--the modern tower of Babel." Psychiat. Quart. 1968, 42, 172-174.

7042. . Tewari,S.N., Harpalani,S.P., and Sharma,S.C. "Separation and identification of the constituents of hashish(cannabis indica Linn.) by thin-layer chromatography and its application in forensic analysis." Chromatographia 1974, 7, 205-209.

7043. Tewari,S.N., Harpalani,S.P., and Sharma,S.C. "Separation and identification of the constituents of hashish(cannabis indica Linn.) by thin-layer chromatography and its application in forensic analysis." Mikrochim. Act. 1974, 6, 991-995.

7044. Texas. Court of Criminal Appeals. "Opinions as to smoking of marihuana." J.A.M.A. 1923, 81, 1553-1554.

7045. Texas. Senate Interim Drug Study Committee. Marihuana in Texas: A Report to the Senate Interim Drug Study Committee. Drug Study Committee, Austin, 1972.

7046. Thacore,V.R. "Bhang psychosis." Br. J. Psychiat. 1973, 123, 225-229.

7047. Thacore,V.R. and Shukla,S.R.P. "Cannabis psychosis and paranoid schizophrenia." Arch. Gen. Psychiat. 1976, 33, 383-386.

7048. Thakkar,A.L., Hirsch,C.A., and Page,J.A. "Solid dispersion approach for overcoming bioavailability problems due to polymorphism of nabilone, a cannabinoid derivative." J. Pharm. Pharmacol. 1977, 29, 783-784.

7049. Thaler,S., Fass,P., and Fitzpatrick,D. "Marihuana and hearing." Can. J. Otolaryng. 1973, 2, 291-295.

7050. Theron,F. "Dagga and the law: a sociological perspective." Crime Punish. Correct. 1973, 2, 43-48.

7051. Thoden,J.S., Mosher,R., MacConaill,M., and Ling,G. "Effects of marihuana on treadmill performance." Med. Sci. Sports 1974, 6, 81.

7052. Thomas,C.W., Petersen,D.M., and Zinggraff,M.T. "Student drug use: A re-examination of the 'hang-loose ethic' hypothesis." J. Hlth. Soc. Behav. 1975, 16, 63-73.

7053. Thomas,J.A., Smith,M.T., and Knotts,G.R. "Current assessment of marihuana." J. Sch. Hlth. 1972, 42, 382-384.

7054. Thomas,R. and Chester,G. "The pharmacology of marihuana." Med. J. Aust. 1973, 2, 229-237.

7055. Thomas,R.B., Luber,S.A., and Smith,J.A. "A survey of alcohol and drug use in medical students." Dis. Nerv. Syst. 1977, 38, 41-43.

7056. Thomas,R.J. "The toxicologic and teratologic effects of delta-9-tetrahydrocannabinol in the zebrafish embryo." Toxicol. Appl. Pharmacol. 1975, 32, 184-190.

7057. Thomison,J.B. "On the pursuit of pleasure." Tenn. Med. Assoc. J. 1972, 65, 1031-1032.

7058. Thompson,G. and Yang,C. "Comparative toxicities of tetrahydropyridobenzopyrans. In Cohen,S. and Stillman, R.(eds.). Therapeutic Potential of Marihuana. Plenum Press, N.Y., 1976, 457-474.

7059. Thompson,G.R. and Braude,M.C. "Chronic oral toxicity of cannabinoids in rats." Toxicol. Appl. Pharmacol. 1972, 22, 321.

7060. Thompson,G.R., Fleischman,R.W., Rosenkrantz,H., and Braude,M.C. "Chronic oral toxicity of cannabinoids in monkeys." Toxicol. Appl. Pharmacol. 1974, 29, 77.

7061. Thompson,G.R., Fleischman,R.W., Rosenkrantz,H., and Braude,M.C. "Oral and intravenous toxicity of delta-9-tetrahydrocannabinol in rhesus monkeys." Toxicol. Appl. Pharmacol. 1974, 27, 648-665.

7062. Thompson,G.R., Mason,M.M., Rosenkrantz,H., and Braude,M.C. "Chronic oral toxicity of cannabinoids in rats." Toxicol. Appl. Pharmacol. 1973, 25, 373-389.

7063. Thompson,G.R. and Rosenkrantz,H. "Neurotoxicity of cannabinoids in chronically-treated rats and monkeys." Pharmacologist 1971, 13, 206.

7064. Thompson,G.R., Rosenkrantz,H., Fleischman,R.W., and Braude,M.C. "Effects of delta-9-tetrahydrocannabinol administered subcutaneously to rabbits for 28 days." Toxicology 1975, 4, 41-51.

7065. Thompson,G.R., Rosenkrantz,H., Fleischman,R.W., and Braude,M.C. "Toxicity of delta-9-tetrahydrocannabinol in rhesus monkeys treated per os or intravenous for 28 days." Proc. 5th Internat'l. Cong. Pharmacol. 1972, 1, 232.

7066. Thompson,G.R., Rosenkrantz,H., Schaeppi,U.H., and Braude,M.C. "Comparison of acute oral toxicity of cannabinoids in rats, dogs and monkeys." Toxicol. Appl. Pharmacol. 1973, 25, 363-372.

7067. Thompson,J. "Doctors and cannabis." Med. J. Aust. 1971, 2, 1342-1343.

7068. Thompson,J.H. "Marihuana--Matter over mind?" Irish Phys. Surg. 1971, 1, 4-15.

7069. THompson,L.J. and Proctor,R.C. "The use of pyrahexyl in the treatment of alcoholic and drug withdrawal conditions." N. Carolina Med. J. 1953, 14, 520-523.

7069a. Thompson,L.S. "'Cannabis sativa' and traditions associated with it." Kentucky Folk. Rec. 1972, 18, 1-4.

7069b. Thompson,R.C. The Assyrian Herbal Luzac and Co., London, 1924.

7069c. Thornton,J.I. and Nakamura,G.A. "Chemistry of the constituents and identification of marihuana." J. Forens. Sci. Soc. 1972, 12, 461-519.

7069d. Thorpe,C.B. "Marihuana smoking and value change among college students." Coll. Stud. J. 1975, 9, 9-16.

7069e. Thunberg,C.P. Travels in Europe, Africa and Asia. F. and C. Rivington, London, 1795.

7069f. Thurlow,H.H. "Brief communications and clinical notes. On drive state and cannabis." Can. Psychiat. Assoc. J. 1971, 16, 181-182.

7069g. Tichborne,R. "Tales of Mexico and marihuana (growing and smuggling operations)." Scanlan's Month. 1970, 1, 6-20.

7069h. Tiegland,J.D. "Marihuana." J. Iowa Med. Soc. 1973, 63, 103-110.

7069i. Tiele,P.A. The Voyage of John Huyghen Van Linschoten to the East Indies(1596). Burt Franklin, N.Y., n.d.

7069j. Timmerman,H. and Buikhuiser,W. "Psychological characteristics of schoolchildren using drugs."(Dut.). Ned. Tijd. Criminol. 1970, 12, 196.

7070. Timmons,M.L., Pitt,C.G., and Wall,M.E. "Deuteration and tritiation of delta-8- and delta-9-tetrahydrocannabinol. The use of trifluoroacetic acid and a convenient labelling reagent." Tetrahed. Lett. 1969, 36, 3129-3132.

7071. Tinklenberg,J. "Drugs and crime." In National Commission on Marihuana and Drug Abuse. Drug Use in America: Problem in Perspective. Gov't. Print. Office, Washington, D.C., 1973, I, 242-299.

7072. Tinklenberg,J. "Marihuana and human aggression." In Miller,L.L.(ed.). Marihuana Effects on Human Behavior. Academic Press, N.Y., 1974, 339-357.

7073. Tinklenberg,J. "Societal features of repetitive drug use: A perspective." In National Commission on Marihuana and Drug Abuse. Drug Use in America: Problem in Perspective. Gov't. Print. Office, Washington, D.C., 1973, II, 771-776.

7074. Tinklenberg,J. "What a physician should know about marihuana." Ration. Drug Ther. 1975, 9, 1-6.

7075. Tinklenberg,J. and Darley,C.F. "A model of marihuana's cognitive effects." In Braude,M.C. and Szara,S.(eds.). Pharmacology of Marihuana. Raven Press, N.Y., 1976, 1, 429-440.

7076. Tinklenberg,J. and Darley,C.R. "Psychological and cognitive effects of cannabis." In Connell,P.H. and Dorn,N.(eds.). Cannabis and Man. Churchill Livingstone, Edinburgh, 1975, 45-66.

7077. Tinklenberg,J., Kopell,B.S., Melges,F.T., and Hollister,L.E. "Marihuana and alcohol. Time production and memory functions." Arch. Gen. Psychiat. 1972, 27, 812-815.

7078. Tinklenberg,J., Melges,F.T., and Hollister, L.E. "Marihuana and memory." Psychopharmacol. Bull. 1971, 7, 20.

7079. Tinklenberg,J., Melges,F.T., Hollister,L.E., and Gillespie,H.K. "Marihuana and immediate memory." Nature 1970, 226, 1171-1172.

7080. Tinklenberg,J. and Murphy,P. "Marihuana and crime: A survey report." J. Psyched. Drugs 1972, 5, 183-191.

7081. Tinklenberg,J., Murphy,P.L., Murphy,P., Darley,C.R., Roth,W.T., and Kopell,B.S. "Drug involvement in criminal assaults by adolescents." Arch. Gen. Psychiat. 1974, 30, 685-689.

7082. Tinklenberg,J., Roth,W.T., and Kopell,B.S. "Marihuana and ethanol: Differential effects on time perception, heart rate, and subjective response." Psychopharmacol. 1976, 49, 275-279.

7083. Tinklenberg,J., Roth,W.T., Kopell,B.S., and Murphy,P. "Cannabis and alcohol effects on assaultiveness in adolescent delinquents." Ann. N. Y. Acad. Sci. 1976, 282, 85-94.

7084. Tinklenberg,J. and Woodrow,K.M. "Drug use among youthful assaultive and sexual offenders." In Frazier,S.H.(ed.). Aggression. Williams and Wilkins, Baltimore, 1974, 209-224.

7085. Tirard,N. "Toxic effects of cannabis indica." Lancet 1890, 1, 723.

7086. Titus,H.W. "Oregon marihuana decriminalization. The moral question." J. Drug Iss. 1977, 7, 23-34.

7087. Tobias,E.S. and Margardia,M. Maconha (cannabis sativa) A Chemical Study.(Port.). Serv. Nac. Educ. Sanit. Rio de Janeiro, 1958.

7088. Tobler,W. "On the diuretic principle in cannabis indica."(Ger.). Zeit. Expt'l. Path. Ther. 1916, 18, 91-98.

7089. Todd,A.R. "The Botany and Chemistry of Cannabis." Book review." Chem. Brit. 1971, 7, 304.

7090. Todd,A.R. "Chemistry of the hemp drugs." Nature 1940, 146, 829-830.

7091. Todd,A.R. "Hashish." Exper. 1946, 2, 55-60.

7092. Todd,A.R. "The chemistry of hashish." Sci. J. Roy. Coll. Sci. 1942, 12, 37-45.

7093. Todd,A.R. "The hemp drugs." Endeavor 1943, 2, 69-72.

7094. Todd,J., Goldstein,R., and Whitehouse,A. "Personality and attitudes of British marihuana users." Psychol. Rep. 1977, 40, 990.

7095. Toffoli,F., Avico,U., and Ciranni,E.S. "Methods of distinguishing biologically active cannabis and fiber cannabis." Bull. Narc. 1968, 20, 55-59.

7096. Toit,B.M. "Historical and cultural factors influencing cannabis use among Indians in South Africa." J. Psyched. Drugs 1977, 9, 235-246.

7097. Tompkins,D.C. Drug Addiction, A Bibliography. Bureau Pub. Admin., Univ. Cal., Berkeley, 1961.

7098. Toohey,J.V. "An analysis of drug-use behavior at 5 American universities." J. Sch. Hlth. 1971, 41, 464-468.

7099. Toohey,J.V. "Marihuana--the evidence begins to grow." J. Sch. Hlth. 1968, 38, 302-303.

7100. Tooth,G. Studies in Mental Illness in the Gold Coast. His Magesty's Print. Office, Colonial Research Publications, London, 1950.

7101. Topp,G., Dallmer,J., and Schou,J. "Changes in the metabolism of delta-9-tetrahydrocannabinol caused by other cannabis constituents." In Nahas,G.G., Paton,W.D.M., Idanpaan-Heikkila,J.E.(eds.). Marihuana. Springer Verlag, N.Y., 1976, 187-195.

7102. Toraude,L.G. "Indian and Greek hemp."(Fr.). Rev. Special. 1923, 3, 737-738.

7103. Torenstra,N. "Use and users of hashish and marihuana."(Dut.). Maandbl. Berecht. 1969, 48, 121-127.

7104. Torres,F. "Importance of cannabis addiction in America."(Sp.). Rev. Tecn. Pol. 1955, 1, 11

7105. Torrington,K.E. "The sentencing of drug offenders." J. Drug Iss. 1977, 7, 339-363.

7106. Town,M.A. "Privacy and the marihuana laws." J. Psyched. Drugs 1968, 2, 105-147.

7107. Town,M.A. "The California Marihuana Possession Statute: An infringement on the right of privacy or other peripheral constitutional rights?" J. Psyched. Drugs 1968, 2, 105-147.

7108. Trachtenberg,S.J. and Paper,L.J. "Marihuana: A further view." Fed. Bar J. 1972, 31, 258.

7109. Tran Van Ky,P., Demailly,A., and Muller,P.H. "Toxicological research on hashish."(Fr.). Med. Leg. Dom. Corp. 1970, 3, 245-250.

7110. Traub,S. "Norm patterns among occasional and regular users of marihuana." Proc. Am. Southwest. Sociol. Assoc. 1970, 18, 41.

7111. Traub,S.H. "Perception of marihuana and its effects: A comparison of users and nonusers." Br. J. Addict. 1977, 72, 67-74.

7112. Traub,S.H. "Rural high school student drug use and the effect of 'Summer Jam, 1973' on drug use patterns: The Watkins Glen case." Internat'l. J. Addict. 1977, 12, 583-590.

7113. Treanor,J.J. and Skripol,J.N. "Marihuana in a tactical unit in Vietnam." U.S. Army Vietnam Med. Bull. 1970, 22, 29-37.

7114. Treffert,D.A. "A transactional analysis approach to the marihuana issue." Contemp. Drug Prob. 1973, 2, 393-400.

7115. Treuting,J.J. "The problem of pot. Pharmacology and chemistry." Southwest. Med. 1970, 51, 166-169.

7116. Trevan,J.J. "Deterrent effects of punishment: subjective measures continued." Can. J. Criminol. Correct. 1976, 18, 152-160.

7117. Trevan,J.J. "Subjective perception of deterrence." J. Res. Crime Delinquency 1976, 13, 155-164.

7118. Triesman,D. "Logical problems in contemporary cannabis research." Internat'l. J. Addict. 1973, 8, 667-682.

7119. Trocchi,A. Cain's Book. Grove Press, N.Y., 1961.

7120. Trolle,H. "Non-specific chemical reactions to detect presence of Indian hemp or hashish and its derivatives."(Fr.). Ann. Falsif. Fraude 1932, 25, 273-280.

7121. Trolle,H. "On the Beam test for identification of hashish."(Fr.). Un. Pharmaceut. 1933, 74, 311.

7122. Trout,M.E. "Marihuana today." J. Leg. Med. 1973, 1, 44-46.

7123. True,R.H. and Klugh,G.R. "American-grown cannabis indica." Proc. Am. Pharmaceut. Assoc. 1909, 57, 843-847.

7124. Truitt,E.B. "Biological disposition of tetrahydrocannabinols." Pharmacol. Rev. 1971, 23, 273-278.

7125. Truit,E.B. "Evaluation of an active metabolite hypothesis for 11-hydroxy-tetrahydrocannabinols." Proc. 5th Internat'l. Cong. Pharmacol. 1972, 1, 236.

7126. Truitt,E.B. "Marihuana vs. alcohol: A pharmacologic comparison." In Majchrowicz,E.(ed.). Biochemical Pharmacology of Ethanol. Plenum Press, N.Y., 1975, 291-309.

7127. Truitt,E.B. "Pharmacological activity in a metabolite of 1-trans-delta-8-tetrahydrocannabinol." Fed. Proc. 1970, 29, 619.

7128. Truitt,E.B. and Anderson,S.M. "Biogenic amine alterations produced in the brain by tetrahydrocannabinols and their metabolites." Ann. N. Y. Acad. Sci. 1971, 191, 68-73.

7129. Truitt,E.B. and Anderson,S.M. "The role of biogenic amines in the central action of tetrahydrocannabinols and their metabolites." Act. Pharmaceut. Suec. 1971, 8, 696-697.

7130. Tuitt,E.B. and Braude,M.C. "Preclinical pharmacology of marihuana." In Gibbins,R.J., Israel,Y., Kalant,H., Popham,R.E., Schmidt,W., and Smart,R.G.(eds.). Research Advances in Alcohol and Drug Problems. John Wiley and Sons, N.Y., 1974, 1, 199-242.

7131. Truitt,E.B., Kinzer,G.W., and Berlo,J.M. "Behavioral activity in various fractions of marihuana smoke condensate in the rat." In Braude,M.C. and Szara,S. (eds.). Pharmacology of Marihuana. Raven Press, N.Y., 1976, 2, 463-475.

7132. Tsao,P.N. and Tai,K. "A preliminary study of cannabis sativa or ta-ma-jen." J. Chinese Pharmaceut. Assoc. 1936, 1, 33-37.

7133. Tschirch,A. "On the secretions of certain plants."(Ger.). Pharmazeut. Zentral. 1886, 27, 496.

7134. Tsien,T.H. Written on Bamboo and Silk. Univ. Chicago Press, Chicago, 1962.

7135. Tsui,P.T., Kelly,K.A., Ponipom,M.M., Strahilevitz,M., and Sehon,A.H. "Delta-9-tetrahydrocannabinol-protein conjugates." Can. J. Biochem. 1974, 52, 252-258.

7136. Tucker,A.N. and Friedman,M.A. "Effects of cannabinoids on L1210 murine leukemia. I. Inhibition of DNA synthesis." Res. Commun. Chem. Pathol. Pharmacol. 1977, 17, 703-713.

7137. Tull-Walsh,J.H. "Hemp drugs and insanity." J. Ment. Sci. 1894, 40, 21-36.

7138. Tull-Walsh,J.H. "On insanity produced by the abuse of ganja and other preparations of Indian hemp, with notes of cases." Ind. Med. Gaz. 1894, 29, 333-334.

7139. Tully,A. The Secret War Against Dope. Coward McCann and Geogehan, N.Y., 1973.

7140. Tunney,R. "Marihuana: just how harmless is it?" Seventeen 1968, 27, 138-139.

7141. Tunving,K. "Cannabis: Use and misuse."(Swed.). Lakartidningen 1976, 73, 3867-3872.

7142. Tunving,K. "Psychoses from cannabis--case reports."(Swed.). Lakartidningen 1976, 73, 3872-3873.

7143. Turk,R.F. "The identification, isolation, toxicity, and tissue distribution of delta-9-tetrahydrocannabinol." Diss. Abs. 1970, 31, 2870.

7144. Turk,R.F., Dewey,W.L., and Harris,L.S. "Excretion of trans-delta-9-tetrahydrocannabinol and its metabolites in intact and bile-duct-cannulated rats." J. Pharmaceut. Sci. 1973, 62, 737-740.

7145. Turk,R.F., Dharir,H.I., and Forney,R.B. "A simple chemical method to identify marihuana." J. Forens. Sci. 1969, 14, 389-391.

7146. Turk,R.F., Forney,R.B., King,L.J., and Ramachandran,S. "A method for extraction and chromatographic isolation, purification and identification of tetrahydrocannabinol and other compounds from marihuana." J. Forens. Sci. 1969, 14, 385-388.

7147. Turk,R.F., Forney,R.B., and Ramachandran,S. "Method for extraction and chromatographic isolation, purification and identification of tetrahydrocannabinol and other components from marihuana." Pharmacologist 1968, 10, 173.

7148. Turk,R.F., Manno,J.E., Nain,N.C., and Forney, R.B. "LD_{50} and distribution of pure(99+%) natural tetrahydrocannabinol in rats." Pharmacologist 1969, 11, 280.

7149. Turk,R.F., Manno,J.E., Nain,N.C., and Forney, R.B. "The identification, isolation, and preservation of delta-9-tetrahydrocannabinol." J. Pharm. Pharmacol. 1971, 23, 190-195.

7150. Turk,R.F., Phillips,R.N., Manno,J.E., Nain,N.C., and Forney,R.B. "Separation of marihuana components by gas-liquid chromatography." Toxicol. Appl. Pharmacol. 1970, 17, 313.

7151. Turkanis,S.A., Cely,W., Olsen,D.M., and Karler,R. "Anticonvulsant properties of cannabidiol." Res. Commun. Chem. Pathol. Pharmacol. 1974, 8, 231-246.

7152. Turkanis,S.A., Chiu,P., Borys,H.K., and Karler,R. "Influence of delta-9-tetrahydrocannabinol and cannabidiol on photically evoked after-discharge potentials." Psychopharmacol. 1977, 52, 207-212.

7153. Turkanis,S.A. and Karler,R. "Influence of anticonvulsant cannabinoids on post tetanic potentiation at isolated bullfrog ganglia." Life Sci. 1975, 17, 569-578.

7154. Turkansi,R.K., Kaymakcalan,S., and Ercan,Z.S. "Antihistaminic action of (-)-trans-delta-9-tetrahydrocannabinol." Arch. Internat'l. Pharmacodyn. Ther. 1975, 214, 254-262.

7155. Turnbull,C. "Hemp." In Ebin,D.(ed.). The Drug Experience. Grove Press, N.Y., 1961, 103-111.

7156. Turner,C.E. "Active substances in marihuana." Arch. Invest. Med. 1974, 5, 135-140.

7157. Turner,C.E. "Chemical analysis of cannabis using gas liquid chromatography and thin layer chromatography." Paper presented at 1st African Internat'l. Conf. Alcohol. Drug Depend., Cape Town, 1974.

7158. Turner,C.E. "Chemical aspects of marihuana." Paper presented at Nat'l. Sympos. on Marihuana, University, Miss., 1974.

7159. Turner,C.E., Fetterman,P.S., Hadley,K.W., and Ubanek,J.E. "Constituents of cannabis sativa L. X. Cannabinoid profile of a Mexican variant and its possible correlation to pharmacological activity." Act. Pharmaceut. Jugoslav. 1975, 25, 7-16.

7160. Turner,C.T. and Hadley,K.W. "Analytical reasons for conflicting pharmacological reports on cannabis sativa." Paper presented at 1st Lat. Am. Cong. Psychobiol., Sao Paulo, 1973.

7161. Turner,C.E. and Hadley,K.W. "Chemical analysis of cannabis sativa of distinct origin." Arch. Invest. Med. 1974, 5, 141-150.

7162. Turner,C.E. and Hadley,K. "Constituents of cannabis sativa L. II. Abscence of cannabidiol in an Africant variant." J. Pharmaceut. Sci. 1973, 62, 251-255.

7163. Turner,C.E. and Hadley,K. "Constituents of cannabis sativa L. III. Clear and discrete separation of cannabidiol and cannabichromene." J. Pharmaceut. Sci. 1973, 62, 1083-1086.

7164. Turner,C.E. and Hadley,K. "Preservation of cannabis." J.A.M.A. 1973, 223, 1042-1043.

7165. Turner,C.E. and Hadley,K.W. "The relationship of chemical analysis to conflicting pharmacological reports on cannabis sativa L." Comm. Prob. Drug Depend. 1974, 2, 1113-1131.

7166. Turner,C.E., Hadley,K.W., and Davis,K.H. "Constituents of cannabis sativa L., V. Stability of an analytical sample extracted with chloroform." Act. Pharmaceut. Jugoslav. 1973, 23, 89-94.

7167. Turner,C.E., Hadley,K., and Fetterman,P.S. "Constituents of cannabis sativa L. VI. Propyl homologs in samples of known geographic origin." J. Pharmaceut. Sci. 1973, 62, 1739-1741.

7168. Turner,C.E., Hadley,K.W., Fetterman,P.S., Doorenbos,N.J., Quimby,M.W., and Waller,C. "Constituents of cannabis sativa L. IV. Stability of cannabinoids in stored plant material." J. Pharmaceut. Sci. 1973, 62, 1601-1605.

7169. Turner,C.E., Hadley,K.W., Henry,J., and Mole, M.L. "Constituents of cannabis sativa L. VII. Use of silyl derivatives in routine analysis." J. Pharmaceut. Sci. 1974, 63, 1872-1876.

7170. Turner,C.E., Hadley,K.W., Holley,J.H., Billets,S., and Mole,M.L. "Constituents of cannabis sativa L. VIII. Possible biological application of a new method to separate cannabidiol and cannabichromene." J. Pharmaceut. Sci. 1975, 64, 810-814.

7171. Turner,C.E. and Henry,J.T. "Constituents of cannabis sativa L. IX. Stability of synthetic and naturally occurring cannabinoids in chloroform." J. Pharmaceut. Sci. 1975, 64, 357-359.

7172. Turner,C.E., Hsu,M.F., Knapp,J.E., Schiff,P.L., and Slatkin,D.J. "Isolation of cannabisativine, an alkaloid, from cannabis sativa L. root." J. Pharmaceut. Sci. 1976, 65, 1084.

7173. Turner,C.E. and Mole,M.L. "Chemical components of cannabis sativa." J.A.M.A. 1973, 225, 639.

7174. Turner,C.E., Mole,M.L., and Beulke,J. "Cardiac toxins of non-polar extracts of cannabis sativa L. roots of Mexican origin." Paper presented at 1st Lat. Am. Cong. Psychobiol., Sao Paulo, 1973.

7175. Turner,J.C., Hemphill,J.K., and Mahlberg,P.G. "Gland distribution and cannabinoid content in clones of cannabis sativa L." Am. J. Bot. 1977, 64, 687-693.

7176. Tylden,E. "The clinical features of cannabis use." Practitioner 1974, 212, 810-814.

7177. Tylden,E. and Wild,D. "A case for cannabis?" Br. Med. J. 1967, 3, 556.

7178. Tytgat,G.N., Saunders,D.R., and Rubin,C.E. "Failure of phenobarbital and marihuana to stimulate the smooth endoplasmic reticulum in the human intestinal absorptive cell." Eur. J. Clin. Invest. 1973, 3, 360-370.

U

7179. Udell,J.G. and Smith,R.S. Attitudes, Usage and Availability of Drugs Among Madison High School Students. Univ. Wisconsin, Bureau of Business Research and Service, Madison, Wis., 1969.

7180. Ueki,S., Fuhiwara,M., and Ogawa,N. "Mouse killing behavior (muricide) induced by delta-9-tetrahydrocannabinol in the rat." Physiol. Behav. 1972, 9, 585-587.

7181. Uelmen,G.F. "California's new marihuana law: a sailing guide for uncharted waters." Cal. State Bar J. 1976, 51, 27-32, 75-86.

7182. Uhr,L. and Uhr,E. "The quiet revolution." Psychol. Today 1967, 1, 40-43.

7183. Ulamec,K. "The problem of the police in the control of drug abuse."(Fr.). Paper presented at Internat'l. Inst. Prevent. Drug Depend., Lausanne, 1970.

7184. Uliss,D.B., Dalzell,H.C., Handrick,G.K., and Razdan,R.K. "Hashish. Importance of the phenolic hydroxyl group in tetrahydrocannabinols." J. Med. Chem. 1975, 18, 213-215.

7185. Uliss,D.B., Handrick,G.R., Dalzell,H.C., and Razdan,R.K. "A novel cannabinoid containing a 1,8-cineol moiety." Exper. 1977, 22, 577.

7186. Uliss,D.B., Razdan,R.K., and Dalzell,H.C. "Stereospecific intramolecular epoxide cleavage by phenolate anion. Synthesis of novel and biologically active cannabinoids." J. Am. Chem. Soc. 1974, 96, 7272-7274.

7187. Ungerleider,J.T. and Bowen,H.L. "Drug abuse and the schools." Am. J. Psychiat. 1969, 125, 105-111.

7188. Union of South Africa. Abuse of Dagga. Report of the Inter-departmental Committee. Gov't. Printer, Union of South Africa, Pretoria, 1952.

7189. Union of South Africa. Dagga Smoking. Dept. of Public Health, Pretoria, 1934.

7190. Union of South Africa. Memorandum of Dagga and its Evils. Dept. of Public Health, Pretoria, 1924.

7191. United Arab Republic. Committee for the Investigation of Hashish Consumption in the Egyptian Region. Research in Progress. I. The Interviewing Schedule: Preparation, Reliability, and Validity.(Arab.). Nat'l. Center Soc. Criminol. Res., Gov't. Print. Office, Cairo, 1960.

7192. United Arab Republic. Committee for the Invetigation of Hashish Consumption in the Egyptian Region. Research in Progress. II. Hashish Consumption in the City of Cairo--a Pilot Study.(Arab.). Nat'l. Center Soc. Criminol Res., Gov't. Print. Office, Cairo, 1963.

7193. United Nations. "A cannabis concoction ('smash')." Bull. Narc. 1968, 20, 55.

7194. United Nations. "A Soviet law." Bull. Narc. 1968, 20, 52.

7195. United Nations. "Cannabis and violence." Bull. Narc. 1968, 20, 44.

7196. United Nations. "Cannabis in early pregnancy." Bull. Narc. 1968, 20, 8.

7197. United Nations. "Coming into force of the Single Convention on Narcotic Drugs, 1961." Bull. Narc. 1965, 17, 1.

7198. United Nations. "Eighteenth session of the Commission on Narcotic Drugs, and thirty-sixth session of the Economic and Social Council." Bull. Narc. 1963, 15, 39-42.

7199. United Nations. "Estimated world requirements of narcotic drugs in 1966: Estimates by the Drug Supervisory Body in pursuance of the 1931 Convention, and including drugs controlled by virute of the 1948 protocol." Bull. Narc. 1966, 18, 49-51.

7200. United Nations. "Estimated world requirements of narcotic drugs in 1968." Bull. Narc. 1968, 20, 58-59.

7201. United Nations. "Professor Joachimoglu retires from internation narcotics control organs." Bull. Narc. 1968, 20, 43-44.

7202. United Nations. "Review of the 20th session of the Commission on Narcotic Drugs and the 40th session of the Economic and Social Council." Bull. Narc. 1966, 18, 63-67.

7203. United Nations. "Review of the 22nd session of the Commission on Narcotic Drugs and the 44th session of the Economic and Social Council." Bull. Narc. 1968, 20, 37-41.

7204. United Nations. "The 15th session of the Commission on Narcotic Drugs, and the 13th session of the Economic and Social Council." Bull. Narc. 1960, 12, 43-46.

7205. United Nations. "The cannabis problem: A note on the problem and the history of international action." Bull. Narc. 1962, 14, 27-31.

7206. United Nations. "The effects of cannabis." Bull. Narc. 1968, 20, 38.

7207. United Nations. "The United Nations narcotics laboratory." Bull. Narc. 1967, 19, 7-15.

7208. United Nations. "Towards a solution of regional narcotics problems: Recent projects of U.N. technical assistance." Bull. Narc. 1968, 20, 41-49.

7209. United Nations. "Twenty years of narcotics control under the United Nations. Review of the work of the Commission on Narcotic Drugs from its first to its 20th session." Bull. Narc. 1966, 18, 1-60.

7210. United Nations. "United Nations consultative group on narcotic problems in Asia and the Near East." Bull. Narc. 1965, 17, 39-46.

7211. United Nations. Commission on Narcotic Drugs. "A program of studies on the cannabis plant and its products. Survey of the situation in Angola." U.N. Doc. E/CN.7/286/Add.9, Apr. 6, 1956.

7212. United Nations. Commission on Narcotic Drugs. "A program of studies on the cannabis plant and its products. Addendum to the survey of the situation in Angola." U.N. Doc. E/CN.7/286/Add.13, Mar. 1, 1957.

7213. United Nations. Commission on Narcotic Drugs. "A program of studies on the cannabis plant and its products. Survey of the situation in Basutoland." U.N. Doc. E/CN.7/286/Add.1, Jan. 18, 1955.

7214 United Nations. Commission on Narcotic Drugs. "A program of studies on the cannabis plant and its products. Addendum to the survey of the situation in Basutoland." U.N. Doc. E/CN.7/286/Add.5, Mar. 11, 1955.

7215. United Nations. Commission on Narcotic Drugs. "A program of studies on the cannabis plant and its products. Survey of the situation in Bechuanaland." U.N. Doc. E/CN.7/286/Add.2, Jan. 19, 1955.

7216. United Nations. Commission on Narcotic Drugs. "A program of studies on the cannabis plant and its products." Survey of the situation in Brazil." U.N. Doc. E/CN.7/286/Add.8, Apr. 19, 1955.

7217 United Nations. Commission on Narcotic Drugs. "A program of studies on the cannabis plant and its products. Survey of the situation in Burma." U.N. Doc. E/CN.7/286/Add.19, Nov. 22, 1957.

7218 United Nations. Commission on Narcotic Drugs. "A program of studies on the cannabis plant and its products. Survey of the situation in Costa Rica." U.N. Doc. E/CN.7/286/Add.17, Apr. 29, 1956.

7219 United Nations. Commission on Narcotic Drugs. "A program of studies on the cannabis plant and its products. Survey of the situation in Cuba." U.N. Doc. E/CN.7/286/Add.25, Oct. 1, 1959.

7220 United Nations. Commission on Narcotic Drugs. "A program of studies on the cannabis plant and its products. Survey of the situation in Cuba." U.N. Doc. E/CN.7/286/Add.27, Feb. 10, 1960.

7221. United Nations. Commission on Narcotic Drugs. "A program of studies on the cannabis plant and its products. Survey of the situation in the Dominican Republic." U.N. Doc. E/CN.7/286, Jan. 20, 1960.

7222 United Nations. Commission on Narcotic Drugs. "A program of studies on the cannabis plant. Survey of the situation in Egypt." U.N. Doc. E/CN.7/286/Add.16, Apr. 15, 1957.

7223 United Nations. Commission on Narcotic Drugs. "A program of studies on the cannabis plant. Survey of the situation in Egypt." U.N. Doc. E/CN.7/286/Add.18, Apr. 29, 1957.

7224. United Nations. Commission on Narcotic Drugs. "A program of studies on the cannabis plant and its products. Survey of the situation in Greece." U.N. Doc. E/CN.7/286/Add.29, Apr. 22, 1960.

7225. United Nations. Commission on Narcotic Drugs. "A program of studies on the cannabis plant and its products." Survey of the situation in Haiti," U.N. Doc. E/CN.7/286/Add.28, Mar. 3, 1960.

7226. United Nations. Commission on Narcotic Drugs. "A program of studies on the cannabis plant and its products." Survey of the situation in India." U.N. Doc. E/CN.7/286/Add.12, Apr. 30, 1956.

7227. United Nations. Commission on Narcotic Drugs. "A program of studies on the cannabis plant and its products." Survey of the situation in India." U.N. Doc. E/CN.7/286/Add.12, Mar. 19, 1957.

7228. United Nations. Commission on Narcotic Drugs. "A program of studies on the cannabis plant and its products. Survey of the situation in Italy." U.N. Doc. E/CN.7/286/Add.15, Mar. 12, 1957.

7229. United Nations. Commission on Narcotic Drugs. "A program of studies on the cannabis plant and its products. Survey of the situation in Jamaica." U.N. Doc. E/CN.7/286/Add.23, Jan. 5, 1959.

7230. United Nations. Commission on Narcotic Drugs. "A program of studies on the cannabis plant and its products. Survey of the situation in Lebanon." U.N. Doc. E/CN.7/286/Add.20, Mar. 14, 1958.

7231. United Nations. Commission on Narcotic Drugs. "A program of studies on the cannabis plant and its products. Survey of the situation in Mexico." U.N. Doc. E/CN.7/286/Add.21, Nov. 11, 1958.

7234. United Nations. Commission on Narcotic Drugs. "A program of studies on the cannabis plant and its products. Survey of the situation in Mozambique." U.N. Doc. E/CN.7/286/Add.10, Apr. 9, 1957.

7235. United Nations. Commission on Narcotic Drugs. "A program of studies on the cannabis plant and its products." Survey of the situation in Mozambique." U.N. Doc. E/CN.7/286/Add.10, Mar. 12, 1957.

7236. United Nations. Commission on Narcotic Drugs. "A program of studies on the cannabis plant and its products. Survey of the situation in Northern Rhodesia." U.N. Doc. E/CN.7/286/Add.6, Mar. 30, 1955.

7237. United Nations. Commission on Narcotic Drugs. "A program of studies on the cannabis plant and its products. Survey of the situation in Pakistan." U.N. Doc. E/CN.7/286/Add.14, Mar. 15, 1957.

7238. United Nations. Commission on Narcotic Drugs. "A program of studies on the cannabis plant and its products. Survey of the sitatuation in Pakistan." U.N. Doc. E/CN.7/286/Add.24, Jan. 5, 1959.

7239. United Nations. Commission on Narcotic Drugs. "A program of studies on the cannabis plant and its products. Survey of the situation in Southern Rhodesia." U.N. Doc. E/CN.7/286/Add.7, Mar. 30, 1955.

7240. United Nations. Commission on Narcotic Drugs. "A program of studies on the cannabis plant and its products. Survey of the situation in Swaziland." U.N. Doc. E/CN.7/286/Add.3, Jan. 20, 1955.

7241. United Nations. Commission on Narcotic Drugs. "A program of studies on the cannabis plant and its products. Survey of the situation in the Union of South Africa." U.N. Doc. E/CN.7/286, Jan. 18, 1955.

7242. United Nations. Commission on Narcotic Drugs. "A program of studies on the cannabis plant and its products. Survey of the situation in the Union of South Africa." U.N. Doc. E/CN.7/286, Feb. 18, 1955.

7243. United Nations. Commission on Narcotic Drugs. "A program of studies on the cannabis plant and its products. Survey of the situation in the United States." U.N. Doc. E/CN.7/286/Add.22, Nov. 25, 1958.

7244. United Nations. Commission on Narcotic Drugs. "Chemical and physical methods of analysis of cannabis resin, by Farmilo,Charles George." U.N. Doc. E/CN.7/304, June 15, 1955.

7245. United Nations. Commission on Narcotic Drugs. "Draft report. The problem of cannabis(Indian hemp)." U.N. Doc. E/CN.7/L.61/Add.3, May 7, 1954.

7246. United Nations. Commission on Narcotic Drugs. "Draft report on the work of the 12th session. V. Abuse of drugs.(drug addiction)." U.N. Doc. E/CN.7/ L.164/Add.16, May 28, 1957.

7247. United Nations. Commission on Narcotic Drugs. "Draft report on the work of the 12th session. VIII. The question of cannabis." U.N. Doc. E/CN.7/L.164/Add.6, May 16, 1957.

7248. United Nations. Commission on Narcotic Drugs. "Draft report on the work of the 13th session. VI. The question of cannabis." U.N. Doc. E/CN.7/L.191/Add.19, May 28, 1958.

7249. United Nations. Commission on Narcotic Drugs. "Draft report on the work of the 14th session. IV. Abuse of drugs (drug addiction)." U.N. Doc. E/CN.7/L.220/Add.10, May 12, 1959.

7250. United Nations. Commission on Narcotic Drugs. "Draft report on the work of the 14th session. VII. The question of cannabis." U.N. Doc. E/CN.7/L.220/Add.6, May 11, 1959.

7251. United Nations. Commission on Narcotic Drugs. "Draft report on the work of the 16th session. IV. Abuse of drugs (drug addiction)." U.N. Doc. E/CN.7/L.237, May 5, 1961.

7252. United Nations. Commission on Narcotic Drugs. "Draft report on the work of the 16th session. VII. The question of cannabis (including scientific research on cannabis)." U.N. Doc. E/CN.7L.237/Add.6, May 5, 1961.

7253. United Nations. Commission on Narcotic Drugs. "Draft report on the work of the 17th session. IV. Abuse of drugs (drug addiction)." U.N. Doc. E/CN.7/249/Add.12, May 29, 1962.

7254. United Nations. Commission on Narcotic Drugs. "Draft report on the work of the 17th session. VII. The question of cannabis (including scientific research on cannabis)." U.N. Doc. E/CN.7/L.249/Add.7, May 25, 1962.

7255. United Nations. Commission on Narcotic Drugs. "Draft report on the work of the 17th session. VII. The question of cannabis." U.N. Doc. E/CN.7/L.249/Add.14, May 26, 1962.

7256. United Nations. Commission on Narcotic Drugs. "Draft report on the work of the work of the 20th session. IV. Abuse of drugs (drug addiction)." U.N. Doc. E/CN.7/L.277/Add.7, Dec. 14, 1965.

7257. United Nations. Commission on Narcotic Drugs. "Draft report on the work of the 20th session. VII. The problem of cannabis (including scientific research on cannabis." U.N. Doc. E/CN.7/L.277/Add.8, Dec. 15, 1965.

7258. United Nations. Commission on Narcotic Drugs. "Draft report on the work of the 21st session. IV. Abuse of drugs." U.N. Doc. E/CN.7/L.287/Add.6, Dec. 16, 1966.

7259. United Nations. Commission on Narcotic Drugs. "Draft report on the work of the 21st session. V. Opium, cannabis and coca leaf." U.N. Doc. E/CN.7/L.297/Add.2, Dec. 12, 1966.

7260. United Nations. Commission on Narcotic Drugs. "Drug addiction: A social problem." U.N. Doc. NAR-AFRI-SEM-DOC.2, Sept. 9, 1963.

7261. United Nations. Commission on Narcotic Drugs. "Incidence of drug addiction." U.N. Doc. E/CN.7/360, Jan. 30, 1959.

7262. United Nations. Commission on Narcotic Drugs. "Illicit traffic in Brazil." U.N. Doc. E/CN.7/R.15/Add.55, July 30, 1965.

7263. United Nations. Commission on Narcotic Drugs. "Narcotic drugs under international control: Multilingual list." U.N. Doc. E/CN.7/436, Mar. 3, 1963.

7264. United Nations. Commission on Narcotic Drugs. "Opium, cannabis and coca leaf; research on opium, cannabis and other substances." U.N. Doc. E/CN.7/497, Sept. 1, 1966.

7265. United Nations. Commission on Narcotic Drugs. "Program of studies concerning the plant cannabis sativa and its products." U.N. Doc. E/CN.7/286/Add.11, Apr. 20, 1956.

7266. United Nations. Commission on Narcotic Drugs. "Research on cannabis." U.N. Doc. E/CN.7/442/Add.1, Jan. 28, 1963.

7267. United Nations. Commission on Narcotic Drugs. "Review of the illicit traffic in narcotic drugs during 1954." U.N. Doc. E/CN.7/292, Apr. 18, 1955.

7268. United Nations. Commission on Narcotic Drugs. "Review of the illicit traffic in narcotic drugs during 1955." U.N. Doc. E/CN.7/309/Add.3, Apr. 13, 1956.

7269. United Nations. Commission on Narcotic Drugs. "Scientific research on cannabis. Note by the Secretary General." U.N. Doc. E/CN/418, Jan 25, 1962.

7270. United Nations. Commission on Narcotic Drugs. "Scientific research on cannabis. Note by the Secretary General." U.N. Doc. 442/Add.1, Mar. 19, 1963.

7271. United Nations. Commission on Narcotic Drugs. "Scientific research on cannabis. Note by the secretary General." U.N. Doc. E/CN.7/418/Add.1, Apr. 6, 1962.

7272. United Nations. Commission on Narcotic Drugs. "Scientific research on opium and cannabis. Note by the Secretary General." U.N. Doc. E/CN.7/476, Sept. 25, 1965.

7273. United Nations. Commission on Narcotic Drugs. "Summary record of the 386th meeting, held at the Palais des Nations, Geneva, May 7, 1958." U.N. Doc. E/CN.7/ Sr.386, Oct. 27, 1958.

7274. United Nations. Commission on Narcotic Drugs. "Summary record of the 387th meeting held at the Palais des Nations, Geneva, May 8, 1958." U.N. Doc. E/CN.7/ Sr.387, Oct. 28, 1958.

7275. United Nations. Commission on Narcotic Drugs. "Terms of reference. Note by the Assistant Secretary General in charge of the Department of Social Affairs." U.N. Doc. E/CN.7/4, Nov. 18, 1946.

7276. United Nations. Commission on Narcotic Drugs. "The possibility of replacing hemp fiber and hemp seed by other crops of similar industrial value or of developing narcotic-free strains of the cannabis plant." U.N. Doc. E/CN.7/297, Mar. 24, 1955.

7277. United Nations. Commission on Narcotic Drugs. "The problem of cannabis. Possibility of developing narcotic-free strains of the cannabis plant or of substituting other crops for hemp fiber and hemp seed: Replies of government to council resolution 588.C." U.N. Doc. E/CN.7/314/Add.2, Mar. 15, 1957.

7278. United Nations. Commission on Narcotic Drugs. "The problem of cannabis. Possibility of developing narcotic-free strains of the cannabis plant or of substituting other crops for hemp fiber and hemp seed: "Replies of governments to council resolution 588." U.N. Doc. E/CN.7/314/Add.1, Apr. 30, 1956.

7279. United Nations. Commission on Narcotic Drugs. "The problem of cannabis. Program of studies." U.N. Doc. E/CN.7/276, Mar. 22, 1954.

7280. United Nations. Commission on Narcotic Drugs. "The problem of Indian hemp." U.N. Doc. E/CN.7/256, Mar. 19, 1953.

7281. United Nations. Commission on Narcotic Drugs. "The question of cannabis. Annex--scientific problems of cannabis research." U.N. Doc. E/CN.7/358, Jan. 20, 1959.

7282. United Nations. Commission on Narcotic Drugs. "The question of cannabis. Cannabinol reactions and pharmacological analyses of the resinous secretions from cannabis cultivated or growing wild in the Northern Caucasus." U.N. Doc. E/CN.7/352, Apr. 3, 1958.

7283. United Nations. Commission on Narcotic Drugs. "The question of cannabis. Further replies from governments regarding scientific research on cannabis." U.N. Doc. E/CN.7/298/Add.6, Mar. 18, 1957.

7284. United Nations. Commission on Narcotic Drugs. "The question of cannabis. Further replies of governments regarding council resolution 548 F11 and scientific research on cannabis." U.N. Doc. E/CN.7/298/Add.5, Apr. 23, 1956.

7285. United Nations. Commission on Narcotic Drugs. "The question of cannabis. Note by the representative of Greece." U.N. Doc. E/CN.7/L.92, Apr. 20, 1955.

7286. United Nations. Commission on Narcotic Drugs. "The question of cannabis. Note by the Secretary General." U.N. Doc. E/CN.7/324, Apr. 26, 1957.

7287. United Nations. Commission on Narcotic Drugs. "The question of cannabis. Note by the Secretary General." U.N. Doc. E/CN.7/399, Dec. 5, 1960.

7288. United Nations. Commission on Narcotic Drugs. "The question of cannabis. Replies of governments regarding Council resolution 548 F11 and scientific research on cannabis." U.N. Doc. E/CN.7/298, Apr. 1, 1955.

7289. United Nations. Commission on Narcotic Drugs. "The question of cannabis. Replies of governments regarding Council resolution 548 F11 and scientific research on cannabis." U.N. Doc. E/CN.7/298/Add.2, Apr. 20, 1955.

7290. United Nations. Commission on Narcotic Drugs. "The question of cannabis. Reply of the government of Austria regarding Council resolution 548 F11 and scientific research on cannabis." U.N. Doc. E/CN.7/286/Add.3, Apr. 22, 1955.

7291. United Nations. Commission on Narcotic Drugs. "The question of cannabis. Scientific information." U.N. Doc. E/CN.7/373, Apr. 15, 1959.

7292. United Nations. Commission on Narcotic Drugs. "The question of cannabis. State Institute of Scientific Research on Medicinal Plants. (Poland)." U.N. Doc. E/CN.7/372, Mar. 17, 1959.

7293. United Nations. Commission on Narcotic Drugs. "The question of cannabis. The merits of antibiotic substances obtainable from cannabis sativa." U.N. Doc. E/CN.7/409, Feb. 17, 1961.

7294. United Nations. Commission on Narcotic Drugs. "Work of the World Health Organization in the field of dependence-producing drugs. The use of cannabis: report of a WHO scientific group." U.N. Doc. E/CN.7/553, Dec. 11, 1972.

7295. United Nations. Commission on Narcotic Drugs. "World trends of the illicit traffic in narcotic drugs during the war 1939-1945." U.N. Doc. E/CN.7/9, Nov. 23, 1946.

7296. United Nations. Conference for the Adoption of a Single Convention on Narcotic Drugs. "Medical use of cannabis drugs. The merits of antibiotic substance obtainable from cannabis sativa." U.N. Doc. E/CONF.34/5, Nov. 24, 1960.

7297. United Nations. Conference for the Adoption of a Single Convention on Narcotic Drugs. "Statement submitted by the Australian delegation. Notes on the cannabis plant and its products." U.N. Doc. E/CONF.34/L.14, Feb. 27, 1961.

7298. United Nations. Department of Social Affairs. "Regional conference on the illicit traffic in drugs." Bull. Narc. 1960, 12, 29-36.

7299. Untied Nations. Department of Social Affairs. "The Midde East narcotics survey mission of the United Nations (Sept.-Oct. 1959)." Bull. Narc. 1960, 12, 37-42.

7300. United Nations. Department of Social Affairs. "The United Nations and the illicit traffic in narcotic drugs." Bull. Narc. 1960, 12, 21-27.

7301. United Nations. Department of Social Affairs. "The work of the permanent central opium board in 1960." Bull. Narc. 1961, 13, 39-41.

7302. United Nations. Economic and Social Council. The Question of Cannabis: Cannabis Bibliography. Office of Public Information, Geneva Switzerland, 1965, (U.N. Doc. E/CN.7/479).

7303. United Nations. Secretariat. "Application of thin-layer chromatography for the analysis of cannabis." (Fr.). U.N. Doc. ST/SOA/SER.3/13, Dec. 6, 1965.

7304. United Nations. Secretariat. "Medical and social problems of drug addiction in West Africa." U.N. Doc. GEN/NAR.65/CONF.2/9, July 20, 1965.

7305. United Nations. Secretariat. "Methods for the identification of cannabis: 1. A study of the specificity of some chemical reactions for the identification of cannabis." U.N. Doc. ST/SOA/SER.S/1, Mar. 15, 1960.

7306. United Nations. Secretariat. "Methods for the identification of cannabis: 2. A study of methods for the identification of cannabis by means of ultra-violet absorption spectrophotometry." U.N. Doc. ST/SOA/SER.S/2, Apr. 29, 1960.

7307. United Nations. Secretariat. "Methods for the identification of cannabis: 3. A study of the behavior of certain plant constituents when tested with chemical reaction for the identification of cannabis." U.N. Doc. ST/SOA/SER.S/5, Nov. 30, 1961.

7308. United Nations. Sectretariat. "Narcotic drug problems in Africa, with particular reference to locally produced drugs." U.N. Doc. NAR/AFRI/SEM/DOC.3, Sept. 18, 1963.

7309. United Nations. Secretariat. "Socio-psychiatric problems of cannabis in Nigeria." U.N. Doc. NAR/AFRI/SEM/DOC.8, Sept. 25, 1963.

7310. United Nations. Secretariat. "Source of production of cannabis and other narcotic drugs entering the illicit traffic." U.N. Doc. GEN/NAR.65/CONF/2-5, June 21, 1965.

7311. United Nations. Secretariat. "The methods used for the identification of cannabis by the authorities in the United States of America." U.N. Doc. ST/SOA/SER.S/3, Nov. 28, 1960.

7314. United Nations. World Health Organization. "Dependence on alcohol and other drugs." WHO Chron. 1967, 21, 219-226.

7315. United Nations. World Health Organization. "Drug dependence." WHO Chron. 1966, 20, 65-67.

7316. United Nations. World Health Organization. "Evaluation of dependence-producing drugs: Report of a W.H.O. Scientific group." WHO Tech. Rep. Ser. 1964, 287, 1-25.

7317. United Nations. World Health Organization. "Expert committee on addiction-producing drugs: 10th report." WHO Tech. Rep. Ser. 1960, 188, 1-16.

7318, United Nations. World Health Organization. "Expert committee on addiction-producing drugs: 11th report." WHO Tech. Rep. Ser. 1961, 211, 1-16.

7319. United Nations. World Health Organization. "Expert committee on addiction-producing drugs: 12th report." WHO Tech. Rep. Ser. 1962, 229, 1-12.

7320. United Nations. Secretariat. "Expert committee on addiction-proudcing drugs: 13th report." WHO Tech. Rep. Ser. 1964, 273, 1-20.

7321. United Nations. World Health Organization. "Expert committee on mental health: 14th report: Services for the prevention and treatment of dependence on alcohol and other drugs." WHO Tech. Rep. Ser. 1967, 363, 1-45.

7322. United Nations. World Health Organization. "List of drugs under international narcotics control." WHO Tech. Rep. Ser. 1962, 229, 13-16.

7323. United Nations. World Health Organization. "Report of a W.H.O. committee." WHO Tech. Rep. Ser. 1965, 312, 1.

7324. United Nations. World Health Organziation. "Research in psychopharmacology." WHO Chron. 1967, 21, 463-467.

7325. United Nations. World Health Organization. "The control of narcotic drugs." WHO Chron. 1960, 14, 309-311.

7326. United States. Bureau of Customs. "Multi-agency force halts contraband." Customs Today 1969, 6, 1, 12.

7326a. United States. Bureau of Narcotics and Dangerous Drugs. Illicit Use of Dangerous Drugs in the U.S.: A Compilation of Studies, Surveys and Polls. Gov't. Print. Office, Washington, D.C., 1970.

7327. United States. Bureau of Narcotics and Dangerous Drugs. Marihuana. Gov't. Print. Office, Washington, D.C., 1972.

7328. United States. Bureau of Narcotics and Dangerous Drugs. Marihuana: An Analysis of Use, Distribution, and Control. Gov't. Print. Office, Washington, D.C., 1971.

7329. United States. Bureau of Narcotics and Dangerous Drugs. Marihuana: Its Identification. Gov't. Print. Office, Washington, D.C., 1939.

7330. United States. Bureau of Narcotics and Dangerous Drugs. Regulations Relating to the Importation, Manufacture, Production, Compounding, Sale, Dealing in, Dispensing, Prescribing, Administering and Giving Away of Marihuana, Under the Act of August 2, 1937. Gov't. Print. Office, Washington, D.C., 1937.

7331. United States. Bureau of Narcotics and Dangerous Drugs. Report on the Marihuana Investigation. Gov't. Print. Office, Washington, D.C., 1937.

7332. United States. Bureau of Narcotics and Dangerous Drugs. Traffic in Opium and Other Dangerous Drugs. Gov't. Print. Office, Washington,D.C., 1935-1951.

7333. United States. Committee of the Judiciary. Senate. Hearings Before the Sub-committee on Improvements in the Federal Criminal Code. Pursuant to Senate Resolution 67, Parts 1 to 10. Gov't. Print. Office, Washington, D.C., 1955.

7334. United States. Committee of the Judiciary. Senate. Hearing Before the Sub-committee to Investigate the Internal Security Act and Other Internal Security Laws. Hashish Smuggling and Passport Fraud: 'The Brotherhood of Eternal Love'." Gov't. Print. Office, Washington, D.C., 1973.

7335. United States. Committee of the Judiciary. Senate. Marihuana and the Question of Personal Security. Gov't. Print. Office, Washington, D.C., 1975.

7336. United States. Committee of the Judiciary. Senate. Sub-committee to Investigate Juvenile Delinquency. Hearings on S.1895, S.2590, S.2637. Gov't. Print. Office, Washington, D.C., 1969.

7337. United States. Committee on Ways and Means. House of Representatives. Control of Narcotics, Marihuana and Barbiturates. Gov't. Print. Office, Washington, D.C., 1951.

7338. United States. Committee on Ways and Means. House of Representatives. Sub-committee on Narcotics. Hearings on H.R. 3490. Gov't. Print. Office, Washington, D.C., 1951.

7338 United States. Committee on Ways and Means. Taxation of Marihuana. Gov't. Print. Office, Washington, D.C., 1937.

7339. United States. Committee on Finance. Senate. Hemp and Marihuana. Gov't. Print. Office, Washington, D.C., 1945.

7340. United States. Select Committee on Crime. Senate. Marihuana. Gov't. Print. Office, Washington, D.C., 1970.

7341. United States. Special Committee to Investigate Organized Crime in Interstate Commerce (Kefauver Committee Hearings). Senate. Gov't. Print. Office, Washington, D.C., 1951.

7342. United States. Sub-committee on Finance. Senate. Taxation of Marihuana. Gov't. Print. Office, Washington, D.C., 1937.

7343. United States. Sub-committee to Investigate the Administration of the Internal Security Act and Other Security Laws. Senate. Marihuana-Hashish Epidemic and Its Impact on United States Security. Gov't. Print. Office, Washington, D.C., 1974.

7344. United States. Committee on Governmental Operations. Intergovernmental Relations sub-committee. House of Representatives. Problems Relating to the Control of Marihuana. Gov't. Print. Office, Washington, D.C., 1968.

7345. United States. Committee on Interstate and Foreign Commerce. House of Representatives. Clarification of Goddard's Views on Marihuana. Gov't. Print. Office, Washington, D.C., 1967.

7346. United States. Committee on Interstate and Foreign Commerce. House of Representatives. Report on Marihuana Control. Gov't. Print. Office, Washington, D.C., 1970.

7347. United States. Internal Revenue Service. Alcohol and Tobacco Tax Division Laboratory: Methods of Analysis. Gov't. Print. Office, Washington, D.C., 1966.

7348. United States. National Commission on Marihuana and Drug Abuse. Marihuana: A Signal of Misunderstanding. Gov't. Print. Office, Washington, D.C., 1972.

7349. United States. National Coordinating Council on Drug Education. Drug Abuse Films. Council on Drug Education, Washington, D.C., n.d.

7350. United States. National Council on Crime and Delinquency. Board of Directors. "Drug addiction: a medical, not a law enforcement problem. A policy statement." Crime Delinquency 1974, 20, 4-9.

7351. United States. President's Commission on Law Enforcement and Administration of Justice. Narcotics and Drug Abuse: Annotations and Consultant's Papers. Gov't. Print. Office, Washington, D.C., 1967.

7352. United States. Report of the President's Advisory Commission on Narcotic Drug Abuse. Gov't. Print. Office, Washington, D.C., 1963.

7353. United States. Secretary, Department of Health, Education and Welfare. Marihuana and Health. Gov't. Print. Office, Washington, D.C., 1971.

7354. United States. Secretary, Department of Health, Education and Welfare. Marihuana and Health. Gov't. Print. Office, Washington, D.C., 1972.

7355. United States. Secretary, Department of Health, Education and Welfare. Marihuana and Health. Gov't. Print. Office, Washington, D.C., 1974

7356. United States. Secretary, Department of Health, Education and Welfare. Marihuana and Health. Gov't. Print. Office, Washington, D.C., 1975.

7357. United States. White House Conference on Narcotic and Drug Abuse. Gov't. Print. Office, Washington, D.C., 1963.

7358. University Committee on Drugs and the Campus. Intoxicant Drugs: Survey of Student Use Roles and Policies of the University. State University of New York, Buffalo, 1968.

7359. Unwin,J.R. "Dissident youth." Can. Ment. Hlth. 1969, 17, 4-10.

7360. Unwin,J.R. "Illicit drug use among Canadian youth. Parts I and II." Can. Med. Assoc. J. 1968, 98, 402-407, 449-454.

7361. Unwin,J.R. "Non-medial use of drugs with particular reference to youth." Can. Med. Assoc. J. 1969, 101, 804-820.

7362. Uppal,R., Dutta,S.N., and Sanyal,R.K. "Influence of cannabis, tetrahydrocannabinol and pyrahexyl on the linguomandibular reflex of the dog." J. Pharm. Pharmacol. 1967, 19, 552-554.

7363. Urban,M.L. "Drugs in Industry." In National Commission on Marihuana and Drug Abuse. Drug Use in America: Problem in Perspective. Gov't. Print. Office, Washington, D.C., 1973, I, 1136-1152.

7364. Urquhart,D. The Pillars of Hercules; or A Narrative of Travels in Spain and Morocco in 1848. Harper and Bros., N.Y., 1855.

7365. Usdin,E. and Efron,D.H. Psychotropic Drugs and Related Compounds. Dept. H.E.W., Washington, D.C., 1967.

7366. Utah Governor's Citizen Advisory Committee on Drug. Drug Use Among High School Dropouts in the State of Utah. Advisory Comm. on Drug Abuse, Capitol Bldg., State of Utah, 1969.

7367. Uyeno,E.T. "Delta-9-tetrahydrocannabinol administered during pregnancy of the rat." Proc. West. Pharmacol. Soc. 1973, 16, 64-67.

7368. Uyeno,E.T. "Delta-9-tetrahydrocannabinol and the competitive behavior of the rat." Fed. Proc. 1974, 33, 2883.

7369. Uyeno,E.T. "Disruption of maze performance by delta-9-tetrahydrocannabinol." Proc. Am. Psychol. Assoc. 1973, 8, 997-998.

7370. Uyeno,E.T. "Effects of delta-9-tetrahydrocannabinol and 2,5,-dimethoxy-4 methylamphetamine on rat sexual dominance behavior." Proc. West. Pharmacol. Soc. 1976, 19, 369-372.

7371. Uyeno,E.T. "Effects of delta-9-tetrahydrocannabinol on the dominance behavior of the rat." Pharmacol. 1973, 32, 725.

7372. Uyeno,E.T. "Effects of delta-9-tetrahydrocannabinol on the viability and behavioral development of the rat." Comm. Prob. Drug Depend. 1973, 1, 167-177.

V

7373. Vachon,L. "The smoke in marihuana smoking." *N. Eng. J. Med.* 1976, *294*, 160-161.

7374. Vachon,L., FitzGerald,M.X., Gould,I.A., and Gaensler,E.A. "Influence of a single dose of marihuana on respiration." *Am. Rev. Resp. Dis.* 1973, *107*, 1099.

7375. Vachon,L., FitzGerald,M.X., Solliday,N.H., Gould,I.A., and Gaensler,E.A. "Single-dose effect of marihuana smoke." *N. Eng. J. Med.* 1973, *288*, 985-989.

7376. Vachon,L., Mathe,A.A., and Weissman,B. "Effect of delta-9-THC on the catecholamine content of the guinea pig lung." *Res. Commun. Chem. Pathol. Pharmacol.* 1976, *13*, 245-248.

7377. Vachon,L., Mikus,P., Morrissey,W., FitzGerald,M., and Gaensler,E. "Bronchial effect of marihuana smoke in asthma." In Braude,M.S. and Szara,S.(eds.). *Pharmacology of Marihuana*. Raven Press, N.Y., 1976, 2, 777-785.

7378. Vachon,L., Robins,A., and Gaensler,E. "Airways response to aerosolized delta-9-tetrahydrocannabinol: Preliminary report." In Cohen,S. and Stillman, R.(eds.). *Therapeutic Potential of Marihuana*. Plenum Press, N.Y., 1976, 111-122.

7379. Vachon,L., Robins,A., and Gaensler,E.A. "Airways response to micro-aerosolized delta-8-tetrahydrocannabinol." *Chest* 1976, *70*, 444.

7380. Vachon,L. and Sulkowski,A. "Attention, learning, and speed in psychomotor performance after marihuana smoking." In Braude,M.C. and Szara,S.(eds.). *Pharmacology of Marihuana*. Raven Press, N.Y., 1976, 1, 449-453.

7381. Vachon,L. and Sulkowski,A. "The effect of beta-adrenergic blockade on acute marihuana intoxication." In Cohen,S. and Stillman,R.(eds.). Therapeutic Potential of Marihuana. Plenum Press, N.Y., 1976, 161-172.

7382. Vachon,L., Sulkowski,A., and Rich,E. "Marihuana effects on learning, attention and time estimation." Psychopharmacol. 1974, 39, 1-11.

7383. Vagnini,L.L. "Some replies to forensic queries in cannabis identification." Am. J. Pol. Sci. 1959, 50, 203-205.

7384. Vaillant,G.E., Brighton,J.R., and McArthur,C. "Physicians' use of mood-altering drugs." N. Eng. J. Med. 1970, 282, 365-370.

7385. Vaille,C. "Cannabis and khat."(Fr.). Nouv. Presse Med. 1976, 5, 1149-1150.

7386. Vaille,C. "International control of narcotics during the last forty years."(Fr.). Nouv. Presse Med. 1968, 76, 939-941.

7387. Vaille,C. and Stern,G. "Drugs: a social plague. Historical."(Fr.). Sem. Med. Profession. Med.-Soc. 1954, 30, 925-932, 1105-1111.

7388. Vakil,F. and Nisbet,C.T. "Some social and economic characteristics of UCLA student marihuana users." Soc. Sci. Quart. 1971, 52, 179-189.

7389. Vale,J.R. "Pharmacological approaches to the study of the cannabis problem." Internat'l. J. Addict. 1969, 4, 623-647.

7390. Valente,L. "Essential oil from cannabis." (It.). Gaz. Chim. Ital. 1880, 10, 479-481.

7391. Valente,L. "On the hydrocarbon extract of Indian hemp."(It.). Gaz. Chim. Ital. 1880, 10, 479-481.

7392. Valentine,J.L., Bryant,P.J., Gutshall,P.L., Gan,O.H.M., Lovegreen,P.A., Thompson,E.D., and Niu,H.C. "High-pressure liquid chromatographic-mass spectrometric determination of delta-9-THC in human plasma following marihuana smoking." J. Pharmaceut. Sci. 1977, 66, 1263-1265.

7393. Valentien,J.L., Bryant,P.J., Gutshall,P.L., Gan,O.H.M., Thompson,E.D., and Niu,H.C. "HPLC-MS determination of delta-9-tetrahydrocannabinol in human body samples." In Willette,P.(ed.). Cannabinoid Assay in Humans. N.I.D.A. Res. Monog. Ser. 7, Gov't. Print. Office, Washington, D.C., 1976, 96-106.

7394. Valic,F. and Zuskin,E. "Effects of hemp dust exposure on nonsmoking female textile workers." Arch. Environ. Hlth. 1971, 23, 359-364.

7395. Valic,F., Zuskin,E., Walford,J., Kersic,W., and Paukovic,R. "Byssinosis, chronic bronchitis, and ventilatory capacities in workers, exposed to soft hemp dust." Br. J. Indust. Med. 1968, 25, 176-186.

7396. Vaili'Cheva,A.I. and Abdukhalikov,F.P. "Pathomorphological alterations in the dog brain resulting from experimental acute hashish poisoning." (Rus.). Ref. Zh. Otd. Vyp. Farmakol. Khim. Sred. Toksikol. 1966, 7, 823.

7397. Valk,L.E.M. "Hemp in connection with ophthalmology." Ophthalmologica 1973, 167, 413-421.

7398. Valle,J.R. "Biogenesis of polycyclic compounds in cannabis."(Port.). Cienc. Cult. 1967, 19, 634-636.

7399. Valle,J.R.D. "Considerations on hemp (maconha or diamba)."(Port.). Inst. Adolfo Lutz 1961, 21, 83-98.

7400. Valle,J.R.D. Studies on Cannabis or Maconha. (Port.). Escola Paulista de Medicina, Sao Paulo, 1966.

7401. Valle,J.R.D., Baratella,J.R.S., Tangary,M.R., and da Silva,N. "Studies on domestic maconha(cannabis sativa L.): II. Use of guarus and lebistes in testing preparations of hemp and effects of some psychotropic drugs."(Port.). An. Acad. Brasil. Cienc. 1967, 39, 445-452.

7402. Valle,J.R.D. and Hyppolito,N. "Study on Brazilian maconha(cannabis sativa L.): I. Planting and determination of pharmacologically active peaks." (Port.). Ann. Acad. Brasil. Cienc. 1964, 36, 549-558.

7403. Valle,J.R.D., Lapa,A.J., and Barros,G.G. "Pharmacological activity of cannabis according to the sex of the plant." J. Pharm. Pharmacol. 1968, 20, 798-799.

7404. Valle,J.R.D., Souza,J.A., and Hyppolito,N. "Bioassay of cannabis preparations based on suppression of the rabbit blink reflex."(Port.). Farm. Ec. Sci. 1967, 22, 27-36.

7405. Valle,J.R.D., Souza,J.A., and Hyppolito,N. "Rabbit reactivity to cannabis preparations, pyrahexyl and tetrahydrocannabinol." J. Pharm. Pharmacol. 1966, 18, 476-478.

7406. Valverde Martinez,A. "Narcotics addicts and trafficking."(Sp.). Pol. Esp. 1970, 9, 53-54.

7407. Van Alphen,J.G. "South Africa's dynamite drug: problem of dagga." Nongqai 1946, 31, 1079-1080.

7408. Van Boven,M. "Determination of cannabinoids in cannabis sativa from Belgium."(Fr.). J. Pharm. Belg. 1976, 31, 215-219.

7409. Vance,J.M. "Marihuana is for the birds." Outdoor Life 1971, 147, 53-55.

7410. Vance,L. and Harrison,J. "Federal reefer rolling factory." High Times 1977, 25, 43-45.

7411. Van Coetsem,M. "Physiological effects of hashish on man."(Fr.). Bull. Acad. Roy. Med. Belg. 1850, 9, 330-331.

7412. Van Dedem,W.K. "Prosecution of narcotic offenders in the District of Amsterdam, during the 1964-1968 period." Lex Scient. 1969, 6, 92-94.

7413. Van den Heuvel,W.J.A. and Zacchei,A.G. "Gas-liquid chromatography in drug analysis." Adv. Chromatog. 1976, 14, 199-267.

7414. Van der Burgh,C. "The incidence of drug use among 4,588 young male subjects with particular reference to dagga: A preliminary report." Paper presented at 1st S. Af. Internat'l. Conf. Alcohol. and Drug Depend., Cape Town, 1974.

7415. Van der Helm,J.J. "Analysis of illicit drugs." In Praag,H.H.(ed.). Biochemical and Pharmacological Aspects of Dependence. De Erven F. Bohn, Haarlem, Netherlands, 1972, 119-122.

7416. Van der Merwe,N.J. "Cannabis smoking in 13th-14th century Ethiopia: Chemical evidence." In Rubin,V.(ed.). Cannabis and Culture. Mouton, The Hague, 1975, 77-81.

7417. Van der Wal,H.J. Opinions on the Use of Drugs; Report of an Investigation Among Members of the Women's Association of the Netherlands Confederation of Trade Unions.(Dut.). Found. for Alcohol and Drug Res., Amsterdam, 1972.

7418. Van Dusen,W. and Metzner,R. "The long term effects of the psychedelics." Clin. Toxicol. 1968, 1, 227-234.

7419. Van Ginneken,C.A.M., Vree,T.B., Greimer,D.D., Thijssen,H.W.H., and van Rossum,J.M. "Cannabinodiol, a new hashish constituent, identified by gas chromatography-mass spectrometry." Paper presented at Internat'. Sympos. Gas Chromatog.-mass Spectrometry, Elba, Italy, 1972.

7420. Van Grunkerbeeck,R. "A social-medical problem in black Africa."(Fr.). Tend. Temps 1961, 19, 19-38.

7421. Van Klingeren,B. and ten Ham,M. "Antibacterial activity of delta-9-tetrahydrocannabinol and cannabidiol." J. Microbiol. Serol. 1976, 42, 9-12.

7422. Van Ky,P.T., Demailly,A., and Muller,P.H. "Toxicological research on hashish. Recent observations made in the North."(Fr.). Med. Leg. Domm. Corp. 1970, 3, 245-250.

7423. Van Nuys,D. "Drug use and hypnotic susceptibility." Internat'l. J. Clin. Expt'l. Hypnosis, 1976, 20, 31-37.

7424. Van Praag,H.M. "Marihuana, folklore and science."(Dut.). Ned. Tijd. Geneesk. 1971, 115, 270-276.

7425. Van Ree,F. "Habit-forming addiction and habituation through use of alcohol, marihuana and LSD." (Dut.). Ned. Tijd. Geneesk. 1968, 112, 707-708.

7426. Van Riezen,H. and Rijk,H. "Do 'loser' rats become 'winners'?" J. Pharm. Pharmacol. 1972, 24, 829-830.

7427. Van Schoor,O. "Preparations of cannabis indica extract."(Fr.). J. Pharm. Anvers 1903, 1, 306-307.

7427a. Vardaris,R.M. and Weisz,D.J. "Delta-9-tetrahydrocannabinol and the hippocampus: Effects on CA1 field potentials in rats." Brain Res. Bull. 1977, 2, 181-187.

7428. Vardaris,R.M., Weisz,D.J., Fazel,A., and Rawitch,A.B. "Chronic administration of delta-9-tetrahydrocannabinol to pregnant rats: Studies of pup behavior and placental transfer." Pharmacol. Biochem. Behav. 1976, 4, 249-254.

7429. Varenne,G. "The concept of drug addiction." (Fr.). Belg. Tijd. Geneesk. 1964, 20, 1236-1255.

7430. Vareene,G. "The hallucinogens, especially the present marihuana problem."(Dut.). Infirmiere 1969, 47, 17-24.

7431. Varlet,T. The Paradise of Hashish.(Fr.). Malfere, Paris, 1930.

7432. Varma,D.R. and Goldbaum,D. "Effect of delta-9-tetrahydrocannabinol on experimental hypertension in rats." J. Pharm. Pharmacol. 1975, 27, 790-791.

7433. Vaschide,N. and Meunier,P. "The poisons of the intelligence--hashish--the experience of Moreau de Tours."(Fr.). Arch. Gen. Med. 1903, 80, 792-800.

7434. Vasconcelos,S. Some Notes on Maconha.(Port.). Serv. Nac. Educac. Sanit., Rio de Janeiro, 1958.

7435. Vaughan,J.G. The Structure and Utilization of Oil Seeds. Chapman and Hall, London, 1970.

7436. Vaughan,P. "Sharp criticism of the English cannabis report."(Swed.). Lakartidningen 1969, 66, 586-589.

7437. Vavivov,N.I. "Centers of origin of domesticated plants."(Rus.). Trud. Prile Bot. 1926, 16, 109.

7438. Vavivov,N.I. "The origin of the cultivation of 'primary' crops, in particular of cultivated hemp." Bull. Appl. Bot. Plant. Breed. 1926, 16, 221-233.

7439. Vavivov,N.I. and Bukinich,D.D. "Agricultural Afganistan." Bull. Appl. Bot. Plant. Breed. 1929, 33, 379-382.

7440. Vazquez,A.J. and Savelli,H.C. "Electrophysiological studies with delta-9-tetrahydrocannabinol." In Singh,J.J. and Lal,H.(eds.). Drug Addiction. Stratton Intercontiental Med. Book Corp., N.Y., 1974, 361-374.

7441. Veiga,E.P. "Contributions to the pharmacological study of maconha."(Port.). Arquiv. Univ. Bahia, 1949, 4, 91-111.

7442. Velasquez,B.L. "Criminogenic action of marihuana or cannabis and, in general, of narcotics." (Sp.). Arch. Fac. Med. Madrid 1965, 7, 131-134.

7443. Velazquez,G.R. "Clinical evaluation of patients addicted of marihuana in Baja California." (Sp.). Salud Pub. Mex. 1975, 17, 487-492.

7444. Veliky,I.A. and Genest,K. "Growth and metabolites of cannabis sativa cell suspension cultures." Lloydia 1972, 35, 450-456.

7445. Veliky,I.A. and Genest,K. "Suspension culture of cannabis sativa." Lloydia 1970, 33, 493.

7446. Venezuela. Ministry of Interior Relations. Marihuana.(Sp.). Nat'l. Print. Office, Caracas, 1961.

7447. Venturi,G. "Five year comparisons among hemp(cannabis sativa L.) cultivators."(It.). Riv. Agron. 1970, 3, 140-154.

7448. Venzmer,G. "Drug offenses: nearly all addicts started with hashish."(Ger.). Zeit. Offentl. Sorge 1971, 68, 24-26.

7449. Verbeke,R. and Corin,E. "The use of Indian hemp in Zaire: a formulation of hypotheses on the basis of an inquiry using a written questionaire." Br. J. Addict. 1976, 71, 167-174.

7450. Verdejo Vivas,G. "Marihuana."(Sp.). Hermandad Farmaceut. Almeriense 1971, 1, 1-111.

7451. Verga,A. "On hashish."(It.). Gaz. Med. Lombard. 1848, 1, 303-308.

7452. Vergely,E. "The influence of short and long days and chemicals on sex expression in hemp."(Ger.). Zeit. Pflan. 1967, 57, 26-57.

7453. Verhoeven,M. and Lundberg,G.D. "Marihuana 'like it is'." N. Eng. J. Med. 1969, 1, 909-910.

7454. Verwey,A.M.A. and Witte,A.H. "A rapid method of preparation of delta-1-THC by isolation of delta-1-THC acid from hashish."(Ger.). Pharm. Weekbl. 1972, 107, 415-416.

7455. Verwey,A.M.A. and Witte,A.H. "Thin-layer and gas chromatographic analysis of illicit hashish samples."(Ger.). Pharm. Weekbl. 1972, 107, 153-162.

7456. Vestergarrd,P., Rubin,V., Beaubrunn,M.H., Cruickshank,E., and Picou,D. "Steroid excretion in chronic cannabis users and matched controls." Act. Pharmaceut. Suec. 1971, 8, 696.

7457. Veylon,R. "Before the hippies. The 'provocateur' ideology according to a sociological study of provos (provokers and provotarianism)."(Fr.). Nouv. Presse Med. 1968, 76, 2123-2126.

7458. Victor,H.R., Grossman,J.C., and Eisenman,R. "Openness to experience and marihuana use in high school students." J. Consult. Clin. Psychol. 1973, 41, 78-85.

7459. Vidal,J.J., Rickles,W.R., Hanley,J., and Buch,M.D. "Effect of acute marihuana intoxication upon the human EEG." EEG Clin. Neurol. 1973, 34, 743-744.

7460. Viehoever,A. "Field tests for marihuana (cannabis)." Am. J. Pharmacol. 1937, 109, 589-591.

7461. Vieira,F.J.A. On the Characterization of the Effects of the Combustion Products of Maconha on White Mice.(Port.). Univ. Ceara, Fortaleza, Brazil.

7462. Viera,F.J.A. and Aguira,M.B. Action of Maconha(Cannabis Sativa) in Cases of Labored Breathing Caused by High Doses of Nesdonal.(Port.). Univ. Ceara, Fortaleza, 1964.

7463. Vieira,F.J.A., Aguiar,M.B., Alencar,J.W., Seabra,A.P., Tursch,B.M., and Leclercq,J. "Effects of the organic layer of hashish smoke extract and preliminary results of its chemical analysis." Psychopharmacol. 1967, 10, 361-362.

7464. Viera,F.J.A., Aguira,M.B., and Filho,F.M.F. "Relation between the anticurare action and the excitatory effects of maconha(cannabis sativa)."(Port.). Paper presented at 16th meeting of Brazilian Soc. for the Progress of Science, Sao Paulo, 1964.

7465. Vieira,F.J.A., Cavalcanti,L.A., Pereira,W.M., and Martins,F. "Nicotinic action of maconha(cannabis sativa)."(Port.). Cien. Cult. 1965, 17, 275.

7466. Vieira,F.J., Abreu,L.C., and Valle,J.R. "On the pharmacology of hemp seed oil." Med. Pharmacol. Expt'l. 1967, 16, 219-224.

7467. Vierth,G. "Psychopathological syndrome following use of hashish. Observations in Morocco." (Ger.). Munch. Med. Woch. 1967, 109, 522-526.

7468. Vigier,A. Contribution to the Study of Cannabis Sativa Seed.(Fr.). Univ. Lyon, Lyon, France, 1933.

7469. Vignole,G. "Essence of cannabis indica."(It.). Gaz. Chim. Ital. 1895, 25, 110-114, 262-268.

7470. Vincent,J. "Experiences of a hashish user." (Fr.). Rev. Paris 1900, 7, 151-165.

7471. Vincent,M.L. "A comparison of the drug habits and attitudes of alcohol and marihuana users." J. Drug Educat. 1972, 2, 149-170.

7472. Vincent,R.J. "A scale to measure attitude toward smoking marihuana." J. Sch. Hlth. 1970, 40, 454-456.

7473. Vincent,R.J. "A ten month comparison of the incidence of smoking marihuana at a midwestern university." J. Alcohol Educat. 1970, 15, 25-34.

7474. Vincent,R.J. "Comparison of incidence of smoking of marihuana." J. Sch. Hlth. 1970, 1, 25-26, 30.

7475. Vincent,R.J. "Marihuana use and non-use. A study of secondary school students' attitudes in Carbondale, Illinois." J. Alcohol Educat. 1969, 15, 21-25.

7476. Vinkenoog,S. "High season." In Andrews,G. and Vinkenoog,S.(eds.). The Book of Grass. Grove Press, N.Y., 1967, 132-134.

7477. Vinson,J.A. and Hooyman,J.E. "Studies in laboratory-use reagents. III. Simplethin-layer chromatographic system for the separation of cannabinoids." J. Chromatog. 1975, 106, 196-199.

7478. Virey,J.J. "On nepenthe; an exhiliarating remedy given by the beautiful Helen to Telemac, according to Homer."(Fr.). Bull. Pharm. 1813, 5, 49-60.

7479. Vitez,T.S., Way,W.L., Miller,R.D., and Eger,E.I. "Effects of delta-9-tetrahydrocannabinol on cyclopropane MAC in the rat." Anesthesiology 1973, 38, 525-527.

7480. Voelksen,W. "Hemp as a drug and narcotic. Detection of marihuana and hashish."(Ger.). Apoth.-Ztg. 1970, 110, 1869-1873.

7481. Vogelgesang,A. "On cannabinon."(Ger.). Allgem. Zeit. Psychiat. 1886, 1, 341-345.

7482. Vogl,A.J. "Marihuana: A bad front in a good war?" Med. Econ. 1970, 47, 33-44.

7483. Volavka,J., Crown,P., Dornbush,R., Feldstein,S., and Fink,M. "EEG, heart rate and mood change ('high') after cannabis." Psychopharmacol. 1973, 32, 11-25.

7484. Volavka,J., Dornbush,R., Feldstein,S., Clare,G., Zaks,A., Fink,M., and Freedman,A.M. "Marihuana, EEG, and behavior." Ann. N. Y. Acad. Sci. 1971, 191, 206-216.

7485. Vollmer,R.R., Cavero,I., Ertel,R.J., Solomon, T.A., and Buckley,J.P. "Role of the central autonomic nervous system in the hypotension and bradycardia induced by (-)-delta-9-trans-tetrahydrocannabinol." J. Pharm. Pharmacol. 1974, 26, 186-192.

7486. Vollner,L., Bieniek,K., and Korte,F. "Hashish XX. Cannabidivarian, a new hashish constituent." (Ger.). Tetrahed. Let. 1969, 3, 145-147.

7487. Von Kobylanski,F. Ecbolic Action of Indian Hemp.(Ger.). Backer, Wurzburg, 1852.

7488. Von Schnizer,V. "Herb of folly."(Ger.). Fortschrit. Med. 1925, 43, 391-392.

7489. Von Schroff,C. and von Schroff,C. Handbook of Pharmacology.(Ger.). Braumuller, Vienna, 1873.

7490. Von Sengbusch,R. "Contribution to the study of the cannabis sativa sex problem."(Ger.). Zeit. Induct. Abstammungs 1942, 80, 616-618.

7491. Von Sengbusch,R. "New contribution to the study of sexual inheritance of hemp as a basis for the cultivation of monoecious hemp."(Ger.). Zeit. Pflan. 1952, 31, 319-338.

7492. Von Sengbusch,R. "New method of hemp cultivation."(Ger.). Das Reich 1944, 9, 23.

7493. Von Sengbusch,R. "Selection of high fiber varieties of monoecious and dioecious hemp."(Ger.). Proc. Internat'l. Flax Hemp Res. Cong. 1956, 5, 9.

7494. Von Sengbusch,R., Hunke,W., Jordan,D., and Neurer,H. "Basis for the cultivation of monoecious hemp."(Ger.). Zeit. Pflan. 1952, 29, 55-75.

7495. Von Sengbusch,R., Neurer,H., and Prieger,E. "Hemp cultivation. Increase of fiber yield."(Ger.). Zuchter 1946, 17, 33-39.

7496. Von Sengbusch,R., Neurer,H., and Prieger,E. "Sexual heredity of hemp and cultivation of monoecious hemp."(Ger.). Zuchter 1943, 15, 49-62.

7497. Votava,A. "Pharmacological problems of drug dependence." Activ. Nerv. Super. 1970, 12, 136.

7498. Vree,T.B. "Mass spectrometry of cannabinoids." J. Pharmaceut. Sci. 1977, 66, 1444-1450.

7499. Vree,T.B., Breimer,D.D., van Ginneken,C.A.M., and van Rossum,J.M. "Gas chromatography of cannabis constituents and their synthetic derivatives." J. Chromatog. 1972, 74, 209-224.

7500. Vree,T.B., Breimer,D.D., van Ginneken,C.A.M., and van Rossum,J.M. "Identification in hashish of tetrahydrocannabinol, cannabidiol and cannabinol analogs with a methyl side-chain." J. Pharm. Pharmacol. 1972, 24, 7-12.

7501. Vree,T.B., Breimer,D.D., van Ginneken,C.A.M., and van Rossum,J.M. "Identification of cannabicyclol with a pentyl or propyl side-chain by means of combined gas chromatography-mass spectrometry." J. Chromatog. 1972, 74, 124-127.

7502. Vree,T.B., Breimer,D.D., van Ginneken,C.A.M., and van Rossum,J.M. "Identification of cannabivarins in hashish by a new method of combined gas chromatography-mass spectrometry." Clin. Chim. Act. 1971, 34, 365-372.

7503. Vree,T.B., Breimer,D.D., van Ginneken,C.A.M., and van Rossum,J.M. "Identification of the methyl and propyl homologues of CBD, THC and CBN in hashish by a new method of combined gas chromatgraphy-mass spectrometry." Act. Pharmaceut. Suec. 1971, 8, 683-684.

7504. Vree,T.B., Breimer,D.D., van Ginneken,C.A.M. van Rossum,J.M., de Zeeuw,R.A., Merkus,F.W.H.M., Witte, A.H., and Verwey,A.M.A. "Chemistry and pharmacokinetics of hashish and marihuana constituents."(Dut.). Chem. Weekbl. 1972, 68, 1-16.

7505. Vree,T.B., Breimer,D.D., van Ginneken,C.A.M., van Rossum,J.M., and Nibbering,N.M.M. "Gas chromatography of cannabinoids. Gas chromatographic behavior of cis- and trans-tetrahydrocannabinol and isotetrahydro-cannabinol." J. Chromatog. 1973, 79, 81-90.

7506. Vree,T.B. and Nibbering,N.M.M. "Phenolic proton transfer to the 1,2 double bond in the molecular ion of trans-1,2-tetrahydrocannabinol." Tetrahedron 1973, 29, 3849-3852.

7507. Vyas,D.K. and Singh,R. "Effect of cannabis and opium on the testis of the pigeon Columba Livia Gmelin." Ind. J. Expt'l. Biol. 1976, 14, 22-25.

W

7508. Wacker,J.R. and Knowles,L. "Victimless crimes: perceptions and attitudes of television critics, high school teachers, and police officers." Police Chief 1975, 43, 38-39.

7509. Wackwitz,J.H., Pelfrey,M.C., and Stenmark,D.E. "The relationship of social and personality characteristics to hallucinogenic use among college females." Addict. Dis. 1974, 1, 189-202.

7510. Wada,J.A., Osawa,T., and Corcoran,M.E. "Effects of tetrahydrocannabinols on kindled amygdaloid seizures and photgenic seizures in Senegalese baboons, Papio papio." Epilepsia 1975, 16, 439-448.

7511. Wada,J.A., Sato,M., and Corcoran,M.E. "Antiepileptic properties of delta-9-tetrahydrocannabinol." Expt'l. Neurol. 1973, 39, 157-165.

7512. Wade,N. "Pot and heroin." New Soc. 1969, 13, 117-118.

7513. Wade,N. "Rise and fall of a research project; sex-pot case." Science 1976, 192, 1086-1087.

7514. Wagley,C. and Galvao,E. The Tenetehara Indians of Brazil. Columbia Univ. Press, N.Y., 1949.

7515. Wagner,E.E. and Romanik,D.G. "Hand test characteristics of marihuana-experienced and multiple-drug-using college students." Percept. Motor Skills 1976, 43, 1302-1306.

7516. Wahlquiest,M., Nilsson,I.M., Sandberg,F., Agurell,S., and Granstrand,B. "Binding of delta-1-tetrahydrocannabinol to human plasma proteins." Biochem. Pharmacol. 1970, 19, 2579-2584.

7517. Waldman,M.M. "Marihuana bronchitis." J.A.M.A. 1970, 211, 501.

7518. Waldo,G.P. and Chiricos,T.G. "An alternative approach to deterrence research." Proc. Am. Sociol. Assoc. 1971, 19, 264.

7519. Waldo,G.P. and Chiricos,T.G. "Perceived penal sanction and self-reported criminality: A neglected approach to deterence research." Soc. Prob. 1972, 19, 522-540.

7520. Waldrop,F.C. "Public enemy no. 1--dope." Hearst's Internat'l. Cosmopol. 1938, 104, 34-35, 152-153.

7521. Walk,D.J. "Marihuana on the campus. A study at one university." J. Am. Coll. Hlth. Assoc. 1968, 17, 144-149.

7522. Walker,B. "Indian hemp poisoning." Br. Med. J. 1896, 2, 1382.

7523. Wall,M.E. "The in vitro and in vivo metabolism of tetrahydrocannabinol(THC)." Ann. N. Y. Acad. Sci. 1971, 191, 23-39.

7524. Wall,M.E. and Brine,D.R. "Identification of cannabinoids and metabolites in biological materials by combined gas-liquid chromatography-mass spectrometry." In Nahas,G.G., Paton,W.D.M., and Idanpaan-Heikkila,J.E. (eds.). Marihuana. Springer Verlag, N.Y., 1976, 51-63.

7525. Wall,M.E., Brine,D.R., Brine,G.A., Pitt,C.G., Freudenthal,R.I., and Christensen,H.D. "Isolation, structure, and biological activity of several metabolites of delta-9-tetrahydrocannabinol." J. Am. Chem. Soc. 1970, 92, 3466-3468.

7526. Wall,M.E., Brine,D.R., and Perez-Reyes,M. "Metabolism of cannabinoids in man." In Braude,M.C. and Szara,S.(eds.). Pharmacology of Marihuana. Raven Press, N.Y., 1976, 1, 93-117.

7527. Wall,M.E., Brine,D., Perez-Reyes,M., and Lipton,M. "Studies on the in vitro and in vivo metabolism of delta-9-tetrahydrocannabinol." Act. Pharmaceut. Suec. 1971, 8, 702-703.

7528. Wall,M.E., Brine,D.R., Pitt,C.G., and Perez-Reyes,M. "Identification of delta-9-tetrahydrocannabinol and metabolites in man." J. Am. Chem. Soc. 1972, 94, 8579-8581.

7529. Wall,M.E., Harvey,T.M., Bursey,J.T., Brine,D.R., and Rosenthal,D. "Analytical methods for the determination of cannabinoids in biological materials." In Willette,P. (ed.). Cannabinoid Assay in Humans. N.I.D.A. Res. Monog. Ser. 7, Gov't. Print. Office, Washington, D.C., 1976, 107-117.

7530. Wallace,D.G., Brown,R.H., and Boulter,D. "The amino acid sequence of cannabis sativa cytochrome-C." Phytochemistry 1973, 12, 2617-2622.

7531. Wallace,G.B. "Summary of sociological, medical, physiological, and pharmacological findings of New York City Mayor's Comittee on Marihuana."(Sp.). Salub. Asist. 1945, 2, 33-41.

7532. Wallach,M.B. and Gershon,S. "The effects of delta-8-tetrahydrocannabinol on the electroencephalogram(EEG), reticular formation multiple unit acitivty (RUA) and sleep of the cat." Fed. Proc. 1972, 31, 250.

7533. Wallach,M.B. and Gershon,S. "The effects of delta-8-THC on the EEG, reticular multiple unit activity and sleep of cats." Eur. J. Pharmacol. 1973, 24, 172-178.

7534. Wallenstein,D. "Marihuana possession as an aspect of the right of privacy." Crim. Law Bull. 1969, 5, 59-93.

7535. Waller,C.W. "Chemistry of marihuana." Pharmacol. Rev. 1971, 23, 265-271.

7536. Waller,C.W. "Growing, extracting and analysis of cannabis sativa." Paper presented at Am. Pharmaceut. Assoc., San Francisco, 1971.

7537. Waller,C.W. "Standardized sources of supply for marihuana research." In Braude,M.C. and Szara,S. (eds.). Pharmacology of Marihuana. Raven Press, N.Y., 1976, 1, 19-21.

7538. Waller,C.W. "Supplies for the marihuana program." Comm. Prob. Drug Depend. 1970, 3, 6394-6396.

7539. Waller,C.W. "The chemistry of marihuana." Proc. West. Pharmacol. Soc. 1971, 14, 1-3.

7540. Waller,C.W. and Denny,J.J. Annotated Bibliography of Marihuana(Cannabis sativa L.) 1964-1970. Univ. Mississippi, Univ., Miss. 1971.

7541. Waller,C.W., Denny,J.J., and Walz,M.A. Annotated Bibliography of Marihuana(Cannabis sativa L.) 1971 Supplement. Univ. Mississippi, Univ., Miss., 1972.

7542. Waller,C.W., Hadley,K., and Turner,C.T. "Detection and identification of compounds in cannabis." In Nahas,G.G., Paton,W.D.M., and Idanpaan-Heikkila,J.E. (eds.). Marihuana. Springer Verlag, N.Y., 1976, 15-31.

7543. Waller,C.W., Johnson,J.J., Buelke,J., and Turner,C.E. Marihuana: An Annotated Bibliography. Macmillan Information, N.Y., 1976.

7544. Waller,C.W. and Scigliano,J.A. "II. The national marihuana program." Drug Depend. 1970, 4, 28-32.

7545. Waller,J.A. "Drugs and highway crashes." J.A.M.A. 1971, 215, 1477-1482.

7546. Waller,J.A., Lamborn,K.R., and Steffenhagen,R.A. "Marihuana and driving among teenagers: reported use patterns, effects, and experiences related to driving.' Accid. Anal. Prevent. 1974, 6, 141-161.

7547. Wallich,G.C. "Cannabis indica." Br. Med. J. 1883, 1, 1224.

7548. Wallis,T.E. Textbook of Pharmacognosy. J. and A. Churchill, London, 1967.

7549. Walsh,E.P. and Frantz,T.T. "The relationship of marihuana smoking and LSD, sex, age, and grades: Setting and rationale for use." J. Coll. Stud. Person. 1972, 13, 18-52.

7550. Walsh,J. "Narcotics and drug abuse: A presidential prescription." Science 1969, 165, 377-378.

7551. Walsh,J.M. and Burch,L.S. "Reduction of the behavioral effects of delta-9-THC by hyperbaric pressure." Pharmacol. Biochem. Behav. 1977, 7, 111-116.

7552. Walters,G.C. and Abel,E.L. "Effects of a marihuana homologue(pyrahexyl) on avoidance learning in the gerbil." J. Pharm. Pharmacol. 1970, 22, 310-312.

7553. Walters,P.A., Goethals,G.W., and Pope,H.G. "Drug use and life style among 500 college undergraduates." Arch. Gen. Psychiat. 1972, 26, 92-96.

7554. Walton,J. "The dagga pipes of Southern Africa." Res. Nat'l. Mus. Bloem. 1953, 1, 85-113.

7555. Walton,R.P. Marihuana; America's New Drug Problem. J.P. Lippincott, Phil., 1938.

7556. Walton,R.P. "Marihuana problems." J.A.M.A. 1945, 128, 383.

7557. Walton,R.P., Martin,L.F., and Keller,J.H. "The relative activity of various purified products obtained from American grown hashish." J. Pharmacol. Exper. Ther. 1938, 62, 239-251.

7558. Wardell,D. and Mehra,N. "Prediction of marihuana usage among students in a university residence." J. Coll. Stud. Person. 1974, 15, 31-33.

7559. Warden,A.J. The Linen Trade. Frank Cass and Co., London, 1864.

7560. Warden,W. "The active principle of Indian hemp." Pharmaceut. J. Trans. 1885, 15, 574-575.

7561. Waring,E.J. Pharmacopoeia of India, 1868. Indian Office, London, 1868.

7562. Waring,G. "Political snafus surround release of LeDain report." Can. Med. Assoc. J. 1970, 103, 117.

7563. Warmke,H.E. "Use of the killfish, fundulus heteroclitus, in the assay of marihuana." J.A.P.A. 1944, 33, 122-125.

7564. Warner,A.M. and Pierozynski,G. "Case report: Psuedocatatonia associated with abuse of amphetamine and cannabis." Postgrad. Med. 1977, 61, 275-277.

7565. Warner,E.B. "Sources of hallucinogenic drugs, including marihuana: The nature and economic significance of the trade." In Wittenborn,J.R., Brill,H., Smith,J.P., and Wittenborn,A.S. Drugs and Youth. C.C.Thomas, Springfield, 1969, 161-167.

7566. Warner,R.W. "Preventing drug abuse: Where are we now?" Person. Guid. J. 1973, 51, 523-529.

7567. Warner,W., Harris,L.S., and Carchman,R.A. "Inhibition of corticosteroidogenesis by delta-9-tetrahydrocannabnol." Endocrinol. 1977, 101, 1815-1820.

7568. Warnock,J. "Insanity from hasheesh." J. Ment. Sci. 1903, 49, 96-110.

7569. Warnock,J. "Insanity from hasheesh." Quart. J. Inebriety 1903, 25, 134-141.

7570. Waser,P.G., Hofmann,A., and Mikes, F. "Marihuana components in smoke and identification of delta-9-THC and two of its metabolites in rats." Act. Pharmaceut. Suec. 1971, 8, 685-686.

7571. Waser,P.G. and Martin,A. "Barbiturate potentiating, temperature reducing, analgesic, and behavioral effects of some synthetic tetrahydrocannabinol derivates in comparison with delta-9-THC." In Braude,M.C. and Szara,S.(eds.). Pharmacology of Marihuana. Raven Press, N.Y., 1976, 331-335.

7572. Waser,P.F., Martin,A., and Heer-Carcano,L. "The effect of delta-9-tetrahydrocannabinol and LSD on the acquisition of an active avoidance response in the rat." Psychopharmacol. 1976, 46, 249-254.

7573. Washburn,B.E. "Ganja smoking." Jamaica Pub. Hlth. 1935, 10, 1-6.

7574. Washington,G. "Diary notes." In Andrews,G. and Vinkenoog,S.(eds.). The Book of Grass. Grove Press, N.Y., 1967, 34.

7575. Waskow,I.E., Olsson,J.E., Salzman,C., Katz,M.M., and Chase,C. "Psychological effects of tetrahydrocannabinol." Arch. Gen. Psychiat. 1970, 22, 97-107.

7576. Wasson,R.G. Soma, Divine Mushroom of Immortality. Harcourt Brace Jonanovich, N.Y., 1975.

7577. Watanabe,K. "A simple method for the field test of cannabis." J. Hyg. Chem. 1970, 16, 101-104.

7577 Waterman,L. Royal Correspondence of the Assyrian Empire. Univ. Mich. Press, Ann Arbor, 1930.

7578. Waters,D.H. and Glick,S.D. "Asymmetrical effect of delta-9-tetrahydrocannabinol(THC) on striatal dopamine and behavior." Res. Commun. Chem. Pathol. Pharmacol. 1973, 6, 57-63.

7579. Watson,C.C. "Drug addiction." Br. Med. J. 1969, 1, 639.

7580. Watt,D.C., Brouckova,V., Bastecky,J., and Velek,M. "Drug addiction--a menace to youth in Great Britain." Activ. Nerv. Sup. 1970, 12, 284-287.

7581. Watt,G. The Commercial Products of India. J. Murray, London, 1908.

7582. Watt,J.M. "Dagga in South Africa." Bull. Narc. 1961, 13, 9-14.

7583. Watt,J.M. "Drug dependence of the hashish type." In Wolstenholme,G.E.W. and Knight,J.(eds.). Hashish: Its Chemistry and Pharmacology. Ciba Found. Study Group No. 21, Little Brown Co., Boston, 1965, 54-69.

7584. Watt,J.M. "Plants and poisoning in man." S. Af. J. Sci. 1937, 33, 702-707.

7585. Watt,J.M. and Breyer-Brandwijk,M.G. "The forensic and sociological aspects of the dagga problem in South Africa." S. Af. Med. J. 1936, 10, 573-579.

7586. Watt,J.M. and Breyer-Brandwijk,M.G. The Medicinal and Poisonous Plants of Southern Africa. E. and S. Livingstone, Edinburgh, 1932.

7587. Watt,J.M. and Breyer-Brandwijk,M.G. The Medicinal and Poisonous Plants of Southern and Eastern Africa. E. and S. Livingstone, Edinburgh, 1962.

7588. Watts,A. "A psychedelic experience: Fact or fantasy?" In Andrews,G. and Winkenoog,S.(eds.). The Book of Grass. Grove Press, N.Y., 1967, 184.

7589. Watts,M.S. and Smith,L.H. "Where we stand on drug abuse." Cal. Med. 1967, 107, 357.

7590. Way,E.L. "Cannabis prelude." Pharmacol. Rev. 1971, 23, 263-264.

7591. Way,E.L. and Isbell,H. "Marihuana and its surrogates." Pharmacol. Rev. 1971, 23, 389.

7592. Wayner,M.J. "The effects of ethyl alcohol and delta-9-THC on the lateral hypothalamus and adjunctive behavior." Paper presented at 1st Lat. Am. Cong. on Psychobiol., Sao Paulo, 1963.

7593. Wayner,M.J., Greenberg,I., Fraley,S., and Fisher,S. "Effects of delta-9-tetrahydrocannabinol and ethyl alcohol on adjunctive behavior and the lateral hypothalamus." Physiol. Behav. 1973, 10, 109-131.

7594. Webb,C.W. "Marihuana use not criminal." N. Eng. J. Med. 1971, 284, 505.

7595. Webb,R.A.J. "Control of marihuana." In Joint Parliamentry Committee on Drugs. Health Commission of New South Wales. Gov't. Printer, New South Wales, 1976.

7596. Webb,S.D. and Colette,J. "Ecological and household correlates of stress-alleviative drug use." Am. Behav. Sci. 1975, 18, 750-770.

7597. Weber,C.M. "'Mary Warner'." Hlth. Dig. 1936, 3, 77-78.

7598. Weber,J.R. "Nutrition and aeration in relation to growth of cannabis sativa." Iowa Acad. Sci. 1951, 58, 221-228.

7599. Webster,C.D., Herring,B., Jupiter,H., and Willinsky,M.D. "The effects of 1-delta-1-tetrahydro-cannabinol on discriminated Sidman avoidance during prolonged sessions." Psychon. Sci. 1970, 21, 289.

7600. Webster,C.D., LeBlanc,A.E., Marshman,J.A., and Beaton,J.M. "Acquisition and loss of tolerance to 1-

delta-9-trans-tetrahydrocannabinol in rats on an avoidance schedule." Psychopharmacol. 1973, 30, 217-226.

7601. Webster,C.D., Willinsky,M.D., Herring,B.S., and Walters,G.C. "Effects of 1-delta-1-tetrahydrocannabinol on temporally spaced responding and discriminated Sidman avoidance behavior in rats." Nature 1971, 232, 498-501.

7602. Wechsler,H. "Marihuana, alcohol and public policy." N. Eng. J. Med. 1972, 287, 515-516.

7603. Wechsler,H. and Thum,D. Drug Use Among High School Youth in the Town of Brookline. Medical Found. Inc., Boston, Mass, 1972.

7604. Wechsler,H. and Thum,D. "Drug use among teenagers: patterns of present and anticipated use." Internat'l. J. Addict. 1973, 8, 909-920.

7605. Weckowica,T.E., Collier,G., and Spreng,L. "Field dependence, cognitive functions, personality traits, and social values in heavy cannabis users and nonuser controls." Psychol. Rep. 1977, 41, 291-302.

7606. Weckowica,T.E., Fedora,O., Mason,J., Radstaak, D., Kyung,S.B., and Yonge,K.A. "Effect of marihuana on divergent and convergent production cognitive tests." J. Abnorm. Psychol. 1975, 84, 386-398.

7607. Weckowicz,T.E. and Janssen,D.V. "Cognitive functions, personality traits and social values in heavy marihuana smokers and nonsmoker controls." J. Abnorm. Psychol. 1973, 81, 264-269.

7608. Weeks,L.E. "Drug usage and drug availability." Cal. Ment. Hlth. Res. Dig. 1965, 3, 118-119.

7609. Weil,A.T. "Adverse reactions to marihuana. Classification and suggested treatment." N. Eng. J. Med. 1970, 282, 997-1000.

7610. Weil,A.T. "Cannabis." Science Journal 1969, 5A, 36-42.

7611. Weil,A.T. "Drugs and the mind." Harv. Rev. 1963, 1, 3-5.

7612. Weil,A.T. "Marihuana." Science 1969, 163, 1144-1145.

7613. Weil,A.T. "Marihuana effects amid great expectations." Science 1969, 165, 204.

7614. Weil,A.T. The Natural Mind. Houghton Mifflin, Boston, 1972.

7615. Weil,A.T. and Zinberg,N.E. "Acute effects of marihuana on speech." Nature 1969, 222, 434-437.

7616. Weil,A.T., Zinberg,N.E., and Nelsen,J.M. "Clinical and psychological effects of marihuana in man." Internat'l. J. Addict. 1969, 4, 427-451.

7617. Weil,A.T., Zinberg,N.E., and Nelsen,J.M. "Clinical and psychological effects of marihuana in man." Ment. Hlth. Dig. 1969, 1, 53-56.

7618. Weil,A.T., Zinberg,N.E., and Nelsen,J.M. "Clinical and psychological effects of marihuana in man." Science 1968, 162, 1234-1242.

7619. Weil,A.T., Zinberg,N.E., and Nelsen,J.M. "Clinical and psychological effects of marihuana in man." Pediatrics 1970, 45, 129.

7620. Weinberg,A.D., Dimen,E., Borzelleca,J.F., and Harris,L.S."Weight and activity in male mice after daily inhalation of cannabis smoke in an automated smoke exposure chamber." J. Pharm. Phamacol. 1977, 29, 477-481.

7621. Weinberg,A.D., Dimen,E.M. , Simon,G.S., and Harris,L.S. "Measurements of weight and activity in male mice following inhalation of cannabis smoke in a controlled smoke exposure chamber." Toxicol. Appl. Pharmacol. 1977, 42, 301-307.

7622. Weingartner,H. "The effect of marihuana and synthetic delta-9-THC on information processing." Proc. Am. Psychol. Assoc. 1972, 7, 813-814.

7623. Weinhardt,K.K., Razdan,R.K., and Dalzell,H.C. "Hashish: Synthesis of (-)-7-hydroxy-delta-1-6-tetrahydrocannabinol." Tetrahed. Lett. 1971, 50, 4827-4830.

7624. Weinrich,J.D. "Marihuana and sex." N. Eng. J. Med. 1974, 291, 309.

7625. Weinstein,R.M. "Interpersonal expectations for marihuana behavior." Internat'l. J. Addict. 1977, 12, 121-136.

7626. Weinstein,R.M. "The imputation of motives for marihuana behavior." Internat'l. J. Addict. 1976, 11, 571-595.

7627. Weiss,J.A. and Wizner,S.B. "Pot, prayer and privacy: the right to cut your own throat in your own way." Iowa Law Rev. 1969, 54, 709.

7628. Weiss,J.L., Watanabe,A.M., Lemberger,L., and Tamarkin,N.R. "Cardiovascular effects of delta-9-tetrahydrocannabinol in man." Clin. Pharmacol. Ther. 1972, 13, 671-684.

7629. Weissbach,T.A., Averbach,B., and Vogler,R.E. "Some social and personality correlates of heroin use." Psychol. Rep. 1973, 33, 755-758.

7630. Weisz,D.J., and Vardaris,R.M. "Effects of delta-9-tetrahydrocannabinol on the slope of auditory generalization gradients in rats." Physiol. Psychol. 1976, 4, 145-148.

7631. Weitman,M., Scheble,R.O., and Johnson,K.G. "Survey of adolescent drug use. I.V. Patterns of drug use." Am. J. Pub. Hlth. 1974, 64, 417-421.

7632. Weitman,M., Scheble,R., Johnson,K.G., and Abbey,H. "Correlations among use of drugs." Am. J. Pub. Hlth. 1972, 62, 166-170.

7633. Weitz,R. and Dardanne,A. "Concerning a chemical test for Indian hemp and its preparations."(Fr.). Bull. Sci. Pharmacol. 1924, 31, 321-330.

7634. Weitzner,M., Smith,A., Pollack,H., Gerver,I., and Figlio,R.M. "A study of the relationship of disposition and subsequent criminal behavior in a sample of youthful marihuana offenders in New York State." In National Commission on Marihuana and Drug Abuse. Drug Use in America: Problem in Perspective. Gov't. Print. Office, Washington, D.C., 1973, III, 798-809.

7635. Weizel,A., Linhart,P., and Heilmann,K. "Hepatitis after taking narcotic and hallucinogenic drugs." (Ger.). Deut. Med. Woch. 1971, 96, 445-448.

7636. Welburn,P.J., Starmer,G.A., Chesher,G.B., and Jackson,D.M. "Effect of cannabinoids on the abdominal constriction response in mice: within cannabinoid interactions." Psychopharmacol. 1976, 46, 83-85.

7637. Welch,B.L., Welch,A.S., Messiha,F.S., and Berger,H.J. "Rapid depletion of adrenal epinephrine and elevation of telencephalic serotonin by (-)- trans-delta-9-tetrahydrocannabinol in mice." Res. Commun. Chem. Pathol. Pharmacol. 1971, 2, 382-391.

7638. Wellisch,D. and Hays,R.J. "A cross-cultural study of the prevalence and correlates of student drug use in the U.S. and Mexico." Bull. Narc. 1974, 26, 31-42.

7639. Wells,B. and Stacey,B. "A further comparison of cannabis(marihuana) users and non-users." Br. J. Addict. 1976, 71, 161-165.

7640. Wendkos,M.H. "Electrocardiographic effects of marihuana." J.A.M.A. 1973, 226, 789-790.

7641. Wenkert,E., Cochran,D.W., Schell,F.M., Archer,R.A., and Matsumoto,K. "CMR spectral analysis of tetrahydrocannabinol and its isomers." Experientia 1972, 28, 250-251.

7641. Wentworth-Rohr,I. "Marihuana flashback: A clinical note." Psychother. Theory Res. Pract. 1970, 7, 236-237.

7642. Weppner,R.S. and Agar,M.H. "Immediate precursors to heroin addiction." J. Hlth. Soc. Behav. 1971, 62, 10-18.

7643. Weppner,R.S. and Inciardi,J.A. "Some problems in decriminalizing marihuana: protection from a devil drug or keeping the status quo?" Paper presented at 28th Meet. Am. Soc. Criminol., Miami, 1976.

7644. Werkman,S.L. "'What next?'--Youth and drugs." Rocky Mt. Med. J. 1969, 66, 32-36.

7645. Werner,G. and Erdmann,G. "Autoradiographic investigation of ^{14}C-tetrahydrocannabinol distribution in the monkey Hapale jacchus." Arch. Pharmacol. 1974, 282, 22.

7646. Werner,J. "Frankish royal tombs in the cathedrals of Cologne and Saint-Denis." Antiquity 1964, 38, 201-216.

7647. Wertlake,P.T. "LSD and marihuana: Where are the answers?" Science 1968, 160, 1064-1065.

7648. West,H.J. "Adolescent drug attitudes: a seven-year study on marihuana and LSD." Diss. Abs. 1975, 35, 5944.

7649. Westen,P.K. "Drugs and the law." Cal. Law Rev. 1968, 56, 1-16.

7650. Wetle,T. and Sengstake,C.B. "The effects of tetrahydrocannabinol on eating behavior of rats." Proc. West. Psychol. Assoc. 1971, 1, 1-8.

7651. Wetz,R. "Youth and drugs."(Ger.). Soz. Welt 1972, 33, 169-187.

7652. Wexler,M. "Personality characteristics of marihuana users and non-users." Cornell J. Soc. Rel. 1975, 10, 1-10.

7653. Whalley,C., Mosnaim,A.D., and Sabelli,H.C. "2-phenylethylamine in rabbit brain and liver: Its synthesis, metabolism and role in the action of imipramine, pargyline and marihuana." Pharmacologist 1973, 15, 258.

7654. Wheals,B.B. and Smith,R.N. "Comparative cannabis analysis. A comparison of high-pressure liquid chromatography with other chromatographic techniques." J. Chromatog. 1975, 105, 396-400.

7655. Wheeler,E.L. "Facts about drug addiction." Nat'l. Educat. Assoc. 1953, 42, 142-143.

7656. Whineray,E. "A pharmacological study of cannabis sativa (being a collection of facts as known at the present date)." In Regardie,I.(ed.). Roll Away the Stone. Llewellyn, St. Paul, Minn., 1968, 69-91.

7657. Whineray,E. "The herb dangerous." In Andrews, G. and Vinkenoog,S.(eds.). The Book of Grass. Grove Press, N.Y., 1967, 69-76.

7658. Whipple,D.V. Is the Grass Greener? Answers to Questions About Drugs. Robert B. Luce, N.Y., 1971.

7659. Whipple,D.V. "What causes more harm, drugs or the laws against them? Excerpt from Is the Grass Greener?" McCalls 1972, 99, 70.

7660. Whiskin,F.E. "An interview with a patient under the influence of marihuana." Internat'l. J. Offend. Ther. Comp. Crim. 1974, 18, 198-199.

7661. Whitaker,R. Drugs and the Law. Methuen, Toronto, 1969.

7662. White,A.C., Munson,J.A., Munson,A.E., and Carchman,R.A. "Effects of delta-9-tetrahydrocannabinol in Lewis lung adenocarcinoma cells in tissue culture." J. Nat'l. Cancer Inst. 1976, 56, 655-658.

7663. White,B. and Cianciarulo,J. "An aid in the biologic assay of cannabis preparations." J.A.P.A. 1924, 13, 813-814.

7664. White,J.R. "The marihuana puff-in." Petition presented to State Supreme Court." Sacremento, 1964.

7665. White,J.S. "Physiological standardisation." Analyst 1923, 48, 303-314.

7666. White,S.C., Brin,S.C., and Janicki,B.W. "Mitogen-induced blastogenic responses of lymphocytes from marihuana smokers." Science 1975, 187, 71-72.

7667. Whitehead,P.C. Drug Use Among Adolescent Students in Halifax. Youth Agency, Halifax, Nova Scotia, 1970.

7668. Whitehead,P.C. "Religious affiliation and use of drugs among adolescent students." J. Scient. Stud. Relig. 1970, 9, 152-154.

7669. Whitehead,P.C. "Student behavior and attitudes toward drugs." Can. Ment. Hlth. 1969, 17, 11-13.

7670. Whitehead,P.C. "The incidence of drug use among Halifax adolescents." Br. J. Addict. 1970, 65, 159-165.

7671. Whitehead,P.C. and Cabral,R.M. "Scaling the sequence of drug using behaviors: A test of the stepping-stone hypothetis." Comm. Prob. Drug Depend. 1974, 1, 707-718.

7672. Whitehead,P.C. and Cabral,R.M. "Scaling the sequence of drug using behaviors: A test of the stepping stone hypothesis." Drug Forum 1976, 5, 45-54.

7673. Whitehead,P.C. and Smart,R.G. "Validity and reliability of self-reported drug use." Can. J. Criminol. Correct. 1972, 14, 21-29.

7674. Whitehead,P.C., Smart,R.G., and Laforest,L. "Multiple drug use among marihuana smokers in Eastern Canada." Comm. Prob. Drug Depend. 1970, 3, 6535-6544.

7675. Whitehead,P.C., Smart,R.G., and Laforest,L. "Multiple drug use among marihuana smokers in Eastern Canada." Internat'l. J. Addict. 1972, 7, 179-190.

7676. Whitehead,P.C., Smart,R.G., and Laforest,L. "Use of other drugs by marihuana smokers in Eastern Canada."(Fr.). Toxicomanies 1970, 3, 49-64.

7677. Whitlock,L. "Marihuana." Crime Delinquency 1970, 2, 363-382.

7678. Whittier,J.G. "The haschish." In Whittier,J.G. Anti-slavery Poems. Boston, 1854.

7679. Whitty,C.W.M. "Cerebral atrophy in young cannabis smokers." Lancet 1971, 2, 1381.

7680. Wichert-Kobas,I. "Effect of gibberellin on growth, maturation, and sexuality of cannabis sativa plants treated with colchicine."(Rus.). Hod. Ros. Aklim. Nasien. 1969, 12, 711-722.

7681. Wickenden,J.W. "The relationships of ego-strength and alienation to extracurricular activity preference and marihuana usage among adolescent girls." Diss. Abs. 1972, 33, 1533.

7682. Wicker,R. The Wicker Report. LEMAR, Detroit, 1965.

7683. Widman,M., Agurell,S., Ehrnebo,M., and Jones,G. "Binding of (+)- and (-)-delta-1-tetrahydrocannabinols and (-)-7-hydroxy-delta-1-tetrahydrocannabinol to blood cells and plasma proteins in man." J. Pharm. Pharmacol. 1974, 26, 914-916.

7684. Widman,M., Dahmen,J., Leander,K., and Petersson, K. "In vitro metabolism of cannabinol in rat and rabbit liver." Act. Pharmaceut. Suec. 1975, 12, 385-392.

7685. Widman,N., Nilsson,I.M., Nilsson,J.L.G., Agurell,S., Borg,H., and Granstrand,B. "Plasma protein binding of 7-hydroxy-delta-1-tetrahydrocannabinol: An active delta-1-tetrahydrocannabinol metabolite." Act. Pharmaceut. Suec. 1971, 8, 706.

7686. Widman,M., Nilsson,I.M., Nilsson,J.L.G., Agurell,S., Borg,H., and Granstrand,B. "Plasma binding of 7-hydroxy-1-tetrahydrocannabinol: An active delta-1-tetrahydrocannabinol metabolite." J. Pharm. Pharmacol. 1973, 25, 453-457.

7687. Widman,M., Nilsson,I.M., Nilsson,J.L.G., Agurell,S., and Leander,K. "Metabolism of cannabis. IX. Cannabinol: Structure of a major metabolite formed in rat liver." Life Sci. 1971, 10, 157-162.

7688. Widman,M., Nordquist,M., Agurell,S., Lindgren, J.E., and Sandberg,F. "Biliary excretion of delta-1-tetrahydrocannabinol and its metabolites in the rat." Biochem. Pharmacol. 1974, 23, 1163-1172.

7689. Widman,M., Nordquist,M., Dollery,C.T., and Briant,T.H. "Metabolism of delta-1-tetrahydrocannabinol by the isolated perfused dog lung. Comparison with in vitro liver metabolism." J. Pharm. Pharmacol. 1975, 27, 842-848.

7690. Wiechowski,W. "Hashish."(Ger.). Verhand. Deut. Pharmakol. Gessell. 1926, 1, 49-50.

7691. Wiechowski,W. "Hashish."(Ger.). Arch. Pharmakol. 1927, 119, 49-50.

7692. Wig,N.N. and Varma,V.K. "Patterns of long-term cannabis use in North India and its effects on cognitive functions: a preliminary report." Drug Alcohol Depend. 1977, 2, 211-219.

7693. Wig,N.N. and Varma,V.K. "The present status of drug dependence treatment in India." Addict. Dis. 1977, 3, 79-86.

7694. Wijbenga,C. Soft Drugs; Social, Medical and Judicial Aspects.(Dut.). Van Bennep, Amsterdam, 1969.

7695. Wikler,A. "Aspects of tolerance to and dependence on cannabis." Ann. N. Y. Acad. Sci. 1976, 282, 126-147.

7696. Wikler,A. "Clinical and social aspects of marihuana intoxication." Arch. Gen. Psychiat. 1970, 23, 320-325.

7697. Wikler,A. "Mechanisms of action of drugs that modify personality function." Am. J. Psychiat. 1952, 108, 590-599.

7698. Wikler,A. "Some implications of conditioning theory for problems of drug abuse." Behav. Sci. 1971, 16, 92-97.

7699. Wikler,A. "The marihuana controversy." In Miller,L.L.(ed.). Marihuana Effects on Human Behavior. Academic Press, N.Y., 1974, 25-42.

7700. Wikler,A. and Lloyd,B.J. "Effects of smoking marihuana cigarettes on cortical electrical activity." Fed. Proc. 1945, 4, 141-142.

7701. Wildes,J.W., Martin,N.H., Pitt,C.G., and Wall, M.E. "The synthesis of (-)-delta-9(11)-trans-tetrahydro-cannabinol." J. Org. Chem. 1971, 36, 721-723.

7702. Wilkins,E.G. "Undesirable effects of marihuana." Br. Med. J. 1967, 3, 496-497.

7703. Willette,P.(ed.). Cannabinoid Assay in Humans. N.I.D.A. Res. Monog. Ser. 14, Gov't. Print. Office, Washington, D.C., 1976.

7704. Wilkinson,P.B. "Cannabis indica: An historical and pharmacological study of the drug." Br. J. Ineb. 1929, 27, 72-81.

7705. Williams,E.G., Himmelbach,C.K., Wikler,A., Ruble,D.C., and Lloyd,B.J. "Studies on marihuana and pyrahexyl compound." Pub. Hlth. Rep. 1946, 61, 1059-1083.

7706. Williams,H.S. "Abuse of American law." In Andrews,G. and Vinkeoog,S.(eds.). The Book of Grass. Grove Press, N.Y., 1967, 223.

7707. Williams,H.S. "An over-dose of cannabis indica." Ther. Gaz. 1885, 9, 18-19.

7708. Williams,R.B., Ng,L.K.Y., Lamprecht,F., Roth,K., and Kopin,I.J. "Delta-9-tetrahydrocannabinol: A hypotensive effect in rats." Psychopharmacol. 1973, 28, 269-274.

7709. Williams,T.I. Drugs from Plants. Sigma, London, 1947.

7710. Williams-Garcia,R. "The ritual use of cannabis in Mexico." In Rubin,V.(ed.). Cannabis and Culture. Mouton, The Hague, 1975, 133-147.

7711. Willinsky,M.D. "Analytical aspects of cannabis chemistry." In Mechoulam,R.(ed.). Marihuana, Chemistry, Pharmacology, Metabolism and Clinical Effects. Academic Press, N.Y., 1973, 137-158.

7712. Willinsky,M.D. "Effects of delta-1-tetrahydrocannabinol on Sidman discriminated avoidance behavior in rats." Paper presented at 7th Internat'l. Cong. Neuro-psychopharmacologia, Prague, 1970.

7713. Willinsky,M.D., de Carolis,A.S., and Longo,V.G. "EEG and behavioral effects of natural, synthetic and biosynthetic cannabinoids." Psychopharmacol. 1973, 31, 365-374.

7714. Willinsky,M. and di Simone,L. "Rapid simultaneous determination of the cannabinoids." Farmaco 1973, 28, 441-448.

7715. Willinsky,M.D., Kalant,H., Meresz,O., Endrenyi, L., and Woo,N. "Distribution and metabolism in vivo of ^{14}C-tetrahydrocannabinol in the rat." Eur. J. Pharmacol. 1974, 27, 106-109.

7716. Willinsky,M.D., Loizzo,A., and Longo,V.G. "EEG spectral analysis for the evaluation of the central effects of delta-6-tetrahydrocannabinol in rabbits." Psychopharmacol. 1975, 41, 123-126.

7717. Willinsky,M.D., Scotti de Carolis,A., and Longo, V.G. "EEG power and spectral analysis in the evaluation of the central effects of the tetrahydrocannabinols in animals." EEG Clin. Neurol. 1973, 34, 787.

7718. Willinsky,M.D., Webster,C.D., and Herring,B.S. "Effects of delta-1-tetrahydrocannabinol on Sidman discriminated avoidance behavior in rats." Activ. Nerv. Super. 1974, 16, 34-38.

7719. Willis,I.P. "Cannabis indica." Boston Med. Surg. J. 1859, 61, 173-178.

7720. Willis,J.H. "Drug addiction--the extent and nature of the problem." Trans. Med. Soc. Lond. 1968, 84, 72-80.

7721. Wilsie,C.R., Black,C.A., and Aandahl,A.R. "Hemp production experiments, cultural practices and soil requirements." Iowa Agricult. Expt'l. Station Bull. 1944, 1, 63.

7722. Wilsie,C.P. and Reddy,C.S. "Seed treatment experiments with hemp." J. Am. Soc. Agron. 1946, 38, 693-701.

7723. Wilson,C.W.M.(ed.). The Pharmacological and Epidemiological Aspects of Adolescent Drug Dependence. Pergamon Press, Oxford, 1966.

7724. Wilson,E. "Crazy dreamers." Collier's 1949, 123, 27.

7725. Wilson,R.S. and May,E.L. "Analgesic properties of the tetrahydrocannabinols, their metabolites and analogs." J. Med. Chem. 1975, 18, 700-703.

7726. Wilson,R.S. and May,E.L. "9-nor-delta-8-tetrahydrocannabinol, a cannabinoid of metabolic interest." J. Med. Chem. 1974, 17, 475-476.

7727. Wilson,R.S. and May,E.L. "The role of 11-hydroxylation in THC activity." In Braude,M.C. and Szara,S.(eds.). Pharmacology of Marihuana. Raven Press, N.Y., 1976, 137-139.

7728. Wiltshire,J.G. "Personal experience in the effect of cannabis indica." South. Clinic 1879, 1, 331-336.

7729. Windscheid,F. "A case for cannabis poisoning." (Ger.). Pharmaceut. Zeit. 1893, 39, 347-358.

7730. Winick,C. "A content analysis of drug related films released during 1971." In National Commission on Marihuana and Drug Abuse. Drug Use in America: Problem in Perspective. Gov't. Print. Office, Washington, D.C., 1973, II, 709-717.

7731. Winick,C. "Marihuana use by young people." In Harms,E.(ed.). Drug Addiction in Youth. Pergamon Press, Oxford, 1965, 19-35.

7732. Winick,C. "The life cycle of the narcotic addict and of addiction." Bull. Narc. 1964, 16, 1-12.

7733. Winick,C. "The use of drugs by jazz musicians." Soc. Prob. 1960, 7, 240-253.

7734. Winn,M., Arendsen,D., Dodge,P., Dren,A., Dunnigan, D., Hallas,R., Hwang,K., Kyncl,J., Lee,Y.H., Plotnikoff,N., Young,P., Zaugg,H., Calzell,H., and Razdan,R.K. "Drugs derived from cannabinoids. 5. Delta-6a, 10a-tetrahydro-cannabinol and heterocyclic analogs containing aromatic side chains." J. Med. Chem. 1976, 19, 461-471.

7735. Winslow,J.J. "Drug use and social integreation." Internat'l. J. Addict. 1974, 9, 531-540.

7736. Winter,K.G.J. "A case of intoxication from cannabis indica extract."(Fin.). Duodecim 1895, 11, 119-124.

7737. Winters,S.R. "Marihuana." Hygeia 1940, 18, 885-887.

7738. Wise,T.A. "Practical remarks on insanity as it occurs among the inhabitants of Bengal." Month. J. Med. Sci. 1852, 14, 500-515.

7739. Wislicki,L. "Alcoholism and drug addiction in Israel." Br. J. Addict. 1967, 62, 367-373.

7740. Wissett,R. A Treatise on Hemp. J. Harding, London, 1808.

7741. Witschi,H. and Saint-Francois,B. "Enhanced activity of benzopyrene hydroxylase in rat liver and lung after acute cannabis administration." Toxicol. Appl. Pharmacol. 1972, 23, 165-168.

7742. Wittenborn,J.R., Brill,H., Smith,J.P., and Wittenborn,S.A.(eds.). Drugs and Youth. C.C. Thomas, Springfield, Ill., 1970.

7743. Wittenborn,J.R., Smith,J.P., and Wittenborn, S.A.(eds.). Communication and Drug Abuse. C.C. Thomas, Springfield, Ill., 1970.

7744. Wogan,M. "Illicit drug use among college students." Coll. Stud. J. 1974, 8, 56-62.

7745. Wogan,M. and Elliot,J.P. "Drug use and level of anxiety among college students." Youth Adoles. 1972, 1, 325-331.

7746. Woggon,A.D.B. "Subjective changes under (-)-delta-9-tetrahydrocannabinol."(Ger.). Internat'l. Pharmacopsychiat. 1974, 9, 138-151.

7747. Woggon,B. Hashish, Use and Effect.(Ger.). Springer Verlag, Berlin, 1974.

7748. Wohlberg,G.W. "Marihuana in junior high school." N. Eng. J. Med. 1970, 283, 318-319.

7749. Wolde-Ab Yisak,M., Widman,J.E.L., and Agurell, S. "Neutral in vivo metabolites of cannabinol isolated from rat feces." J. Pharm. Pharmacol. 1977, 29, 487-490.

7750. Wolf,A.S. "New views on an old drug." Alaska Med. 1972, 14, 9-10.

7751. Wolf,W. "Uncle Sam fights a new drug menace... marihuana." Pop. Sci. Month. 1936, 128, 14-15, 119-120.

7752. Wolff,P.O. "Drug addiction, a universal problem."(Sp.). Bol. Of. Sanit. Panam. 1933, 12, 30-44.

7753. Wolff,P.O. "Drug addiction and criminality." (Sp.). Rev. Psiquiat. Criminol. 1941, 6, 433-453.

7754. Wolff,P.O. "Drug addiction and war."(Sp.) Rev. Psiquiat. Criminol. 1943, 8, 456.

7755. Wolff,P.O. Marihuana in Latin America. The Threat it Constitutes. Linacre Press, Washington, D.C., 1949.

7756. Wolff,P.O. "Pain and euphoria. Pharmacological progress."(Sp.). Cienc. Invest. 1948, 4, 186-198.

7757. Wolff,P.O. "Problems of drug addiction in South America." Br. J. Addict. 1949, 46, 66.

7758. Wolff,P.O. "The treatment of drug addicts." Bull. Hlth. Organ. League Nations 1945, 12, 451-682.

7759. Wolfson,E.A. Survey of Drug Abuse in Six New Jersey High Schools. I. Methodology and General Findings. Baywood Pub. Co., N.J., 1972.

7760. Wolk,D.J. "Marihuana on the campus. A study at one university." J. Am. Coll. Hlth. Assoc. 1968, 17, 144-149.

7761. Wolk,D.J. "Youth and drugs: guidelines for teachers." Soc. Educat. 1969, 33, 667-674.

7762. Wollner,H.J., Matchett,J.R., Levine,J., and Loewe,S. "Isolation of a physiologically active tetrahydrocannabinol from cannabis sativa resin." J. Am. Chem. Soc. 1942, 64, 26-29.

7763. Wollner,H.J., Matchett,J.R., Levine, J., and Valaer,P. "Report of the marihuana investigation." J.A.P.A. 1938, 27, 29-36.

7764. Wolmer,B. "Cannabis laws." New Soc. 1976, 35, 333-334.

7765. Wolstenholme,G.E. and Knight,J.(eds.). Hashish: Its Chemistry and Pharmacology. CIBA Found. Study Group No. 21, Little Brown and Co., Boston, 1965.

7766. Women's Christian Temperance Union. Marihuana. WCTU, Evanston, Ill., 1928.

7767. Wong,K.C. and Lien-Teh,W. History of Chinese Medicine. National Quarantine Service, Shanghai, China, 1936.

7768. Wood,F.C., Elkinton,J.R., Farnsworth,D.L., Brill,H., and Robitscher,J. "Drug abuse: Legal and ethical implications of the non-medical use of hallucinogenic and narcotic drugs." Trans. Stud. Coll. Phys. Phil. 1968, 36, 63-95.

7769. Wood,G.B. and Bache,F. "Extractum cannabis, U.S. secondary, extract of hemp." In Dispensatory of the United States of America. Lippincott, Grambo, and Co., Phil., 1854, 338-340.

7770. Wood,G.B. and Bache,F. "Extractum cannabis. U.S." In Dispensatory of the United States of America. J.P. Lippincott and Co., Phil., 1869, 379-382.

7771. Wood,H.C. "On the medical activity of the hemp plant, as grown in North America." Proc. Am. Philosoph. Soc. 1869, 11, 226-232.

7772. Wood,H.C. "Tannate of cannabine." Ther. Gaz. 1885, 9, 379.

7773. Wood,H.C. and Smith,R.M. "Poisoning by cannabis indica." Ther. Gaz. 1884, 5, 514-515.

7774. Wood,T.B., Spivey,W.T.N., and Easterfield,T.H. "Cannabinol." Proc. Chem. Soc. 1898, 14, 66-67, 153-154.

7775. Wood,T.B., Spivey,W.T.N., and Easterfield,T.H. "Cannabinol." J. Chem. Soc. 1899, 75, 20-36.

7776. Wood,T.B., Spivey,W.T.N., and Easterfield,T.H. "XL--Charas. The resin of Indian hemp." J. Chem. Soc. 1896, 69, 539-546.

7777. Woodhouse,E.J. "Confirmation of the presence of 11-hydroxy-delta-9-tetrahydrocannabinol in the urine of marihuana smokers." Am. J. Pub. Hlth. 1972, 62, 1394-1396.

7778. Woodside,A.G., Bearden,W.O., and Ronkainen,I. "Images on serving marihuana, alcoholic beverages, and soft drinks." J. Psychol. 1977, 96, 11-14.

7779. Woody,G.E. "Visual disturbances experienced by hallucinogenic drug abusers while driving." Am. J. Psychiat. 1970, 127, 683-686.

7780. Woody,R.H. "Therapeutic techniques for the adolescent marihuana user." J. Sch. Hlth. 1972, 42, 220-224.

7781. Wooton,B. "Cannabis is not heroin." Sci. Journ. 1969, 5, 3.

7782. Work,T.S., Bergel,F., and Todd,A.B. "The active principle of cannabis resin. I." Biochem. J. 1939, 33, 123-127.

7783. Worm,K., Morkholdt Andersen,J., Nielsen,E., Schou,J., and Steentoft,A. "Studies on the metabolism and disposition of delta-9-THC in Danish pigs before and after prolonged intravenous administration of delta-9-THC." Act. Pharmaceut. Suec. 1971, 8, 690-691.

7784. Wrenn,J.M. and Friedman,M.A. "Inhibition of hydrocortisone induction of mouse liver tyrosine amino-transferase(TAT) activity by delta-9-tetrahydrocannabinol." Pharmacologist 1976, 18, 297.

7785. Wright,J.D. "Knowledge and experience of young people regarding drug abuse." Proc. Roy. Soc. Med. 1970, 63, 725-729.

7786. Wright,P.L., Smith,S.H., Keplinger,M.L., Calandra,J.C., and Braude,M.C. "Reproductive and teratologic studies with delta-9-tetrahydrocannabinol and crude marihuana extract." Toxicol. Appl. Pharmacol. 1976, 38, 223-235.

7787. Wurmser,L. "Myths and facts about marihuana." Alumnae Mag. 1970, 69, 3-5.

7788. Wurmser,L., Levin,L., and Lewis,A. "Chronic paranoid symptoms and thought disorders in users of marihuana and LSD as observed in psychotherapy." Comm. Prob. Drug Depend. 1969, 3, 6154-6177.

7789. Wursch,M.S., Otis,L.S., Green,D.E., and Forrest,I.S. "^{3}H-delta-9-tetrahydrocannabinol(THC) metabolism in rhesus and squirrel monkeys." Proc. West. Pharmacol. Soc. 1972, 15, 68-73.

7790. Wyman,L.C. "Examples of marihuana crimes." Congress. Rec. 1968, E2753-E2754.

7791. Wyzanski,C.E. "It's up to the young to solve the problem." New Repub. 1967, 157, 115-116.

Y

7792. Yablonsky,L. The Hippie Trip. Pegasus Pub., Pegasus Pub., N.Y., 1968.

7793. Yagen,B. and Mechoulam,R. "Stereospecific cyclizations and isomerizations of cannabichromene and related cannabinoids." Tetrahed. Lett. 1969, 60, 5353-5356.

7794. Yagiela,J.A., Gibb,J.W., and Karler,R. "Investigation of the hypothermic effects of 1-delta-9-tetrahydrocannabinol." Pharmacologist 1973, 15, 200.

7795. Yagiela,J.A., McCarthy,K.D., and Gibb,J.W. "The effect of hypothermic doses of 1-delta-9-tetrahydrocannabinol on biogenic amine metabolism in selected parts of the rat brain." Life Sci. 1974, 14, 2367-2378.

7796. Yagnitinsky,B. and Mechoulam,R. "Stereospecific cyclizations of cannabinoid dienes." Israel J. Chem. 1969, 7, 18.

7797. Yakuskina,N.I. and Chuikova,L.V. "Effect of growth related factors on physiological changes in hemp."(Rus.). Izvest. Voron. Otdel. Botan. Obsh. 1963, 1, 79-85.

7798. Yamauchi,T., Shoyama,Y., Aramaki,H., Azuma,T., and Nishioka,I. "Tetrahydrocannabinolic acid, a genuine substance of tetrahydrocannabinol." Chem. Pharmaceut. Bull. 1967, 15, 1075-1076.

7799. Yamauchi,T., Shoyama,Y., Matsuo,Y., and Nishioka, I. "Cannabigerol monomethyl ether, a new component of hemp." Chem. Pharmaceut. Bull. 1968, 16, 1164-1165.

7800. Yanishevskii,F.B. "Effect of gibberellin on nitrogen metabolism in hemp."(Rus.). Fiziol. Rast. 1962, 8, 529-532.

7801. Yarmolenko,A.V. "Cannabis in Komarov." Flora U.S.S.R. 1936, 5, 383-384.

7802. Yawger,N.S. "Marihuana. Our new addiction." Am. J. Med. Sci. 1938, 195, 351-357.

7803. Yisak,W.A. "Neutral in vivo metabolites of cannabinol isolated from rat feces." J. Pharm. Pharmacol. 1977, 29, 487-490.

7804. Yolles,S.F. "Men, money and marihuana." Am. J. Psychoanal. 1971, 31, 153-163.

7805. Yoshimura,H., Fujiwara,M., and Ueki,S. "Biochemical correlates in mouse-killing behavior of the rat: Brain acetylcholine and acetylcholinesterase after administration of delta-9-tetrahydrocannabinol." Brain Res. 1974, 81, 567-570.

7806. Yoshimura,H., Fujiwara,M., and Ueki,S. "Effect of delta-9-tetrahydrocannabinol on brain acetylcholine levels in rats." Jap. J. Pharmacol. 1974, 24, 54.

7807. Yost,O.R. "Marihuana." In Yost,O.R.(ed.). The Bane of Drug Addiction. MacMillan Co., 1954, 50-51.

7808. Young,J.R. Tests for Marihuana. Bureau Internal Revenue, Alcohol Tax Unit, Washington, D.C., 1951.

Z

7809. Zacone,V.P. "Marihuana and ethanol: Effects on sleep." *Psychiat. Med.* 1973, *4*, 201-212.

7810. Zaehner,R.C. "Mysticism: Sacred and profane." In Andrews,G. and Vinkenoog,S.(eds.). *The Book of Grass.* Grove Press, N.Y., 1967, 183.

7811. Zaks,M.S., Hughes,P., Jaffe,J., and Dolkart,M.B. "Young people in the park: Survey of socio-cultural and drug use patterns of Yippies in Lincoln Park, Chicago Democratic convention 1968." Paper presented at Am. Orthopsychiat. Assoc., New York, 1969.

7812. Zalcman,S., Liskow,B., Cadoret,R., and Goodwin,D. "Marihuana and amphetamine: The question of interaction." *Am. J. Psychiat.* 1973, *130*, 707-708.

7813. Zaltsman,G.I. and Lenskii,G.P. "Effect of hashish on the mind."(Rus.). *Zdrav. Kazak.* 1962, *22*, 30-35.

7814. Zamir-ul Haq,M., Rose,S.J., Deiderich,L.R., and Patel,A.R. "Identification and quantitative measurement of some n-heterocyclics in marihuana smoke condensates." *Anal. Chem.* 1974, *46*, 1781-1785.

7815. Zane,M. "Turning on in society." *Nation* 1970, *211*, 595-596.

7816. Zarco,R.M. and Almonte,M.P. "Drug abuse in the Philippines." *Addict. Dis.* 1977, *3*, 119-128.

7817. Zeidenberg,P. "Defense of 'Marihuana: Deceptive Weed'." *N. Eng. J. Med.* 1973, *289*, 1151.

7818. Zeidenberg,P., Bourdon,R., and Nahas,G.G. "Marihuana intoxication by passive inhalation: Documentation by detection of urinary metabolites." *Am. J. Psychiat.* 1977, *134*, 76-78.

7819. Zeidenberg,P., Clark,W.C., Jaffe,J., Anderson, S.W., Chin,S., and Malitz,S. "Effect of oral administration of delta-9-tetrahydrocannabinol on memory, speech, and perception of thermal stimulation: Results with four normal human volunteer subjects. Preliminary report." Comp. Psychiat. 1973, 14, 549-556.

7820. Zeigler,W.H. "The intraperitoneal injection of certain drugs." J.A.M.A. 1925, 14, 86-93.

7821. Zelepuka,S.I., Ravinovych,A.S., Pochynok,P., Nerash,A.K., and Kudryasvtsev,V.A. "Antibacterial properties of a hemp preparation."(Ukr.). Mikrob. Zhurn. Akad. Nauk Ukrain. 1963, 25, 42-46.

7822. Zerbetto,R. "An overview on drug abuse in Italy." Addict. Dis. 1977, 3, 43-50.

7823. Zetterstrom,K. "Bena Riamba. Brothers of the hemp." Stud. Ethnog. Upsal. 1966, 26, 151-165.

7824. Zhatov,A.I. and Kovalenko,V.M. "Effect of presowing gamma-irradiation on germination and viability of hemp seeds."(Rus.). Radiobiologia 1969, 8, 769-772.

7825. Zhukovsky,P.M. Cultivated Plants and Their Wild Relatives. Commonwealth Agricultural Bureau, Farnham Royal, Bucks, England, 1962.

7826. Zimmer,B.D., Bickel,P., and Dittrich,A. "Changes of simple somatic parameters by delta-9-trans-tetrahydrocannabinol in a double-blind study." Arz.-Forsch. Drug Res. 1976, 26, 1614-1616.

7827. Zimmerberg,B., Glick,S.D., and Jarvik,M.E. "Impairment of recent memory by marihuana and THC in rhesus monkeys." Nature 1971, 233, 343-345.

7828. Zimmerman,A.M. and Zimmerman,S.B. "The influence of marihuana on eukaryote cell growth and development." In Nahas,G.G., Paton,W.D.M., and Idanpaan-Heikkila,J.E. (eds.). Marihuana. Springer Verlag, N.Y., 1976, 195-207.

7829. Zimmerman,D.H. "You can't help but get stoned: Notes on the social organization of marihuana smoking." Soc. Prob. 1977, 25, 198.

7830. Zimmerman,S., Zimmerman,A.M., Cameron,I.L., and Laurence,H.L. "Delta-1-tetrahydrocannabinol, cannabinol and cannabidiol effects on the immune response of mice." Pharmacol. 1977, 15, 10-23.

7831. Zinberg,N.E. "A study of social regulating mechanisms in controlled illicit drug users." J. Drug Iss. 1977, 7, 117-133.

7832. Zinberg,N.E. "Against hysteria." Internat'l. J. Psychiat. 1972, 10, 69-73.

7833. Zinberg,N.E. "Amotivational syndrome." Psychol. Today 1976, 6, 45-47.

7834. Zinberg,N.E. "Marihuana and heroin use in Vietnam: A report." Act. Pharmaceut. Suec. 1971, 8, 697-698.

7835. Zinberg,N.E. "Marihuana and sex." N. Eng. J. Med. 1974, 291, 309-310.

7836. Zinberg,N.E. "Narcotics in the U.S.: A brief history." Harvard Rev. 1963, 1, 56-62.

7837. Zinberg,N.E. and Robertson,J.A. Drugs and the Public. Simon and Schuster, N.Y., 1972.

7838. Zinberg,N.E. and Weil,A.T. "A comparison of marihuana users and non-users." Med. Sci. Law 1970, 10, 194.

7839. Zinberg,N.E. and Weil,A.T. "A comparison of marihuana users and non-users." Nature 1970, 226, 119-123.

7840. Zinberg,N.E. and Weil,A.T. "Cannabis: The first controlled experiment." New Soc. 1969, 13, 84-86.

7841. Zinberg,N.E. and Weil,A.T. "The effects of marihuana on human beings." Addictions 1969, 16, 26-43.

7842. Zitko,B.A., Howes,J.F., Razdan,R.K., Dalzell, B.C., Dalzell,H.C., Sheehan,J.C., and Pars,H.G. "Water-soluble derivatives of delta-1-tetrahydrocannabinol." Science 1972, 177, 142-144.

7843. Zufall,C.J. "Marihuana in Indiana." Purdue Pharmacist 1938, 1, 20.

7844. Zuger,V. "A new type of hashish."(Ger.). Kriminalistik 1974, 28, 129-130.

7845. Zuk,J. and Heslop-Harrison,J. "The role of tapetum in microsporogenesis of cannabis sativa." Genet. Pol. 1964, 5, 140.

7846. Zunin,L.M. "Marihuana. The drug and the problem." Milit. Med. 1969, 134, 104-110.

ADDENDUM

A

7847. Abel,E.L. "Comparative effects of delta-9-tetrahydrocannabinol on thermoregulation." In Paton,W.D.M. and Crown,J.(eds.). Cannabis and its Derivatives. Oxford Univ. Press, London, 1972, 120-140.

7848. Abelson,H. and Atkinson,R.B. Public Experience with Psychoactive Substances. Response Analysis Corp., Princeton, N.J., 1975.

7849. Abelson,H. and Fishburne,P.M. Nonmedical Use of Psychoactive Substances. Response Analysis Corp., Princeton, N.J., 1976.

7850. Abbott,B.J., Fukudam,D.S., and Archer,R.A. "Microbiological transformation of cannabinoids." Exper. 1977, 33, 718-720.

7851. Ackerman,N.R. "The lack of an effect of delta-9-tetrahydrocannabinol on pulmonary smooth muscle function in the guinea pig." Toxicol. Appl. Pharmacol. 1977, 41, 321-328.

7852. Adams,M.D., Earnhardt,J.T., Martin,B.R., Harris, L.S., Dewey,W.L., and Razdan,R.K. "A cannabinoid with cardiovascular activity but no overt behavioral effects." Exper. 1977, 33, 1204-1205.

7853. Adler,P.T. and Lotecka,L. "Drug use among high school students: Patterns and correlations." Internat'l. J. Addict. 1973, 8, 537-548.

7854. Agarwal,A.K., Sethi,B.B., and Gupta,S.C. "Physical and cognitive effects of chronic bhang(cannabis sativa)." Ind. J. Psychiat. 1975, 17, 1-5.

7855. Aldrich,M.A. "Acapulco Gold." Marihuana Rev. 1968, 1, 11.

7856. Aldrich,M.R. "Artificial paradises." J. Psyched. Drugs 1971, 3, 107-109.

7857. Aldrich,M.R. "California marihuana initiative analysis." Marihuana Rev. 1973, 9, 1-64.

7858. Aldrich,M.R. "Fitz Hugh Ludlow, the hasheesh eater." Marihuana Month. 1975, 5, 24-25.

7859. Aldrich,M.R. "High court frees high priest, opens way for new marihuana laws." Marihuana Rev. 1968, 1, 3-5.

7860. Aldrich,M.R. "It's time." Marihuana Rev. 1968, 1, 16.

7861. Aldrich,M.R. "Marihuana smoking in the U.S." Marihuana Rev. 1968, 1, 15-17.

7882. Aldrich,M.R. "New investigations and research." Marihuana Rev. 1968, 1, 9.

7883. Aldrich,M.R. "Notes on the big pot chart." Marihuana Rev. 1968, 1, 4-5.

7884. Aldrich,M.R. "Operation intercept." Marihuana Rev. 1968, 1, 4-6.

7885. Aldrich,M.R. "Pot research." Marihuana Rev. 1968, 1, 8-9.

7886. Aldrich,M.R. "Scythia hemp purification ceremonies." In Stone Mountain (ed.). Pot Art and Marihuana Reading Matter. Apocyrpha Press, Tucson, 1970, 15-16.

7887. Aldrich,M.R. Speakers' Handbook for California Marihuana Initiative. California Marihuana Initiative Statewide Steering Committee, San Francisco, 1972.

7888. Aldrich,M.R. "Street THC: A shuck, a burn, a down." Marihuana Rev. 1968, 1, 2.

7889. Aldrich,M.R. "Tantric cannabis use in India." J. Psyched. Drugs 1977, 9, 227-233.

7890. Aldrich,M.R. "The Rastafarians: A meditation on immortality." Marihuana Month. 1976, 1, 11-12.

7891. Aldrich,M.R. "Three ancient species of pot." Marihuana Month. 1976, 2, 10-12.

7892. Aldrich,M.R., Mikuriya,T.H., Schneider,B., and Brownell,G.S. "Costs of California marihuana law enforcement: A preliminary study." In California Legislature, Senate Select Committee on Control of Marihuana. Final Report, Marihuana: Beyond Misunderstanding. Cal. Legislature, Sacremento, 1974.

7893 Aldrich,T.B. "Hascheesh." In Poems of Thomas Bailey Aldrich. Houghton Mifflin Co., Boston, 1882, 35-36.

7894. Alexander,J.B. "The Rastafarians." High Times 1974, 1, 61-62, 67

7895. Allwart,W.H. "Photochemical studies of marihuana (cannabis) constitutents." J. Pharmaceut. Sci. 1972, 61, 1994-1996.

7896. Alva Correa,J.J. "The problem of marihuana." (Sp.). Medicina 1973, 33, 309-314.

7897. Ananth,J. "Drug problem: Marihuana" Addiction Therapist 1975, 1, 26-30.

7898. Anonymous. "A marihuana note with impact on race for White House." U.S. News Wld. Rep. 1972, 73, 50.

7899. Anonymous. "A new test for marihuana." J.A.M.A. 1972, 221, 722.

7900. Anonymous. Cooking with Pot. Sacred Mushroom Press, Gable Gulch, Cal., 1969.

7901. Anonymous. "DHSS supports marihuana law changes." Wisconsin Ment. Hyg. Rev. 1976, 10, 2.

7902. Anonymous "Driving ability not impaired by pot." Marihuana Rev. 1968, 1, 13.

7903. Anonymous. "Drugs and driving." Traffic Laws Commentary 1965, 65, 1-17.

7904. Anonymous. "Identification of drug abuse." Can. Ment. Hlth. 1968, 16, 25-27.

7905. Anonymous. "Intoxicants of the Orient."(Fr.). Vichy Medical 1937, 8, 9.

7906. Anonymous. "Joint rolling around the world." High Times 1974, 4, 28-29.

7907. Anonymous. Mary Jane Superweed. Stone Kingdom Syndicate, San Francisco, 1970.

7908. Anonymous. "Non-medical use of drugs, with particular reference to youth." Can. Med. Assoc. J. 1969, 101, 804-820.

7909. Anonymous. "On selling marihuana." In Goode,E. (ed.). Marihuana. Atherton Press, N.Y., 1969, 92-102.

7910. Anonymous. "Playboy's student survey." Playboy 1971, 18, 208-216.

7911. Anonymous. "Research on marihuana." N. Eng. J. Med. 1972, 287, 994-995.

7912. Anonymous. "The drug generation." Newsweek 1969, 107-108, 110.

7913. Anonymous. "Some thoughts on marihuana and the artist." In Goode,E.(ed.). Marihuana. Atherton Press, N.Y., 1969, 177-183.

7914. Anonymous. "The Brotherhood of Eternal Love: the Senate report." High Times 1974, 2, 36-37, 56.

7915. Anonymous. "The marihuana menace." Changing Times 1951, 1, 12-14.

7916. Anonymous. "The sexual effects of marihuana." High Times 1974, 5, 64-65.

7917. Arafat,I. and Yorburg,B. "Drug use and sexual behavior of college women." J. Sex. Res. 1973, 9, 21-29.

7918. Arthur,G.L., Sisson,P.J., Nix,G.C. "Three year follow-up survey of high school youth in a typical Georgia school." J. Drug Educat. 1977, 7, 43-52.

7919. Ashley,R. "Hash oil." High Times 1977, 18, 66-68.

7920. Ashley,R. "How we got our dope laws." High Times 1976, 11, 43-46, 54, 72.

7921. Ausbel,R. "The psychology of marihuana." In Goode,E.(ed.). Marihuana. Atherton Press, N.Y., 1969, 17-19.

B

7922. Bailey,F.L. and Rothblatt,H.B. *Handling Narcotics and Drug Cases*. Lawyers Co-operative Pub. Co., Rochester, N.Y., 1972.

7923. Bailey,K., Legault,D., and Verner,D. "Identification of synthetic cannabinoids by gas chromatography." *Chromat*. 1973, *87*, 263-266.

7924. Barber,B. *Drugs and Society*. Russell Sage Foundation, N.Y., 1967.

7925. Barnes,G.C. and Noble,P. "Deprivation and drug addiction: A study of a vulnerable sub-group." *Brit. J. Soc. Work* 1972, *2*, 299-311.

7925. Baselga,E. "Young drug users: sociological study of one sample." *Bull Narc*. 1972, *24*, 17-22.

7926. Battegay,R., Ladewig,D., Muhlemann,R., and Weidmann, M. "The culture of youth and drug abuse in some European countries." *Internat'l. J. Addict*. 1976, *11*, 245-261.

7927. Bowles,P. "Kif making in Morocco." *High Times* 1976, *13*, 43-46.

7928. Becker,H.S. "Consciousness, power and drug effects." *Trans-Action* 1973, *10*, 26-31.

7929. Benetowa,S. *Hemp in Belief and Popular Customs*. (Fr.). Nakladen Towarzystwa Naukowego Warszawskiego, Warsaw, 1936.

7930. Berlet,C. "The smoke-filled room. Where the candidates stand on dope reform." *High Times* 1976, *9*, 41-43.

7931. Bernheim,D. *Defense of Narcotic Cases*. Matthew Bender, N.Y., 1975.

7931. Bertsch,W., Shunbo,F., Chang,R.C., and Zlatkis,A. "Preparation of nickel high-resolution open-tubular columns." Chromatog. 1974, 7, 128-134.

7932. Besley,M.A. "A national strategy for drug control." J. Drug Iss. 1977, 7, 319-331.

7933. Bethards,J.M. "Parental support and the use of drugs." Humboldt J. Soc. Rel. 1973, 1, 26-28.

7934. Biasucci,P. "Harry J. Anslinger. Interview." High Times 1977, 21, 27-29, 42.

7935. Bigwood,J. "The secret hash factories of Mexico." High Times 1977, 18, 60-61.

7936. Binzer,S.V. "The Hollywood story." Marihuana Month. 1976, 2, 23-25.

7937. Blackford,L. Student Drug Use Surveys--San Mateo County, California 1968-1976. Dept. Pub. Hlth. Welfare, San Mateo, 1976.

7938. Blizard,J. "Marihuana, cigarettes and alcohol." Med. J. Aust. 1977, 2, 228.

7939. Blum,R.H. and Funkhouser,M.L. "Legislators on social scientists and a social issue: A report and commentary on some discussions with lawmakers on drug abuse." J. Appl. Behav. Sci. 1965, 1, 84-112.

7940. Blum,R.H. "Drugs, behavior and crime." Ann. Am. Acad. Polit. Soc. Sci. 1967, 374, 135-146.

7941. Blum,R.H. "To wear a Nostradamus hat: Drugs and America." J. Soc. Iss. 1971, 27, 89-106.

7942. Boeren,E.G., Elsohly,M.A, Turner,C.E., and Salemink,C.A. "b-cannabispiranol: A new non-cannabinoid phenol from cannabis sativa L." Exper. 1977, 33, 848.

7943. Bogdanoff,B., Rorke,L.B., Yanoff,M., and Warren,W.S. "Brain and eye abnormalities. Possible sequelae to prenatal use of multiple drugs including LSD." Am. J. Dis. Child 1972, 123, 145-148.

7944. Bonzani Da Silva,J. "Chromatographic determination of cannabinol in blood, urine, and saliva of cannabis sativa addicts."(Port.). Rev. Fac. Farm. Bioquim. 1967, 5, 205-214.

7945. Boolsen,M.W. "Drugs in Denmark." Internat'l. J. Addict. 1975, 10, 503-512.

7946. Borg,J. "Dose effects of smoked cannabis upon human cognitive and motor functions." Diss. Abs. 1973, 34, 5-13.

7947. Borland,L. "Ganga in Samatra." High Times 1974, 4, 32.

7948. Bowker,L.H. Drug Use Among American Women, Old And Young: Sexual Oppression And Other Themes. Reed and Eterovich, San Francisco, 1977.

7949. Bowles,P. "Kif making in Morocco." High Times 1976, 13, 43-46.

7950. Bradford,L.W. and Devaney,J. "Scanning electron microscopy applications in criminalistics." J. Forens. Sci. 1970, 15, 110-119.

7951. Brandenberger,H. "Role of the mass spectrometer in the toxicological-chemical laboratory."(Ger.). Deut. Lebensmitt. 1974, 70, 31-39.

7952. Brown,R.A. "A preclinical survey of drug use among law students in New South Wales: Attitudes and habits." J. Drug Iss. 1977, 7, 439-455.

7953. Brehm,M.L. and Back,K.W. "Self-image and attitudes toward drugs." J. Personal. 1968, 36, 299-314.

7954. Briscoe,R.G. "Educational implications of differences of perceptions by drug-using and non drug-using students at Davis high school." Diss. Abs. 1971, 31, 3767-3768.

7955. Bro,P., Schou,J., and Topp,G. "Cannabis poisoning with analytical verification." N. Eng. J. Med. 1975, 293, 1049-1050.

7956. Brook,J.S., Lukoff,I.F., and Whiteman,M. "Correlates of adolescent marihuana use as related to age, sex, and ethnicity." Yale J. Biol. Med. 1977, 50, 383-390.

7957. Brown,J.E., Kassouny,M., and Cross,J.K. "Kinetic studies of food intake and sucrose solution preference by rats treated with low doses of delta-9-tetrahydrocannabinol." Behav. Biol. 1977, 20, 104-110.

7958. Brown,J.K., Shapazian,L., and Griffin,G.D. "A rapid screening procedure for some 'street drugs' by thin-layer chromatography." J. Chromatog. 1972, 64, 129-133.

7959. Bruce,P.D. and Ferraro,D.P. "Learned tolerance to delta-9-tetrahydrocannabinol in pigeons." Paper presented to Rocky Mt. Psychol. Assoc., Salt Lake City, 1975.

7960. Brunel,R. "Excerpt from the 1890 report of Health Council of Greece on the effects of hashish."(Grk.). _Greek Agriculture_ 1892, _1_, 525-529.

7961. Brunswick,A.F. "Health and drug behavior: a study of urban black adolescents." _Addict. Dis._ 1977, 3, 197-214.

7962. Buikhuisen,F.P.H., Dijksterhuis,J.J., and Hemmel,J.J. _Drug Use in Girten_.(Dut.). Inst. Criminol. Groningen, Netherlands, 1971.

7963. Buikhuisen,W. and Timmerman,H. "Drug use among secondary schoolchildren."(Dut.). _Ned. Tijd. Criminol._ 1970, _12_, 173.

7964. Buikhuisen,W. and Timmerman,H. "Hash users: Characteristics and policy. An empirical investigation."(Dut.). _Sociologica Neerlandica_ 1971, _7_, 73-87.

7965. Buikhuisen,W. and Timmerman,H. "The development of drug use among secondary schoolchildren."(Dut.). _Ned. Nijd. Criminol._ 1971, _13_, 193.

7966. Burkett,S.R. "Religion, parental influence, and adolescent alcohol and marihuana use." _J. Drug Iss._ 1977, _7_, 263-273.

C

7967. California. Bureau of Criminal Statistics. Drug Diversion 1000 P.C. in California 1974. Bureau Crim. Stat., Sacremento, 1976.

7968. Carlin,A.S. and Trupin,E.W. "The effect of long-term chronic marihuana use on neuropsychological functioning." Internat'l. J. Addict. 1977, 12, 617-624.

7969. Carlini,E.A., Lindsey,C.J., and Tufik,S. "Cannabis, catecholamines, rapid eye movement sleep and aggressive behavior." Br. J. Pharmacol. 1977, 61, 371-379.

7970. Carr,R.H. and James,C.M. "Synthesis of adequate protein in the glands of the pigeon crop." Am. J. Physiol. 1931, 97, 227-231.

7971. Carranza-Acevedo,J. "Pharmacological aspects of drug abuse in Mexico."(Sp.). Gac. Med. Mex. 1972, 103, 381-384.

7972. Cash,D.K. "Marihuana." Med. Leg. Bull. 1970, 212, 1-7.

7973. Cates,W. and Pope,J.N. "Gynecomastia and cannabis smoking. A nonassociation among U.S. army soldiers." Am. J. Surgery 1977, 134, 613-615.

7974. Cavers,D.F. "The legal control of the clinical investigation of drugs. Some political, economic and social questions." Daedalus 1969, 98, 427-448.

7975. Central Limburg Youth Welfare Foundation. Drugs in Central Limburg.(Dut.). Youth Wel. Found, Roermand, Netherlands, 1971.

7976. Chakravarty,I. and Ghosh,J.J. "Effect of cannabis extract on uterine glycogen metabolism in prepubertal rats under normal and estradiol-treated conditions." Biochem. Pharmacol. 1977, 26, 859-862.

7977. Champion,R.A. *Trends in Marihuana Use in New South Wales 1971 to 1973*. Div. Health Services Research, New South Wales, 1976.

7978. Charne,A. "Hash rubbing in Kashmir." *High Times* 1974, *3*, 41-42.

7979. Charney,S. "Hash in the U.S.S.R." *High Times* 1974, *1*, 31-32.

7980. Chazan,J.B. and Ourisson,G. "Tetrahydrocannabinol analogs and related compounds. II. Syntheses in the xanthene series."(Fr.). *Bull. Soc. Chim.* 1968, *1*, 1384-1393.

7981. Choate,G. and Lloyd,P. "Does marihuana cause male breast growth?" *High Times* 1974, *6*, 50-51.

7982. Clarke,R.C. *The Botany and Ecology of Cannabis*. Pods Press, Ben Lomond, Cal., 1976.

7983. Cohen,F. *Psychology, Social Psychology and Sociology of Drug Abuse*.(Dut.). Inst. Soc. Med., Amsterdam, Netherlands, 1969.

7984. Cohen,G.M. "Pulmonary metabolism of inhaled substances and possible relationship with carcinogenicity and toxicity." In Junod,A.F. and de Haller,R.(eds.). *Lung Metabolism*. Academic Press, N.Y., 1975, 185-200.

7985. Cohen,S. "Therapeutic aspects." In Petersen,R.C. (ed.). *Marihuana Research Findings: 1976*. N.I.D.A. Res. Monog. Ser. 14, Dept. H.E.W., Rockville, Md., 1977, 194-225.

7986. Consroe,P.F. and Wolkin,A.L. "Anticonvulsant interaction of cannabidiol and ethosuximide in rats." *J. Pharm. Pharmacol.* 1977, *29*, 5-0-501.

7987. Conte,M.J. and Fergusun,L.W. "Rated effectiveness of antidrug letters by users and nonusers." *J. Psychol.* 1974, *86*, 335-339.

7988. Copetas,A.S. and Foldes,M. "Keith Stroup, the great weed hope." *High Times* 1976, *10*, 18-24.

7989. Craig,D.S. "Dope war crimes in Mexico." *High Times* 1977, *21*, 45-49.

7990. Crommelin,L. *A Essay Towards Improving of the Hempen and Flaxen Manufactures in the Kingdom of Ireland*. R. Owen, Dublin, 1734.

D

7991. Daniels,P. How To Grow Marihuana Hydroponically. Sun Magic Pub., Seattle, Wash., 1977.

7992. Darley,C.F., Tinklenberg,J.R., Roth,W.T., Vernon, S., and Kopell,B.S. "Marihuana effects on long-term memory assessment and retrieval." Psychopharmacol. 1977, 52, 239-241.

7993. Davalos,S.F., Boucher,F., Fournier,G., and Paris, M. "Analysis of a population of cannabis sativa L. originating from Mexico and cultivated in France." Exper. 1977, 33, 1562-1563.

7994. Delamer,E.S. Flax and Hemp, Their Cultures and Manufacture. Routledge, Warner and Routledge, London, 1859.

7995. De Monfried,H. "The great charas: fighting the drug ring." High Times 1974, 4, 57-64.

7996. DiBenedetto,M. "Cannabis and the peripheral nervous system." Br. J. Psychiat. 1977, 131, 361-365.

7997. Dichter,M.S. "Marihuana and the law: The constitutional challenges to marihuana laws in light of the social aspects of marihuana use." Villanova Law Rev. 1968, 13, 851-879.

7998. Dick,R.B. and Brown,L.T. "A comparison of drug users and non-users on a mid-western university campus." Internat'l. J. Addict. 1974, 9, 903-907.

7999. Dickson,D.T. "Bureaucracy and morality: An organizational perspective on a moral crusade." Soc. Prob. 1968, 16, 143-156.

8000. Dike,S.Y. "A new one-step systhesis of hexahydrocannabinoid analogs." Exper. 1977, 33, 985.

8001. Dixit,V.P. "Testicular degeneration and necrosis induced by chronic administration of cannabis extract in dogs." Endokrinologie 1977, 69, 299-305.

8002. Dodge,D.L. "Dimensions of marihuana use in a midwest Catholic university: subcultural considerations." Internat'l. J. Addict. 1977, 12, 971-978.

8003. Dodson,N. "Sociocultural factors of nonopiate drug abusers: A comparative study." Paper presented at Southwest. Sociol. Assoc., Tulsa, 1971.

8004. Dolby,T.W. and Kleinsmith,L.J. "Cannabinoid effects on adenylate cyclase and phosphodiesterase activities of mouse brain." Can. J. Physiol. Pharmacol. 1977, 55, 934-942.

8005. Dott,A.B. "Effect of marihuana on aggression and risk acceptance in an automotive simulator." Clin. Toxicol. 1974, 7, 289.

8006. Dren,A.T., Bopp,B.A., and Ebert,D.M. "Nitrogen-containing benzopyran analogs; reduction of intraocular pressure in rabbits." Pharmacologist 1975, 17, 267.

8007. Drug Abuse Council. Survey of Marihuana Use and Attitudes: State of Oregon. Drug Abuse Council, Washington, D.C., 1975.

8008. DuPont,R.L. "Marihuana--our next step." Paper presented at Psychiatric Inst. Foundation, Washington, D.C., 1977.

E

8009. Eastland, J.O. "Marihuana--hashish epidemic and its impact on U.S. security." Polygraph 1974, 3, 355-372.

8010. Elinson, J. "Antecedents and consequences of teenage drug behavior." Paper presented at Conference on Strategies of Longitudinal Research in Drug Use, Puerto Rico, 1976.

8011. Ellner, M. "Marihuana use by heroin abusers as a factor in program retention." J. Consult. Clin. Psychol. 1977, 45, 709-710.

8012. Erickson, P.G. The Marihuana Arrest: Examining the Coincidence Hypothesis From the Offenders Perspective. Addiction Res. Found., Toronto, 1977.

F

8013. Farmilo,C.G. "Scientific research on cannabis. 4. A review of some recent results on the chemical analysis of cannabis." U.N. Doc. ST/SOA/SER.S/4, April 27, 1961.

8013a. Farmilo,C.G., McConnell Davis,T.W., Vandenheuvel,F.A., and Lane,R. "Scientific research on cannabis. 7. Studies on the chemical analysis of marihuana, biogenesis, paper chromatography, gas chromatography, and country of origin." U.N. Doc. ST/SOA/SER.S/5, March 12, 1962.

8014. Federn,E. "Drug misuse in adolescents from a socio-educational standpoint."(Ger.). Prax. Kinderpsychol. Kinderpsychiat. 1971, 20, 219-225.

8015. Fejer,D. and Smart,R. "The use of psychoactive drugs by adults." Can. Psychiat. Assoc. J. 1973, 18, 313-320.

8016. Feldman,B.H. "Drug use by college students and their parents." Addict. Dis. 1977, 3, 235-242.

8017. Fennessy,M.R. and Taylor,D.A. "The effect of delta-9-tetrahydrocannabinol on body temperature and brain amine concentrations in the rat at different ambient temperatures." Br. J. Pharmacol. 1977, 60, 65-71.

8017a. Fernandez Guardiala,A. "Thermocutaneous threshold for pain in man."(Sp.). Cuadernos Cientificos 1974, 1, 23-34.

8017b. Ferraro,D.P. "Some effects of (-)-delta-9-tetrahydrocannabinol on delayed matching-to-sample performance in chimpanzees." Proc. 5th Internat'l. Cong. Pharmacol. 1972, 1, 67.

8017c. Fetterolf,D.J. and Ferraro,D.P. "Retardation of the acquisition of a successive discrimination by delta-9-tetrahydrocannabinol in rats." Paper presented at Rocky Mt. Psychol. Assoc., Salt Lake City, 1975.

8017d. Fischer,M.L. "Drug usage in rural, small town New England." J. Altered States Conscious. 1975, 2, 171-183.

8017e. Fish,F., Wells,B.W.P., Bindeman,S., Bunney,J.E., and Jordan,M.M. "Prevalence of drug misuse among young people in Glasgow 1970-1972." Br. J. Addict. 1974, 69, 343-355.

8017f. Fletcher,J.M. "A methodological commentary on the Egyptian study of chronic hashish use." Bull. Narc. 1977, 29, 29-34.

8017g. Ford,R.D. and McMillan,D.E. "Further studies on the behavioral pharmacology of delta-8- and delta-9-tetrahydrocannabinol." Fed. Proc. 1972, 31, 506.

8018. Forrest,I.S., Green,D.E., Otis,L.S., and Wursch, M.S. "Excretion of ^{3}H-delta-9-tetrahydrocannabinol in rhesus and squirrel monkeys." Fed. Proc. 1972, 31, 506.

8019. Freidman,E. and Gershon,S. "Tetrahydrocannabinols: Inhibition in acetylcholine synthesis in regional rat brain slices." Pharmacologist 1974, 16, 286.

8020. Freidman,M.A. "In vivo effects of cannabinoids on macromolecular biosynthesis in Lewis lung carcinomas." Cancer Biochem. Biophys. 1977, 2, 51-54.

8021. Freidrich-Fichtl,J. and Spiteller,G. "New cannabinoid--1." Tetrahed. 1975, 31, 479-487

8022. Frisch,J.R. "Our years in hell: American addicts tell their story 1829-1914." J. Psyched. Drugs 1977, 9, 199-207.

8023. Frizza,J., Chesher,G.B., Jackson,D.M., Malor,R., and Starmer,G.A. "The effect of delta-9-tetrahydrocannabinol, cannabidiol, and cannabinol on the anaesthesia induced by various anaesthetic agents in mice." Psychopharmacol. 1977, 55, 103-107.

8024. Fuerta,G.C. "Marihuana and its dangers."(Sp.). Antioquia Med. 1961, 11, 23-74.

8025. Fujita,M., Shimomura,H., Kuriyama,E., Shigehiro, J., and Akasu,M. "Cannabis 2. "Study of narcotic and related ingredients in cannabis by gas-liquid and thin-layer chromatography."(Jap.). Shoyaku. Zas. 1967, 21, 57-64.

8026. Fujiwara,M. and Ueki,S. "Correlation of delta-9-THC induced muricide and biogenic amines in the rat brain." Jap. J. Pharmacol. 1974, 24, 54.

G

8027. Gallagher,J.A. "A comparison between students' and teachers' attitudes toward adolescent alcohol and marihuana users and dogmatism." *Diss. Abs.* 1973, *34*, 3057-3058.

8028. Gallup Opinion Index. *Marihuana in America.* Amer. Inst. Pub. Opin., Princeton, N.J., 1977.

8029. Gebler,H. "Rapid method for identification of toxic agents and drugs of abuse."(Ger.). *Pharmazeut. Ztg.* 1973, *118*, 1949-1951.

8030. Gildea,M.L. and Bourn,W.M. "The effect of delta-9-tetrahydrocannabinol on barbiturate withdrawal convulsions in the rat." *Life Sci.* 1977, *10*, 133-140.

8031. Giusti,G.V. "Muscular dystrophy in mice after chronic subcutaneous treatment with cannabinoids." *Forens. Sci.* 1977, *10*, 133-140.

8032. Gray,L.C. *History of Agriculture in the Southern United States to 1860.* Peter Smith, Gloucester, Mass., 1958.

8033. Greaves,G. "Level of conceptual system functioning in experience of sex with drugs." *Psychol. Rep.* 1971, *28*, 130.

8034. Green,K., Kim,K., Wynn,H., and Shimp,R.G. "Intraocular pressure, organ weights and the chronic use of cannabinoid derivatives in rabbits for one year." *Expt'l. Eye Res.* 1977, *25*, 465-471.

8035. Grlic,L. "A study of infra-red spectra of cannabis resin." *U.N. Doc.* ST/SOA/SER.S/10, Nov. 24, 1965.

8036. Grlic,L. "Scientific research on cannabis. 10. A study of some chemical characteristics of the resin from experimentally grown cannabis of various origins." U.N. Doc. ST/SOA/SER.S/11, Feb. 5, 1964.

8037. Grlic,L. and Tomic,N. "Scientific research on cannabis. 8. Examination of cannabis resin by means of the ferric chloride test." U.N. Doc. ST/SOA/SER.S/14, Jan. 31, 1963.

8038. Groff,S.H. "Marihuana and the 'O' effect." In Andrews,G. and Vinkenoog,S.(eds.). The Book of Grass. Grove Press, N.Y., 1967, 176-177.

8039. Grossman,D.S. "Academic variables associated with marihuana use in a Catholic college." Diss. Abs. 1973, 34, 392-393.

8039a. Grupp,S. "Deterrence and the marihuana smoker." Paper presented to 2nd Inter-American Conference on Criminology, Caracas, 1972.

8039b. Gustav Fritz,L., Weimann,J., and Dirner,Z. "A pharmacological study of fibrous ca-nabinacae grown for industrial purposes in Hungary." U.N. Doc. ST/SOA/SER. S/5, Oct. 8, 1964.

H

8040. Hager,D.L., Vener,A.M., and Stewart,C.S. "Patterns of adolescent drug use in middle America." J. Counsel. Psychol. 1971, 18, 292-297.

8041. Halpin,G. and Whiddon,T. "Drug education: Solution or problem?" Psychol. Rep. 1977, 40, 372-374.

8042. Hamburg,B.A., Kraemer,H.C., and Jahnke,W. "A hierarchy of drug use in adolescence: behavioral and attitudinal correlates of substantial drug use." Am. J. Psychiat. 1975, 132, 1115-1163.

8043. Hanneman,G.J. and McEwen,W.T. "Televised drug abuse appeals: A content analysis." Journelism Quarterly 1973, 50, 329-333.

8044. Hanus,L. "The present state of knowledge of the chemistry of substances of cannabis sativa L. IV. Nitrogen containing compounds." Act. Univ. Palack. Olom. 1975, 73, 241-244.

8045. Harper,J.W., Heath,R.G., and Myers,W.A. "Effects of cannabis sativa on ultrastructure of the synapse in monkey brain." J. Neuroscience Res. 1977, 3, 87-93.

8046. Harvey,D.J., Martin,B.R., and Paton,W.D.M. "Identification of di- and tri-substituted hydroxy and ketone metabolites of delta-1-tetrahydrocannabinol in mouse liver." J. Pharm. Pharmacol. 1977, 29, 482-486.

8047. Harvey,D.J., Martin,B.R., and Paton,W.D.M. "Identification of metabolites of delta-1-and delta-1(6)-tetrahydrocannabinol containing a reduced double bond." J. Pharm. Pharmacol. 1977, 29, 495-497.

8048. Harvey,D.J., Martin,B.R., and Paton,W.D.M. "In vivo metabolism of cannabinol by the mouse and rat and a comparison with the metabolism of delta-1-tetrahydrocannabinol and cannabidiol." Biomedical Mass Spectrometry 1977, 4, 364-370.

8049. Harvey,D.J. and Paton,W.D.M. "In vivo metabolites of delta-1(6)-tetrahydrocannabinol produced by the mouse via the epoxide-diol pathway." J. Pharm. Pharmacol. 1977, 29, 498-500.

8050. Havens,J. "A working paper: Memo on the religious implications of the consciousness changing drugs." J. Scientific Study Religion 1964, 3, 216-226.

8051. Hembree,W.C. "Effects of marihuana on gonadal function in man." Paper presented at 6th Internat'l. Cong. Pharmacol., Helsinki, 1975.

8052. Hendriks,H., Malingre,T.M., Batterman,S., and Bos,R. "Mono- and sesqui-terpene hydrocarbons of the essential oil of cannabis sativa." Phytochemistry 1975, 14, 814-815.

8053. Hindmarch,J. "Drugs and their abuse--age groups particularly at risk." Br. J. Addict. 1972, 67, 209-214.

8054. Hollister,L.E. "Myth of the perfect orgasm may lead to gilding the lily with drugs." Sex. Behav. 1972, 2, 49.

8055. Huszar,L.A., Greenberg,J.H., and Mellors,A. "Effects of delta-9-tetrahydrocannabinol on lymphocyte and synaptosomal lysophosphatidylcholine acyltransferases in vivo." Mol. Pharmacol. 1977, 13, 1086-1091.

8056. Huth,M.J. "Drug abuse and American youth." Sociol. Sympos. 1971, 6, 23-37.

I

8057. Itokawa,H. "Biotransformation of cannabinoid precursors and related alcohols by suspension cultures of callus induced from cannabis sativa L." Chem. Pharm. Bull. 1977, 25, 1941-1946.

J

8059. Joachimoglu, G. "Studies on the distribution and excretion of ^{14}C tetrahydrocannabinol in rats." *U.N. Doc*. ST/SOA/SER.S/8, Sept. 25, 1967.

8060. Johnson, K.M., Ho, B.T., Dewey, W.L., and Harris, L.S. "In vitro induction of ^{3}H-reserpine binding to subcellular components of the rat forebrain by delta-9-tetrahydrocannabinol." *Neuroscience Abs*. 1975, *5*, 241.

8061. Johnson, W.T., Petersen, R.F., and Wells, L.E. "Arrest probabilities for marihuana users as indicators of selective law enforcement." *Am. J. Sociol*. 1977, *83*, 681-700.

8062. Joscelyn, K.B. and Maickel, R.P. *Drugs and Driving: A Recent Review*. Nat'l. Technical Inform. Service, Springfield, Va., 1977.

K

8063. Kaestner,E., Rosen,L., and Appel,P. "Patterns of drug abuse: Relationships with ethnicity, sensation seeking, and anxiety." J. Consult. Clin. Psychol. 1977, 45, 462-468.

8064. Kamali,K. and Steer,R.A. "Polydrug use by high-school students: involvement and correlates." Internat'l. J. Addict. 1976, 11, 337-343.

8065. Kasachkoff,A.R. "Effect of marihuana on the human spatial distortion threshold." Diss. Abs. 1974, 35, 1023.

8066. Kelner,M. "Drug users as people: Some observations on youthful drug use." Paper presented to Can. Sociol. Anthrop. Assoc., Toronto, 1971.

8067. Khavari,K.A., Humes,M., and Mabry,E. "Personality correlates of hallucinogen use." J. Abn. Psychol. 1977, 86, 172-178.

8068. Kinder,B.N. "Attitudes toward alcohol and drug use and abuse. I. Demographic and correlational data." Internat'l. J. Addict. 1975, 10, 737-760.

8069. Kline,N.S. "The future of drugs and drugs of the future." J. Soc. Iss. 1971, 27, 73-87.

8070. Klinge,V., Vaziri,H., and Lennox,K. "Comparison of psychiatric inpatient male and female adolescent drug abusers." Internat'l. J. Addict. 1976, 11, 309-323.

8071. Kohler,J.E. "The highs and lows of marihuana legislation in the United States." Ohio Northern Univ. Intramural Law Rev. 1971, 1, 60-76.

8072. Koval,M., Babst,D.V., and Lipton,D.S. "Development of drug involvement classification for residents of New York State." Drug Forum 1977, 6, 153-176.

8073. Kraatz,U. and Korte,F. "Synthesis of 8-methyl-delta-8-tetrahydrocannabinols." Chem. Berichte 1976, 109, 2485-2489.

8074. Krakowski,M. Drug Content in Popular Magasines. Addiction Research Found., Toronto, 1977.

8075. Krejci,Z. and Vybiral,L. "Thin layer (aluminum oxide) chromatographic isolation of biological active substances from cannabis sativa L. and the biological retnetion of antibacterially active substances." Scr. Med. Brno. 1962, 35, 71-72.

8076. Krohn,M.D. "An investigation of the effect of parental and peer associatons on marihuana use: An empirical test of differential association theory." In Reidel,M. and Thornberry,T.P.(eds.). Crime and Delinquency: Dimensions of Deviance. Praeger, N.Y., 1974, 91-103.

8077. Kupperstein,L.R. "Assessing the nature and dimensions of the drug problem." Ann. Amer. Acad. Polit. Soc. Sci. 1975, 417, 76-85.

8078. Kurtn,H.J., Kraatz,U., and Korte,F. "Synthesis of thio-cannabinoids." Chem. Berichte 1976, 109, 2164-2174.

8079. Kvalseth,T.O. "Effects of marihuana on human reaction time and motor coordination." Percept. Motor Skills 1977, 45, 935-939.

L

8080. Ladner,R., Page,W.F., and Lee,M.L. "Ethnic and sex effects on emergency ward utilization for drug-related problems: a linear model analysis." J. Hlth. Soc. Behav. 1975, 16, 315-325.

8081. Langer,J. "Drug entrepreneurs and dealing culture." Soc. Prob. 1977, 24, 377-386.

8082. Larsen,F.F. and Pryor,G.T. "Factors influencing tolerance to the effects of delta-9-THC on a conditioned avoidance response." Pharmacol. Biochem. Behav. 1977, 7, 323-329.

8083. Lecorsier,A., Hoellinger,H., Hoang-Nam,N., and Fournier,E. "Allergic characteristics of delta-9-tetrahydrocannabinol, the active principle in Indian hemp (cannabis sativa var. indica)."(Fr.). C. R. Acad. Sci. 1977, 285, 1351-1353.

8084. LeMay,M.L. and Penn,J.R. "Drug usage trends in college living units during a three-year period." Drug Forum 1973, 2, 309-315.

8085. Leon,J. "Trends in drug use among young people in Oshawa: Prevalence and responses." Can. Ment. Hlth. 1977, 25, 6-10.

8086. Leuw,E. Cannabis and Schoolchildren; An Investigation Into The Background And Significance Of The Use And Nonuse Of Cannabis Among Pupils For General Secondary Education In The Province Of South Holland. Foundation for Alcohol and Drug Research, Amsterdam, 1972.

8087. Lewis,S. and Trickett,E.J. "Correlates of differing patterns of drug use in high school populations." Am. J. Community Psychol. 1974, 2, 337-350.

8088. Libman,E. "Cannabis effects related to cutaneous sensory perception and personality measures." Diss. Abs. 1977, 37, 5873.

8089. Llewellyn,G.C. "Examination of fungal growth and aflatoxin production on marihuana." Mycopathologia 1977, 62, 109-112.

8090. Lockwood,R.S. "The United States drug problem and international trafficking. I. The need for more rigorous controls." Internat'l. J. Addict. 1977, 12, 633-650.

8091. Love,A.J. and Killorn,L.H. Drug Use Among Adolescents in Prince Edward Island. Addiction Found. of Prince Edward Island, Charlottetown, P.E.I., 1973.

8092. Lucas,W.L. "Initiation of marihuana use: An analysis of panal data in a predictive model framework." Diss. Abs. 1977, 37, 5376.

8093. Lucas,W.L. "Longitudinal research and marihuana smoking: A successful approach." Criminol. 1974, 3, 315-327.

M

8094. Malit,L.A. and Smith,T.C. "Research on marihuana." N. Eng. J. Med. 1972, 287, 994-995.

8095. Marks,V. and Chapple,P.A.L. "Hepatic dysfunction in heroin and cocaine users." Brit. J. Addict. 1967, 62, 189.

8096. McBroom,P. "Marihuana on the medical campus." New Physician 1974, 23, 24-25.

8096a. McCann,H.G., Steffenhagen,R.A., and Merriam,G. "Drug use: A model for a deviant sub-culture." J. Alcohol Drug Educat. 1977, 23, 29-45.

8096b. Maccannell,K., Milstein,S.L., Karr,G., and Clark,S. "Marihuana-produced impairments in form perception. Experienced and non-experienced subjects." Prog. Neuropsychopharmacol. 1977, 1, 339-343.

8097. Mechoulam,R. and Gaoni,Y. "The isolation and structure of cannabinolic, cannabidiolic and cannabigerolic acids." U.N. Doc. ST/SOA/SER.S/9, May 5, 1965.

8098. Miczek,K.A. "A behavioral analysis of aggressive behaviors induced and modulated by delta-9-tetrahydrocannabinol, pilocarpine, d-amphetamine and l-dopa." Activ. Nerv. Super. 1977, 19, 224-225.

8099. Miller,R.H., Dhingra,R.C., Kanakis,C., Amat-y-Leon,F., and Rosen,K.M. "The electrophysiological effects of delta-9-tetrahydrocannabinol (cannabis) on cardiac conduction in man." Am. Heart J. 1977, 94, 740-747.

8100. Milman,D.H. "Multiple drug use by children." N.Y. State J. Med. 1972, 72, 2793-2796.

8101. Milman,D.H. "Warning to drug users." N. Eng. J. Med. 1966, 274, 167.

8102. Milzoff,J.R., Forney,R.B., Stone,C.J., and Allen,D.O. "The cardiovascular effects of delta-9-THC in vagotomized rats." Pharmacologist 1971, 13, 247.

8103. Miras,C.J. and Coutselinis,A. "The distribution of tetrahydrocannabinol-^{14}C in humans." U.N. Doc. ST/SOA/SER.S/7, Nov. 2, 1970.

8103a. Miras,C.J. and Coutselinis,A. "The presence of cannabinols in the urine of hashish smokers." U.N. Doc. ST/SOA/SER.S/2, Nov. 4, 1970.

8104. Mitosinka,G.T., Thornton,J.I., and Hayes,T.L. "Examination of cystolithic hairs of cannabis (sativa) and other plants by means of the scanning electron microscope." J. Forens. Sci. Soc. 1972, 12, 521-529.

8105. Moerkhold,I., Andersen,J., Nielsen,E., Schou,J., Steentoft,A., and Worm,K. "Specific method for the demonstration of cannabis intake by TLC of urine." Act. Pharmacol. Toxicol. 1971, 29, 111-112.

8106. Monti,J.M. "Hynotic-like effects of cannabidiol in the rat." Psyhcopharmacol. 1977, 55, 263-265.

8107. Murphy,H.B.M. "The cannabis habit." Addictions 1966, 13, 3-25.

N

8108. Naditch,M.P. "Relation of motives for drug use and psychopathology in the development of acute adverse reactions to psychoactive drugs." J. Abnorm. Psychol. 1975, 84, 374-385.

8109. Nagle,B.T., DiGregorio,G.J., and Chernick,W.S. "The influence of delta-9-tetrahydrocannabinol on pilocarpine induced parotid secretions of the rat." Pharmacologist 1974, 16, 259.

8110. Nahas,G.G., Schwartz,I.W., and Adamec,J. "Immunosuppression and tolerance development to delta-9-tetrahydrocannabinol." Fed. Proc. 1973, 32, 756.

8110a. Nakazawa,K. and Costa,E. "Induction of methylcholanthrene of delta-9-tetrahydrocannabinol metabolism in rat lung." Pharmacologist 1971, 13, 297.

8110b. Nargel,M.D., Zagury,D., and Nahas,G.G. "Induction of lymphoblastic transformations in mice by delta-9-tetrahydrocannabinol."(Fr.). C. R. Acad. Sci. 1973, 276, 1089-1091.

8110c. Nazar,B., Kairys,D.J., Fowler,R., and Harclerode,J. "Effects of delta-9-tetrahydrocannabinol on serum thyroxine concentrations in the rat." J. Pharm. Pharmacol. 1977, 29, 778-779.

8110d. Neuninger,H. "Chemical analysis of narcotics." (Ger.). Oester. Apoth. Zeit. 1973, 27, 91-96.

8110e. Nichols,D.E., Mason,D.L., and Jacobsen,L.B. "Allylbenzene analogs of delta-9-THC as tumor growth inhibitors." Life Sci. 1977, 21, 1245-1248.

8110f. Noirfalise,A. "Toxicological analysis of hallucinogenic drugs."(Fr.). J. Pharm. Belg. 1966, 23, 287-399.

8110g. Noirfalise,A. "Toxicological problems from drugs of abuse."(Fr.). Arch. Belg. Med. Soc. Hyg. 1971, 29, 281-302.

8110h. Nowlis,H.H. "Communicating about drugs." In Hollander,C.(ed.). Background Papers on Student Drug Involvement. Nat'l. Student Assoc., Washington, D.C., 1967, 61-68.

8110i. Nowlis,H.H. "Marihuana." Current Issues Higher Educat. 1969, 24, 113-122.

8110j. Nowlis,H.H. Drugs On The College Campus: A Guide For College Administrators. Nat'l. Assoc. Student Personnel Administrators, Detroit, 1967

O

8111. Okamoto,K. "Constituents of Japanese cannabis." (Jap.). Kagaku Keisatsu Kankyusho Kokoku 1967, 20, 109-116.

8112. Oliver,B. Medical Plants in Nigeria. Nigerian College of Arts, Science, and Technology, Lagos, 1960.

8113. Olsen,O. "Cannabis sativa."(Dan.). Gartner Tidende 1967, 39, 12-13.

8114. Osgood,P.F. and Howes,J.F. "Delta-9-tetrahydrocannabinol and dimethylheptylpyran induced tachycardia in the conscious rat." Life Sci. 1977, 20, 1329-1336.

8115. Ostalenko,V. "Hereditary change of sex in hemp resulting from electrical stimulation of soil."(Rus.). Tsent. Genet. Lab. Michurina 1962, 8, 139-144.

8116. Ottersen,T., Rosenquist,E., Turner,C.E., and El-Feraly,F.S. "The crystal and molecular structure of cannabinol." Act. Chem. Scand. 1977, 31, 781-787.

P

8117. Papavassiliou,M.J. and Liberato,S.N. "Beam's reaction for hashish." J.A.P.A. 1937, 14, 194.

8118. Parry,H.J. "Patterns of psychotropic drug use among American adults." J. Drug Iss. 1971, 1, 269-273.

8119. Pastor Quesada,L. "Marihuana and its psycho-physical influence on individuals."(Sp.). Criminalistica 1959, 6, 27.

8120. Paton,S. "Depressive mood and adolescent illicit drug use: a longitudinal analysis." J. Genet. Psychol. 1977, 13, 267-289.

8122. Pearlman,S. "Drug experiences and attitudes among seniors in a liberal arts college." J. Assoc. Deans Admin. Stud. Affairs 1967, 4, 121-126.

8123. Pechmeja,A. "Hashish."(Fr.). Manetiseur 1868, 1, 443.

8124. Peck,D.G. "Belief, deterrence and marihuana use." Diss. Abs. 1977, 37, 5376-5377.

8125. Penuelas Hera,E. "Historical note on hemp disease."(Sp.). Rev. Clin. Espan. 1946, 22, 124-128.

8126. Perchine,G.N. "The pharmacology of cannabis." Pharmacol. Toxicol. 1949, 2, 12, 37.

8127. Perez Cadavid,J. "Marihuana intoxication." (Sp.). Antioquia Med. 1952, 2, 738-743.

8128. Pernambuco Filho,P. and Botelho,A. The Diamba Vice.(Port.). Libraria Francisco Alves, Rio de Janeiro, 1924.

8129. Perry,D.C. "Street drug analysis and drug use trends. 1969-1975. Pt. I." Pharm. Chem. News. 1977, 6, 1-4, 13.

8130. Perry,D.C. "Street drug analysis and drug use trends. 1969-1975. Pt. II." Pharm. Chem. News, 1977, 6, 1-4, 9.

8131. Personne,J. "Report on the progress relative to the analysis of cannabis."(Fr.). J. Pharm. Chim. 1855, 28, 461-463.

8132. Pfefferbaum,A., Darley,C.F., Tinklenberg,J.R., Roth,W.T., and Kopell,B.S. "Marihuana and memory intrusions." J. Nerv. Ment. Dis. 1977, 165, 381-386.

8133. Phalen,J.M. "The marihuana bugaboo." Milit. Surg. 1943, 93, 94-95.

8134. Pio Correa,M. Dictionary of Useful Plants of Brazil and Exotic Cultivated Specimens.(Port.). Imprensa Nacional, Rio de Janeiro, 1926.

8135. Piotrowski,G. "Concerning the action of tobacco, opium, and hemp."(Pol.). Wszechswiat 1884, 3, 185-188.

8136. Pittenger,P.S. "Comparative activity of male and female cannabis." Proc. Penn. Pharmaceut. Assoc. 1919, 42, 173.

8137. Poliscuk,M. "Hemp as a medicinal plant."(Pol.). Vest. Czazv. 1959, 6, 168-170.

8138. Pollaci,G. and Gallotti,M. "Indian hemp cultivated in Lombardy."(It.). Ebenda 1940, 15, 324.

8139. Porcino,F. "Antagonistic effect of Indian hemp on isonicotinoyl hydrazide-induced convulsions." (It.). Farmaco 1954, 9, 278-281.

8140. Posey,H.T. Marihuana. Tulane Univ., New Orleans, 1937.

8141. Postma,W.P. "Observations on the cytology of normal hemp plants and those treated with colchicine." (Ger.). Rec. Trav. Bot. Neerland. 1939, 36, 672.

8142. Prebles,A.S.M. and Mann,H.V. "Ganja as a cause of insanity and crime in Bengal." Ind. Med. Gaz. 1914, 49, 295.

8142a. Prioreschi,P. "On the abuse of marihuana and other drugs." Med. Hypotheses 1977, 3, 265-266.

8143. Pryor,G.T., Larsen,F.F., and Carr,J.D. "Interactions of delta-9-tetrahydrocannabinol with phenobarbital, ethanol and chlordiazepoxide." Pharmacol. Biochem. Behav. 1977, 7, 331-345.

8144. Pusinelli,A. "On cannabis poisonings."(Ger.). Deut. Med. Woch. 1886, 12, 815-816.

R

8145. Radosevic,A., Kupinic,M., and Grlic,L. "Scientific research on cannabis. 6. Antibiotic activity of various types of cannabis resin." U.N. Doc. ST/SOA/SER. S/10, Jan. 25, 1962.

8146. Rose,S.E. "The effect of delta-9-tetrahydrocannabinol on the absolute visual threshold of the albino rat." Diss. Abs. 1977, 37, 5876-5877.

8147. Rosenberg,J.S., Kasl,S.V., and Berberian,R.M. "Sex differences in adolescent drug use: recent trends." Addict. Dis. 1974, 1, 73-96.

8148. Rosenthal,M.P. "Dangerous drug legislation in the United States: Recommendations and comments." Texas Law Rev. 1967, 45, 1037.

8149. Rota,J. and Diaz,V. "Relationship between interpersonal and mass media communication and some aspects of drug addiction in high school students in Mexico City."(Sp.). Cuadernos Cientificos 1974, 1, 99-138.

S

8150. Salgado,A. and Ayala,F. "Psychophysiological study of the interaction between alcohol and marihuana in man."(Sp.). Cuaderno Cientificos 1974, 1, 35-48.

8151. Salisbury,H. "A survey of student attitudes toward drug use." West. Carolina Univ. J. Educat. 1976, 7, 5-13.

8152. Samrah,H. "A preliminary investigation of the occurence of cannabis components in the various parts of the plant." U.N. Doc. ST/SOA/SER.S/8, Dec. 1, 1970.

8153. Samrah,H. "A preliminary investigation on the possible presence of alkaloidal substances in cannabis." U.N. Doc. ST/SOA/SER.S/9, Dec. 11, 1970.

8154. Schou,J. and Nielsen,E. "Cannabinols in various United Nations samples and in cannabis sativa grown in Denmark under varying conditions. Experiments with Korte and Sieper's thin layer chromatographic method." U.N. Doc. ST/SOA/SER.S/12, Oct. 19, 1970.

8155. Segal,B. "Reasons for marihuana use and personality: A canonical analysis." J. Alcohol Drug Educat. 1977, 22, 64-69.

8156. Sethi,V.K. "Chemical investigation of wild cannabis sativa L. roots." Planta Med. 1977, 32, 378-379.

8157. Siegel,P., Siegel,M.I., Krimmer,E.C., Doyle, W.J., and Barry,H. "Fluctuating dental asymmetry as an indicator of the stressful prenatal effects of delta-9-tetrahydrocannabinol in the laboratory rat." Toxicol. Appl. Pharmacol. 1977, 42, 339-344.

8158. Smart,R.G. "Effects of legal restraint on the use of drugs: A review of empirical studies." Bull. Narc. 1976, 28, 55-65.

8158a. Smart,R.G. "Perceived ability and the use of drugs." Bull. Narc. 1977, 29, 59-63.

8159. Snow,M. Youth and Drugs: A Pilot Study of Use, Attitudes, and Knowledge of Drugs among Students in Two New York City Schools. Narcotic Addiction Control Commission, N.Y., 1970.

8160. Sobrino Lazaro,G. "Marihuana drug dependence in Quintana Roo."(Sp.). Salud Publica Mexico 1977, 19, 431-435.

8160a. Sofia,R.D., Dixit,B.N., and Barry,H. "The effect of repeated administration of delta-9-tetrahydrocannabinol on serotonin metabolism and the rat brain." Arch. Internat'l. Pharmacodyn. Ther. 1977, 229, 52-58.

8161. Sorosiask,F.M., Thomas,L.E., and Balet,F.N. "Adolescent drug use: an analysis." Psychol. Rep. 1976, 38, 211-221.

8162. Soueif,M.I. "The Egyptian study of chronic cannabis use: a reply to Fletcher and Satz." Bull. Narc. 1977, 29, 35-43.

8163. Spulak,F., Claussen,U., Fehlhaber,H.W., and Korte,F. "Hashishs XIX. Tetrahydrocannabitriol cannabidiol-carboxylic acid ester, a new constitutent of hashish." (Ger.). Tetrahed. 1968, 24, 5379-5383.

8164. Stanton,M.D. "Drugs, Vietnam, and the Vietnam veteran: An overview." Am. J. Drug Alcohol Abuse 1976, 34, 557-570.

8165. Stillman,R.C., Wolkowitz,O., Weingartner,H., Waldman,I., DeRenzo,E.V., and Wyatt,R.J. "Marihuana: Differential effects on right and left hemisphere functions in man." Life Sci. 1977, 21, 1793-1800.

T

8166. Takahashi,R.N., Zuardi,A.W., and Karniol,I.G. "Chemical composition and importance of various constituents in Brazilian cannabis sativa."(Port.). Rev. Bras. Pesquis. Med. Biol. 1977, 10, 379-385.

8167. Taylor,D.A. and Fennessy,M.R. "Biphasic nature of the effects of delta-9-THC on body temperature and brain amines of the rat." Eur. J. Pharmacol. 1977, 46, 93-99.

8168. Todd,J., Goldstein,R., and Whitehouse,A. "Personality and attitudes of British marihuana users." Psychol. Rep. 1977, 40, 990.

V

8169. Valle,J.R. "Pharmacological approaches to the study of the cannabis problem." Internat'l. J. Addict. 1969, 4, 623-647.

8170. Vane,N.W. "The eradication of cannabis sativa L. with herbicides in the Hunter River Valley, New South Wales, Australia." Bull. Narc. 1973, 25, 49-50.

W

8171. Wand,M. and Mather,J.A. "Diphenylhydantoin intoxication mimicking botulism." *N. Eng. J. Med.* 1972, *286*, 88.

8172. Wechsler,H. and Thum,D. "Teen-age drinking, drug use and social correlates." *Quart. J. Stud. Alcohol* 1973, *34*, 1220-1227.

8173. Wolk,D.J. "Marihuana on the campus: A study at one university." *J. Am. Coll. Hlth. Assoc.* 1968, *17*, 144-149.

8174. Wurmser,L. "Drug addiction and drug abuse--a synopsis." *Maryland State Med. J.* 1968, *17*, 68.

Z

8175. Zanini,A.C., DeCamargo Fonseca Moraes,E., Akerman,B., Aizenstein,M, and De Toledo Salgado,P.E. "Concept and use of psychoactive drugs among university students in the Sao Paulo area." Drug Forum 1977, 6, 85-99.

8176. Zinberg,N.E., Jacobson,R.C., and Harding,W.M. "Social sanctions and rituals as a basis for drug abuse prevention." Am. J. Drug Alcohol Abuse 1975, 2, 165-182.

8177. Ziomkowski,L., Mulder,R., and Williams,D. "Drug use variations between delinquent and non-delinquent youth." Intellect 1975, 104, 36-38.

INDEX

Books

ABOUT THE COMPILER

Ernest L. Abel is a Research Scientist at the Research Institute on Alcoholism in Buffalo, New York. His books include *Drugs and Behavior, The Scientific Study of Marihuana*, and *The Handwriting on the Wall* (Greenwood Press, 1977).